P9-DNT-159

BY ARTHUR HERMAN

How the Scots Invented the Modern World

*To Rule the Waves: How the British
Navy Shaped the Modern World*

*Gandhi & Churchill: The Epic
Rivalry That Destroyed an
Empire and Forged Our Age*

*Freedom's Forge: How American
Business Produced Victory
in World War II*

*The Cave and the Light: Plato Versus
Aristotle, and the Struggle for the
Soul of Western Civilization*

THE
CAVE
AND
THE
LIGHT

THE CAVE AND THE LIGHT

Plato Versus Aristotle, and the Struggle for the Soul of Western Civilization

Arthur Herman

 RANDOM HOUSE TRADE PAPERBACKS
NEW YORK

2014 Random House Trade Paperback Edition

Copyright © 2013 by Arthur Herman

All rights reserved.

Published in the United States by Random House Trade Paperbacks,
an imprint of Random House, a division of Random House LLC,
a Penguin Random House company, New York.

RANDOM HOUSE and the HOUSE colophon are
registered trademarks of Random House LLC.

Originally published in hardcover in the United States by Random House,
an imprint and division of Random House LLC, in 2013.

Image credits:
© iStockphoto.com/Vgm6 (p. 47)
© iStockphoto.com/zakkum5 (p. 78)
© iStockphoto.com/mmac72 (p. 126)
Wellcome Library, London (p. 222)
© iStockphoto.com/HultonArchive (p. 384)
akg-images/Fritz Eschen (p. 511)
akg-images/Anna Weise (p. 539)
From K. Clinton, *Myth and Cult: The Iconography of the Eleusinian
Mysteries: The Martin P. Nilsson Lectures on Greek Religion,
Delivered 19–21 November 1990 at the Swedish Institute at Athens*
(ActaAth-8°, 11), Stockholm, 1992, p. 88. (p. 565)

LIBRARY OF CONGRESS CATALOGING-IN-PUBLICATION DATA

Herman, Arthur
The cave and the light: Plato versus Aristotle, and the struggle for
the soul of Western civilization / Arthur Herman.
p. cm.
Includes bibliographical references and index.
ISBN 978-0-553-38566-3
eBook ISBN 978-0-553-90783-4
1. Civilization, Western—Greek influences. 2. Plato—Influence.
3. Aristotle—Influence. 4. Philosophy, Ancient. I. Title.
CB245.H4286 2010 909'.09821—dc22 2010008230

Printed in the United States of America on acid-free paper

www.atrandom.com

1 2 3 4 5 6 7 8 9

For Beth, the light of my life

PREFACE

An editorial in *The New York Review of Books* recently asked: "Do the Classics Have a Future?" The real question is: Will the classics ever leave us alone? This books tells the story of how everything we say, do, and see has been shaped in one way or another by two classical Greek thinkers, Plato and Aristotle.

Far from being "dead white males," they've been powering the living heart of Western culture from ancient Greece to today. Their influence extends from science and philosophy and literature, to our social life and most cherished political institutions—and not just in the West but increasingly in the rest of the world, too, including the Muslim world. And at the center of their influence has been a two-thousand-year struggle for the soul of Western civilization, which today extends to *all* civilizations: a struggle born from an act of rebellion.

It came around 360 BCE, when the young Aristotle, son of the court doctor of the Macedonian kings, turned against the ideas of his famous teacher, Plato of Athens, and set out to create a school of his own. The clash of ideas that then sprang up between Plato and Aristotle is summed up in this book's title.

The Myth of the Cave appears in Book VII of Plato's most famous work, the *Republic*. Plato used it to represent his most fundamental idea: that man is destined by his creator to find a path from the dark cave of material existence to the light of a higher, purer, and more spiritual truth. It's when we rise above the merely human, Plato insisted, and enter the realm of "the everlasting and immortal and changeless" that we achieve wisdom.

As readers will learn, Aristotle disagreed, and his dissent from his famous teacher would have enormous consequences.

"All things have a specific nature," he would argue in his *Physics*, based on a union of form *and* matter. Instead of trying to rise above mundane reality, Aristotle believed the philosopher's job was to explain how the world works, and how as human beings we can find our proper place in it. There is no cave; only a world made of things and facts. "The *fact* is our starting point," he once said, and that insight permeated his thinking on everything, from science to politics and drama.

For the next two thousand years Aristotle would become the father of modern science, logic, and technology. Plato, by contrast, is the spokesman for the theologian, the mystic, the poet, and the artist.

One gave us a view of reality as multiform and constantly evolving; the other, as eternal and One.

One told us we have to learn to deal with things as they are, including each other. The other said we need to think about how things ought to be, including ourselves and our society.

One shaped the contours of Christianity; the other, the ideas of the Enlightenment.

One gave us modern economics; the other, the Reformation.

One inspired Europe to lift itself out of the Dark Ages; the other inspired the greatest artistic works of the Renaissance, including Michelangelo's Sistine Chapel ceiling.

One gave us the U.S. Constitution, the Manhattan Project, and shopping malls. The other gave us Chartres Cathedral, but also the gulag and the Holocaust.

Aristotle asks, "How do you fit into the world that already exists?"

Plato asks, "Why does that world exist at all?"

How this split happened, and how Western culture came to develop this strange dual face, forms the narrative of this book. So do the events and thinkers and personalities who perpetuated that struggle between the two ancient rivals, as well as the strange twists and ironies that arose along the way. This is neither a history of philosophy nor a history of Western civilization. It is an account of the interaction of both, and of how the legacies of Plato and Aristotle live on around us and continue to shape our world.

May 7, 2013

CONTENTS

Raphael, *The School of Athens*, Stanza della Segnatura, The Vatican

THE SCHOOL OF ATHENS

*There are Plato and Aristotle, and around them
is a great school of philosophers.*
— Giorgio Vasari, "Life of Raphael of Urbino"

He was a provincial boy, a painter like his father. Everyone recognized that
Raphael Sanzio had extraordinary artistic talent: talent, as his fellow painter
Vasari later said, more like a god than a man.[1] At sixteen and with his father's
encouragement, he moved from his sophisticated but small hometown of
Urbino to work with the Umbrian master Pietro Perugino, and then to Flor-
ence, the city of the Medici.

What he found there was a visual and artistic feast. Raphael spent days
and nights examining the works of his two great elders, Michelangelo and
Leonardo, which, according to Vasari, "inspired him to study even more intensely" so he could raise his skills closer to their exalted level. However,
Raphael's big break came in 1508, when a letter arrived from another Urbino
native, the architect Bramante, inviting him to work for the pope in Rome.

In 1508, Rome was western Europe's most revered city. It was the former
capital of an ancient empire and the center of the contemporary art scene.
Pope Julius II had come to the throne of St. Peter five years earlier determined to remake the city in his own grandiose image and to use the revived
classical style of the ancient Greeks and Romans to do it. He had commissioned Bramante to create a design for the new St. Peter's Basilica, which was
to be larger and more ornate than any church in Christendom.

Bramante also supervised a host of other artistic projects at the behest of Pope Julius. In 1508, money and an appetite for grand artistic visions were plentiful in Rome. That meant big opportunities for a talent like Raphael.

Bramante and the pope had already engaged the best artists in Italy. When Raphael arrived in the Eternal City, Michelangelo Buonarroti was just starting to set up the scaffolding for painting a series of frescoes for the ceiling in the Sistine Chapel. The bearded, brooding Florentine was thirty-four, in the prime of life and at the height of his creative powers. He was still furious that Pope Julius had pulled him off the project on which Michelangelo's heart was set, the pope's tomb and its almost forty life-size marble statues, and instead put him to work in the chapel. Michelangelo had no inkling he was about to start work on his greatest masterpiece. Nor did he realize that the slim youth from Urbino to whom Bramante introduced him was about to create something that would be as much a landmark of Western civilization as his own Sistine Chapel ceiling.

In addition to the morose Florentine, Julius's stable of artists included Luca Signorelli and Raphael's old master Perugino; the enigmatic Venetian Lorenzo Lotto; and an eccentric character whose scandalous sexual habits earned him the nickname "the Sodomist" (Il Sodoma).* However, unlike these temperamental and even tempestuous artists, Raphael was easygoing and easy to work with. Life at the court of Urbino had taught him what today we call the power to make friends and influence people. After the stormy negotiations with Michelangelo over painting the Sistine ceiling, the pope was delighted to deal with someone with charming manners and a winning personality.

But where to put the young man to work? Julius's mind drifted to his papal apartments in the Vatican Palace. He hated them.[2] Their splashy gilt decorations and dated lifeless frescoes served only to remind him of his predecessor the infamous Pope Alexander Borgia and Alexander's poisonous children Cesare and Lucrezia. Julius already had Il Sodoma, Lotto, and the rest hard at work redecorating key rooms on the first and second floors. He had something else in mind for Raphael.

The room he was thinking about was on the third floor and offered more

---

*Born in Vercelli in Piedmont, he was christened Giovanni Antonio Bazzi. The origins of the nickname are disputed, although Vasari leaves no doubt that it originated with his sexual tastes. Bazzi was also renowned for his paintings of intimate same-sex scenes. What is remarkable is that he signed some of his works as Il Sodoma and that he should have been employed by the pope himself.

than five hundred square feet of wall space. It had high, arched ceilings and a mosaic pavement set with geometric designs. The rest stood bare except for some ceiling frescoes Julius intended to replace. So at some point in the winter of 1508, he and Raphael and Bramante would have wandered inside, passing teams of artists and assistants laboring in the halls with paintbrushes and trowels. They would have seen their breath as they stood in the frigid air. Their words would have echoed in that soaring empty space.

"This shall be our personal library," Julius probably said, gesturing toward the empty walls. "Give us a design suited to that purpose."

Raphael had little experience painting frescoes and none conceiving an artistic program comprehensive enough to fill such a space. But Julius knew how to handle men, and he knew artists. He sensed that if this young provincial, whose reputation was built on his charming but rather anodyne portraits of the Madonna and Child, was turned loose to decorate the papal library— what would be the center of Julius's intellectual life—the result would be a masterpiece.

He was correct. We can see it today, just down the hall from the Sistine Chapel. Like Michelangelo's ceiling, Raphael's *Stanza della Segnatura** is a triumph of skill and intellect. In Vasari's words, "By the genius shown in this work, Raphael clearly demonstrated his determination to be the undisputed master" of Renaissance painting, the equal of both Michelangelo and Leonardo da Vinci.[3]

We know that the complete artistic program of the *Stanza*, with its allegorical representations of Philosophy, Theology, Law, and the arts, was drawn up not by Raphael but probably by the pope's librarian, with the help of the humanist Giovanni Pico della Mirandola.[4] But Raphael brought his own gift for pictorial drama to the task, and it permeates the *Stanza*'s centerpiece. *The School of Athens* is a grand summing-up of Western civilization's debt to the ancient world at midcareer, and to that world's two greatest and most influential minds, perhaps the two greatest minds of all time: Plato and Aristotle.

The painting shows the two philosophers larger than life size in an architectural setting of unparalleled splendor, with other philosophers arrayed on either side until they fill the entire wall.

Plato stands slightly to the left and points heavenward toward a transcen-

---

* So called because after Julius II's death, the library was moved out and the chamber was used for meetings of the papal tribunal to oversee appeals to the Holy See, the Segnatura della Grazia (or Council of Grace).

dent reality. Next to him stands his great teacher Socrates, and below him sits the mathematician Pythagoras. Alongside are Plato's closest disciples, his nephew Speusippus and Xenocrates, but also the ancient thinkers who emphasized the importance of intuition, the emotions, and speculative philosophy. Scholars have identified Plotinus, the father of Neoplatonism, and Epicurus, the founder of Epicureanism, as well as an Arab philosopher, Averroës; and a woman, the pagan priestess Hypatia. At their feet sits another philosopher, Heraclitus, which is in fact a portrait of Michelangelo. Over all their heads stands a statue of Apollo, the god of the arts and divine inspiration.

On the opposite side, on the right side, is the vigorous bearded figure of Aristotle, which we know Raphael drew from ancient busts of Aristotle in order to make it as accurate and lifelike as possible.[5] Beside him are the representatives of science and empirical thought. There is Eudemus, the historian of mathematics, and Aristotle's student Theophrastus, the father of botany. There are the scientists of the ancient Alexandrian school who were heavily influenced by Aristotle, like Ptolemy the astronomer and Euclid the geometer, which is actually a portrait of Raphael's mentor Bramante ("portrayed so realistically," Vasari says, "that he almost seems alive"). There is the geographer Strabo[6] (which some argue is actually a portrait of Leonardo da Vinci, who had arrived in Rome just as Raphael was finishing), Diogenes the Cynic with his famous begging bowl, and others who cannot be identified. Above *their* heads Raphael has placed a statue of Pallas Athena, the goddess of reason and wisdom.

Raphael's painting offers in visual form an idea that Pico and the Renaissance inherited from the Roman statesman and thinker Cicero: that Plato and Aristotle serve as the twin fountainheads of Western reason, intellectual coequals who sum up the entire scope of human knowledge.[7] It is a historical view that permeated not only the Renaissance, but Western education for centuries until our own time. It lives on in old-fashioned textbooks that talk about the "wisdom of the Greeks" when they really mean Plato and Aristotle, and in sound bites from cultural arbiters who refer to "the classical mind" and "Plato and Aristotle" as if they were virtually interchangeable.

Now it's time to look deeper.

Today we see that as a painting, *The School of Athens* not only sums up the legacy of Plato and Aristotle as the progenitors of ancient philosophy and Western thought, it also captures the dual character of Western culture almost from its start.

On one side there is Plato the idealist, who became the guiding spirit of Western idealism and religious thought. In Plato's arms Raphael has put his famous dialogue the *Timaeus*, which inspired a thousand years of theologians, mystics, and students of the occult.

On the other side stands Aristotle, the man of science and common sense, who points earthward in contrast with Plato's gesture toward the heavens. In Aristotle's arms Raphael put Aristotle's *Nicomachean Ethics*, which St. Thomas Aquinas used to rewrite the Catholic Church's understanding of morality and which Cicero believed was the finest guide on how to live free in a free society. Twenty-five hundred years later, Aristotle's *Ethics* may still be the single most decisive influence on our modern understanding of politics, morals, and society just as Aristotle remains the father of modern science.

Mysticism versus common sense; religion versus science; empiricism versus idealism: *The School of Athens* is in fact an allegorical painting about two contrasting but highly influential worldviews that have shaped our world, in a perpetual struggle for the soul of Western civilization.

Seen in this light, the West's greatest thinkers, theologians, scientists, artists, writers, and even politicians have found themselves arrayed on one side or the other in a twenty-four-centuries-old battle between the ideas of Plato and Aristotle and the two paths to wisdom they represent. At certain critical junctures of history, thinkers have tried to knit the two together into a single system. But each time, the old antagonism reasserts itself and the battle is renewed from generation to generation, century to century.

One path—Plato's path—sees the world through the eyes of the religious mystic as well as the artist. It finds its strength in the realm of contemplation and speculation and seeks to unleash the power of human beings' dreams and desires.

The path of Aristotle, by contrast, observes reality through the sober eyes of science and reveals the power of logic and analysis as tools of human freedom. "The fact is our starting point," he said, and meant it.

Over the centuries, Plato's and Aristotle's ideas have managed to pull and tug Western civilization in conflicting directions.

The battle molded classical culture in ancient Greece and Rome and helped to trigger the emergence of Christianity in ancient Rome. In the Middle Ages, it not only shaped the contrasting worldviews of St. Augustine and St. Thomas Aquinas, but pervaded the works of the greatest minds of the age, from Peter Abelard and Abbot Suger to William of Ockham, and dictated the terms of the first cultural interface between Christianity and Islam.

The clash between Plato and Aristotle is visibly inscribed on the stones of Chartres Cathedral and Notre Dame de Paris. It sparked the first idea of the national state and nearly brought the medieval papacy crashing to the ground.

As we will see, it inspired new thinking about politics, art, and science in the Renaissance and touched thinkers as diverse as Leonardo da Vinci, Machiavelli, Martin Luther, and William Shakespeare. It explains why Raphael and Michelangelo became the most influential painters of their age, why Sir Thomas More wrote his *Utopia* and Machiavelli *The Prince*, and why the violence of the religious wars helped to inspire the scientific revolution.

The battle between Plato and Aristotle raged on into the modern age. It shaped the ideas of Galileo, John Locke, Isaac Newton, and Louis XIV, not to mention Adam Smith, Thomas Jefferson, and Jean-Jacques Rousseau. It lived on in the age of Romanticism and in the thought of Karl Marx, John Stuart Mill, and Friedrich Nietzsche. It even shaped modern science and the Cold War. It still determines how we think about human nature and global warming.

The English poet Samuel Taylor Coleridge once said every person is born either a Platonist or an Aristotelian.[8] In fact, Platonists and Aristotelians are not born but made. We are all part of Raphael's *School of Athens*, standing on one side or the other.

In the end, however, it is the enduring tension between these two different worldviews that distinguishes Western civilization from its predecessors and counterparts. It explains both the West's perennial dynamism as a culture, and why at times it presents such a confusing dual face to the rest of the world. The West has been compassionate, visionary, and creative during certain periods of history, yet dynamic, hardheaded, and imperialistic in others—even at the same time.

Its technologies have saved millions and killed hundreds of thousands of others at a single press of a button. Its theologies have inspired some of the greatest works in human history, and also burned helpless victims at the stake. Its ideologies have created the freest and most dynamic societies in the world, and also the most brutal tyrannies in the history of man.

Why? Much, if not all, the answer lies in the perpetual struggle bewtween Plato and Aristotle.

To a modern audience, permeated by the Internet and an ongoing cult of the new, they may seem dim, distant figures. In an age of political correctness, they are presented as the quintessential "dead white males" and apologists for slavery as well as the subjection of women.

This book will show that Plato and Aristotle are alive and all around us. Their influence is reflected in every activity and in every institution, including our universities and laboratories and governments, as well as on the Internet. They have taken us to the moon and probed the innermost secrets of the human heart. And contrary to modern misconception, their influence served to abolish slavery, not only in the West but around the world, and to grant equality to women.

It is the greatest intellectual and cultural journey in history. Yet it all began in a jail cell, twenty-five centuries ago.

THE
CAVE
AND
THE
LIGHT

After Jacques-Louis David, *The Death of Socrates*

One

THE FIRST PHILOSOPHER

True philosophers make dying their profession.

—Socrates

They were young and free, and did not like to think of him in prison.

They had visited with him until late the previous evening. Then, before the sun was up, they gathered again near the courthouse at the foot of the Acropolis and stood shivering in the predawn gloom.

The jail porter greeted them with a solemn face. Their hearts sank as he said:

"The Eleven"—those were the Athenian judicial officials—"are taking off his chains, and giving orders that he is going to die today."

Grief-stricken, the young men stumbled down the damp stone steps to their teacher's cell. Inside was a small, strongly built squat man with a white beard, bald pate, and pug nose. He was sitting on his narrow bed, rubbing his legs where the shackles had been. Despite his impending death sentence, he looked calm and collected. In the opposite corner of the cell was his wife. She was surprisingly young, with a small boy on her knee. It was the prisoner's son, even though the prisoner was seventy years old.

His name was Socrates.

When the younger men appeared, the woman sprang to her feet. On the verge of hysteria, she blurted out: "Oh, Socrates, this is the last time that you will converse with your friends, or they with you." Then she burst into tears.

The squat old man spoke calmly to the leader of the group and he gestured toward his wife, Xanthippe.

"Critias," Socrates said, "let someone take her home." One of Critias's slaves took Xanthippe away as she wept unconsolably.

Watching her leave, Socrates smiled with a serene expression that amazed Critias and the others. They were struck with how "the Master seemed quite happy," as one of them said later, and how he seemed to face certain death "nobly and fearlessly."

His students knew Socrates had been convicted by a jury of his peers of blasphemy and "corrupting the youth of Athens." But they also knew that the charge had been politically motivated and the conviction a foregone conclusion. They knew Socrates's real crime had been daring to think for himself and convincing others to do the same.

All the same, his calmness—his cheerfulness, almost—in the face of death made them uneasy. When they finally asked why he was so relaxed, Socrates gave them his answer.

"The real philosopher has reason to be of good cheer when he is about to die," he said, especially since "he has the desire for death all his life long."

They asked what he meant. So he told them.

It was a story some had heard from Socrates many times before. It was about how if a man freed himself from the distractions and false pleasures of the body, and dedicated himself single-mindedly to the pursuit of truth, he must eventually find his elusive quarry.

It was a story about how everything that exists in the world we see, taste, feel, and hear is only an imperfect copy or reflection of a much higher reality, a realm of perfect standards of all the virtues, including manliness, health, strength, and beauty, and absolute justice and goodness as well.[1]

These absolute ideal standards constitute "the essence or true nature of everything," Socrates told them. They shared a perfection with our own soul. All the same, grasping that higher reality is not easy.

By now his disciples had found seats around the cell or leaned against the wall, eager to hear more.

"When using the sense of sight or hearing or some other sense," Socrates explained, "the soul is dragged by the body into the realm of the changeable, and wanders and is confused." However, when the soul returns to reflect upon its own nature, "then she passes into the other world, the region of purity, and eternity, and immortality, and unchangeableness, which are her kindred, and with them she ever lives. . . . And this state of the soul," he concluded, "is called wisdom."

It was this wisdom, he went on, that made possible the practice of courage and self-control and goodness, because in this state the soul rules the body just as the gods rule the lives of men. For, Socrates pointed out, "the soul is the very likeness of the divine, and immortal, and intellectual, and indissoluble and always good, while the body is the very likeness of the human, and mortal, and multi-form and changeable, and prone to evil."[2]

This meant that no soul, including his own, could achieve the highest wisdom and virtue as long as it was encumbered by its physical body.

Therefore, this life "is a sort of pilgrimage," Socrates had told the jury of his fellow Athenians before they sentenced him to death. On that journey, the "soul is a helpless prisoner," Socrates now told Crito and the others, "chained hand and foot in the body, compelled to view reality not directly but through its prison bars, and wallowing in utter ignorance."

Now that he was about to die, Socrates said, he could look forward to meeting the True, the Good, and the Beautiful as they really were, in the invisible world of perfection. Just as the jailer had released the shackles that bound his legs, so death would free his soul from its body altogether. Finally he would find the knowledge he had sought all his life as a lover of wisdom, or (literally in Greek) as a *philosopher*.

Outside the cell, the dawn had heaved itself into day. Normal life in Athens had begun. Farmers were gathering in the marketplace to sell their olives, figs, and other produce; goats and small boys were running underfoot; fishermen were hauling out their baskets of fish down at the harbor of Piraeus. Beneath the Acropolis and the temple to Athena, men and women were setting out their wares outside shop doors and artisans' studios. Litigants were running to present their cases to the law courts; priests were preparing their sacrifices at the Parthenon and other temples on the Acropolis mount. Wealthy citizens walked arm in arm, trying to decide how to amuse themselves for the day; and old men found seats for themselves in the shade to escape the noonday sun.

Inside Socrates's cell, however, all was dark and silent as they contemplated a wisdom beyond this world and a life beyond death.

Still his disciples were astounded. How could a man like Socrates, the wisest and gentlest and happiest they had ever known, accept the end of life so willingly? Surely he knew, they protested, that he had been wrongly prosecuted, that he was the innocent victim of a vendetta directed at a ring of pro-Spartan collaborators, including his former student Alcibiades, once the glamour boy of Athenian politics and now disgraced as a traitor. His friend Crito had even told him they were ready to bribe his guard and get him out of prison to escape a death sentence he knew was unjust.

But Socrates had just smiled and shook his head. To break the law, he told Crito, *even a law that he knew was unjust*, would be wrong. As he told his disciples many times, "one must not do wrong even when one is wronged."[3] By doing wrong, a man did injury to his soul. Doing right, by contrast, makes his soul healthy and strong. A life of virtue is a life without compromise, Socrates believed, in which the goal is perfection according to an eternal standard.

Besides, "do you imagine that a city can continue to exist and be turned upside down, if the legal judgements which are pronounced in it have no force but are nullified and destroyed by private persons?"[4] A true philosopher knows that one's country is to be valued and held more holy than any father or mother or ancestor. Its laws must be treated as sacred.

No, Socrates concluded. A man who had devoted himself to freeing his mind and soul from the distractions of the body, who had labored to "deck his soul with self-control, and goodness, and courage, and liberality, and truth," was bound to wait for death not with fear, "but with pleasure. Fair is the prize, and hope great!"[5]

The disciples had listened with quiet attention. They had listened so long, in fact, that they failed to notice that the sun had nearly set. The moment they dreaded had come.

"We shall try our best as you have taught, " Crito finally blurted, "but how shall we bury you?"

"Any way you like," Socrates joked, "but you must get hold of me, and take care that I do not run away from you," meaning that his soul was about to depart for a higher and better world.

Socrates wandered into an adjacent room to take a final bath so that his body would not have to be washed before burial, as was the Greek custom. When he returned, he found his jailer waiting for him.

The man had come to say good-bye and to apologize for Socrates's incarceration. "I have come to know during this time," he said with great emotion, "that you are the noblest and gentlest and bravest of all men that have ever come here, and now especially I am sure you are not angry with me, because you know who is responsible." Then the jailer burst into tears and walked away.[6]

Socrates was moved and turned back to the others, many of whom were also on the verge of tears. "How generous of him to shed tears for me," he exclaimed with genuine pleasure. "But now, Crito, let us do as he says. Someone had better bring in the poison, if it is prepared."

Then the man in charge of administering the poison, made from the juice of the hemlock plant, appeared. This was a standard form of Athenian execution; jars of hemlock were even kept at the ready at the courthouse, in case some passerby decided to take his own life.

The man handed Socrates the lethal dose in a cup.

"You have only to walk about until your legs are heavy," he said, "and then lie down, and the poison will act."

Socrates took the cup "quite readily and cheerfully," one of the disciples remembered, and drained it in a single motion.

Now his visitors, who had held back their tears, exploded in a flood of wails and lamentation. "What is this strange outburst," Socrates admonished them. "I sent away the women mainly in order that they might not misbehave in this way. Be quiet, then, and have patience."

This calmed his disciples, and the tears and cries ceased. Socrates matter-of-factly walked up and down the room for a few minutes, then stopped.

"My legs are heavy," he announced, then lay back on the bed.

The man with the hemlock cup pinched Socrates's foot hard. He asked if Socrates felt anything.

"No," Socrates said. Then he slowly pulled his sheet over his face.

From time to time, the man checked to chart the poison's progress. When the numbness had spread to his waist, Socrates uncovered his face and said:

"Crito, I owe a cock to Asclepius. Will you remember to pay the debt?"

Crito swallowed hard. He knew this was Socrates's final gesture of contempt for death. Asclepius, the god of medicine, normally received a sacrifice from those who had been suddenly cured of disease. It was Socrates's way of announcing that he had finally been cured of life, meaning life in a world filled with lies and illusion.

The world that had sentenced him to death.

Crito asked if Socrates wanted anything, but there was no answer. After a few minutes, he pulled back the sheet. Socrates's eyes stared back, unseeing. Slowly Crito closed his beloved teacher's eyes and mouth, and replaced the sheet.

A few days later, one of Socrates's friends asked Phaedo, an eyewitness: "Who was actually there?"

Phaedo, still shaken, pulled himself together and listed the names, including Crito and Apollodorus and half a dozen others. The friend asked about two more, Aristippus and Cleomdorus.

"No," Phaedo said, "they were said to be in Aegina."

"Anyone else?" the friend asked.

"I think that's about all."[7]

There was one name he did not mention. A disciple who was not present when the great Socrates died, on a summer day in "the year of Laches" in 399 before the Christian era. Someone who for reasons of illness missed the last dramatic moments of the "bravest and also the wisest and most upright man we knew in our time," as Phaedo put it, but who would spend the rest of his life making that man immortal.

His name was Plato.

Plato made Socrates into the single most influential thinker in history. The Socrates we meet in Plato's dialogues is indeed the first philosopher, the man who, as the Roman statesman Cicero said three centuries later, "pulled philosophy down from the heavens and sent it into the cities and homes of man." Socrates is why we still praise the power of reason in human affairs today: a power we praise more than we practice. And the fact is, we know a lot more about Socrates as a historical figure than about his famous disciple.

We know, for example, Socrates was born in Athens in 470 BCE, nine years after Athens and the other Greek city-states decisively smashed the Persian invasion of their homeland at the battle of Plataea. We know he was the son of Sophroniscus, a man of considerable stature in his *deme* or district o

Athens (the old story that Socrates was the son of a stonecutter seems to be largely untrue), and a woman of good family named Phaenarete, whom Plato says in the dialogue *Theaetetus* enjoyed fame as a midwife.

By every account, Socrates was a typical Athenian in habits and outlook. He obeyed its laws; he attended its religious festivals; he voted and served on trial juries (in Athens a jury might number in the hundreds). He married an Athenian woman, Xanthippe, who bore him a son and two children who were infants in arms when he died—perhaps surprising for a man approaching seventy. He was also intimate with some of Athens's most blue-blooded families, a fact that ultimately sealed his doom.

Still, for all his learning and intelligence and sophisticated circle of friends, Socrates remained a hometown boy. Athens was all the world he needed to see and experience. As he tells us in the *Crito*, he had never left the city's environs, not even to visit Delphi or attend the Olympic games, until in middle age compulsory military service in the Peloponnesian War took him to northern Greece.[8]

In Socrates's day, Athens was Greece's largest city. It was rich, sophisticated, and commercially active. After the defeat of the Persians, it became the deadly rival of fellow Greek city Sparta. Like Elizabethan England or Gupta India, Athens in the fifth century BCE witnessed intellectual ferment and pathbreaking creativity in the arts—but also great violence and ruthless conquest. It was the home of dramatists Euripides, Sophocles, Aristophanes, and Aeschylus, as well as the statesman Pericles and the sculptor Phidias, principal decorator of Athens's temple to its patron goddess, Athena, the Parthenon.

But those were also the years of the Peloponnesian War (431–404). It was the Great War of the Greek city-states, except it lasted a quarter century. It saw Athens and Sparta clash for hegemony of the eastern Mediterranean with hoplite armies and fleets of warships, until the war devoured Athens's power and prestige. It wiped out a Lost Generation of Athenian citizens and shattered the city's confidence in its own institutions, including its democracy— the freest form of government on the planet.

Socrates lived through it all and saw it all. When he was born, Sophocles and the great Pericles were still very young men, and when the Peloponnesian War broke out, Socrates was already forty.

By then, Socrates was something of a minor celebrity in Athens. He became the subject of an early play by the satirist Aristophanes called *The Clouds*, which shows him as a teacher surrounded by his disciples much as

Plato's dialogues do, but which also casts him as a bit of a quack. Socrates is a leading character in the writings of another Athenian, the soldier and author Xenophon, who composed a *Symposium* and an *Apology* to set beside the more famous ones by Plato.

We even know what Socrates looked like: short, squat, and physically robust. Quite apart from his active military service,[9] we see him in Plato's *Symposium* drinking all the younger men under the table. He famously lacked the conventional masculine beauty so prized by Athenians. His homely appearance was the frequent butt of jokes, including his own.

Finally, we know Socrates was sentenced to death for blasphemy and corrupting Athens's young men, just as Plato described; and that the sentence was largely trumped up for political reasons. Thanks to modern archaeology, we think we even know where his prison cell was (on the east side of the city, not far from the Areopagus) and where the hemlock was stored that ultimately sent him to his death.

In short, Socrates is a vivid historical figure, foursquare and three-dimensional. Plato is another matter.

Even the name is not his real one. His given name was Aristocles. Plato, from the Greek for "wide" or "broad," was probably a family nickname. Did Plato have a weight problem? No one knows. His life before the age of sixty is a virtual blank.[10] What evidence there is suggests he was born around 428–27 BCE and that noble blood flowed through his veins. His father, Ariston, could trace his family lineage back to the old kings of Athens, long before democracy was established in the city. Ariston died when his son was still very young. Plato's stepfather, in whose house Plato was raised, seems to have been a conscientious and civic-minded politician, but without Ariston's social pedigree. Neither man is mentioned in any of their son's writings.

Plato's mother, Perictione, on the other hand, came from a family active in the highest levels of Athenian politics for more than two hundred years. Her great-uncle had even been an intimate of the great Solon, Athenian democracy's George Washington and Thomas Jefferson rolled into one. Solon may be the inspiration for Plato's ideal rulers described in his *Republic*, the so-called Philosopher Rulers. Certainly having a family connection to Athens's most revered statesman was something in which Plato could take pride, unlike his stepfather's connections to the politician Plato most detested—namely, Pericles.

Yet beyond this we know almost nothing about Plato except for what he

tells us in passing in his writings.* Apart from a handful of letters written
when he was a very old man, those writings focus almost exclusively on the
figure of Socrates, his friend and teacher. Since Socrates was on close terms
with Plato's uncle Charmides and Plato's mother's cousin Critias, Plato probably knew the philosopher most of his life. Socrates became his mentor, his
role model. He was certainly a surrogate father. Yet Plato himself never appears in any of his dialogues, just as he was absent from the most important
scene of all, the death of Socrates.

The twenty-eight dialogues are Plato's tribute to his dead friend and
teacher. Each is set and organized like a play. Athens was home to many great
literary dramatists: Aeschylus, Sophocles (author of *Oedipus Rex*, the world's
first detective mystery), and Euripides. Plato is not far behind. However, what
makes the dialogues such exciting reading (and I read my first one, the
Laches, when I was still in grade school), and what has made them so influential, isn't just Plato's literary and dramatic flair.

It is also their leading character, Socrates: the first philosopher and first
intellectual hero. Plato made him as vivid as any figure from literature and
used him to open a new chapter in the Greek world's unprecedented effort to
understand the world and reality through the use of reason.

---

*Or what his former students tell us, above all Aristotle.

Two

THE SOUL OF REASON

The soul is like an eye: when it sees that on which truth and Being shine, the soul perceives and understands, and is radiant with intelligence.

—Plato, *Republic*, Book VI

The adventure began more than one hundred years before Socrates's birth, in the sun-baked commercial town of Miletus on the coast of Asia Minor, or modern-day Turkey. In about 585 BCE, a man named Thales amazed his fellow Milesians by correctly predicting an eclipse of the sun. A few years earlier or later (the record is scanty and unclear), Thales also made a trip to Egypt, where he calculated the height of a pyramid by measuring the length of its shadow at the same time of day that his own shadow equaled his actual height.[1]

With these two feats, Thales signaled a major change in Greek thinking and world thinking. A new, rational way of understanding reality was born, as opposed to one tied to myth or religious ritual—as still prevailed in two much older civilizations, Egypt and Babylon. It was a major shift, and a radical one. Quite suddenly, Greeks of the sixth century BCE lost faith in the ancient legends about the origins of the world told by Homer, Hesiod, and other early poets; about how Uranus had fathered the Titans with Mother Earth and how the Titans fought and lost to Zeus and the other gods for dominance of the world. They no longer seemed believable; they even seemed deliberately misleading (one reason Plato bans poets from his *Republic*). Instead, the question that every Greek sage before Socrates wanted to answer was: "What is *real* about reality?" More specifically, what is the stuff from which everything else in the world is made?

Thales and his fellow pre-Socratics, as they are called, came up with a variety of answers, some more speculative than others. Only fragments of their words have survived. Reconstructing their thought process involves a certain amount of guesswork. But almost all agreed that water, air, fire, and earth were the key constituents of material reality—although which came first, or which held sway over the others,* was a matter of long and intense debate. Thales himself opted for water as the first element from which all things, even the sun and stars, were made (a notion he may have picked up from Egyptian cosmology).[2] Anaximenes proposed air instead.

Democritus and Leucippus were willing to take another tack. They insisted that all four elements, and everything else, were actually made up from tiny indivisible particles they called *atoms*—an astonishing anticipation of the modern atomic theory to come twenty-four centuries later.[3] At the time, however, the atomists were only one more voice in the fierce debate over the true nature of reality, which still raged when Socrates was growing up.

In the end, two theories stood out, each in direct opposition to the other. As it happened, both would decisively affect Socrates's views and Plato's.

Heraclitus is the wild card of the pre-Socratic pack. Other Greek thinkers wanted to find some fixed principle around which a stable, predictable way to understand reality could be built (especially the Pythagoreans, about whom we will say more later). Heraclitus threw out the whole concept of stability. His mottoes "War is the father of all things," "Strife is justice," and "Good and evil are one" show just what he thought of most men's desire for a peaceful, harmonious life and a harmonious universe.

Instead of stability, Heraclitus said, there is only change: ceaseless, relentless, and without end. In the desperate watercourse of existence, any notion

---

*Thales's pupil Anaximander, for example, seems to have considered the balance among the four elements as a matter of proportion and cosmic justice. It may be the first time proportion and justice were linked in Greek thought.

we have of permanent or fixed values, even of our own body, is pure illusion. Instead, everywhere we look, everything we see is in constant flux and change. "The world is a living fire," Heraclitus is supposed to have said, while his most famous sayings of all, "All things change" (*Panta rhei*) and "You cannot step into the same river twice," make him the father of relativism: a relativism that teeters on the brink of embracing chaos.[4]

On the brink, but not quite. The one principle Heraclitus did embrace was that of the *Logos*, which can be variously translated as the Word or the Spirit or the Reason or even the Way—in fact, the parallels between Heraclitus's *Logos* and the Chinese Tao are striking. By following the *Logos*, Heraclitus affirmed, which he saw as a kind of spark or breath (*psyche* in Greek) that resides in each of us as individuals and also permeates the world, we can achieve peace. For Heraclitus, the discovery that nothing is permanent was meant to be a source not of nihilistic despair but of understanding, as we come to realize that the physical reality around us—buildings, trees, mountains, other people, the entire works—is not actually "real" at all, but merely the playing out of opposites, "an attunement of opposite tensions, like a bow or lyre."

Heraclitus's theory of the *Logos*, his cryptic sayings (which resemble those of the famous Oracle at Delphi, revealing how much philosophy and religion were still intermingled), and his love of paradox earned wide respect, if not exactly acceptance. They were so clever, in fact, that the only way to answer the Heraclitean riddle of existence seemed to be to challenge its entire foundation. This another thinker from one of the Greek cities in southern Italy, Elea, proceeded to do during Socrates's own lifetime. His name was Parmenides, and in answer to Heraclitus's claim that *everything* changes, Parmenides countered by arguing that *nothing* changes.

Far from permanency being an illusion, as Heraclitus claimed, it is *change* that is the illusion. To do this, Parmenides scrapped the whole elusive search for the first of the four elements. Everything that exists, he argued—air, fire, and the rest—forms a single perfect whole. We watch the boy grow into a young man and then grow old and die, but it is still the same man. We watch the leaf on the tree turn from green to brown, but it is still the same leaf. Even when it falls to the ground and withers and crumbles, it never becomes *nothing*. It is still part of a reality that to our imperfect eyes and ears seems full of change and transformation, but which our reason realizes is never changing at all, since Being as such is all there is. Try to think of Non-Being—that is

Nothing. It's impossible: we live in a world in which "No Thing" can never exist.[5] Hence our own experience teaches us that Being, which is the opposite of Nothing, actually unites everything: "complete, immovable, and without end."[6]

Two powerful early thinkers; two mutually exclusive views of reality and the world. Yet it was Socrates's, and Plato's, great accomplishment to combine these two views into one and give birth to history's first great rational system.

Socrates could do this because he starts with a different question from "What is real?" (although eventually he gets there, too). Socrates was the first also to ask: "What am I?"

That question touched a deep chord in the culture of his time. Every educated Greek was familiar with the cryptic commandment issued by the Oracle at Delphi: Know thyself. Socrates was merely asking the next obvious question. What is the self? Who is this self who is observing all this change going on around me—or, if I happen to be Parmenides, the lack of change? Who is it who watches the birds and stars and changing seasons, who predicts eclipses and propounds theories about fire and water, and who tames horses and trains dogs but greets other men as creatures like himself?

Socrates's answer was astonishing. As far as we know, it was without precedent.[7] It was that this "I" was a soul, something existing apart from my body, which was the true seat of normal waking intelligence and moral character: "my" fundamental identity, in fact. The word Socrates used for this soul, *psyche*, or "breath," was a common one in Greek. Homer and other poets had used it for that part of the human being which survives death and passes into the underworld (Odysseus meets many of them, including those of dead friends, when he visits the underworld in the *Odyssey*).

Still, Socrates gave the term a new status and importance. He may have borrowed Heraclitus's notion of *psyche* as sharing the same essential nature as the *Logos* that permeates the world. In any case, it was a surprising twist for the thought of the time, which was still obsessed with unlocking the secrets of physical material reality. His fellow Greeks and Athenians were astonished to be told that this *psyche* was far more important than the body, and was the original home of man's moral and intellectual faculties.[8] All the same, the idea soon caught fire. Thanks to Plato, Socrates's notion of the individual rational soul would become an integral part of Western thinking for the next two thousand years.

"The idea of man," wrote Plotinus, one of Plato's most distinguished disciples, three hundred years after his death, "is formed after that which is the prevailing and best part of him," namely his soul.[9] This assumption bridged the classical culture of the Greek and Roman world and the Christian culture of the Middle Ages. It permeated the humanism of the Italian Renaissance and animated the great debates of the Reformation and the early modern era. Even today, when scientists try to reduce all forms of consciousness to bioneural states, the existence of the self remains an elusive mystery. From every angle—historical, philosophical, religious, and cultural—the soul of Socrates is the starting point for everything to come.

To be a human is to have a soul, Socrates and Plato tell us. Our soul is our true essence, our true identity. It is the soul that actively seeks to unlock the mysteries of the world, including the truth about reality.

Reality turns out to have a dual nature. Yes, Socrates said, the world is one of constant change and flux: as Heraclitus said, that's the visible world around us. In Socrates's and Plato's terms, it's the world of Becoming. But there is also a realm of Permanence that Parmenides described, a higher reality that we grasp not through our senses, but through our reason alone. This is the world of Being, which is divine, "the realm of the pure and everlasting and immortal and changeless," just as Socrates told visitors in his prison cell.[10]

Our soul serves as the essential bridge between these two worlds. Like Being, it is (Socrates says) immortal and rational. But it also dwells in the world of Becoming, because of its adherence to the body. On one side of the bridge lies a world of error and illusion; on the other, of wisdom and truth. Yet for most people—indeed, for all but a very few people—that bridge has been washed out.

Here the metaphor Plato preferred was not that of a bridge but that of a cave. It appears for the first time in Book VII of his most famous dialogue, the *Republic*, although there is a foreshadowing of it in the *Phaedo*, where the condemned Socrates compares the soul of the ordinary man to someone viewing existence "through the bars of a prison . . . and wallowing in utter ignorance."[11] Indeed, the cave is like Socrates's own cell, a place of confinement from which we seek to be set free. The only question is how to do it.

For nearly forty years before his death, Socrates wandered through the streets of Athens and its marketplace, the Agora, with his students in tow, talking and arguing. He showed them that the people of Athens, like people everywhere, were badly confused about their own values and virtues. Socrates had revealed generals who could not define courage (in the *Laches*), good friends who could not define friendship (in the *Lysis*), religious men who could not define piety (in the *Euthyphro*), and political experts who could not define justice (in the *Gorgias*). Even those who were paid to think about and teach such lofty matters, the so-called Sophists, some of whom made immense fortunes in Athens as political consultants, turned out to have no clearer idea of what constituted true wisdom than ordinary citizens.

"It seemed to me," Socrates would say, "that the people with the greatest reputations were the ones who were most deficient [in true knowledge], while others who were supposed to be their inferiors were much better in practical intelligence."[12] No wonder Socrates roused the ire of his fellow Athenians!

Socrates had taken his students into the streets of Athens. Today, we just have to turn on the TV news or E! TV. Everywhere we look, we see mediocrity, stupidity, and base selfishness of the most embarrassing kind. But Socrates was compassionate as well as shrewd. If human beings do not understand the true nature of things, and principles like beauty and justice and goodness, he explained, then no one can expect them to live by those principles in their own lives. The world we live in, in other words, is a world created by our systematic ignorance—and our unwillingness to see things as they really truly are.

The metaphor of the cave explains how this works. It occurs in Book VII of Plato's *Republic*, where Socrates describes the world around us as a darkened cavern, across the back of which a puppet show is flashed with the figures of men, animals, and objects cast as shadows. For a modern audience, the description has an eerily familiar ring. It's the world of television and the media at its most flimsy and superficial.

Imagine, Socrates says, that everyone inside the cave had been born there and had been forced to watch the puppet show since birth without being allowed to take their eyes off the screen. "If they were able to talk to one another," Socrates asks his listeners, "would they not assume that the shadows they saw were the real things?"

"Inevitably," his young student, Glaucon, replies.

"And so in every way they would believe that the shadows of the objects we mentioned were the whole truth."

"Yes, inevitably," Glaucon says.

We can imagine Socrates now leaning forward and speaking very softly.

"Then think what would happen to them if they were released of their bonds and cured of their delusions," he says. Imagine one of them suddenly slipping his bonds and seeing for the first time the lights used to make the shadow play. Think how they would dazzle him and make him doubt his own eyes.

And then if he were told "what he used to see was so much empty nonsense and that he was now nearer reality and seeing more correctly," would he immediately affirm the truth? Or is it more likely that he would return with relief to the original shadows as his familiar "reality" even though he has just learned they are only illusions flashing across the screen of consciousness?[13]

For Glaucon, the answer is easy. Most people retreat from uncomfortable truths about themselves. They dismiss these occasional insights into reality ("I'm wasting my time playing video games all day" or "This job makes me a peddler of lies" or "Politics is a farce") as impractical or unrealistic and subside back into their mundane existence among the shadows in the cave.

So does Socrates's prisoner. But then, Socrates goes on, warming to his point, "what if he were forcibly dragged out into the sunlight?" There "he would be so dazzled he would be unable to see a single one of the things he was now told were real."

"Certainly not at first," Glaucon adds.

"Because of course he would need to grow accustomed to the light before he could see things in the upper world outside the cave," Socrates says. But gradually he would begin to see clearly, and see things as they are for the first time. First he would make out the heavenly bodies and the stars at night, then the moon, and finally the sun itself. After a time, he would be able to "gaze at it without using reflections in water or any other medium, but as it is itself"—and realize it is the source of all true light and reality.

And having seen the light of the sun and the truth, Plato has Socrates say, "when he thought of his original home" in the cave, "and what passed for wisdom there . . . don't you think he would congratulate himself on his good fortune?" He would never again be satisfied with that illusory world; he would never rest again until he finally reached the ultimate source of all reality: the Good in Itself.[14]

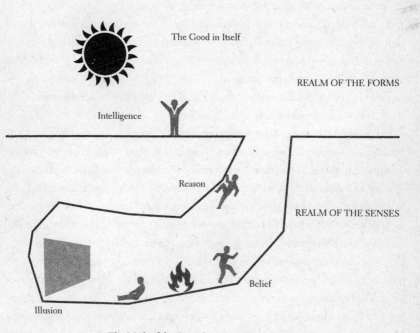

The Myth of the Cave, from *Republic*, Book VII

· · ·

It was a startling, even puzzling concept, then as now. When we say, "I just played a good game of tennis," and, "Our company's prospects are good," and, "He's been a good husband," does the use of the word *good* in all those statements have something in common? Most would say no, if we think about it at all.

Socrates, however, says yes. For Socrates and for Plato, finding what they do have in common, that single standard of excellence they all share, is what true knowledge is all about. For every quality in life—goodness, justice, courage, beauty, loyalty—there has to exist a single standard, a model of perfection of which, Socrates says, "all equal objects of sense . . . are only imperfect copies."[15] This model naturally stands apart from its many individual instances in the world, since it is the standard by which we judge all individual instances—which are only pale, dim copies, like shadows in a cave.

How do we discover that standard? We could look at all the different examples of courage or beauty or loyalty and try to find out what they have in common (that's the "inductive method"). Or we can save time by realizing that all of them reflect to a greater or lesser degree a single ideal of perfection, which is impossible to know through our senses, but is knowable through the soul of reason. If we can concentrate our minds instead on that higher standard, or what Socrates calls the *Idea* or *Form* of that virtue, defined as Courage or Beauty or Justice in Itself—or even Goodness, which is the highest Form of all, setting the standard of perfection for all the rest—then true wisdom will be ours.

For Plato, then, all certain knowledge requires an element of abstraction from concrete reality. Through Socrates, Plato tells us to constantly reach for the highest level of knowledge beyond mere individual examples, toward a universal standard for judgment that will give us a stronger, more confident position for acting in the world. Our slogan should be "Where there's a Good and a Better, there must be a Best." And when we finally reach the Best that sets the standard for all the others, Plato says, we've entered the realm of the Forms.

The Greek word he has Socrates use for these Forms or ideal models is *idean*, or ideas (sometimes he also uses *eidos*, a mold or form—which is the term most scholars use in English).[16] For centuries philosophers have worn themselves out, and their readers, debating whether the Forms are really

Socrates's idea (sorry) or Plato's, and what Plato "really" meant by insisting that these Forms were the true objects of knowledge. In the *Parmenides*, a youthful Socrates is even asked: Are there *Idean* for the opposites of Beauty and Goodness as well, which we must also seek to know in order to understand Ugliness and Evil? Are there ideal forms of Man, or even Mud and Hair?

Plato has Socrates admit he doesn't know. Perhaps at a certain level he didn't care. What mattered most to Plato, and to us, is not what the Forms are but what they are *not*. They are *not* just collective definitions (like the famous example "A man is a featherless biped") or universal propositions ("All men are featherless bipeds"). The Forms have a real existence, Plato tells us in the dialogues, but outside time and space. They are *not* part of the realm of the senses or the world we normally describe as reality. They are the models from which that world is built; so they must be prior to, and higher than, that world we engage in on a daily basis.

They are also what keep us from sinking into that world. Plato's Forms keep us from becoming absorbed into the Heraclitean flux of daily phenomena that appear and disappear from our consciousness with pointless persistence—in short, the world of the cave or what we see on CNN and E! TV. By remaining eternal and unchanging, the Forms offer us the light and power of permanence.

And far from being a crutch or an intellectual convenience, Plato's Forms are remarkably *inconvenient*. They remind us that there is always a higher standard, a model of excellence by which everything we do or say or encounter must be measured—and inevitably be found wanting. At one level, we all become Platonists when we are conscious of our own shortcomings and weaknesses. We move through life aware we could be, or should be, someone different: someone more honest, more courageous, more compassionate. In Plato's terms, this higher self is our own soul reflected in the light of the Forms.

The American satirist H. L. Mencken once said that conscience is the voice that says, "Someone might be looking." For Plato, that someone is the higher self. We may resent its presence, but it's hard to ignore. Being true to that self, the soul, means living up to those models of perfection in thought, word, and action.

This is hard, because they are by definition invisible to our ordinary senses. For Plato, what makes the Forms invisible is their flawless perfection, requiring perception by an equally pure receptor, namely the soul. Their knowledge comes to us instead in a kind of introspective mental seeing in which clarity and truth suddenly come together as one. As Socrates observes in the *Phaedo*, "If the thing is plain and clear, then there is no need to look further."[17]

Now, it is clear that Plato himself had an incredibly vivid imagination. It is reflected in his powerful use of imagery, allegory, and metaphor in all his dialogues. No one should be surprised that he should think it possible to perceive a thing through the eye of the mind and perceive it as true. He did *not* go to the next step, however, of arguing that whatever is vivid and clear must therefore also be true. He was not what philosophers call an intuitionist; but he will point many followers from Plotinus to René Descartes down that road in the future.[18] It is one of the major points that will separate Plato from his Neoplatonist imitators. All the same, they form part of Plato's legacy, and their pictures belong next to his in the Platonist family album.

No one can ever know true Justice or Beauty in his mortal lifetime. He can, however, make the search for that higher knowledge his life's work, just as Socrates did. He can be a lover of wisdom or *philosopher* in the truest, widest sense—even if that love is always, until our final breath, unrequited. As a result, the life devoted to reason can take on an almost heroic dimension. The shining reflected light of the Forms, in the words of the great Plato scholar Benjamin Jowett, comes to fill "not only the intellect, but the whole man."[19]

By talking this way, Plato and Socrates compelled their fellow Greeks to confront a crucial question: What is the good life? By what standards do we arrange our conduct and judge that of others so that we earn the plaudits not just of the crowd, but of ourselves? How do we achieve that sense of inner well-being that the Greeks called *eudaimonia* and we call happiness: the sense of waking every morning and facing the world with confidence, energy, and expectation rather than loathing and dread?

The standard Greek answer was that the key to happiness was cultivating virtues like courage, wisdom, and justice. How do we get those virtues? Plato gives his answer through Socrates: through knowledge of the Forms. Just as there are many chairs, there are many acts of charity; and just as there is only one "real" chair, its ideal Form, there can be only one ideal standard of charity, by which we measure all the imperfect copies.[20] The Forms reveal to us what a true equilateral triangle looks like, or a perfect game of tennis, or a perfectly turned urn, so that we can judge the less-than-perfect examples in our midst. However, they also teach us what loyalty is, as well as disloyalty, and allow us to understand the true nature of justice and laws. They lead us to do what we *know* is right and to avoid doing what is clearly wrong—in short, to make virtue an exact science.

This point is fundamental for Plato and his legacy to the West. Knowledge is always the prerequisite of virtue, just as ignorance always leads us into evil. For Plato and all Platonists who come after him, grasping a standard of perfection is what we need in order to be virtuous and ultimately happy.

But how do we that? Especially since, as we have seen, the Forms do not exist in time and space, and none of us ever really knows them until we are dead.

In fact, Plato says, it's easier than we think. We (or rather our immortal part, the soul) have actually met all the Forms before, in the afterlife. Plato was a firm believer in the theory of transmigration of souls, and another key dialogue, the *Meno*, aims to convince the reader that all knowledge is actually a process of recollection. This is why sometimes we seem to know the answer to a question before we're finished asking it—just as the slave boy in the *Meno* is able, with Socrates's prompting, to figure out for himself that the area of a square is proportional to the second power of the length of the sides.

Yet Socrates "tells" him nothing. The working of the boy's own reason fills in the gaps and makes the connections, "for seeking and learning are in fact nothing but recollection."[21] The reason is, Socrates suggests, that his soul and ours knew it all along before we were born. We just need a refresher course to jog our postnatal memory.

Still, even if we accept Plato's reincarnation of souls, the effort to present all knowledge as a matter of déjà vu seems unconvincing. It works best with mathematical proofs, as in the *Meno*. But Socrates also supplies a surefire method for "recovering" that knowledge lost at birth—to grasp truth as if we knew it all along. That is, through questioning and applying reason to the answers. This is the Socratic method, which Socrates used first to test our ignorance ("What is friendship?") and then to present a solution to our ignorance. The Greek name for Socrates's method is *elenchus*, which means a test or trial. Later, Plato elaborated the method into a formal procedure, a kind of sustained mental workout for the soul to prepare it to receive the truth, called the *dialectic*.

Plato was not the first Greek to see thinking as a kind of winnowing process: of asking questions in order to get rid of what we know is false, so that what is left must be true.[22] However, he is the first to say that this process gets us to the one true Reality. The dialectic is in effect our ticket out of the cave. For example, we discover through dialectical reason that the husband who cheats on his wife, or the man who allows a friend to break the law, or the law that unfairly punishes the innocent, *can't* be good husbands or true friends or just laws by definition, since all three violate a higher standard our minds perceive as the essence of fidelity or friendship or justice. Dialectic teaches us that contradiction is the essence of the false, just as consistency with first principles is the essence of the true.*

For Plato, this kind of reasoning before getting enmeshed in the details of individual experience, or a priori reason, keeps the illusions and imprecisions of one part of daily experience (just ask anyone trying to pick out a mugger in a police lineup) from distracting us from a higher perfection. And the process of distinguishing the false from the true is made easier when we assume, as Plato does, that our reasoning self—the soul—shares the same perfection for which we want to strive.

"When one tries to get at what each thing is in itself," Plato has Socrates say in the *Republic*, by asking the inconvenient questions, sifting through the answers, and "relying on reason without any aid from the senses," then he has mastered the dialectic. He will stand "at the summit of the intellectual realm," just like the man who stood on the mountaintop after escaping from the cave and saw the sun, and see "the Good in Itself" by an act of pure thought.[23] Not only will he know the truth, he will be prepared to act on it. He will be ready to change the world in the light of truth and a higher reality.

Still, for Socrates himself, the final escape from the cave comes only with death. The soul is finally free of the imperfections of the body and can reunite itself with all the categories of knowledge in their abstract perfection. In this sense, Socrates's philosopher truly does make "dying his profession" and death a joyous moment of release from ignorance as well as life.

In this, he may find others willing to help. Socrates asks Glaucon to imagine what others will say when the man who finally sees things in their true light returns to the cave, returns to the world of ignorance and illusion.

Wouldn't they say "that his visit to the upper world had ruined his sight, and that the ascent was not worth even attempting?"

---

*For example, the statement, "One of my black swans is white" is a clear contradiction in terms and obviously false, even if we've never met any of your swans.

Glaucon nods.

"And if anyone tried to release them and lead them up, they would try to kill him if they could lay their hands on him."

Glaucon seems to pause, and then says, "They certainly would."

Already, Plato hints, the hemlock is waiting.

The soul of reason. The light of truth. The path of dialectic leading to understanding, even of goodness itself. These are Plato's great ideals. Still, the Myth of the Cave reveals a bitter truth: Most people prefer life in the cave. The world and institutions around us reflect it—and as Glaucon realized, people get upset and even furious when someone challenges their fondest illusions— what Francis Bacon would call the Idols of the Tribe—especially if everything else is collapsing around them.

That sense of collapse came to Athens with the defeat by Sparta in the Peloponnesian War. As with the fall of France to the Nazis in 1940, the humiliating defeat brought into power collaborators with the victors, a junta of thirty pro-Spartan politicians known as the Thirty Tyrants. Most came from blue-blooded families. Critias, leader of the most radical pro-Spartan faction, was a cousin of Plato's mother. Her brother, Charmides, was one of the principal figures in the reign of terror that the Thirty Tyrants brought down on their democratic opponents.[24]

Socrates—the real Socrates, not the spokesman in Plato's dialogues— was caught in the crossfire. He knew many of the Thirty well. He was certainly no fan of the machine-style democratic politics Pericles had used to dominate Athens and which led the city into the disastrous war with Sparta in the first place. In the *Gorgias*, Plato even has Socrates say that Pericles made Athenians "idle, cowardly, talkative, and greedy"—a far cry from the kind of praise modern commentators usually heap on the father of Athenian democracy.

But Socrates drew the line when Critias and his colleagues began arresting and executing opponents without trial. He commented sardonically that he had never heard of a herdsman who took pride in thinning his own herd.[25] Even this mild criticism enraged the Thirty Tyrants, who turned against him. Later, they summoned him to lead a citizens' committee to arrest a former pro-democrat admiral, Leon of Salamis, on patently false charges. Socrates refused. "Powerful as it was," Socrates explained later, "the government could not terrify me into committing a wrong action."[26] Instead, he went home, fully expecting he would be arrested the next day.

Fate intervened—as it happened, fate with a cruel sense of humor. A fresh revolution came to Athens, and the Thirty Tyrants were swept from power. The hunters became the hunted, and those they had persecuted took over the city and launched a counterterror of their own. By his actions, Socrates should have been one of the revolution's heroes. But the democrats remembered only his earlier critiques of Athenian popular rule and his previous associations with some of the Thirty. Socrates made a convenient scapegoat, and the charges that he had "corrupted the youth of Athens" and trained traitors masked a desire for political vengeance.

The accusations were brought not by the Athenian government, but by three private citizens. Socrates tried to deflect their charges, including atheism and impiety, with his usual caustic sense of humor. He even suggested that his "punishment" should be receiving a pension from the city of Athens for services rendered: "for I spend all my time going about trying to persuade you, young and old, to make your first concern not your bodies or your possessions but the highest welfare of your souls" and teaching them that goodness is the true wealth both for the individual and for the state.[27]

The jury members were not amused. They chose to condemn to death the man who for decades had harassed and harried them with his inconvenient questions.

As the condemned man, Socrates spoke last. He remained quietly defiant. He warned the jury that his ultimate responsibility was not to them, but to his conscience, or what he called his "inner voice": his own soul. For his soul's sake, he would not stoop to servility in serving the Thirty Tyrants. Now he would not stoop to indignity by pleading for his life. "But I suggest, gentlemen, that the difficulty is not so much to escape death; the real difficulty is to avoid doing wrong, which is far more fleet of foot"—as their own verdict evidently proved.

As for death, Socrates told the jurors (in words that were probably as close as Plato came to giving an exact transcript of his master's words), "nothing can harm a good man either in life or after death; and his fortunes are not a matter of indifference to the gods." If Socrates was right, death would even be a blessing. "I [go] to die, and you live," he said as a farewell, "but which of us has the happier prospect is unknown to anyone but God."[28]

A month later he was dead.

Three

THE MIND OF GOD

God is always doing geometry.

— Saying attributed to Plato

Socrates insisted that it was better to suffer wrong than inflict it, and his last days proved it. It's why Cicero dubbed Socrates "the wisest and most upright of men" and why centuries later, Mahatma Gandhi took him as a personal role model and called him "a soldier for Truth." Socrates's quest to lead his fellow citizens to a higher vision of themselves and their society, while living that example himself, even when it cost him his life, raised him to the level of the heroic, where he has stayed more or less ever since.[1]

Plato, his heartbroken disciple, took things a step further. The fact that Athens had sentenced Socrates to death was more than an unjust act. It was final proof that human institutions were flawed by their nature, even those ostensibly concerned with democracy and justice, because they are all based on opinion and illusion. The fate of Socrates proved to Plato that true knowledge lay permanently beyond the reach of the masses. Indeed, as he implied in the Myth of the Cave, they are instinctively hostile toward its devotees. Truth on Plato's terms is destined to be a quarry reserved for a tiny minority, those trained in the rigors of dialectic and who are ready to make the same arduous climb out of the cave that Socrates made, in order to discover how to lead a virtuous life and show others how to do the same. For the purposes of this philosophical safari, he created his famed Academy in Athens, and composed his dialogues to serve as basic texts for his students. Through their dramatic settings and vivid characters, Plato turned Socrates's insights into a complete theory of ethics (as in the *Philebus*), of love and friendship (the *Symposium*), of language (the *Phaedrus*), and of politics (the *Gorgias* and *Republic*).

As one would expect from an Athenian, Plato returns to politics again and again. Even late in life when his own thinking had moved on to questions like the origin of the universe, he still found time to write about the practical side of running a fair and wise government in his *Laws*. The *Gorgias*, *Republic*, *Statesman*, and *Laws*: All reveal Plato's political thinking in different stages. The one common thread is Plato's desire to avoid the kind of disastrous democratic politics he had seen wreck Athens and kill his teacher. Politics on Plato's terms always involves the search for a foundation more elevated and certain than custom or public opinion or majority rule, because all of them reflect, to a greater or lesser degree, the realm of ignorance and error. It would be one of the major sources of conflict with his student Aristotle.*

Yet none of this—not even Plato's politics—would be possible, or even imaginable, without Plato's God.

Socrates talked a lot about God and the gods. He even told his jurors that "God orders me to fulfill the philosopher's mission of searching into myself and other men," and he seems to have believed that his inner voice that kept urging him to ask questions and seek knowledge was indeed the voice of God.[2] Ironically, one of the charges against Socrates was atheism. It was so evidently false that Socrates brushed aside the accusation. But the fact remains that Socrates's God was clearly very different from the ones ordinary Athenians were used to: Zeus, Apollo, and the other deities of the classical

*For more on Plato's politics, see chapter 5.

pantheon with their superhuman powers and more than human appetites and foibles. It was even different from the impersonal divine forces explored by secret societies like the Orphic and Pythian mystery cults.[3]

The God that Socrates presented to his disciples stood above and beyond the familiar myths and rituals. Socrates's God shares the same transcendent immortality as the soul and lies beyond all material space and time. He dwells naturally in the same afterlife as the Forms: indeed, Socrates's entire doctrine of recollection depends upon it.

In some of the later dialogues, Plato has Socrates give us a pretty clear picture of this afterlife.* At the end of the *Republic*, for example, he outlines how the just and the unjust receive their rewards and punishments after death, in which every wrong we have committed against others requires a tenfold punishment, and "those who are responsible for many deaths, for betraying a state or army, or have cast others into slavery" must pay ten times for each offense.[4]

Socrates describes souls on the march through a mighty chasm past judges and guardian spirits, who snatch away the guilty, skin them alive, and impale them on thorns along the roadside, prior to being cast into Tartarus, or hell. The souls of the just, by contrast, move across a meadow to a realm of splendor where they are assigned new bodies by lot, all under the dome of the sky supported on a "shaft of light stretching from above straight through heaven and earth, like a pillar [and] resembling a rainbow, only brighter and clearer."[5]

It is striking how much Plato's vision resembles later Christian accounts of heaven and hell; nor is it entirely coincidental. But serious questions remain about this afterlife, and the soul's place in it, that Socrates never answers. Plato's Socrates never takes time to flesh out the relationships between God and the soul, the afterlife and the Forms—and never explains how these Forms actually shape the material reality of appearances in this world.

Toward the end of his life, however, Plato himself did. And the answer he arrived at was so astonishing, so complex, and yet so persuasive that it formed the bedrock of Western religious *and* scientific thinking for the next thousand years. Without it, Christianity as we know it might not exist. Neither would modern physics or astronomy.

Plato's startling vision appears in the most enigmatic of his writings and

---

*Much of it, apparently, derived from the view of the underworld conveyed by the Orphic mystery cult.

one of his last: the *Timaeus*. It must have been written when he was seventy.[6] Compared with earlier dialogues, it is a strange, almost impenetrable work. The *Timaeus* is made even more mysterious because it opens with a long description of a lost civilization and a lost continent, which Plato called Atlantis. It's kindled the imagination of thinkers and writers—even moviemakers—ever since.* But Atlantis plays little part in the main thrust of the dialogue.

Like most of Plato's other late writings, the *Timaeus* pushes the figure of Socrates into the background. We have to assume that Plato is no longer giving an account of his teacher's doctrines, but reveals his own thoughts. In this case, Plato chooses a wandering scholar named Timaeus to act as his spokesman. Timaeus, as it happens, is from Italy—a crucial clue to understanding the radical new direction Plato's thought was about to take.

What Timaeus offers his listeners, and the reader, is nothing less than a complete account of the creation of the universe. It is a vision of creation (the Greek word is *genesis*) dominated by a rational God, acting as Supreme Creator. In the process, Plato demonstrates that the ideal Forms, the models of perfection out of which God has fashioned the visible world, are actually numbers. To do this, Plato turns to the most enigmatic of Socrates's predecessors, and the one whom Plato would make into the most influential of the pre-Socratics: the mystical mathematician Pythagoras.

By Plato's time, the name Pythagoras was already shrouded in legend. There is no doubt he had been an actual person, and although details of his life are skimpy, he was probably alive c. 530 BCE.[†] Apart from a few snippets preserved by other writers, absolutely nothing survives of his writings—assuming he wrote anything at all. However, we do know that while living in the Greek colonies of southern Italy, Pythagoras established a secret brotherhood of fellow mathematicians, who preserved his famous theorem (the one that the slave boy in the *Meno* discovers, with Socrates's help, that the square of the hypotenuse of any right-angle triangle is equal to the square of the opposite two sides), and his experiments in music theory. (Pythagoras was the

---

*For more on Atlantis, see chapter 4.

[†]According to Herodotus, he was born in Samos and fled to the city-state of Croton in southern Italy to escape the tyranny of his home island's ruler. In Croton, Pythagoras is said to have risen to a position of considerable authority, but eventually he was overthrown and left for Metapontium, where he died.

first to discover the mathematically proportioned intervals of the harmonic scale.) But above all, Pythagoras was convinced that number was the secret language of nature.[7]

Where did Pythagoras get this idea?

Possibly from the Babylonians, who were the masters of mathematics in the early ancient world. Perhaps also from the Egyptians, who pretty much invented geometry to survey and resurvey landholdings after periodic floodings of the Nile.[8] Pythagoras's contribution was to take their geometry (literally "earth measure") in a new, more abstract direction. He wanted to show that geometry was not just a way to measure things like land or build monuments like the Pyramids, but a way to understand the fabric of reality. "Figures as archetypes, not figures for profit," he is supposed to have said. The Pythagorean program was to prove that math and geometry are the starting points of Being itself, and that "all things are numbers."[9]

Pythagoras started with the number one—literally a pebble in the sand. One (the Monad) forms the starting point for all numbers and geometry, while two pebbles (the Dyad) generate the line and spatial extension—literally the base line of all subsequent forms.[10] Putting one and two together gives us three. The Triad serves as the three points of the triangle, Pythagoras's first geometric surface and (thanks to Pythagoras's theorem) the basis of the square and every other geometric figure.

Then Pythagoras added an imaginary fourth pebble standing above the other three. This creates the pyramid, or geometry's first solid form, as the relations between the numbers and their ratios move into the realm of three-dimensional actuality.[11] The number four also served for what later Pythagoreans called the Tetrad, the sign of harmonious completion. Just as four intervals form the musical scale, so there are four seasons in the year and so on.[12]

In the digital age, Pythagoras's belief in a number-generated reality might seem less far-fetched than it used to.[13] Plato certainly didn't find it far-fetched. By his time, a mathematician named Archytas was reviving the Pythagorean teachings at a school in Tarentum (modern-day Taranto), on the inside heel of the boot of south Italy. We know Plato went to Italy at about the same time and made contacts with members of Archytas's circle and learned of their

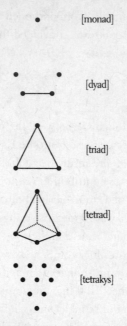

• [monad]

[dyad]

[triad]

[tetrad]

[tetrakys]

Pythagoras taught Plato that number was the language of nature.

belief that nature, like man himself, is governed by a permanent geometric and mathematical order.

It is also tempting to argue that what Plato found in Pythagoras was the kind of anchor that had been missing in his life with the death of Socrates.* In the world he knew, the values of the traditional Greek *polis* and city-state, and the moral and social consensus on which they rested, were falling apart. Everywhere Plato looked, he saw nothing but chaos and disorder.[14]

In Pythagoras, by contrast, he found a reassuring vision of the opposite: a mathematically harmonious cosmic order. After his Pythagorean encounter, Plato became obsessed with unlocking the final secrets of a sacred geometry that would bind human beings to the cosmos and the starry heavens—a cosmic order graspable by the workings of Socrates's a priori reason.[15]

Any informed reader opening the pages of the *Timaeus* has to admit that

---

*Pythagoras's belief that reality was essentially dual, split between the Limit (one) and the Unlimited (two), and that the soul was immortal and transmigrated after death, also surfaces in Socrates's view of the world as reflected in the dialogues.

Pythagoras had a decisive impact on Plato, so decisive that one ancient writer accused him of outright plagiarism.[16] Be that as it may, the *Timaeus* is the crucial Platonic dialogue, preserved through the centuries. It firmly embedded mathematics and geometry in the Western understanding of reality and allowed Plato to solve the questions about the soul and God that Socrates had raised but never fully answered.

In the dialogue, Timaeus (who is an obvious stand-in for Plato's friend Archytas) gives an account not simply of how creation takes place, but, just as important, why. Timaeus admits that giving "a consistent and accurate account" of God's purposes through reason alone is impossible. Still, he says, our understanding must be rooted in the fact that, being the supreme source of all goodness and perfection, God would want all things to be as like Himself as possible and therefore as perfect as possible. Thus, "finding the visible universe in a state not of rest but inharmonious and disorderly motion, [He] reduced it to order from disorder, as He judged that order was in every way better" than disorder.[17]

To do this, God decided to use as His model "the highest and most completely perfect of intelligible beings," namely Himself. If the world "were manufactured according to [that model's] pattern," then the universe would be not only the most perfect creation possible, a union of body and soul, but also unique—indeed, *our universe is and will continue to be His only creation*.[18]

It is the relation between number and figure, Timaeus affirms, that allows God to do this: "In the first place it is clear to everyone that fire, earth, water, and air are bodies, and all bodies are solids. All solids again are bounded by surfaces, and all rectilinear surfaces are composed of *triangles*."[19] The two basic forms of triangles, right angle and equilateral, form for God (and Plato) the basic architecture of matter, from squares to the first solid figure, the pyramid—which is also the form of fire. The cube (made up of four squares or eight triangles) forms earth; the eight-sided octahedron (eight squares) defines air; the next elaboration of square and triangle, the twenty-sided icosahedron, is the basic building block of water.

The most complex of all is the dodecahedron, a multisided solid that defines the sphere. It alone is made not from triangles, but from the pentagon—which also happens to be Pythagoras's own figure for the irrational numbers like the square root of 2 or the square root of 3, from which a mathematician can generate the so-called Golden Section, traditionally the most harmonious physical scale for everything from architecture to pictorial landscapes.* From Plato's perspective in the *Timaeus*, the sphere is the most perfect shape of all, with which God "embroidered the heavens" and the earth itself.[20]

Out of these five geometric solids, which mathematicians still refer to as the Platonic solids, God goes on to generate the cosmos, which in turn is fitted within the copy of Himself He has already made, the World Soul. The *Timaeus* gives us an extraordinary picture of God literally cutting strips of "soul stuff" in proportion with the intervals of the musical scale (4:4:2:1) and then laying them crosswise, into a +. Then God bends each strip into a circle, so that He ends up with two circles at right angles to each other, which eventually encompass the entire sky.[21]

"And he made these circles revolve in contrary senses relative to each other," Timaeus says; some according to the same invariable motion—which is the motion of the fixed stars—and others according to variable but harmoniously proportioned motions—the motion of the planets and the sun. Within this great spherical arena, the God of the *Timaeus* "proceeded to fashion the whole corporeal world within it, fitting it center to center." Then He created the human soul and its three parts—reason, emotion, and appetite—in order to fit them into the human body.[22]

And so it goes. It is without doubt the most grandiose vision of ordered creation the ancient world had ever seen or ever would see. The material world acts as a kind of receptacle into which a plan of divine perfection is steadily poured. At each step, we see how everything fits into the cosmos as a totality, extending from the "music" of the heavens (so called because the planets are spaced in the *Timaeus* according to musical harmonies) to the specifications of the human body, right down to every living and nonliving thing. As Plato puts it, where "we can trace divine goodness [that is, perfection] we can trace divine purpose"; and where we see material creation, we see the conscious, ordering mind of God.[23]

What God has put into the world, a preordained mathematical order, we

---

*This is when the ratio between the two parts of a divided line are equal to the ratio of the longer section to the entire line. When used to turn a square into a rectangle, as the Greeks often did (for example, in designing the Parthenon), the result was said to be so visually pleasing it had to be of divine origin.

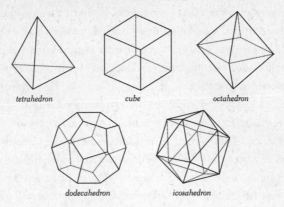

tetrahedron   cube   octahedron

dodecahedron   icosahedron

The Platonic solids described in the *Timaeus* were God's building blocks of the cosmos.

can trace back to God through that same order. Like Leonardo da Vinci's famous drawing of the man standing in the square and circle, divine geometric proportion turns out to be written into every feature of our lives and is only waiting to be revealed like a crucial message inscribed in invisible ink. Thanks to Pythagoras's mystical math, Socrates's cave suddenly comes alive in the divine order and meaning.

Still, did Plato really mean for the *Timaeus*, with all its fantastic imagery, totally unprovable but dogmatically persuasive, to be taken at face value? His most famous pupil, Aristotle, certainly thought so. Unlike some modern scholars who insist Plato never meant the *Timaeus* literally, Aristotle also had the advantage of hearing Plato's own lectures on the subject. But it really doesn't matter. Over the centuries Plato's followers, and to a large extent Greek as well as Latin Christendom, would accept the *Timaeus* as the authoritative account of the creation of the cosmos and a precious insight into the workings of the mind of God.[24]

This is a cosmology in which the same Platonic dualities keep recurring, in chapter after chapter of the *Timaeus*. There is the division between the Same and the Other, and between the Limit and the Unlimited drawn from Pythagorean sources. There is also the division between Divine Mind and physical matter that appears in other Platonic dialogues but which the *Timaeus* raises to new cosmic significance.

It is a universe that we *perceive* as multiform and constantly changing, but which is, in the clear light of reason, actually eternal and One.[25]

And presiding over this complete and ordered cosmos is a God unlike any that has appeared in Greek thought, or indeed anywhere in history. It is a God who is a rational, beneficent Creator, who is pure spirit and pure mind. He is a Creator who occupies no existence in space yet presides over all things that occur in space and time. He is a God who demands from us not worship through ritual and sacrifice, but our mind's assent to the laws and principles He has laid out for His creation.[26]

The influence of Plato's image of God as a rational Creator knowable through our reason would be immense, and not only in ancient Greek thought. It would shape the whole notion of God in early Christianity. In fact, the word Plato uses for his ordered creation, *genesis*, will become the title of the first book of the Greek translation of the Hebrew Bible. In time, early Christian and medieval commentators will carefully stitch together Plato's version of creation and Moses's into a harmonious whole, so that spiritual-theological and rational-scientific elements of both the Old Testament and the *Timaeus* could emerge as one coherent system we still call Intelligent Design.

In addition, the *Timaeus*'s insistence that physical matter is simply inert material waiting for the imprint of *nous*, or reason, in order to have any significance or motion became a central theme of ancient and medieval science. Even Plato's rival Aristotle will make it a starting point for his own work.[27] Likewise, the idea of planetary motion as a harmonious system of circles or spheres (later called "the music of the spheres"), and of man as a microcosm of the universe with a body, mind, and soul in tune with the larger harmonies of creation, marks the start of long, influential chapters in Western thought.

The sacred geometry of the *Timaeus* would reach across the Middle Ages to the Renaissance. It leaves its mystic imprint on the philosopher Nicholas of Cusa (one of whose disciples will be a Polish astronomer named Nicolaus Copernicus), on Leonardo da Vinci, and even on the Sistine Chapel ceiling. It is not for nothing that Raphael has Plato offer the *Timaeus* as his most representative work in *The School of Athens* or that Pythagoras himself appears in the painting sketching a diagram of the *tetraktys*, which Pythagoras proposed, and Plato accepted, as the symbol of the created eternal realm. Still later, Plato's often expressed view that "God is always doing geometry" and "Where there is number there is order; where there is no number there is nothing but confusion, formlessness, and disorder" would decisively shape the scientific views of Copernicus, Kepler, and Galileo, not to mention Isaac Newton and Albert Einstein.*[28]

Long before that, however, the *Timaeus* occupied pride of place in the school Plato founded in Athens to carry on his ideas. We don't know exactly when Plato decided he needed a formal school to pass on his ideas or acquired a parcel of land a mile outside the walls of Athens near a grove sacred to an Athenian hero, Academus, as the place to build it. It was probably just before or just after his first trip to Italy in 388–86, when he was nearly forty. When he returned, he devoted himself to organizing an entire course of study for his growing number of students, and eventually the *Timaeus* joined a batch of other lengthy later dialogues—the *Laws*, *Philebus*, and *Statesman*—as a central textbook for Plato's disciples.

It is important to see these not as replacing the earlier works, like the *Republic* or the *Phaedo*, which students almost certainly continued to read. Instead, the new works highlighted features of the old and gave them a new significance as Plato's fascination with number as the architecture of reality seemed to explain what had, like the Forms, been puzzles before.

In the *Philebus*, for example, Plato applies his mathematical theories to ethics. He shows, or tries to show, that virtue itself is a matter of harmonious proportion, not unlike the intervals of the musical scale: that all human activities involve finding the right measure between the Unlimited and Indeterminate and the stabilizing Limit, and that the good life depends on the permanent establishment of right and definite measure or proportion.[29] In effect, the Forms, even the Good in Itself, turn out to be nothing more than mathematical formulae for virtuous living—even if the actual calculations remain vague and elusive.

Still, the fact that studies at the Academy involved no less than ten years of mathematics, and that the motto over the door read, "Let no one ignorant of Geometry enter here," suggests just how powerful that Pythagorean impulse remained in Plato's program. It may explain why Plato taught his students that numbers cannot be added together. If we are talking about numbers as arithmetical figures, the statement is obvious nonsense. But if we are talk-

---

*Einstein never lost sight of this idea of a cosmos as a totality and devoted his last years to finding the common mathematical pattern that would (for example) tie together gravitation and the forces of electromagnetism. It made him resentful of the suggestion of the randomness of nature embedded in quantum theory and made him keep reminding his fellow physicists, "God is not malicious," and, "God does not play dice." Finally, Niels Bohr (who was something of a Platonist himself) retorted, "Stop telling God what to do."

ing about number as an abstract Form representing a class of objects (a notion very close to modern mathematics), then it takes on a more profound meaning.[30] No wonder the leading mathematician of the age, Eudoxus of Cnidus, moved his entire school to Athens to make common cause with the Academy—an intellectual collaboration that laid the foundation for Euclidean geometry.[31]

Meanwhile Plato's Academy would become the model for every monastery and university on the Western model. Students lived in small huts scattered around the property and shared common meals in Plato's house, while Plato himself seems to have regularly held classes in the garden or in the park.[32] Plato's school became the Greek world's principal training ground for two types of graduates: mathematicians and geometers, and public policy legislators who knew how to turn the principles of sacred geometry into the principles of the perfect State.

The juxtaposition seems startling, yet in Plato's ordered world, perfection in one should be reflected in the other. And others seemed to have agreed with him. For example, Plato's student Phormion went to Elis to straighten out its laws and institutions; Aristonymus to Megalopolis; and others to other city-states. The Cyrenaeans asked Plato to come to them in person, but he refused. However, when Perdiccas, king of Macedonia, asked him for a trained counselor, Plato dispatched another Academy student, one of his cleverest, named Euphraeus.

Euphraeus exhorted the members of the Macedonian court "to study geometry and philosophy."[33] What Macedonia's aristocracy, who devoted themselves to drinking when they weren't breeding horses or fighting, thought about this advice isn't recorded. However, Euphraeus did convince King Perdiccas to give his royal heir a special province to rule so he could learn the skills of kingship. The experiment worked better than anyone could have imagined. Perdiccas's heir, Prince Philip, would become Macedonia's greatest king and within two decades conqueror of Greece. In fact, Philip's entire meteoric career—later overshadowed by the fame of his own son Alexander and *his* tutor Aristotle—owed its start to Euphraeus and indirectly to Plato.

This intermingling of philosophy and high policy is in keeping with the spirit of Plato's Academy. Anyone imagining that the philosopher's life would be one of serene contemplation of the Forms would be amazed by Plato's later years at the Academy.

It was a bustling place. Students flocked from every part of Greece, as

Plato presided as moderator over seminar-style discussions of the most important dialogues. The rest of his time was spent lecturing. These lectures were open to the general public, and people turned up in droves to hear Plato on topics like "The Nature of the Good." Plato grew so busy that for nearly twenty years he did not write a word except the *Philebus*. When he finally pulled himself away from his hectic routine, he managed to sit and write the *Sophist, Timaeus, Statesman*, and the other late dialogues. Not bad for a man approaching eighty.

Yet even at the end Plato never put himself in his own work. Nor would he acknowledge himself as author. "There never is and never shall be any treatise by Plato," he wrote in a revealing passage in one of his letters, "what now bears the name belongs to Socrates beautified and rejuvenated." Until the end of his life, everything he wrote or did, including founding the Academy, was a tribute to his dead friend and teacher: the greatest monument of any disciple ever left to his master.

After Plato's death in 347, the Academy continued to flourish. Under his successors, it drew the best and the brightest students for nine hundred years, until it formally closed its doors in 529 CE.

But the most famous Academy student of all was the one who rejected it all.

Aristotle (384–22 BCE)

Four

THE DOCTOR'S SON

*All men by nature desire to know. An indication of this is the delight
we take in our senses.*

—Aristotle, *Metaphysics*

The Academy's most famous dropout was raised in Macedonia, the Texas of
ancient Greece. A wild, rugged country of hardy horsemen and splendid warriors, Macedonia came into its own in the fourth century BCE as city-states
like Athens and Sparta went into decline. Macedonia's king Philip (the same
Philip who had been the pupil of Plato's student Euphraeus) would unite all
of Greece under his rule. His son Alexander, known to posterity as Alexander
the Great, would become the ancient world's greatest conqueror.

Aristotle's life and career revolved around the kingdom's royal house, in
more ways than one. Aristotle's own father, Nicomachus, was the Macedonian royal physician. The son would go on to become Alexander's tutor. A
few years later, that extraordinary figure would launch a career of conquest

that eventually extended from Greece and Egypt to Afghanistan and the Punjab.

Evidence suggests that teacher and pupil were closer than some—remembering Alexander's ruthless, bloodthirsty career—would like to think. All the same, it is Aristotle's relationship with Plato, not Alexander, that defined and determined the course of his career. Although he absorbed many of its elements and assumptions, Aristotle turned foursquare against the elaborate system of philosophy his mentor had carefully crafted. That act of rebellion explains the key features of Aristotle's own thought and defines his place in the making of Western civilization.

Legend says Aristotle, like Socrates, was short but strongly built. It also says he spoke with a lisp.[1] The most authentic portraits reveal a man with a broad brow and a firm jaw, with intense, watchful eyes. It's a face that doesn't tolerate nonsense or prevarication. It is the face of robust common sense.

Aristotle is no woolly-minded, dreamy-eyed philosopher. He is the realist and empiricist compared with Plato the mystic and idealist. Aristotle believed his teacher's dismissal of the material world as a realm of illusion and error was a major mistake, and he devoted himself to analyzing that world in all its rich multiplicity. If Plato tells us to leave the cave in order to find a higher truth beyond the senses, Aristotle retorts: Don't be in such a hurry. What happens in that cave is not only important, but the only reality we can truly know.

They began as student and master. They ended as rivals. Plato is supposed to have said, "Aristotle kicked me, as foals do their mothers when they are born."[2] All the evidence, however, suggests the crucial break between them came after Plato's death. Aristotle entered Plato's Academy in Athens at age seventeen, probably in 367 BCE. When he left, he was in his forties. Plato was the formative influence in Aristotle's life, just as Socrates was in Plato's. In fact, Aristotle wrote his earliest works (now lost) in the same dialogue form.

Exactly when Aristotle broke with his mentor is less important than why and even where it happened, and what fault lines it left behind. Most accounts agree he left Athens after Plato died in around 347 BCE and moved to Atarnaeus, a small town in Asia Minor directly opposite the island of Lesbos. Why did he leave? Philip of Macedon had just crushed the armies of the Greek city-states at the battle of Olynthus. It may not have been a good time for a Macedonian to hang around Athens. Aristotle may also have been disappointed that he, Plato's most brilliant pupil, was passed over as the great man's successor and that leadership of the Academy went to Plato's nephew

Speusippus—an example of the nepotism rife in ancient Greece, even at the philosophical level.*

In any case, Aristotle made a new life for himself in Atarneus, and later on Lesbos. He married the niece of the local ruler, Hermias. He taught classes and met a student, Theophrastus, who would carry on Aristotle's life's work after his death. In his spare time, he walked the white sandy beaches and climbed the hills around the town and the island. He observed the rich variety of fish and mollusks found in tidal pools and the clear open waters, and the birds and small animals and tiny insects that wandered through its groves. The experience gave him a lifelong fascination with nature and a passion for analyzing and understanding its seemingly bewildering teeming life. It was on Lesbos that Aristotle probably made his first attempts to dissect biological specimens.

These experiences coincided with, and reinforced, the doubts he had already had about Plato's successor at the Academy, Speusippus, and eventually about Plato himself. Speusippus had largely given up on Plato's theory of Forms and the mystical theory of ideal numbers outlined in the *Timaeus*.[3] But Plato's nephew still clung to the notion that the truth about reality had to be found in mathematical formulae. However, Aristotle saw at once that even if the proposition that math is a certain and exact science is true, and even if the proposition that the first principles in philosophy must be certain and exact is also true, that did *not* prove that those first principles must be mathematical. The Pythagorean belief that "all things are numbers" was one of the first assumptions Aristotle's own work would overturn.[4] Aristotle had even less patience with the lingering Pythagorean emphasis on secrecy and cryptic aphorisms, which flew in the face of Aristotle's overriding conviction that philosophy must necessarily be an open book, with everything as clear, organized, and straightforward as possible even for the slowest student.

That same insistence would ultimately make him impatient with Plato's reliance on allegory and myth to convey truths he considered too profound to be expressed in ordinary language. The Myth of the Cave in the *Republic*, the Myth of Atlantis in the *Timaeus*: Aristotle made it clear he had no time for tall tales like these, which obfuscate more than they reveal. "Plato raised up the walls of Atlantis," Aristotle wrote, "and then plunged them under the waves,"

---

*It is also possible that Speusippus sent Aristotle and his colleague Xenocrates to Assos to ope branch of the Academy. We simply do not know.

meaning that the whole story was an obvious fabrication and nothing more. "About those who have invented clever mythologies," he added in the *Metaphysics*, "it is not worthwhile to take a serious look."[5]

In the end, he also rejected the most powerful myth Plato ever created: the myth of Socrates himself.[6] Socrates does appear in Aristotle's writings, but he is not a heroic figure or a philosophical role model. He is simply one more object of analysis and criticism like all Aristotle's other predecessors, including Plato. Everyone and everything were becoming bricks in the comprehensive and complex edifice Aristotle was determined to build in order to reach the most profound truths. Those truths, as he made clear,* come not in a sudden moment of intuitive insight or from some inner contemplative process. They are the result of hard work and thought. Of course it would be nice, Aristotle tells us, to be as certain about everything as we can be about mathematical truths. It would be lovely to know the answer almost the instant we ask the question, as when we say $2 + 2 = 4$: in other words, to know truth a priori. All of Aristotle's works point out, however, that the most vital knowledge we have comes a posteriori, meaning "after the fact" or from experience, as we link up a given visible effect to its preceding cause.

This was a profound shift—not just away from Plato, but away from the whole direction of Greek philosophy since Thales. Aristotle decided that Reality with a capital R is not (for the most part) something ultimately above or behind the world we see and hear and smell and touch. It *is* that world. What Plato had dismissed as the illusions of the cave, Aristotle set out to prove were the keys to ultimate understanding all along.

After all, it seems improbable that some all-knowing Divine Mind would spend so much time and energy generating the world around us, from the sun and moon and heavens and man down to the tiniest flowers and fleas, unless that world had some intrinsic significance. That is, unless it contained important truths that man's reason was only waiting to discover: "We must trust the evidence of the senses rather than theories," Aristotle says, "and theories as well, as long as their results agree with what is observed."[7]

Aristotle, we must remember, was a doctor's son. Although he was very young when his father died, his family were longtime members of the medical guild of the Asclepiades. Using one's eyes and ears and sense of touch to diagnose ailments and complaints, and judge the course of a disease or its

---

* Especially in his *Categories* and the two parts of the *Analytics*.

cure, was in a sense a family tradition. According to the great Greek doctor Galen,* Asclepid families also taught their sons dissection.[8]

So those walks along the beach were not idle time. They must have confirmed for Aristotle what he already suspected, that reason must be linked to the power of observation. Reason steps in *after*, not before, experience; it sorts our observations into meaningful patterns and arrives at a knowledge as certain and exact as anything in Plato's Forms. Aristotle's term for this knowledge of the world was *epistēmē*, which later Latin commentators translated as *scientia*, or science.

Aristotle is the true father of science and scientific method, by which we still mean a methodical process of observation, classification, and discovery.[9] In this, Aristotle was his own best student. In the *History of Animals*, he describes cutting open a chameleon to see what goes on inside; and he gives us a concise but wholly accurate description of the life cycle of the gnat. In his biological writings alone, Aristotle names over 170 species of birds, 169 species of fishes, 66 types of mammals, and 60 types of insects, making him the father of ichthyology and entomology as well as biology. His writings contain references to the internal organs of more than 100 creatures from cows and deer to lizards and frogs, and most in such detail that the dissector could only have been Aristotle himself.[10]

He is also the inventor of the language of science. Words like genus and species, hypothesis and analysis, all find their first and still current use in the works of Aristotle. So do the names of the principal physical and natural sciences. With almost unbelievable discipline and energy, Aristotle invented and wrote the pioneering treatises of all the following fields: biology, zoology, gerontology, physics, astronomy, meteorology (meaning the study of meteors and comets), politics, and psychology, not to mention logic and metaphysics.† He was the first to use the observation that ships sailing out to sea seem to vanish over the horizon hull first, then masts and sails, to draw a far-reaching conclusion: that the earth must be round.[11]

But biology always remained for him the model of true science. The observation, collection, and classification of specimens in order to discern how they differ and how they are alike; noting how the same species can show different characteristics based on different stages of maturity and develop-

---

*Fl. second century CE.
†At least the study of metaphysics. The term itself comes from one of his later editors as a way to refer to the work that comes after Aristotle's *Physics*—quite literally, "after the *Physics*."

ment; above all, the delight in dealing with tangible objects made of flesh, fur, shell, and bone and the firm feel of organic life instead of the disembodied abstract Forms of the Platonists or numbers of the Pythagoreans: These were fundamental to Aristotle's way of seeing the world and seeking the truth. They have remained fundamental to the scientific outlook right down to today.

All this observable data, as we would call it, had to be classified and arranged in order to make sense of it. So Aristotle provides the basic analytic principles by which to do it. There are the treatises on logic, the *Prior Analytics* and *Posterior Analytics*; the *Topics* and *On Sophistical Refutations*, which show us the pitfalls of faulty logic and reasoning; and the *On Interpretation* and *Categories.* *

There is indeed far more to Aristotle's philosophy of science, however, than just an impulse for tidy-mindedness—or, in Bertrand Russell's famous phrase, "a common-sense prejudice pedantically expressed."[12] Aristotle's bias toward observation and classification also led him to break completely with the concept of Plato's Forms. He did so not only because they seemed too abstract and logically unwieldy,[13] but because they missed certain essential features of reality.

Take the example of a puppy, a chocolate brown Labrador retriever. For Plato, what makes our puppy real is not the fur we see, the paws we touch, or the wet muzzle we stroke, but his participation in the ideal Form of Puppiness; or perhaps Chocolate Lab Puppiness as opposed to Yellow Lab Puppiness and Black Lab Puppiness, all of which are subsumed under the Form of Labrador Retrieverness, which is in turn a subset of Dogness (not to mention Retrieverness, along with all the other retriever breeds). In other words, all the dogs and puppies we see are only copies of an ideal standard, which defines what and who they are.

Aristotle says, Look again. Our puppy, Rover, is not just a puppy. He is also essentially something out of which *something else* will eventually emerge: a mature dog. That mature Labrador retriever is not separate or distinct from Rover: it *is* Rover, our puppy, at a later stage, in the same way the man is in

---

*The last purported to reveal the ten ways in which everything that exists can and should be scientifically classified: by substance, quantity, quality, relation, place, time, position, state, action, and affection.

A Labrador retriever puppy reveals a lot about Aristotle's theory of nature.

the boy. Adulthood is the final form into which Rover, and all individuals, will ultimately evolve.

"Evolution" is not a bad word for the version of nature that Aristotle brings to the philosophical table.[14] It is a world in which all things, puppies, men, plants, and animals, are constantly altering and changing, a nature in which all of us emerge from something and grow into something else without losing our identities, either as individuals or as part of a class of individuals (so even if Rover grows up to look nothing like his earlier puppy self, he is still Rover).

That continuously becoming *something* is what Aristotle called *substance*. Every substance for Aristotle is a compound of physical matter with an intelligible structure or form—a collusion of matter and form of which the individual is the point of intersection. All substances in nature come with attributes that appear in *this* puppy, *this* horse, *this* man, but they are attributes that are determined by their final form (for example, there are chocolate Labs and white Labs, but no pink Labs).

And not just for animate or living beings. Aristotle's own example is of an artisan forging a bronze sphere. Bronze is the matter, but sphericity is the form, a form imposed by its maker, just as nature imposes its forms on physical matter. For Aristotle, our visible world is not an illusion or a pale imitation of something else. It is substantial in a literal sense: it is *real*, and therefore worth knowing on its own terms.

This is a crucial point, which Plato missed in two ways. First, Plato's theory of knowledge leaves out the possibility of change. Back at the Academy, Aristotle's teacher constantly stressed that true Reality is by definition changeless and eternal. In fact, Aristotle was able to answer, change is part of what makes the world what it is and what allows form to reach its full potential. There are no mature dogs without puppies; no men and women without boys and girls; and no certain knowledge that doesn't take those facts into account.

The puppy as it grows; the house as it is being built; the vase as it is being turned: All show us at different stages distinct attributes that also point to their final form. By analyzing substances, we begin to think about how the potential turns into the actual. In short, the philosopher and scientist deal not with an ideal Reality, but with a constantly evolving reality with a small r. It's a reality firmly rooted in the here and now, and what we see, hear, and touch.

Second, Aristotle restores the reality, even the dignity, of the individual. Aristotle's forms, unlike Plato's Forms, do not exist separately from individuals. They appear only *through* the individual. We would know nothing about dogs without individual dogs in the world to observe and study; we would know nothing about justice without individual examples to examine and analyze.

One could say that Aristotle had turned Plato on his head. Instead of the individual being a pale copy of a more real abstract form, the universal is less real (indeed only a copy) of the individual.[15] This reversal left Aristotle's philosophy with a built-in bias in favor of the individual: in science, in metaphysics, in ethics, and later in politics.

What's true of substances such as puppies and vases is also true of men and women, with one additional feature: that of the mind. Thinking is as essential to our form and function as barking or swimming is for the dog. However, it also links us to a much higher level of being. Aristotle's version of

Plato's God is pure *nous*, or pure thought. The human soul is not; it includes other faculties or powers, like the senses and the passions. But there is still enough *nous* left to figure out what is going on.

If Aristotle's world is the conquest of matter by form, then the study of the world and nature requires figuring how and why this works. Fortunately, as human beings we come with the equipment to do it. Reason allows us to sift through the multitude of matter and tease out the essential forms and functions that give it all life and meaning.

I go for a walk through the forest near my house, just as Aristotle walked along the beach at Assos. All around me are trees and plants and flowers of bewildering variety and in various stages of growth. Some trees are mere saplings, others lie dead and rotting on the ground. Still others stand towering toward the sky. Some plants are in bloom and others are about to bloom. Insects crawl or fly in all directions. Birds, including ones I've never seen before, flit among the branches; other creatures scurry through the dead leaves or slither through the grass. The wind blows as clouds of constantly changing patterns pass overhead.

This is nature, the real world buzzing and blooming around us. But we are not overwhelmed or intimidated by it. Aristotle teaches us that certain basic principles underlie all this rich variety and all the change and motion, however strange or bizarre. In addition, these principles are not separate or mysterious but embedded in the things themselves, together with their form and function. The world is a *system*. Our contemporary notion of an "ecosystem" neatly captures this element of interconnectedness of Aristotle's view of nature, just as our belief in the power of science to unlock that system is its most important offshoot.

For Aristotle, nature is no insubstantial mystery, just as no system is entirely static. Like the puppy and like us, systems naturally incorporate change. Aristotle's term for nature's built-in bias toward change and motion is *energeia*; he also uses the word *dynamis*, which translates as "power." Aristotle's worldview is dynamic. Everything I see on my forest walk exhibits that *dynamis* of nature: growing to maturity, struggling to realize its form, pushing to perform its due function, and then dying. All things exist in a matrix of space *and* time. All things that are and were and will be must appear in that matrix. They surface either here and now, as in the forest or the beach at Assos, or in the past, as causes, or in the future, as results or actualities.

So instead of Plato's philosophy of *transcendence*, in which everything is a reflection or a sign of something higher and more real, Aristotle gives us a philosophy of *causation*. Everything that is, has been caused to be or made to happen; and when we discover the cause or causes of a thing, we learn what it is supposed to do and be. We "possess unqualified scientific knowledge of a thing," Aristotle declares in his *Posterior Analytics*, "when we think that we know the cause on which the fact depends, as the cause of that fact and of no other."[16]

Causes for Aristotle come in clusters of four. In his house at Assos, there was probably an amphora sitting in the corner, waiting for a delivery of wine or olive oil. Aristotle could see that its material cause was the clay from which it was fashioned; that the potter's wheel and potter's hands had been its efficient cause; that the shape of an amphora that was standard all across Greece was its formal cause; and the final cause is what the potter had in mind when he created the amphora in the first place.

The same cluster applied to natural objects, like our puppy Rover. Flesh and fur are the material causes; Rover's father and mother are the efficient causes; the physical shape of Labrador retrievers is the formal cause; and the final cause for Aristotle is what Labs are intended to do: to serve man in helping to hunt waterfowl and to be a faithful companion. In Aristotle's science as it persisted down through the Middle Ages, function is always directly related to form and part of a thing's essence.

Today, our thinking runs in a very different direction. We would reserve the word *cause* to only one of the cluster, the efficient cause.[17] No one today ventures to suggest that the end or purpose of a thing is somehow its cause; that part of Aristotle's science of nature has dropped away. We prefer and expect a scientific view that is less teleological and more provisional and open-ended, with *telos*, or purpose, left to the human creator or the public, or even to chance.

But Aristotle himself wanted to see all phenomena as part of a great chain of causation that leads inevitably to the one great final cause. He was determined to establish the essential role of a divinity who is the final cause of everything, the one who sets the whole system in motion, the master engineer.

Aristotle's term for this God is the Unmoved Mover or Prime Mover, since He presides over everything that changes or moves in the universe, without changing or moving Himself. He alone has already achieved His actuality, or *energeia*, simply by being. He thinks, and everything moves.

Aristotle's God borrows many of the characteristics of Plato's God. He exists outside time and space; He is knowable only through the effects of His rational presence. But He is also more remote. Aristotle's God is pure Mind, with no material component or even a point of entry for such a component. Because God is perfect, and thinking is the best and most perfect activity, He can think only about Himself. The intrusion of thoughts about His creation and the creatures in it would not only break His concentration, it would overthrow the very principle on which (for Aristotle) His existence depends: His perfection. Aristotle's God "cannot care for the world; he is not even aware of it."[18]

It is a frigid, not to say theologically barren, point of view that will get some of Aristotle's Christian admirers in trouble in the Middle Ages. Still later, it is that very frigidity that will appeal to Enlightenment Deists like Voltaire and Thomas Jefferson.[19] Aristotle, however, did not care. There is no sign that he had any interest in the notion of a divine providence, as Socrates and Plato did, or in divine rewards and punishments. Even his theory of the soul includes no mention of immortality. Nature, as he says in many passages, does nothing in vain.[20] That seems to have been enough for Aristotle. Like many of his modern scientific successors, he showed little concern for what God does, or more precisely, what God thinks.

Still, even under the big tent, after analyzing God as Unmoved Mover of the universe in the *Metaphysics*, Aristotle wants us to come back down to individuals as examples of form, and on individuals' potential form in the future. In Aristotle's world, what the puppy was, or the amphora (a shapeless lump of clay), matters less than what it does now and what it will become. The same applies to people. If we want to know what a man really is, we need to focus not on where he came from or what he left behind, but on what he can do now and in the future, as part of his own dynamic nature.

What applies to individual dogs and men can be extended to human beings in general. For Aristotle's disciples in the eighteenth century such as Adam Smith, it even applies to entire societies. In the Aristotelian mind-set, it is the future that counts, not the past.

Here we arrive at one of the most crucial differences between Plato and Aristotle, and one of the most important for the future shape of Western culture. Plato's philosophy looks constantly *backward*, to what we were, or what we've lost, or to an original of which we are the pale imitation or copy. In that past original, Plato will say, we find the key that unlocks our future. Later that most Platonist of epochs, the Renaissance, would look back to classical antiquity for its model of perfection, just as the Romantics—Platonists almost to a man and woman—would look back to the Middle Ages.

Aristotle, by contrast, looks steadily *forward*, to what we can be rather than what we were. His outlook is by its nature optimistic: "The universe and everything in it is developing towards something continually better than what came before," including ourselves. It is truly a "philosophy of aspiration," as scholar F. M. Cornford once dubbed it, and for Aristotle the world we make for ourselves continually reflects that constant striving toward improvement. In that sense, Aristotle is the first great advocate of progress—and Plato, creator of the vanished utopia Atlantis, the first great theorist of the idea of decline.[21]

This is why Aristotle was prepared to take a second look at the mechanical, practical arts of his day, or what we call technology. All forms of knowledge, he declares in his usual categorical way, are either theoretical, technical, or practical. Pure theory (*epistēmē*) is concerned only with knowing and understanding, like biology, metaphysics (or "first philosophy"), and theology. Practical knowledge, *praxis*, has to do with doing. Interestingly, he puts politics and ethics in that category.

But *technē*, the third kind of knowledge, has to do with *making*. Its goal is not understanding but production. The potter at his wheel, the blacksmith at his forge, the shipwright in a Piraeus boatyard, are not interested in discovering some new scientific principle or adding to the sum of human knowledge. The art of making, Aristotle declares, only imitates nature rather than inventing something new. But in Aristotle's system, this too makes *technē* a valid, even dignified, form of action, because it involves the systematic use of knowledge in order to advance human action—one could even say to advance human purpose.

By giving activities like pottery making and metallurgy a comparable (albeit inferior) status to pure contemplation, Aristotle highlighted the value of everyday human activities that yield practical material benefits. *Technē*, Aristotle wrote, is one of the crucial ways by which "the soul arrives at truth," since it involves "a reasoned productive state . . . concerned with bringing something into being," based on certain rational principles, such as making a vase or a suit of armor, or building a house.[22]

In this way, Aristotle opened the door for a future technological society.* The Platonist looks at nature and says, "What does it mean?" So does the Aristotelian, but then he poses an additional question: "What's it good for?" That's why Ralph Waldo Emerson called him the first of the "moderns." Ayn Rand, of all people, would have agreed. Without Aristotle, there would have been no Archimedes and no Steve Jobs. There probably wouldn't have been a Hiroshima, but neither would there have been gene splicing or laser surgery. We can complain about where technology has taken us. However, we can't ignore how we got started on the journey: a few brief lines in a book on ethics written more than twenty-three centuries ago.

It is characteristic that Aristotle's remarks on technology should surface in a book on ethics. The same practical outlook shaped Aristotle's approach to the other key question every Greek had asked since Socrates: "What is the good life?"

On one side, Aristotle's starting point is the same as Plato's. The best life is the one in which we follow our reason, not our passions or emotions. But man's function is not just to *think*—which Aristotle admits to be the highest of all human activities—but also to *do*.

Aristotle outlines his approach in his *Nicomachean Ethics*.† It takes us down from Plato's mountaintop and puts us back on the street, where merchants are selling and families and slaves are passing by; where prostitutes and money changers are looking for customers and mothers are looking for their children; where some men are making deals and running for office and others are trying to decide whether to go to work or go to a *taberna*. This is not a realm of illusions or shadows in a cave. This is real life.

So what do we find there? Some people are stupid and ignorant and behave badly, just as Plato pointed out. But the vast majority are simply doing their jobs, raising families and paying the bills and trying to be good husbands and citizens—in Aristotle's terms, performing their function and fulfilling

---

*It also opened the door wide enough for mathematics to get back into Aristotle's theory of science and knowledge, as a way to calculate and measure changes and results.

†So called because his son Nicomachus edited the first published version.

their potential as human beings. Their problem is learning how to do it better. The job of ethics, Aristotle asserts, "is not that we may know what virtue is, but that we may become virtuous," especially in our daily dealings with others.

We can see the difference in outlook in the famous last scene in the movie *The Bridge on the River Kwai*, when the British doctor, played by James Donald, watches the violent denouement from the hill overlooking the bridge. He sees the men frantically killing one another, mortars and rifles firing blindly, the sudden spectacular explosion of the bridge, and the train crashing into the Kwai River. It's over in a few breathtaking minutes. The doctor's only comment from his lofty perch is "Madness, madness!"

This is the Platonic view of human action, the view looking down from the mountaintop back into the cave. Aristotle's response is that this isn't madness at all. Anyone seeing the entire movie realizes everyone is following his own separate agenda from the start. The Japanese colonel has his bridge to build; the British colonel sees building it as a way to restore his men's morale; others, however, have a mission to blow it up. From the lofty Platonic perch, it all looks like chaos. But from the Aristotelian point of view of the individuals involved, every action has its reasonable—if at times violent—point.

So it is with life. We live in a world of separate individuals, each following his or her agenda and narrative. Moral questions necessarily arise when we interact with others, and we have to make decisions about what to do. The problem is not knowing an ideal right from an ideal wrong, Aristotle insisted, but knowing how to behave toward others in the real world and still uphold certain timeless moral standards.

This is why for Aristotle ethics is not a science. We aren't looking for moral perfection. "In fact, such a life is not possible for man," Aristotle states. "If it were, he would be a God."[23] Instead, we look for advantage and improvement. From that point of view, Aristotle assures us, learning to be virtuous is not that hard. It's all a matter of practice and learning the habits that go with it.

At times, Aristotle sounds like the behaviorist B. F. Skinner—and just as Aristotle is the original father of science and technology, so he opens the path to the calculus of Western behaviorism. "The whole concern of both morality and political science must be pleasures and pains," is how he states it in the *Ethics*. The key is teaching people how to take pleasure in doing the right thing and experience pain in doing the bad thing. We teach our children to brush their teeth and share their toys and save their allowance by rewarding them if they do and punishing or scolding them if they don't. We do this for their sake, not ours, in order to teach the habits that will make them be happy, healthy human beings.

Adults are no different. "Moral goodness is the result of habit," he writes, pointing out that the words for character and custom are the same in Greek: *ethos*.[24] A large share of the laws and customs in a city like Athens was set to inculcate the kinds of personal virtues Plato and Aristotle wanted their fellow citizens to have. Aristotle's point was that learning those virtues took more than laws. It took building habits based on a relative calculus of pleasure and pain.

However, unlike modern behaviorists like Skinner, the eighteenth century's Jeremy Bentham, or today's Richard Dawkins, Aristotle doesn't rest on a purely mechanical or materialist view of either nature or man. The transformative power of good habits, and Aristotle's principle that practice makes perfect, rests on our essential spiritual purpose. The goal of man from the start is to be happy, and "it is virtuous activities that determine our happiness."[25] As human beings, we have an inborn disposition to virtue; if we want to cultivate that disposition, which most of us do (who really revels in being evil?), we need to cultivate the habits that go with it.

Aristotle's formula seems very simple. Yet how different from Plato's! For Plato, true knowledge, including the knowledge of the true nature of pain and pleasure, solves everything. For Aristotle, it is possible to be good *even if we don't know exactly what we are doing*, or why. The habit, and the behavior that flows from it, is enough to do the job.

This is why, in a notorious passage in Book Five of *Ethics*, Aristotle concedes that a good man could be a bad citizen, and vice versa. In fact, most people are geared this way. Few meet the standard of doing the right thing because they know it's the right thing in all matters and at all times. No one, that is, except Aristotle's so-called great-souled man, the man who is good to the highest degree in everything and knows it and is proud of it—but who is, perhaps thankfully, in short supply.

And yet, as Aristotle notes, the world is basically a good, not an evil, place. This is true especially on the day-to-day matters that really count in the life of a family or a community. Most people want to be loved; most people want to be admired. "In every community there is supposed to be some kind of justice and some kind of friendly feeling." Most people even "wish what is good," if only for themselves.[26] Even bank robbers will sometimes carry out the garbage or send Mother's Day cards—if only because habits, including good ones, are hard to break.

As a rationalist, Aristotle was willing to concede that doing good is not as optimal as knowing the good. In fact, practice makes perfect applies to bad habits as well as good. As human beings, we have the potential for both. It all boils down to a question of the choices we make: not just at the start of the journey, but at every point along the way. If we resolve to be alcohol-free but have a drink every time it's offered, we will never get there. Choice and intention are the dynamic elements in our moral life, and "intention is the decisive factor in virtue and character."

This is how Aristotle ends up with his most famous, and most misunderstood ethical doctrine—that of the mean. He states it simply enough:

> Virtue aims to hit the mean. . . . It is possible, for example, to feel fear, confidence, desire, anger, pity, and pleasure and pain generally, too much or too little; and both of these are wrong. But to have these feelings at the right times on the right grounds toward the right persons for the right motive and in the right way is to feel them in an intermediate, that is the best degree; and that is the mark of virtue.[27]

Hence, the courageous man is neither cowardly (shunning all dangers) nor foolhardy (embracing all dangers); the generous man is neither a miser nor a man who gives away everything so that his family has nothing; and so on.

Stated in this way, Aristotle's theory of the mean seems simple-minded; or to quote Bertrand Russell again, common sense pedantically expressed. However, if we change the word *mean* to *proportion*, we get closer to what Aristotle must have meant—and large parts of his *Ethics* as well as his *Politics* make more sense. The mean represents not so much a literal middle point as striking a balance between conflicting impulses and choices, and seeing our way through to the other side.

That balance differs depending on where we are in terms of time and situation, and who we are. This is one reason Aristotle believed that the practice of virtue was different for different social classes, or for masters and for slaves: not (or at least not entirely) because Aristotle was a snob, but because he recognized that our status and occupation put us in different real-life situations that require a nice judgment (*sophrosyne*, or prudence), rather than a rote formula of right versus wrong, in order to arrive at what to do.

Again, virtue is an activity, not a state of mind. Like all dynamic action, physical or otherwise, it demands a sense of balance, of *centeredness*, which no single set of rules can supply. Socrates had asserted it was better to suffer wrong than to do wrong. Aristotle wants to ask: Are you sure? Aren't there circumstances when it is better to do wrong to someone—say, knock an elderly blind lady to the curb—in order to prevent a greater wrong—say, letting her get run over by a truck? The decisive issue in moral action for Aristotle is always our intention—in this example, our desire to save someone from certain death. It does not lie in the nature of the action itself.

Socrates and Plato, to their credit, did recognize that circumstance and intention can complicate moral judgments.* Aristotle's point was that *all* forms of morality are situational, because morality takes place in a real, live-fire environment, and in virtual time, just like all the forms in the rest of nature.

So in the end we are back where we started, in a constantly evolving world of actualities and potentialities. We all have the potential to be good and the potential to be bad. But which we become depends on the choices we make as rational beings and the dispositions that arise over time from those choices.

In the dialogue *Phaedrus*, Plato brilliantly compares human beings to charioteers driving the two horses of our human nature: our soul of reason and our irrational animal passions. The charioteer's task "is difficult and troublesome," he says, as we try to give the lead to the one and rein in the other. But if we do it well, we will live a virtuous life and reach the goal of every wise man and "in the course of [our] journey" behold "absolute justice and discipline and knowledge" before the soul "withdraws again within the vault of heaven and goes home."[28]

Aristotle's soul, by contrast, is like the bareback rider. She has only one horse, herself. She needs to stay balanced on that horse with subtle adjustments of her body to keep her seat and stay in control as she takes in the scene, adjusting her pace to the road and terrain, going neither too fast nor

*For example, in Book I of the *Republic*.

too slow, but never falling off or throwing the horse into confusion—and never losing sight of the final goal.

Those who wish to be virtuous, Aristotle concludes, "are compelled at every step to think out for themselves what the circumstances demand, like a navigator on a ship at sea or a physician."[29]

Not a surprising view from one who saw Plato's moral absolutism as contrary to human happiness—and not a surprising turn of phrase from a doctor's son.

Was Athens in the fifth century BCE a model for how men should govern themselves?
Aristotle said yes; Plato said no.

Five

GOOD CITIZEN OR PHILOSOPHER RULER?

> *There will be no end to the troubles of states, or indeed, my dear Glaucon, of humanity itself, until philosophers become kings in this world.*
>
> —Plato, *Republic*

> *It is not the nature of the polis to be a unity as some thinkers say that it is, [and] what is said to be the supreme good of the polis is actually its ruin.*
>
> —Aristotle, *Politics*

Despite their differences, Plato and Aristotle agreed on many things.

They both stressed the importance of reason as our guide for understanding and shaping the world. Both believed that our physical world is shaped by certain eternal forms that are more real than matter. The difference was that Plato's Forms existed outside matter, whereas Aristotle's forms were unrealizable without it.

Both shared the typical Greek chauvinism about non-Greeks, treating them as barbarians and unfit for serious study. Both condoned the pedophilia prevalent in upper-class Greek circles and the subordinate role of women.

And neither uttered a word of condemnation of slavery. Later Western intellectuals would specifically quote Aristotle in its support.*

But they did clash bitterly over how men should be governed.

Aristotle's politics is like his ethics. It is rooted in real life, the Greek *polis* as he knew it, especially Athens, for which he wrote a description of its constitution that we still have. Aristotle believed that the goal of political institutions was man's improvement rather than his perfection. He believed the way to do this was by encouraging each individual to realize his potential, rather than force him to submit to a collective order.

By contrast, the most famous Platonic dialogue, the *Republic*, is all about raising that collective order to the highest-pitched perfection. Plato explicitly made the individual's health and happiness dependent on the larger political community.[1] Whereas Aristotle looked to Athens as his basic political model, Plato preferred Sparta, Athens's great rival.

Plato's outspoken admiration for Sparta reveals a lot about his ultimate political agenda. That state's regimented and austere values (Sparta was more of a collection of agricultural villages than an urban city) stood in sharp contrast with sophisticated, freewheeling, commercial Athens. However, Spartans could beat any opponent on the field of battle, even when outnumbered, and no one questioned a Spartan's courage or his word—or dared to.

Spartan citizens were not allowed to use money, practice a trade, make a statue, or write a poem. Neither are Plato's Guardians in the *Republic*. For all its limitations, in his *Republic* and the *Laws*, Sparta was proof to Plato that freedom was a function of solidarity and unity of purpose.[2] Aristotle, by contrast, saw Athens as proof that men can be free only if they are individuals and are allowed to live their lives as they, not others, see fit. "Freedom from any interference of government," rather than submitting to its dictates, no matter how just, is one of Aristotle's hallmarks of a democratic society.[3]

Over the centuries, Aristotle's politics will lead the way for Western advocates of individualism and democracy, including America's Founding Fathers. Plato's communitarian vision points very much in the other direction, with ugly consequences. Yet curiously, both drew their arguments from the same vision of freedom in the Greek *polis*. Their disagreement arose over how to fulfill that ideal—and Western political thinking has been split down the middle ever since.

*See chapter 25.

In this sense, Aristotle's view was more parochial and traditional. If Aristotle saw Athens as a largely positive example of the *polis* ideal, Plato's politics was a biting critique of Athenian democracy. This was not just because it had put his beloved teacher, Socrates, to death. It was a negativism shared by nearly everyone in Greek intellectual circles in the mid–fourth century BCE. Democracy, and the *polis* generally, had proved to be a disappointment. Its troubles were reflected in factional strife and declining economies, plus the weakness of the Greek states in confronting the emerging colossus from the north, the kingdom of Macedonia. As one scholar put it, "The fourth century was suffering from political evils which many of the more thoughtful men of the time regarded as incurable, and the sight of which only too often induced a feeling of pessimism and despair."[4]

Plato's antipathy may have run deeper than that. His stepfather had been heavily involved in Periclean politics. In the house where he had been raised, Plato must have witnessed some of the sordid behind-the-scenes deal making and clubhouse politics that permeate every democracy, even ancient Athens. Having seen how the democratic sausage was made, Plato was in no mood to sit at the feast. Instead, his impulse was to start over, more or less from scratch.

This is what we get when we open the pages of his most important and influential treatise, the *Republic*. It is a blow-by-blow account of what the world might look like if it were run by men of knowledge and virtue instead of ignorant, grasping politicians—that is, if a true philosopher like Socrates came down from the sunlit mountaintop back into the cave and set about straightening out the mess in front of him.

So not surprisingly, Socrates is the *Republic*'s main character, and on this all-important topic for the first time he speaks to the reader in the first person. He describes to his listeners the outline of an ideal government that, although unrealizable in reality, can serve as a model for implementing future change. "It makes no difference whether it exists now," Socrates says at one point, "or will ever come into being." By studying the laws of an ideal state, Plato argues, men will learn how to order their lives better in the real ones.[5]

The ten books of the *Republic* are the centerpiece of Plato's vision, both politically and (as the Myth of the Cave shows) philosophically. But there is a kind of prelude in a much earlier dialogue, the *Gorgias*, where he shows us what he saw as the bleak alternatives to his visionary brand of politics. In it Socrates meets a visiting teacher of rhetoric, Gorgias of Leontini. Gorgias preens himself as a teacher of virtue because he teaches men how to speak

persuasively on "the most important of human concerns," as he calls it—
namely, politics. However, harried by Socrates's polite but relentless questions, Gorgias has to admit that as a political consultant, he is concerned only
with presenting a persuasive message, even if that message is evil rather than
good.

"On Gorgias's own admission," as A. E. Taylor explains, "oratory is a device by which an ignorant man persuades an audience equally ignorant" as
himself, especially in democratic Athens.[6] It is precisely this kind of political
circus and its inherent dangers that a true Platonic science of politics strives
to rise above, whether it's in Plato's hometown or later in revolutionary Paris
or St. Petersburg.

Socrates's other antagonist is the younger and more sinister Callicles. Instead of Gorgias's moral evasion, Callicles offers a chilling version of might
makes right. "Philosophy, Socrates, is a pretty toy," he tells the older man
dismissively, but the real world is governed by power and power alone. Conventional notions of right and wrong are drawn up by the weaklings who form
the majority of mankind in order to bamboozle their stronger betters. The
only truly free man is the one strong or ruthless enough to do as he pleases,
Callicles concludes.

Still, Callicles is forced to admit under questioning that might makes
right *still* presupposes that some people know better how to rule than others.
Even a Hitler or a Saddam Hussein has to know how to do *some* things that a
wise and just ruler would do, like policing the streets and making sure there
is food on the shelves, if only to hold on to his ill-gotten power. Likewise, even
an out-and-out hedonist—and Callicles is a proud hedonist—soon realizes
that not everything that gives pleasure is automatically good (smoking crack
cocaine, for example).

So, Socrates says, when talking about what's right and wrong, we are still
operating in the realm of knowledge. Indeed, he insists, we never left it. What
ultimately makes for the good life is not power or money or the pursuit of
pleasure, but *knowledge*—knowledge of what harms and what benefits us (for
example, knowing that courage is useless if it leads us to risk our lives needlessly); knowledge of what harms or benefits others; knowledge, finally, of
good and evil.

"Let us then allow ourselves to be led by the truth . . . which teaches that
the best way to live is to practice righteousness and virtue. And what is true

for the individual, his listeners are forced to concede, must be equally true for society.[7]

Moral relativism, nihilism, hedonism: In the *Gorgias*, Socrates takes them all on and demolishes them one by one. It's a spectacular tour de force. What emerges from this demolition is Plato's secure foundation on which a good society can be built: the pursuit of virtue based on knowledge of the good. Politics is as much about applying that knowledge of the good to the state, as a doctor's job is administering medicine to the body. (It's not clear what Aristotle, the doctor's boy, might have thought of this formula the first time he encountered it at the Academy.) And just as "badness of soul is the very greatest evil to which a man is exposed," so true justice consists of using our knowledge to guide men to virtue, so that they do good instead of evil.

"Ought we not then," Socrates concludes, "to set about our treatment of the state and its citizens on this principle, with the idea of making the citizens themselves as good as possible?"[8]

Plato composed the *Gorgias* when he was just beginning to think about alternatives to the politics of his day. The *Republic*, by contrast, was written when Plato was at the height of his powers. It is by far the richest of all his works, with plenty to appeal to many different kinds of readers. It is Plato's masterpiece, and the most influential of his works, with the exception of the *Timaeus*. At the same time, moralists can admire the *Republic* for its rout of ethical relativism in Book I, where Socrates demolishes the "might makes right" arguments of Thrasymachus (the *Republic*'s updated version of Callicles) and concludes once again that it is better for our soul's sake to suffer wrong than to do wrong.

Ancient Pythagoreans and medieval astronomers were enraptured by his description in Book X of the music of the celestial spheres, with angels guiding the orbits of the seven planets so that each sustains one note in a perfect harmonic scale.[9] Modern historians enjoy pointing out how many features of Plato's ideal republic—its community of property and dormitory living for its Guardians, its ban on all forms of art and poetry (these being, after all, illusions based on illusions)—reflect those of actual Sparta.

Likewise, Socialists can take pleasure in Plato's insistence that the perfect political community must have no private property: the *Republic* is in effect the first Communist state. Feminists can point to the fact that his class of Philosopher Rulers makes no distinction between men and women. "We must pick suitable women to share the life and duties of Guardians with men," Socrates tells his listeners, "since they are capable of it and the natures of men and women are alike."[10]

Meanwhile, Book VII sets forth the original Myth of the Cave, while Book X offers Socrates's dazzling vision of the afterlife drawn from Pythagorean as well as Orphic sources, and heaven as the final dwelling place for the soul's contemplation of the Forms.

One big question about the *Republic* remains. Was it intended as a blueprint for creating the perfect society or (as some have argued) as a blueprint for totalitarianism? It is unlikely its author meant either one. Instead, the *Republic* is Plato's answer to a single question, "What is justice?" meaning, how are we to regulate our dealings with others? A more colloquial way to put it would be "Why should I be good?"

His short answer is that no one is an island unto himself. Our ethical choices, such as whether to suffer wrong rather than to do wrong, all have social consequences. If we live in a society in which people consistently do evil to themselves (like the crack addict) and to one another, eventually we end up with no society at all. A society that has fallen into this position, as he believed Athens had, is sick, in Plato's sense almost literally so. It desperately needs a doctor to restore it to spiritual health.[11]

Like a medical doctor, the political healer must wield absolute authority, at least at the start. "When one is advising a sick man who is living in a way injurious to his health," Plato asks, "must one not first of all tell him to change his way of life and give him further counsel only if he is willing to obey?"[12] The idealized society he offers us in the *Republic* is in effect Plato's master prescription on which all future real-life cures of social ills should be based.

The first step is establishing a clear division of labor. Plato's ideal republic is divided into three distinct groups. There are the common householders of farmers, tradesmen, blacksmiths, and other craftsmen, who are essential for the services of the city and who make up the majority of the population (we need to remind ourselves that Plato's ideal commonwealth probably numbers no more than five thousand people). Then there would be the Guardians, or soldiers, who are trained to defend the republic from foreign enemies.

Finally, there is the class of Rulers, who are also the city's philosophers, the moral and administrative keepers of the state; the people who make sure everything else in society works. This third class is, not surprisingly, the main focus of the *Republic*. Socrates tells his listeners how the Rulers will use their knowledge (he carefully describes the mental and physical training they will undergo, including a thorough grounding in mathematics) to harmonize the other two parts of society, just as reason keeps the other two elements of the soul (courage and the appetites) in check.

The class of Rulers are above all a class of legislators and lawmakers. Through good laws, even the lowest and least-educated citizens will be able to learn to be just and virtuous, even if they do not understand justice and virtue themselves. In this way, an ideal society and even an ideal people will result—especially since Plato's plan includes a rudimentary form of eugenics, with the Rulers making sure the best breed with the best.[13]

At this point, Socrates's listeners get a bit skeptical. Does Socrates think such a society could ever be set up in reality? No, Socrates admits, he does not. But at least it can serve as "the ideal pattern" (the word he uses is *paradeigma*, or paradigm), which the more closely any society approximates it, the happier and more virtuous it will become.[14]

At this moment, two-thirds into Book V of the *Republic*, an important impulse for Western culture is born—and a clever Greek pun. It is the utopian impulse, after the Greek word *utopia*, which can mean either the best place to live (*eutopia*) or nowhere (*u-topia*), since experience (and Aristotle) will teach us that they are one and the same. Still, in various guises over the centuries, in settings large and small, men and women will try to bring their version of Plato's *Republic* to fruition. Some, like Sir Thomas More (who first coined the term *utopia*) and Sir Francis Bacon, will confine their efforts to paper. Others will take up the task more literally with varying and sometimes hilarious, and sometimes horrifying, results. From New Harmony, Indiana, to Pol Pot's Cambodia, they are all efforts to create a brand-new society according to Plato's basic premise, that through laws based on the highest and most certain knowledge, we can create if not the perfect society, at least a pretty fair copy.*

Indeed, without a model of perfection, Socrates affirms, "there is no other road to real happiness, either for society or the individual."[15] Of course, Plato's own formula involves what we would see as excessive regimentation. It abolishes private property and marriage for Rulers and Guardians alike. Instead, the Rulers will decide who will breed with whom, in order to produce

---

*It is said that, after the Koran, Plato's *Republic* was the favorite book of the founder of Iran's Islamic republic, the Ayatollah Khomeini.

the best specimens for each class. Plato dictates what kind of food each class will eat and even what kind of music each group will be allowed to hear (stirring martial music for the Guardians and serene, contemplative tunes for the Rulers).

However, the purpose of all these rules and regulations was to end what Plato saw as the worst aspect of normal Greek politics: the bitter class conflict and clashes among competing factions. In the average Greek city, rich and poor were literally out for each other's blood, as historian Michael Rostovtzeff has pointed out in his description of what politics was like in one city-state, the home of the philosopher Thales:

> At Miletus the people were at first victorious and murdered the wives and children of the aristocrats; then the aristocrats prevailed and burned their opponents alive, lighting up the open spaces of the city with live torches.[16]

In his stepfather's household, he had seen the typical Athenian politician who sought to exploit rather than end these ancient antagonisms. The mission of Plato's Philosopher Ruler was to end this kind of madness.

On his mother's side he had an ancestor who could serve as his model statesman. This was the legendary legislator Solon, whose laws ended the civil strife that had divided Athens in the sixth century BCE. Solon's reforms, which embodied "his preference for an ordered life, with its careful gradations giving its class its proper place," earned him pride of place among the Seven Wise Men of Greece. They also made Solon the real-life paradigm for Plato's Philosopher Rulers in the *Republic*, where "those we call kings and rulers really and truly become philosophers, and political power and philosophy come into the same hands."[17] A truly utopian hope, we might say—but amazingly, Plato got the chance to try it himself in 367 BCE, when he was nearly sixty. Twenty years earlier during his trip to Italy, he had visited Syracuse, Sicily's largest city-state, and made fast friends with the brother of its ruler, a man named Dion. Two decades later Dion invited him to return as political adviser to Syracuse's new ruler, Dion's nephew Dionysius II.

The offer seemed irresistible to Plato. He had just finished the *Republic*, or was nearly finished. What better opportunity to transform his theory into action—to see the principles of law, virtue, and justice he had set forth achieved in reality? "Now is the time to try," Plato told himself, so he set off by ship for Syracuse, hoping he might be following in the footsteps of his illustrious ancestor Solon.[18]

As soon as he landed and met Dionysius II, however, he learned that legislating perfect justice is not so easy. His friendship with Dion went back twenty years. "I imparted to him my ideas of what was best for men," Plato later tells us in one of his letters, "and he listened with a zeal and attentiveness I had never encountered in any young man."[19] Dion now encouraged Plato to cleanse Syracuse of her luxuries and vices "and put on her the garment of freedom," along with laws to make the citizens orderly and virtuous. Plato may even have contemplated abolishing private property as he had in the *Republic*, or at least imposing limits on wealth. Certainly he hoped to train the young Dionysius to become the kind of conscientious ruler a true Platonic state would need to maintain order: in short, a living Philosopher Ruler.

Plato's hopes were quickly dashed. Dionysius II had every gift except good sense; he was also an incurable alcoholic. He soon lost patience with his two would-be political tutors and threw them out. Stuck in exile in Athens, Dion devoted himself to raising money and troops to liberate his native land and expel Dionysius. Many Academy students joined in, possibly with Plato's encouragement, and sailed with Dion's expedition to Syracuse. Although outnumbered, they managed to topple Dionysius's tyranny. Now it was Dion himself who seemed poised to realize Plato's dreams.

However, as the people of Syracuse soon observed, "we have only exchanged a drunken tyrant for a sober one."[20] Dion proved to be just as corrupt as his unlamented nephew, and eventually he, too, had to be driven out by force.

Plato watched the unfolding of these events from his Academy in Athens. They also made him sadder and wiser. When some of Dion's former friends asked Plato for advice on a future constitution for Syracuse, he gave them far more modest advice than the grandiose vision he had set forth in the *Republic*. It involved a mixed constitution of democratic and monarchical elements, with a warning: "Do not subject Sicily or any other state to the despotism of men, but to the rule of laws; this at least," he adds timidly, "is my doctrine."[21]

The vision of a perfect commonwealth united in virtue and justice that seemed so dazzling in theory proved much messier in practice. The utopian impulse requires some regard for reality. And thanks to the Syracuse experience, Plato's late political writings like the *Statesman* and the *Laws* make more concessions to reality than his earlier masterwork.

All the same, they are animated by the same beliefs. Good laws will make good men, and the best laws are forged not in the heat of crisis or the give-and-take of ordinary political debate, where men's appetites take over, but through the exercise of knowledge and reason. Self-interest must learn to yield to the common interest; and men must be united if they are to be free. Taken together, that remains Plato's most important political legacy.

Here, the final word belongs to Socrates. "The society we have described," he says in the *Republic*, "can never grow into a reality or see the light of day." Nonetheless, "there will be no end to the troubles of states, or indeed, my dear Glaucon, of humanity itself, until philosophers become kings in this world."[22]

As we might expect, Aristotle's approach is very different. Aristotle's *Politics*, like his *Metaphysics*, turns Plato's system upside down. For Plato, we find our true freedom only when we find our proper place within the political community. Aristotle, by contrast, concludes that community exists to serve the individuals who make it up, not the other way around. Plato's *Republic* celebrates a communitarian ideal based on men's dreams. It will give us Jean-Jacques Rousseau and Karl Marx, but also Martin Luther King. Aristotle's *Politics*, by contrast, will give us Thomas Aquinas and Thomas Jefferson, as well as Boss Tweed. It marks the birth of a democratic individualism that draws its pragmatic principles from sometimes hard-won experience.

This is because Aristotle's philosopher is always an observer of reality, not the creator of it. Instead of laying out the perfect blueprint, then turning reluctantly to the real world, Aristotle starts with the real world itself.

When he wrote his *Politics*, which is more a collection of essays than a single treatise, that real world was the Greek city-state. The original *Politics* was accompanied by something like 158 constitutions from actual Greek cities, of which only the Athenian example survives. These constitutions were for Aristotle the biological specimens for his political laboratory. As he had done with the fish and mollusks he had collected, he intended to probe inside to find out how they worked, in order to arrive at a general picture of how *all* political societies worked, or should work.

Political science on Aristotle's terms is about observation and analysis, or induction: very much what goes on in political science departments in universities today. Aristotle knew that a political science on Plato's terms, based on an exact knowledge of how to create the perfect laws, might be a worthy goal. Plato's writings, Aristotle says, "show ingenuity, novelty of view, and a spirit of inquiry."

But perfect laws cannot stand up to the lessons of experience in actual cities and societies, "in which these things [advocated by Plato] would not have gone unnoticed if they had really been good." As with ethics, in Aristotle's politics it is the practice, not the vision, that counts.[23]

Like Plato, Aristotle accepts that the goal of politics is to make the members of the community good. "The end of political science is the highest good; and the chief concern of this science is to endow the citizens with . . . virtue and the readiness to do fine deeds."[24] However, the way to get there is not from the top down, as in Plato's *Republic* and the *Laws*, but from the bottom up.

Aristotle reveals that the essential building block of every political community must be the individual household, consisting of the citizen and his family (including household slaves). From the household springs every other type of human association, starting with the clan or tribe. The final realization of all *these* associations is the self-governing city-state, the *polis*.

But that community still exists, Aristotle argues, in order to make the householder happy, rather than the other way around. This is why Aristotle describes man, in his most famous phrase, as a "political animal." We are *zoon politikon* by nature, but we join together to realize our own ends as individuals, not to serve the ends of others. In order to do this, men require some freedom from government interference, and in a democracy like Athens, they require equality before the law. In his *Politics* Aristotle set out the essential prerequisites of democratic liberty pretty much as they remain today.[25]

This is why Aristotle becomes so impatient when he turns to the *Republic*. Plato's goal is unity, a laudable one. But Aristotle says that this kind of unity equals the death of the *polis* and freedom. Plato's authoritarian, even arbitrary, rules reduce the community to the outlook of a single household or family, whereas a truly free society requires an aggregate of families and, as he says, "different kinds of men."

For Aristotle, diversity is the keynote of the free society, and free exchange lies at its heart. In the true (as opposed to the ideal) political community there must be a diversity of social roles, like the differing arts and crafts and social types we find along the street, from pot makers and carpenters to sea captains and merchants and wealthy landowners. This also entails a diversity of individual talents and abilities and a growing diversity of individual interests. A free society "necessarily requires a difference of capacities among its members," Aristotle writes in Book II, "which enables them to serve as complements to one another, and to attain a higher and better life by the mutual exchange of their different services."[26]

The political character of the citizenry must reflect that same diversity. Instead of one group monopolizing political power—even if that monopoly, as in the case of the *Republic*, is for everyone's good—"the natural equality of all the citizens" in a free state requires human beings to share power and to experience ruling and being ruled in turn. Aristotle's free society is one in which the citizens participate in their government rather than submit to it. *All* will be rulers in one way or another, at one time or another. "This means some rule, and others are ruled, in turn, as if they had become, for the time being, different persons."[27]

Some citizens will run for office, like the magistrates, or *archons*, chosen annually in Athens. Others will sit in the councils elected by the tribal districts, or *demes*; still others will vote by a simple show of hands in the assembly. All need some role to play, and the job of a constitution is to devise a system for doing that. Because if some lose their turn at ruling and being ruled or are systematically excluded, Aristotle concludes, we all lose out, "which again proves that difference of kinds is essential to the constitution of a *polis*."[28]

The same is true with the economic life of the *polis*. The diversity of crafts and exchanges is what gives it its energy and dynamism; it is what makes the self-governing community self-sufficient. Plato's ban on certain crafts, like statue making or writing poetry, and restrictions on others seemed absurd to Aristotle. However, Aristotle recognized that some will do better at their jobs and professions than others. Diversity of interests means inequality of results, even a division between rich and poor.

That division, and the resulting class conflict that infected all the Greek city-states, is the sign of a free society. It is one reason Aristotle stands so opposed to Plato's communism. Enforcing economic equality is not just a violation of common sense. It also flies in the face of why the *polis* exists at all.[29]

For Aristotle, class conflict is inevitable. He spends nearly half the *Politics* talking about it. But this conflict is not a source of despair, as it was for Plato. Nor is it a sign that political disaster is looming. Instead, Aristotle's science of politics is about learning how to build a harmony out of these competing existing parts through balance and moderation, rather than trying to *impose* order and harmony through rational legislation, as Plato tried to do in his *Republic.*

So the basis of Aristotle's secure and stable order is not the Philosopher Ruler, but the good citizen who participates actively in the political, social, and economic life of his community. He takes his turn in office and in voting; he leads his own life with his family; and he pursues his own interests at work every day. In his values and orientation, Aristotle's citizen is a true "political animal." To borrow a word that will be freighted with other meanings later on, he is *bourgeois.*

In his daily interactions, he practices that peculiar mixture of prudence and virtue that enables him to hit the mean and keeps his family and his *polis* on an even keel even as it complements the same virtues of his neighbors. He is no visionary or crusader. Aristotle would have little patience with those we call political activists. The good citizen's life is not about achieving one single goal, however laudable, or doing one thing perfectly. It is about doing all things well enough to be a happy man—and be an integral part of a happy free society.

Still, Aristotle holds out for certain principles that were traditional to the Greek *polis.* He still believes that the goal of self-government must be cultivating the good life as defined by our nature, not just self-defense or the protection of property (that will occur to other Aristotelians later).[30] He also believes that justice within the city must be based on what we deserve by our contributions; in other words it must be distributive, meaning the wealthy get more and women and slaves have no political identity.

But in Book III, Aristotle confronts the weightiest issue of all. Plato had raised it in the *Republic:* "Who should rule?" In modern political parlance, this is the issue of sovereignty. In the end, after examining the best constitutions and the conditions on the ground, Aristotle concludes that power belongs best with the people. This may be difficult to achieve, he points out. It may fly in the face of Plato's claim that laws should be made by those who know best.

But "there is this to be said about the Many," Aristotle remarks. "Each of them by himself may not be of [much] quality; but when they all come together it is possible they may surpass—collectively and as a body, not individually—the quality of the few best."[31] Those who argue that only experts know best are wrong. In politics, as in house building, the best judge of what works is the user, not the maker. Aristotle's support for the rule of the people, backed by "rightly constitutional laws" that must be ultimately sovereign, becomes a crucial legacy for the future of the West. Democracy on the Athenian model may not be ideal, Aristotle says, but it may be the best we can hope for.[32]

By the time we close the last pages of the *Politics*, we realize we are standing on the brink of two different ways of thinking about governing human beings. Politics on Plato's terms becomes *prescriptive*, a series of formulae for shaping man and society into what they should be rather than accepting things as they are. Politics on Aristotle's terms will be largely *descriptive*, in which the more we discover about human nature, the more we recognize our powerlessness to effect real change.

Ironically, that point was rammed home by Aristotle's own experience with real-life politics when he became tutor to Philip of Macedon's son Alexander.

Plato was sixty when he took his stab at high politics. Aristotle was about forty. He was not yet famous, and his own views were still developing. Despite his urban bias, Aristotle was not indifferent to the heroic, even Homeric, virtues this headstrong virile athletic youth seemed to represent. He may even have hoped that he could turn the sixteen-year-old Alexander into a real-life version of his "great-souled man" outlined in the *Ethics*.

Alexander and Aristotle were together for four years. When they parted company, it was as if they had never met. "Men who are utterly superior" to others, Aristotle says at one point in the *Politics*, are "a law unto themselves."[33] Perhaps the one thing Alexander got out of his lessons with Aristotle was the sense of natural Greek superiority to other barbarian races, and that if Greeks ever truly unified, they could crush anyone, even the Persian Empire. Alexander, of course, proceeded to do just that. But this was a chauvinist view he could have learned from almost any Greek writer in the mid–fourth century BCE, even Plato.

As for Aristotle, his links to Alexander and the royal family certainly did not hurt his career. He and the regent Alexander left behind in Greece, Antipater, seem to have been on fairly intimate terms.[34] Aristotle's nephew and disciple, Callisthenes, actually went with Alexander on his conquests. But in the end, Alexander remained the same ruthless barbarian his father had been. Teaching him had been like petting a lion in the zoo, Aristotle learned. It is better to take your hand out of the bars too soon rather than too late. Alexander eventually turned on Callisthenes and had him executed on trumped-up treason charges. Faced with the decision to defend his nephew against Alexander's unjust attacks, Aristotle thought it wiser to do and say nothing.

It is an instructive story. Since World War II, political theorists have been all too aware of the dangers of Plato's approach to politics, of reaching too high and too fast to make our utopian hopes a reality.* The Philosopher Ruler can turn out to be Cambodia's Pol Pot or the Ayatollah Khomeini.

But there are dangers inherent in Aristotle's approach as well. They involve an acceptance of the status quo that can shade into timidity, and rationalizing injustices with a casual shrug of "that's the way things are." Aristotle's philosophy emphasizes the necessity of change, even progress. Yet paradoxically, his insistence on being the detached observer, on analyzing rather than influencing events, winds up providing the excuse for institutional inertia and apathy. This is what happened when his influence grew too strong in the universities of medieval Europe and when scholars turned to Aristotle to justify appalling episodes like the slave trade and the conquest of the New World.[†]

The necessary antidote to Aristotelian indifference appears, appropriately enough, in Plato's *Republic*. There he lists the qualities he most esteems in the Guardians of his imaginary state, one of which is *thymos*. It is not an easy word to translate. Most commentators describe it as spirit or courage. For Plato, it is the natural ally of reason rather than the appetites.[35]

We can also translate *thymos* as righteous anger, the burning indignation we feel at the sight of a parent abusing a helpless child, or any wrongdoing and injustice. *Thymos* is the fire that burns in the heart of the activist, the reformer, the revolutionary, and the intellectual rebel. All the truly great reformers had it: Mohandas Gandhi, Emmeline Pankhurst, William Wilberforce, Bishop Desmond Tutu. It's what distinguishes a Martin Luther from an Erasmus; a Rousseau from a Voltaire; a Martin Luther King from a

---

*The centerpiece of this critique is Karl Popper's *The Open Society and Its Enemies*, which was first published in 1945 but which Popper began writing the day Nazi Germany occupied Austria in the *Anschluss* of 1938. For more on this, see chapter 29.

[†]See chapter 25.

Booker T. Washington; and a Lenin from a Kerensky. It's a quality that can land us all in trouble; but sometimes it also springs us out of servitude.

More than once in history, Aristotle's writings will offer a pretext around which brutal practices like slavery and imperialism, and narrow-minded and rigid orthodoxies, will be justified or built. And more than once in history, it will take a renegade Platonist to knock them down.

From politics and ethics to theories of knowledge and nature, then, the battle lines between Plato and Aristotle were drawn. They would strengthen and intensify, as disciples and admirers took over the struggle. The best would borrow from both, but none could evade the fact that Greek, and then Western, thought was now set on a double, rather than a single, track. And it would move in directions and toward places neither Plato nor Aristotle could ever have imagined.

In 335–34, Aristotle returned to Athens. He was now the foremost living philosopher in Greece. He had not seen the city since Plato's death. As he walked the streets, however, he would have wandered past the Academy, where he had spent most of his young adulthood. The man who had squeezed him out as director, Plato's nephew Speusippus, was dead. But the members had chosen as his successor a man who was just as opposed to Aristotle's theories as Speusippus had been. So Aristotle decided it was time to found his own school.

The place he found for it was on the eastern side of town, in some rented buildings close to a grove sacred to the god Apollo Lykeius. Later, when he had some buildings of his own constructed on the site, the name stuck. The Lyceum was Aristotle's answer to the Academy and its mirror image. There was a large garden and a temple dedicated to the Nine Muses, or museum, just as there was in the Academy. There were also lecture rooms, large billboards on which were mounted maps of Greece and the world, and a room set aside for a growing collection of books and scrolls (as far as we know, the first formal library in the ancient world).

There were also rooms with tables for collecting and dissecting biological specimens. As we would expect, Aristotle made sure his Lyceum students had a thorough training in the natural sciences. His student Theophrastus's *History of Plants* and Aristotle's own *History of Animals* were the fruits of the Lyceum laboratory. Aristotle also created the first real medical school, which became famous all across Greece. Aristotle deserves the title of father of medicine as least as much as Hippocrates does.

Aristotle lectured regularly just as his teacher Plato had, usually on the more difficult philosophical topics in the mornings and on rhetoric and dialectic in the afternoons. Most of what survive as Aristotle's writings were probably lecture notes preserved by his listeners. And since Aristotle liked to walk as he talked, with his pupils following behind and on either side of him, the students of the Lyceum became known as the "wanderers," or *peripatetikoi* — the Peripatetics.

The productive routine of the Lyceum and Aristotle's last years was shattered by a single event: the death of Alexander the Great in 323 BCE. Overnight, it turned the Greek world upside down. Those who had been out of favor as opponents of Macedonian rule were in; those who had collaborated or benefited from the Alexandrian order found themselves in danger. Aristotle himself fled Athens for Chalcis in Euboea, where his mother had owned property and where in his last years he was able to find some shelter from the storms around him.

One of his last pieces of writing that survives is his will. It mentions which sister will take custody of his son and daughter and which gets the house and garden. He names which slaves are to be set free and asks that money be set aside for a modest memorial statue to Zeus. He never mentions the Lyceum or his old students and friends. It is, as his biographer Werner Jaeger pointed out, the will of a lonely man.[36]

He passed on in his sixty-second year, in 322, a year after Alexander, his most famous pupil. Aristotle died alone and isolated, almost in disgrace. Even Delphi had stripped him of the honors it had heaped on him during his lifetime. Although his portrait bust remained in the museum of the school he had founded, his own writings sat in the Lyceum's library for nearly a century, largely forgotten.

All the same, under his former pupil Theophrastus the Lyceum was about to take on a life of its own. Its work and the patient inquiries of its Peripatetics would spread far beyond the interests of its founder, even as Plato's Academy did. In fact, the clash between Plato and Aristotle's legacies was just beginning.

Diogenes (412?–323 BCE)

Six

THE INHERITORS: PHILOSOPHY IN THE HELLENISTIC AGE

It is vain to ask of the gods what a man is capable of supplying for himself.

—Epicurus (341–270 BCE)

Aristotle's greatest pupil died in 323 BCE, convinced he had conquered the world. He had come back from his campaigns beyond the Indus River to die in Babylon. Someone asked Alexander on his deathbed what he wanted for his funeral. He whispered, "I see great games."

His prediction proved right. At his death, his empire flew apart. His generals fought war after war for the spoils that were left. Greece entered a period of constant turbulence, even as new cities like Alexandria, Antioch, and Pergamum and new kingdoms rose to prominence. This was the Hellenistic age, a diverse multicultural world in which Greeks and peoples newly assimilated into Hellenic culture found new ways to flourish and compete for power.

Much the same happened in philosophy. Thanks to Plato and Aristotle, Athens remained the center of Greek intellectual life. Alexander's success had neutered the old free *polis* ideal that Athens had epitomized since the battle of Marathon. The irony was that for all its impotence, Athens was more affluent than ever and home to a philosophical talking shop unlike any before or since.

Plato's Academy and Aristotle's Lyceum soon found themselves besieged by rivals on every side. In 306, a man named Epicurus came to Athens to found a school of thinking that quickly bore his name and was based on the pursuit of pleasure and avoidance of pain. Five years earlier, a Phoenician from Cyprus named Zeno preached a doctrine of moral austerity under the porch, or *stoa*, of the city's marketplace. That gave his followers the name of Stoics, and a school of thought that would soon spread from one end of the ancient Mediterranean to the other.

Meanwhile, the poor son of an Athenian citizen and a Thracian slave named Antisthenes had been instructing students to renounce all material possessions at the Cynosarges, a gymnasium used by working-class Athenians. Under his disciple Diogenes, Antisthenes's doctrines, dubbed Cynicism after the gym where he had held classes, would shape the outlook of the Greek and Roman classical worlds.

Epicureans, Stoics, Cynics, and Skeptics (another group who flourished in Athens in the century after Aristotle, arguing that nothing can be known for certain): All of these schools live on as part of our language today. Of course, when we describe someone as cynical or stoical or skeptical, we usually mean their general outlook on life rather than a formal set of philosophical doctrines.

Yet this was precisely what the Hellenistic philosophers wanted. They hoped to move philosophy beyond the bounds of formal discussion that Plato and Aristotle had laid down. They encouraged their students to cultivate a distinct attitude toward themselves and the world that would reflect an intellectual "brand" based on their teachings. They were also hungry for the age's equivalent of media attention. Publicity brought them fame and students from every corner of the Greek-speaking world. They would have been as at home on Facebook or Twitter as any contemporary blogger. They even wanted to look different from other people, growing long beards (just like Plato and Aristotle in their portrait busts) instead of being clean-shaven like the rest of Hellenistic Greece's ruling class.

Some of these new schools appeared during Plato's time, like the Cynics, and some after. Adding to the confusion, most stood in direct opposition to the orthodoxies of the Academy and the Lyceum, even when they drew from the same sources. Epicureans, for example, looked back to pre-Socratic thinkers like Democritus and Heraclitus. There was even a revival of Pythagorean thought (Epicurus came from Pythagoras's home island of Samos) that would effervesce across the Mediterranean until quite late in antiquity.[1]

Nonetheless, everyone's starting point was the same that Socrates had set out, and that Plato and Aristotle in their different ways had made famous. Every Hellenistic philosopher insisted that life was about the soul's search for the one crucial thing it did not have but which, once it was found, would make it happy. But what was that one thing? That's where the battle began.[2]

The students who flocked to Athens from all over the Greek world, in the years after Alexander's death, all wanted an answer to the same question. Where do we find the key to living a moral life that will protect our souls from vice and corruption, they asked, especially when the traditions we have inherited from the past no longer seem to have any meaning? It's a question that makes the immediate heirs to Plato and Aristotle still relevant today.

It's also what cut them off from Plato and Aristotle. Greeks of that earlier age still believed in a familiar and more or less ordered cosmos, which (as the *Timaeus* said) was writ large in the heavens and writ small in man himself. Aristotle could confidently assert that the free Greek city-state was the ultimate expression of man's essential nature and be believed.[3]

One hundred years later, no one believed it. In the messy multicultural world Alexander's conquests had stirred up, Greeks found themselves outnumbered. They rubbed shoulders on every street corner with non-Greeks, who now spoke the same language but whose cultural roots lay with strange gods and even stranger traditions. Even the Academy would end up being led by a Carthaginian,* a people whom Plato had dismissed as hopeless barbarians. Hellenistic Greece triggered a cultural revolution that turned every tradition inside out. The heirs to Plato and Aristotle wanted answers Plato and Aristotle could no longer give. However, they could not escape the way the quarreling pair had framed the questions.

The godfather of the Epicureans, Aristippus of Cyrene, had actually been a student of Socrates. The *Phaedo* tells us that he, like Plato, was absent from the final death scene in Socrates's prison cell. However, he and Plato took very different lessons from their dead master's teachings. They demonstrated

---

*This was Cleitomachus, who took over the Academy in 127–26 BCE.

that when they met again almost thirty years later at the court of Dionysius II in Syracuse where, the story goes, at one drunken banquet Dionysius asked both men to dance for him in purple robes.

Plato thought the robes and gesture unseemly and effeminate, and he refused. Aristippus, however, happily agreed to this festive cross-dressing, quoting back to Plato a Greek couplet:

> *Even in Bacchus's wild alarm,*
> *The modest woman suffers still no harm.*

True or not, the story reveals Aristippus's formula for happiness: Enjoy the good life, including food and drink, because pleasure is all that counts. His disciple Epicurus systematized this hedonistic impulse into a genuine philosophical doctrine. Aristippus, like Socrates, wrote nothing. Epicurus, who left behind some three hundred separate treatises, probably wrote too much. As one writer puts it, "It is curious that the great advocate of ease and comfort should have cared little for the comfort of his readers."[4]

Epicurus's doctrines and his parties in Athens attracted, not surprisingly, a rather wild crowd. He himself seems to have taken little interest in the more obvious examples of pleasure, including sex. The comparison with Andy Warhol seems irresistible. But Epicurus had a loftier goal. It was to get his followers to concentrate their minds on the one sure thing in life, pleasure, so they could achieve a constant state of detached well-being, instead of overindulging in pleasure's more obvious manifestations. Epicurus even defined pleasure as the absence of pain: not exactly a formula for a life of sex, drugs, and rock and roll.

Still, the underlying principle of his philosophy—that the one thing all nature seeks to avoid is pain, and the one thing it seeks to gain is pleasure, and men should do the same—was only an extreme version of Aristotle's theory of knowledge based on our senses. Plato had stated that sensation and knowledge were direct opposites. Epicurus, like Aristotle, disagreed. However, Epicurus's conclusion that sensation must be the source of *all* knowledge (since the sensation of pain is the *only* evil and that of pleasure the *only* good) would have horrified Aristotle, not to mention Socrates himself.[5]

For Epicurus, our one friend is our body and the knowledge of the world it provides through the senses. Our one enemy is religion, especially any that promises rewards and punishments in the afterlife in order to keep us on the straight and narrow, instead of allowing us to seek happiness in this world. For in the end, we are nothing but atoms, like the universe itself, and we pass randomly once through this life. Even death is simply oblivion—right where we started in the first place. So live for the moment, Epicurus concludes, "and never shall you be disturbed waking or asleep, but you will live like a god among men."[6]

Epicureanism will be the hardy perennial among the Hellenistic philosophical plants. The idea that sensation is the source of all knowledge would find a congenial home in the age of John Locke, and his ideas have commanded front and center seats for every debate on morality until today. Certainly Epicureanism enjoyed a fertile flowering in the Greek and Roman worlds, especially among its upper classes.* For all its celebration of the good life, however, Epicureanism as a doctrine was rather chilly and comfortless: an indifferent God; an empty sky above; a random meaningless world below. Beyond that, Epicureanism trumpeted its open declaration of war on both the Lyceum, since it denied Aristotle's assertion that the universe is immortal and without end, and the Academy, since it overthrew the rule of reason and substituted the kind of hedonism Plato and Socrates had been at pains (a forgiveable pun) to refute.

Plato's Academy certainly felt philosophical pressure from the Epicureans. But it faced an even greater challenge from the Stoics. They swung in the opposite direction to Epicurus's disciples. Beginning with their founder, Zeno, the Stoics taught that the key to the happy life is adhering to a strict sense of virtue and a rigid duty toward others rather than indulging in pleasure, and a renunciation of, or at least an indifference to, all worldly goods.

"I leave you what is of far more value than earthly riches," the Roman Stoic Seneca told his family before he died, "I leave you the example of a virtuous life."[7] Another Stoic master, the ex-slave Epictetus, lived his own version of the Golden Rule: "What you wouldn't want to suffer, don't make others suffer"—words one might expect from a man who had lived a life in bondage.[†8]

---

*The best-known example is probably Gaius Cassius Longinus, Brutus's friend and fellow plotter against Julius Caesar, who is immortalized in Shakespeare's *Julius Caesar* with the line "The fault, dear Brutus, is not in the stars, but in our selves . . ." Good Epicurean advice, although Brutus himself, despite his obvious Stoic leanings, was an alumnus of the Academy.

†The story is that Epictetus had once had a sadistic owner who left him permanently lame. When his master was twisting his leg, Epictetus only smiled and said, "You will break it." And when it broke, "I told you so." This indifference to physical pain would be a hallmark of Stoicism, particularly the

To some, this must have seemed like an extension of Plato's own teachings. Zeno, after all, had been inspired to go to the Academy after reading Plato's *Apology*. And in the deep background of Zeno's belief that an all-powerful *Logos* animates the material universe and makes all men brothers was the notion of the World Soul in Plato's *Timaeus*.[9]

Still, the Stoic indifference to pain and adversity and worldly success sprang from a deep fatalism—"Fate leads the willing," Epictetus says at one point, "and drags the unwilling"—that is foreign to both Plato and Aristotle.* Stoics were even more resolutely convinced than the Epicureans that everything we know, or can know, must come entirely from our senses—in other words, out of the very depths of the cave. It certainly was not geared to win the Stoics many friends at the Academy, which fought the men of the *stoa* with a passionate intensity that lasted for nearly a century.[10]

The Cynics, too, had Socratic roots. Their founder, Antisthenes, had known both Socrates and Plato personally. He lived in Athens's port at Piraeus, and legend has it that he walked the forty furlongs every day up to the Agora to hear Socrates speak.[11] Antisthenes created his school at the Cynosarges, or "Dog Pond," after the death of the man he considered his mentor. Above all, he seems to have taken from Socrates the notion that man's freedom depends completely on the state of our soul, not on some physical or material condition; and on our capacity to endure adversity and to be indifferent to our outward fate.

This sounds very Stoic. But Antisthenes took his Cynic doctrines to the next radical step. He rejected any and all social conventions, including all forms of property and government. He also violently turned his back on Plato's theology and even more violently his theory of Forms. "A horse I see," Antisthenes is supposed to have exclaimed, "but not horseness": words that would echo in the works of the medieval philosopher William of Ockham.

Cynicism really took off, however, with the arrival of a rather scruffy young man who told Antisthenes that nothing would keep him from learning from him, even after Antisthenes beat him repeatedly with a stick. The young man's name was Diogenes. He came from a small town called Sinope, and when people asked him if it was true that his fellow citizens had condemned

---

Roman kind. It persists in the most familiar Stoic character from television, the pointy-eared Vulcan hero Mr. Spock of *Star Trek*.

*This quotation is often credited to the Roman Stoic Seneca (see chapter 9). Epictetus, however, gave it its original Greek formulation, quoting Zeno's successor Cleanthes (c. 330–231 BCE).

him to exile, he would reply, "Yes, and I condemned them to remain in Sinope."[12]

Diogenes's quick wit and, dare we say it, cynical outlook disguised a first-class intellect focused on proving a single principle: that we have to own nothing, *absolutely nothing*, to be truly free. Diogenes was the first homeless philosopher. He chose to live instead in a great water jar outside an Athens temple, to beg for food in the street, and to freely defecate and urinate in public.

Naturally, this drew an enormous audience and great publicity. The ruder Diogenes behaved, in fact, the more his sophisticated Hellenistic audience loved it. In an age when philosophy was being reduced to sound bites, Diogenes provided the juiciest of all. Most people have heard of his walking the streets of Athens with a lantern, looking (he said) for an honest man and never finding one. Someone else once found him begging for food from a statue. When they asked him why, he said, "I'm learning to deal with rejection."

At one point he met the greatest celebrity of the age, Alexander the Great himself. The great king had heard about the famous Cynic and on a visit to Corinth wanted to meet him. Alexander found Diogenes sunning himself in an outdoor court of the local gymnasium.

"I am Alexander the king," the conqueror said.

"I am Diogenes the Cynic," replied the philosopher, and continued to sun himself.

"Is there any favor that I may bestow upon you?" Alexander asked.

Diogenes looked up with a frown. "Yes," he said. "Stand out of my light."

Later Alexander said if he could not be himself, he would want to be Diogenes. As a later scholar pointed out, no one asked Diogenes if he would prefer to be Alexander.[13]

But behind Diogenes's clowning lay a serious purpose. He wanted to show that man has to return to his most basic nature in order to discover his true self and that everything that is not part of that self, including property and normal social and political obligations, was a useless distraction. His model was still Socrates: not the dialectician or mystical visionary into which Plato had turned his teacher, but the man from the *Apology* who described himself as a gadfly stinging his fellow Athenians to the path to virtue. Diogenes wanted to shine the light of truth on the people and institutions sheltering in Plato's cave, whether they liked it or not. Diogenes also revved up

Socrates's gentle yet caustic sense of humor into a powerful tool for doing that.

Diogenes's goal, he said, was "to deface the coinage," meaning strip away the false conventions on which society was built and expose the raw reality underneath.[14] He is not only the first homeless philosopher, but the first deconstructionist. Before he died in 323 BCE—the same year as Alexander, an irony he would have appreciated—Diogenes had given Cynicism a respectable position in the field of literature as well as philosophy. His mordant wit inspired the major creators of Greek satire and parody and founded a Western comedic tradition that has lasted until today.[15]

All this, of course, was a far cry from the kind of rigorous dialectical and metaphysical training offered at the Academy or the Lyceum. The sight of Diogenes's urn, with its constant crowd of curious onlookers, must have grated on every serious teacher and student who walked past it. Plato's and Aristotle's heirs were finding themselves at war, not just with each other, but with the Cynics and Stoics and all the rest. The Academy fought back with a host of weapons, even using the arguments of the Skeptics to challenge the notion that our senses are the only source of real knowledge.

The philosophy wars in Athens between 300 and 200 BCE weary readers and scholars alike. What matters here is that they knocked mathematics and science out from the pride of place they had occupied in Plato's Academy. Plato had wanted all his students to be master mathematicians and astronomers, as well as exemplars of virtue, especially since he believed knowledge of the one pointed the way to understanding of the other.

Early Academicians, for example, made enormous contributions to the field of astronomy. Plato's friend Eudoxus devised a working model for showing the movement of the planets and the heavens. Heraclides, another Plato student, may have been the first person to propose that the earth rotated on its axis. He also used calculations of the orbits of Venus and Mars to show that they must be revolving not around the earth, but around the sun—literally an earthshaking hypothesis.*

Later there would still be Academy-trained geometers; Euclid was one. There would still be Platonic astronomers. But as the Academy's battles with other schools over what makes for the best life intensified, time spent dealing

---

*Heraclides never lost sight of Platonic astronomy's ultimate goal and liked to quote Pythagoras: "Beatitude is the knowledge of the perfection of the numbers of the soul."

with empirical scientific questions shrank away.[16] Platonism became more and more focused on ethical and metaphysical questions: in other words, what lies either outside or beyond the scope of the physical sciences. In a few short decades, the future trajectory of Plato's influence on Western culture was set.

The opposite happened at the Lyceum. It had a rocky time in Hellenistic Athens. The school's "collaborationist" connections to the Macedonian regime caused Aristotle's pupils considerable problems. At one point its director, Theophrastus, had to close the Lyceum's doors. In 287 BCE, there were even anti-Lyceum riots. One of the lecture halls was set on fire; the statue of Aristotle was destroyed or stolen, as were other statues. Even so, the school continued to churn out graduates who were employed and honored across the Greek world. Peripatetic scholars wrote treatises on physics, astronomy, politics, poetry, and even history that earned the respect of a small but educated audience.[17]

Perhaps for that reason, the Lyceum had little impact on the more popular philosophies of the age. It was also facing an identity crisis. The turning point came in 287–86, when Aristotle's personal disciple Theophrastus died, and Strato of Lampsacus was named as his successor.

Strato, to judge from the sources, was entirely self-directed—a true self-starter. Born in a small town facing the Black Sea, he is one of science's forgotten heroes. He was nicknamed, significantly, Strato the Physicist. His appointment sent a clear signal that the natural and physical sciences would be the Lyceum's focus in the future, just as ethics and formal philosophy would be the future focus at the Academy.

As a member and then director of the Lyceum, Strato made two crucial decisions for the future of Western thought. The first was to insist that scientific research had to be free from any restraints by theology (he himself seems to have been a materialist and atheist) or philosophy, including ethics. Instead, according to a knowledgeable ancient authority, "[Strato] devoted himself entirely to the investigation of nature."[18] It is under Strato that the heirs of Aristotle took the first tentative steps toward the idea of pure science, that an investigator must be free to pursue his work regardless of where it leads or what inconvenient truths it discovers—or even what comfortable worldviews it upsets, including Aristotle's own.

It is hard to believe this is what Aristotle intended.[19] He had seen his natural philosophy, including his physics and astronomy, as a complete and unshakably true picture of reality. But by stressing the power of observation as the main source of knowledge, he had let the genie run free. His students, even the loyal Theophrastus, felt compelled to question his theories based on new data or new observations. Strato contrived physical tests to bring Aristotle's fondest assumptions under scrutiny. His work on creating an artificial vacuum, which Aristotle had said was impossible, may be the first true scientific experiment.[20]

In this way and almost in spite of himself, from the moment he first picked up a lungfish on the beach and wondered what was inside, Aristotle had created a Western scientific method that was destined to be permanently open-ended. It would be based on observation, analysis, and making fine distinctions (*diairein*) or divisions, instead of worrying about the Big Picture. It became the vehicle for research into every aspect of nature. It would lead in directions Aristotle himself never imagined, and not just in Athens.

Becoming an advocate of pure scientific research was Strato's first momentous decision. We don't know exactly when he came to his second, which was to leave Athens for Alexandria in Egypt. We do know it was before 287 BCE and came at the invitation of Egypt's ruler, Ptolemy I, who wanted a tutor for his son and heir, Ptolemy Philadelphus. In any case, Strato's arrival in that thriving port city was a landmark event in the history of Greek science. At one stroke Strato was leaving Athens, the ancient city of philosophers, intellectuals, and cosmopolitan aristocrats, for Alexandria, a new city of international businessmen, mathematicians, and engineers.

Before Alexander founded the city at the mouth of Nile thirty or so years earlier in 332, there had been nothing but sand dunes and swamps and scattered fishing villages. But the area formed a natural harbor, and in a couple of decades Alexandria became one of the richest urban centers on the Mediterranean.

In a sense, it was the first modern city. It stood at the confluence of three ancient cultures: Greece, Egypt, and the Middle East, including Babylon. People of every color and religion from Syria, Asia Minor, Iberia, Phoenicia, Nubia, the Arabian peninsula, Persia, and India swarmed its streets, did business in its shops, and unloaded their goods in its warehouses. Its Jewish quarter (according to the historian Josephus, Jews started arriving shortly after Alexander's death) covered two of the city's five principal districts. Jewish Alexandria became the home of shopkeepers, craftsmen, and artisans and a dozen synagogues.[21] Jewish relations with Greeks and Egyptians alike were respectful and amiable. People were too busy making money to fight over religious or ethnic differences.

No other ancient city demonstrated so powerfully Aristotle's assertion that "a difference of capacities among its members enables them to attain a higher and better life by the mutual exchange of their different services." From that point of view alone, Alexandria was already Aristotle's city.

Its ruler was the Macedonian king of Egypt Ptolemy I, one of Alexander's former generals, a tough, vigorous man who continued to command armies in the field until he was in his eighties. Ptolemy had always wanted his capital city to have a strong connection with Aristotle and the Lyceum. Perhaps he had learned on his campaigns with Alexander the value of Aristotle's kind of precise scientific research—and the value to a ruler of this kind of intellectual patronage.[22] Ptolemy had asked Aristotle himself to set up a library in Alexandria. Later, he invited Theophrastus to do the same.

In the end, he had to be satisfied with Strato of Lampsacus as his son's tutor. However, that was enough. Strato saw the situation clearly as soon as he got off the boat. Here was a rich, thriving city, a metropolis (as the Hellenistic Greeks termed it) teeming with alert, intelligent people from every part of Europe, Africa, and Asia. And here was a rich, powerful patron, Ptolemy I, determined to make Alexandria the most glorious city in the world and to bring his own reputation out from under the shadow of its illustrious founder.

Strato must have smiled at his good fortune. The Ptolemies father and son were the perfect foils for his plan to give the Lyceum a new importance and freedom. Alexandria was also the perfect place to give Aristotle a new boost as the godfather of Western science.

Seven

KNOWLEDGE IS POWER

Give me a lever and a place to stand, and I shall move the earth.
—Archimedes (287–12 BCE)

It was shortly after arriving in Alexandria that Strato of Lampsacus became King Ptolemy's principal adviser on all matters intellectual and scientific. Over the next several years, he would use that position to create the ancient world's most important research center, Alexandria's Mouseion, or Museum. Just as Alexandria was Aristotle's city, so its Museum would be the centrifuge for spreading Aristotle's methods and ideas across the ancient world.

We have no record of when or how Strato suggested creating the Museum and no idea when Ptolemy, the wily old general, gave his approval. Still, Strato clearly meant it to be a kind of branch campus of the Lyceum. Alumni of the Lyceum in Athens, the so-called Peripatetics, flocked to Alexandria to pursue their scientific research. Since, as its name implied, the Museum was dedicated not just to science but to all the Muses, its Peripatetic staff also

launched the first systematic study of Greek literature and language (following in the footsteps of Aristotle's own work in his *Rhetoric* and *Poetics*).*
Under Strato's former pupil Ptolemy II Philadelphus, the Museum grew still larger and more prestigious. It was the Hellenistic world's equivalent of Harvard, Oxford and Cambridge, and MIT all rolled into one.

The rules of the Museum itself seem to have been based on the Lyceum, with students and scholars taking meals together and living under the same roof. The salaries of its teachers and officials were even tax-exempt.[1] And Strato and his staff not only had all of Greek learning at their fingertips, they could also draw on Egypt's two-millennia-old tradition of study of mathematics and geometry, as well as astronomy and medicine.

Soon Alexandria's Museum was a busy hive of intellectual labor, even as Strato and his Peripatetic colleagues provided the impetus for another act of Ptolemaic patronage, the Great Library. It was probably inspired by Aristotle's library at the Lyceum and embodied a key Aristotelian principle: that the starting point of all true knowledge is not (contrary to Plato) abstract reasoning, but the collection and comparison of individual specimens, whether they be plants and shellfish or books and manuscripts.[2]

Like that of the Museum, the Great Library's history is shrouded in conflicting accounts and legend. We can be reasonably sure its first director was Demetrius of Phalerum, a shrewd and strong-willed figure with deep connections to the Lyceum in Athens. Demetrius seems to have brought a heavy influx of Peripatetic influence into the choosing of the library's collections and in the selection of its staff. In the end, Demetrius assembled no fewer than 120,000 separate titles, arranged in room after room of neatly rolled papyrus scrolls, including thousands of precious Egyptian and Babylonian texts. The Great Library was a treasure trove for research not only for science but for history, literature, philosophy, and theology. At some point (according to the ancient scholar Athenaeus), a former student of Theophrastus's sold Ptolemy II his teacher's complete library, including many works Aristotle himself had collected. In this way, the Great Library of Alexandria became Aristotle's physical as well as intellectual legacy to the ancient world.[3] Tapping into these unmatched resources, including forty separate rolls of Aristotle's *Ana-*

---

*The Muses were the nine Greek female deities supposed to inspire the most important learned arts: Euterpe (lyric poetry), Thalia (comedy and idyllic poetry), Melpomene (tragedy), Calliope (epic poetry), Terpsichore (choral dance and song), Clio (history), Erato (love verse and mimicry), Polyhymnia (sacred song), and Urania (astronomy). For more on Aristotle's literary legacy, see chapter 23.

Library of Alexandria

lytics,[4] scholars in Alexandria could now conduct research on a scale never imagined by Aristotle or his heirs in Athens, or indeed anyone else.[5] It triggered a transformation of Greek science, beginning with medicine.

The heroic figure in ancient medical research between Hippocrates and the great Galen is Herophilus of Chalcedon. Galen's own work would be unimaginable without him. Born around 335 BCE, Herophilus's first teacher came from Cos, the home island of Hippocrates and long a center of medical studies. However, Herophilus's most important work was all done in Alexandria, probably in connection with the Museum. Certainly his students taught medicine there.

Herophilus pioneered the study of the neurovascular system. He proved, for example, that the nervous system's center was (contrary to Aristotle's own teaching) the brain. He explored the prognostic possibilities of taking a patient's pulse, and he helped to create a standard medical vocabulary based on Greek words like *haima* for blood, as in hematoma (*toma* from the Greek *tumma*, or *oma*), and *gaster* for stomach, as in gastritis that is still used today.[6]

His biggest contribution, however, was in the study of anatomy. Following Aristotle's example with animals, he turned to dissection to discover what was going on inside the human frame. His curiosity was insatiable. Some ancient sources claim he turned to human vivisection in his work, including experiments on criminals handed over to him by the Ptolemaic government.[7]

Are the stories true? Given the fact that a couple of centuries later Galen mentions testing new poisons on condemned criminals, and the fact that slaves were routinely tortured to extract information in legal cases, there is no reason to doubt them. Centuries later, the Christian critic Origen blamed Herophilus for carrying free scientific inquiry too far and called him "that butcher who cut up innumerable human beings so that he could study nature." It was a first hint of the battles to come between religion and science over what we call medical ethics.[8]

It may be unfair to Herophilus to have Jack Kevorkian or Josef Mengele hovering over his reputation. Certainly the corpus of his anatomical writings might have been scientific Alexandria's greatest gift to posterity, if it had not perished in the great fire that devastated large portions of the Great Library in 48 BCE.*[9]

Meanwhile, one of Strato's pupils, Aristarchus of Samos, was busy transforming astronomy. He set out to study the summer solstice, that day in the calendar when daylight hours are longest. Aristarchus's observations led him to propose a completely new model of the universe and solar system, based on the hypothesis that the planets revolved around the sun and that the earth itself revolved every twenty-four hours around its axis. Aristarchus was also a formidable mathematician, who made calculations of the distance from the earth to the sun and the diameter of the sun based on solar eclipses.

Aristarchus's heliocentric theory was an astonishing leap into the future. However, it found no buyers among other Hellenistic astronomers. They

---

*The fire was set inadvertently by Julius Caesar and his Roman legionnaires, the wreckers of ancient Greece's legacy in more ways than one. And watching helplessly from the royal palace as those centuries of learning went up in smoke would be Ptolemy I's great-great-great-great-granddaughter Queen Cleopatra.

took a straightforward geometric, rather than dynamic, view of motion. As orthodox Aristotelians, they couldn't understand the idea of force or acceleration except in terms of something pushing something else (it will take Galileo and Newton to set that issue straight). Nor could they understand why, if the earth really did rotate, everything not tied down or rooted in the ground did not eventually fly off in the opposite direction.[10]

It's not known how Aristarchus answered what, given the assumptions of the time, were reasonable objections backed by the authority of Aristotle himself, or even if he did. In the end, Greek astronomers preferred to stick to Aristotle's "celestial spheres" to explain the movement of the planets and the stars.* The earth remained the center of the universe for another two thousand years. Even so, the mathematical computations of Alexandrian astronomy remained at a very high level. The philosopher of mathematics Bertrand Russell has called them "works of astonishing genius."[11]

This amazing—if ultimately misleading—work culminated in the treatises of the great Ptolemy (no relation to the ruling dynasty) in the first century CE. Ptolemaic astronomy was Alexandria's last word on the geocentric view of the cosmos. It would remain Europe's principal guide to astronomy until the Renaissance. Ptolemy's greatest claim to authority, his firm reliance on Aristotle, was also his greatest limitation and foreshadowed a pattern that would become all too familiar later on.

Ptolemy and other Aristotle disciples would find themselves having to "save the appearances," as the commentator Simplicius called it a couple of centuries later: in other words, reinterpreting any new empirical evidence so that it shored up, and never contradicted, Aristotle's own assumptions about the universe and nature.[12] The Aristotelian schoolmen of medieval Paris would do the same thing. Still later, the poet John Milton would mock them all in *Paradise Lost*:

> *Hereafter, when they come to model Heav'n,*
> *And calculate the stars, how they will wield*
> *The mighty frame: how build, unbuild, contrive*
> *To save appearances; how gird the sphere*
> *With centric and eccentric scribbl'd o'er,*
> *Cycle and epicycle, orb in orb . . .*

*According to Aristotle's *Metaphysics*, no fewer than fifty-five separate spheres.

The limitations of Aristotle's teachings were becoming apparent just decades after his death. It was only after scientists began rigorously applying his *methods* instead of his doctrines that astronomy and physics and ultimately biology would begin to turn themselves around.

Thanks to Strato, Greek science in Alexandria bore the heavy imprint of Aristotle, and with it the future of science. All the same, there were two outstanding figures in Alexandria with undeniable Platonic roots—men who were harbingers of a still larger notion of science yet to come.

The first was the geometer Euclid. We know almost nothing about his life. He may have been from Athens; he may even have studied at Plato's Academy. We do know he was teaching mathematics in Alexandria about the time Strato arrived and that Ptolemy I once asked him if there wasn't an easier way to study geometry than by taking Euclid's classes. Euclid is supposed to have answered, "There is no royal road to geometry." Anyone who has read his or her way through the *Elements* knows what he meant.

As a textbook, Euclid's *Elements* is peerless in its clarity and majesty of progression from first principles, or axioms, to particular demonstrations, or proofs. They move from the definition of line and point on the first pages to Pythagoras's famous theorem and beyond. For more than two thousand years, they have been the model of a priori reasoning at its most dignified.

The subtext of the *Elements* is also the principle Euclid may have absorbed from his teachers at the Academy: that mathematics and geometry are reason's direct insight into the mind of the "supreme geometer," God Himself. Indeed, Euclid's principal works could almost have served as textbooks for Plato's Rulers in the *Republic*. They were the *Elements* for arithmetic and geometry; the *Conic Sections* for the study of proportion and harmony; and his *Phaenomena* as a guide to astronomy, since it focuses on the theory of uniformly rotating spheres.[13]

Still, as a work the *Elements* is pure Aristotle: one reason Raphael set Euclid firmly in Aristotle's camp in his *School of Athens*. The book's layout, with definitions, postulates (for instance, "All right angles are equal" and "Any line segments can be extended indefinitely in either direction"), and axioms, follows precisely the guidelines of Aristotle's logic of science in the *Prior Analytics*.[14]

Euclid's aim was also the same as Aristotle's for all science, and for all good pedagogy. Any mathematician in Alexandria in the third century BCE could point out that his *Elements* contained nothing new.[15] What Euclid did was to set out principles that *were* known so clearly and elegantly that it became the most reproduced book in the ancient and medieval world, even more than the Bible.[16] It remained the fundamental textbook for teaching geometry to young minds right through the nineteenth century. Minds as diverse as René Descartes, Thomas Hobbes, and Charles Darwin would get their first whiff of what scientific reasoning is all about from the pages of the *Elements*.

Euclid demonstrated that geometry could not only be rigorous, but also beautiful and inspiring—a lesson the later builders of Chartres cathedral would raise to the sublime.

The other Platonic figure was Eratosthenes the geographer, a sometime Academy student who came to Alexandria and became director of the Great Library around 267. His nickname in the ancient world was Pentathlos, the all-around scholar-athlete. Indeed, his writings show an impressively wide range of interests, from geometry, astronomy, and mathematics (including a work on the philosophy of mathematics that he called, strikingly, the *Platonicus*) to history, metaphysics, and poetry. Using his observations of the different shadows cast by sundials along the same meridian and a little number crunching, Eratosthenes made a calculation of the earth's diameter that was amazingly accurate: 7,850 miles, only about 60 off the actual mark.

It was in the study of geography, however, that Eratosthenes made his most amazing discovery. While working at the Great Library, he grew fascinated by a manuscript left by an intrepid mariner named Pytheas from the Greek colony of Massalia (today's Marseilles). Beginning around 320 BCE, Pytheas had made several voyages at the far end of the western Mediterranean, including beyond the famed Pillars of Hercules, or Strait of Gibraltar. Pytheas also sailed around the coast of Spain and made at least one trip across the English Channel, including circumnavigating the British Isles. In addition, he gathered what information he could about lands lying still farther west.

Pytheas had published his extraordinary voyages as the *History of the Ocean* (now lost). His account fit none of the accepted conceptions about the shape of the world, and Aristotelian scholars in particular branded him a liar.

Eratosthenes, however, instantly saw its value. He already understood that Alexander's conquests had changed the Greeks' traditional map of India and Asia (Eratosthenes's own map was the first to divide the globe into meridians of longitude and parallels of latitude).[17] Assumptions about what new inhabited lands might exist, and where, had to change as well. Perhaps Plato's account in the *Timaeus* of a great continent lying to the west, Atlantis, encouraged the Academy-trained geographer to keep an open mind.

In any event, Eratosthenes took Pytheas's book and did some quick calculations based on his own estimate of the earth's diameter. He concluded that if the Indian Ocean was not a landlocked sea, as most Greeks supposed, but opened up onto a still larger ocean extending to the shores of the Pillars of Hercules, as Pytheas's voyage indicated, then it might be possible for a sailor to sail west from Spain to India, although Eratosthenes calculated it would take at least thirteen thousand miles.* Furthermore, he speculated, perhaps there was even another "inhabited world" (*oikoumenē*) to be found *between* Spain and India, one that covered at least part of the western hemisphere of the globe—a hemisphere that mathematics proved had to exist since the earth was round, but which was still entirely unknown.[18]

His Aristotelian colleagues scoffed. How could one predicate the existence of something no one had ever seen, especially an inhabited landmass; and when everyone knew the Indian Ocean ended at the western shores of India? So Eratosthenes's stunning thesis of a possible New World located between Europe and Asia never caught on, even after the Romans discovered there was indeed an ocean on the far side of India. His idea of a western continent faded from the science books. It would take Columbus's accidental discovery in 1492 to finally prove that the Aristotelians at Alexandria had been wrong and Eratosthenes right all along.

In some ways, this was not surprising. For all their formidable brainpower, the Alexandrians were content to work inside the box, as we would say, instead of trying to think outside it. Like good Aristotelians, they were content to be specialists in the true modern sense: more concerned with uncovering the *how*, whether it was in geography or astronomy or medicine, than pondering the *why*. They fit perfectly the character of the modern scientist as described by philosopher Thomas Kuhn: expert puzzle solvers, for whom the

---

*Eighteen centuries later, Ferdinand Magellan would show that the distance was much shorter, 5,734 miles.

challenge of the puzzle, not a thirst for breakthough discoveries, is the name of the game.[19]

A passion for solving puzzles certainly describes Alexandria's most famous scientist, who probably came to the city around 265 BCE. He almost certainly studied mathematics with a leading figure there, Conon of Samos, and he may have created his first important invention in Alexandria as well.

He is the founder of Western technology as an intellectual discipline—one might even say as a passion.

He was Archimedes of Syracuse.

As with most ancient scientists, details on his life are scanty. It's generally agreed that Archimedes was born in Syracuse in 287, the same city where Plato had launched his failed utopia a century before. He was the son of an astronomer named Pheidias and related by blood (so it is alleged) to the city's ruler Hiero II.[20] At some point, it is clear that Pheidias's son went to Alexandria to study with the distinguished array of scientists and scholars at the Museum.*

It must have been a dazzling, exciting experience. When the young Archimedes arrived, he would have found eminent mathematicians like Aristarchus and Eratosthenes and his future teacher Conon of Samos meeting under Alexandria's covered walks to escape the hot Egyptian sun or taking their ease in the Museum's arcade with its stone benches and recessed seating along the walls. Nearby was the Great Library, with its daunting collection of scientific and literary works, where its director, Callimachus of Cyrene, had recently finished his largest and most Aristotelian project, the *Collection of the Wonders of the World,* a veritable encyclopedia covering topics from geography and history to the miraculous properties of plants and minerals.[21]

The spirit of Aristotle was alive in another way, which seized Archimedes's attention from the start. Aristotle's praise for technology, or *technē,* knowledge for a practical purpose rather than just theoretic understanding, had found a congenial audience in Ptolemaic Alexandria. Researchers there were working on a host of practical technologies. The most important was the science of ballistics, indispensable for siege warfare in the age of the warring states of Hellenistic Greece.

---

*Although direct evidence is lacking, he describes Conon of Samos as his teacher and friend, and at least some of his writings were dedicated to Eratosthenes, suggesting personal contact with that formidable mathematical brain.

The key figure was yet another former Strato student named Ctesibius, who was devising a series of improved catapults, including one that worked on the principle of compressed air. We don't know how practical Ctesibius's machines were; in a historical sense it doesn't matter. The point is that in Archimedes's day, Alexandria was becoming the center of Greek military technology research, and technicians like Ctesibius were as renowned as the city's great theoretical mathematicians.[22]

The result was a conceptual revolution—not the last time a military industrial complex has served as the spur to intellectual and technological growth. Plato had seen it coming in his own lifetime. According to the historian Plutarch, he had violently opposed it, objecting that the best geometers were giving up pure philosophy in order to work on material projects and "instruments which require much base and manual labor."[23] Aristotle's own reservation about purely technological knowledge was that it didn't encourage the discovery of any new principles of nature but only applied what was already known.

His heirs in Alexandria were now proving him wrong. By constantly devising new formulae for calculating the angle of falling catapult shot, including the shot's speed and direction, the city's geometers were reinventing the theory of mechanics. Thanks to men like Ctesibius, the use of mechanical demonstrations to establish new scientific principles had come to stay. And one of those caught up in the new science of applied mathematics and geometry was Archimedes, who watched and learned and picked up principles and tricks he would use to create his own set of high-tech weapons for the most famous siege in the history of technology: the siege of Syracuse in 214 BCE.

The other area of technical study in Alexandria that drew Archimedes's attention was hydraulic engineering. This was essential for keeping the wheat and cotton fields of the Nile valley irrigated and keeping the city of Alexandria clothed and fed. The reigning figure, again, was Ctesibius, who wrote an important treatise on hydraulics and created a working water clock.[24] It was probably in Alexandria that Archimedes came up with the invention that bore his name throughout the ancient world: the Archimedes water screw. Called "the snail" because of its shape, the screw enabled farmers to move water over long distances and even uphill by means of its continuous twisting motion. The ancient historian Diodorus asserts that Archimedes's invention enabled the Ptolemies to irrigate most of the Nile Delta.[25] It has remained in use in the poorer parts of rural Egypt until today.

When Archimedes returned to Syracuse, his interest in things aquatic did not stop. He continued his research in the principles of hydraulics and another field he largely invented, hydrostatics, or the study of fluids at rest. This is the origin of the most famous story about Archimedes. It tells how the king of Syracuse, Hiero II, once asked him to figure out the gold content of a certain sacrificial wreath or crown. Archimedes was pondering the problem as he eased himself into his morning bath, noticed the water spilling over the sides of the bath, and realized that by weighing the volume of water displaced by an object, he could determine how much gold or silver it contained. According to the story, he then leaped out and ran down the street stark naked, shouting: "I have found it! I have found it!" (*Eureka! Eureka!*)[26]

A charming story, which dates back at least to the Roman architect Vitruvius. Most modern scholars doubt it happened, which doesn't mean it isn't true. What is far more revealing is that Archimedes, in his own treatise on hydrostatics, never mentions it or tells us anything about how he discovered or researched any of his amazing works.

This is a striking omission, but typical of the Aristotelian spirit of the ancient Greek scientist. What ultimately fascinates us most about the history of science is its Platonic side—the dramatic process of discovery and intuition, when what is true is at once clear and vice versa; those moments of insight that Socrates and Plato would recognize as seeing with the inner eye. What fascinates us most interested the scientist of the Alexandrian age least.

Instead, all the emphasis in Greek science is on laying out new mathematical or scientific proofs, including using visual diagrams, so logically and so beyond contradiction that there could be no possibility of dissent. This is precisely what all of Archimedes's writings do. That is why they are so important, and so boring. What Aristotle had formalized and Euclid codified—the power of clear, logical reasoning and presentation—Archimedes made his intellectual slave and the servant of science.

And as his research continued in Syracuse, Archimedes made sure word of what he was doing got back to friends in Alexandria. Among his correspondents was a former Croton pupil named Dositheus* to whom Archimedes would send one major treatise after another that would revolutionize mathe-

---

*Dositheus is a Jewish name (the Greek for Matthew, or Matityahu). Alexandria had a large Jewish community, so it's not surprising that Jews would have studied at the Museum or used the Great Library. If Dositheus was a Jew, then his correspondence with Archimedes is the only one between a Greek and a Jew to survive from the ancient pagan world.

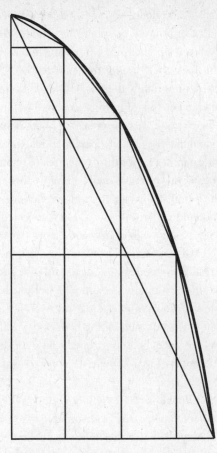

By dividing volumes and areas into infinite numbers of smaller pieces, Archimedes worked out
the principles of integral calculus nineteen hundred years before it was invented.

matics. There was *Quadrature of the Parabola*, then two books on *Sphere and Cylinder*, one on *Spiral Lines*, and finally a treatise on *Conoids and Spheroids*.[27]

Taken together, they laid the future cornerstone of what comes to be called *calculus*, or the mathematics of infinity (Archimedes was the first mathematician to use the concept of infinity in his work). Without it, modern math and science as we know it would not exist.

In one sense, the impetus to Archimedes's math research was proving that Plato had been wrong: you can't form a sphere out of a series of triangles or pentagons, as Plato claimed in the *Timaeus*, any more than you can form a circle out of a square. Archimedes showed this by demonstrating that you can't measure the area of a circle or sphere or cylinder using any kind of straight line. However, you *can* measure it by slicing it into pieces that can be bounded by straight lines, then slicing that part left over into measurable pieces again and again, until finally there is nothing left unmeasured.[28] This is what calculus, and the concept of infinity, enabled Archimedes to do.

He discovered, for example, that the area of a sphere is four times the area of its greatest circle; and that the area of a parabola (like the one described by a stone flung from a catapult) is four-thirds the area of the triangle enclosed within it. Archimedes's work was also establishing in passing another scientific landmark for the future. If you can't measure something, then *it probably doesn't exist*. It's a notion that Aristotle would have rejected at once. It was, however, another logical outgrowth of his own scientific method.*

Archimedes also liked to lay traps for the unaware and the uninitiated. He enjoys leading the reader to a conceptual dead end in order to force him to go back and reassess his own original assertions. Archimedes even seems to have sent out fraudulent proofs to mathematical rivals for their approval in order to expose them as fools. In spite of the bath story, he can't have been a very lovable man. All the same, he fully grasped a basic Aristotelian principle from his years at Alexandria—that knowledge is power—and he was determined to live by it.

This is why, despite Plutarch's later disclaimer that Archimedes "regarded the business of engineering as a base and sordid activity," he remained so fascinated with technology. He invented a working hydraulic musical organ. He also created a working mechanical planetarium, an enclosed globe in which replicas of the sun, moon, and planets performed the same motions relative to the moving sphere of the stars that they do in the sky, so that astonished observers could even watch the successive phases of the moon.[29]

He experimented with pulleys, by which he demonstrated his famous leverage principle, "that with any given force it was possible to lift any given weight." This enabled him to stage one of his most famous coups de théâtre in front of King Hiero and the entire city of Syracuse. Archimedes tied a series of pulleys to a dry-docked three-masted ship loaded with cargo and passengers, and then, to the crowd's stunned amazement, he lifted it into the harbor by himself. This led Hiero to declare, "From this day forward, Archi-

*See chapter 19.

medes is believed no matter what he says," which led Archimedes to reply in the full flush of triumph, "Give me a lever and a place to stand, and I shall move the earth."[30]

As the applause stopped and the crowd went home, no one in Syracuse could have doubted Archimedes's superhuman genius and skill. Still, even his most devoted admirers could not have imagined that his miraculous machines were about to spell the difference between life and death for their city.

As a city-state, Syracuse had survived many crises. It had survived tyrants like Dionysius II and Dion; it had survived sieges by the Athenians (led by Socrates's friend Alcibiades) and the Carthaginians. It had even survived Plato's disastrous hopes of creating a real-life *Republic* out of its laws and citizens.

Shortly after Archimedes's masterful show in Syracuse harbor, however, the city faced the deadliest threat of all. There was a new regional power in the central Mediterranean basin, the imperial republic to the north: Rome. Breaking Syracuse to its will was the key to Rome's hegemony over Sicily and the rest of Italy, and in 214 BCE an enormous Roman fleet and army gathered at the entrance to the harbor. Syracuse went to battle stations, and its most famous citizen, now in his seventies, sprang into action.

The best description of what happened next is by the Greek historian Polybius. He wrote it not long after the siege of Syracuse, when some of the participants may still have been alive. He tells us how the Syracusans put Archimedes in charge of constructing their defenses and how he laid them out so that "they would have everything ready to hand, and could respond to any attack by the enemy with a countermove."[31]

The Romans were hardly amateurs when it came to besieging cities. Their plan was a simultaneous land and sea assault, with boats equipped with massive mobile siege towers rowing up to storm Syracuse's walls. However, as Polybius relates, "Archimedes had constructed artillery which could cover a whole variety of ranges, so that while the attacking ships were still at a distance he scored so many hits with his catapults and stone-throwers" that the Roman general Marcus Claudius Marcellus had to call off the attack before his men reached the walls.

On the landward side, the Romans fared no better. Their main objective was the eastern Hexaply gate. But every attempt to get scaling ladders and grappling hooks up to the gate's walls met a hailstorm of fire from the catapults and other war engines Archimedes had devised. Stunned and exhausted, the Roman legionnaires finally had to retreat.[32]

The desperate Romans then tried a night attack. Archimedes was waiting for them. As the Roman triremes glided up in the darkness, great wooden beams suddenly swung out from the walls of the harbor and hovered over the water. A rain of catapult stones drove the Roman marines back from the bows of their ships, while grappling irons attached to chain pulleys dropped from the hovering wooden beams. At Archimedes's command, each engineer in charge of a beam then seized the prow of a ship, like an eagle or hawk seizing its prey.

When Archimedes's engineers were sure they had a good grip, they pulled down on the lever controlling the beam's pulley. With a powerful jerk, each Roman ship was lifted by its prow and made to stand on its stern. As the Romans on board jumped for their lives, the pulleys would suddenly be released.

"The result was that some of the vessels heeled over and fell on their sides," Polybius relates, "and others capsized," while still others hit the water so hard that they began to flood and became useless to steer.[33] All the same, a few intrepid Roman ships managed to get close enough to the walls to avoid the catapult barrage, and Roman troops made ready to jump ashore and begin their attack.

It was a tragic mistake. Archimedes had carved out a series of loopholes along the city walls, and as the Romans scrambled for shore, Syracusans opened up with "scorpions," or iron dart Gatling guns, another Archimedes invention, which fired one devastating volley after another into the Roman ranks.

Men screamed as they died under the deadly curtain of fire. The handful who reached the foot of the walls found themselves bombarded by rocks and beams thrown from above. Marcellus, realizing his attack had once again failed, sounded the retreat.

Thanks to the efforts of a single old man, the Romans were beaten and demoralized. "The Romans began to believe they were fighting a supernatural enemy," Polybius says, "as they found themselves constantly struck down by opponents whom they could never see."* Each time they tried to move

---

* So did Archimedes also deploy his most legendary weapon, a series of convex mirrors to focus the rays of the sun and set Roman ships and rigging on fire? The best ancient sources, Polybius and Plutarch, make no mention of it. The oldest account is by the first century CE philosopher Lucian, who merely mentions Archimedes setting Roman ships on fire by artificial means; he says nothing about mirrors. The best modern scholars doubt the story. This is not to say Archimedes wouldn't have found a way to make such a "death ray" work, if he had thought of it.

their siege engines toward the walls, volleys of catapult arrows and stones greeted their advance. Each time their ships entered the harbor, the great grappling hooks swung down and scattered the mighty triremes as if they were toy boats. When they fell back to count their losses, Archimedes's machines continued to harass their retreat.

According to Marcellus's biographer Plutarch, things got so bad that each time the Romans saw a piece of timber or rope appear above Syracuse's walls, they would cry: "Look! Archimedes is aiming one of his machines at us!" and turn and run.[34] Marcellus decided there was no way to take the city by storm. "Archimedes uses my ships to ladle sea-water," he grumbled to his officers. He decided instead that the Romans would wait it out and hope a blockade of the harbor would finally starve Syracuse into submission.

They did not have to wait long. Few ancient sieges ended by taking the city by force. Most ended with the besieged population starved into cannibalism and then submission or betrayed by one of their own, usually at night. The lock on a crucial gate left deliberately open; a party of enemy soldiers entering by a side door in the walls or a barred window opened from inside in the dead of night; a local prominent citizen who decides the enemy's victory will be his opportunity for gaining power and who bribes a guard to look the other way.

That was how most ancient sieges ended, and so it happened with Syracuse. "Marcellus noticed a particular tower which was carelessly guarded [perhaps deliberately?] and into which he could infiltrate men unobserved."[35] One night, as the Syracusans were celebrating a feast day in honor of the goddess Artemis, the Romans stormed the tower and burst into the city. Archimedes's triumph had been short-lived.

Marcellus had wanted to spare the magnificent ancient city and capture it intact. His men and officers, however, were hungry for loot and blood and demanded their age-old right to plunder a captured city. Marcellus gave way, although "he wept at the thought of [Syracuse's] fate," according to Plutarch, "and of how its appearance would be transformed in a few hours as his soldiers plundered it." On one point, however, he was absolutely adamant: Take Archimedes alive.

So as Roman legionnaires poured out into Syracuse's streets and looted, raped, and murdered their way across the city, a handful of picked soldiers passed along the smoke-filled, blood-strewn alleys looking for Archimedes's house. They found it in a quiet corner and bounded up the steps.

Archimedes had not heard the screams of his panicked fellow citizens. He was not even aware that the city he had defended so skillfully had fallen to the enemy. He was sitting in a chair, absorbed in a difficult geometric problem that he had drawn in the sand table (or *abacus*) on his desk. He did not even notice the Roman soldiers entering the room.

A legionnaire stood behind Archimedes's chair and prodded him with his bloodstained sword.

The old man looked up, startled and angry. "Do not disturb my circles!" he shouted.

The soldier snapped. Perhaps he was exhausted from the terrible siege and carnage; perhaps he was pumped with adrenaline from the sudden Roman victory. Perhaps he had seen too many friends and comrades killed by Archimedes's volleys of iron darts or thrown down and drowned by his great grappling hooks. Whatever the reason, with a single lethal lunge he killed the old man where he sat.[36]

When he heard the news that Archimedes was dead, Roman general Marcellus bitterly regretted the passing of the man who—had he been taken alive—might have raised Roman siege warfare to a whole new level. "He abhorred the man who had killed him as if he had committed an act of sacrilege," Plutarch tells us, "and sought out Archimedes' relatives and treated them with honor."[37] Science had its first hero martyr, and the power of technology to move and shape events was fixed firmly in the Western imagination.

The death of Archimedes and the fall of Syracuse also marked the end of an independent Hellenistic world. A new power now ruled the Mediterranean: Rome.[38]

As it happened, the rise of Rome would also give the rivalry of Plato and Aristotle a whole new lease on life.

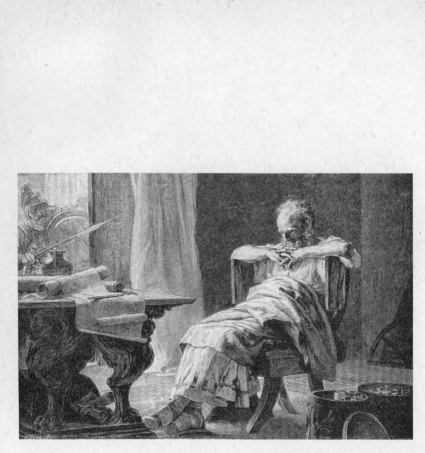

The Death of Archimedes, 212 BCE

Eight

HOLE IN THE SOUL:
PLATO AND ARISTOTLE IN ROME

The study of history is . . . the only method of learning to bear with dignity the vicissitudes of Fortune.

— Polybius (200–118 BCE)

At last he had found it.[1]

He had sworn he would. Finally, near the gate of Archradina, the vow was fulfilled. He could feel a deep sense of personal, even national, satisfaction. One hundred and forty years earlier, the ground around him would have been strewn with the bodies of his fellow Romans, soldiers killed during the siege of the city of which he was now Rome's *quaestor*, or tax collector.

Because the once-proud city-state of Syracuse was now capital of the Roman province of Sicily. When he arrived from Rome, Marcus Tullius Cicero was barely thirty-two and on the verge of a brilliant political career.

One desire, however, had consumed him when he wasn't counting revenues or assessing taxes. In his spare time he had searched the city from end to end, until he came to this neglected corner overgrown with brushwood and thorns. It was a cemetery, and in the shadows stood row after row of marble columns and funerary monuments. Cicero must have wondered which was the right one.

Then, "I observed a small column standing out a little above the briars," he wrote later, "with the figure of a sphere and a cylinder upon it." Cicero immediately turned to his Syracusan guide and the laborers with him and cried, "I think I've found it!"

The men set to work with scythes, cutting a path through the briars and thorns so Cicero could get close enough to examine the column. The marble was mottled with lichens and neglect. Along the base of the pedestal he could barely make out a faded inscription, "although," he wrote afterward, "the latter parts of all the verses were effaced almost half away."

Still, there was no doubt about it. This was the tomb of the great Archimedes.

Cicero must have glowed with satisfaction. The Syracusans had had no idea where their most famous citizen had been laid to rest 140 years earlier. Some had even sworn the tomb didn't exist. Cicero, however, had learned from dusty ancient sources that Archimedes had asked that his funerary monument, or *stele*, be inscribed with the sphere and cylinder, as a tribute to what the canny old scientist regarded as his greatest discovery: that the volumes of these two solids share a 3:2 ratio.

Cicero's discovery of Archimedes's tomb was a first-class piece of detective work, perhaps the world's first example of applied archaeology. On the whole, however, the Romans made bad detectives. They were perhaps the least curious people in history, as well as the most acquisitive. Cicero himself barely mentioned Archimedes or mathematics again, either in his books or in his plentiful letters.* Instead, "an Archimedean problem" became Cicero's pet phrase for any dilemma of insoluble complexity.[2] For most Romans, that meant virtually any problem for which neither Plato nor Aristotle offered a clear answer.

Although they professed to despise the Greeks as a people, the Romans developed a strange dependence on Greek culture and on its two greatest thinkers. Rome had begun as a rough, rather crude agricultural community with a keen taste for war, not unlike the Spartans. Then around 380 BCE,

---

*In fact, today we still have no idea where exactly the tomb was.

just as on the other side of the Mediterranean Plato was composing the *Republic*, they overthrew their more sophisticated neighbors the Etruscans, and things began to take off.

In less than two hundred years they had conquered the entire Italian peninsula, driven northward into the Celtic kingdoms of Gaul, overwhelmed the Greek colonies of Sicily including Syracuse, and absorbed the empire of their only rival in the western Mediterranean, Carthage. Although Romans saw their serial conquests as proof of their master-race status, the fact was Greeks were instrumental in their success, then and later. Greek science and technology helped their armies and navies move and fight, just as Greek art filled their homes and villas and Greek literature their libraries.

By Cicero's time, any Roman of distinction could speak Greek as well as he did Latin. Many traveled to Greece to receive their education at the Academy or the Lyceum, or both. Others like Cicero were raised by Greek tutors who taught them the basic tenets of Plato's ethical doctrines and Aristotle's treatises on logic and rhetoric.[3]

Later Greek engineers built their fortifications and temples, including the famous Pantheon. Greek philosophy provided the rational framework for understanding their own laws and history; Greek artisans kept them supplied with consumer goods; and Greek gladiators and charioteers kept them entertained in the Colosseum and the Circus Maximus.

The Romans mastered Greek culture and made it essential to the functioning of their empire. But they never went beyond it or challenged it. Like the vast majority of classical statues we see in museums today, everything was a Roman copy of a Greek original. Even distinctly Roman contributions to the history of architecture, like the dome, arch, and barrel vault, were only extensions of Greek engineering principles.

In that sense, the civilization the Romans inhabited remained forever foreign and opaque to them—like the codes of software applications the average person installs on his or her iPad and uses every day. When the software hits a glitch, most of us are helpless without a manual to help. And the manuals the Romans increasingly relied on for understanding the glitches in Greek culture, as well as their own, were Plato and Aristotle.

Of course, they admired and absorbed a wide range of other Greek authors and thinkers, including thousands of works that are now lost. Roman law, drama, and political thought, including Cicero's, would be unimaginable without the input of the Stoics. The greatest philosophical poem of the ancient world, Lucretius's *De Rerum Natura* (*On the Nature of Things*) owed a huge debt to Epicurus.

All the same, taken together, the works of Plato and Aristotle dealt with such a wide range of subjects, and offered such a sense of completeness and comprehensiveness, that Roman readers found them reassuring. You couldn't go wrong, it seemed, if you relied on one or the other to understand some issue, whether it was astronomy* and physics or politics and poetry.

Everyone from leading politicians to the best chefs read Plato's dialogues. Aristotle's presence loomed over Roman politics as well as science. As scholars Jonathan Barnes and Miriam Griffin write, Plato and Aristotle "formed an integral part" of an educated Roman's mental equipment; they were "tools for thinking analytically and making rational decisions."[4] It is not too far-fetched to say that it is the Romans who permanently etched Plato and Aristotle into the grain of Western civilization, just as they made them the governing intellects of their empire.

Yet ironically, thanks to one man, Plato had sealed the fate of that empire almost before it got started.

He was Polybius, a native of Megapolis in the wild country of Arcadia in western Greece, but his education was as sophisticated as any young man of status from Athens or Alexandria. He arrived in Rome in 167 BCE and soon found work as a tutor to the sons of the most prominent Roman politician of the age, Publius Aemilius Paulus. Paulus was determined to give his boys the best possible education, including philosophy and rhetoric, sculpture and drawing, as well as a thorough grounding in Greek grammar and literature.

There was, however, a major point of contention between Polybius and his Roman patron. In 168, Paulus had led Roman legions in crushing the Macedonians at Pydna, signaling the end of an independent northern Greece. Polybius's hometown had been allies of Macedonia, and Polybius himself had been involved in the anti-Roman resistance. Taken prisoner, he had originally been transported to Italy for interrogation and probably execution. Only a chance conversation with one of Paulus's friends saved him and landed him an interview with his country's conqueror. Whatever his true feel-

---

*Cicero's account of the making of the universe in the last book of his *De Re Publica* (the so-called *Dream of Scipio*) is taken almost entirely from Plato's *Timaeus*. For many later medieval scribes and scholars, it was the one source for knowing anything about Plato at all.

ings about the Romans, Polybius realized that with his education and background (he could not only write history and read philosophy, but ride and hunt all day), he could make a new life for himself as tutor and mentor to the sons of Rome's most powerful politician.

The one who fell most under his spell was the youngest, Publius Scipio Aemilianus. He also happened to be heir to the same Scipio who had repelled Hannibal's invasion of Italy.* Polybius proved to be more than just a pedagogue to young Publius. The former Greek resistance fighter became the young man's friend and confidant. He went with him on his first military campaign in Spain. Seven years later in 146, he watched as his protégé led a Roman army against Carthage in the third and final war between the two great rivals. It is even possible Polybius donned a helmet and shield and joined in the final assault and breaching of Carthage's walls.[5]

He certainly watched the savage retribution Publius Scipio Aemilianus meted out to its former enemy, in which every Carthaginian inhabitant was either killed or sold into slavery and every trace of the city was obliterated, with salt sown on the razed site so that nothing would ever grow there again. Carthage's former territories were turned into the Roman province of Africa. Then, shortly afterward, word arrived at the jubilant camp that Rome's Senate had displaced the heirs of Alexander and turned the former kingdom of Macedonia into a Roman province as well.[6]

For Polybius, it was a moment of revelation, but also inspiration. There is no record of his feelings at that moment, when the power he had fought all his life became the supreme power of the civilized world. But surrounded by the stench of dead bodies and with the ruins of Carthage still smoldering in the background, he now decided he would write a complete account for posterity of how the Romans succeeded in just fifty-six years[†] in making themselves virtual masters of the civilized world, "an achievement," as Polybius wrote, "without parallel in human history."[7]

He brought to the task many gifts. One was a boundless curiosity so typical of the Aristotelian mind but entirely lacking among the Romans. He traveled to Italy to retrace Hannibal's march across the Alps, pausing in mountain passes to contemplate the great Carthaginian general's feat and how it nearly brought Rome to the brink of destruction. He interviewed the elderly Numid-

---

*P. Scipio Africanus (so called because of his crushing victory over Hannibal at Zama on the North African plain in 202 BCE) was young Aemilianus's grandfather.

†That is, from the final defeat of Hannibal in 202 BCE to the fall of Carthage in 146.

ian king Masinissa, who had known Hannibal and who helped Polybius to reconstruct the politics of the period. He even convinced his former pupil Scipio to lend him ships and money to explore the African coastline beyond the Pillars of Hercules.[8]

Polybius also had the Platonist's thirst for a unifying theory that rises above mere contigencies and appearances. Previous historians like Thucydides and Xenophon had written about their own times or from the perspective of their own people and culture. Polybius wanted to write an entirely new kind of history, one with a universal theme—the role of the unexpected or Fortune in the making of human events. He meant to turn history into a science based on clear rational principles backed up by observation. Inevitably, he turned to both Aristotle and Plato for help. It was a intellectual breakthrough—and a model for all historians in the future.

Polybius used Aristotle first of all in order to explain why the Romans had managed to remain a strong and free and stable republic despite catastrophes like Hannibal's invasion and the sacking of the city by the Gauls a century and half before. Aristotle's *Politics* classified all governments as rule by either the One (monarchy), the Few (aristocracy), or the Many (democracy). Each had its characteristic problems, Aristotle said, and none was destined to prosper forever. However, a "mixed constitution" that included elements of all three would hold up best over time.[9]

Polybius concluded that was exactly what the Romans had done. The republic had its monarchical element with its two consuls, who enjoyed absolute authority, or *imperium*, on the battlefield and in times of national crisis. It had its aristocratic element with the Roman Senate, which was not elected but chosen instead from Rome's best families and most distinguished heroes and which made the major decisions for the city's foreign policy, including signing treaties and deciding to go to war.

Finally, Rome had its democratic element in its various popular assemblies, where the Roman people, or *plebs*, voted "or bestow offices on those who deserve them," including the two consuls, and "who have the right to award both honors and punishments, the only bonds whereby kingdoms, states, and human society in general are held together."[10]

Taken as a unit, the consuls, Senate, and assemblies formed in Polybius's mind the perfect "mixed constitution," meaning a mixture of the best features of all three standard forms of government. "The result is a union which is strong enough to withstand all emergencies," Polybius wrote; "this peculiar form of constitution possesses an irresistible power to achieve any goal it has set itself." Following this analysis, Polybius had to conclude, "It is impossible to find a better form of constitution than this."[11]

In short, this rude and crude city built on the banks of the Tiber had managed to craft a political system more perfect than that of the Athenians or Spartans. Yet how could Rome maintain that living perfection and make sure that the judicial mixture of three elements "unite and work together" in the future?

Here Polybius turned to the second of his authorities, Plato. And here the answer was not so encouraging.

Polybius went back to the *Republic*, where in Books VIII and IX Plato gives us his most trenchant analysis of politics as it actually works, as opposed to the utopian ideal he outlined earlier in the work. Socrates warns his listeners that every political system that fails to live up to those ideal principles must eventually be overtaken by an inevitable cycle of decay and collapse. It is a chilling story, made more chilling by the sober, matter-of-fact way Socrates tells it.

For example, Socrates explains that the dissolute freedom of democracies like that of Athens, "which treats all men as equals whether they are equal or not," must lead inevitably to moral corruption, civic disorder, and mob rule. He implicitly dismisses Aristotle's notion that a system based on the idea that those who rule are ruled in turn, if only by the rule of law, will ever work in practice. Instead, democratic man "lives from day to day, indulging in the pleasures of the moment" and refusing to accept any order or restraint, including the restraint of law. The chaos that results will lead inevitably to one-man rule, he says, in order to restore calm.[12]

At first, one-man rule will be accepted and even invested with the legal trappings of kingship. However, "the man who tastes a single piece of human flesh," Socrates says, "is fated to become a wolf." As the ruler's appetite for power grows, kingship, too, "degenerates into its corrupt but associated form, by which I mean tyranny" (this is Polybius, not Plato, writing). Tyranny triggers resentment, revolution, and violent overthrow again. Out of the rubble of the rule of One emerges the rule of those who have led the revolt against it, namely a jealous and self-interested aristocracy.

Yet this, too, eventually decays into something corrupt and ugly, namely the naked rule of the rich, which breeds a bitter wave of resentment among the underprivileged masses. According to Plato, society now splits "into two factions, the rich and the poor, who live in the same place [but] are always plotting against each other."[13] When this class struggle reaches its climax, the poor rise up in their massive numbers to claim power for themselves, and so "democracy is born" again.

And so it goes, at least according to Plato. As he explains it, the same dreary process repeats itself over and over, an endless cycle (in Greek, the term is *anakuklosis*) of political birth, decay, revolution, and renewal without end or purpose. This is the dismal cycle, the *Republic* explains, that all those condemned to live in the cave are fated to repeat. It is this cycle, that only rule by philosophers can ever interrupt or break.

For the Romans, Polybius argued, this had to be a sobering wake-up call. His *Histories* subtly transformed Plato's cycle from a specific theory of government into a general theory of history. This pointless cycle, "described in greatest detail by Plato," Polybius wrote, had evidently doomed Greece to impotence, as the free city-states of Greece had yielded to the power of Alexander and the Macedonians, which then decayed into warring petty kingdoms and acrimonious intercity feuds, making Rome's rise to power inevitable.* Could Rome expect to evade the same fate? Mixed constitution or not, Polybius regretted to conclude it could not.

"For this state, [which] takes its foundation and growth from natural causes, will pass through a natural evolution to its decay." Sooner or later, doom would come to the greatest empire in the world. This is "a proposition which scarcely requires proof," Polybius grimly wrote, "since the inexorable course of nature is sufficient to impose it on us."[14]

It was a heart-stopping prophecy, in part because Polybius's picture until then had been so positive and reassuring. In a profound way, Polybius's prophecy was Greece's revenge on its Latin conqueror. Polybius had cunningly turned Plato into a dagger that plunged into the heart of Rome's hopes for the future.

On the one hand, Rome had the most perfect constitution in history. In fact, Aristotle's notion of the mixed constitution as distilled by Polybius would pass down from the Romans into the mainstream of Western political thinking, including America's Founding Fathers.† On the other, Rome was doomed to failure, as Plato turned Aristotle's formula for constitutional success into a

---

*Polybius was certainly thinking of a figure from the Lyceum and the Great Library, Demetrius of Phalerum, who had predicted Macedonia's decline as a matter of fate.
†See chapter 28.

warning. A mixed constitution required every group in society pulling its appropriate weight. Allowing any one element—the monarchical, the democratic, or the aristocratic—to gain undue influence over the other parts became a death knell of doom, and the end of any self-governing republic.[15]

The point of Plato's cycle of conflict and Polybius's *Histories* was that sooner or later this overbalancing must happen. There was nothing Romans could do to stop it. The best they could hope for was to learn to "bear with dignity the vicissitudes of Fortunes" and accept their own impotence to control the future. And that is what Roman thinkers, philosophers, and historians for the next four hundred years would try to do. A hole had appeared in the soul of the Romans, which made it impossible for them to enjoy anything they did.

It may seem incredible that a single idea could have such a devastating impact. However, it appeared to have the unimpeachable authority of both Plato and Aristotle behind it—and the Romans were great believers in authority. In addition, Polybius had hit upon the Romans' one fatal weakness: their fascination with politics.

They were obsessed with the subject. The city's noble families kept competitive score of how many members had been elected as consul or tribune and spent their time speculating which son or grandson was likely to be the next. Everyone else wanted to know who had the most clout in the Senate; who had the most momentum in the next election; and which *princeps* (head of the Senate) or great man was in the voters' favor and which was not.

Roman politics was not for the faint of heart. It was the story of endless feuds and bloody partisan battles among great families reminiscent of the movie *The Godfather*. In the years after Polybius's *Histories* appeared, from 133 to 85 BCE, seven consuls and four tribunes of the *plebs* were murdered in street violence.[16] Yet those were the same years in which Rome completed its domination of Spain, conquered Gaul (France), and brought the rest of Asia Minor, Syria, Cyrene (Libya), and Cyprus under its sway.

It was a strange juxtaposition. It looked even stranger to Rome's political elite and finest minds, who, after reading Polybius, could see in Rome's unprecedented growth to power only the seeds of corruption and destruction. The idea that Rome's good old days—including that marvelous mixed constitution—were vanishing blinded men to the possibility that something new, better, and stronger might be emerging. Instead Rome's ruling class became obsessed with decline and inured to an indifferent fate. "Now we are suffering the evils of too long a peace. Luxury, deadlier than any armed invader, lies like an incubus upon us still, avenging the world we brought to heel," Juvenal wrote in Satire VI.

The first to sense that something was wrong was Marcus Porcius Cato (234–149 BCE), and he knew just where to point the finger of blame: "The Greeks are a most wicked and undisciplined people," he argued, whose philosophy and literature were spreading the same corruption into Rome.

Cato singled out Socrates as the main source of the difficulty, that "windbag who did his best to tyrannize over his country by undermining its established customs." Cato spent his life trying to get Greek teachers and tutors expelled from the city, to keep them from doing the same to Rome.[17] Yet Cato's great-grandson would go to study in Athens and become Rome's leading Stoic voice.

Grit your teeth and bear it. Keep your temper. Remain indifferent to pain and accept your fate, whatever it may be. These are hallmarks of the Stoic outlook, and the younger Cato (95–46 BCE) hoped that cultivating the parallels between traditional Roman values and Greek Stoicism could restore its ruling class. He was wrong. Instead, by his time, the age of Pompey and Julius Caesar, the demoralization of Rome's elite had become a self-fulfilling prophecy.

Gaius Sallustius Crispus (86–35 BCE) was typical. Bright and able, he came from a Roman family with hopes of a political career. He soon found himself in over his head. In 50 BCE, the censors of the Senate swept him out of the consulship on charges of vice and accepting bribes.

Sallust took his revenge by retiring to the country to write history—increasingly the way in which Rome's losers managed to get their revenge on the winners. Sallust describes how he tried to make his honest way into politics. However, "there I found many things against me. Self-restraint, integrity, and virtue were disregarded; unscrupulous conduct, bribery, and profit-seeking were rife."

Sallust had read and absorbed Polybius's *Histories*. Like Polybius, he chose the final defeat of Carthage in 146 BCE as the moment when "Fortune turned unkind" against Rome, the world's greatest power. Before that, Romans had been better and more noble. "To such men no toil came amiss; no ground was too steep or rugged, no armed foe too formidable; courage taught them to overcome all obstacles." Their only goals in life were honor and glory; "at home they lived frugally and never betrayed a friend."[18]

However, as Rome's empire grew, "growing love of money, and the lust for power which followed it, engendered every kind of vice." Today, Sallust declared, Romans were surrounded by "universal robbery and pillage." Yet even as he wrote this sentence circa 50 BCE, the city's power and influence in the world were still growing, from Julius Caesar's conquest of Gaul to his rival Pompey's suppression of piracy across the Mediterranean and subjugation of Egypt and the Levant.

Rome, it seemed, was never in worse shape; and never more powerful. Sallust and his literary successors ignored the contradiction. Instead, the overall pattern of writing Roman history was set, from the last days of the republic straight through the empire. The story would be presented as the story of Rome's steady slide from virtue to vice—in Sallust's words, "the steady degeneration of its noble character into vice and corruption"—of which the chief sign was, paradoxically, its imperial growth and steady advance over its foreign rivals.[19]

On the one hand, Rome enjoyed a power without equal or limits. On the other, the glory surrounding that power would seem increasingly hollow—even a sign of imminent dissolution and moral collapse. The fact that the one seemed to contradict the other never bothered the Romans. Plato and Polybius made them immune to material success, just as they were resigned to moral failure. "Here in the city nothing is left," wrote one of Sallust's contemporaries, "the real Rome is gone forever."[20]

It had taken an outsider using Plato and Aristotle to get Rome into this jam. It would take another using Plato and Aristotle to try to get it out.

He was born north of Rome in 106 BCE, in the small town of Arpinum. Marcus Tullius Cicero lacked the aristocratic connections of a Cato or Julius Caesar, or the ruthless will of a Pompey or Crassus. To this day, hardheaded historians of Rome treat him with disdain, even contempt, while the Middle Ages and Renaissance revered him, even though they barely understood him. Entirely self-made, Cicero learned to rely on his gifts as an orator and a lawyer to get ahead. They were considerable enough to land him his position as *quaestor* in Syracuse at age thirty-two and consul, the republic's supreme office, at forty. In 50 BCE, the year Sallust was swept from office and noisily denounced the violence and corruption infecting Roman politics, Cicero was proconsul in the province in Cilicia. He was poised to return to Rome to take a leading part in its political debates—and in his own mind, to save the city single-handedly from political breakdown and disaster.

As educated as any philosopher, Cicero saw that trying to use sheer force of will and reason to uphold the old standards of courage and integrity, as Stoics like Cato were trying to do, would never be enough. On the other side, engaging in a steady dirge lamenting lost Roman virtue, as Sallust and others were doing, was pointless. Polybius had used Plato to turn Aristotle's politics, and Rome's, inside out. Cicero subtly sought to reverse the process.

He had grown up with Greek tutors and had traveled to Athens to study at the third or new Academy under the philosopher Carneades, which Cicero believed came closest to Socrates's own methods. He admired Plato more than any other thinker: "the prince of philosophers," was Cicero's title for him. Indeed, Cicero's *De Re Publica* is closely modeled on the *Republic*, and it follows Plato's dialogue form. Cicero's goal was the same as Plato's: to offer a picture of the ideal state.[21] But Cicero's state is not a utopian dream but a real place—republican Rome. Its main character is not a philosopher but a politician, as it happens a figure from Polybius's past, not Cicero's: the Greek historian's long-dead master, Scipio Aemilianus. He is a symbol of Rome as it once was—and might be again.

Cicero endorsed Polybius's view that Rome's mixed constitution was the cornerstone of its success. Rome's future, he affirmed, would depend on maintaining that proper balance between the Senate, the consulate, and the Roman people, all pulling together in their respective roles.[22] But Cicero rejected Polybius's prediction of Rome's doom and Plato's inevitable cycle of political degeneration. Instead, he had Aristotle come to Rome's rescue not in just one but two powerful ways.

First, Cicero made Aristotle's ethics the core of his projected Roman revival, and his *res publica*. The Latin term means literally "the public thing," and for Cicero the Roman republic is far more than just its constitution or system of government—what mattered most to an analyst like Plato. Instead, the republic is the place where citizens learn and practice the virtues they need in order to be happy, as a matter of civic habit. The chapters of *De Re Publica* where Cicero talks about the qualities needed for the ideal citizen and statesman are lost.[23] However, we get some hint of them in the titles of some of his other works: *On Friendship* (*De Amicitia*); *On Moral Obligations* (*De Officiis*); and in his writings on piety and respect toward the gods, *On the Laws* (*De Legibus*), and on respect for one's elders, *On Old Age* (*De Senec-*

tute). And his chief moral tenet certainly echoes Aristotle's: "Never go to excess, but let moderation be your guide."

Above all, Cicero wanted Rome's citizens to keep an Aristotelian sense of proportion between their responsibility toward family and friends and their responsibility toward the state. No relationship should be more important to us than the one with our *patria*, our country. "Our parents are dear, our children are dear," Cicero writes, "our friends and relatives; but our *patria* alone embraces all our deepest feeling. What good man would hesitate to meet death for its sake, if he could?"[24]

At the same time, Cicero also echoed Aristotle by noting that the individual household is "the seed-bed of the State." By Cicero's reckoning, government must respect our personal sphere of responsibilities and connections, including our property, in order to win our respect and loyalty. Indeed, Cicero straightforwardly states that the reason men create states and cities is to protect private property—a momentous step beyond Aristotle's own views and toward those of John Locke fifteen centuries later.[25]

In short, there must be another balance to match the one that maintains a free and fair constitution. This is the balance between the state and the citizen, between the needs of the community and what Romans called *libertas*, or individual liberty. For Cicero, maintaining that balance represents the future of all free men. In this way, Polybius's mixed constitution will have a firm moral foundation in the mutual obligations that tie us together as individuals (much as Aristotle would have pointed out), as well as those that bind us as a community (as Plato would have insisted).

But how to do this? To understand Cicero's solution, and Aristotle's next major contribution to the Western political tradition, we also have to understand that politics in late republican Rome was above all a performance a⸱
Like the audience at a cineplex, every citizen and politician, even those fr⸱
the most exalted patrician families, expected it to be as dramatic and th⸱
cal as possible. And center stage was Rome's Forum, the hub of civic ⸱

On any given day, Cicero could wander down to the Forum and
through throngs of people gathered around one elevated rostrur⸱
other. On some were candidates for office haranguing voters; on
major debates in front of one of Rome's many plebeian assem⸱
others were law trials, where both budding and experienced po⸱
their oratorical skills, just as Cicero himself had done, by def⸱
clients before a jury—or prosecuting their enemies.

Cicero had built his career arguing such cases, and liked to compare practicing law with acting in front of a theater audience.* He knew Roman crowds were always looking for the most exciting law case or political dispute. One could easily spot the oratorical superstars by the size of their *corona*, literally "crown," or circle of admiring listeners.[26] The same was true of politics. *Eloquentia* was the quality most highly prized among Roman statesmen, and every politician had to be able to sway a crowd with the kind of emotionally charged language and operatic gestures—even as he might be dodging brickbats or flying missiles or fending off an enemy's dagger—that we usually associate today with a Verdi or Puccini aria.

It was precisely this kind of politics that Plato most despised. He had seen plenty of it in the Athens of his day. As he made clear in his *Gorgias*, Plato had learned to hate all orators, just as he hated all theater and all representational art. Oratory, Plato says, has the same relation to justice as cosmetology does to bodybuilding: "a mischievous, swindling, base, servile trade which creates an illusion by the use of . . . makeup and depilation and costume, and makes people assume a borrowed beauty to the neglect of the beauty that is the result of training and discipline."[27] And for the same reason: both politics and makeup appeal to the emotions instead of reason.

The orator lurks in the dark like the artist in the Republic's cave, the realm of opinion and illusion (art and theater were the worst, since they created an *illusion* of the material world, which is already an illusion). In Plato's view, the democratic politician's verbal dexterity is a direct index to his level of moral corruption.

Aristotle, as we might expect, took a different and more moderate position. Yes, orators don't use the same rigorous arguments as the philosopher or dialectician; and yes, sometimes demagogues misuse their rhetorical skills to convey lies or to lead their audience into evil and vice, like a Hitler or a Huey ... But eloquence in the hands of a Winston Churchill or a Martin Luther ... can also be used to lead men and women to do good instead of evil. For everything depends on the character of the orator *and* the integrity of speaking itself. Given the right rules and restraints, Aristotle argued, Cicero would affirm, rhetoric can be a way to guide human beings

---

... s the formal term Roman law designated for the plaintiff, just as the different ... known as acts, almost as if they were parts of a play.

Cicero believed Roman orators, like the one portrayed in this Etruscan statue, could use Aristotle to save the Republic.

to practice virtue and wisdom almost, if not quite, as surely as philosophy itself.

This is what Aristotle set out to do in his *Rhetoric*. It offered all the rules a speaker needed so that he could appeal to an audience's emotions and its common opinions (*topoi* in Greek) in order to get the audience to do the right thing—namely, to make a moral judgment or draw a logical conclusion.

This was, Aristotle warned, a method for arriving at the truth less rigorous and certain than scientific demonstration.[28] The speaker in a political debate or legal case has to deal with particular facts rather than universal propositions, and with future probabilities rather than the formal necessities of a science like physics. However, Aristotle devised a set of rules that adapted the formal rules of logic to suit a popular audience*—the very people, in fact, who in a free society will be voting on a jury or in an election. By following Aristotle's rules for organizing the material for a speech, a speaker learns how to build a compelling case that allows no contradiction, while excluding cheap emotion or false reasoning. At the end of his speech, he will be able to say to his audience, "You all have heard; you have the facts; give your judgment," and sit down confident that he and justice will have won the day.[29]

Aristotle's *Rhetoric* showed how public oratory could be a creative force for virtue and truth instead of prevarication and "spin." It had a compelling influence on teachers of rhetoric in both Greece and Rome, including Cicero. Cicero hailed Aristotle as the mighty river of which all subsequent theories of rhetoric, including his own, were only minor tributaries.[30] However, Cicero's interest was more than theoretical. Cicero seized on Aristotle's notion of the orator turning his audience's emotions into a force for good rather than evil with the desperation of a drowning man clinging to a spar. With violence and civil war looming, Cicero turned Aristotle's ideal orator into the savior of the Roman state.

Aristotle's orator had to have a philosopher's knowledge of right and wrong in order to distinguish good from evil and truth from falsehood. But above all, he had to know his country's laws, "for the salvation of the state is in its laws."[31] For Cicero, the core of those laws was Rome's mixed constitution. Echoing Polybius, he insisted that Rome's constitution was not like Plato's ideal republic: it was "the product not of one genius but of many . . . the work of several men in several generations." The task of future Roman statesmen had to be exhorting the Senate, the magistrates, and the people to carry out their different duties in order to preserve the republic's balanced mixture and to prevent Rome from falling into Plato's cycle of decay and dissolution, which Cicero now believed could be evaded or at least indefinitely postponed.[32]

Cicero's *De Oratore* (*On the Orator*) is the essential companion piece to

---

*For example, Aristotle's classic syllogism of three elements, such as "All men who commit murder deserve the death penalty; Archias has committed murder; therefore Archias deserves the death penalty," is simplified for rhetorical purposes to just two: "Archias has committed murder; he deserves the death penalty."

his *De Re Publica*. One is useless without the other. Cicero's orator is a man built to heroic proportions. He must be a man of *eloquentia*, with the speaking skills necessary to move great crowds. He must be a patriot whose profound love of country allows him to identify with his audience, to feel what they feel and understand their needs and desires. And he must be a man who understands the true nature of good and evil.

As with Aristotle, this last is the most important quality for a great statesman and orator. Like Archimedes's lever, the statesman's ability to draw moral distinctions allows him to lift up the hearts and minds of his fellow citizens, to show them that they are all in this together, as citizens in a free commonwealth: a "coming together of men united by a common agreement about laws and rights," Cicero says, "and by the desire to participate in mutual advantages."[33] Once they realize they have a common destiny, they will be ready to do the right thing. And by doing the right thing, they will save their country.

It is Cicero who made public speaking one of the essential tools of Western self-government and democracy. His own orations would be studied over the centuries to teach the skills of the trade to everyone from trial lawyers and presidents to high school debating societies. Together with Aristotle, he created a civic tradition founded on the heroic image of the orator, who inspires his countrymen by a combination of eloquence, rational argument, and moral vision, and by doing so rallies his nation in a time of crisis. From Washington's farewell speech to Lincoln's Gettysburg Address and Kennedy's inaugural, Cicero and Aristotle would inspire a vital part of American political culture.

In his own time, however, Cicero's plea for the creative power of civic eloquence had an air of desperation. As he himself said, "Advice is judged by results, not intentions." In 54 BCE, when he began *De Re Publica*, Rome was dominated by an uneasy troika of ruthless power brokers led by Julius Caesar. Street brawls and assassinations plagued every election; bitterness and cynicism were everywhere. In a few short years, Rome would be plunged into civil war.

The hole in the Roman soul was growing wider. Cicero believed that his Aristotelian formula represented the republic's last best hope.

His reward would be ignominy and death.

Like other Romans, Marcus Aurelius (emperor 161–80 CE) could find
no solace in ruling the world.

Nine

DANCING IN THE LIGHT:
THE BIRTH OF NEOPLATONISM

I have tried everything, and it's no good.
—Attributed to Emperor Alexander Severus, c. 230 CE

Aristotle had shown how the Roman republic could save itself, or so it seemed to Cicero. Cicero had worked out the means to do it. His ideal common-wealth built on the free association of citizens inspired by great men to do great deeds would be rediscovered with delight by the buoyant age of the Renaissance and be passed along down to America's founders.[1]

Cicero's fellow Romans, however, paid no attention to his program of re-form. Leading statesmen turned their backs on him. Although Cicero had held Rome's highest office, they blocked his entry into the Senate. Men like the younger Cato, Julius Caesar, and his rivals Pompey and Crassus all knew something was seriously wrong with the Roman political system: it was suited to running a small city-state, not a vast empire. Each simply assumed he could ride out the coming chaos and emerge on top. Instead, all four would die violent deaths—while the republic itself, much as Polybius had predicted, passed into history.

As Cicero pointed out, Rome's rot was moral and self-inflicted, and it started at the top. Julius Caesar proved that it was not just intellectuals who felt the chill of Polybius's pronouncement of doom. He was descended from an ancient noble family, fluent in Greek, and widely read. As a young man, he set out to study the art of rhetoric on the island of Rhodes, an important center of Aristotelian learning.

On the way, however, he had been captured by pirates. By sheer force of personality, Caesar virtually took over the band of brigands. He made them applaud his speeches and admire the poems he wrote for them. After thirty-eight days his ransom was paid and the pirates released him, pledging to be friends forever. Caesar returned to Rome, raised a vigilante force of men and ships at his own expense, and sailed back to capture and crucify the pirates to the last man.

This was the kind of ruthless alpha male destined to rise to the top of Roman politics. Caesar did this in short order by crossing the Rubicon River north of Rome with his legions in order to bend the Senate to his will in 49 BCE; then by crushing his rival Pompey at the battle of Pharsalus two years later; and finally by being named dictator for life by the Senate two years after that, in 45 BCE.

It was a remarkable success, unprecedented in Roman annals. Still, Caesar suffered as much as anyone from the hole in the soul Plato and Polybius had left. There was no inward sense of triumph to match the outward of becoming sole ruler of Rome. When he stood and gazed out over the field of enemy dead at Pharsalus, which included the fine flower of Rome's aristocracy, he said bitterly, "They would have it thus."[2] Caesar knew that his new extraordinary powers would only provoke jealousy and hatred (one of those he hoped would cooperate, Cato the Younger, chose suicide instead). He took them anyway because, "for all his genius," as a friend later said in a striking remark, "Caesar could see no way out."

During his dictatorship, Caesar sometimes spoke about carrying out important social reforms, especially relieving the crushing debt on Rome's working families. In the end, he did little or nothing. As for himself, "my life has been long enough," Caesar said at the height of his fame and adulation, "whether reckoned in years or in renown." Victory had left the taste of ashes— and cost him a taste for living.[3]

On March 14, 44 BCE, Julius Caesar attended a dinner party at a friend's house. At the height of the banquet, as the dishes were cleared away and the wine cups were refilled, the conversation turned to death.

Someone asked what kind of death would be best. Before anyone could speak, Caesar gave his answer. "An unexpected one," he said.

The next day, on the ides of March, he got his wish.[4]

We don't know if Caesar read Polybius's *Histories*. We know his killer, Marcus Brutus, was steeped in it. While campaigning in Greece, he wrote a digest of Polybius's work (now lost). He was also familiar with Cicero's reform proposals, concocted out of Aristotle. Cicero's own son was part of Brutus's circle. However, as the descendant of one of Rome's most illustrious houses, Brutus convinced himself something more drastic was needed to restore *libertas* as well as the *mos majorum*, the upright ways of Rome's ancestors. He chose action over words, a dagger rather than a speech.

Caesar's murder has been immortalized by Shakespeare's play *Julius Caesar*. This is appropriate, since the assassination was itself a piece of performance art in the tradition of Roman politics. Brutus and the other Liberators, as they dramatically called themselves, had no plans or strategy once Caesar was dead. They assumed the gesture would be enough to restore the old system. Instead, Caesar's former allies Mark Antony and Caesar's adopted son, Gaius Octavianus, rallied the Roman army and herded the Liberators out of the city. To paraphrase the French statesman Talleyrand, the murder of Caesar proved to be worse than a crime. It was a blunder—and the last act of the old Roman republic.

In that sense, the murder of Cicero five days later was the first act of the new Roman Empire. It came on the orders of Mark Antony, who had been the subject of some of Cicero's most excoriating speeches (indeed, Antony demanded that the executioner bring him not just Cicero's head, but also his hands, which had written them. With Cicero died the last hopes of a revived republic. After Brutus's defeat at Philippi in 42 BCE, he and his fellow Liberator Cassius took their own lives. Twenty-one-year-old Octavianus, grandson of Caesar's sister, emerged as the dictator's heir in political as well as personal terms. His decisive victory over Egypt's queen Cleopatra and Mark Antony at the battle of Actium in 31 BCE put the last touch on his supreme power.

Still, the decades of mob violence, gangster politics, and fashionable despair were finally over. Octavianus took the name Caesar Augustus, and the title *princeps et imperator*. However, Augustus was shrewd enough to see that the best way to secure his reign was to present it not as the establishment of something new, namely a Roman empire, but as the restoration of something old: Polybius's and Cicero's balanced constitution.

Augustus was like the architect who renovates an old apartment building by keeping the original Gilded Age façade but putting in completely brand-new fixtures. The façade included the conveniently dead figure of Cicero, who would be posthumously elevated to the status of a Roman Socrates—the virtuous man made impotent by the viciousness of his enemies, including the hated Mark Antony. It was a reputation Cicero would retain without interruption through Victorian times.

The façade also included the Roman Senate and the consulate, although the latter was now reduced to a merely ceremonial office. The new fittings included taking personal command of Rome's legions, the largest army in the world, as *imperator*, or emperor—the key to stabilizing Rome all along—and taking personal control as *princeps*, or head of the Senate, of the provinces of Rome's increasingly far-flung empire. The finished product, or *principate*, would be reviled by Romans who yearned for a return to the republic and also by some historians. But it worked. For almost three hundred years, the Augustan system maintained a solid and steady *Pax Romana* that protected one generation of critics after another from Rome's enemies, even as those critics devoted their energy to trying to tear it down.

To his credit, Augustus sensed what was coming. He assembled a stable of writers, poets, and propagandists to convey the image that his *principate* had halted Plato's cycle of inevitable decay and dissolution in its tracks. The poet Virgil composed an entire epic poem in the manner of Homer, the *Aeneid*, to persuade readers that everything in Rome's history since its founding had been leading up to this magic moment:

> Caesar Augustus, son of a god,* destined to rule
> Where Saturn ruled of old in Latium, and there
> Bring back an age of gold: his empire shall expand
> Past Garamants and Indians to a land beyond the zodiac
> And the sun's yearly path . . .

*That is, since he had defied Julius Caesar and built a temple to his memory.

> *To these I set no bounds, in space or time;*
> *Unlimited power I give them.*

"A great new cycle of centuries begins," Virgil proclaimed. For Romans, "the lords of creation," a bright new future had started.[5] The problem was, no one believed him.

However, Rome's educated elite remained plunged in gloom. "Too happy indeed, too much of a 'Golden Age' is this in which we are born," wrote one with genuine bitterness.[6] Augustus died in 14 CE. Literary Rome proceeded to portray his successors as corrupt and incompetent monsters, from Tiberius and Nero and Caligula to Domitian and Caracalla (the emperor who appears in all his malignant splendor in the film *Gladiator*). Gifted writers like Catullus and Juvenal painted imperial Rome as a cesspool of moral depravity. The image has persisted to this day. The historian Tacitus made his reputation, then and later, by tracing how the "trickle down" of corruption at the top by Tiberius, Nero, and Caligula triggered a decay of private morals and a blank passivity among Rome's leading families in the face of tyranny.

The poet Lucan, who mourned rather than celebrated Caesar's victory in his epic *Pharsalia*, wrote: "Of all the nations that endure tyranny our lot is the worst: we are ashamed of our slavery." The satirist Propertius proclaimed that proud Rome was being destroyed by its own prosperity.

That remark is unintentionally revealing. The truth was that Augustus's successors, even Nero and Caligula, presided over an unprecedented expansion of both the empire and its wealth. The *Pax Romana* protected one generation of its critics after another from the dark forces threatening the ancient world. Some of its rulers may have been mentally unstable and incompetent. In a brutal age, purges and bloodshed at the top were not unknown, and *severitas* was the rule more than the exception in dealing with outsiders. "You Romans bring a desolation," Tacitus quotes one Briton complaining to his conquerors, "and call it peace."[7]

All the same, what is remarkable is how this great empire managed to carry on and prosper, regardless of who was in charge. Far from being cowed by tyranny, the Roman Senate actually exercised far more power and influence than it liked to pretend. Diplomacy under Nero helped to establish peace along Rome's frontiers; the emperors Tiberius and Claudius rendered important reforms to Roman provincial government.[8] Meanwhile, the old

Roman elite, having decimated itself in the civil wars of the republic, was steadily replaced by new men from the provinces, including Greece. They brought new energy and enthusiasm to the empire, just as Roman rule brought a new level of settled life to outlying areas around the world, from Britain to the desert reaches of Algeria and Mesopotamia.

The result was a strange duality in Roman culture under the empire. On one side, for three centuries legions marched, roads were built, and new provinces were conquered and plundered. Triumphs were celebrated, emperors were deified, and great temples were consecrated in their memory. Great monuments like the Colosseum and the Circus Maximus rose on the Roman skyline, as the empire's citizens enjoyed an unparalleled prosperity and splendor. Yet Rome's finest minds and spirits found it all empty and meaningless, even a sign of approaching doom.

A later age would develop a term for this disaffection: alienation.

But we can find its origin in Plato's cave, when we realize all we do and see is a meaningless illusion, and we seem permanently shut out from the light and truth. *Alienatio mentis* became almost the occupational disease of Rome's intelligentsia. In any case, Tacitus, Rome's greatest historian, certainly suffered from it. He despised the imperial system even though he was writing under what posterity recognized as one of Rome's best and most enlightened rulers, the emperor Trajan. Tacitus had to admit, "The interests of peace require the rule of one man," and since Augustus, "all preferred the safety of the present to the dangers of the past." Still, as historian M. L. Clarke puts it, Tacitus's head was with the empire, but his heart was with the republic.[9] He could not shake off the feeling that the reign of Augustus's successors, which he savagely chronicled in his most widely read work, the *Annals*,* was only symptomatic of a deeper loss of Roman moral integrity and vitality. It was not just Caligula and Nero who were cruel and corrupt. The decay had infected all of Roman society.

In Tacitus's eyes, the only place where you could find courage, manliness, and honor anymore was not in the Roman Empire, but on the other side of its frontiers. The naked, blue-painted natives of far-off Britain (Tacitus's father-in-law had been governor there) and the Germanic tribes that crowded

---

*They would inspire Robert Graves's *I, Claudius,* with their picture of Rome at its most vicious and X-rated.

close to the Roman watchtowers along the Rhine seemed to Tacitus to display the kind of free manly virtues Romans once had and had lost.

The shame was that the Britons and Germans didn't realize they had it so good. When they began to adopt Roman ways, like going to the baths and building villas and attending dinner parties, Tacitus sneered, "they call it civilization when in fact it is only slavery."[10]

Tacitus is the first romantic anthropologist. His sentiments will reappear in the writings of Jean-Jacques Rousseau on the "noble savage," among other places. But its roots are to be found once again in Plato and his Myth of Atlantis: the idea that at some primeval stage of humanity, long before the cycle of man's degeneration began, men knew the truth clear and pure and obeyed the laws of God.

Atlantis's inhabitants were such a people, Plato writes. But "when the divine element in them became weakened," Plato says in the *Timaeus*, the former super-race of Atlantis became merely human. "To the perceptive eye," Plato wrote in the *Timaeus*, "the depth of their degeneration was clear enough, but to those whose judgement of true happiness is defective they seemed, in their pursuit of unbridled ambition and power, to be at the height of their fame and fortune."[11] Zeus and the gods knew the truth, Plato says; and together they plotted the doom of Atlantis—a doom so devastating it vanished forever.

Once men knew the truth; one day they might know it again. But not before the cycle of decay and dissolution was complete, and not before existing institutions had dissolved away into nothingness.

It was precisely that nothingness which more and more Romans were yearning for.

By the time Tacitus died around 117 CE, the Roman Empire bore little resemblance to the one Polybius had known. It covered more than 2.5 million square miles from the Grampian Hills of Scotland to the Tigris and Euphrates and contained 65 million inhabitants. A network of 50,000 miles of stone-laid roads connected its most distant frontiers to its capital. It was also thoroughly Hellenized. Trajan's successor, the emperor Hadrian, had been born in the Roman province of Spain but preferred speaking Greek to Latin. His boyhood nickname was "the little Greek," and he became an honorary citizen of Athens. Emperors after Hadrian did most of their correspondence in Greek; Marcus Aurelius would even write his memoirs in Greek.

The migration of Greek families and Hellenized Asians into the Roman Senate that began under Augustus was now a tidal wave. Indeed, Rome could not have managed without them. Imperial Rome's finest physicians were Greeks like Galen, who explained the functions of the human body, and Asclepiades (c.124–40 BCE) the mysteries of the human mind. The Greek Strabo established its map of the world while Ptolemy explained the movements of the stars and heavens. The famous jurists Papinian and Ulpian, who codified Rome's laws, were also born and bred Greeks.

Alexandria, Cleopatra's former capital, was fast becoming the intellectual center of the Roman world much as it had been the center of the Hellenistic one. The very fact that the great battles that decided the birth of the empire, from Pharsalus to Philippi to Actium, were all fought in Greece was proof that a shift of the center of gravity had been under way for more than a century—a shift that the building of a new imperial capital at Constantinople in 323 CE made official.

The presence of Greek thought and philosophy in Roman culture was more palpable than ever. Plato's dialogues and Aristotle's treatises, plus the innumerable commentaries on their works by generations of students, were part of the fabric of daily intellectual life. The graduates of Plato's Academy remained active all through the empire, as were their Stoic, Epicurean, and Skeptic rivals; while the traditions of Aristotle's Lyceum lived on in a multitude of scholars' studies and laboratories, including Alexandria's restored Library and Museum.

All the same, the trend was a self-defeating one. Even as the city by the Tiber crowned herself "mistress of the world," the hole in the Roman soul yawned even wider. Under the dual impress of Plato and Polybius, all Greek philosophy managed to do was convince generations of Romans that the happiness of the human spirit depended on being indifferent to everything that their reality offered.[12] Epicureans taught that men were happiest when they moved through the world like random atoms, just as the world itself was only a heap of atoms that had come together by chance, with no deeper meaning or purpose. The Skeptics (or Pyrrhonists) taught "that which is truly good is unknowable," and since we have no means of knowing which of our judgments about the world are true and which are false, "therefore we should not rely upon them but be without judgements"—the perfect formula for a moral relativism that knows no bottom.[13]

The Stoics should have done better. They had understood that men and women had to live in the world, and came equipped, as Aristotle would have pointed out, with the moral and mental tools to deal with that fact. Man's reason gives him the power to shape nature according to his needs, Polybius's friend Panaetius the Stoic had told his patrons. The arts of civilized life, including building, tools, machines, and farming, were proof that humans were destined to build a future for themselves based on benevolent interdependence with others, under the protection of a divine providence.[14]

This softer, socially optimistic side of Stoicism made a deep impression on Cicero's *On Moral Obligations*, where it mixed easily with Aristotelian notions of man as "political animal," in other words born with an instinct to cooperate with others to achieve a common good.*

All the same, it is the "hard" side of Stoicism that dominated the life and work of its most famous Roman exponent, the philosopher Seneca (4 BCE–65 CE). Seneca's wise man is indifferent to pain and suffering; he has no fears and no hopes. He never gets angry, even when he sees his father killed and his mother raped.[15] Seneca believed in humane virtues like gratitude and clemency, including toward slaves, and writes eloquently about their lasting benefit to others.

In the end, however, Seneca loved humanity more than he cared for human beings. He preached abstinence even while he owned one of the most sumptuous homes in Rome. Once, he attended the spectacles in the arena of which the Romans took great pride, with its gladiatorial combats and slaughter of wild beasts. He came back, he said, a worse person, because he had been among his fellow men. Roman society itself, he concluded, was nothing more than a collection of wild beasts.[16]

The characters in Seneca's plays, which resemble *The Texas Chain Saw Massacre* in their taste for blood and horror, suffer unspeakable torments. However, the characters learn to bear their suffering with what Seneca called *fortitudo* and *constantia*, or constancy. They prefer to endure the "slings and

---

*Similarly, the Stoic notion that all men are brothers because they share the same nature (*logos*) paid huge dividends in the development of Roman law and of how basic principles of justice can have universal application to all peoples everywhere—a development that is still going on in international law today.

arrows of outrageous Fortune," in the words of Shakespeare (whose tragedies were heavily shaped by Seneca's), rather than try to fight back.

Seneca's solution to life's inevitable cruelties was to withdraw. It was an increasingly attractive reaction in the later imperial age. The wise man must shun unnecessary human contact and connections, Seneca said. He must live within, and for, himself. He must cultivate the virtue of *apatheia*, literally an indifference to the fate of others—apathy even, in the last moment, to his own fate (faced by unjust accusations by the emperor Nero, Seneca and his wife chose suicide).[17]

Remain indifferent to pain and accept your fate. Consider yourself already dead, and live out the rest of your life according to nature. These Stoic lessons also fill the pages of Marcus Aurelius's *Meditations*, written a century after Seneca's death and the one piece of serious philosophy to come from the pen of a Roman emperor.

From the watchtowers of Hadrian's Wall in northern England, and the army camps along the Rhine and Danube frontiers, Marcus Aurelius could see the forces of barbarian darkness already gathering. He would spend his reign fighting to shore up the frontiers from attack, from the Germanic tribes in the north to the Parthians in the east. He would die on campaign along the Danube in 180 CE, worn out and without hope.

The *Meditations* were probably written during the bloody wars of the 170s, when it really did seem as if Rome might not survive. However, they tell us nothing about the tumultuous events taking place outside the emperor's tent. Instead, they reflect a resigned state of mind that is influenced not only by Stoicism, but by the figure of Socrates. Socrates was a particular hero for Marcus Aurelius, as the man who accepts his mortal fate; a symbol of a philosophy that is indeed a "meditation on death."

What are Alexander and Pompey and Augustus, Marcus Aurelius asks, compared with Socrates and Diogenes and Heraclitus—the man who said that nothing in the world is permanent? "This is the chief thing: be not perturbed, for all things are according to the nature of the Universal; and in a little time you will be nobody and nowhere. . . ." So leave this life satisfied, because He who releases you is also satisfied.[18]

Strange words to come from a man who was ruler of the known world. Socrates, Plato, Diogenes, and even Pythagoras appear several times in the *Meditations*. Aristotle, never. Aristotle's outlook was precisely the one Marcus Aurelius wanted to warn against: the idea that man is born to take charge of his existence and solve problems in a practical way, by building a better house or a more efficient machine; to make a better empire and a better life. Man's impulse toward *energeia*, considered action toward a desired end, was precisely the way of life the *Meditations* rejected.

"You have been a citizen of this great world," Marcus Aurelius says to himself in his last meditation. "What difference does it make if it is for five years or one hundred?" Of course, for millions it was a very great matter. Sixty years after Marcus Aurelius's death, from 245 to 270, every Roman frontier collapsed.[19] For those who lived through it, the Stoic message of "bear and forbear" was very cold comfort. However, another thinker arose who would offer comfort, at least to those who had time and energy to devote to books and philosophy. He showed men that if they could not control the great disasters of the third century, they could rise above them. And if they could not save the empire, they could at least save their souls.

His name was Plotinus. He is without doubt the most important and influential thinker to appear between Aristotle and Saint Augustine. Yet we know almost nothing about him. His life is an enigma wrapped in a mystery. He declined to tell his disciples any details about his life. He even refused to have his portrait painted or a bust made of his likeness.

Plotinus was also the most relentlessly antimaterialist thinker in history. He taught his disciples that everything we see or imagine to be real is actually only a series of faded images of a higher realm of pure ideas and pure spirit, intelligible only to the soul. According to his student Porphyry of Tyre, he was even sorry that his soul had to live inside a physical body.[20]

That sounds a great deal like Plato, and Plato was always the central figure in Plotinus's cosmic vision. But Plotinus had also read his Aristotle, and by putting the two together in a thoroughly original way, he transcended the traditional limits of ancient thought. It was a major breakthrough. From the last days of the Roman Empire through the Middle Ages and the Renaissance, Plotinus's "Neoplatonism" offered a new dimension for the European intellect to explore, and a new challenge: how to make the rational soul one with the Absolute.

Plotinus appears to have been born in Lyco in Egypt, a city that was founded on the Lower Nile by priests of Osiris, probably around 205. Whether Plotinus had any family connection with the rites of Osiris, the Egyptian god symbolizing man's hope for immortality, we will never know.[21] When he came to Alexandria to study at age twenty-eight, his interests were not religious at all but philosophical. He set up with a teacher, Ammonius Saccas, who immersed him in Plato and also Aristotle.*

Later Plotinus became part of Emperor Gordian III's entourage on his disastrous expedition against the Persians in 238. Gordian's army suffered a crushing defeat; the survivors scattered in all directions, while the hapless Gordian, still in his teens, was murdered by his courtiers. Among the refugees was Plotinus, who found shelter first in Antioch and then in Alexandria. The whole experience must have confirmed Plotinus's conviction that what we call "real life" is actually a realm of meaningless pointless suffering. Still, Plotinus refused to surrender to the usual Roman impulse toward bitter alienation. Instead he decided he was going to set up a school of philosophy to examine the alternatives—this time not in Alexandria or in Athens, but in Rome itself.

It was a momentous decision—and symbolic of a momentous break. What Plato's Academy had done in the nearly five centuries since Plato's death held no interest to Plotinus. He and his followers always called themselves "Platonists," never "Academics."[22] The long tussles between the Academy and the Epicureans, Stoics, and others had led the formal heirs to Plato further and further away from Plato's original ideas and doctrines. Now Plotinus brought them back to where they were supposed to start: the dialogues, including the *Timaeus*, which Plotinus read not just as a handbook for understanding astronomy or physics, as Cicero and others had, but as the key for understanding existence itself.

Since Socrates, thinkers had been obsessed with the question "What is the good life?" Plotinus decided it was time to revert to the earlier question, "What is reality?" What he discovered is that once we get the right answer to that question, it also provides the key to the other one. In other words, no truly virtuous or happy life is possible until we realize that everything, including ourselves, has its rightful place in a single spiritual realm: the Absolute One, Goodness or Being in Itself.

This may sound like Plato, but then Plotinus veers in a very different direction. Plato had seen reality as *dual*, with the spiritual and the material as

---

*Another student of Ammonius Saccas was a sharp-eyed, intense young man named Origen, who would use his master's lessons very differently. See chapter 10.

totally separate and distinct realms. Plotinus wanted to treat them as a single totality, embracing Being in Itself *and* the smallest and most insignificant part of creation and everything else in between.

Plotinus's universe doesn't just exist. Like Aristotle's, it forms a living system, a continuous spiritual emanation from the Being in Itself's own perfection, like water cascading down the steps of an enormous pyramid or ziggurat. Its life-giving force flows down the steps, level by level, and then spreads across the rest of creation. Plotinus taught that the material world is *not* distinct from the spiritual. The cave still reflects the distant light of truth, no matter how dimly.

Instead, all things exist in a carefully ordered sequence, a sequence not only of time but of value, running from the purest and most spiritual—the One and its animating principle, *Nous*, or Being in Itself—down to the basest and most material, just as the steps of the ziggurat lead from one to the next.

Where did Plotinus get this idea? Obviously it comes from Plato and his vision of the Good in Itself, which not only is the summit of all knowable things, but also gives the rest of the Forms (and everything else knowable by reason) their very existence.[23] But it also owes a debt to Aristotle's *Metaphysics*. Plotinus saw at once that Aristotle had provided him with a built-in scale for ordering all reality. At the top sits pure Form, Aristotle's invisible Prime Mover. Then comes the visible but imperishable realm of the planets and heavens. Next comes the realm of substances, informed matter, starting with man, then animate animals and inanimate plants, followed by the inorganic world of rocks, dirt, and water, as Aristotle's life-giving, purpose-giving form gradually loses out to matter.

Finally, at the bottom, Aristotle put Prime Matter itself: without form, unlimited, and without extension, with no positive properties.[24] Like pure Form, it is invisible to the human eye, but it remains a necessary component for everything sandwiched in between.

So far so good, if you are an orthodox follower of Aristotle. But Plotinus now put this together with Plato's picture of God the Demiurge from the *Timaeus*, the Supreme Creator who crafts the universe out of the image of His own perfection, so that each element reflects the perfection of the whole. All of a sudden, Plotinus gave his generation a whole new luminous way of seeing the world and humanity's place in it.

To understand its impact, we need to go back on our first Aristotelian walk through the woods but this time see it through Plotinus's eyes. We see the same trees and shrubs and stones in the path and the clouds overhead, we hear the same creatures scurrying in the leaves and insects buzzing around our head, and we feel the same sun on our face and the same breeze blowing through our hair.

But now we see that everything expresses, to an exact lesser or greater degree, the animating life-giving spirit of mind and Being, which connects everything to everything else. From God Himself in the heavens and the sun in the sky, to me and Rover the chocolate Lab with his humanlike alertness and curiosity, the watchful deer in the shadows, the chipmunks and squirrels, the bees and other insects, and then the trees and other flora, down to the dirt and dead leaves: All form an ordered hierarchy of Being.

I curl a baby lizard in my hand, so transparently orange that it seems made of plastic. But then it moves, its tiny limbs reminding me that it carries the breath of divinity within it, less than that of my own soul but more than the twigs and leaves from which I extracted it—and all in harmonious proportion with one another. When the eighteenth-century poet William Blake spoke of seeing eternity in a grain of sand, he was speaking the language of Plotinus and Neoplatonism.

"All things follow in continuous succession," Plotinus told his disciples, "from the Supreme God to the last dregs of things, mutually linked together and without a break." At the top is the One and the Good, beyond knowledge and description. "As the One it is the first cause, and as the Good the last end, of all that is."[25] As part of its own perfection, the One produces *Nous*, or Being in Itself, which contains all the perfect intelligible forms necessary for creation. *Nous* in turn gives birth to the World Soul, just as in Plato's *Timaeus*: it is both the generator and the container of the rest of creation, the means by which life flows out into the rest of existence, including the human soul, our direct point of contact with the source of all goodness and perfection.

The One's spiritual giving does not stop there. It flows down uninterrupted through the animals and plants, down to the smallest speck of dust and least significant bits of matter, all of which still reflect to some infinitesimal degree the perfection of the whole. From one end to the other of the hierarchy, everything participates in a constant diminishing series of divine emanations.

These emanations, and the connections they forge, form what comes to be called the Great Chain of Being. Any time a thinker of the Middle Ages or Renaissance talks about "a scale of being" or "the ladder of perfection," he is

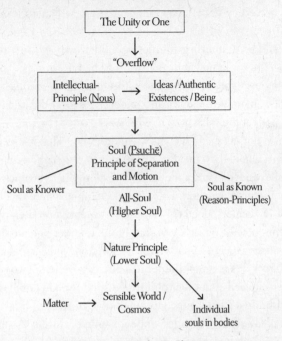

The cosmos according to Plotinus

borrowing from Plotinus.[26] And just as all things spiritual and material form rungs along the ladder, so God "fills them all with life . . . this single radiance [which] illumines all and is reflected in each, as a single face might be reflected in a series of mirrors."[27]

In his search for an ordered intelligible guide to existence, Plotinus had managed to fuse Aristotle's regard for the material world as the work yard of form with Plato's Demiurge as the procreative fountainhead of all truth. Yes, Plotinus says, we are born in a cave. But it's not hard to find our way out. There's a trail provided for us, because the links in the Chain of Being not only go down, like the steps of a ziggurat, they also lead *up.* The downward flow of divine perfection is matched by an equal upward striving of all things back toward their original source.

The human soul, which bears the largest share of that spiritual radiance that fills all material creation, feels that upward tug the most. We don't have to be dragged forcibly out of the cave to see the light, either, as Socrates seemed to suggest in the *Republic.* Instead we are gently pulled out by our own innate attraction to perfection: because that perfection is our own true self.

This would be Plotinus's great message to his own age and to the future. All of us, whether we know it or not, want to be one with perfection—or as later Neoplatonists will say, to be one with God. No one *wants* to live in the cave. We all want to see the light; and once we discover the true trail, we can retrace the path of the spirit back to whence it came.

Of course, finding the trail is the great difficulty. That is why Plotinus set up his famous school in Rome. For a time, it was more famous than the Academy. Plotinus resided in a Roman mansion belonging to two rich aristocratic women, mother and daughter, both called Gemina. There he drew to himself a circle of senators, doctors, well-to-do students, and literary types with whom he conducted a nonstop seminar in the manner of Plato's dialectic.

The discussions seem to have gone on for days. They also—and this was unique in Greek or Roman philosophical circles—included women students and children (indeed, a number of distinguished Roman families made Plotinus their children's guardian). His students were part of a last despairing generation of Romans. They desperately wanted answers. As the emperor Alexander Severus (who was an avid fan of Plato's *Republic*) said, they had tried everything else and had found it was a waste of time. So they looked to their teacher, Plotinus, their guru almost, to explain how to find their way back to truth and spiritual health.

He, on the other hand, was content to take his time. As we know from the *Enneads*, the discussions ground on day after day, topic after topic. Increasingly, Plotinus realized that no dialectical process, no matter how rigorous, was going to lead to the big breakthrough he wanted: to see the truth for itself and grasp the last mysteries of existence.

Plato had written about the inadequacy of mere words to express reality—one reason he often turned to myth and allegory.[28] The Pythagorean alternative had been to turn to the eternal truths of number and mathematics. But to Plotinus mathematical reasoning, too, seemed a series of clumsy symbols or signs, just as language did, compared with the raw truth of spirit and the One.

The trail out of the cave suddenly seemed a dead end. Plotinus decided there was only one way out: a leap of mystical illumination.

According to his student Porphyry of Tyre, Plotinus experienced this mystical union at least four times in the six years Porphyry studied with him.

Plotinus's description of what it was like stretched the normal boundaries of language—proving again to Plotinus the inadequacy of words to capture the most essential features of reality.

"Often I have woken to myself out of the body," Plotinus wrote, "[I] had become detached from everything else and entered into myself." Plotinus found himself surrounded by "beauty of surpassing greatness" and felt assured that "I belonged to the higher reality," which lay beyond the realm of Intellect and belonged directly with the Divine.[29]

In the end, Plotinus's system is less of a philosophy than a religion.[30] At its core is a mystical, even ecstatic, union with God, the final leap in which we transcend all the limitations of matter, time, and space and become one with the One. The closest metaphor Plotinus could find to capture its delight was of a dance with eternity:

> On looking on [the One] we find our goal and our resting-place, and around Him we dance the true dance, God-inspired, no longer discordant. . . . In this dance, the soul beholds the wellspring of Life, and wellspring of Intellect, the source of Being, [the] cause of Good, and root of Soul. . . .

In the divine dance, these highest spiritual qualities appear in themselves, undiluted by their presence in material creation. "They themselves remain, like the light while the sun shines."[31]

For Plotinus, the task of the wise man is the same as it was for Socrates. It is to prepare the soul for the final revelation of truth. But no one has to wait to die to achieve it. Wisdom can be found here and now, through mystical union with the One that takes us "from this world's ways and things" to a higher reality.

All around him and his school, the Roman Empire was steadily coming apart. Plotinus ignored it. He proposed to the emperor Philip creating a new city to be called Platonopolis, where Plotinus and other philosophers could find peace and shelter and study the nature of the universe. Unlike Plato's original version in the *Republic*, this utopian city would be set up not to remake the world, but to escape from it.

Philip listened politely, but nothing came of the plans. With Germans streaming across the Rhine, Goths plundering cities in Greece, and the Parthians hammering away from the east, the emperor had other things to worry about. With Plotinus we have come to the last loosening of the ties of loyalty between the empire and its best and brightest. "The wise man," Plotinus said, "will attach no importance to the loss of his country."[32] True happiness (*eu-daimonia*) requires a flight from all worldly connections toward a higher end, the final union of the soul with God.

Plotinus had finally found the cure for the hole in the soul of his world-weary countrymen. The price was any commitment to, or belief in, the value of the Roman Empire or any other kind of politics. Don't worry about those things, Plotinus said. Stay on the steep ascent to the One, and keep the soul focused on its ultimate goal. On his deathbed his last words were, "Strive to lead back the God within you to the Divine in the universe."[33]

There was only one problem. Plotinus's solution worked fine for those with the money and leisure to retire to a Roman villa to contemplate the eternal verities. What about everyone else?

Strangely enough, the answer lay just outside Plotinus's door.

Raphael, *St. Paul Preaching in Athens*

Ten

CHRIST IS COME:
PLATO AND CHRISTIANITY

Since the Logos has opened the eyes of our soul, we see the difference between light and darkness and in every way prefer to stand in the light.

—Origen of Alexandria, c. 240 CE

In the fourth year of the emperor Claudius's reign, more than two centuries before Plotinus's birth, the city of Athens had an unexpected visitor.

He came from the busy port city of Tarsus on the Asia Minor coast. This man, however, did not come to Athens on business. Nor did he come to visit Plato's Academy, already in its fourth century of existence, or the other venerable schools of philosophy in the city, although they were very much on his mind.

His name was Saul. He had come to Athens to deliver a message. A Jew by birth and a Greek by language and culture, Saul of Tarsus was also a Roman citizen. In fact, it is by his Romanized name, Paul, that we know him best. His message would be delivered in the language of ancient philosophy, in Greek, and would shake the ancient world to its foundations.

He spoke from the top of the Areopagus, a hill that sat slightly north of the Acropolis. As Paul climbed up, he would have scattered the goats grazing on its rock-strewn slopes. Below him were the buildings of the Academy in their sacred grove; the red marble-columned portico of the *stoa*; and the Agora, where Socrates had once argued with his fellow Athenians about wisdom and virtue. If he had looked harder, Paul could also have made out a long, low stone building with narrow grilled windows. This was Athens's municipal prison, where Socrates had drunk his fatal cup of hemlock four and a half centuries before.

Meanwhile, a crowd of curious onlookers gathered around the tent maker from Tarsus.

"What will this babbler say?" they were asking themselves. A number of them, we are told, were "certain philosophers of the Epicureans and Stoics," who had already heard Paul say a few words in the Agora about some strange god and a man from Galilee who had risen from the dead. They and others then followed Paul to the Areopagus to hear more. As our source tells us, the one thing Athenians enjoyed more than talking was hearing someone else talk, especially about some new and exciting philosophical doctrine.[1]

"May we know what this new doctrine of yours is?" they asked Paul.

Paul told them.

He told them about a God who had made the world and all things. He told them about a God who was Lord of heaven and earth "and hath made of one blood all nations of men." But he warned them this Lord God did not dwell in any temple made by human hands. He then pointed below to a building he had seen on his way up the hill, dedicated "To the UNKNOWN GOD."

He cried out, "Whom therefore you ignorantly worship, him I declare unto you." That alone must have created a sensation in the crowd, but Paul plunged on. If the people would seek out this Lord God, he said, they would find that He was closer than they thought: "For in Him we live, and move, and have our being; as certain also of your own poets have said, 'For we are also His offspring.' "

And now this God "has appointed a day, in the which He will judge the world in righteousness." Paul said this would happen through the man whom He had raised from the dead as a sign that all shall rise from the dead on the day of judgment.[2]

At that point, the New Testament tell us, Paul began to lose his audience.

The dead are going to rise up again and be alive? the Athenians asked one another. Some started to snicker. Whom did he think he was kidding? The crowd drifted away. One or two did stay around to hear more about the need for repentance and about having "faith toward our Lord Jesus Christ."* But on the whole, Paul's stay in Athens was a disappointment.

He would move on, first to Corinth and then to other Greek cities. He would even go to Assos, where Aristotle had once walked along the beach, and to Miletus, the city of Thales and the birthplace of rational Greek thought.[3] Eventually he ended up in Rome. He would not leave that city alive.

Before he died, however, Saint Paul the Apostle would transform the ancient world. His journeys and his letters turned Christianity from a small heretical Jewish sect into a major presence among the Hellenized and Romanized populations of the Mediterranean basin.

Although Paul was a Jew, he devoted himself to preaching to non-Jews— that is, to the Gentiles. The secret of his success was crafting a message that resounded with the deepest emotional needs of a sprawling empire, including its finest minds.

Here are the answers, he proclaimed, for which you have been searching all your life. Here is a sense of belonging, in an empire where the bonds of community and traditional identities were dissolving.

Here is a permanence, in a world where bewildering change had become the rule. Here is a sense of moral purpose, where all other institutions seemed to have lost their way.

Above all, Paul's Christian message replaced the prevailing pessimism among Rome's governing classes with a message of hope and confident expectation. "God is able to provide you with every blessing in abundance," he wrote to the church he founded in Corinth, "in order that you will always have enough of everything and provide an abundance in all your good work." Even though Christ's resurrection and the day of judgment seemed only a short time away, the tone of all of Paul's letters is always upbeat, full of energy and joy. "Am I not an apostle?" he told the Corinthians. "Am I not free?"[4] It was a feeling that many, if not perhaps all, in the Roman Empire might envy.

This was, in the end, the real secret to Christianity's success in the late Roman and Greek world. It supplied, or claimed to supply, the answers to all

---

*With momentous consequences for one of them, Dionysius the Areopagite. See chapter 13.

the questions Plato, Aristotle, and their disciples had been asking for nearly five hundred years. By accepting the person of Jesus as the son of God and savior, by absorbing His words and life lessons, man's soul would finally grasp the timeless wisdom that every previous philosopher had said was the key to happiness. Through Christianity, what Socrates had called "the realm of the pure and everlasting and immortal and changeless" was suddenly, amazingly accessible—not only to the trained and disciplined minds of the Academy and Lyceum (or, later, Plotinus's seminars), but to every human being.

It was an idea, and a movement, whose time had truly come.

The Sermon on the Mount, the third-century Christian Apologist Irenaeus told listeners, takes over where Plato's dialogues left off. Every Christian would realize the elusive goal that Plotinus was seeking in vain: the joyful reunion of the soul with God. He or she could confidently say with Paul, "O Death, where is thy sting? O grave, where is thy victory?" and hear the answer echo all the way back to Socrates's prison cell.[5]

Not everyone believed it, of course. Greek and Roman traditionalists, including Plotinus's disciples, fought back with everything they had. The Christian tide, however, proved irresistible.

By the time Paul died around 65, Christian congregations had sprung up in every corner of the empire. There were already enough Christians in Rome to allow the emperor Nero to blame them for the Great Fire.[6] A century later, Marcus Aurelius took time away from fighting barbarians and writing his *Meditations* to order authorities in Lyon to put to death anyone adhering to the Christian faith.

A century after that, even as Plotinus was unraveling the secrets of Plato in his Roman villa, Christian congregations numbered in the millions. After years of fighting on Rome's frontiers, the emperor Diocletian set up his palace at Nicomedia in 287. An old-fashioned pagan, he was horrified to see a Christian *basilica* sitting on the opposite hill. Sixteen years later he learned that Christians had penetrated his court, even his wife's entourage. His savage persecutions, however, failed to diminish their numbers or their esprit de corps. Just eight years later, rivals for the imperial throne would be vying for support from the empire's Christians, who now numbered in the millions.

Today, historians point to social and economic factors to explain Christianity's amazing spread. But the key factor was its skill in seizing the high ground of Greek thought, especially Plato. Other schools had their role to play. The Stoics had spoken of a brotherhood of man not very different from

Paul's vision of the brotherhood of Christians, as he very well knew.[7] Aristotle's theory of substance would come in handy when Christians had to explain how a spiritually all-powerful God could become flesh and blood and how a holy offering of bread and wine could turn into the real presence of a resurrected Jesus Christ.

But Plato was crucial. His works provided a framework for making Christianity intellectually respectable, while Christianity in turn gave Plato's philosophy a shining new relevance. The supreme light of truth that had hovered outside Plato's shadowy cave was now revealed to be the light of Christ.[8]

The triumph of Christianity does *not* mark the end of ancient philosophy, let alone a closing of the Western mind, as some critics like to claim.[9] Instead, it deepened and broadened the Greek imprint on Western culture. It allowed familiar features to stand out in striking new ways. As the song has it, "Everything old is new again." The same was true of Plato under Christianity. And that imprint was headlined, splashily enough, in the very first words of the Gospel According to St. John: "In the beginning was the *Logos*."

Logos is Greek for "word." As far back as Heraclitus, it was used to refer to a divine essence pervading the universe: "immortal, Logos, Aeon, Father, Son, God, and justice . . . ruler of the universe."[10] The evangelist John, a Hellenized Jew like Paul (he was also writing in Greek, not Hebrew), made it clear that the Christian God was precisely this same *Logos* who had made everything in the world and is "the true light, which comes into the world to light every man." In the same way, John said, God's begotten son, Jesus, "who dwelt among us full of grace and truth," was that Word, or *Logos*, made flesh.[11]

John wasn't the first to connect the Hebrew deity and the highest truths of the Greeks. More than fifty years earlier, a Jewish thinker from Alexandria named Philo established the same link. However, Philo then took the next leap by identifying this *Logos* as the offspring of Plato's Demiurge from the *Timaeus*, the creative source of all being and intelligibility in the universe. Philo even said that the *Logos* was God's firstborn son. It was almost certainly this Platonized *Logos* that John had in mind when he wrote his Gospel.[12]

The consequences were huge. Anyone with an ounce of training who had read the *Timaeus* could see what Philo and John were up to. By using Greek philosophy to explain essential features of an alien creed like Judaism, not only were they laying out a blueprint for a Christian theology that would make sense to Greco-Roman culture. They were also offering a God who transcended the limitations and boundaries that previous thinkers, including Plato and Aristotle, had imposed on the conception of the divine.

The result was a God who was "beyond Being," eternal and uncreated.[13] He was a God more powerful and pervasive than Plato's Demiurge but also more actively involved in His creation than Aristotle's Prime Mover. He had, after all, sent His son to earth as the *Logos*, a figure who finally reconciled the eternal split between spirit and matter, between divinity and mortality.

This Platonized Christian God also made Plato's Forms seem more real, as the eternal patterns existing in the mind of God out of which He built heaven, earth, and the rest of His creation. When Saint Paul wrote that "the invisible things of God" are to be understood through "the visible things that are made," his words struck home with every reader of dialogues like the *Timaeus* and the *Meno*. Christianity also offered a hereafter, in which every soul would be judged according to its merits, just as Plato related in his *Republic*: except that the judges were not mythic figures from a shadowy pagan underworld, but the awesome team of Father and Son and Their heavenly angels.

The similiarity to Plotinus and his Neoplatonic mysticism was even more striking. Christianity offered a God who drew together all life and diversity as One just as Plotinus insisted, not simply in a series of ever-diminishing spiritual emanations, but in a single swift decisive moment, through the incarnation as Christ. Another never-to-be-repeated moment in the future, the Second Coming, would then fulfill that creation's entire destiny, including man's resurrection (which Saint Augustine in his *City of God* asserted that Plato would have endorsed if he had ever heard the Gospels).[14]

No more pointless repetitive cycles, no more meaningless drift, no more dreams of nothingness. Instead, at the Second Coming Christians shall see "the invisible things of the world" as they really are; "we shall see the material forms of the new heaven and the new earth," Augustine says, "and see God present everywhere. . . ."[15] There will God be in His final glory, "Alpha and Omega, the beginning and the end, the first and the last," along with the souls of His servants, "for the Lord God giveth them light, and they shall reign forever and ever."[16]

It was a grandiose vision, breathtaking in its comprehension and scope. So while Judaism and the Bible gave Christianity its weight and matter, its flesh and blood, Plato and Neoplatonism became its conceptual spine.

For example, just as Plotinus's God came in three emanations—the transcendent Godhead or One; the Divine Intellect, or *Nous*; and the World Soul—so Christianity ended up with its Holy Trinity, with God the Father bringing forth his Son, or *Logos*, who in turn draws together the divine essence in all things through the Holy Spirit. Likewise, Christianity revealed an individual human soul as immortal as Plato's and with the same yearning for truth. However, this soul did not appear in the world as an unhappy prisoner, "chained hand and foot in the body" just as Socrates's had been.[17] On the contrary, by living in the here and now, by sharing in the goodness of the Lord's creation and obeying His commandments, Paul and his successors insisted the soul is able to realize its destiny through union with Christ.

As for Holy Scripture, the Bible was the *Logos* in the truest sense, the Word of God set forth "in order that you may believe that Jesus is the Christ," John the Evangelist wrote. "So believing, you will have life in His name"—along with that final wisdom generations of philosophers had sought in vain.[18]

For the Lord's message was not just for the lovers of wisdom, but for all mankind. Christianity put what had been the privilege of the few within the grasp of everyone, even those who lived beyond the pale of empire. "Thanks to the Logos, the whole world is now Greece and Rome."[19]

Those words were written around 170, little more than a century after the apostles Paul and Peter were martyred. They reflect the growing confidence among Christians that the cultural tide had already decisively turned in their favor. Earlier Christian leaders, including both Paul and Peter, had endured scorn, persecution, and martyrdom (in a few decades, they would endure them again). Their early converts had tended to be people on the margins of Greco-Roman society, the socially or economically displaced or those, like women and slaves, who were seen as devoid of the virtues necessary for true culture (*paideia* in Greek), but who could find a path to fulfillment through a belief in Christ.

Clement, by contrast, came from a well-to-do Athenian family. He was as much at home with his society and culture as an Ivy League graduate. He had come to the great intellectual talking shop in Alexandria early in the reign of Marcus Aurelius to study and learn, but in a specifically Christian context. To Clement and his generation, Christianity was not the enemy of philosophy, but its finest and last expression.

Its doctrines, and the teachings of Jesus in particular, were in Clement's mind the perfect summing up of all the doctrines about nature, justice, and truth that Plato had laid out. Hadn't Socrates taught there was one God, and hadn't he been persecuted for his beliefs, just as Christians were?[20] The wisdom Socrates had brought to the Greeks, Clement asserted, Jesus had brought to the Jews and other barbarians. In fact, Socrates and Jesus were spiritual brothers. Just as Plato and Aristotle founded schools to teach disciples, so now Christ was the new "schoolmaster" of the human race. In fact, mosaics and statues of the time even showed Christ as the Great Teacher, seated on his teacher's chair, or *cathedra,* as if he were a professor at the Academy itself, surrounded by well-groomed students.

For Clement and the other so-called Christian Apologists of the third century, the future was a win-win situation. Old Testament Judaism and Greek philosophy had come to flow into the same great river, Christianity. The wisdom Plato and Aristotle had been forced to search for on their own could now be brought unmediated to the followers of Christ. The great search for wisdom and truth on which Plato had set the ancient world was finally at an end.

Not everyone, however, bought the formula. Traditional Platonists found themselves like MIT graduates being confronted by people who claim to have learned plasma physics taking an Internet class over the summer. They were furious about what was happening and fought back hard.

Plotinus's students in particular were outraged at this vulgarization of Plato and their master.[21] One was a Greek writing during Clement's lifetime who composed the most damaging of all attacks on Christianity, then or since. His name was Celsus, and he titled his work (in Greek) *The True Logos*—a direct challenge to the Christianized *Logos* of his opponents.

Celsus ripped aside the veil of intellectual respectability Christian Apologists had tried to give their faith. He gleefully exposed its roots in a Judaism that most Romans and Greeks despised and proved that Christianity had little or nothing in common with the elitist philosophy of Plato. The whole idea of a poor Jewish boy being the son of God was ridiculous. "Did not Plato say that the Architect and Father of the universe is not easily found?" How likely would it be that His son would turn up in a despised corner of the world like Galilee?

Celsus also rebuked the Christian claim that God's return was imminent. "God would never come down to earth to judge mankind. Why would he do this? He already knows all things."[22] He mocked a faith that turned followers into cannibals by insisting that they eat the body and blood of their god, and a faith that actually celebrated the god's death as a common criminal. Plato's God had been the epitome of refined reason. This Christian deity was clearly fit only for the gutter.

It was time for Christians to put aside their vain illusions, Celsus concluded. The vagabond and charlatan who called himself Messiah had only led his followers to disaster. He promised them prosperity and dominion over the world, "and yet," Celsus sneered, "you do not have one yard of ground to call your own." How could such a misbegotten mob possibly claim to be Plato's heirs?

Celsus's attacks were so stinging and devastating that they went unanswered for nearly a century. Even Clement of Alexandria felt inadequate to the task. Instead, it fell to Clement's most famous pupil to take up the cudgels on behalf of Christianity and to use Plato to stand Celsus's arguments on their head.

He was born around 185 in Alexandria to a Greek father and Egyptian mother, who named him Origen, meaning "the son of Horus." He was built like a boxer or wrestler, with an aggressive personality to match. This earned him the nickname of "The Untamed."[23] He brought the same reckless quality to his Christianity. In fact, Origen was so self-assertive and so clearly gifted that he took over Clement's school of theology at age eighteen when the older scholar left.

Plotinus's student Porphyry once said that Origen "lived like a Christian but thought like a Greek."[24] In fact, Origen was steeped in Plato: in Alexandria, he and Plotinus shared the same teacher, the great Platonist Ammonius Saccas. As a result, Origen brought the fusion of Christianity and Platonism to an entirely new level — one could say a more urgent level. More than any other thinker before him, Origen used a Platonized Christianity to address the pressing issues of his age. In doing so, he permanently shaped its character in ways that only one other Church Father, St. Augustine, would begin to match.

Unlike his rival Plotinus, Origen could not shut himself off from the world. Nor could he be complacent about it. Like his teacher Clement, he had felt its cruelty firsthand. When he was seventeen, Origen had watched his father being dragged through the streets to be executed for his Christian faith in one of the periodic pogroms pagan officials were beginning to use to intimidate their Christian rivals. His father and other Christian prisoners were put into a building near the city's necropolis for a time, then moved into the temple of the pagan god Serapis, where a cheering, jeering mob had gathered. Origen managed to squeeze into the crowd unobserved, and there, in the fading dusk, he saw his father being beheaded. Then the executioners threw the body to one side, next to the other bodies, and in the torchlight made a hideous pyramid out of the severed heads.[25]

A man "should take each moment and hold it tenderly in his hands," Origen later wrote, in order "to examine what other possible meaning it may hold, what other purpose or end." His father's martyrdom became the defining moment in Origen's life. In fact, he would spend his life facing the same fate from Roman persecutors—in effect, with a death sentence hanging over his head.[26]

This led him to ask a question: If I were to die tomorrow, and had to stand before my God for judgment, what would I say to Him? Socrates had said that the unexamined life was not worth living. The same was true for Origen and, he believed, for every Christian.[27] The task of Christianity had to be to prepare believers for that awful moment and to show them how to live a life that reflected the light of divine truth in every aspect.

Origen was the first Christian thinker to make the conscience, Socrates's *daimon*, or inner voice, the focus of moral life. For Origen, the conscience is all that separates the human being from the savage beasts who lynched his father. His teacher Clement had praised the ancient Stoic virtue of *apatheia*, emotional detachment. Origen never does.[28] If Christianity was to have any larger meaning in the lives of the faithful, Origen believed, it had to cultivate that inner conscience, to make it the guide all our dealings with the world and others. By combining Plato's *thymos*, that sense of moral outrage, with the teachings of Jesus, Christianity could scour away the cruelty and savagery of the age.

Today, we are vaguely if uncomfortably aware of that side of Roman life. We see movies like *Gladiator* about the bloody spectacles of the Colosseum and read about how Nero had Christians torn apart in the arena by wild dogs for the delight of the crowds or "made into torches to be ignited after dark." The sexual and moral license of the empire's elite has been portrayed ad nauseam in Hollywood's images of Roman orgies.

But the reality was far more brutal. Roman arenas that are still standing, like the Colosseum and the ones in Arles and Verona, were settings for a daily bloodbath. From Spain to Antioch, the mass murder of prisoners and thousands of caged animals was standard public fare. In Roman homes, slaves and children were considered nonpersons. Their physical and sexual abuse, including castration, was accepted without question, as was the abuse of women. Exposing unwanted children and infanticide were commonplace— so much so that scholars speculate infanticide may have helped to doom Rome's population and prosperity to permanent decline.

At the same time, the empire's leisure class celebrated a sexual adventurism that knew no limits and spared no one in its taste for the bizarre, running the gamut from prostitution and homosexuality to incest, bestiality, and child sodomy, "a vicious cycle of agitation, quest, satiation, exhaustion, ennui."* As for Rome's governing institutions, its prisons were nonstop horrors, where men accused of plotting against the emperor or of using witchcraft, or taxpayers who no longer had the money to pay (taxes under Diocletian routinely took one-third to one-half of gross income), were routinely tortured to death. If they were of low birth, they would be roasted over a slow fire—as were, of course, Christians.[29]

As Origen pointed out, the wise man as defined by Plato and Aristotle and other philosophers would never participate in any of these horrors. Like Socrates, he would avoid inflicting pain on any living thing; prefer suffering wrong rather than doing wrong to others; and avoid the gross temptations of sexual license. Like Seneca, he would turn away from the blood theater of the games in disgust. Like Plotinus, he would proclaim the sanctity of all life, including animals, and keep his soul pure until his dying day.

The same was true of the first Christians, Origen pointed out; and the people whom Celsus affected to despise most, the Jews. "The Jewish people never found delight purely in games," Origen wrote, "or the theater, or horse races. Their women never sold their beauty. . . . They always believed in the immortality of the soul, and are indeed wiser than those philosophers who, after their most learned utterances, continually fall back upon the worship of idols and demons."

What was the secret of the Jews' strength and virtue? Origen offered the answer. First of all, their Scripture with its power to transform multitudes,

---

*Romans even had a special verb, first used in poetry by Catullus, to describe the fluttering movement of the passive partner's buttocks in sodomy. The verb had two forms: one for males and one for females.

"making the coward the hero, and the wicked good." Then there was their faith: a faith more powerful than human reason alone, because it was based on still higher wisdom, the wisdom of God.

And what the Jews had done, Origen affirmed, Christians could do. They could spearhead an assault on the moral turpitude of the age and bring forth the inner voice in every believer. Justin Martyr had already pointed out how conversion to Christianity could bring about a moral transformation:

> We who heretofore conversed with loose women, now strictly con-
> tain within the bounds of chastity; we who devoted ourselves to magic
> arts, now consecrate ourselves entire to the one unbegotten God....
> We who were consumed with mutual hatred and destruction, now live
> and eat together [in peace], and pray for our enemies.[30]

Origen saw the need for this kind of transformation of society as more urgent than ever. It is the message underlying his polemical masterpiece, his *Against Celsus*. It was a devastating rebuttal of the era's most erudite anti-Christian critic, and reflected Origen's new confident, even defiant, stance. Christianity no longer just summed up ancient civilization's highest aims, as Justin and Clement had argued. It now had the power to *save* that civilization, Origen proclaimed, by bringing the highest moral principles down to earth right here.

Origen saw this as both necessary and natural. The one great lesson Origen learned from his Neoplatonist teachers was that every human being was made in the image of God, in the same way Plato described all material objects as made in the image of the Forms.[31] Of course, the most perfect of God's images was Jesus Christ himself, His only begotten son. However, everyone of every race, sex, age, or creed, from the lowest slave to the emperor himself, carried that same reflection of perfection.

It was what made God knowable to man: "Only like can know like" was a basic Platonic principle (as, for example, the soul's knowledge of the Forms).[32] The more man developed his own reflection of that perfection, by living his life in conformity with God's will, the more ready he would be to receive the grace of true knowledge and wisdom. And to deny or sully that perfection by behaving like a beast was a direct insult to God and the goodness of His creation.

In short, Origen saw us all like the slave boy in Plato's *Meno*. We are souls equipped by our nature to follow the path to the truth, once someone points us along the way.* The role of the Christian Church in Origen's eyes was to provide that guidance, to uphold that reflection of perfection into every aspect of life, for every Christian.

This was a new way of casting the relationship between the church and the faithful. Churches at the time still saw themselves largely as centers of worship rather than moral instruction. Christians like Origen's father had gathered to receive the Eucharist (already a firmly established religious ritual by the second century), pray, and perform baptisms.[33] Origen's passion was to turn these churches into centers of moral rearmament, starting with his own in Caesarea in Palestine, where he moved when he was forty-eight. Caesarea became his religious laboratory, where he instructed the faithful through his homiletic writings and his public sermons.[34]

More than any other Church Father, Origen established the sermon as a principal focus of Christian service and the Bible as the central subject for discussion. He was also one of the first Christian thinkers to treat the New and the Old Testaments as forming a single work. He taught his students to read the Bible *allegorically*, in order to see how every event in the Old Testament foreshadows later events in the New, like the Jews' exodus from Egypt foreshadowing the flight of the Holy Family, and Joseph's run-in with Potiphar foreshadowing Christ before Pilate. This would then lead them to read the events and images *symbolically*, as reflecting the highest spiritual truths or "mysteries" of Christianity, and *morally*, meaning its connection with the inner life of the believer.[35]

Because Plato had taught him that the visible is always the reflected image of the invisible, even the visible written word, Origen transformed the Bible into a new kind of spiritual treasure trove, including the Old Testament. Beyond the actual words of God, and underneath the literal narrative of law, history, and even geography, Origen could discern timeless truths waiting to be pointed out and explained. This way of reading the Bible, called *exegesis*, would become standard during the Middle Ages. Indeed, the Mid-

*See chapter 2.

dle Ages came to interpret just about everything morally, symbolically, or allegorically and sometimes all three.*[36] It was a direct legacy from Origen. But it sprang ultimately from Plato's insight that symbols and allegories can sometimes lead men to the highest truths more powerfully than reason—including to a knowledge of God.

Plato, it seems, watches constantly from the wings of Origen's great treatises. Christianity, Origen sometimes implies, is nothing less than Platonism for the masses.[37] However, the figure at the center of his sermons and his pastoral work was Jesus. Origen devoted more of his attention to Jesus as a person than any previous Christian thinker. He saw him not only as the son of God and the Messiah (the principal theme of Saint Paul's epistles), but as a role model and inspiration for the individual Christian. Jesus served as a walking, talking example of how anyone could live in conformity with the highest moral principles: in short, as the consummate Socratic philosopher.[38]

By his example, "[Christ] rescues us from all irrationality," Origen wrote. Jesus reveals how, by dedicating even activities like eating and drinking to the glory of God, we are raised up and illuminated and "become rational beings in a divinely inspired manner." For "Christ is all Wisdom."[39]

This is what later figures like Thomas à Kempis or Erasmus of Rotterdam, a keen admirer of Origen, will mean when they speak of living a life in Christ: " 'He that followeth Me, walketh not in darkness,' saith the Lord. These are the words of Christ, by which we are taught to imitate His life and manners, if we would be truly enlightened, and be delivered from blindness of heart."[40] Today, when ministers or even politicians feel it necessary to quote from the Sermon on the Mount to inspire or admonish us, it is Origen's distant example they are following.

In the end, Origen's Platonized Christianity added up to more than a cleverly argued theology. It signaled a cultural revolution. Its overt moral absolutism smashed all the cherished myths and institutions of mainstream ancient culture, from its temples and gods, including the emperor worship that underpinned the Roman Empire, to its games and spectacles and

---

*Take this classic example from a letter by the poet Dante Alighieri on the passage "When Israel came out of Egypt and the House of Jacob from among a strange people, Judah was his sanctuary and Israel his dominion." The *literal* meaning is the exodus of the Jews from Egypt; the *allegorical* meaning is man's redemption by Christ. The *moral* sense is the conversion of the soul from sin to a state of divine grace; and the *anagogical* meaning is the journey of man's soul from the corruption of this world to the liberty of eternal glory.

sacrifices—all in the name of Greek wisdom and reason. It triggered a systematic process of deconstruction, both literal and symbolic, that would reach its climax in Saint Augustine's *The City of God*. Nothing, absolutely nothing, would survive Origen's withering blast—not even Celsus's brilliant anti-Christian polemic of a century before.

In *Against Celsus*, Origen overturned Celsus's claims that Christianity rested on strange and bizarre religious rites (such as eating bread and wine as the body and blood of Christ), irrational superstitions, and unverifiable and unscientific miracles like raising Lazarus from the dead. Pagans had no business casting stones. What could be more improbable than the story of Athena's birth from the head of Zeus? What could be more contemptible than the sexual promiscuity associated with certain pagan sects? What could be more absurd than the mystery cult of Cybele, which demanded that adherents castrate themselves, or more barbarous than a religion that not only demanded the shedding of innocent blood to consecrate religious festivals, but condoned it in the arena to gratify the sadism of the masses?

The claim that paganism somehow embodied the best and Christianity the worst of Greco-Roman civilization was an obvious lie to Origen. He ripped aside the veil of respectability with which the ancients had clothed their traditional gods and goddesses and exposed the sordid reality underneath. What Socrates and Plato had started, the overthrow of the pagan pantheon, Origen's Christianity finished.

In the end, however, Origen's principal argument for the validity of his faith was its own success. Christianity's spread, he implied, was a kind of democratic referendum on the elitist institutions of the ancients. The philosophy of the ancients and the Stoics had reserved final wisdom for a chosen few. Christianity delivered those same truths, and the moral virtues that went with them, to the many, right down to slaves and the homeless. Plato was like a chef at a five-star restaurant, Origen said, who only knew recipes that appealed to his handful of wealthy diners. Jesus, by contrast, Origen says, "cooks for the multitudes"—and the multitudes have responded.[41]

As Origen's biographer Joseph Trigg concludes, in the end Origen's most compelling argument for the truth of Christianity was not its logical consistency, but the fact that it worked.[42] By 250, Christianity had spread from Palestine across the Roman empire. Was this purely an accident, Origen asked, or was it in fact a sign of divine providence? The impact of Christian faith was palpable in the lives of ordinary men and women, who had embraced sexual continence, willingly set their slaves free, and in martyrdom displayed the highest form of courage. Again, was this coincidence, or was it a sign that man's divine nature had finally truly been awakened?

Now the task of Christian churches was to ensure that this process of moral reformation deepened and spread. Origin vigorously opposed Rome's blood sports. A century later, Saint Ambrose (another Origen admirer) argued for removing the pagan altar of Victory from the Roman Senate partly on the grounds that it was soaked in the blood of generations of innocent animals sacrificed to gratify the bloodlust of the pagans and their gods. Other Christian bishops would fight to ban gladiatorial games and wage an ultimately unwinnable war against the institution of slavery.

Origen's Platonized theology marks the birth of the Christian humanitarian conscience. It will bear its final fruit not only in the Catholic antiabortion movement, but in the Quaker Society of Friends, in the Mennonites, and in a secularized form in groups like PETA and Greenpeace. It ultimately stems from Origen's conviction that every aspect of our lives and our interactions with others must reflect a set of moral convictions that we may not be able to prove, but to which we must be unshakably loyal. It also reflects Plato's moral absolutism: the insistence that the human soul has an eternal destiny and that the rational order of the universe set up by God must be reflected in our present character and conduct.

Unlike Platonism, however, Christianity bases its moral absolutism less on abstract reason than on an inner *faith*. It rests more on Socrates's inner voice, that spiritual conviction that cannot be denied without giving up the most essential part of our identity, than on any set of rational arguments.

For Origen, this included sex. No aspect of the early Church has been more systematically, and at times deliberately, misrepresented than its attitude toward women and sexuality.* Of course, the early Christians were rigidly puritan by modern standards. But then so were all the great schools of ancient thought, starting with Socrates and Plato. Apart from Epicurus, it is hard to find a single serious thinker who did not regard the human body with regret, as the tomb of the soul or a pointless encumbrance to the soul's purity. It's also hard to find a philosopher who did not regard sexual desire as "dirty,"

---

*Made worse by the huge popularity of *The Da Vinci Code*, which suggests that early Christianity was essentially matriarchal in nature until the emperor Constantine let the mysogynists take over. For a corrective, see chapter 11.

the disgusting epitome of the body's gross impure materiality—precisely what the soul had to overcome on its forward march to enlightenment.[43]

As the great scholar E. R. Dodds once pointed out, Christian and Neoplatonist ethics on this point were almost indistinguishable.[44] Like his Neoplatonist rival Plotinus (who wondered aloud why something as pure as the soul had to inhabit the body in the first place) and like Socrates, Origen saw freeing his body from the pangs of sexual desire as a primary form of liberation for the soul. As a young teacher in Alexandria, surrounded by female coeds from well-to-do Christian families, that challenge to his resolve became such a distraction that when he read a passage from the Gospel of Matthew, "There are some eunuchs . . . who made themselves so for love of the kingdom of heaven," he took matters into his own hands, as it were, in order to free himself from his libidinal energies.[45]

Ever since, Origen's ordeal of self-castration has marked him as a religious fanatic of the worst sort. All the evidence, however, suggests Origen came to regret his rash decision, and to see that Holy Scripture interpreted in an overliteral manner can be as dangerous and misleading as no Scripture at all. Instead, Origen wanted chastity and virginity (he seems to have been the first theologian to teach the perpetual virginity of Jesus's mother, Mary) to be voluntary acts of giving oneself to God, a sacrifice like martyrdom itself. Origen saw marriage, too, as a sacrifice, a voluntary giving of oneself to another that, like the vow of celibacy, raised men and women above gross carnality to a state of divine grace and love.[46]

In the end, however, all these relationships had to endure the flame test of Christian conscience. Conscience in Origen's view, sears away our desire for sin as our soul moves toward assimilation with God. "If you are a good Catholic," the conscience says, "you will do certain things and avoid doing others for the good of your soul." It is that flame which the Church has to labor to keep alive and burning, Origen believed—a mission the Catholic Church has tried to maintain ever since, almost notoriously so.

Today we live under the shadow of the Enlightenment. As we will see, we operate under very different, more Aristotelian, assumptions about individual behavior and the choices we make.

Still, the forerunners of the stereotypical nuns with steel rulers are Plato's Guardians in the *Republic*. They serve the same Platonic principle Origen extolled, that the Church, like the ideal *polis*, exists for the betterment of man.[47] The Church's job was to train our inner voice to answer to our faith, *not* as an alternative to our reason, but as its highest expression. It is that conviction that will give the Christian the courage to speak truth to power, whether we are speaking of Origen or Martin Luther King.

Origen lived his life under the ax edge of power and persecution. In 250, the rounding up of Christians started again. Origen was caught in the dragnet. Every morning, jailers dragged him from his cell and beat him with whips and chains. Eusebius, church historian and Origen's admirer, describes how for months Origen was chained to the rack by his tormentors, suffering tortures that left him permanently crippled, and how he still refused to recant his faith. What kept him sane, Origen later wrote, were memories of his martyred father, who had after all endured worse, and a saying from his old rival Plotinus, that when bodily pain seems beyond endurance, it can lead to a spiritual cleansing, "that it obliterates the face of time until whole eons fall away like dead leaves from a tree."[48]

When the emperor Decius died, Origen was released. After months of recuperation, he was able to walk again with the help of a cane, one hundred yards at a time. Origen died in Tyre around 253–54, at age seventy. He left behind a letter from Christians in Alexandria, clamoring for him to come back to take them under his pastoral care.

No figure since Saint Paul left a greater stamp on his Church and his faith. Origen left behind more than six hundred written treatises (most now lost), hundreds of letters, plus sermons and homilies. "Who," asked Saint Jerome, another admirer, "can ever read all that Origen wrote?"[49] For the first time in history, through Origen, Christian theology had been elevated to the level of philosophy. After his death, some of his Neoplatonic notions (for example, the preexistence of souls as emanations from the Divine Intellect) would land him and his followers in trouble. To this day, he is denied sainthood in the Catholic Church.

Still, no other thinker brought about a more thoroughgoing synthesis between Christian revelation and ancient reason, between Plato and Jesus, than Origen. He challenged the Catholic Church to be like Plato's *Republic*: a community dedicated to the perfection of wisdom as well as salvation. In one way or another over centuries, it has tried to remain faithful to Origen's vision.

When Origen died, that vision seemed only a dream. Yet in just fifty years, events would give it a new, astonishing reality.

"In this sign you will conquer." The labarum that Constantine and his soldiers wore to victory at the Milvian Bridge, 312 CE.

Eleven

TOWARD THE HEAVENLY CITY

Cicero and Plato said many wise things. But I never heard them say,
"Come unto me."

—Saint Augustine

He was an unlikely Christian hero. Hard and muscular, he had answered since childhood to the nickname "Bullneck." He had been born in dark, fog-bound Britain, far from the Mediterranean world that nurtured early Church Fathers like Origen. When the emperor Diocletian retired in 305, however, Constantine son of Constantius Chlorus rushed his legions down from Britain to join in the struggle for power.

He also displayed a ruthless cunning in working to secure his title. He married the daughter of Diocletian's co-emperor, Maximian, then in 310 had his father-in-law arrested and strangled. The next year he allied himself with one rival, Licinius, in order to declare war on the other, Maximian's son, Maxientius.

In late October 312, the two rivals' armies converged on the outskirts of

Rome. A single bridge across the Tiber River stood between them. Constantine was outnumbered; his men were exhausted after a grueling march up the spine of Italy. Maxentius's troops were fresh and confident. Their mood had been buoyed by a pagan oracle that had announced as they marched out of the city that "an enemy of Rome would be killed" in the coming battle.

However, Constantine was not worried. In his tent a night or two before the battle (the accounts differ on the details), he had had a dream. He saw a glowing object in the dark, a cross with a loop at the top. Then he seemed to hear a voice say, "In this sign you will conquer."[1]

By the measure of the age, Constantine was not a superstitious man. Like many in the army he chose to worship a god called the Sol Invictus, an all-powerful sun god based loosely on Plato's Demiurge from the *Timaeus*. But also like most men of his time and place, Constantine believed dreams meant something. On the eve of what might be the decisive battle for the Roman Empire, he was not about to take any chances. The next morning, he told his troops to paint the cross with the loop on their shields. Astonished but obedient, they did as ordered.

The two opposing armies finally met at a place called Saxa Rubra. Constantine rode at the head of his heavy cavalry and at the first charge sent Maxentius's forward rank of armored horsemen flying back in disorder. Horses reared and screamed, men fought and died, the air was filled with cries of pain and triumph. Maxentius's left and right flanks, guarded by troops from his African provinces, collapsed. His soldiers in between, hard pressed on three sides, wavered, then broke and ran.

The fleeing men reached the banks of the Tiber and the bridge. The original stone bridge, the Milvian Bridge, had been destroyed before the battle.[2] However, Maxentius had lashed together a line of boats into a makeshift pontoon bridge, on which his troops had advanced into action. Now, panic-stricken, they scrambled onto it in their retreat. The bridge swayed and buckled under the weight of yelling, running refugees, horses, and wagons. Their commander, Maxentius, tried to restore order but found himself caught in the jam.

The tethers holding the bridge to the bank snapped. The boats pulled apart under the force of the current, and with a tremendous rending crash the whole thing gave way, plunging soldiers and horses, the emperor and officers, into the foaming Tiber. Constantine's troops watched, fascinated, as their enemies were swept away in the torrent.

Later, soldiers found the body of Maxentius half-submerged in the sand along the shore, and still clad in his magnificent armor. They fished it out, cut off the head, and brought it back on the end of a spear to Constantine. He had his men then carry it at the front of his triumphant march into Rome — along with his new battle standard, or *labarum*, decorated with the miraculous looped cross.

Amid the round of congratulations after the battle, Constantine's officers expressed their amazement. How had he managed to pull off this victory? He told them about the dream and the sign but confessed that its meaning was still a mystery to him.

Then, it seems, one of Constantine's Christian officers spoke up. That wasn't a cross you saw, he said. It must have been a Greek letter *khi* (X) superimposed not on a loop, but on another Greek letter, *rho* (P). As every Greek-speaking Christian knew, these were the first letters of *Khristós*, or Christ. The voice you heard, Constantine was told, must have been that of God Himself.[3] Later, someone also pointed out that the X looked exactly like the cross that Plato described in *Timaeus* as the basic shape into which God fashioned the World Soul. In short, Constantine's new *labarum* had the authority not only of Christ behind it, but of Plato as well.[4]

Constantine was impressed. He knew Christians had become an important constituency in the Roman Empire, especially in the thriving commercial cities of the East like Antioch and Alexandria. He and his ally Licinius had both appealed for Christian support, promising a new era of toleration after a decade of brutal persecution by Diocletian and his colleagues.

Now, it seemed, their god had intervened decisively in his favor. It was time for Constantine to make a decisive intervention of his own. He cast aside his invincible sun god without a second thought. From this point on, he would consider himself a Christian in belief and deed. A month or two later, he issued his imperial Edict of Milan, which brought religious toleration to everyone in the empire, including Christians.

Nothing like it had ever been promulgated in the ancient world before — or ever was again.[5] For the first time, Christians were free to rebuild their churches (Constantine also ordered confiscated Christian lands and property to be restored), spread their dioceses, and worship as they pleased in public. Overnight they turned from being a hunted minority into a sect on equal footing with their former persecutors.

However, the Christians did not stop there. They saw in the new emperor more than just a patron and protector. Constantine's victory proved that he was God's Chosen One, the ruler selected to lead humanity to a new era of peace and harmony. "Light was everywhere, and men who once dared not look up greeted each other with smiling faces and shining eyes."[6] Constantine would be the emperor who would finally make the world safe for Christianity.

This loyalty to the empire marked a major change in Christian attitudes. Until now, the Christian Church had viewed the fate of the Roman Empire with indifference and its rulers with contempt. The emperors had been among Christianity's worst tormentors. They were also worshipped as pagan gods themselves: a clear act of blasphemy. To Origen and his generation, the idea that Christians had anything to gain, spiritually or materially, by supporting Rome's governing institutions would have seemed absurd. "I owe no allegiance to any forum, army, or Senate," wrote one of them, Tertullian, "All secular powers and dignities are not merely alien from, but hostile to, God. . . ."[7]

Thanks to Constantine, there was now the opportunity to reverse the controls. The Church seized it eagerly. The pagan Celsus had once sneered, "If all men wanted to be Christians, the Christians would not want them." A century and a half later, the situation had completely changed. By 300, Christianity was ready to embrace the entire civilized world, along with the empire that held it together.[8]

Two Christians in particular used their position in Constantine's inner circle to bring that about. The first was a Greek bishop named Eusebius; the other was a Latin-speaking royal tutor named Lactantius. They set out to persuade an empire that Christians, pagans, and Constantine himself had reached a unique moment in human history. One turned to Plato, the other to Aristotle, to cement their case.

Eusebius and Lactantius are now forgotten figures. No one except those in pursuit of a doctoral degree ever opens their works. But their rereadings of Plato and Aristotle would reset the horizons of the Western political imagination and present civilization with an entirely new problem: finding a workable dividing line between man's religions and political impulses. Such a dividing line would never have occurred to the ancient Greeks or the Romans. Early Christians had other, more urgent things to worry about. Christ's dictum "Render unto Caesar that which is Caesar's" meant little to men and women whom Caesar was trying to kill.

It was the men of Constantine's generation who put the issue of Church and State on the cultural map for the first time. The impact was momentous and almost immediate. A bishop in North Africa, Saint Augustine, would dream of a heavenly empire to replace an earthly one and write *The City of God*. Four centuries after that, on a cold Christmas Day, a barbarian Frankish king, Charlemagne, would be crowned as Holy Roman Emperor by another bishop, that of Rome. Men would fight and die in the struggle between empire and papacy in the Middle Ages; in the Reformation they would fight over the divine right of kings in the same way. Today we debate abortion, aid to parochial schools, and teaching evolution with less violence but with almost as much fervor.

It was Eusebius and Lactantius who set it all in motion, by trying to tell the bullnecked victor of Milvian Bridge how he came to power and why.

Neither man was a true Roman. Lucius Caecilius Lactantius came from North Africa and Eusebius from Caesarea in Syria, where he had studied under a pupil of Origen. Eusebius was a Christian Neoplatonist in Origen's image: at one point he composed the vigorous *In Defense of Origen*, supporting what some in the Church saw as Origen's runaway rationalism.[9] After Milvian Bridge, however, Eusebius had found a new hero. Writing his *History of the Church* while sitting as bishop of Caesarea, he recast the entire history of Christianity so that it culminated in a single dazzling moment of Neoplatonic epiphany: the emperorship of Constantine.

It was a conclusion that would have surprised Origen, not to mention Saint Paul and Jesus. Eusebius, however, felt no compunction in explaining how everything that had happened in the Christian Church since the Crucifixion—all the apostolic labors, all the sudden conversions, all the persecutions and martyrdoms—had led inexorably to this miraculous event. Eusebius knew his biblical exegesis from Origen (who is a seminal figure in his *History of the Church*). He drew pointed parallels between Constantine leading Christians to victory and Moses leading the Jews to the Promised Land, and between the battle of Milvian Bridge and pharaoh's armies being swept away by the Red Sea.[10]

The real weight of Eusebius's argument, though, was that God, Supreme Creator and Governor of the universe, had deliberately chosen Constantine to be prince and sovereign in His name—in effect to be God's living image on earth. Just as God's only begotten son, Jesus, had drawn together all humanity with the promise of ultimate salvation, so God had deputized "an Emperor so great that all history had not reported his like," in order to unite all the nations of the world under a single authority. Just as for a Platonist every visible material object is a copy of an invisible original Form, so Constantine's imperial authority was a direct visible copy of God's invisible but absolute power.

Constantine, "having the whole Christ, the Word, the Wisdom, the Light impressed upon his soul . . . frames his earthly government according to the pattern of the divine original, feeling strength in its conformity with the monarchy of God . . . for surely monarchy far transcends every other constitution and form of government. . . ."[11] Constantine's imperial presence is like the rising sun itself, Eusebius enthused, radiating truth from the imperial palace "as though ascending with the heavenly luminary" and shedding "upon all who came before his face the sunbeams of his generous goodness."[12]

One empire under one absolute God, with one absolute ruler as His image on earth. The ancient Greco-Roman ideal that human government exists to serve human ends suddenly disappears from the scene. Instead, a luminous new image of political authority had arrived, which over time would radiate out from Constantinople and Rome across all of Christian Europe, from the shores of the Atlantic to the Urals.

This was an ideal of government serving *divine* ends, with God appointing and anointing a ruler to exercise supreme authority in His name. A coin from Constantine's reign shows a great hand emerging from a cloud to place a crown on the emperor's head—the very model of royal coronations from Charlemagne and the kings of England and France to the czars of Russia.[13]

This is kingship Neoplatonist style: the ruler as earthly image of God Himself. Not surprisingly, it was the model of rule Constantine's successors enthusiastically embraced. The emperor Justinian will call himself *Autokrator* and *Kosmokrator*, literally "Ruler of the Cosmos." He will sign documents with a special divine red ink. Royal officials receiving imperial documents (like his famous law code) would bow and reverently kiss the parchment as if it were Holy Scripture.[14]

Of course, absolute rulers had existed before. However, Near Eastern civilizations and the pagan Roman Empire had given their ruler absolute power because they were actual gods. After Eusebius, monarchs are Platonic copies of a higher invisible perfection. Not being God may seem a limitation to some, but exercising an earthly version of God's omnipotence is certainly not bad. It was only much later, when the bishops of Rome as successors of St. Peter stepped up *their* claim to be God's deputy, or *vicarius* (literally "vicar of Christ"), that the distinction stood out. Then what had seemed an asset, namely divine sanction, suddenly seemed a liability. Much of the political history of the Middle Ages will be spent trying sort out the balance sheet left behind by Eusebius.

At the time, however, his insistence that just as there is one absolute God, so there must be one absolute emperor was all that Constantine could have asked for and more. It would be passed down over the centuries to become the property of European monarchs from Charlemagne to Charles I of England and would be dazzlingly reflected in the images of the Sun King in Louis XIV's Hall of Mirrors at Versailles.

Eusebius had traced out this imperial theology from a Neoplatonist perspectve. His rival Lactantius attempted to do the same thing from the Aristotclian end, with similar momentous results. If Eusebius used Neoplatonism to explain to Constantine and his successors what their powers were, Lactantius used Aristotle to tell them what to do with them.

When Constantine came to the imperial throne in 312, Lucius Caecilius Lactantius was already renowned as "the most cultivated mind in the Empire," according to his admirer Saint Jerome. He had arrived in Rome after teaching rhetoric in the North African town of Sicca Verentia (El Kef in modern-day Tunisia), a bustling commercial center on the road to the great port at Hippo Regius. Lactantius's earlier conversion to Christianity had once cost him his job and almost his life. Under Constantine, however, it brought him favor and advancement as tutor to Constantine's son.

The books and treatises Lactantius wrote were largely for the edification of the imperial heir. We know Constantine himself looked over their pages and pondered their arguments. Virtually everything Constantine knew about Christian doctrine he probably got from Lactantius.[15] As we would expect from a teacher of the ancient rhetorical tradition, Lactantius attempted to describe the new Christian empire in terms a Cicero might recognize: Cicero's *On Moral Obligations* was in fact the model for his great *Divine Institutes*.[16] However, in the background of Lactantius's ideas there lurks another earlier figure, namely Aristotle.

Like every good Aristotelian, Lactantius began his discussion of political power by looking first at the society it governs. Yes, Constantine's victory was a sign from God; and yes, he is the image of God, and therefore his authority is absolute. All the same, Lactantius explained, that authority is underpinned by a larger process, which was the emergence of a distinctly Christian society to replace the earlier pagan one.

Lactantius observed that religion (*religio*) comes from the verb *religare*, meaning "to tie or bind." Religion is about bonds between God and man, but also between man and man. Like Aristotle's *polis*, Lactantius's Christian *societas* is a partnership made up of families who have come together in order to work together. "A kind God wants us to be social animals," he wrote, echoing Aristotle's definition of man as *zoon politikon*, "because all humans need mutual support."[17] The difference is that these Christian families have come together not to get rich or practice a craft, but to practice the virtues of their faith. They seek to achieve their destiny not only as social creatures, but as divine ones made in the image of God.[18]

Lactantius's Christian society doesn't stand in the way of human nature. It *is* human nature operating at its highest pitch. Even before Constantine appeared on the scene and Lactantius was still studying at Sicca, one of his Christian professors, Arnobius, had taught how Christianity was already making the world more civilized and wars less violent, because its teachings had softened men's hearts and awakened their consciences. One day, the old man predicted to Lactantius, wars will be unnecessary. Swords really will be beaten into plowshares, just as Scripture predicted; and mankind would realize its full potential through virtue, self-restraint, justice, and excellence.

Christian society achieves its self-actualization, as Aristotle might say, through the union of faith and reason. At a quick glance, this *societas* resembles the Roman *res publica*, the classic commonwealth. But it is not one in which Cicero or Aristotle would find many landmarks. The politics of persuasion, on which so much depended for both Aristotle and Cicero, withers away. There will be no need for it (a strange position for a former professor of rhetoric to take). Individual choice and social distinctions have no place, either. Indeed, Lactantius seeks to abolish them both, especially the division between rich and poor. And instead of consisting of five thousand citizens as in Plato's *Republic*, this Christian republic will be universal, stretching out to encompass all humanity.

The concept of Christendom as a universal (in Greek, *katholikos*) community of shared values and ideals, living together in peace and harmony, had arrived.[19] It comes about not through men obeying nature (as Aristotle would have framed it), but through obeying God. Or rather it will come about someday in the not-too-distant future, when all men everywhere follow His community. Until then arrives, Lactantius admits, men still need laws and a lawmaker, the emperor. But this political power in its new Christian form must be directed toward a higher end than simply maintaining public order and the *Pax Romana*. Constantine and his successors serve a higher constituency, namely all of humanity. Their task is to create a world fit for Christians to live in, and one that eventually they will take over.

Constantine took up the challenge with enthusiasm. He announced that he was the agent whose services God had deemed suitable for the accomplishment of His will (this was after he had driven Licinius, his only remaining rival and a pagan, from the scene). "With the aid of divine power, I banished and destroyed every form of evil which prevailed, in the hope that the human race, enlightened by my instruction, might be recalled to a due observance of God's holy laws. . . ."[20] By 323, he established a brand-new capital for himself at Constantinople, to be a truly Christian capital free of any lingering pagan stain from Rome.

Constantine promulgated edicts banning gladiatorial games and establishing Sunday as a day of compulsory Christian worship. Another edict outlawed homosexuality.[21] In 325, he summoned more than three hundred bishops to the city of Nicaea and personally presided over the first universal church council, where he made sure that a Neoplatonized Trinity became part of the Christian creed as a matter of sworn oath for all Christians.

The Council of Nicaea was a major step toward making religious orthodoxy compulsory under imperial law—just what Lactantius wanted and predicted. Thirteen years after Constantine's Edict of Milan, the empire's once persecuted Christians were poised to become the new persecutors. The emperor's successors would increasingly apply the standards of a Christian *societas* against the non-Christians in their midst. The place left in the public square for pagans and Jews would steadily diminish until it vanished.[22]

For now, however, the rise of Christian intolerance seemed a matter of celebration rather than regret. Once, Christianity and empire had been enemies. Now they were one. As the thirtieth year of his reign drew to a close in 336, Constantine issued new coins celebrating himself as *Victor Omnium Gentium* ("Victor over All the Nations"). His last major military campaign crushed the Goths along the lower Danube, reestablishing a Roman province his pagan predecessors had lost. He had founded a series of new magnificent churches both in Rome and in Constantinople, including one for the bishop of Rome at Saint John Lateran. His treasury was flush, his people peaceful and grateful.[23]

He could hardly have guessed that his son's distinguished tutor had already doomed him to irrelevance.

This was because with his Aristotelian turn of mind, Lactantius saw the emergence of Christendom as a largely self-perpetuating process. He had been as devoted to Constantine as Eusebius and just as lavish in his praise of Constantine's role in establishing a true Christian society. But in the final analysis Constantine himself was not essential to it. The victory at Milvian Bridge, however welcome, was just another step in a process that would have gone on without him—and which God's will would extend even if future emperors were not Christians.

The test came when the last of Constantine's sons died in 361. Constantine was born a pagan and died a baptized Christian. His nephew Julian went the opposite route. Julian had lived in Athens, where pagan disciples of Plotinus taught him the old Hellenic tradition of literature and philosophy along with Neoplatonism's criticism of Christianity, including the works of that now-despised figure, Celsus. Julian's conversion was as complete as his uncle's had been. He shed his family's faith, grew a long beard in the manner of his Greek teachers, and came to the imperial purple in 361 determined to return the Roman Empire to its pagan glories and Neoplatonism to its pre-Christian roots.

It was hopeless from the start.

Julian the Apostate, as he is known to history, lived the highest virtues of a Greek sage. He was merciful and modest (in the imperial palace he insisted on sleeping on the floor), temperate and sexually continent (he left no children). Even Christians, noted the historian Edward Gibbon, had to acknowledge that Julian wielded his authority for the happiness of his subjects; that he was "a lover of his country, and that he deserved the empire of the world."[24]

By casting off his office's Christian moorings, however, Julian cut off all connections with the emerging society around him. The great palace at Constantinople became deserted as courtiers and lobbyists realized they would only get the cold shoulder from this paragon of virtue. Julian reopened the old pagan temples and made himself sit in the imperial box at the Hippodrome, although he despised sports as intensely as any Christian bishop. But the whole thing had an air of artificiality and insincerity. In the three short years of his reign, Julian became a cold, incomprehensible figure even to would-be supporters.

The same thing happened with his brand of Neoplatonism. Julian wanted to return to the serene pre-Christian world picture of Plotinus. He described his authority as emperor as an emanation of the Absolute, which "has been preserved in my hands pure and immaculate."[25] By now, however, Christianity had given that lofty system a solid grounding in human experience. It was lived every day in the churches across the empire and underscored in every reading of Holy Scripture. Once that was stripped away, what was left (to quote Gibbon again) was "solemn trifling" and "impenetrable obscurity." When Julian tried to reinterpret pagan myths like the birth of Venus with the same allegorical subtlety that Origen and Eastern Church Fathers had brought to the Old and New Testaments, not only was the result unconvincing, it looked positively ridiculous.[26]

The truth was that Greco-Roman culture, even in its highest ideals, was no longer going anywhere without Christianity. When Julian realized this, it shattered his spirit. He died in 363 leading a reckless campaign against the Parthians in Mesopotamia. His last words were, "Man of Galilee, thou hast won." The brief but spectacular failure of Julian's reign guaranteed the triumph of Christian civilization. It also hastened the doom of the Roman Empire.[27]

Constantine's Christian empire began with a battle. Sixty-six years later, it ended with one. In 378, the emperor Valens confronted roving war bands of Germanic Goths at Adrianople near Constantinople. With a massive cavalry charge, the Goths shattered Valens's army and killed the emperor. It was a disaster of the first order.[28] The capital managed to shut its gates against the German invader. However, the price of the Eastern Empire's survival was the loss of the West.

One Germanic tribe after another—Goths, Vandals, Franks, Allemanni, Burgundians—shot westward through the Balkans, overrunning the Rhine frontier and the Roman provinces on the other side, including Italy. The basic framework of imperial government, like the Roman road system dating back to Caesar Augustus, collapsed under the strain. So did law and order.

Only the Church held firm. In virtually every town, starting with Rome itself, its leaders became symbols of resistance. Like the young Genovefa (later canonized Saint Genevieve) in Paris, they rallied citizens to stand fast and defend their cities; like Pope Leo I with Attila the Hun, they struck deals with the invaders to spare their congregations. When negotiations failed they organized humanitarian relief for the devastated areas and offered words of comfort and hope when everything looked its bleakest.

The Catholic bishop became the one upholder of a social and cultural order to which the people living in his diocese, including pagans, could still cling. His basilica (originally an imperial building), where he administered the sacraments and offered sanctuary to refugees; his collection of holy relics left by illustrious predecessors; and his books, like the pope's library in the Vatican, which included his personal copies of the ancient classics—these were often all that was left standing in the flood.

What Lactantius had predicted had come true. The empire was finished, at least in the West. Christendom was here to stay. The proof is that the diocese as an imperial administrative unit vanished after the fourth century; as a unit of church administration, it survives to this day.

This is due in large part to the intrepid figures who took it upon themselves to save what was left of their civilization, along with their faith. One of the most intrepid, and the most influential, was the reluctant bishop of the wealthy North African town of Hippo Regius, the man we know as Saint Augustine.

"I desire to have knowledge of God and the soul. Nothing else? No, nothing else whatever."[29]

With Saint Augustine, we come to the end of the road as far as the Greco-Roman world is concerned. Before becoming a bishop, he had been brilliantly trained in that tradition of ancient rhetoric stretching back to Aristotle, with its ideal of using the power of speech and language to shape the good life.[30]

It was Augustine's curse to live in an age when that ideal, and the texts and authors who formed it, seemed a superfluous luxury. Augustine and his contemporaries were like men in a lifeboat: they had to make hard choices about what they needed to survive and what they had to jettison to stay afloat.

In the end, that meant throwing overboard the great ancient schools of thought. "What does Athens have to do with Jerusalem?" One of Augustine's fellow Christian Africans, Tertullian, had posed that question in the third century. His meaning was all too clear. What do Plato, Aristotle, and the rest really tell us about wisdom and salvation, compared with the Bible and

Christianity? More than a century later, Augustine bleakly answered: Not much.

Certainly, Augustine's writings contrast sharply with the buoyant optimism of the great Christian Apologists. There are plenty of reasons for this. There were the barbarian invasions, the collapse of imperial institutions, economic dislocation and depression, and all the things that usually come under the heading "Decline and Fall of the Roman Empire."

Another reason, however, was Augustine's deep awareness of original sin. Lactantius had written about man's natural impulse to virtue as if he had never heard of the doctrine.[31] Augustine had felt the hidden corrosive effect of Adam's Fall, like the worm in the apple, firsthand. He tells us about it in the most fascinating work to come out of the end of the ancient world, but also the one I find the most harrowing, his *Confessions*.

It tells of growing up in the small North African town of Thagaste, where his working-class Christian mother sacrificed everything to get him the finest classical education, including Cicero, Virgil, and especially Plato. He paid her back by partying, stealing, drinking, womanizing, and denigrating his mother's church and faith. He did this, Augustine remembers, not because he didn't know better, but precisely because he *did:* "I loved . . . not the things for which I committed wrong, but the wrong itself."[32]

So much for Plato's assertion that knowledge is the key to virtue. Like the boy from the expensive prep school who becomes a drug dealer, or the evangelist preacher who steals from his congregation, Augustine had discovered that simply *knowing* right from wrong was not enough. What's needed is a deeper emotional commitment to rightness and truth. Augustine saw it coming not from our reason or from our conscious will, which bears the stain of Adam, but from our faith.

Most people know the quotation from the *Confessions* "O God, make me good, but not yet!" But few realize the tension and despair underlying that famous bon mot. Like Aristotle, Augustine believed that the quality of life we lead depends on the choices we make. The tragedy is that left to our own devices—and contrary to Aristotle—most of those choices will be wrong. There can be no true morality without faith and no faith without the presence of God.

It was that presence he discovered in 384 when he traveled to Milan in northern Italy. It was the new imperial capital for the West, where grim, armor-clad emperors were trying to get a handle on a steadily dissolving frontier. Augustine went to find a political career. Instead, he found God, and the man who would be his mentor, Milan's bishop Saint Ambrose. It was Ambrose who brought Augustine back to his mother's faith and who personally baptized him in Milan's basilica in 387. Augustine was thirty-three.

Conversion changed Augustine's life in more ways than one. He learned that his Christian faith offered not only a steady anchor but a set of priorities. He could see them in Ambrose himself. Spare, elegant, exquisitely educated in the Greek as well as Latin classics, Ambrose had been a provincial governor and a major figure at court. He was not a priest at all, but when the people of Milan called on him to become their bishop and protector, Ambrose never looked back.

The ancient classics and the values they represented became dead to him. The time has come to move on, Ambrose taught Augustine. Ours is a new, far more volatile and dangerous world. When we look through Saint Ambrose's surviving letters, we can see that everything he did was focused on reforming and strengthening his congregation and building the bonds of Lactantius's great ideal, Christian society. Augustine would follow Ambrose's example when he returned to Africa in 396 and the people of Hippo Regius made a similar urgent call to him to be their bishop.

For mentor and pupil, the ancient authors were reduced to a box of useful tools, nothing more. Ambrose's celebrated manual on the duties of priests, which became a standard textbook for the medieval Church, was based on Cicero's *On Moral Obligations*, but only in the sense that *West Side Story* is based on Shakespeare's *Romeo and Juliet*. Augustine would make the same use of Plato and Neoplatonism when he found himself dealing with the single most unimaginable event in the empire's history.

In the late summer of 410, the Western Goths (or Visigoths) arrived at the gates of a defenseless Rome. Their king Alaric wanted to cooperate with Rome in finding a permanent home for his people within the empire. He knew what Romans did not, that a far more dangerous and menacing foe was on the move in the hinterlands behind him: the Huns.

Alaric and other barbarian chieftains would gladly have joined forces with the Romans against these Asian marauders. However, the king of the Visigoths decided that Rome's officials were playing tricks on him. On August 24, he ordered his troops to take the city and pillage it, which they did for three days.

The physical damage the Visigoths did was minor. However, the psychological damage was felt from one end of the empire to the other. Rome, mistress of the world, had fallen to the blast of trumpets and the howling of the Goths, as one eyewitness described it. Constantinople held three days of mourning at the news. "If Rome can perish," Saint Jerome wrote from distant Palestine, where he was struggling to translate the Hebrew Old Testament into usable Latin, "what can be safe?"[33]

Refugees from Rome brought the horror stories of the siege and sack to Hippo Regius that winter: stories of murder and rapine, even cannibalism. Their listeners shivered and wondered when the forces of destruction would reach them. Already there were whispers about how for seven hundred years the pagan gods had protected Rome; then the Christians forced the emperors to close the gods' temples and remove their altars. Rome's fall, some began to say, was the awful price of embracing Christianity.

Augustine decided he had to meet the rumors head-on. When he entered his basilica, he addressed his congregation with all the skill and eloquence he could muster from his years as a teacher of rhetoric. "Do not lose heart, brethren," he told them, "there will be an end of every earthly kingdom." He told his astonished listeners that the fall of Rome was not actually bad news, but good news. It was merely another step in God's construction of His new Jerusalem.

"Do not hold on to the old man, the world. . . . The world is passing away; the world is losing its grip; the world is short of breath. Do not fear, *thy youth shall be renewed as an eagle.*"[34] The sermons Saint Augustine composed to reassure his congregation would be the basis of his most influential work, *The City of God.*

The very title (*De Civitate Dei*) was a direct slap in the face of the classical ideal of the *polis.* According to Augustine, all societies built around earthly ends, the needs and desires of human beings, are doomed to destruction—including Rome. The first half of *The City of God* is a devastating survey of the history of the city by the Tiber. It begins with Romulus murdering his brother Remus in founding Rome and continues through one gruesome scene of bloodshed, murder, cruelty, and betrayal after another.

To those who claim Rome had been the home of ancient virtue, Augustus could quote Sallust back in their faces. Yet Sallust lied when he praised the early republic, Augustine said, since he knew full well Rome had been governed then by the same pack of killers and thieves who governed it later. Even the veneer of Christianity under Constantine, Augustine had to conclude, could not save an empire whose foundations were rotten from the start.[35]

This is what happens, he explained, when a community tries to survive with human virtue as its only protection. The Earthly City may be founded on an ideal of liberty, but it ends in a "blood lust for domination and glory." It may claim to uphold justice as its ultimate aim, as did Plato's *Republic*. However, "true justice has no existence save in that republic whose founder and ruler is Christ. . . ."[36]

This will be the new and true *res publica* that will emerge from the current rubble of Rome, Augustine proclaimed. A Heavenly City will replace the Earthly City with a genuine community of hearts and minds united under God.

What are the tools Christians will use to build Rome's replacement? First of all the Christian faith, an unshakable belief in Jesus Christ as Savior and Lord. However, there is also a role for man's reason: for if Augustine was ready to throw away the entire tradition of Greek thought, he was keen to hang on to its most important discovery. Augustine was no philosopher. However, he recognized his debt both to Plato (whose philosophy comes closest to Christianity and who would have been a Christian, Augustine affirms, if he had had the opportunity) and to the man who was Augustine's principal interpreter of Plato, the great Plotinus.[37]

From Plotinus, Augustine had learned that man's reason is like the soul's flashlight, beaming out into the surrounding gloom. It is able to identify the shape and nature of the material objects around it; but when its beam falls on those objects that share the same God-derived incorporeal essence as our soul, they flash out with a sudden luminosity and meaning that we recognize instantly as truth.[38]

In Neoplatonist terms, our reason picks out the trail of divine emanation like a phosphorescent glow in the dark, which eventually leads our soul out of the cave, toward the ultimate source of the light of reason and everything else, God Himself. This is what Saint Augustine means (or seems to mean) when he speaks of "the divine illumination of the intellect."[39] Man's reason is not superfluous to Augustine's relationship with God. Fused together with faith, it is essential to it. It is just that reason *alone* gets us nowhere; it remains stuck at the cave's exit. Faith provides that needed extra boost, by affirming the supreme immutable truth imbedded in the Word of God, which no

Saint Augustine (354–430 CE) shown in a fourteenth-century Italian manuscript. At his feet, lying prostrate, is Aristotle, who had asserted, contrary to Christian doctrine, that the universe was immortal. The inscription is from Aristotle's *Physics*: "We conclude the world is immortal, having neither a beginning nor an end."

human being could hope to discover in this mortal life by himself. We see the luminous trail for what it really is, the path to salvation.

"Understanding is the reward of faith," Saint Augustine says. "I believe, in order that I may understand" will be the catchphrase of the early Middle Ages. It is the summing-up of Augustine's final authoritative fusion of Neoplatonism and Christianity. In his name, it will have a sweeping impact on Western culture for the next thousand years and beyond.[40]

However, there will be a price to pay for this belief that the ultimate meaning of reality can be found in our own spiritual nature. Our interest in the outside physical world, the realm of nature and science, by necessity drops to second place. What vital truths does the world of sensory experience offer us? The Augustinian Christian will answer as Plato does in the *Theaetetus*: None. "It is not necessary to probe into the nature of things," Augustine will write, "as was done by those whom the Greeks called physicists." There is nothing there to interest the searcher after wisdom, only more shadows and gloom.*

Greek science on Aristotle's terms, which had already fallen into decrepitude under the late Roman Empire, will take a long hiatus during the Middle Ages. For most Christians, it will be enough to mark down the material world as simply one more part of God's creation and the Great Chain of Being. They have more important things to think about, including discovering their place in the age to come.

For the future belongs to the Heavenly City, the republic founded by Christ. It will bear little relation to the one proposed by Plato. However, it achieves the same goals Plato sought, because at its foundation are the ultimate truths of God. It is where "there shall be no evil things; where no good thing shall be hidden, where we shall have leisure to utter the praises of God, which shall be all things in all!"[41]

Instead of justice for the few, it will offer justice to all human beings, men and women, masters and slaves. Instead of uniting men by power or a love of glory, it will unite them by the bonds of love, derived from love of God. Instead of the fragile liberty of the Greek *polis*, it provides the true liberty of the Christian soul that comes through doing God's will and being united with Him. "For what other thing is our end, but to come to that kingdom of which there is no end?" And instead of vanishing into dust, like all earthly empires and dominions, it will live on, beyond space and time, eternal and forever.

It is important to realize that for Augustine, this Heavenly City was *not* the Catholic Church as he knew it, let alone the Catholic Church as it would become in the Middle Ages. Augustine's City of God is a kind of Platonic ideal, of which Christendom can become an earthly reflection only if it strictly follows God's word and laws and embeds them in men's hearts. Augus-

---

*But not number. The Neoplatonist notion derived from the Pythagoreans that numbers can be formulae for grasping the reality of being never lost its fascination for Augustine. His works would keep the Pythagorean spirit alive in medieval philosophy, where it will pop up in surprising contexts—not least of which is in the building of Chartres Cathedral. See chapter 13.

tine's formula, with its conscious echoes of Plato's *Republic*, remains the basis of the Western idea of a church to this day: Catholic or Protestant, Methodist or Mormon. This is the idea of the church as a *community*, whose members share the same values and beliefs and who are bound together in their dedication to love God as they love one another; and to serve His commands rather than those of some bureaucrat or politician.

For Augustine, all true community depends on God's grace. Someday, perhaps Christianity and Christendom will be the same. But not yet, he said to himself, scanning the horizon from the walls of Hippo Regius. Cities and provinces in turmoil; wars and chaos everywhere. At the end of his life, Augustine watched armed Vandal tribesmen sailing into Hippo's broad harbor to besiege and loot the town. He died in 430, four years after finishing *The City of God*, even as the Vandals were pounding on his city's gates. To the congregation he left behind, the hopes of the New Jerusalem must have seemed a very long way off.

Still, Saint Augustine proved more right than wrong. When the last Roman emperor in the West was finally deposed in 476, hardly anyone noticed. A new civilization was already taking shape: not the Heavenly City exactly, but something very different from what had come before.

No one could have guessed that this new civilization would find its first intellectual hero in almost exactly the same place the ancient world had, namely in a stone-walled prison cell—or that after four centuries of Plato and his admirers dominating the conversation, he would triumphantly restore Aristotle's place at the cultural table.

Boethius (475?–525 CE) used Aristotle to save Europe from the Dark Ages.

Twelve

INQUIRING MINDS:
ARISTOTLE STRIKES BACK

Through doubting we question, and through questioning we perceive the truth.

—Peter Abelard

He was a dignified, slightly pompous man, as his full sonorous name, Anicius Manlius Severinus Boethius, might imply. Contemporaries viewed him with awe as the last Roman. We can think of him as the first medieval man, and the man who reintroduced Aristotle to the West.

Boethius was born fifty years after Augustine's death to an ancient Roman aristocratic clan, the Anicia. The family library was one of the wonders of Rome. Boethius was a Christian; he counted a pope as well as two emperors among his ancestors. Still, the proudest day of his life came in 522, when his two sons were elevated to the consulship, the state's highest office, on the same day—an honor unique in the history of the ancient city.[1]

Two years later Boethius found himself in a prison cell, awaiting death from the same man who had granted him that signal honor, King Theodoric of the Ostrogoths. As he looked around his cell, the old senator must have smiled bitterly to himself. He should have known the bond of trust between Roman and barbarian, orthodox Catholic and Arian heretic,* would not last. When the Ostrogoths had swept into Italy, Theodoric looked for the best and brightest Roman for advice on how to govern. He turned to Boethius. For nearly two decades, Boethius had acted as Theodoric's chief political adviser and mentor—his surrogate father, almost.

Theodoric was dazzled by Boethius's shrewd advice, by his icy calm in times of crisis, but above all by his knowledge of Greek literature, philosophy, and science. Once when Theodoric needed a gift for a fellow barbarian king, he asked Boethius, who built him a magnificent mechanical water clock and sundial.

"In your hands Greek philosophy has become Roman doctrine," an amazed Theodoric said through a letter composed by one of his secretaries (Theodoric himself was illiterate). Aristotle and Plato, Archimedes and Pythagoras—all had found a new home in Rome, the letter gushed, thanks to Boethius.[2]

However, as Aristotle had discovered with Alexander, under the outward charm of a semicivilized ruler like Theodoric lay a streak of ruthless paranoia. Their differences over religion and Arianism may have sowed the seeds of suspicion. Or Theodoric may have simply calculated that by taking out the most eminent figure from Rome's remaining elite, he would terrify any future opposition into silence.

In any case, there were charges of a plot, and evidence was produced to implicate Boethius. Boethius could not take the charges seriously. He probably dismissed the flimsy evidence with less urgency, and fewer pleas for mercy, than he should have. Theodoric had him arrested. The barbarian then coerced the Roman Senate into finding their former colleague guilty of treason. The Senate cravenly complied. Now in the grim Ostrogothic fortress of Pavia, Boethius awaited his death sentence and the horrible tortures he knew would accompany it.

In the dungeon's silence, Rome's finest scholar, gaunt and white-haired,

---

*The Ostrogoths, like other Germanic tribes, were converted to Christianity by a disciple of a priest from Lybia named Arius (256–336), who preached the existence but not the divinity of Jesus Christ. Arianism was denounced as a heresy several times, most famously at the Council of Nicaea in 325. The fact that the German tribes (except the Franks) remained loyal to this heretical brand of Christianity did more to sour relations between Roman and barbarian than any other issue.

took up his pen one last time. "Fickle Fortune gave me wealth short-lived," he wrote with a trembling hand, "then in a moment all but ruined me." What did it all mean? He was pondering this when he was suddenly aware of someone standing behind him.

Startled, he turned. Out of the surrounding gloom stepped the figure of a woman. "She was of awe-inspiring appearance," he tells us, "her eyes burning and keen beyond the usual power of men." Her dress was from the finest materials, although Boethius could see its color had faded and it was covered with a fine film of dust. Along the bottom hem he could barely make out an embroidered Greek letter *pi* and at the top the letter *theta*.*

Suddenly he realized who she was. She was Philosophy, "my old nurse in whose house I had been cared for since my youth." Amazed to see her in these dismal surroundings, Boethius asked why she had come.

Philosophy answered, "To protect you and keep your strength unimpaired." This is not the first time wisdom had been threatened by men's evil, she added. "Before the time of my servant Plato, I fought many a great battle against the reckless forces of folly. And then in Plato's own lifetime, his master Socrates was unjustly put to death." Yet it had been a victorious death, because Philosophy had been at his side.

Boethius was too moved to answer. But "as she spoke she gathered her dress into a fold and wiped from my eyes the tears that filled them." The conversation continued long into the night. Before it was over, "the night was put to flight, the darkness fled, And to my eyes their former strength returned. . . . The clouds of my grief dissolved and I drank in the light."[3]

Boethius's death row conversation had, of course, been imaginary. His account of it is not. It fills the pages of his *Consolation of Philosophy*: philosophy, we note, *not* Christianity. An extended allegory about the ultimate meaning of life and death, it makes references solely to ancient Greeks and Romans—not a single Christian author or figure appears in it, not even Jesus. Yet Boethius was an unshakably orthodox Catholic; he wrote numerous tracts on theology, including an influential one on Augustine's favorite subject, the Trinity.[4] The old idea that Boethius might somehow have been a cryptopagan who, faced by death, decided to cast aside any further Christian pretense will not bear up to serious scrutiny.

---

*The letters stand for the distinction Aristotle made between "practical" philosophy, like ethics and political science, and the "theoretical" or speculative philosophy, like metaphysics, natural science, and theology. In Greek, *pragmatika* begins with a *pi* and *theoretika* with a *theta*.

So Boethius's decision to turn to Socrates, Plato, and Aristotle for guidance and assurance rather than Jesus Christ in his last moments of life seems puzzling: puzzling, that is, until we realize what he was up to.

Boethius was four years old when the Roman Empire in the West ended. He grew up under the growing shadow of what we call the Dark Ages. He watched the spread of barbaric chaos, and the slow extinguishing of civilization, with deep alarm. He came to realize that Christian society *by itself* was not going to survive. The death of the Earthly City had led not to the creation of the Heavenly City, but to something far worse. To live in a dangerous world, people needed something more than the Bible and the Church Fathers—or the advice to simply turn the other cheek to our enemies.

Boethius is the first Christian thinker to realize that Plato and Aristotle were still indispensable to Western civilization. They still provided an essential and rational framework for dealing with the real world—and also dying in it.

Philosophy as "a preparation for death" was no moot point for Boethius. Soon after he finished the *Consolation*, his guards led him away. He was forced to kneel on the stone floor, and a cord was tied around his temple and across his eyes. On Theodoric's order, the executioner wound the cord tighter and tighter until the Roman's eyes popped loose from their sockets. Then, in unbearable agony, he was bludgeoned to death with iron rods.

Back in his cell sat the abandoned manuscript. It read:

> *Happy the man whose eyes once could*
> *Perceive the shining fount of good:*
> *Happy he whose unchecked mind*
> *Could leave the chains of earth behind.*[5]

The Consolation of Philosophy became an imperishable part of Boethius's legacy to the emergent culture of the Middle Ages. During the Renaissance, his reputation fell on hard times. All the same, it was Boethius who demonstrated that Western civilization would not survive if it forgot its classical roots. He singled out three figures as summing up that vital contribution: Plato, Aristotle, and Socrates.* By and large, that valuation has stuck ever since.

---

*With Cicero coming in a respectable fourth. As he makes clear in the *Consolation*, Boethius considered the Stoics and Epicureans as lightweights, essentially derivative figures.

Above all, Boethius treated Plato and Aristotle as the essential anchors of a civilized education. It's a point of view that linked Boethius not only to the Middle Ages, which read his works with passionate devotion, but indirectly to every college and university today that still teaches what his world, and ours, call the liberal arts. Still, it is important to realize that this view of education marked a sharp break from the cultural direction toward which Augustine had pointed, with huge implications.

Augustine was a keen believer in education, too, including the seven liberal arts.[6] But in his mind, all learning was directed toward a single goal: reading and analyzing the Bible and bolstering our faith. That vision of education seemed too stifling to Boethius. So did Augustine's assertion that man's supreme freedom was to be found in following God without fear of social or political constraints and in doing the right thing with the confidence that everything we do is in accord with His supreme all-knowing will.

To Boethius, Augustine's "Christian liberty" grated against more ancient ideals of liberty. For one thing, it seemed to strip men of the power of free will.[7] If we are going to be happy, we have to be free to act in the world, even if that means we make mistakes.

Boethius's reassessment of the importance of freedom was *not* the result of living in a more settled world than Augustine's. If anything, the sixth century had even more reason for despair. The empire in the West was gone for good; its fate was entirely in the hands of barbarian tribesmen like Theodoric. For another intelligent, educated Roman Christian, Saint Benedict, the only recourse seemed to be a complete retreat from a world grown too hostile and savage to endure. Benedict would found his monastery at Monte Cassino three years after Boethius's death, in 527.

That same year, the emperor Justinian ordered the last pagan schools in Athens to close. After nine hundred years, Plato's Academy had to shut its doors for good. Eighty years after that, the armies of Islam would sweep over the southern and eastern shores of the Mediterranean, isolating Constantinople and sealing off the West from the ancient sources of its culture.

Boethius understood the dangers his civilization faced and the odds against its survival. It was to shore up those odds that he dedicated his life and scholarship. If we are going to deal with a complex and dangerous world, he believed, we had better be prepared. That means above all reading Aristotle.

It was Plato who prepared him for facing death. This was the real Plato, not the yeasty mystical concoction of the Neoplatonists. Boethius was probably the last Western thinker for nine hundred years who knew all the dialogues of Plato, not just the *Timaeus*, backward and forward. Of course, he also knew the *Timaeus* intimately and summed up its grand cosmic vision in the *Consolation* with approval.*

At the same time, Boethius was deeply aware of the practical, humanistic side of Plato's thought in dialogues like the *Republic*, the *Gorgias*, and the *Crito*. He embraced Plato's belief that men need wisdom in order to confront and deal with evil in this world, as well as to prepare for the next. The proof is the reverence with which he invokes the name of Socrates. Socrates, who endured death for crimes he never committed, was Boethius's role model for obvious reasons. But Socrates had also refused to yield to the baseness and corruption around him, and his bold refusal had inspired others to follow the path to enlightenment. Life is bound to be stormy for the virtuous man, Boethius wrote, whose "chief aim in the sea of life is to displease wicked men." In those rough waters, we want Socrates on our bridge.[8]

So Plato was a powerful presence in Boethius's thought. The most famous line from his *Consolation*, "God is to be found in goodness itself and nowhere else," might have been written by Plato himself. But Aristotle held a deeper interest for Boethius. With the knowledge of Greek steadily disappearing from western Europe, the need for a Latin version of Aristotle seemed more urgent. In fact, Boethius made it his life's work.

"I wish to translate the whole work of Aristotle," Boethius wrote when he turned thirty. "Everything Aristotle wrote on the difficult art of logic, on the important realm of moral experience, and on the exact comprehension of natural objects, I shall translate in the correct order."[9] Boethius never finished the mammoth project he had set for himself (prison and death also interrupted his plans to translate Plato's dialogues). Aristotle's writings on politics, ethics, and rhetoric, along with his central work, the *Metaphysics*, had to wait another six centuries before they saw the light of day in the West.[10]

But Boethius did manage to turn Aristotle's main works on logic into everyday usable Latin. He also translated the commentaries on them by Plotinus's old student Porphyry of Tyre, who showed how Aristotle's view of logic,

---

*For many medieval scholars, Boethius's summary was all the Plato they ever knew. The *Timaeus* did survive in two late Latin translations, but they were garbled and missing important passages. Cicero's *Dream of Scipio* (a fragment of his lost *De Re Publica*) also borrowed heavily from Plato's *Timaeus*, but it, too, was only a summary. It would not be until 1464 that Plato's own writings once again became part of the Western cultural arsenal. See chapter 17.

reason, and language fit into the larger Neoplatonist vision. Boethius rounded these off with his own set of commentaries, plus original works on logic and music theory and translations of Euclid and Ptolemy. *The Consolation of Philosophy* completed the set.

To appreciate the value of Boethius's legacy to Western culture, we need to remember that for the next thousand years, everything Europeans counted as knowledge had to be copied out painstakingly by hand. In a largely illiterate society, the disappearance of a precious manuscript from fire or vandalism or official disapproval, or simply the failure to make a fresh copy, could wipe out knowledge of a subject for a generation, possibly forever.

By Boethius's time, Greek was already a dead language in western Europe. During the barbarian invasions and the Dark Ages that followed, the power to read and write Latin became the privileged property of a tiny few. It was only the relentless reproduction of Boethius's works, by generations of forgotten monks and scribes from Subiaco and Monte Cassino in Italy to Kells in Ireland, that allowed some fragments of that Greek legacy to enter the Western consciousness. When writers talk about the monks of Ireland "saving civilization," this is what they mean: how from the age of Charlemagne to the Crusades, they copied and recopied the manuscripts of Boethius, alongside Saint Augustine, Cicero and Virgil, and Saint Jerome's Latin Bible.[11]

Because in the end, it was Boethius who counted most for the future of Europe and its reeducation, once the worst of the barbarian disruptions were over. His translations of Aristotle's logic were crucial.* Boethius revealed that logic is not some remote ivory tower discipline. Instead, it thrusts us into the real world, by focusing on what we can say with certainty about the world around us and the necessary relationship between language and truth.

Aristotle's logic grew out of Plato's dialectic, that relentless process of "asking questions and giving answers, affirming and denying" that Socrates had said was necessary to arrive at truth.[12] But how does the process really work?

---

*Boethius did translations of the *Categories*, *On Interpretation*, the *Topics*, and the *Prior Analytics* and *Posterior Analytics*, plus "On Sophistical Refutations" (in Latin, *De Sophisitici Elenchi*). In addition, he wrote five independent treatises on logic. What was available on a regular basis to medieval scholars, and in readable form, is another matter. The Boethius version of the *Posterior Analytics* was so garbled by multiple miscopyings as to be almost unusable. It wasn't until the twelfth century and Gerard of Cremona's translation of 1187 that this crucial text on inductive logic finally entered the mainstream. See chapter 14.

Plato and his Neoplatonist followers tended to treat dialectic as a rather mysterious discipline, an inward turning of the soul that allowed it to join up with a transcendent and abstract reality. Aristotle, by contrast, set out to dispel the mystery by bringing logic down to earth. Finding out how one true assertion (all human beings die) leads to another (someday I will die) turned out to be a straightforward process based on a set of rules: the rules of *inference*.

Those rules, Aristotle pointed out, rest on certain self-evident laws, such as the law of identity (whatever else it is, A is always A), the law of contradiction (A cannot be both B and not B), and the law of "excluded middle."* But in the end, all inferences that are true have to come in two forms.

They are either deductive, meaning that given one or more true premises, the conclusion we draw is *necessary*; or they are inductive, meaning that given one or more facts—such as the things we know through observation— the conclusion we draw is *reasonable*. The classic deductive inference (actually taken from Aristotle's *Categories*) is "All men are mortal; Socrates is a man; therefore Socrates is mortal." Usually a good deductive inference goes from greater generalities to lesser ones: "All dogs are mammals; all Lab retrievers are dogs; therefore all Lab retrievers are mammals." By contrast, inductive logic usually (though not always) goes from the lesser to the greater. "I have five friends who have white beards; all five are over fifty years of age; therefore all men with white beards are over fifty years of age.".

Inductive logic offers a source of *new* knowledge, based on empirical observation. Aristotle recognized the value of induction; his own sciences were founded on it.[13] Still, his real focus was always the logic of deduction. How can we be sure that what we say about the world and the things and people in it is necessarily, and without fear of contradiction, true? After all, there might be men under fifty with prematurely gray hair who end up with white beards.

On the other hand, Socrates's mortality, like the dog's status as a mammal and the frog's nature as an amphibian, becomes part of the definition of who they are (what Aristotle called their *essence*). Aristotle called these true deductive inferences *syllogisms*. All syllogisms follow the same basic structure as the "Socrates is mortal" example. Each contains two premises or assumptions (called major and minor) and the inescapable conclusion we have to draw from them.

---

*That is, either Des Moines is in Iowa, or it's not in Iowa; either Edith is pregnant, or she's not pregnant. There is no third, or middle, possibility.

> *All human beings are rational.*
> *Some human beings are Americans.*
> *Therefore, some Americans are rational.*

Or:

> *No horses have claws.*
> *All Appaloosas are horses.*
> *Therefore, no Appaloosas have claws.*

Aristotle showed that every valid syllogism fit one of four basic patterns, although his followers in the Middle Ages claimed to discover more than four. Far more important, Aristotle showed (or seemed to show) that by linking one valid syllogism to another regarding a single subject, such as biology or ethics or even the nature of God, one could build a conceptual chain of reasoning that would inevitably lead, link by link, from one set of necessary truths to another, all the way to the highest truths of all.

In effect, Aristotle's logic offered the possibility of creating a universally true science out of anything—or of deconstructing claims of being a science. Aristotle had used his logical arguments to challenge Plato's theory of Forms or Pythagoras's assertion that all things were made from number, on the grounds (as the third man argument showed, for example) that *they made no logical sense.* Not everything that makes deductive sense may be true.* But if it doesn't fit into a syllogism, Aristotle concluded, then don't bother asking if it's true or not.

Thanks to Boethius, Aristotle's logic was now available to apply the same test to Christianity's weightiest assertions about God, heaven and hell, and the Church's most cherished views about human beings and nature.

At first, this seemed a positive development. Indeed, the first man to use Boethius and Aristotle to open the mind of the Dark Ages would become pope in 999 as Silvester II. Before assuming the papacy, Gerbert of Aurillac embodied the new spirit spreading across Europe as it approached the landmark date of 1000 CE, thanks in large part to Boethius. Men like Gerbert had

---

*For example, "No puckatoos eat sudsy snacks; all puckatoos are flibberdegibbets; therefore no flibberdegibbets eat sudsy snacks" is pure nonsense but a valid deductive syllogism. On the other hand, later logicians would point out that not every valid deduction fits the syllogism form. Mathematical deductive truths, like 2 + 2 = 4, very rarely do.

realized that they were witnessing not the end of the world, as some had feared, but a new beginning.[14]

The last wave of barbarian attacks on Europe, including the Vikings, had finally receded. Charlemagne's Holy Roman Empire, which came apart with his death in 814, had been successfully restored, with the imperial title in the hands of strong Saxon kings (one of them made Gerbert pope). Life was returning to a settled pattern for the first time in centuries. Europeans were finally free to wake up, look around, and sift through the rubble to find what was valuable and useful for building the new future.

Gerbert was the greatest teacher and scholar of his generation. He was an avid collector of ancient manuscripts (he traveled to the rough borderlands of Muslim Spain to find texts he wanted), and endlessly and confidently curious. He was also the first man in western Europe to lecture on Boethius's logical treatises. As the scholar R. W. Southern has put it, it was Gerbert who made Boethius "the schoolmaster of medieval Europe" and made Aristotle's logic the centerpiece of an education based on the seven liberal arts.[15]

The idea of the "liberal arts" (so called because it was the education fit for *liberi*, or free men, as opposed to slaves) was a late Roman invention.*[16] Gerbert had a deep interest in its more advanced elements, the so-called *quadrivium*. For arithmetic, he revived that lost ancient calculator the abacus. For the study of music, he invented a stringed instrument, the monochord, for demonstrating to students the Pythagorean precision of musical intervals. For geometry, Gerbert wrote a commentary on Euclid and helped to revive an interest in astronomy in the West by telling friends about a marvelous Arab device he had discovered on his travels to Spain, the astrolabe.[17]

However, Gerbert's first loves were the subjects of the *trivium*, especially rhetoric and logic. His insistence that students learn the rules of logic before embarking on anything else made Aristotle the founder of the medieval university curriculum.[18]

Aristotle turned out to be particularly valuable to teachers. His logic gave them a clear and orderly way to present unfamiliar material to students, by boiling everything down to a series of easy-to-learn syllogisms: If A is true, then B must also be true; if B is true, then C must be true; and so on. It also left plenty of room for what every teacher loves or should love, namely tests of memorization and brainteaser-style exercises—and all with the confidence

---

*The seven were grammar, rhetoric, and logic; astronomy, music, geometry, and arithmetic.

that everything that was being presented was deductively, and therefore necessarily and indisputably, true.

So why not theology and Christian dogma? Christianity, after all, offered a feast of rational truths of the highest order: Every important thinker since Augustine had said so. So it is hardly surprising that by 1050, Aristotle's logic had found a home not only in the liberal arts curriculum, but at the desks of Europe's most influential theologians.

Berengar of Tours was the student of Gerbert's most distinguished pupil, a priest named Fulbert. Fulbert had founded one of the first and most influential medieval schools in the cathedral town of Chartres. Many called him the Socrates of France—a sign of how an interest in things classical and Greek was already reviving. For his part, Berengar proclaimed logic to be "the art of arts" and asserted that it was the true sign of a great mind to turn everything into syllogisms. Reason could decide any and every issue, he said, including matters of Christian doctrine. Anyone who failed to apply the test of reasoned logic to the assertions of religious dogma was denying his own nature, Berengar said, "for it is by his reason that man resembles God."[19]

Few were willing to be as bold as Berengar. The most famous Christian thinker to apply the techniques of logical demonstration directly to his understanding of God was the bishop of Canterbury named Anselm. Anselm was always careful to present his work as harmonizing, not testing or challenging, the teachings of Scripture and the Church Fathers. Still, he loved the thrill of the intellectual chase as much as any scientist. When he was working out his groundbreaking logical proof for the existence of God, his medieval biographer tells us, he lost all taste for food or drink or even attending Mass—until the truth broke through "and filled his whole being with the greatest joy and exaltation."[20]

Anselm's famous "ontological" proof is a model of clarity and simplicity (I was able to memorize it as a child of four).[21]* But like Anselm's other syllogisms, it is also a model of religious orthodoxy, blending cold logic with heartfelt piety. Taken together, they extend the Church's assumptions about the Trinity and the Incarnation of Christ. They never challenge them. It was Anselm who coined the most famous phrase of the Middle Ages: "I believe

---

* "If that than which nothing greater can be conceived exists in the understanding alone, the very being than which nothing greater can be conceived is one than which a greater can be conceived. But obviously this is impossible. Hence there is no doubt that there exists a being than which nothing greater can be conceived, and it exists both in the understanding and in reality."

[in God] in order to understand." He was not devaluing reason or logic: just the opposite. He was simply reminding readers of where his, and their, priorities needed to be.

Berengar died in 1088 and never earned a sainthood. Anselm, who died at Canterbury in 1109, did. Yet the truth was, he and everyone else were playing with fire. The problem with Aristotle's logic is that once it gets started, it is very hard to stop. It can become a kind of compulsion as it moves from examining one set of conventional beliefs and assumptions after another, overturning everything in sight. Logic is, to borrow William Blake's phrase, self-delighting. The experience can be so exhilarating that we fail to notice where we are headed.

In Peter Abelard's case, it led him right to the brink of disaster and cost him a more terrible price than even his many enemies would have wished.

If Aristotle had had a younger son, he might have wanted him to be like Peter Abelard. Abelard was born in Brittany in 1079, the home of quick-tempered, quarrelsome Celts and a land not so different from Aristotle's Macedonia. His father was a feudal lord, a chain-mail-clad warrior like the ones we see in the Bayeux Tapestry.

Well built and fit, Peter would almost certainly have become the same except that Abelard *père* had a strong respect for book learning. In an age and a region where nearly every layperson was illiterate, Lord Abelard of Le Pallet was an exception. So in between practice sessions with sword and buckler, he sent seven-year-old Peter for lessons with a local *grammaticus*, a cleric who taught Latin.[22]

What had been interesting to the father became a passion for the son. By the time he was a teen, Peter Abelard imbibed enough Cicero, Seneca, Virgil, and Ovid to decide to exchange "Mars for Minerva," as he later put it, and begin serious study for a career in the Church. Like the other boys, Peter would have squatted on the stone floor in a large unheated room day after day, shivering in the cold while their teacher unveiled for them the mysteries of the *trivium:* first Latin grammar, then Latin rhetoric, and finally Aristotle's logic, or dialectic, as contemporaries called it.

It fascinated the quick-witted teenager. In a school like his, books (like chairs) were scarce. Memorization was the rule of the day, and before long

Peter had stocked his brain with a lifetime's arsenal of quotations and rules from the major texts of early medieval logic, above all Aristotle's *Categories* in Boethius's translation.[23]

"I preferred the art of dialectical exercise," he later wrote, "among all the teachings of philosophy, [so] I exchanged literal arms for these, and sought instead of the trophies of war those of disputation." His role model was Aristotle himself, and his classmates nicknamed him the Peripatetic of Pallet.[24] In fact, Peter Abelard became a kind of intellectual knight-errant, wandering the countryside wielding his syllogisms like a razor-sharp sword in order to slice and dice his opponents one after another, starting with his own teachers.

His instructor at Loches was a distinguished scholar named Roscelin. After a few months, Roscelin became so frustrated with his insolent, arrogant pupil that he sent Abelard along to Paris to irritate another famous master, William of Champeaux. William also got fed up with being beaten in every argument—"by logic I compelled him to change his opinion," Abelard wrote proudly, "indeed to abandon it"—and finally expelled Abelard from his school at the Notre Dame Cathedral. Peter Abelard found himself on the street, armed only with his mind and his Aristotle, wondering what to do next.

With entrepreneurial bravado, Abelard decided to open his own school. He was confident that the very qualities that infuriated his superiors—his insolence, his precocious abilities, his flashing charisma—would attract him to students. He was right. Within a couple of years, Abelard had drawn enough pupils eager to learn the rules of logic that by 1108, at age twenty-nine, he became the dominant intellectual figure in the city.

Young men from across France came to Abelard's classes. These were held outside the city limits on the Left Bank of the Seine near the Abbey of Ste. Genevieve so that his rival William of Champeaux, now archdeacon, could not invoke the bishop of Paris's authority to shut him down. However, it was still close enough to Notre Dame "that I could lay siege, as it were," Abelard later explained, "to him who occupied my [rightful] place," namely William of Champeaux.[25] Students abandoned his rival's school to flock to the Left Bank (the home of French students ever since), listening and arguing, disputing and quoting favorite one-liners as they wandered the narrow streets, their minds filled with Aristotle, Boethius, Porphyry—and Abelard.

He was without doubt a superstar. No one was quicker on his feet in handling a difficult logical problem, no one was more devastating in his critique of a rival (Abelard at one point sat in on William of Champeaux's classes just to heckle and torment him). And no one was more eloquent in his praise of the value of Aristotle's logic for arriving at truth.

Abelard told his students that the word *logic* came from *Logos*, the divine Word in St. John's Gospel. "In the beginning was the Logos"; but logic obviously came a close second.[26] By using logic and dialectic, he told them, they could open new vistas in the study of theology. In fact, he seems to have been the first to coin the term *theologia* (logic plus *theos*, or God) in the modern sense. He was also the first to create the techniques by which theology could become as rational and logically disciplined a subject as philosophy—the techniques later called scholasticism.[27]

Abelard encouraged students to collate the Church Fathers' different opinions, or *glosses*, on specific passages from the Bible. Then they compared those with the original passages to arrive at a definite conclusion as to who had been right and who had been wrong. Nothing is infallible outside Scripture, he told them; even the apostles and Church Fathers sometimes err.[28] It was up to his students to decide, based on the evidence and their own reason. After all, Abelard proclaimed with echoes from Berengar of Tours, man's reason was what made him the image of God. "In fact," Abelard once told his class, "you *are* gods!" The students yelled and cheered. Then they hoisted Abelard on their shoulders and carried him through the streets.

Some worried about where all this was heading, but not Abelard. "My students clamored for human and philosophical reasons," he wrote later in his defense. "They did not need affirmation but rather intelligible explanations." In the end, Abelard concluded, "no one can believe something which he has not first understood."[29] As for whether all this cold-eyed logical examination might lead minds astray into skepticism and doubt, Abelard replied: Never fear. "Careful and frequent questioning is the basic key to wisdom." He added what is probably his most famous maxim: "By doubting we come to question, and by questioning we perceive the truth."[30]

Anselm said I must believe so that I can understand. Abelard now reversed the formula: I must understand so that I can believe. Faith without reason was merely supposition, an opinion or guesstimate (*aestimatio*). Abelard's most famous work, *Sic et Non*, compared 150 passages from Scripture and the Church Fathers that contradicted one another. The only way to sort out the mess, Abelard was saying, was through reason and logic. The only way

Christianity could make itself a believable faith was by responding to our natural inclination to question its foundations.[31]

Given all this, what is amazing is not that Abelard got into trouble with the authorities, but that he didn't get into more trouble sooner. In fact, he might have been left alone altogether if, in the spring of 1119, he hadn't made a fatal mistake. A canon of Notre Dame named Fulbert (no relation to Gerbert's famous pupil) needed a private tutor for his niece Héloïse. He asked Peter Abelard. Abelard agreed.

Abelard was forty. Héloïse was seventeen. She was attractive, extremely well-read (she seems to have memorized more Latin poetry, including Virgil and Ovid, than Abelard had), and vivacious. He was tall, well dressed (since Abelard held no church office, he was free to dress in the latest male fashions), charismatic, and famous. It's not clear who seduced whom. But it is clear from Abelard's own description that the private "classes" soon became nonstop steamy sex sessions. "Under the cloak of study, we freely practiced love," he wrote in *The History of My Calamities*. "My hands more eagerly sought her breasts than the books before us." Things even took an S/M turn. "I sometimes beat her in love rather than in anger, not for wrath but for pleasure that surpassed all ointments in sweetness."[32]

The secret affair did not remain a secret for long. One day, Héloïse announced she was pregnant. When her uncle found out what had been going on in his upstairs study while he was at church, his rage was understandable. However, when Abelard offered to marry the girl, Fulbert accepted. The thought of having the famous Abelard as a son-in-law helped to ease Fulbert's humiliation.

But after a son was born in 1121 (named Astrolabe after the astronomical device) and the pair were secretly married at his parents' house, Abelard insisted that Héloïse enter a nunnery. He was still afraid that if the story of their affair and marriage came out, it would ruin his career not as a Catholic cleric (many in 1122 still had mistresses or even wives), but as France's most glamorous philosopher.

Héloïse agreed and went to a monastery at Argenteuil, close to Paris. Unable to help himself, Abelard began paying her secret meetings. Soon they were having sex again.

That was when Fulbert snapped. He hired a band of thugs to visit Abelard in his chambers in the rue St. André des Arts. They bribed one of Abelard's servants to let them enter his room while he slept. The men seized him, tied him down, and then with a knife "cut off those parts of my body with which I had done the deed they deplored." Hearing Abelard's screams, another servant ran out into the street to call for help. His assailants were caught and tried; with a kind of rough justice, two of them were sentenced to be castrated as well. That meant little to Abelard. Not only had he been robbed of his genitals, he had also been robbed of his reputation and his fame.[33]

Things went quickly downhill for Abelard. Over the next several years, he would show a series of failures of judgment almost equal to his decision to seduce the teenager Héloïse. All the while his many enemies, sensing his sudden vulnerability, gathered for the kill.

"Feeling the embarrassment more keenly than the injury," as he tells it, "more afflicted by the shame than by the pain," Abelard decided to shut himself away in the monastery at Saint Denis. It was a cry for help as well as an act of penance. Peter Abelard was temperamentally unsuited to the cloistered life. Soon he was up to his old dialectical tricks again and after a couple of years had to flee the wrath of his fellow monks.* He then tried heading his own monastery in Brittany. That proved to be a disaster. It was only when he returned to teaching in Paris fifteen years after his terrible castration that Abelard came back into his own. He drew the usual hordes of students (one was John of Salisbury) and published his theological treatises, including *Sic et Non*.

This time his enemies were ready for him. Back in 1121, they had forced him to publicly burn his treatise on the Trinity for daring to imply that Plato and Plotinus had a clearer understanding of the idea than Moses thanks to their reason alone. Now twenty years later, at a church synod in the new cathedral at Sens, he was summoned to defend his views once again in public, this time under the disapproving eye of the great theologian and monastic reformer Bernard of Clairvaux.

Bernard was nearly ten years younger than Abelard. In the old days, Abelard would have treated him with magisterial condescension. Instead, the once invincible dialectical knight-errant lost his nerve and, in effect, forfeited the match. His condemnation at Sens was the final humiliation. He died worn out but still defiant two years later in 1142 under the protection of the monastery at Cluny and its prior, Peter the Venerable. Venerable Peter sent

---

*For the reasons why, see chapter 13.

the news to Héloïse, who was still a nun at Argenteuil, with comforting words: "He was renowned the world over for the weight of his learning, and his fame was universal." The Cluny prior promised her that one day she and Abelard would be reunited, "one day beyond these voices where there is peace."[34] The Middle Ages' most restless intellect was gone.

What was his legacy? As another brilliant logician, Bertrand Russell, pointed out, Abelard tended to overrate the value of Aristotelian logic and of deduction as the only path to truth. Abelard had no interest in the one sphere where inductive reasoning is most important to yielding new knowledge, namely science.[35] Aristotle's writings on that subject were still unavailable to him. Reason for Abelard and his followers was a tool for understanding what was already known, especially about God and the Bible, not opening new vistas for human investigation.

Nor did Abelard's skepticism and rationalism ever lead him to doubt the truth of Christianity. "I will never be a philosopher," he wrote after his con-demnation, "if this is to speak against Saint Paul; I would not be an Aristotle, if this were to separate me from Christ."[36] He saw logic as the buttress of the-ology and his faith, not a substitute for them. If this earns him impatience from later skeptics and freethinkers, it does fit him into his own time and place. Peter Abelard's Aristotle points down the road to Thomas Aquinas, not the Enlightenment.

All the same, Abelard opened the mind of the Middle Ages in new and startling ways. He gave the name of Aristotle and Aristotle's logic an edgy glamour it never entirely lost. Aristotle had said: All men desire to know. Abelard now added: All men need to question and doubt in order to know. These were important signposts for the future. For now, medieval civilization was about to swing down another path, one emblazoned by the Neoplatonist imagination.

Rose window, Chartres Cathedral, south transept

Thirteen

CELESTIAL HARMONIES: PLATO IN THE MIDDLE AGES

Man may rise to the contemplation of the divine through the senses.
—Abbot Suger

"As the third year that followed the year one thousand drew near," wrote medieval chronicler Raoul Glauber, "there was to be seen over almost all the earth, but especially Italy and France, a great renewal of church buildings. It was as if the world had shaken itself, and, casting off the old garments, had dressed itself again in every part in a white robe of churches."[1]

One of those white-robed churches was in Sens, a town southeast of Paris on the river Yvonne, which had grown rich with the revival of the wool trade in the former Roman province of Gaul, or France. In 1130, its archbishop laid the foundations for a new cathedral, something larger and more splendid than its Romanesque predecessor. Ten years later, construction was still under way. When bishops, abbots, prelates, and other church officials arrived in the spring of 1140, they had to step over piles of masonry and dodge ropes from cranes as they assembled in the cathedral's new choir. They were there for a church council, the most important in France ever. In terms of the history of Western civilization, perhaps the most important of all.

The Sens council had been summoned to hear Peter Abelard defend his strange new doctrines. His judges included a monk in his early fifties who was a particular friend of Sens's archbishop and the acknowledged leader of Europe's most dynamic new monastic order, the Cistercians. He was Bernard of Clairvaux, later to be canonized as Saint Bernard.

Under his leadership, the Cistercians had grown from a handful of monasteries to more than 350 houses by 1140. Although he was ten years younger than Abelard, Bernard was already the single most influential churchman of the age. He was an intimate adviser and friend to one pope, Innocent II, and the mentor and teacher of another, Eugenius III. Bernard was determined to cleanse from the Church all forms of corruption, including intellectual corruption. That meant a return to first principles, especially those of Saint Augustine, that "from this hell on earth there is no escape except through the grace of the Savior Christ, our Lord and God."[2] Bernard had heard a great deal about Abelard's teachings. He didn't like what he had heard.

"[Abelard] casts what is holy before dogs," was how Saint Bernard put it in a letter, "and pearls before swine."[3] *Sic et Non* and Abelard's other works "run riot with a whole crop of sacrileges." Bernard was especially offended by how Abelard had held the Church's great authorities up to logical scrutiny, criticizing their conflicting views on the Trinity and the Incarnation as if they had been ignorant students instead of divinely inspired Fathers and Doctors of the Church.

"The garments of Christ are being divided," Bernard raged, "the sacraments of the Church torn to shreds." Abelard "corrupts the integrity of the faith . . . and oversteps the landmarks placed by our Fathers" in the name of reason. A new gospel was being forged and a new faith being founded, the great Cistercian argued: a faith based on Aristotle. "Outwardly, [Abelard] dresses as a monk but inwardly he is a heretic."[4]

Thus far, Abelard had been allowed to get away with his defiance, Bernard told Pope Innocent, "there being no David to defy him." That is, until that summer of 1140, when at the church council at Sens they would finally meet. "Where all have fled before him," Bernard wrote with a wry smile, "he calls me out . . . to single intellectual combat." However, Bernard would be ready. "With the Lord to aid me, I have no fear of the worst man can do."[5]

The square outside Sens's cathedral was jammed.[6] People had come to see the twin combatants clash like jousting knights in a tournament. The carnival-like atmosphere continued inside, where dozens of churchmen and dignitaries gathered under the soaring ribbed stone vaults and arches. Even King Louis VII was present. Everyone wanted to witness the headline bout between Aristotle's most outspoken champion and the stern warrior for the faith of Saint Augustine.

Abelard was on his feet almost at once, ready for battle. The archbishop, however, insisted that the charges against him be read first. Disgruntled, Abelard sat down while Bernard, in a low, clear voice, began reading aloud the nineteen heretical propositions that authorities said were in Abelard's writings.

"Number 3: That the Holy Spirit is the World-Soul. Number 4: That Christ did not assume flesh to liberate us from the devil." As Bernard read, Abelard became more and more agitated. When Bernard got to the fifth accusation, that he had denied the Trinity, Abelard had reached his limit.

"He refused to listen and walked out," Bernard remembered later. Abelard said he would appeal any decision by the Sens council, even though he himself had chosen his judges, "which," Bernard noted with some asperity, "I did not think was permissible."[7] The much publicized match was over before it began. The crowd, including the king, was disappointed. Bernard, however, could be satisfied. He had faced his most dangerous adversary, and his adversary had retreated without a fight. The Sens council duly denounced *Sic et Non* and Abelard's other works, and a furious but defeated Abelard was forced to throw his own books in the fire. Now it was up to Bernard to consolidate his victory not just over Abelard, but over the entire Aristotelian worldview.

What had offended Bernard most was how Abelard had tried to use the ancient pagan philosopher to pry open the most delicate divine mysteries. "He trie[d] to explore with his reason what the devout mind grasps at once with a vigorous faith." The prophet Jeremiah had said, Unless you believe, you shall not understand. But Abelard, "apparently holding God suspect, will not believe anything until he has first examined it with his reason." Philosophy had no business trying to lift the veil from mysteries beyond human understanding. The way to get to those, Bernard affirmed, was not through the mind but through the heart.[8]

From the point of view of Plato—not to mention Socrates—this was a shocking downgrading of reason. But Bernard was only following Plato's hierarchy of knowledge as adopted and adapted by Saint Augustine. Just as reason is superior to opinion (*doxa*), so Saint Augustine taught that faith is superior to reason because it rests on the highest wisdom of all, the truth of God's revelation.[9] Faith of this potent kind is more than belief. When we say, "I believe the Pittsburgh Steelers will win the Super Bowl," or, "I believe the person who stole my car will get caught," we are talking about probabilities— or indulging in wishful thinking. Real faith is a matter of an unqualified emotional commitment, what Saint Augustine called love, or *caritas*: a fierce spiritual force that binds man to God and (as proved by the sacrifice of the Crucifixion) vice versa. "Faith avails not," Bernard wrote, "unless it is actuated by love." Love for Bernard was the gift of the Holy Spirit. It was the heartfelt token of salvation.[10]

To modern scholars, Saint Bernard does not strike a very sympathetic figure. They have tagged him as a puritan bigot who mercilessly hounded Abelard ("perpetual silence should be imposed on that man," he urged one of the cardinals in Rome, "whose mouth overflows with curses, calumny, and deceit") in the name of a narrow-minded Catholic orthodoxy.[11] He fought hard to keep women out of the Cistercian order; he believed females to be sexual temptresses by their nature. It was one of the few battles he lost.[12]

All the same, it was Saint Bernard who put the image of the Virgin Mary, the nurturing Mother of God, at the center of the Catholic faith and who made the loving human heart the key to exploring religious truth—even the key to discovering God.[13] Even more than Augustine, he is the first great religious psychologist—therapist, almost. Bernard's goal was to lay bare the deepest recesses of the soul and bring man to a spiritual simplicity and humility. Looking forward, his theology prefigures the teachings of the most tenderhearted of medieval saints, Saint Francis of Assisi. Looking backward, Bernard's goal was that of Augustine and, at one remove, Plotinus: the self-sacrificing, unwavering love that raises knowledge of ourselves to a mystical union with God.

This, Bernard decided, had been Abelard's problem. He knew all about his rival's dealings with Héloïse and deeply disapproved. But he also sensed that they sprang from the same pride that Abelard took in his own reason. Abelard's love for Héloïse was actually a form of self-love, even self-obsession. "He is a man who does not know his limitations," Bernard confided to a friend. "Nothing in heaven or on earth is hidden from him, *except himself.*"

It was a shrewd observation. For Saint Bernard, self-love is the root of all evil, and the Achilles' heel of the Aristotelian mind. Not only does it block us from grasping the true nature of love, and hence of God. It also prevents us from realizing the relative *un*importance of human reason.[14]

Without faith, Bernard affirmed, intellectual inquiry is doomed to run off the track. Worldly wisdom, he liked to point out, teaches only vanity.[15] By contrast, by making God the center of our lives instead of ourselves, we are spiritually transformed. Through love of God, "he who by his former life and conscience was doomed as a true son of perdition to the eternal flames," he wrote, "draws new life and hope beyond all expectation." He is "rescued from a most deep and dark pit of horrible ignorance, and plunged into a pleasant region bright with eternal light."[16]

Later, this spiritual transformation will be called being born again. It is in fact a Christian variant on Plato's Myth of the Cave. "Once I was blind," as the hymn says, "but now I see." It was Saint Bernard's goal to turn the Catholic Church into an instrument to enable people to see the world and themselves in the true light of God; in the phrase of William Blake, who shares a good deal with Saint Bernard, to see not with but *thro'* the eye. Bernard wanted to draw people out of the cave and into the light of God, not by imposing new rules and regulations (although Bernard had no problem with those), but by appealing to human beings' most basic feelings.

One way was through sermons. Saint Bernard transformed the art of sermons and elevated their importance in the medieval Church by introducing a rich evocative Latin style that appealed to listeners' senses and touched their hearts. For those without Latin, Bernard saw the importance of using religious imagery like the cross, and figures like the Virgin Mary, as a way to speak directly to the emotional needs of the listener, even the simplest and least educated. The cross was the only decoration he allowed in his monasteries, as the symbol of God's willing sacrifice of His only son to save humanity: a sacrifice born of true undying love. "Let no one who loves God doubt that God loves him"—and the sign of the cross is the proof of that promise.[17]

He also made the Virgin Mary a powerful symbol of the Church's role as loving mother and intercessor with God. Thanks to Saint Bernard, the anonymous *The Miracles of the Virgin* became one of the most popular books of the Middle Ages. One new church after another would be dedicated to her, including two of the most famous: Notre Dame in Paris and Notre Dame in Chartres. Meanwhile, religious painters and sculptors of the age turned to depicting the tender scene of Virgin and Child as a way to reflect the compassionate face of Bernardine Christianity. They succeeded in establishing a genre that would reach its climax in the Renaissance and the paintings of Botticelli and Raphael—all due to the influence of the supposedly misogynist Bernard.[18]

Then there was music. Plato had always been aware of the power of music to stir human emotions, both for good and for ill. Pythagoras had also made Plato and the Academy aware of how music expressed the same divine order of number and proportion as in geometry. Plotinus had passed this Platonic fascination with music and number to Saint Augustine, who saw both as reflections of a divine order catastrophically disrupted by Adam's Fall.[19]

Augustine then passed that same fascination to Saint Bernard and his followers. For the Middle Ages, music seemed to offer a new series of proofs of the existence of God, uncovered not through logic, but intuitively through the senses. Oddly, the medieval followers of Neoplatonism saw another of the liberal arts, astronomy, the same way. The phrase they coined for the coordinated precision of the heavenly bodies was "the music of the spheres." No one in the Middle Ages actually hears the music of the spheres. But they could see and *feel* it as they watched the starry night move overhead month by month, season by season.

"Music," Augustine wrote, "is the science of moving well."[20] Likewise, music was more than just a pleasing sound to Bernard. It was the divinely proportioned audible trace of God's presence. Bernard was more involved in the creation of liturgical music than any Church Father since the creator of the Gregorian chant, Pope Gregory the Great. Bernard was convinced that the bliss of heaven itself was an eternal concert conducted by choirs of singing angels.[21]

Of course, any notion of perfect proportion must also have a visual component. And to see it requires something that Bernard believed also opened the heart to a knowledge of God beyond reason and logic. This was light.

Augustine and his Neoplatonist mentors had said that the light of nature was a reflection of God's own radiance. It was what made the world intelligible to reason, "the divine illumination of the mind," and had deep significance in the theology of Saint Bernard. But the Middle Ages owed its deepest debt for the importance of light in the Neoplatonist universe to an obscure Syrian monk who had lived centuries before—and to a shocking case of forged identity.

. . .

Shocking, because the perpetrator managed to escape detection for nearly one thousand years. Only Peter Abelard came close to guessing the truth. Even today, monks at the remote monastery at Mount Athos in Greece celebrate every October 3 as the forger's feast day. Amid clouds of incense and the glow of oil lamps, they chant hymns of praise in front of his icon and recite his works aloud in order to understand the divine secrets of the universe.[22]

To them, he is still St. Dionysius the Areopagite, the first bishop of Athens, who had been converted by Saint Paul himself. To scholars, however, he is the Pseudo-Dionysius, one of the cleverest fakes of the late Roman Empire and without a doubt the most influential.

Who was he, really? No one has a clue. It is possible he bore the same first name as the man mentioned in Acts 17:34: "Certain men came to believe [Paul the Apostle] and came to him, among them Dionysius the Areopagite." All his works were penned under that name. Yet all the evidence suggests he lived at least four hundred years later. Some suspect he was a Syrian, but no one knows for certain. He was certainly a monk, one heavily immersed in the Eastern traditions of Neoplatonism with its ideal of monastic life (passed down by a fourth-century admirer of Origen named Evagrius) as a single-minded contemplation of the divine.

Maybe he thought the pen name Dionysius the Areopagite would give his startling synthesis of Christian and Neoplatonist ideas more authority and credibility. He may even have believed that his words really *were* the kind of grand vision Saint Paul and the other early apostles had shared but never bothered to write down.[23]

Whatever his motivation, working day by day, year after year, quietly in his cell, the Pseudo-Dionysius wrote some of the most compelling and evocative treatises on theology ever written and fobbed them off as works by Saint Paul's most famous disciple. Even after his act of forgery was discovered, his insights proved too valuable to be discarded. In fact, no one who enters a church today or visits a museum, no one who gazes at a landscape or buys a picture to hang on his living room wall, is entirely free from the influence of the Syrian monk and the startling new twist he gave to Plato's influence on Western thought.

The Pseudo-Dionysius begins with a seeming paradox. We see God nowhere, and yet God is everywhere. The skeptic and atheist get stuck at the first obvious truth; they fail to push on to the second. The secret is that God's presence is made visible to us not directly but *symbolically*, in a material world that bears the faint but still perceptible trace of a higher intelligible and spiritual realm.

The Pseudo-Dionysius's God makes His impression on matter as (to borrow a metaphor from the author's later admirers) a signet ring presses into a blob of hot wax. The signet lifts away and moves on; only the wax seal is left. Yet the impression that gives the seal shape and meaning still carries the trace of its original maker. That trace is a symbol, not because it stands for another thing, but because it *is* that thing in a different form—just as the world reveals God's handiwork in a material form rather than His (and Plato's) immaterial Forms.

In fact, at the deepest level of contemplation, the Neoplatonist Dionysius argues that we will no longer *see* the wax seal at all. Instead, what contemplation of the material world finally reveals to us is what made the impression in the first place: the hand of God Himself.[24]

Of course, moving from looking at a wax seal to looking at God is not so simple. As any good Neoplatonist knew, God's presence in the world proceeds downward through a series of spiritual emanations, from the realm beyond Being and Non-Being to the perfect and intelligible, to finally the material and imperfect. Likewise, man's knowledge proceeds upward along the same track, the Great Chain of Being.*

What the Pseudo-Dionysius did in his cell was work out the entire map of the universe of spirit in detail, from the top all the way down. He laid out the Great Chain of Being in an exquisitely defined series of gradations for which he coined a new term, the Celestial Hierarchy.

Like the Jacob's Ladder in the Bible, Dionysius's Celestial Hierarchy is a spiritual elevator that human beings can catch going both up and down. The hierarchy runs down by regular stages from God through His angels to intelligible realms like the Forms; then through the rational soul to the world of material bodies, including our own. It also carries us upward by the same gradations toward a mystical union with God, drawing us irresistibly stage by stage toward the One. "The aim of hierarchy is the greatest possible assimilation to and union with God . . . to become like Him, so far as is permitted, by contemplating intently His most Divine Beauty."[25]

---

*See chapter 9.

However, we can never get to that final mystical union entirely by ourselves. Our consciousness must be coaxed along, drawn in a great procession stage by stage from matter to mind to spirit, by the mediating presence of higher beings like angels, who bear the impression of God's truth more immediately than we do.

Once we start the journey in earnest, Dionysius pointed out, we realize that the world around us is not some darkened cave devoid of meaning, as followers of Plato liked to claim.[26] It offers a rich pageant of sights and sounds, a forest of symbols that constantly trigger new insights and urge us along toward a higher reality. And "every divine [movement] of radiance from the Father, while constantly flowing bounteously to us, fills us anew with a unifying *power*, recalling us to things above, and leading us to the unity of the Shepherding Father and to the Divine One."[27]

The most important mediating force for the Pseudo-Dionysius was the Church. To the Syrian monk, the clergy, the liturgy, the sacraments, and even the Bible itself were nothing more than symbols to coax and guide us to that highest knowledge, the knowledge of God Himself. However, his more potent point was that *everything* in life is a mediating power to one degree or another. Nothing is entirely devoid of God's spiritual beauty: "As the true Word says, all things are beautiful." Indeed, without the presence of material things, especially beautiful things, the mind will never get started on its upward spiritual journey.

What opens the door for the journey and makes it possible? The answer is light: nothing more or less than the radiance of God's presence in the world. Neoplatonists had always been fascinated by Plato's remark in the *Republic* that the Good in Itself was the source of all light in the material realm.[28] The Pseudo-Dionysius made creation of the visible world itself an act of illumination. His followers pointed out that we would not exist without light. In their eyes, all men are "lights" in that their existence bears witness to that one unifying Divine Light bathing them in the same penetrating radiance. In the final analysis, it is the presence of physical light that God uses to draw His creation toward Him—but above all, man.[29]

The Pseudo-Dionysius's works were a triumph of the Neoplatonist imagination. In an age of science like our own, they seem wildly fanciful. The lists of seraphim, cherubim, thrones, powers, and the other grades of angelic beings seem like an elaborate fantasy game. However, in an age of faith like the early Middle Ages, with monastic imaginations starved for new stimuli, they were a stunning revelation. The first Latin translation of *Celestial Hierarchy* appeared at the court of Charles the Bald. It quickly became a Christian classic, along with the learned commentary provided by its Irish translator.* Readers were compulsively fascinated by the book's elaborate angelology, but also by its budding theology of light. This struck a deep harmonious chord with followers of Saint Augustine, including Saint Bernard.[30]

All the same, the Pseudo-Dionysius's promise of a knowledge of God achieved through the senses rather than the mind and reason found its most lasting home in the realm of stone rather than words and parchment. It is still visible today in the Gothic churches at Saint Denis and at Chartres.

In a purely technical sense, Sens Cathedral is probably the first Gothic church. When Abelard and Bernard met there in the spring of 1140, they probably did not notice that an architectural revolution was taking place over their heads. Its builders pioneered many of the characteristic elements of the Gothic style, from ribbed interior vaults and a three-part elevation, to the famous pointed Gothic arch for its windows.[31]

The pointed arch came from the East, from Islamic builders. Its rival the standard semicircular arch was the product of Aristotelian and Roman engineering. The pointed arch, by contrast, is the product of Platonic geometry. It results from the intersection of two arcs drawn on the same straight line— for French builders like the ones who built Sens and Saint Denis, essentially two quick swipes of a compass. Any builder worth his pay could then use a set of calipers to reproduce a series of those same arcs within the regular rectangle of the church's outside wall, or crisscross a pair of pointed vaults inside a series of perfect squares in the interior, enabling him to prop up the roof with far less stress than the old barrel vault of the Romans.

In truth, a good master mason could build an entire Gothic cathedral with just a compass and a T square, a device he borrowed from Greek mathematicians for lining up perfect vertical and horizontal lines. This dazzling command of practical geometry made the cathedral builders of the Middle

---

*This was John Scotus Erigena, one of the very few intellectuals in the Dark Ages West who could read Greek. Erigena was a Neoplatonist of some distinction. At some point, he may have left the Carolingian court for England to work as an adviser to King Alfred the Great. There, according to tradition, Erigena's students became so frustrated with his lessons that they stabbed him to death with their pens. The story is a salutary warning to every boring teacher. Alas, it is probably untrue.

Ages truly independent businessmen. By the fourteenth century, they were already calling themselves *free* masons.* Some would claim their knowledge reached back to the Pyramids. In fact, the Pyramids employed a far cruder geometry than the Gothic cathedrals.[32] The latter's real designers were Plato and Pythagoras, via Euclid and Boethius. And certainly no Freemason would have been allowed near a church site if his practical geometry had not measured up to the sacred geometry of the twelfth century's Platonic revival.

The man most active in bringing together these twin forces for divine order and proportion was Abbot Suger, head of the famous abbey of Saint Denis near Paris. Saint Denis had been the burial place of French kings since the early sixth century. It was one of the historic treasures of France. Although he had been tonsured and trained as a monk, Suger was more politician than churchman. He had served as the king's ambassador at the papal court and handled secular affairs for his boyhood friend Louis VI for years.

Then, beginning in the 1130s, he launched a thoroughgoing reform of the Saint Denis abbey inspired by Saint Bernard's Cistercian principles.[33] With his single-minded drive and energy, Suger also supervised the rebuilding of the abbey church. The result was a startling new approach to church design both inside and out. Later ages would call it the Gothic. Suger himself called it simply "the new style" or, more precisely, "the style of continuous light."

Once again, Saint Bernard was his inspiration. The great reformer had bitterly criticized the kind of twisting sculptural forms and garbled ornamentation that cluttered up Romanesque churches. He wanted his Cistercian abbeys to be as clean and pure to the eye as they were for the spirit. "There must be no decoration," he said, "only proportion."[34]

There were to be no painted frescoes or floor mosaics, no elaborate hangings. Instead, everything would reveal a clear geometric simplicity, using pure forms (the square, cube, rectangle, and that most potently Pythagorean of all geometric figures, the pentagon) to emphasize the principle of harmonious proportion. Suger would do the same with his plan for Saint Denis.

Its floor plan closely resembles the geometric simplicity of Bernard's Cistercian churches.[35] Painting and figurative sculpture disappeared from the church's interior. The human figures carved on the outside, especially around and above the church's entrance or portal, achieved a new monumental stillness, which is also strongly present in the west portal at Chartres.[36] The Gothic sculptor and mason concentrated on cutting stone with clean precise lines and blank smooth surfaces. As for Saint Denis's interior, it reveals a harmonious structure built entirely around bare walls and open bays. If architecture is frozen music, then Saint Denis is a visual hymn to divine perfection.*

The Neoplatonist theology of light was crucial for Suger. Here patriotic reasons played their part as well. In French, Saint Dionysius was Saint *Denis*. Since the first bishop of Paris and founder of the abbey c. 300 had been named Denis, it was all too easy to believe he had been the same Dionysius who had been Saint Paul's disciple, as well as the author of the *Celestial Hierarchy*. In fact, Abelard's problems with the monks at Saint Denis began when he dared to cast doubt on this triple misidentification. How likely was it, he pointed out, that a Latin-speaking saint living in France would write his most important theological tracts in Greek?[37]

The monks were outraged and drove Abelard out of the abbey. The assertion that the *Celestial Hierarchy* had been written by a Frenchman and the founder of Saint Denis became a matter of national dogma, one might almost say national theology. "Among ecclesiastical writers" in France, enthused one late-twelfth-century author, "Dionysius is believed to hold the first rank after the Apostles."[38] Abbot Suger turned his church into a radiant tribute to the abbey's famous founder and to his celebration of light as the radiance of God.

Suger installed windows everywhere, great pointed arch windows lining the aisles appearing along the church's upper floor, literally the "clear story," or clerestory. He also put the first Gothic rose windows over the west portal and at the rear of the church, over the sanctuary. Stained glass had been used in churches before, but for Suger it became a fascination, almost an obsession. The Church of Saint Denis glowed with great kaleidoscope mosaics of colored glass showing scenes from the Bible and church history. There was even a stained glass portrait of Abbot Suger himself, kneeling at the feet of Bernard of Clairvaux's favorite saint, the Virgin Mary.

The result was dazzling. When the sunlight poured in through Saint Denis's windows, it would cast glowing patterns of blue, red, green, and amber

---

*The music metaphor is appropriate since these spaces were filled with the sound of Gregorian chants, which were written to a musical scale made from the same Pythagorean proportions.

gold set bright against the black of their lead frames. Transformed into rainbows of color, the light streamed and shimmered across the stone floor. If a church's interior should be an image of heaven for the faithful, then entering the Church of Saint Denis meant entering a heaven of light and color and a radiant, eternal divine proportion.[39]

When Suger first stepped in his sun-filled church, he described his feelings: "It seems to me I see myself dwelling, as it were, in some strange region of the universe." This was a region that "neither exists entirely in the slime of the earth nor entirely in the purity of Heaven." However, "by the grace of God, I can be transported from this inferior to that higher world" thanks to the mediating power of light—or what later will be called the beauty of holiness. "The dull mind rises to the truth through material things," Suger said, echoing the *Celestial Hierarchy*, "and having seen the light, [the mind] arises from its former submergence."[40]

In 1144, the finished choir at Saint Denis was consecrated in an elaborate ceremony. The king of France was there and his queen Eleanor of Aquitaine. So was Bernard of Clairvaux. All around them was evidence of a new Neoplatonic spirit arising in the Catholic Church, inspiring a fresh appreciation of the physical world. It was the result of a synthesis of Saint Augustine's belief in the power of love and faith and Neoplatonism's belief in the power of visible order to bring the human soul closer to God.[41]

Thanks to Suger, Neoplatonism became virtually the property of the French monarchy and a lasting cultural legacy for France. All the most nearly perfect Gothic cathedrals until about 1230 would be built in France. Today, it is hard to find much trace of Suger's original Gothic church at Saint Denis. Only part of the ambulatory at the far eastern end, or *chevet*, still survives. If we want to see the Gothic in its full original Neoplatonic splendor, we need to travel southwest of Paris by about fifty miles, to the town of Chartres.

There had been a bishop of Chartres, and a basilica, since Carolingian times. However, in about 1100 a group of scholars set up shop in the wealthy market town in order to teach local boys Latin and theology, but also to examine the complex mysteries of Plato's one surviving text in the West, the *Timaeus*. When the old cathedral burned down in 1020, and then caught fire again in 1194, the so-called school of Chartres would have a direct hand in its reconstruction, including its plan and decorative sculptures.

The new Chartres was rebuilt with all the features of the Gothic style. There are the pointed arch windows and circular rose windows (including one donated by the queen of France, Blanche of Castile) and ribbed interior vaults. There is the soaring spire, almost 350 feet high, symbolizing the soul's aspiration to be one with God. As for Chartres's famous flying buttresses, the first ever constructed, they were built to relieve stress on the cathedral's walls, so that windows could be available for yards and yards of glittering stained glass.

At the same time, the scholars at Chartres also gave Suger's "style of continuous light" (they too were avid fans of the Pseudo-Dionysius) a new richness and complexity, thanks to their reading of the *Timaeus*. Later, some would claim they tried to replace theology with geometry.[42] All they were really doing was using Plato and the Gothic style to offer a new insight into the nature of the existing world—not just to prepare for union with God in the next.

The God of Plato's *Timaeus* is the Demiurge, the Architect of the Universe—in a profound sense, the Master Builder. Plato tells us He constructs the physical world from the five Platonic solids by incorporating the four physical elements—earth, air, fire, and water—in proportions to ratios such as 1:2:4:8 and 1:3:9:27. What holds Plato's world together is literally "geometrical proportion."[43] Thanks in large part to the school of Chartres, by 1150 the image of God as Geometer was appearing everywhere, in medieval manuscripts and in statuary. And the most important geometric form of all was the cube, the only figure with a 1:1:1:1 ratio, which every student of Plato or Pythagoras knew was the symbol of divine unity or Oneness.

Just such a cube forms the central crossing of Chartres Cathedral. This is no great surprise. However, tipping a cube at a forty-five-degree angle will also produce a hexagon. A hexagon is constructed out of six equilateral triangles, another figure charged with Pythagorean significance. It also formed the basic figure that medieval builders used to generate their system of continuous proportion, called *ad triangulum*.[44]

Too confusing and esoteric? Not to the builders and scholars at Chartres. A mind trained by the Pseudo-Dionysius was always open to mediating symbols. The very existence of such complexity would be ipso facto proof of the work of a divine hand: proof that the order of nature enjoys a geometric perfection that must bring us closer to God.

And so, as scholar John James recently proved, the builders of Chartres Cathedral expanded the cubic space of the central crossing into a hexagonal

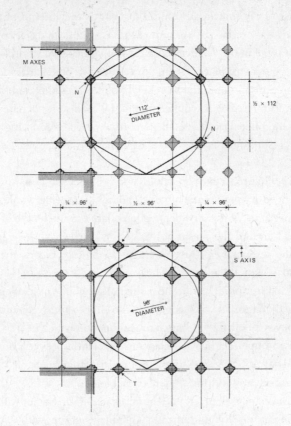

Chartres Cathedral interior, with hexagons forming the central crossing

matrix of intersecting triangles, using the vaults and pillars of the adjacent bays. These then grew out, triangle by triangle, to the next set of bays and then the next, all according to the *ad triangulum* formula and all in perfect proportion to one another.

The hexagons that result do much more than define the line of columns across the transepts of Chartres. When the diagonals of the overall scheme are linked up, the position of every column in the entire building suddenly emerges. Those positions then define the positions of the windows within the rectangle of the church interior; those in turn define the height of the windows and walls; and so on. The *ad triangulum* principle, like a hologram, runs through every individual subunit that forms the interior of the cathe-dral—a dynamic exercise in proportion that is almost an exact copy of how Plato's Demiurge in the *Timaeus* built the visible material world.[45]

Platonic geometry plays its part in the outside of Chartres as well. As scholar Otto Simson notes, the total height of the cathedral and the western portal, with its magnificent sculpted figures, follow a series of ratios based on the square and once again the equilateral triangle. (The resulting rectangles are called "golden rectangles," since all their sides are related as a ratio of 1:2:4:8.)[46]

Likewise, Chartres's famous statues of kings, queens, saints, and scholars are all arranged proportionately to one another and to the whole, since the elbow of each figure forms a golden section relative to the length of the entire figure.[47] And around the portal of the Virgin Mary in Majesty are arrayed figures of the seven Liberal Arts, including Geometry, clearly the queen of the arts just as Mary is the queen of heaven.

In the Chartres portal, as in the cathedral's school, these allegorical fig-ures summed up human knowledge from the Gothic and Neoplatonic points of view. They symbolize the Church's reconnection with the West's classical heritage as an imperfect but still necessary revelation of God's divine order. In the words of Abbot Suger's friend the mystic Hugh of Saint Victor, "All human learning can serve the student of theology."[48]

There is a female figure representing Dialectic or Logic, with Aristotle busily writing at his desk underneath. There is Rhetoric, with Cicero, simi-larly engaged; and Grammar, with a Roman author, Priscian, who taught countless medieval boys their lessons in Latin. In fact, one boy is shown dili-gently copying under Grammar's direction, while another boy mischievously pulls his classmate's hair.

Arithmetic is teamed with a portrait of Boethius, just as Euclid is teamed with Geometry and Ptolemy with Astronomy. Pythagoras, meanwhile, poses with the allegorical figure of Music, who chimes out her perfect melodies with a harp and a set of hanging bells.

So where is Plato? The answer is, nowhere and everywhere. At once the most famous but also the most unknown of Greek thinkers, he was trans-formed by the school of Chartres in the twelfth century into the great unify-ing intelligence of the High Middle Ages. The Gothic mind saw him as the one philosopher capable of drawing all human and divine knowledge into a harmonious whole.

Abelard had made Aristotle the greater intellectual polarizer. The anti-Aristotle backlash led by Saint Bernard put Saint Augustine in a similar polemical position. To scholars like William of St. Thierry, who knew both warring scholars, only Plato and Neoplatonism seemed to offer the possibility of an orderly synthesis, where mind, body, and spirit "have each been ordered and disposed in its rightful place," as William wrote, "and a man may begin perfectly to know himself."[49]

It was a brilliant prediction, but wrong. At the beginning of the twelfth century, one of the chancellors of the Chartres school had declared that scholars of his generation were "dwarfs standing on the shoulders of giants"— meaning antiquity. By the end of the century, the men at Chartres began to realize just how gigantic those Greek and Roman minds really were. A flood of new learning was sweeping over western Europe from strange and unexpected sources. A grand synthesis was indeed in the works.

Its pivotal figure, however, would turn out to be not Plato, but Aristotle.

Aristotle, from the western portal of Chartres Cathedral. Thanks to the Arabs, he was about to become the philosopher for the Middle Ages.

Fourteen

AT THE SUMMIT:
ARABS, ARISTOTLE, AND
SAINT THOMAS AQUINAS

Although grace is more efficacious than nature,
yet nature is more essential to man.
—St. Thomas Aquinas

Allah Akbar!

The high, thin cry to prayer split the early morning air of Toledo. God is Great! The first time the young man from Italy had heard it, the sound must have seemed like an audial illusion, like the cry of a bird that you briefly mistake for a human voice.

Then he heard it again. The ritual of Islam was asserting itself against the natural sluggishness of the city as it lay half-asleep in the postdawn chill. *Hayya ala salaah, hayya ala salaah.* Come to prayer, come to prayer, repeated twice. Then twice again: A *salaatu khairun min-an-naum.* Prayer is better than sleep.

Every morning, every year, the same exotic process had unfolded itself before his eyes. Muslim men in colorful caftans and women in silken chadors threading their way through the streets to Toledo's central mosque; Jews in their high-crowned hats emptying the bazaar to go to synagogues in the Jewish Quarter; Spanish Christians headed toward services at the cathedral. And as the young man wandered Toledo's narrow alleyways, he could see the massive towers of the former Moorish fortress, the Alcázar, looming over all of them. —

Ever since the legendary El Cid took back Toledo from the Moors in 1067, its citizens had lived under Christian rule. Castile's king Alfonso had upheld the customs of his Muslim predecessors and worked to preserve Toledo as a city in which Jews, Christians, and Muslims could live and work side by side. This tradition of official toleration and interreligious harmony, called *conviviencia*, had resulted in a rich cultural and commercial interface between East and West that made Toledo Europe's first cosmopolitan capital.

It was also what drew the young man from Cremona in Italy. He had been bored with his teachers and set out for Spain in search of something new. He had arrived in Toledo in 1140—the same year that Abbot Suger was hard at work on his church at Saint Denis and Peter Abelard was being condemned to the priory of Cluny, still grumbling and complaining about his fate.

None of this meant much to the young man from Cremona, whose name was Gerard. He had come to Toledo in search of certain secret books. Now, finally, they were within his grasp.

He knocked at the stout, iron-studded door of a large house. It opened to reveal a servant, who silently beckoned him in. Gerard stepped into the cool, dark courtyard. It had taken him months of searching to track down the books, and it would take many more months of study to be able to read them. He had met with nearly every important scholar in Toledo, Muslim, Christian, and Jew alike, including the great Jewish theologian Abraham ibn Ezra. It may have been Ibn Ezra himself who taught Gerard how to read Arabic, in order to unlock the secrets the books contained.[1]

For there, on the table, were the precious manuscripts. Gerard opened the first, its parchment pages turning crisply in his trembling fingers. The title page read: "On the Heavens." He opened to another page and read:

> The evidence of the senses further corroborates the fact that the earth is round. How else would eclipses of the moon show segments shaped as we see them? In eclipses the outline is always curved; and since it is the interposition of the earth that makes the eclipse, the

form of this line will be caused by the form of the earth's surface, which is therefore spherical. . . .

The text was in Arabic, but the author was a Greek.[2] The man's name, Gerard noted, was Aristotle. He read on.

"Again, our observations make it evident, not only that the earth is circular, but also that it is of no great size." Even as he read Aristotle's words with growing excitement, Gerard was reaching a decision that would have huge consequences for the history of civilization.

Gerard decided that his life's work would be to translate all these lost texts and make them available once again to the Christian West. He had everything he needed here in Toledo: lots of time, lots of help from other scholars, and lots of texts to translate. All around him were stacks of books in Arabic on mathematics, astronomy, astrology, physics, and philosophy by various Greek and Arabic authorities. They included many works by Aristotle that no one in western Europe had opened in six hundred years.

Gerard would also need an eager and grateful audience for his translations. Fortunately he had that already, thanks to that most disreputable event in medieval history, the Crusades.

Most people who have taken a high school history class know that the Crusades, that long-standing effort by medieval Christendom to retake Jerusalem from the Muslims, were a political and religious disaster. The First Crusade did manage for a brief time to capture the city in 1099, after which Crusaders went on a spree of murder and mayhem until the blood, an eyewitness said, splashed up to their horses' reins.[3] Then the city where Jesus had been crucified, buried, and resurrected was lost to the Muslims again in 1187 and Christian Europe never got it back. Saint Bernard of Clairvaux had given up everything in order to preach in favor of what became the Second Crusade to regain lost territory in the Holy Land. Its failure shattered Bernard's reputation (his friend Abbot Suger had silently disapproved) and probably hastened his death.

The Third Crusade (1187–92) is probably the most famous, since its participants included two great national heroes, King Richard the Lion-Hearted of England and King Philip Augustus of France. But it proved no more successful than the ones that preceded it or the ones that followed with steadily diminishing effort and enthusiasm, until the French king Louis IX, or Saint Louis, died a miserable death from fever and disease on the last one in 1270.

The Crusades were a notorious waste of lives and reputations. However, economically and culturally they were an undeniable success. They opened up Latin Christendom to trade with the more affluent world of Byzantine Greece and Islam. New goods and products entered ports and cities. A new affluent lifestyle caught the imagination of Europe's nobility. They began wearing silk gowns and perfume, eating food laced with Asian spices, playing chess and polo, listening to music played on lutes and rebecs, and reading new forms of poetry and literature—as well as taking regular baths, a custom borrowed from the East.[4]

The Crusades also triggered an interest in the intellectual riches of the same world. The original warriors against Islam were interested in loot, not books or information. But the crusading spirit opened the frontier between Islam and Christendom to a steady trickle of scholars who traveled to Sicily and southern Italy, Asia Minor, and above all Spain.[5]

Their names should be better known than they are. Adelard of Bath risked starvation and death to travel to Sicily and Antioch, where he translated the works of Euclid and various Arab writers on astronomy and mathematics and wrote his own treatise on the astrolabe. Around 1150, James of Venice put together the first Latin translation of Aristotle's *Metaphysics* and *On the Soul*.

Dominic Gundisalvi or Gonzalez was a converted Jew who rose to become archdeacon of Segovia. He translated key works by Islamic philosophers, on and about Aristotle. In fact, Gundisalvi respected the ancient Peripatetic master so much that he proposed that Aristotle should be the basis for a complete revision of Europe's intellectual culture—a sign of things to come.

The most dedicated and most important, however, was Gerard of Cremona. Until his death in 1187, he translated no fewer than eighty-seven books from the Arabic, including Ptolemy and Euclid, and a precious hoard of texts by Aristotle. These included the *Posterior Analytics*, which completed the West's knowledge of Aristotle's works on logic.* Gerard also turned out

---

*Aristotle's other texts on logic, including the *Prior Analytics* and his treatise on logical errors, *De Sophistici Elenchi*, found translators a little earlier. The mature Abelard was aware of this "New Logic" of Aristotle, in addition to the "Old Logic" via Boethius. By the thirteenth century, they were a standard part of the medieval curriculum.

Latin versions of Aristotle's pathbreaking scientific treatises, not only *On the Heavens* but the *Physics, On Generation and Corruption,* and *Meteorology,* as well as Arab commentaries on the *Metaphysics* and *On the Soul*—the key texts of Aristotle's entire philosophy. Aristotle's *Politics, Nicomachean Ethics,* and *Rhetoric* had to wait a few more years to find a suitable translator.

Plato was not entirely neglected. Latin versions of the *Phaedo* and the *Meno* saw the light of day for the first time in 1156.[6] But the rediscovery of Aristotle's lost works was far more momentous. It gave him an entirely new lease on intellectual life, as did the idea that man has an obligation to search out the truth about the natural realm as well as the divine one. From astronomy and medicine to biology, mathematics, and physics, the entire scientific framework of Western culture took on a fresh robust shape, thanks to Aristotle's intrepid translators and their Muslim hosts.

For the fact remains that without Arab help, western Europe would never have recovered its knowledge of Greek science and mathematics—still the foundations of modern science today—or understood how to interpret it.[7] Arabs supplied Europe with a new scientific vocabulary, with words like algebra, zero, cipher, almanac, and alchemy; and a new system of recording numbers that we still call Arabic numerals. Arab tables of astronomic observation and mathematical calculation, as well as manuals on medicine, introduced the Western mind to the great discoveries of the Greeks—as did the works of Arab commentators on Aristotle.

For almost a century the Christian and Islamic worldviews overlapped, especially their view of nature. The seam along that overlap was Aristotle, whom Arab scholars dubbed the Master of Those Who Know and whom Christian scholars would come to know as the Philosopher, as if there were no others of any lasting value.

No one contributed more to this new appreciation than Ibn Rushd, whom the Christian West knew under his Latinized name of Averroës. Born in Córdoba in Spain in 1126, Averroës was not only personal physician to the all-powerful caliph, but a devoted disciple of Aristotle. "Let us praise God," he wrote, "who set this man apart from all others in perfection, and made him approach very near to the highest dignity humanity can attain." The teaching of Aristotle was the supreme truth, Averroës affirmed, because Aristotle's mind was the final expression of the human mind.[8] If Aristotle said it, then it was true. Certainly no one had to look further than Aristotle's great catalog of works to understand how the world worked. Nor could anyone who read Aristotle's works doubt any longer that the world around us offers a direct path to understanding reality.

For medieval thinkers, this was an eye-opening revelation. Side by side with divine truth, Averroës was saying, lay another truth, that of the natural world. This insight earned Averroës an admiration equaled by no other living non-Christian. It is why Dante praises him in his *Divine Comedy* and why Raphael gives him a prominent place in his *School of Athens*. It is also why the rediscovered texts of Aristotle had so sweeping, even revolutionary, an impact on minds still conditioned by a Neoplatonized Christian theology.

For the first time, scholars saw in Aristotle a great thinker who did not see the world of the senses as an illusion or a vale of sin and suffering or even a complex forest of symbols. Here was a thinker, one undeniably of the highest order, who seemed unaware of the need for a Savior and Redeemer or of a better, more perfect world to come. Aristotle's universe is whole and complete. He is entirely comfortable with it.[9] To the surprise of everyone who read him, and to the delight of many, his empirical scientific approach offered a new series of vistas and a new series of tasks, more than a lifetime's work, and a truth, as Averroës said, as certain and complete as that of divine revelation.

If this made certain theologians in Spain and elsewhere more than a little nervous, Averroës hastened to offer reassurance. Not to worry, he said. There is no real conflict between reason and faith (Christian or Muslim, it didn't matter). He distinguished among three levels of reason and three ways of attaining the truth. The first was that of the uncultured ordinary person, whose mind is largely closed to reason and who can be moved either by emotional appeals like those outlined in Aristotle's *Rhetoric* or by arguments from authority. That person's desire for knowledge is easily satisfied by parables and injunctions from the Bible or the Koran.

Then there is the educated man, who wants something more than the literal Word of God. He turns to theology and dialectic; he seeks to reconcile his reason with his faith but ultimately is content if faith wins out. However, the third level of truth belongs to the true man of reason. Nothing short of Aristotle's logic with its system of necessary rational demonstration, and nothing short of Aristotle's science of substance and potentiality, will satisfy his quest for knowledge.[10]

This man of reason Averroës described was a startling proposition in the

Europe of Saint Bernard and Suger. Here was someone who doesn't worry if what he learns about how the world works (for example, the process of biological reproduction) conflicts with religious belief (for example, the Virgin Birth). He respects the truths of revelation and theology, but he also knows what he knows. No outside religious authority will ever shake his inner conviction or overturn any truth that pure reason has reached with the help of Aristotle.

For example, reason will never accept the idea that God could somehow create the universe on His own, literally making something out of nothing. Clearly, Aristotle's idea of an Unmoved Mover is much closer to the truth. Likewise, the notion of the soul's immortality violates every principle of science and nature. The soul is better understood as the potential intellect Aristotle described in *De Anima*. It comes into existence at birth, the moment we come into contact with the outside sensory world. However, at death it passes along to rejoin the universal intelligence, Averroës asserted, like a drop of water returning to the ocean.[11]

At this point, the Catholic Church had had enough. In 1210, it issued its first condemnation of Averroës and his disciples in the West; for good measure, it extended the ban to the works of Aristotle. It was already too late. Just fifteen years after the ban was issued, Aristotle's greatest medieval expositor was born. To his family and neighbors, he was Tommaso D'Aquino. To history, he is Saint Thomas Aquinas, the single greatest creative mind of the Middle Ages.

Aquinas was no Averroist. His life's work would be an implicit repudiation of Averroës's idea that reason has a higher claim to truth than faith does.[12] Instead, Thomas Aquinas's reading of Aristotle led him in a different direction. He would conclude that faith and reason are actually two sides of the same coin. His writings would try to persuade his age that men are part of both a divine *and* a human order, and both have valid standing in their lives.

Like Peter Abelard, Aquinas was born to a noble family. Unlike Abelard, though, he was no warrior. His father, Landulf, was a count and vassal of German emperor Frederick II Hohenstaufen. Frederick was the first Western ruler to take up the trappings of Europe's imperial past (he even commissioned a statue of himself in a Roman toga). He was also the first to assume an openly secular stance regarding political power. When the pope demanded that he launch a Crusade to retake Jerusalem, Frederick instead signed a treaty with Muslim rulers who then gave Christians free passage to the city.*

Frederick welcomed Jewish and Saracen scholars to his court and founded a university at Naples. It soon became a major conduit for Aristotle's works to enter the medieval mainstream because Frederick encouraged his scholars to ignore the earlier papal ban. Nowhere else, as scholar Josef Pieper notes, was it possible to encounter Aristotle so comprehensively as in the city of Naples.[13] And it was in Naples that young Thomas Aquinas first learned Aristotle's logic and first read Aristotle's *Metaphysics*.

When Thomas was five, Count Landulf of Aquino took a hard look at his youngest son. The boy was fat and slow moving, with fair, delicate skin. His father tried to imagine him wielding a sword or lance, or dodging a flying missile on the battlefield, and gave up. However, the famed monastery at Monte Cassino was nearby; it seemed the perfect place to put him. Besides, his father and mother had several other sons to carry on the warrior tradition. Tubby little Tommaso seemed destined to pass his life in cloistered obscurity.

Exactly why that did not happen, we'll never know. We do know that Tommaso was fourteen or fifteen when he left Monte Cassino to begin studying in Naples and that in 1244 he turned in his Benedictine robes to take up the rough, white habit of one of the new orders of preaching friars, the Dominicans. His father had died some months before. When his mother heard what Tommaso had done, she was furious. Having abandoned her son to the Benedictines for more than ten years, Countess Theodora suddenly took an almost hysterical interest in her son's future and how it might reflect on her.

The Benedictines were a long-established religious order; Monte Cassino was their founding house. The Dominicans, on the other hand, had been in existence for only twenty years. Members wandered Europe's cities under a strict vow of poverty, preaching and teaching. Like their Franciscan brothers, the Dominicans were "mendicants": literally, a begging order. The idea of her son begging food from strangers was more than Countess Theodora could stand.[14]

She convinced the pope to offer her son the abbacy of Monte Cassino itself. He would even be allowed to wear his Dominican habit. Thomas turned

---

*The outraged pope excommunicated him.

the pope down. Theodora then sent a letter to her two other sons in the emperor's entourage, which had pitched camp at Acquapendente in Tuscany.

But their brother was no longer in Naples. He had set off on foot with his teacher and three other Dominican friars for Paris, where he was slated to continue his studies in theology. They had stopped in a village in Tuscany and were quietly refreshing themselves at a fountain when they realized they were surrounded by armed men. It was the D'Aquino boys, clad in chain mail and wielding swords, and they were fighting mad. They roughly shoved aside the other friars, seized their brother, hoisted him up over a horse, and galloped off so that he could face their mother's righteous wrath.

By turns the countess begged, threatened, and cajoled her son to give up the Dominican order. He refused. There were tears and shouts and bellowed threats (at one point, one of his brothers seems to have smuggled in a prostitute to make him violate his oath of chastity). Thomas was unmoved. Instead, he instructed his sisters in sacred literature and converted his eldest sister to become a nun.[15] He calmly read the Bible and Aristotle's *Metaphysics* and waited.

His family kept Thomas Aquinas prisoner for nearly two years. Finally they released him and let him go on to Paris. He had won. Why did he do it? Certainly the incident reveals a calm determination underlying Aquinas's lethargic girth and soft-spoken modesty. On that point, he never changed. His scholarship reflects it. Let's hear what everyone else thinks first, he begins each chapter of his *Summa Theologica*. Then I'll get back to you with what I think. And he always does, quietly cutting through the static and chatter to get to the heart of the matter.

There may also be another reason Aquinas was so determined to become a Dominican. The order of friars was heavily involved in combating and converting heretics living outside the bounds of the Catholic Church. Aquinas's first important work was a manual for debating non-Christians, including Muslims. Still later, the pope would appoint him to head a commission to explore a reunion of the Catholic and Greek Orthodox Churches.[16]

Far more than Bernard or Abelard, Thomas Aquinas was aware of the larger world around him, and he was fascinated by it. By joining the Dominicans, he would see how the other half lived, people from a variety of lands and speaking a variety of languages: peasants, knights, merchants, parish priests and university students, prostitutes and day laborers.

At the end of his life, Aquinas wrote, "All I have written seems to me so much straw compared to all I have seen and what has been revealed to me."[17] Aristotle became his compass for figuring out how to understand that larger world.

Paris was a good place to begin.

When Aquinas arrived in that city in 1245, it was the busy commercial center of France as well as France's political capital. It also boasted the leading university in Europe. What Abelard had started little more than a century ago had exploded into a major center of teaching and learning. Paris had become a city of students.[18] In 1200, the French king granted the schools established there a royal charter with special privileges, which were later confirmed by the pope. For anyone in Europe interested in getting a bachelor's degree in the seven liberal arts, or a master's degree in medicine, canon law, or theology (the College of the Sorbonne was officially set up in 1257), Paris was the place to go.

Commercial cosmopolitan cities had always been receptive to Aristotle: Alexandria in the ancient world; Toledo in the early Middle Ages; later Georgian London and Edinburgh. In the 1200s, Aristotle's city was Paris. Despite the official papal ban, his works were everywhere. Aristotle's logic was accepted as the basis of nearly every university textbook. His other formerly lost works had an equal appeal. They explained every subject clearly and simply and logically, from meteors to the nature of time, in terms that were easy to memorize and in a sequence that was easy for teenage medieval minds to absorb.

The problem was getting unfettered access to them. All the papal ban had done was increase students' fascination with Aristotle.* The same was true of the works of Averroës. The Arab's biggest champion, Siger of Brabant, arrived at the university shortly after Aquinas's second stay in Paris as a teacher ended in 1259. Still, when he first arrived Aquinas could meet confirmed Averroists in every classroom and in every seminar.

They passionately believed that human beings had the right to learn everything they could about the natural world, including human nature, with-

---

*When Aquinas arrived in Paris, the University of Toulouse was circulating placards boasting of their Aristotle expertise. Come to Toulouse, they read; we've got here what's been forbidden to you in Paris.

out worrying about whether it contradicted Scripture or church doctrine. The "truths" of divine revelation might satisfy the curiosity of some, they alleged. The genuine intellectual, however, won't be satisfied until he gets to the bottom of those truths revealed by his own reason.

Aquinas was impressed by their arguments and acknowledged the validity of their passion. But he was put off by their air of certainty, not to mention their arrogance. Leave revealed religion to the mob, the hoi polloi, the Averroist says. Knowledge and wisdom really belong only to the privileged few who can see through the façade of simple faith but are discreet enough to say nothing about it. In this sense, Averroism will be the taproot of Enlightenment Deism and is summed up perfectly by Voltaire more than five centuries later: "I don't believe in God, but I hope my valet does so he won't steal my spoons."

Aquinas was unconvinced. The message of revealed religion contained in the Bible and church doctrine was meant for everyone, not just the rednecks among us. Likewise, every human being deserved to know the whole truth, not just a chosen elite. To fall for the notion of a "double truth" and argue there was one set of truths for reason and another for faith and never the two shall meet made nonsense of the idea of truth itself.[19]

There had to be a better way to reconcile the battle between reason and faith that Abelard and Bernard had started under the respective banners of Aristotle and Augustine. Thomas began to tease out clues from the lectures of his teacher Albertus Magnus, or Albert the Great.* From his chair as regent master, Albertus patiently led Aquinas page by page through Aristotle's major texts, including the *Metaphysics,* and wrote prodigious commentaries on them—thirty-eight volumes' worth in the modern edition. However, he was also deeply respectful of Saint Augustine and all those Church Fathers who had stressed the primacy of faith. His own theology was heavily influenced by Dionysius the Areopagite.[20] If the great Albert never felt it necessary to address any conflict between reason and faith, Aquinas concluded, perhaps there never really was one.

The problem was, Albert never made that lack of conflict explicit. For all

---

*Albert was a Dominican, like Aquinas. The other teaching order at Paris, the Franciscans, were devotees of Saint Augustine. Since they were not formally subject to the papal regulations of the university, the Dominicans were free to pursue the study of Aristotle—one reason their classes were always popular and why the conflicts between university authorities and the Dominicans became so bitter. Albert finally left Paris in 1248 for Cologne, and Aquinas went with him, returning only in 1252.

his staggering erudition, he was never tempted to join up the two great existing systems of wisdom in the Western world: the school of Aristotle and Greek
science and that of Plato and his Christian disciples, including Saint Augustine. That was the task Aquinas decided to undertake once he received his
license to teach at the University of Paris in 1256.

The work Aquinas did in the next sixteen years changed the face of Western Christianity *and* philosophy. He wrote commentaries on virtually everything Aristotle wrote; he wrote on the Book of Job, the Gospel of John, and
Paul's epistles; he wrote a seminal treatise on the nature of evil and another
on building aqueducts and on military siege operations.[21] Above all, he also
wrote the two works that would earn him the title of Universal Doctor of the
Catholic Church: the *Summa Contra Gentiles* and *Summa Theologica*.

These last two alone total a stupefying two million words. They are a
monumental fusion of learning and faith, and a reconciliation of ancient
philosophy and Christian theology, without parallel even in the works of
Saint Augustine. In fact, together they make Aquinas the one Christian
thinker whose system can stand beside those of Aristotle and Plato—in part
because it is a brilliant synthesis of the best of both thinkers.

What was more stunning is that both works were written by a man who
was still largely underestimated by his contemporaries. With his wide girth,
slow-moving manner, and soft-spoken, self-effacing style, Thomas Aquinas
had never looked like an intellectual superstar. His fellow students at Paris
had called him "that dumb ox from Sicily." Albert Magnus had overheard
them during a class and warned, "That dumb ox is going to surpass all of you,
and one day his bellowings are going to be heard around the world."[22]

Except that Thomas Aquinas never bellows. This becomes a problem for
modern readers. Anyone who picks up a copy of the *Summa Theologica*, or
even an editor's selection of choice bits, expecting to be dazzled and enthralled will quickly put it down again (as I did as a college student with the
original Latin edition).

Aquinas's prose style seems passionless and without personality—certainly when he is compared with Saint Augustine. In this, they reflect something Aquinas picked up from Aristotle's lost writings: the value of an
objectivity based on logic, which doesn't worry about one's own feelings or
preconceptions or the readers' but stays completely focused on a single question: "Is what I have just said true or not?"

In page after page of the *Summa*, Aquinas will calmly and tentatively assert a position. Then he looks around at all the counterpositions and objections. He examines whether they hold up under scrutiny; if not, he quietly refutes them and moves on to the next question. At one stroke, a Christian dialectic was born, more sophisticated than Abelard's and more all-embracing than Anselm's, because it stands on a reading of Aristotle's entire corpus.

The overriding issue for Aquinas is, "Is it true?" His Averroist colleague Siger of Brabant had asserted that if it was in Aristotle, then it *must* be true. Not necessarily, Aquinas says. He cites the Philosopher (as he calls Aristotle in both *Summas*) more often than any other non-Christian thinker. But he also finds powerful insights in Plato, in Saint Augustine, and in Dionysius the Areopagite.* Citations from the Bible always clinch the argument.

Aquinas's point is always that we humans are down here, while the ideas and celestial beings and the supreme eternal truths are all up there. Everything that Plato and Neoplatonists and Saint Augustine said were the most intelligible and true are also the most removed from our experience. Why? Maybe because the human mind tends to be dazzled and confused by too much divine wisdom.[23] Maybe that's why God decided to put us in the cave in the first place, Aquinas is hinting. He didn't want us overwhelmed by too much light at once.

Since we are human beings, then, we have to start with what we know in order to get our bearings. That means the Bible and divine revelation, of course. But it also means the realm of the senses, and here Aristotle points the way. "As Aristotle himself shows," Aquinas writes in the *Summa Contra Gentiles*, "man's ultimate happiness consists of seeking the knowledge of truth" through reason.[24] Then as we move forward, we discover that truths human and divine, the objects of reason and those of faith, actually reinforce each other. They don't form parallel tracks, as Averroës claimed. They ultimately converge: not just in God their Supreme Creator, but in ourselves as human beings.

Aquinas's God is not Aristotle's Prime Mover. He is a beneficent Creator and creative Architect, a composite figure from Scripture and Plato's *Timaeus*. However, Aquinas's God shares one important characteristic with Aristotle's Unmoved Mover: He is the ultimate source of all movement and change. "Whatever is done by nature must be traced back to God as its first

---

*Albert the Great had a strong interest in the Pseudo-Dionysius, which he passed on to his most famous pupil. Aquinas even did a commentary on the *Divine Names*, and the Dionysian idea of hierarchy would be very important in Aquinas's own thought.

cause."[25] In fact, we live in a world blessed by the very act of creation. Quoting Aristotle again, "Nature creates nothing in vain"—and neither does God.[26]

God's supreme reason dictates the structure of both the supernatural *and* the natural order, since both reflect His eternal purpose. Truths about the first are revealed to us in the form of divine law, which means Scripture. Truths about the second are revealed to us through our senses, by means of the laws of nature.

Lex naturalis, natural law, is a cornerstone of Aquinas's system and his most consequential contribution to Western thought. Natural law, he says, is apparent in the regular workings of nature, including the movements of the planets and in the growth and formation of living things; in the self-evident truths of mathematics and geometry; and in the logical workings of the human mind.

However, it takes reason to see them and recognize them *as* laws. Dogs and cows live their lives in accordance with the laws of nature, from birth to death. But they lack the power to wonder why or how. Human beings, on the other hand, do. "The natural law is nothing else than the rational creature's participation in the eternal law. . . . Human reason cannot have a full participation of the dictate of the divine reason," Aquinas writes, "but [only] according to its own mode, and imperfectly." That imperfect way of seeing, however, supplies us with enough common principles so that we can understand the phenomena around us and see how God's creatures divide into separate species and genus; notice how the planets are different from the stars; understand why murder is wrong and why justice is necessary in every human community; and recognize the place of each within the whole. In short, the laws of nature are the foundation of all our knowledge and conduct in the world.

Take natural law away, and we are helpless to do anything or find happiness, even with divine revelation at our elbow (just as some people never bother to open the Gideon Bibles in their hotel rooms). Take up the laws of nature and study them, and suddenly every aspect of existence is bathed with a new significance that eventually our reason traces back to God.

Aquinas fully endorsed Aristotle as our guide for grasping and analyzing those laws. Like Aristotle, Aquinas believed that to fully know something means understanding its essence; *that* in turn depends on discovering its purpose by observing its interactions with everything else. This applies to objects both man-made and made by nature. We learn that God has designed a horse for riding, for example, and a bird's wing for flying, and man's sexual organs for reproduction, just as the carpenter makes a chair for sitting.

This is a long way from our idea of science today. But for Aquinas, who was a theologian and not a scientist, the crucial point was that Aristotle had made substance and essence the point at which the material and the ideal meet. This includes man. Human beings cannot escape their corporeal nature, nor should they try. The isolated soul is not enough. It cannot actually exist except through something else, namely a material body. The human being is a soul *within* a body, the junction point of the two halves of divine creation, body and spirit. He is (in a true sense) the man in the middle.

Aquinas's vision of creation turned Aristotle's ordered nature into a Neoplatonist hierarchy in which "a wondrous linkage of beings" connects each and every creature to its Divine Creator. For Aquinas, every link in the chain marks a distinct advance toward divine perfection over the one just below.[27] As we run down the hierarchy from spirit to mind to matter, God is more perfect than the angels, and the angels are more perfect than human beings. Running up the same hierarchy, we perceive that the bee is more sentient than the flower; the bird is more sentient than the bee; the pig is more sentient than the bird; the dog is more sentient than the pig; and so on.

And in the middle is man, the highest and most rational of material beings but also the lowest of the spiritual beings, "the boundary line of things corporeal and incorporeal." Human beings occupy a crucial place in Aquinas's ordered nature. They are the one material being gifted with a soul. They are also the one spiritual being gifted with a mind, meaning an active intelligence ready to take on the challenges the material world offers.

To deny the power of our own reason is in effect throwing away one of God's greatest gifts. So would be refusing to take on the challenges life offers, from riding a horse and studying the planets to balancing a checkbook. Our goal must not be to retreat from the world. Aquinas the former monk left room for a life of renunciation and contemplation as an expression of divine grace and the highest faith. For everyone else, however, our goal must be to bring man's unique fusion of body, mind, and spirit to its highest perfection.

The Thomist vision is appealing, even inspiring. Aquinas's works are a landmark not only in medieval thinking, but also for the future. Being human means understanding the reality around us not because God commands us to, but because that is what our mind does as part of its nature. The Augustinian and the Neoplatonist mind passively contemplates the world and waits for a connection to a higher truth to be revealed. Aquinas saw the mind as Aristotle did, as actively analyzing that world in order to forge those connections for itself.

The Aristotelian and Thomist mind *works:* it doesn't just wait around to recover something hidden or something lost. This includes the laws governing nature as understood by science and the laws that govern our own behavior in terms of morality and ethics. By 1240, Aristotle's *Ethics* had finally found a translator not from Arabic but the original Greek; and Aquinas made heavy use of it.[28]

Just as Aquinas deployed Aristotle's science of substance to shed new light on the Christian doctrine of the Eucharist, so he used Aristotle's ethics to understand the nature of sin.* In order to commit murder or commit adultery, he concluded, we have to *intend* to commit that action. It must be an active choice made voluntarily, free from compulsion (someone is holding a gun to our head or our children hostage) and error (I didn't realize the woman I was having sex with was not my wife).

Although a good intention cannot redeem a bad action, like stealing from the rich to give to the poor, it can redeem an action's unintended consequences, as when the man defending his own life ends up killing his attacker.[29] For Aquinas as for Aristotle, human freedom boils down to the power to make choices. In the end, the morality of our actions must always be judged by the active will and the intentions behind them. It also implies the freedom to choose good over evil and the mental capacity to know the one from the other (which is why dogs and infants can't commit mortal sins).

From Aquinas's point of view, the pagan virtues outlined by Plato and Aristotle, and Christian virtues like charity and humility, are mutually reinforcing. Both reflect a knowledge of God's laws for men. The difference is merely that one was and is learned in the natural realm; the other is learned in the divine realm of God's Revealed Word.

In other chapters of his *Summa Theologica,* Aquinas demonstrates how the laws of nature could unlock the mysteries of why and how human beings

---

*This is his famous doctrine of transubstantiation, later adopted by the Church as official dogma. The bread and wine in the Eucharist remain what Aristotle would have called *accidents*, meaning in appearance only. Their actual Aristotelian *substance* has been transformed by the priest into the body and blood of Jesus Christ. This was a change unlike any other in nature, Aquinas added, and quite irreproducible in other circumstances—all of which seemed to prove its miraculous character.

built communities, how and why they framed laws, and how they interacted with one another in society. His analysis of the role of natural law in politics would set off a revolution that had huge consequences for the future.*

In all his works, however, Aquinas refused to simply recycle Aristotle, as the Averroists had. He pointed Aristotle in entirely new directions and raised him to a higher, more relevant level for the Western future. For Aristotle, it was man's nature to know things. For Aquinas, to know is to *be* in an existential sense; to know the world is to be part of the world ourselves. God has put us into the world for a purpose, His purpose. We need to use and understand that world to catch a glimpse of that purpose, and thus a glimpse of God Himself.

Through the study of natural law, Aquinas believed, science and philosophy could arrive at a theological truth through reason alone, namely the existence of God. "It was necessary for man's salvation," Aquinas wrote, "that there should be a knowledge revealed by God [by] the philosophical sciences [to be] investigated by human reason."[30]

Far from being a distraction from holy things, as St. Bernard had claimed, this earthly order is their complement. The fact that man has two aspects, the material and the spiritual, does not mean conflict or compromise: "Grace does not replace nature, it perfects nature." It's Aquinas's most famous aphorism, and it simply means we *can* merge the two halves of ourselves into a single higher whole—just as Thomas Aquinas had merged Aristotle and Christianity into a single system.

The *Summa* was unfinished at Aquinas's death in 1274, and the gaps show. For all his genius, his grasp of the physical sciences remained fairly primitive. Aquinas never used his analysis of natural law to shed new light or open new directions in biology or astronomy or physics. In the phrase of the great Thomist scholar Étienne Gilson, he did not have the heart for the task. Perhaps if he had, his followers could have helped to reconcile the Catholic Church with the major revolutions in scientific thinking that would come during and after the Reformation.

All the same, Aquinas had achieved what no one had before or since: a fusion of Platonized Christianity with Aristotle's science of man. It is one of the great achievements of Western civilization. But it didn't last. Even before Aquinas's death, the old opposition would reassert itself. He would be forced

*See chapter 20.

to leave the University of Paris and die in his former home of Naples while the intellectual battle raged around him.

Exactly three years later in 1277, on the third anniversary of his death, the teachings of Aquinas came under a formal ban along with those of Averroës and Aristotle. The clash between Aristotle and Plato was about to enter a new, more critical phase, as it passed beyond the cloisters and the universities. Its new battleground would be the field of politics, with the fate of the papacy and the Church itself hanging in the balance.

Fifteen

THE RAZOR'S EDGE

What can be explained on fewer principles is explained needlessly by more.

—William of Ockham, *Sum of All Logic*

From God and nature all mortals born free and not subject to anyone else have the power voluntarily to set a ruler over themselves.

—William of Ockham, *A Short Discourse on Tyrannical Government*

I walk into a pub in Ockham in Surrey, England, population 391—not many more than when Ockham's most famous son was born there in 1290. I order a pint of ale, leave a five-pound note on the bar, and go to use the toilet. When I come back, the barkeep has left me my change and my beer, poured into two half-pint glasses.

I look at him, and he says, "There's your pint, mate."

I reply, "I don't understand. *Why use two glasses when one will do?*"

I've just employed Ockham's razor, the most useful philosophical discovery of the fourteenth century. It's also one of the most important for the future of the Western mind. Ockham's razor has nothing to do with shaving, although its inventor, William of Ockham, did use it to slash to ribbons some of the Middle Ages' most cherished notions. In an age when manuscripts were made from dried lambskin or parchment, scribes used a straight-edge razor to scrape mistakes off the parchment surface. Ockham's razor is in effect a kind of eraser, to rub out the unnecessary duplication of ideas or principles or entities.

Why use two (or more) when one (or fewer) will do, is the principle that William of Ockham introduced into the medieval thought process. It grew out of his refinement of Aristotle's logic and set off a revolution not only in philosophy, but in politics and religion. Before he died, Ockham's razor would undercut the foundations of the medieval Church.

Ockham was an Englishman. In the 1200s, Paris had been the central battleground between the legacies of Aristotle and Plato. By 1300, the scene had shifted across the English Channel, to the University of Oxford.

In Paris, Franciscan friars had led the charge on behalf of a Neoplatonism inherited from Saint Bernard as well as Saint Augustine. They demanded that Aristotle be condemned anew in 1271, along with Averroës and Aquinas. They even managed to get Aquinas's religious order, the Dominicans, expelled from the university.[1]

At Oxford, by contrast, it was the Franciscans who were Aristotle's champions. Their leader was Robert Grosseteste, the first Englishman to read through and absorb all of Aristotle's writings in the original Greek.* This enabled him to make more accurate translations, including the first complete Latin edition of the *Nicomachean Ethics*. When Grosseteste died in 1253, he had turned Oxford into an Aristotelian stronghold. Two subsequent Franciscans would use Aristotle to push secular knowledge to new intellectual altitudes Thomas Aquinas never imagined.

The first was Roger Bacon. He was born around 1215, the same date as the Magna Carta. Many legends surround his life. One is that he discovered the secret of flight (not true, although he closely studied the mechanics of birds' wings). Another is that he invented gunpowder: also not true, although Bacon's writings do describe a mysterious explosive powder that had come from China and which he believed would increase its power if it were packed into a container.[2]

Bacon's real story was interesting enough. He was the most compulsively curious man of the Middle Ages, a kind of English-speaking Leonardo da

---

*Despite his Germanic name, Grosseteste was born in Suffolk around 1168 and studied at Paris as well as Oxford. When he returned home from Paris, he set up the first Franciscan school at Oxford in 1229.

Vinci who found every aspect of nature, from birds' wings and the manufacture of magnifying glasses to alchemical stoves and the planets, obsessively fascinating. He wanted to know everything about everything, including the history of the Bible. At one point he applied himself to studying Hebrew, Arabic, and Chaldean in order to unlock its hidden secrets of religion.[3]

Bacon wrote seminal works on astronomy, alchemy, geography, optics, mathematics, geometry, and the nature of language. He helped to reform the Gregorian calendar. He speculated about the possibility of using giant reflecting lenses to burn Saracen ships at sea and was arrested by the idea that Archimedes may have discovered the same thing.[4] He threw himself into studying anatomy and did a study of the human optic nerve and lens that is probably the most accurate piece of medical research of the entire Middle Ages.

Bacon's curiosity makes him sound amazingly modern, and in many ways he was. But his writings look back as much as they look forward, and the figure to whom he owes his greatest debt is without doubt Aristotle, whom he discovered through his admiration for Grosseteste.[5] Aristotle's works unlocked for Bacon a world of scientific investigation, above all a method of exploring the wonders of nature and understanding its underlying principles that sustained him until his death.

In some ways, Bacon also looked beyond Aristotle. First, he believed that no natural or physical science could get anywhere without a firm foundation in mathematics. He called it the "gate and key" to all science. He quoted Boethius in his support, thus anticipating Galileo three centuries later. Second, more than any previous medieval thinker, Bacon grasped the empirical aspect of Aristotle's thought: that knowledge ultimately comes to the knower via the senses, which supply the raw data that reason sorts and disentangles in order to arrive at the truth. "There are two modes of acquiring knowledge," he wrote, "namely by reasoning and experience. Reason draws a conclusion . . . but does not make it certain [but] the mind may rest on the intuition of truth when it discovers it by the path of experience." It's a sentence that might have been written by John Locke or even David Hume.[6]

His belief in the experimental method led him, despite his Franciscan vow of poverty, to raise huge sums to buy scientific instruments, alchemical equipment, and to collect unusual natural specimens—creating in effect Europe's first laboratory. Bacon could also be scathing about the complacent ignorance of his own day. He once declared that he wanted every Latin edition of Aristotle burned because the translations were so inadequate. Above all, he excoriated the failure of the Church and universities to embrace the wisdom of the past, including Greek science. "The whole clergy is given up to pride, luxury, and avarice," he writes at one point. "Their quarrels, their contentions, their vices are a scandal to laymen." In short, the English Franciscan managed to anticipate the spirit of the Reformation as well as the scientific revolution.[7]

Living as he did in the 1200s, Roger Bacon sometimes seems almost too good to be true. Still, it is worth noting that his magnum opus on how to reconcile Aristotle's observation of nature with traditional theology was written at the behest of a friend who also happened to be pope. Bacon never doubted that the greatest discoveries of the sciences and the arts would be impossible without the revelation of God. "All that which our intellect is able to understand and know is small," he writes, "compared with those things which in the beginning in its weakness it is bound to believe, such as the divine verities. . . . "

At its heart, Roger Bacon's vision of science owes a great deal to the Neoplatonist inheritance or even Saint Augustine. For Bacon, it was the inner light of reason that stirs our desire to unlock the mysteries of nature and art, including the divine light around us: one reason Bacon was so fascinated with the science of optics.[8]

Roger Bacon, then, was a powerful Janus figure. He looks forward to the age of Galileo and Descartes and empirical science but also back to the Pseudo-Dionysius with reason's divine illumination drawing man closer to God through the wonders of His creation. He hoped to bring about a complete reform of Christian education based on mathematics and science, a project that earned him an impossibly grandiose condemnation and papal house arrest, in 1277—oddly, the same year as the condemnation of Aquinas. Yet Bacon was clearly too oddball a figure to concern church authorities that he might one day lead a movement or cause them serious anxiety.

That cannot be said of William of Ockham. Born a few years before Bacon's death in 1294, he carried the Aristotelian legacy of the Oxford Franciscans into direct conflict with the Church's most powerful figure, the pope himself.

In retrospect, it seems bizarre that Ockham did not get himself into more trouble than he did. But the truth is that Ockhamism took hold of many of Europe's best universities in the later 1300s and 1400s. "Some would profess it," writes historian Étienne Gilson, "others would refute it, but nobody was allowed to ignore it."[9] The impact of his thinking would stretch far beyond the Middle Ages. Far more than Thomas Aquinas or even Bacon, Ockham is the true forerunner of the modern era.

He started his studies at Oxford around 1310. Ockham* quickly made a name for himself as a master of Aristotelian logic and for solving one of the most troubling problems the medieval philosopher faced, namely the question of universals.

What's in a name? Shakespeare asked later. What indeed, medieval scholars wanted to know. Is a name more meaningful, or is something more true, when we utter it about an entire class of objects and persons instead of a single individual in that class? "All men are mortal" and "Socrates is mortal" are both true; so are "All dogs have four feet" and "Rover has four feet." But while I can see and point to Socrates and Rover, who am I talking about when I mention "men" and "dogs"?

In other words, do universal terms like men and dogs and feet (or souls or saints) refer to something genuine and real? Or do they operate merely as terms of convenience when we want to talk about multiple dogs instead of just one?

Those medieval scholars steeped in Neoplatonism answered that universal terms or concepts do indeed refer to something real: the ideal Forms of which the individual instance is a material copy. To say "All men are mortal" *is* saying something different from saying that some individual man is mortal. A universal statement reveals a higher level of truth and knowledge, the Platonist affirms, than what we can know about individuals.

Others said no. Universals, they said, were merely collective names with no larger significance. Any name (*nomen* in Latin) is nothing more than an utterance of the voice; reality is confined to the realm of individual men and dogs about whom we speak and refer. Before he died, Peter Abelard had refined this so-called nominalist position slightly. He said universals did refer to something genuine, namely the shared resemblance between men and dogs that we see and name. "When we maintain that the likeness between things

---

*There is some dispute about exactly where he actually came from. There is also a village named Ockham in northern Lincolnshire; some claimed he hailed from there instead of the tiny hamlet in Surrey on the road to Portsmouth, between Wisley and Riply.

is not a thing," he wrote in his *Treatise on Logic* in 1140, "we must avoid it seeming as if we were treating them as having nothing in common." All men and all dogs do in fact have certain characteristics in common; it is that commonality, one could even say the Aristotelian essence of a thing, to which the universal name "man" and "dog" and "animal" referred.

This was the position on universals that Thomas Aquinas accepted (more or less), along with John Duns Scotus, the reigning Aristotelian at the time William of Ockham began his academic career. And it was this moderate realist position that Ockham proceeded to overturn, thus opening a new chapter in medieval thought and pushing the reliance on Aristotle in a radical new direction.

No, Ockham concluded, there is no common nature shared by individual dogs or men that we call by a common name. No universal exists outside the mind; everything that is real exists *only* as individuals. When I say, "All men are mortal," this is shorthand for saying, "Socrates is mortal," "Plato is mortal," and so on.

Universals are nothing more than signs to Ockham—useful shorthand. They mean nothing in themselves, but as signs they empower us to manipulate concepts and form general hypotheses in our mind, without bothering to refer to every individual who makes up the class, whether it's men or dogs or meteors or souls. In an important sense, the world we understand through reason is a *fiction* (at one point in his early writings, Ockham even uses the word). It is a mental construct that we have built up from the raw data supplied by our perception of those individual men and dogs and meteors that form the stuff of reality.

Ockham didn't use the term *fiction* to suggest that what we say about the world isn't true; just the opposite. Science deals with real life; and logic is the language of science. But we shouldn't mistake the logical gymnastics going on inside our heads for the reality going on outside. Science is about real things; logic, surprisingly perhaps, is not.[10] Ockham saw this discovery as a return to the genuine Aristotle, shorn of the Neoplatonic excrescences of previous scholars like Aquinas and Duns Scotus. Getting rid of the notion that classes of objects and persons have some meaningful existence outside the individuals who make it up will be liberating, Ockham said. It makes life, and truth, simpler.[11]

Ockham's famous "razor" principle extended the same principle to every branch of knowledge. If any idea or proposition is not required either as a matter of observation and demonstration *or* as a matter of religious faith, then scratch it out. Don't clutter our brains with unneeded baggage; and don't clutter our discussion about the world with them, either.

Ockham's razor cut to shreds everything that was left of Plato's Forms and Neoplatonism's metaphysics. For example, why assume that God must have created a World Soul in order to carry out the rest of creation, as Plotinus and Christian Neoplatonists always did? Why assume two Gods when one will do? Why assume a Great Chain of Being or a Celestial Hierarchy of divine emanations, if there is no direct evidence for them around us and we can talk about and understand the world without reference to either one? The same reasoning went for Thomas Aquinas's notion that everything has an essence, which the *Summa* says stands separate from existence and is nature's way of revealing the thing's divinely designed purpose. Cut out the essence talk, and suddenly we can discuss individuals as they appear before us, whole and complete.

Once Ockham's razor got started, in fact, not much was left standing. That included Averroës's "double truth."[12] We need only one truth, Ockham affirms, the one reason derives from our senses. Religious faith, including faith in God, is an entirely separate matter. Religion is a matter of belief and will, not of reason or logical truth. Ockham took it for granted that absolutely nothing could be *proved* about God in the light of reason, not even His existence.[13] At best, we get probable hints of His existence when we examine nature. Otherwise, nature is a closed book as far as theology and dogma are concerned.

Those are best left to the Church and those who control its doctrines, Ockham affirmed. As for the rest of us, let's get on with life: freed of the burden of trying to reconcile faith with reason, we can plunge into the world with a new optimism and gusto—but also with the sense that we have been left pretty much to ourselves.

This was a radical new position for the mind of the Middle Ages. The intimate connection between God and nature, and God and reason, had finally, decisively been severed.[14] The prospect seemed both exhilarating and nerve-racking. Ockham, however, was unworried. We'll let the Church worry about matters above, he told his followers. Let's concentrate on understanding the world down here. Accordingly, there was a sudden new burst of interest in natural philosophy and science in Europe's universities in the 1300s.

Then events forced Ockham to come out of his deliberate detachment into the open. He was forced to choose sides in the biggest battle to sweep through the Church until the Reformation—and in so doing opened a new chapter in Western political thinking.

In 1305—the same year the English captured and executed the Scottish warrior William Wallace, and the same year the French king Philip IV arrested the Knights Templar on charges of heresy—a new pope was elected, a Frenchman as it turned out, who took the name Clement V. His most urgent task was to clean up the mess left by an ugly two-decade conflict between his predecessor and the king of France over taxation of church revenues, the same king who had overthrown the Templars. That battle had already left one pope dead and Philip IV and his chief minister excommunicated. The battle was not going to be as easy to resolve, however, as Clement and his advisers liked to pretend.

"The Lord says in John that there is one sheepfold and one shepherd. . . . Therefore there is one body and one head of this one and only church, namely Christ and Christ's vicar, Peter and Peter's successor." Pope Boniface VIII had written this three years earlier in 1302, and it was that claim of papal sovereignty over Christendom that was the source of all the trouble.

Ever since the emperor Constantine had invested dominion over the Church in the bishop of Rome,* successive popes had borrowed his Neoplatonist vocabulary of imperial authority to describe their own. The Catholic Church saw itself as a Platonic copy of the true Universal Church, the Body of Christ. And just as the Body of Christ has only one head, went the argument, so also must Christian society. God had indeed conferred the image of His own fullness of power (*plenitudo potestatis*) on his deputy or "vicar," just as Eusebius and his colleagues had proclaimed: except that in this case the true *vicarius Christi* was the pope.

When the last emperor disappeared from the West in 476, the bishop of Rome's claim to that fullness of power seemed even stronger.[15] On a chilly Christmas morning in 800, he was able to crown Charlemagne Holy Roman Emperor as if the empire were his to give, and no one questioned it—least of all Charlemagne. Indeed, any emperor or king who dared to challenge that

*Or so it was believed; the Vatican had documents to prove he had. No one guessed in 1302–05 that the so-called Donation of Constantine was a forgery.

papal sovereignty ran the risk of excommunication or a papal interdict suspending the sacraments within his territories and subjects. As the emperor Henry IV of Germany discovered in the 1100s and King John of England in the 1200s, getting out from under the cloud of papal disapproval could be a costly business—not only in time and money but in civil war. Still, as time went on and Europe's secular authorities became more powerful, the claim that all final authority in Christian society belonged to the successors of Saint Peter began to grate. So when King Philip IV of France and Pope Boniface locked crowns over the question of who controlled the revenues of France's churches, the king or the pope, far more was at stake than just money. Philip considered Boniface's assertion of his authority an unwarranted intrusion on his own as God-bestowed ruler of his kingdom, and he said so.

Boniface struck back with the most far-reaching declaration of papal sovereignty that anyone, even the great popes of the Dark Ages, had ever conceived. It came in a papal bull entitled *Unam Sanctam* or One Holy Realm, which stated that God had decreed that the world be ruled by two swords, one of temporal power and the other of spiritual power. The first was relegated to kings and other temporal rulers; the other belonged to the supreme pontiff and his priests.

Boniface had no doubt about which was more important. "One sword ought to be under the other," he proclaimed, "and the temporal power under the spiritual power." He even stated that as spiritual intermediary, the lowliest parish priest was a higher power than the greatest king or emperor, and he quoted the Pseudo-Dionysius to that effect.[16]

King Philip IV did not appreciate being relegated to the lower rungs of a pope-dominated Great Chain of Being. He also had a weapon the pope did not: an army. And so in 1303 he sent troops to the papal retreat at Agnani to arrest Boniface and bring him back to France for trial. Outraged and mortified, the elderly pope died on the way. Philip ignored the ensuing uproar; in his mind he had won his fight, and now he intended to make sure something like it never happened again.

Through a combination of arguments and threats, he persuaded Boniface's successor, Clement V, to move the entire papal government to the town of Avignon in France—ostensibly for the pope's protection but in reality so he could keep Christendom's supreme pontiff under his thumb. Clement reluctantly agreed, and so began what Italians called (understandably) the Babylonian Captivity and historians the Avignon papacy. For sixty-nine years

Des fanctes Cermonies.

Coronation of an emperor by a pope, from a fifteenth-century manuscript. This gesture
of divine benediction turned out to be a two-edged sword.

Avignon—a city of ancient walls and bridges—was home to the papal curia
and Holy See, while the Vatican sat vacant. In 1324, Avignon also became
William of Ockham's home, when he was summoned to teach philosophy
there at the local Franciscan school.

For four years Ockham dutifully conducted classes and worked on his
logical studies within earshot of the papal court. Then one day, the head of
the Franciscan order, Michael of Cesena, came to town with a problem.
Pope John XXII (the elderly Clement had died in 1314) had ordered Cesena
to Avignon to defend himself against charges of heresy, specifically the claim
that the Franciscan friars' vow of poverty had followed the example not only

of Saint Francis himself, but of Jesus Christ and the apostles, including Saint Peter.

Cesena asserted that it was perfectly orthodox to teach that Jesus and the apostles owned nothing as their own. So why should his successors not do the same? The pope, for reasons obvious to any visitor to Rome or the sumptuous papal palace at Avignon, thought this a dangerous heresy and innovation. Cesena wanted to know, what did Brother William think? Ockham promised to look into the matter and get back to him.

When he returned with his answer, he stunned both the pope and Cesena. There was no doubt, Ockham concluded, that the doctrine of apostolic poverty was sound. To Ockham, this was not a matter just of theology and belief, that realm "up there" in which the man of science avoids involving himself. This was a matter of empirical fact, confirmed by Scripture and other church sources. Therefore, Ockham explained, by daring to impose papal authority over a matter outside his jurisdiction, namely a matter of provable fact, it was Pope John XXII who was the *real* heretic, not Michael of Cesena or his fellow Franciscans.

Cesena was delighted. Then his smile vanished. It was all too easy to imagine the pope's reaction when news of Ockham's opinion leaked out— and it would leak out in a small, self-absorbed world like papal Avignon. Shakespeare's phrase about discretion being the better part of valor hadn't been invented yet, but Cesena managed to persuade Ockham of the importance of the concept. That night, on May 26, 1328, Ockham, Cesena, and another Franciscan companion slipped out of their rooms, mounted horses, and lit out of Avignon for the border.

The trio did not stop until they crossed into Bavaria, where the Holy Roman Emperor Ludwig IV was engaged in his own dispute with the pope. They met in Munich, where according to legend William of Ockham said to the emperor, "Defend me with your sword, and I will defend you with my pen." Ludwig accepted the offer. For the rest of his life, William of Ockham would devote himself to defending not only the emperor's autonomy but every other secular ruler's from the presumptions of Saint Peter's successors.[17] He found an eager audience.

Ludwig had already assembled a team of experts on ancient Roman law to help him assert his rights against the pope, including a shrewd Italian ex-doctor named Marsilius of Padua. Marsilius was working on a treatise called *Defensor Pacis* (Defender of the Peace), which was redrawing the conceptual boundaries between secular and sacred power, which had barely budged since the era of Constantine. But with his usual incisive skill, Ockham cut to the heart of the matter with a simple but significant question: Why does the papacy exist in the first place?

The answer came to him from reading Aristotle's *Politics*, where Aristotle asserts that a ruler, *any* ruler, must promote and defend the welfare of all those subject to his rule. Clearly the same obligation applied to the pope. This was why Christ had told Saint Peter, "Feed my sheep" (John 21:17). As shepherd of Christ's flock, Ockham wrote in late 1339, the pope "has authority from God only for preserving, not for destroying" the Catholic Church and faith.[18]

Therefore, if a particular pope proved unable to do his job; if his actions or behavior brought the Church into danger or disrepute, as Pope John XXII's clearly had—and Pope Benedict's before him—then, Ockham concluded, the Church could dictate that he must go and have someone else take his place. By its nature as a community (the term he used was *congregatio*), the Catholic Church retained the power to "judge and depose" a pope, even against his will or express command.[19]

Pope John XXII, of course, had read "Feed my sheep" very differently. Like Boniface, he saw it as enshrining papal authority over the sheep of secular society, including its secular rulers. So William of Ockham proceeded to take his famous razor to Boniface's arguments.

The pope had no such plenitude of power, Ockham replied; the faithful are neither sheep nor slaves. Nor are there *two* swords, as Boniface had claimed. There is only one, the one that kings and magistrates use to govern and protect their subjects. In fact, Christ had specifically forbidden his apostles from exercising the same kind of authority over the faithful that kings exercised over subjects (Matthew 20:25–27).[20]

By claiming broad authority, as Boniface had done, popes had in effect turned their office into an illegitimate enterprise. What could the congregation of the faithful (*congregatio fidelium*) do about it? To Ockham, the answer was clear. Because it exists in the temporal realm, the rules of that realm as described by Aristotle must apply. If those appointed to head the Church fail to do their job, then the members of the *congregatio* have the power to choose a new one—just as they have the power to invest every ruler with his authority over them.

"To understand this it must first be known that the power of making human laws and rights was first and principally in the people," Ockham wrote in 1328, "and hence the people transferred the power of making the law to the emperor," or whomever else they choose to exercise authority over them.[21] All mortals who are born free have the power voluntarily to put a ruler over themselves, including the Church and the pope. *But the final power remained with the people.* So having put the pope in office, the people were now free to end "his raging tyranny over the faithful" and push him out.[22]

Not surprisingly, Ockham's writings earned him an excommunication. But since he was living under the protection of an emperor who was himself excommunicated, the sentence did not affect him much.* At the same time, the more Europe's secular rulers looked at Ockham's arguments, including the emperor Ludwig, the more compelling they seemed—at least on the question of the pope's authority over them. The emperor Ludwig put this to the test in 1328 when he traveled to Rome for his coronation and announced he was deposing Pope John XXII, residing in Avignon. Instead, Ludwig designated an elderly city father as Pope Nicholas V and proudly had himself crowned Holy Roman Emperor.

It was a daring move, but largely a bluff. Ludwig and Pope John XXII managed to patch up their differences, and the "papacy" of Nicholas V was over almost as soon as it began. However, the deeper issues raised by Ockham's *A Short Discourse on Tyrannical Government* remained. A new battle line had been drawn between the heirs of Aristotle and the heirs of Plato, this time over the power of the papacy. All that was needed was an excuse to sound the charge.

It came in the early spring of 1378. The Church's cardinals assembled in Rome for the first time in three-quarters of a century, to elect a new pope. The last, a Frenchman, had died at Avignon. The cardinals who met were bitterly divided between Frenchmen, who took pride in having the Holy See on French soil, and Italians, who did not.

The mood in the Eternal City was ugly. Chanting crowds had gathered outside the Church of Saint John Lateran, where the cardinals were meeting. Over and over the mob shouted: "Choose a Roman! Choose a Roman!" At one point, exasperated by the delays and fearful that yet another Frenchman would be chosen as supreme pontiff, the crowd broke through the church's

---

*It was officially rescinded by an Avignon pope, Innocent IV, in 1359.

great bronze doors and charged into the conclave chamber. The terrified cardinals hastily proclaimed that they had indeed chosen a Roman and adjourned to escape the mob's wrath. *

Over the summer, the disgruntled French cardinals met again in Avignon. There they proclaimed that their vote for Pope Urban VI had been coerced and was therefore illegal. On September 20 they chose their own pope, a Frenchman who took the name Clement VII.† The Great Schism was on.

Europe had two popes, each claiming his share of church tithes and revenues; each claiming the power of appointment to church offices; each insisting that Catholics treat him as sole supreme pontiff. Two popes, in other words, when one would do. To many, that sounded like a problem for the Invincible Doctor himself, William of Ockham. Unfortunately, he had died in 1348, when the Black Death swept across Germany. However, his Ockhamist followers were free to bring up his solution to papal tyranny as a way to solve the problem of the Great Schism—namely, a general church council.

A church council was hardly a novelty. The emperor Constantine had summoned the first back in 325 at Nicaea. For centuries, however, it was the supreme pontiff who called church councils into existence and ordered them to carry out the papal agenda, as part of his "fullness of power" over the Church. Certainly no bishop or abbot or professor of theology who attended one had ever thought of himself as an elected representative of the faithful, let alone as empowered to depose a pope if he felt so inclined.

Yet that was exactly what William of Ockham claimed they were empowered to do. Council members were ex officio intermediaries between the faithful and the pope, acting on behalf of the body of the Church to protect it from harm. This was why if a pope was a notorious heretic, "a general council can be summoned without the authority of the pope to judge and depose" him, Ockham had said.[23]

In the turmoil of the Great Schism, Ockham's disciples took this a step further. Since the Church is "greater than the Pope," wrote Jean Gerson, chancellor of the University of Paris, this meant the power to make decisions on the Church's behalf "remains at all times within the body of the Church" or anyone it delegated to act in its name, including a church council.

---

*They had lied. They did choose an Italian, however, the archbishop of Bari, who took the name Urban VI.
†Not to be confused with a late Medici pope, Clement VII (1523–34).

Therefore, "a General Council can be summoned without a pope," Gerson declared, since its powers and its members come directly from the *congregatio fidelium*, or the people themselves—a power the people never relinquish as long as they exist and which no pontiff, no matter how exalted, can take away from them.

It was a sweeping and revolutionary concept. In 1378, medieval Europe had more than its share of what we call representative institutions, the most famous being England's Parliament. These were all, however, outgrowths of feudal society and seen as articulations of its hierarchy and separate functions. No one had spoken of these bodies as somehow embodying the will of the people. For the first time, Europeans had a clear notion of a body of representatives chosen to act for the *entire* community, including the power to depose a ruler and replace him with another.

After much negotiation and debate, in March 1409 a general council met in Pisa to resolve the schism according to the new formula. The members were not elected by any democratic means we would recognize. Most were chosen outright by the Holy Roman Emperor and other crowned heads. Still, the church council at Pisa did have the power to make all decisions by a simple majority vote.[24] After it voted to depose the two popes in Rome and Avignon and declare the papacy vacant, it appointed Pope Alexander V to fill the post. When the delegates went home, it looked as though the Catholic Church had become Europe's first constitutional monarchy.

However, the two popes in Avignon and Rome refused to be deposed. So instead of two popes, the Pisa council had now given Europe three. The arguments and bickering continued, and what was now called "the conciliarist movement" fell apart almost as quickly as it had started. The kings of France and England, and the Holy Roman Emperor, struck their own private deals with the quarreling popes, promising to reinforce papal authority in exchange for control over their own national churches. When the next church council met at Constance in 1414, it resolved the schism by affirming rather than denying the pope's absolute sovereignty over his Church. The heretic Jan Hus, whose religious views were a kind of theological outgrowth of conciliarism, was brought to Constance and burned at the stake.

Europe returned to a single pope as well as the idea of the successor to Saint Peter as supreme head of the Church. Today it is popes who summon and dismiss church councils, not the other way around. Still, for a few crucial years a weak and divided Catholic Church came very close to being rebuilt along the principles of Aristotle's *Politics*, thanks to Ockham and his disciples. Later, their arguments offered powerful ammunition to religious reformers during the Reformation.[25]

Even more ironical, the notions of Ockham, Gerson, and Marsilius of Padua about the importance of popular consent and elected bodies acting for the people would boomerang back at the very same crowned heads who had used them to humble the Holy See. Ockham himself had said that protecting the public interest was the primary function of any government, not just the Catholic Church. If the pope's powers were granted only as a matter of convenience, not as a permanent handover of sovereignty, then the same principle applied by analogy to lay rulers. In 1518, Ockham's admirer Jacques Almain would write, "*All* sovereignty, lay as well as ecclesiastical, is instituted for the benefit not of the ruler but of the people." The power to decide what that benefit is ultimately belongs to the people themselves. For a "free people is not subjected to anyone," Almain would affirm, nor can anyone take away that fundamental freedom.[26]

A century after Pisa, the monarchies that had used the arguments of Ockham and the conciliarists to beat the Catholic Church into submission would end up having the very same arguments used against *them*. A full-fledged theory of popular sovereignty broke surface for the first time in the sixteenth century in the writings of Almain and his colleague John Mair and then more explosively during the Reformation. It resurfaced again in the seventeenth century in authors like John Locke.

Thus over time, the idea slowly took root that "governments are instituted among men deriving their just powers from the consent of the governed." However, its advocates argued, "whenever any form of government becomes destructive of those ends, it is the right of the people to alter or abolish it" through their representatives "and institute new government," organizing it as they see fit to provide for their safety and happiness.

If these words have a familiar sound, it is because they are not from Ockham or Gerson, but from Thomas Jefferson. They come from the most influential summary of medieval conciliarist doctrine in its secular form: the American Declaration of Independence.[27]

Even with the eclipse of conciliarism, the fact remained that by 1400, Aristotle reigned supreme in Europe's universities and its intellectual life. Plato and the great exponents of Neoplatonism were still treated with enormous respect, especially Saint Augustine and Saint Bernard. University schoolmen would read Aristotle's *Metaphysics* or *On Interpretation* inside buildings built in an international Gothic style like Merton College at Oxford, the stone-and-stained-glass tribute to the theology of light.

All the same, "only Aristotle," wrote Roger Bacon, "together with his followers, has been called The Philosopher in the judgment of all wise men." Aristotle was the figure who dominated every part of the university curriculum, from Salerno and Toledo to Paris and Oxford and Louvain, from the seven liberal arts to medicine, law, and especially theology. Aristotle was, in the Arab phrase made famous by the poet Dante, "the Master of Those Who Know."

He was also the supreme teacher of all those who wanted to know. The standard way to learn any subject was first to read Aristotle's own works on it line by line from cover to cover, then pore over the commentaries on the work by Boethius, Duns Scotus, Peter Lombard, and Thomas Aquinas (whose works were rehabilitated when he was canonized in 1323). Finally, the student would write up his own series of *quaestiones*, or logical debating points, that seemed to arise from the text, and which were themselves reflections on past scholars' debates on Aristotle.[28]

All this not only prepared the student for attaining his own academic degree, it also prepared him for passing down that same knowledge and the same commentaries to the next generation of students. Aristotle may have been dull to read, but he was easy to memorize. The same was true of his equally dull commentators. In this way, the insights of Duns Scotus and Porphyry and Averroës and many lesser minds were preserved alongside Aristotle's own writings, as pillars of an unchallengeable intellectual tradition.*

By 1400, the authority of Aristotle closed virtually every argument. Once a student learned his view on a subject, whether it was a fine point in logic or the number of planets or the functions of body organs, there was no point in going any further. Someone wanting to know how many udders a cow had would be pointed to the relevant passage in Aristotle instead of being sent out to a field to count for himself.

Aristotle had become so indispensable to the life of the European mind

---

*Peter Lombard's *Sentences*, written in 1148–51, remained the standard textbook on theology at the Sorbonne until the end of the seventeenth century.

that it seemed impossible he could ever be yanked out. However, what the medieval mind gained in certainty, it gave up in terms of curiosity and innovation. The study of nature was reduced to a science of final causes, and the last word on that subject, as on all subjects, was Aristotle, now dead for one thousand years. Imagination and creativity fled. The Aristotelian empirical spirit of Ockham and Roger Bacon was replaced by the dead letter of Aristotle himself. By the end of the Middle Ages, it had hardened into an arid virtuosity without passion or piety or joy. When Adam Smith arrived at Oxford in the 1740s, he was stunned to discover that students were using the same textbooks that William of Ockham had known four centuries before.

Two spheres of late medieval life, and two spheres only, managed to escape Aristotle's dry encyclopedic grasp. The first was the papacy in Rome. The defeat of conciliarism meant that popes could still speak of their absolute power, or *plenitudo potestatis*, in Neoplatonic terms, as an emanation from a celestial hierarchy giving them unquestioned sway over the community of the faithful. Even under the Borgias and the Medici, when the papal curia sank to new lows of corruption, no one dared to question the spiritual vision embodied in the Holy See. It was an intellectual environment in which, for all its hypocrisies and limitations, the soaring imagination of a Michelangelo and a Raphael could suddenly catch fire.

The other place was the mystical tradition of Christian Neoplatonism. Driven from the universities, it found refuge in a totally unexpected place: the homes and hearts of Europe's working families.

C. Amberger, *A Patrician Lady:* the new face of Neoplatonist piety

Sixteen

ARISTOTLE, MACHIAVELLI, AND THE PARADOXES OF LIBERTY

The Florentine people thought there could never be a life for them without liberty.

—Leonardo Bruni, 1403

The fact is that a man who wants to act virtuously in every way necessarily comes to grief among so many who are not virtuous.

—Niccolò Machiavelli, 1513

We see their faces in the paintings of the Flemish masters Jan van Eyck, Hugo van der Goes, and Rogier van der Weyden. Sober, intelligent, and pious faces: the faces of merchants, shopkeepers, minor nobles, and sturdy city fathers—and city mothers. They are the faces of the *devotio moderna*.*

Starting in the early 1300s, Europe's Low Countries—today's Belgium, Netherlands, and northern Germany—became the epicenter of a lay religious movement that eventually swept as far south as Italy. Newly enriched by the rebirth of trade and industry in their corner of Europe, every port and

---

*"Modern devotion," as distinct from a pro forma sacraments-based Christian worship. The term was coined by a leader of the group Brethren of the Common Life, *devotio moderna*'s most famous offshoot.

market town saw the same unprecedented explosion of private piety, even religious mysticism. The most fervent advocates and most popular authors were clerics like the German mystic Meister Eckhart (1260–1327). But its "silent majority" were laypeople, both men and women. They were the hardworking beneficiaries of Europe's reviving commercial prosperity, and they used their affluence and social networks to build churches, found schools for boys and girls, and organize little reading groups in their homes—because with commerce and industry had come literacy for Europe's new urban middle class.

What did they read? Works of personal devotion and religious mysticism mostly, the majority fewer than a hundred pages. But almost all carried a strong Neoplatonist message. They read Eckhart, for example, and learned how the soul passionately seeks reunion with God. They read the anonymous mystical tract *The Cloud of Unknowing*. And they read Thomas à Kempis (1380–1471) and his little pamphlet *The Imitation of Christ*, the unexpected bestseller of the late Middle Ages that spelled out how to live day by day the "life in Christ" Origen had spoken of centuries earlier.

The burghers of Ghent, Bruges, Beauvais, Nürnberg, and Pisa were learning that religion was about something more than rites and rituals. As Saint Bernard and his followers had taught, it rested on an inner spiritual disposition based on the love of God and the heart's most ardent affections. People also learned that mystical union with Him belonged not just to an elite but was the normal aspiration for every soul. Well before the printing press had appeared, they understood that Holy Scripture should be the main source of meditation and inspiration for all Christians.[1]

For the most part, these were quiet unassuming men and women. They went to work in their shops and counting houses, raised their children to be good Catholics, and gave generously to their local parish. If some made fortunes, they never dreamed of rising above their station or challenging existing authority. All they asked was to be left alone to pray and read their devotional tracts and follow the orthodoxies of the Church.

Yet they also could not forget the devastating critique of the papacy and the church hierarchy unleashed in the previous century. That critique would surface in the works of the *devotio moderna*'s most sophisticated offspring, Erasmus of Rotterdam.[2] It would reach critical mass in 1517, when the storm over papal indulgences forced these devoted and sober citizens to realize that the Church was either too timid or too arrogant to change, or both. The resulting explosion would be the Reformation. It would knock the schoolmen's Aristotle off his throne and open a new era for the European mind.

Until then, however, Aristotle had one vital legacy to leave.

By a strange turn of events, Italy's cities had been left largely to govern themselves since the Dark Ages. No great barbarian chieftain or king had managed to gain control over them, as Clovis and the Franks had in Gaul, although several had tried. Instead, merchants in these towns had formed self-governing communes to protect their wealth from marauders large and small and to secure their farms and lands. Florence, Venice, Bologna, Padua, Pisa, Genoa, and the rest had enjoyed virtual sovereignty over their territories, in defiance of both the pope in Rome and the Holy Roman Emperor.

The coming of the Crusades had made them rich as well as independent, and made each city envious of its equally affluent neighbors. The 1200s saw fierce wars for hegemony, as when Genoa challenged Venice for control of the eastern Mediterranean and Florence crushed Pisa in battle in 1265. Not since the days of Athens and Sparta had Europe seen an era of violent civic pride like the one that covered the Italian peninsula in the age of Dante and Marco Polo.

But then the trend changed. The days of affluence and confidence ebbed away. The coming of the Black Death in 1348, which killed off at least one-third of Italy's population, was the coup de grâce. The wars became more desperate and the mercenary captain or *condottiere*, who led a city's army to plunder its neighbors, more necessary. In one city after another, economic depression triggered social unrest and polarized communal politics. Self-government gave way to government by a single individual—the *condottiere*, who turned his success on the battlefield into absolute power, sometimes even a reign of terror, over the local citizenry. By the time of the Great Schism, Italy had descended back into gangster politics, as in the days of Caesar and Pompey.

Milan was a classic case. Since the early 1300s the Visconti family had ruled the city like Mafia dons murdering their rivals and terrorizing opponents into submission. The most ruthless, and the most ambitious, of the Visconti was Gian Galeazzo. In 1385, he overthrew and murdered his uncle Bernarbò Visconti. Five years later, he decided to transform his autocratic power over the city of Milan into autocratic control of all of northern Italy.

In swift succession his army took over the major cities of the Po River valley: Verona, Vicenza, and Padua. He paid one hundred thousand florins to the emperor for the title Duke of Milan—the first step to becoming recognized as king of Italy. For the first time since the Caesars, the boot-shaped peninsula was about to submit to the rule of a single individual: one more powerful, and more ruthless, than any pope or previous feudal figure.

The one city that stood in Visconti's way was Florence. By 1395 it was, with the exception of Venice, the last self-governing republic in Italy. The Florentines cherished their tradition of self-government. The city's *gonfaloniere*, or mayor, its Council of Ten, and its various popular assemblies still kept the old communal ideal alive. And despite a long century of troubles, Florence was also still relatively rich. It had a strong army and a commanding presence in Tuscany. As long as Florence retained its liberty, Visconti's plans could go nowhere.

The Visconti coat of arms was a serpent eating a man. In the same way (or in what might be called Machiavellian fashion,) Gian Galeazzo Visconti set out his coils to encircle and devour his enemy. Florentines sensed something was up when Visconti took over Pisa to their west in 1399 and Perugia to the south in 1400. That same year, Visconti signed a nonaggression pact with the other surviving Italian republic, Venice, to the east.

The Florentines pleaded with the Venetians not to sign. "This could cast the Florentine people into despair," they explained, "they would feel wholly abandoned and left a prey to the tyrant." The Venetians signed the treaty anyway.[3] Florence stood alone against the Visconti threat.

At the same time, Visconti was waging a propaganda war by portraying himself on coins and in pamphlets as the true successor to the Caesars. There had been a revival across Italy of interest in Roman history and literature since the poet Petrarch had first rediscovered the lost letters of Cicero. Visconti cast himself as the man who would bring back the stability and glory of the ancient Roman Empire. Hired propagandists compared him with Julius Caesar and talked of Visconti uniting Lombardy and Tuscany under one natural lord. They condemned Florence "in the name of every true Italian" for upholding the "enemy of quietude and peace, which they call liberty."[4]

After years of turmoil, it was a hard message to resist, even for Florentines. So Florence's city manager, or chancellor, Coluccio Salutati, looked for ways to counteract Visconti's propaganda and to inspire the Florentines with a renewed respect for that *libertas*: the right to run one's affairs as one sees fit.

Salutati was a learned man with a large library. He finally found what he needed in the works of Aristotle.

Salutati's Aristotle was not the Aristotle of Abelard or the scholastics, the Aristotle of logical distinctions and final causes. This was the Aristotle of the *Politics* and *Ethics*, the spokesman for the ancient *polis* who cast his political vision in direct opposition to Plato, and who had inspired Cicero. This triggered a major break from medieval thinking. When Thomas Aquinas read in Book III of the *Politics* that Aristotle considered monarchy to be the ideal state, he assumed it was an endorsement of an institution like the Holy Roman Empire. So did Aquinas's admirer Dante, who wrote a treatise on the subject.

Unlike Aquinas, however, Salutati read Aristotle in the original Greek— as did his successor as chancellor, Leonardo Bruni. Together they realized that Aristotle's ideal state was simply that: an abstraction no more applicable to real human beings like the Florentines than it was to ancient Athenians. What they found in Aristotle instead was a picture of the self-governing *polis* as the way of life most conformable to human nature.

The highest form of life, Aristotle said, was that of the householder, who "as a citizen shared in the civic life of ruling and being ruled in turn."[5] That certainly sounded a lot like life in 1402 Florence as well as fifth-century BCE Athens. Furthermore, the citizen contributed to this free self-governing community in not one but two ways.

First, he practiced the virtues of the free man, including cultivating and growing the fruits of his economic freedom—something the average Florentine merchant or shopkeeper certainly understood. Second, he contributed by becoming an active part of civic life. He voted; he ran for and held municipal office; and he entered into the honest deliberation of issues of common concern, out of which emerged laws that were binding on everyone since they enjoyed everyone's formal consent. In Aristotle's balanced constitution of the One, the Few, and the Many, *all* citizens have their role to play. All help to realize a larger goal: because "the end of the state is not mere life," Aristotle wrote, "it is, rather, a good quality of life."[6]

In short, a democracy like Athens or a republic like Florence was a cooperative partnership, in which men agree to be the best they can be in both their public and their private lives, instead of (as in Plato's *Republic*) having those rules imposed from above. Only under liberty could men realize their true nature as human beings *both* as free individuals and as part of a greater whole.[7] This was why the ancient Athenians had defied the tyranny of Persia against all odds. This was why the early Romans had risked everything to overthrow their kings, so that they could live free or die. And that was why the Florentines had to be ready to die to defend their liberty, Leonardo Bruni concluded—because without liberty, "life [has] no meaning for them."

This powerful Aristotelian message also meant that the Florentines weren't just defending their own particular liberty; they were standing up for the principle of liberty itself as it applied to humanity everywhere. As they had told the Venetians, "to us it seems all those in Italy who are anxious to live in freedom, must band together. . . . For it is a mistake to believe that, if one of us should fail, the other would survive. . . . The defense of Florence is also the defense of Venice." Beyond that, it was a defense of the idea of civic freedom as a universal human value.[8]

Fine words. But fine words didn't prevent the Venetians from signing their pact with the tyrant of Milan, and they weren't going to defeat Gian Galeazzo's advancing juggernaut. In July, his army crushed a combined Florentine-Bolognese force, and Bologna was forced to throw open its gates to the conqueror. As August began, Gian Galeazzo's knights and pikemen were concentrating along the border of Florence. Like Britain in 1940, Florence stood completely alone.

No one thought of surrender. "Even though the troops which we had at Bologna were destroyed," said one council member at the height of the crisis, "we must courageously go on." Another spoke in Churchill-like tones as the Florentines braced for the final blitz and invasion: "Let our minds not be subdued, but roused" by the danger ahead, and "face it with courage rather than fear."[9]

On August 10, Gian Galeazzo called together his war council. He appeared pale and distracted. He was ill with a fever; his doctors told him to take to his bed. The invasion was postponed. Over the next several days Visconti took a turn for the worse; and on September 3, 1402, the would-be king of Italy died. His heirs quarreled over their inheritance. Within weeks Gian Galeazzo's empire crumbled away, and his armies scattered into the countryside. Florence was saved.

To the Florentines, it was obvious what had happened. They had been saved by a divine miracle. But it was also a divine judgment: a vindication of their way of life and liberty itself. Everything that made Florence a free society—from its constitution to its trade and commerce, along with its arts and scholarship—had received a powerful sanction. "To be conquered and become subjects," wrote historian Gregorio Dati, recalling his hometown's great crisis, "this never seemed to the Florentines a possibility."[10] And now God had put His stamp of approval on their resolve.

The result was a sudden upsurge of confidence and energy in all aspects of Florentine life. That same year, Filippo Brunelleschi and his friend Donatello went to Rome to study the beauties of classical architecture and sculpture. Upon his return Brunelleschi began work on his great dome for Florence's cathedral, and in 1403, Lorenzo Ghiberti started casting the great bronze doors for the baptistry. The following years saw the arrival of a new, classically based architecture designed by Brunelleschi and Leon Battista Alberti; new works of history by Bruni and Gregorio Dati; a new figurative style of painting in the works of Masaccio; and a new lifelike classicism in the sculptures of Donatello.

All this creative outflow—the product of a post-1402 generation of Florentines eager to celebrate their political liberty and its unleashing of human potential—we call the Renaissance. Thanks to the Florentines' reading of Aristotle, a new way of seeing the world had been born, and with it a new appreciation of civic freedom.

Of course, it drew from deeper sources than just the crisis of 1402. Florentine traditions of pictorial realism dated back at least to Giotto, and classical architectural elements had been preserved in Italian city life since the fall of the Roman Empire. A tradition of political freedom had been preserved as well, in the works of Cicero, which scholars in Italy had been reading since the 1100s.[11]

Italy was also home to the rediscovery of Roman civil law during the Middle Ages, which had given Italians a version of liberty that was summed up in the phrase coined by the great legal scholar Bartolus (also a key figure in the conciliarist debate along with William of Ockham) that "a free people is its own prince."[12]*

All the same, what was missing from Roman law, and even from Cicero, was the idea that living in freedom was a *universal* human value transcending all local traditions and historical contexts. It was precisely this sense of free-

*From freedom's point of view, however, Roman law proved to be a double-edged sword. Nothing prevented a single figure from claiming to exercise that power in the name of the people, as the ancient Roman emperors claimed to do. Visconti could recite just as many passages from the Justinian Code reinforcing his claim to absolute rule as the Florentines could find protecting civic liberty.[13]

dom as an essential part of human nature and potentiality that the Florentines had discovered in Aristotle and passed on to subsequent generations. The conclusion was clear: to be human was to desire to be free. Being free in turn meant living under a constitution in which men "rule and are ruled in turn" and by choosing their own leaders, chose their own collective destiny.

The Florentine rediscovery of Aristotle's politics of freedom signaled the birth of a new ideal for Europe.[14] It asserted that the highest form of human life was that of the free active citizen, just as the free self-governing republic is the form of political life most suited to human nature. In this way, it was believed, liberty opens the door to a standard of excellence in both public and private affairs unknown to those living in servitude or unfree societies. In short, a republic built on Aristotle's model will allow men to achieve their highest potential not only as political animals, but as complete moral beings.

The Florentines saw this happening in their own city. They had a constitution (they felt) that achieved the kind of balance between the One, the Few, and the Many that Aristotle made the hallmark of successful self-government. They were witnessing a flourishing of the arts and a standard of aesthetic perfection in the works of Donatello, Brunelleschi, and Masaccio not realized since ancient Athens, while Florentines also led the rest of Italy in the study and recovery of classical texts, including the works of the ancient Greeks.*

In Florence "liberty exists for all," wrote Bruni, and "the hope of winning public honors and ascending is the same for all." This equality of opportunity awakens the talents of the citizens, "for where men are given the hope of attaining honor in the state, they take courage and raise themselves to a higher plane" so that "talent and industry distinguish themselves in the highest degree."[15]

When asked why all the key ingredients of Renaissance culture first appeared in Florence, the artist Vasari said it was due to the city's freedom, which inspired the spirit of criticism: "the air of Florence making minds naturally free, and not content with mediocrity."[16] The ultimate goal was summed up by the title of a work of another Florentine scholar, Giannozzo Manetti, *On the Dignity and Excellence of Man*, meaning the dignity and excellence of the free individual.

Renaissance Florence did not forget about the importance of Christianity

---

*Ironically, among them Aristotle's great rival Plato. See chapter 17.

and sacred values. It was said that Manetti knew three works by heart: the *Ethics* of Aristotle, Saint Paul's letters, and Augustine's *City of God*.[17] Still, the Florentines did insist that education needed to reflect the new secular emphasis on human freedom and the pursuit of excellence for its own sake. Leonardo Bruni's term for this new program of learning suitable to the free active citizen was *studia humanitatis*, literally "the study of humanity." We call it the humanities, and the humanists who devoted their lives to it managed to lift the traditional liberal arts of their scholastic morass like a submerged yacht being pulled out of the mud.

Instead of the old *trivium* and *quadrivium*, the Renaissance humanist focused on only four subjects. The first was the study of history, in order to understand free nations in the past, especially ancient Greece and Rome. The second was the study of rhetoric in order to make men fit to lead a free society—not surprisingly, since the typical humanist saw Cicero as well as Aristotle as his ancient mentor. Then there was Greek and Roman literature to raise men's standard of eloquence, and finally moral philosophy, which meant above all Aristotle's *Ethics*.[18] *Studia humanitatis* were the four parts of the essential tools of freedom, training the minds of men to see the pursuit of excellence as an expression of their essential nature, whether in the past or the future.

"To you is given a body more graceful than other animals," Leon Battista Alberti enthused, "to you most sharp and delicate senses, to you wit, reason, memory like an immortal god." Excellence was humanity's birthright, and thanks to liberty, Alberti concluded, "a man can do all things if he will."[19]

There was only one problem. The liberty did not last.

Leonardo Bruni died in Florence in 1444. His body was interred with great ceremony in the Church of Santa Croce. The motto inscribed over his tomb was, "History is in mourning."

Well it might have been. By that date, a short, rather soft-spoken former wool merchant turned banker named Cosimo de' Medici had been secretly controlling the city for almost a decade. Bruni and other humanists had watched with dismay as he took control of the Florentine constitution. In less than a generation, Florence had its own "soft power" version of Visconti's tyranny.

There was no *coup d'état*. Cosimo and the Medici family never drew a sword against anyone. They never tortured or murdered enemies,* as previous tyrants had done and were doing in other parts of Europe. Far from enriching themselves, they spent lavishly to give Florence a new civic splendor and became great patrons of the arts.

Still, beginning in 1434 and until the death of Lorenzo the Magnificent in 1492, the Medici family and their banking interests became indispensable to the running of Florence. Only their friends and cronies ever rose to high political office. Anyone critical of their methods and their political machine found himself frozen out of politics, at times even sent into exile. Florence flourished under the Medici and enjoyed unprecedented peace with their neighbors. The city was still the center of the arts, and humanist scholarship flourished as never before. But in their hearts, the citizens of Florence knew they were no longer free.

How had this happened? The Medici were certainly rich. There had been rich Florentines before but none had enjoyed the kind of power Medici did. The real question was, why were Florentines willing to take their money in the first place? A generation of agonized humanists asked, why had Florence let its freedom slip away?

Not everyone collaborated with the Medici regime. In 1433, when the city council feared Cosimo's power too much, they had him arrested and driven into exile—but in less than a year, they called him back. It was also true that Leonardo Bruni had secretly joined with others to try to overthrow Cosimo's power—but the plot never came off. Then in April 1478, a group of young men, inspired by the example of Brutus and the other ancient Romans who slew Caesar to restore liberty, tried to do the same to Lorenzo the Magnificent in Florence's cathedral. They managed to stab his brother to death, and Lorenzo himself narrowly escaped. However, instead of joining in, the Florentine citizenry lynched the assassins and publicly congratulated Il Magnifico on his escape.[20]

It was a stinging reproach to everything the generation of 1402 had stood for. It also raised a more general point. If Aristotle had been right and it was man's destiny to be free, if our nature as human beings makes us fit to govern our lives as we see fit, then why is it that everywhere we look human beings are unfree and submit to various forms of tyranny and slavery, including now

*After their return to power in 1512, they made an exception. See below.

in Florence? Why did freedom fail, not only in Florence but throughout history—even ancient Greece and Rome?

The man who developed the authoritative answer to this question would become the Italian Renaissance's most famous, even most notorious, thinker—in part because his answer was so startling and so disturbing.

The journey to his answer began on a cold and gray dawn in May 23, 1498. A long raised scaffold had been built leading from the doors of Florence's city hall, the Palazzo della Signoria, to a great mound of bundled sticks and lumber in the center of the square. A great throng of people had gathered, and all eyes turned as three barefoot figures in the white robes of penitents stumbled along the elevated walkway toward the mound and the stark wooden stake looming over it in the shape of a cross. ,

The three men could barely walk. Armed guards had to half carry them to their doom. They had been tortured for hours and days on the rack; only the right arm of the lead figure, a lean, hook-nosed man with dark, flashing eyes, had been left unbroken so that he could sign his final confession, admitting to blasphemy and heresy and conspiring against the Florentine republic.[21]

His name was Girolamo Savonarola. Ironically, he had once been hailed as the republic's savior. Lorenzo the Magnificent had died suddenly in 1492, the same year the Genoese explorer Christopher Columbus sailed to the New World. Savonarola had been a popular Dominican preacher, and from his pulpit he told the Florentines that they had regained their liberty through the grace of God, just as in 1402: but only if they now proved worthy of it.[22]

Citizens cheered as Savonarola rewrote the constitution to empower Florence's lower middle class. He organized a systematic purification of the city, closing bars and brothels, and set up the famous "bonfire of the vanities," where Florentines burned hundreds of carnival disguises, wigs, fancy ladies' undergarments, playing cards and musical instruments, books of poetry and rare manuscripts, and portrait paintings, including several by Botticelli. In a sardonic twist of irony, the bonfire had been on the very spot where Savonarola would now mount the scaffold to be hanged and burned at the stake.[23]

Savonarola had tried to secure his power by allying Florence with France. But the pro-Spanish pope Alexander VI imposed economic sanctions on the

The burning of Savonarola, from a painting by an unknown artist, circa 1500

city that hurt Florence's wealthy merchants. The urban mob grew tired of Savonarola's puritanical regime and turned against him. By the time the papal Inquisition's sentence was pronounced, Florentines were eager to see the end of their once revered messiah.

So the crowd cheered as one by one Savonarola and his two former aides were hanged. Soon their corpses hung lifeless from their chains. Men moved below to set the stacked dry wood to the torch. As the flames consumed the dangling bodies, the ropes binding Savonarola's arms burned away. The crowd gasped as the fire's blast seemed to raise his hand in a gesture of final ironic benediction to the city.

"A miracle! A miracle!" some cried out. But then the flames reached higher and consumed everything. As the smell of roasting flesh grew more intense and the cloud of black smoke rose higher and higher, the crowd dispersed. The deed was done; Florence's experiment with God-directed democracy was over.[24]

Only one man continued to watch from the shadows, a lean, ferret-faced man with tears in his eyes.

Niccolò Machiavelli watched and wondered. Savonarola had promised that God would save Florence's freedom. In the end, the Dominican friar hadn't been able to save himself. To the twenty-nine-year-old Machiavelli, it was a shattering revelation. It marked the turning point in his life—and a pivot point in the evolution of Western political thinking.

We have been trained to think of Machiavelli as the apologist for power politics. In fact, his passion for the ideal of liberty was so strong, it cost him his career and almost cost him his life. It had made him a follower of Savonarola; paradoxically, it also made him the author of his most notorious work, *The Prince*. Some would insist that the book was inspired by the devil.[25] But Machiavelli was only a close student of Aristotle's version of civic liberty, which led him in the wake of Savonarola's fall to ask some uncomfortable questions.

What if God really *didn't* care whether Florence survived as a republic or not? What if God didn't really care whether men lived as free men or slaves? And what if human nature suits us as much for servitude as it does for liberty?

Machiavelli had never known a time when the Medici had not run the city. He was born in 1469, the year Lorenzo de' Medici assumed power from his uncle Cosimo. Young Niccolò had been bred to read the classics and believe in the ideal of civic humanism, even though that ideal was contradicted everywhere he looked.[26] Then came 1492 and Savonarola. The republic had been reborn; it even managed to survive the disgrace and death of its would-be messiah. Ironically, the fall of his former hero brought good fortune to Machiavelli. Friends in the new government offered him an important municipal post, which he accepted.

This is a vital point for understanding Machiavelli's works. The writer was no armchair strategist. For fourteen years he loyally served the restored Florentine republic, traveling and negotiating with the leading political personalities of his day, including the pope, the kings of France and Spain, and the sinister Cesare Borgia.

In 1498, the reborn republic found itself again surrounded by the enemies of liberty, much as in 1402. What could save it? Machiavelli had seen divine grace fail with Savonarola. He had, however, one other hope. It came once again from the pages of Aristotle, in the *Ethics*, where the Greek philosopher observed that mercenary soldiers (like the ones who fought for Italy's city-states) will fight only if they think they can win.

Otherwise, "they are the first to flee," Aristotle declared, "while citizen troops die at their posts" because they know that when one is fighting for one's homeland, "flight is disgraceful and death preferable to safety." Courage in battle comes to the citizen not merely as a matter of professional skill, the Master of Those Who Know concluded. It was a matter of civic pride; one more positive fruit of liberty.

Thus was born the modern citizen soldier ideal, which would loom large down through the modern centuries, and in Florence. Aristotle's argument had impressed Leonardo Bruni enough to inspire his treatise *On the Militia*, demanding reestablishment of Florence's citizen militia, which had been abolished in 1351.[27] Now Machiavelli agreed. The free active citizen had to be an armed citizen as well, like the Spartan hoplites who fought at Thermopylae and the Athenians at Marathon, or the Roman legionnaires of old. Machiavelli pushed his friend Piero Soderini, the head of the post-Savonarola republic, to organize a citizen militia for Florence. "You need to understand," he wrote, "the best armies are those of armed peoples: and they cannot be resisted except by armies similar to themselves."[28]

Soderini put Machiavelli in charge, and for nearly six years beginning in 1506, Niccolò Machiavelli (who had no military experience) oversaw the recruiting, arming, and training of bakers, weavers, shoemakers, and other Florentine citizens into a fighting force. They drilled and practiced Roman legion maneuvers, even as a large Spanish army advanced on the city to restore the Medici once and for all.

It was the summer of 1512. For Florence, it was the crisis of 1402 all over again—except that this time no miraculous illness cut down their enemy. This time the Florentines would have to fight. Still, Machiavelli had his doubts. "At the beginning we thought we would not put our soldiers in the field," he wrote later, "because we did not think they were powerful enough to resist the enemy." It was not until August that Machiavelli was forced to deploy his citizen militia at Prato, about ten miles from Florence.[29]

Machiavelli had raised nearly three thousand men for Soderini to command. None had ever faced an enemy in battle, including Machiavelli. The Spanish were paid professionals to a man, hardy veterans who had fought their way across Italy. The Florentines managed to beat off their first attack. Then, at the second assault, the Florentines dropped their swords and pikes and fled.[30]

Prato fell to the Spaniards, and then Florence. Soderini resigned and fled into exile. The Medici agreed to return as private citizens, but everyone knew that they would dominate the city more harshly than ever. By November, they had forced Machiavelli out and disbanded his ill-fated militia.

Florence's tyrants were not yet finished with him. They imposed a thousand-florin fine and restricted his movements outside the city. Then when rumors circulated of a plot to overthrow the Medici, Machiavelli was one of the first to be arrested.

In prison his hands were tied behind his back, and he was then lifted to the ceiling by rope and pulley. At a command, he was dropped straight down until the rope stopped him with the jerk. The term for this torture was *strappado*. One drop was usually enough to loosen a prisoner's tongue; four were enough to dislocate a person's shoulders, perhaps permanently.

Machiavelli endured six drops of the *strappado* but still refused to name names. Instead, he was left to rot in prison. "The walls were full of lice so big and fat they seemed like butterflies," Machiavelli would remember later; the stench was almost unbearable. Day and night, he could hear the sound of clanking chains and the cries of other prisoners being tortured.[31] Then, after twenty-two days of wondering whether he would live or die, Machiavelli was set free.

He returned to his house and farm outside Florence, where every evening, as he told a friend in a letter, "at the door I take off the day's clothing, covered with mud and dirt, and put on garments regal and courtly," in order to read his favorite ancient authors, including Aristotle.[32]

His goal was to find out why freedom had failed.

History, people like to say, is written by the winners. The truth is, some of the most profound works on the past were written by those who considered themselves history's *losers*. They are men and women trying to figure out what went wrong; what was the turning point when optimistic hopes were dashed and the forces of doom and destruction inevitably closed in.

This was true of ancient historians like Thucydides; Tacitus and Sallust (widely read in Medici Florence); and to a degree Polybius. It was certainly true of Machiavelli. We think of his books, particularly *The Prince*, as works of political theory. They are above all works of history. History was always for Machiavelli a rich storehouse of the past experience of others, far richer than anything anyone could accumulate in a single lifetime. And for the student of Aristotle, the touchstone of understanding reality must be experience.[33]

History teaches us what human beings are like in reality rather than what we would like them to be. And when we deal with the sum total of history's record, high-minded ideals like those of Plato's Philosopher Rulers have to be pushed off over the side. Reality teaches a very different set of lessons about politics—and Machiavelli's ambition was to present them to posterity.

That at least was Machiavelli's goal. What he did in reality was to plug Aristotle's formula for understanding civic liberty into Polybius's time machine, the inevitable cycle of historical rise and decline.* The result was the *Discourses*, a much longer work than *The Prince* but crucial for understanding that more celebrated book. For in writing the *Discourses*, Machiavelli discovered a basic paradox: When it comes to liberty, nothing fails like success.

The freer a society becomes, the more prosperous and more arrogant it becomes as well. Like ancient Rome or Renaissance Florence, it sows the seeds of its own servitude. Although self-government and liberty are the highest forms of political life, Machiavelli revealed that human nature also makes them the most unstable.[34]

Machiavelli's fusion of Polybius and Aristotle yielded a future of gloom. The Romans had read Polybius to discover how a great empire would be doomed if it failed to keep Aristotle's balance of monarchy, aristocracy, and democracy—the One, the Few, and the Many. Machiavelli's reading was far more pessimistic. Not just Rome, but every free society is doomed from the start. Real republics exist in real time, not on some eternal plane like Plato's literary version. "All human affairs are ever in a state of flux and cannot stand still," the *Discourses* explains, meaning that every society will experience either constant improvement or decline.

When a republic organized around Aristotle's principle of balance expands its power and place in the world, as it must, it becomes rich and powerful. But in the process, the balance is lost: a free society's "basic principles will be subverted," Machiavelli declared, and it will soon be faced with ruin."[35]

To Machiavelli, the very things that give a free republic like ancient Rome or Athens or pre-Medici Florence verve and energy—prowess in war, a vigorous politics, the accumulation of riches from trade and empire—ultimately turn back on themselves. Prosperity and success turn men's passions toward self-enrichment rather than service to the State. The battle of conflicting in-

---

*See chapter 8.

terests between rich and poor, which Machiavelli shrewdly points to as the real source of the Roman republic's dynamism,[36] degenerates into bitter factionalism.

Under these circumstances, the very things that are supposed to preserve liberty become a trap. Each group in the mix of One, Few, and Many is determined to gain power at the expense of the other. Politics becomes a cycle of vendetta and payback.[37] Meanwhile, the habits of wealth and luxury undermine the important virtues necessary to sustain free institutions, including honor and service in arms—even the passion for freedom itself. Men become soft and effeminate, like the bakers and tinkers of Machiavelli's failed militia.[38] People prefer the comfortable life to the stern sacrifices of their forefathers.

New legislation on Plato's model won't help, either: "The modification of the laws did not suffice to keep men good." On the contrary, Machiavelli declared, "the new laws are ineffectual, because the [society's] institutions, which remain constant, are corrupt."[39]

Once a free people have reached this point, Machiavelli concluded, there is no hope left. Their empire may expand, as Rome's did under the emperors. The wealth can continue to pour in. The arts may flourish; the political factionalism makes for dramatic entertainment, while people ignore the underlying rot. But such a society is doomed, unless a major crisis forces a change in its thinking.

"Hence it is necessary to resort to extraordinary methods, such as the use of force and the appeal to arms, to become a prince in the state so that one can dispose of it as one thinks fit" and thus save it from extinction.[40] This is where *The Prince* comes in. He is the instrument of last resort, the man who pulls a corrupt society out of its self-destructive rut and puts it back on the road to political health. However, he is no Platonic soul doctor; no high-minded Philosopher Ruler. As Machiavelli noted in the *Discourses*, such a man will not be greeted as a messiah.

"Very rarely will there be found a good man ready to use bad methods in order to make himself prince," Machiavelli wrote. There are also plenty of bad men who are willing to take power without bothering to reform the society they lead.[41]

Nonetheless, history shows that some men are willing to do evil in order to accomplish good. They are in fact history's great heroes, like Alexander the Great and Julius Caesar and even Moses, who raised the Hebrews out of their slothful servitude, mercilessly crushed their enemies, and then led them into the Promised Land. "Fortune, as it were, provided the matter but [these men] gave it its form," Machiavellii wrote, echoing Aristotle; "without opportunity their prowess would have been extinguished and without such prowess the opportunity would have come in vain."[42]

The Prince explains that such a man must not let success go to his head, as it does to citizens in a free society. He has to constantly watch his back; he must not allow his followers to become too powerful on the one side or too resentful on the other. He must above all train his mind and body to stay focused on the state of his military: "The first way to lose your State is to neglect the art of war." He must learn from the example of both the lion and the fox, Machiavelli wrote, since at times he will be forced to act like a beast as well as a human being.[43]

Machiavelli understood "that such a ruler, especially a new ruler, will be forced to act treacherously, ruthlessly, or inhumanely, and disregard the precepts of religion" in order to maintain his power and thus save the State. He shouldn't worry about a reputation for cruelty since that will discourage others from resisting his will: "It is better to be feared than loved if one cannot be both."[44] Yet such a man can still save the state, and preserve its liberty.

Now, it's a rare event in history when a figure like this appears. But when he does, Machiavelli argues, it's a sign a society can protect itself from both its enemies *and* its own vices. This was still Machiavelli's hope for Italy, even a figure like Cesare Borgia.* "What people would fail to obey him?" Machiavelli asks at the end of *The Prince*. "What Italian would deny him homage?"[45]

These were questions a Leonardo Bruni would have been ashamed to ask. A century later, Machiavelli would have considered himself derelict *not* to ask them. However, no such superman appeared. Cesare Borgia died broken and discredited; when Machiavelli himself died in 1527, the outlook for Italy seemed bleaker than ever. But his point in *The Prince* was a more general one, which gets obscured if we treat the work as nothing more than a treatise on power politics. For Machiavelli had uncovered the final paradox of liberty on Aristotle's model.

Aristotle's *Politics* is built on the back of his *Ethics:* The good life presupposes the virtuous life. However, in order to survive, free societies sometimes have to violate the very values they profess to uphold. They have to wage war

---

*Oddly, Machiavelli never mentions Gian Galeazzo Visconti in *The Prince*.

and kill innocents; they have to imprison enemies and sometimes torture them. In extreme situations, they have to suspend civil liberties, even shut down traditional institutions—all to prevent something worse.

To the just belongs injustice. All the same, Machiavelli knew there was no guarantee that people will put up with the measures that are meant to save them from themselves. At the battle of Prato, the Florentines preferred to run away and lose their liberty rather than die to save it. The masses can suddenly turn on their savior, just as they turned on Savonarola. Most rulers prefer not to run that risk. Instead, they will maintain the status quo, the false façade of normal politics, just as the Medici did in order to dupe the public into believing they were still free when in fact they were not.

This had happened to ancient Rome under the emperors; it had happened to Florence under the Medici. It's the risk that free governments run anywhere. It is ultimately why Machiavelli concluded that "it is difficult, or rather impossible, either to maintain a republican form of government in states which have become corrupt or to create such a form afresh." Instead, the old vitality simply ebbs away. Final disaster comes not from outside, but from within.[46]

Freedom is doomed to fail. This was the final dismal conclusion Machiavelli reached by the time he finished *The Prince*. By then Florence and Italy, the cradle of modern European liberty, were bowing down to foreign tyrants and their armies. Machiavelli called the situation a stench in the nostrils of humanity at least for now.[47] But the political will for liberty had collapsed. If men wanted to be free and to realize their highest nature, they were going to have to look somewhere other than politics.

Botticelli, *The Birth of Venus*: the fusion of divine and secular love, thanks to Plato's *Symposium*

Seventeen

THE CREATIVE ASCENT: PLATO AND THE HIGH RENAISSANCE

Aristotle's genius is purely human, but Plato's is both human and divine.

—Marsilio Ficino, *Platonic Theology*

Love wakens, rouses, puts the wings in feather,
As a first step, so the soul will soar
And rise to its Maker.

—Michelangelo Buonarroti, Sonnet 258

At dawn on May 25, 1453, the bells of Constantinople's churches rang out an urgent appeal. Rich and poor, old men, women, children, priests, and nuns crowded into the Church of Holy Wisdom—the largest church in the world—to pray, receive communion, and await the inevitable. Armored soldiers clambered to their posts along the city's fabled walls—walls that had withstood sieges by Goths, Avars, Persians, and Arabs for one thousand years.

This time it was the Turks who were coming, fierce warriors from the steppes of Asia and followers of the religion of Muhammad. This time there were not enough soldiers, not enough cannons and ships, and nowhere to run. Nothing could save the Roman Empire's last capital.

A faint breeze rising from the Bosphorus stirred the emperor's banners for the last time. Silently the weary Greek soldiers watched as wave after wave of attackers rushed toward the walls, shouting and brandishing swords while the Turkish sultan's mercenary guards herded them on with whips and battle maces. The sultan's great cannons belched enormous stones' (one that fell short dug a pit six feet deep), punching hole after hole through the massive walls.[1] After desperate fighting, the outer wall fell. The gatehouse leading to the inner wall became a scene of mass confusion and slaughter.

The last emperor tried to rally his fleeing troops. Finally he threw off his imperial regalia, seized a sword, and plunged into the melee, never to be seen alive again (later his body was identified by his imperial purple slippers).

By the time the triumphant Turkish sultan Mehmet reached the scene, the city was being sacked. All around him priests were being killed, nuns were being raped, and the other inhabitants were being herded together to be sold into slavery. The streets were bathed in blood mingled with hot soot from burning houses and shops.

At the battered entrance to the Church of Holy Wisdom, the sultan dismounted and poured a handful of dirt over his red silk turban as a sign of humility and gave solemn thanks to Allah for his victory. As he did so, the historian Edward Gibbon tells us, he sang a Persian song softly to himself: "The spider has wove his web in the imperial palace, and the owl has sung her watch-song on the towers of Afrasaib."[2]

Constantinople, the largest city in the world and capital of the Byzantine Roman Empire (Rum to Arabs and Turks), had fallen. Europe's last surviving link to the age of the Caesars would be remade as a Muslim city and renamed Istanbul. It would remain the headquarters of the sultan's descendants for the next 460 years. The greatest church in the world would become a mosque and its magnificent mosaics of biblical scenes and images of the saints would be whitewashed into oblivion, where they remain to this day.

Meanwhile, Greek refugees scattered in all directions to escape the chains of slavery or worse. These included scholars fleeing with their last precious possessions: their books. Unaccustomed to life outside their quiet studies, they looked for places where they could read, write, and meet other intellectuals in peace—and discuss the rich knowledge they brought with them, much of it still unknown in the West.

Most of them found safe haven in Italy, and many of their manuscripts found their way to the library of the monastery of San Marco in Florence. Cosimo de' Medici had helped to build the library and patronized its collection. More than anyone, he was responsible for bringing the refugees and their books, with their cursive Greek script and strange illuminations, to Florence.

One day Cosimo came to visit the precious texts in the airy, light-filled room. He had brought along the six-year-old son of his doctor. "Someday," Cosimo said to the awestruck boy, pointing, "you will grow up to translate those works and reveal their secrets to the world."[3]

Cosimo's prediction proved correct. Because the books in the San Marco monastery contained intellectual gold. They were the lost dialogues of Plato. And thanks to the doctor's boy, almost within a single generation the original Plato once again became a major force in European civilization.

The boy's name was Marsilio Ficino. His last portraits before his death in 1499 show an austere, rather sad-faced man, a dreamer and scholar rather than the robust citizen soldier of the Aristotelian civic humanist ideal.

The Florentines of the generation of 1402, men like Bruni and Alberti, had wanted to use the rediscovery of the ancient Greeks and Romans to change the world. Marsilio Ficino wanted to use it to change the self. His translations of Plato and the founding of a new Platonic Academy in Florence in 1463 signaled a major reorientation of the Renaissance, and of European thinking. If freedom in terms of political liberty was proving to be a dead end in Italy and elsewhere, Plato offered a different path to freedom: freedom through the creative spirit.

Through their reading of Plato, Ficino and his followers believed they had unlocked the secret of human creativity. Artists, poets, writers, and even scientists have followed their lead ever since. If historians are right and the Renaissance truly marks the birth of the modern world, then Ficino and his translation of Plato's dialogues acted as midwife.

It's a metaphor Plato himself would have appreciated.[4] The Middle Ages had known Plato's *Timaeus* in various versions; its cosmology was unimaginable without it. The rest of his works, however, were a closed book for nearly five hundred years. In the 1100s, Arab libraries yielded up a sprinkling of Platonic dialogues, which found Latin translators. Leonardo Bruni himself did several, including the *Phaedo* and the *Laws*, which were widely admired.[5]

But none of this was enough to shake loose Aristotle's iron grip on the Western mind. It was the influx of Greek scholars into Italy in the 1400s, both before and after the fall of Constantinople, that finally woke the West from its dogmatic scholastic slumbers.

Gemistos Plethon, for example, came to Florence in 1439 and lectured on Plato to a large and fascinated audience, including Cosimo de' Medici. Another, John Argyropoulos, barely escaped the siege of Constantinople. He would become a fixture at the University of Florence and later in Padua. Among his listeners would be the young Leonardo da Vinci.

Thanks to these Greek refugees, Westerners realized for the first time that the Platonic dialogues formed a system of thought as coherent and profound as that of Aristotle, in which every work from the *Parmenides* and the *Republic* to the *Sophist* and *Timaeus* had a significant place. However Plato's appeal was not just that his works were fresh and engaging to read, compared with the dogmatic stuffiness of Aristotle and his medieval commentators.

It was also that these supposedly unknown works had a strange ring of familiarity: and no wonder. At the end of the Roman Empire, Christian Neoplatonism had given Plato a shining new relevance. Now the reverse happened. The rediscovery of Plato in the fifteenth century reopened issues that had consumed Christian thinkers since Origen and Saint Augustine, such as the relationship between mind and spirit, and between God and the individual soul; the nature of rational truth and understanding the structure of the cosmos; and issues about mysticism and divine love—all with a stunning new force.

"Platonism," writes historian Sem Dresden, "became *the* Renaissance philosophy."[6] This was in part because it came with the shock of the familiar. And no one contributed more to pointing out what was familiar but also what was new in Plato than Cosimo's studious protégé Marsilio Ficino.

He was born in Florence in 1433. He studied at the University of Florence, taking classes in philosophy, the humanities, and medicine, but does not seem to have completed a degree. In fact, Ficino would make formal university degrees largely irrelevant to the life of the mind for the next three hundred years. He turned to Greek on his own just three years after the fall of Constantinople and began writing about Plato's philosophy shortly after that.

Ficino offered the age a new intellectual master. "Aristotle's genius is purely human," he wrote, while "*Plato's is both human and divine.*" After all, it was Plato who first taught the doctrine of the immortality of the soul, even Saint Augustine had pointed out that he was the pagan philosopher who came closest to the doctrines of Christianity.

Indeed, everyone in the ancient world, Ficino pointed out, from Greeks and Jews to early Christians and Zoroastrians, had recognized that Plato's writings were divinely inspired. It was time for modern Florentines to note the same fact.[7] Cosimo de' Medici was so impressed that in 1462 he gave Ficino a large house in Careggi outside Florence, and provided money for creating a Platonic Academy there to carry on the mission of presenting the wisdom of "the Father of Philosophers" to a Latin-reading audience.

In 1464, Ficino was able to come to Cosimo's deathbed and read aloud passages from his translation of Plato's *Philebus*, with its message that the soul never ceases its pursuit of the highest good because the desire for truth is part of its very nature. Translations of the other dialogues soon followed. Cosimo's son Piero kept Ficino supplied with more Greek texts and urged him to publish his translations.[8]

Those translations duly appeared in 1469, along with a commentary on the Platonic dialogue that had most impressed Ficino with its freshness and originality, not to mention its relevance to contemporary Florence. That was the *Symposium*—certainly the only major work of philosophy that takes place at a drunken party.

The characters in the *Symposium*, including Socrates, have gathered for a festive soirée complete with large cups of wine and flute girls. The theme of the evening is praise of the goddess Love in all her physical and sensual aspects, including homosexual love. One by one, the speakers (among them the comedic playwright Aristophanes) rise unsteadily to their feet to make their speech. Socrates's is the last. Not surprisingly, it is also the most profound.

His theme is "Love Is Desire Aroused by Beauty." Socrates reveals to his fellow revelers that the greatest form of love is actually the one that rises above carnal and physical desire and aspires to spiritual truth. Love's most potent trigger, physical beauty, turns out to be the direct material copy of Goodness in Itself, in the same way that material objects are copies of the Platonic Forms. Once we realize that what arouses our desire for a beautiful boy or woman (and it is striking that Socrates tells the *Symposium* guests that the true spiritual nature of love was revealed to him by a woman, the priestess Diotima) is actually only a glimpse of a higher perfection, then our love of beauty must eventually lead us forward toward a love of truth and goodness, and eventually to God.

Can we really go from a *Playboy* centerfold (or *Playgirl*, for that matter) to an understanding of the mind of God? Socrates says yes, provided we look beyond the physical object that aroused our love and desire. Instead, we must ask the question "What do all beautiful objects, whether women or boys or vases or sculptures, have in common that makes them beautiful to our eyes?"

In due course, the answer to that question will lead us to "see that each type of beauty is closely related to every other." Suddenly the *Playboy* centerfold is no longer enough, either on paper or in the flesh. We want something more meaningful, as our soul realizes that the appearance of perfection in the world matches its own spiritual nature: "Instead of this low and petty-minded slavery, [we] will be turned towards the great sea of beauty" and the abundance of riches that can be found in its depths.[9]

Slowly, love and desire move from the merely physical to the higher spiritual realm. The result, Socrates tells his audience, is "that [we] will regard beauty of body as something petty" compared with beauty of the mind and spirit. Finally, we will want to know Beauty in its purest form, as the source of all physical perfection: in other words, we want to catch "a sight of divine beauty itself," which is the highest kind of knowledge—and love—there is.

"Like someone using a staircase," Plato writes, "[we] should go from one to two and from two to all beautiful bodies, and from beautiful bodies to beautiful practices, and from beautiful practices to beautiful knowledge." It's an ascent that ends finally in the highest enlightenment possible for man. "This is why every man should hold Love in respect," he has Socrates say in the end, "and why on every occasion I praise the power and might of Love!"[10]

The *Symposium* is by far the strangest of all Plato's dialogues. The modern classicist will tell us that it belongs very much to the homoerotic atmosphere of Athens in the early fourth century BCE, which Plato in the guise of Socrates seeks to downplay.[11] However, to any reader of Plotinus (Ficino also translated the complete works of Plotinus into Latin) or the Pseudo-Dionysius, Plato's reference to "a staircase" would have triggered immediate thoughts of heavenly hierarchies and the Great Chain of Being. So would the notion of a movement of the soul from lower to higher, as part of its processional return to its heavenly realm. Clearly, love as Plato described it in the *Symposium* had the same higher spiritual goal as his later Neoplatonist admirers: that of final mystical union with God.

"For whatever subject [Plato] deals with," Ficino would write, whether it was ethics or physics or politics or mathematics, "he quickly brings around . . . to the contemplation and worship of God."[12] So it must be with his doctrine of love, despite its origins in a drunken orgy and in the realm of the carnal sexual side of human nature.* This love that manages to rise above the merely carnal and physical to a higher spiritual level, Ficino termed "Platonic love." The term has stuck ever since. Platonic love is supposed to be about far more than two friends not sleeping together. As the great Ficino scholar Paul Oskar Kristeller explained, "There can never be two friends only; there must always be three: two human beings and God."[13]

By a mental sleight of hand, Ficino effortlessly merged Plato's theory of love with Christian Neoplatonist ideas about divine love derived from familiar authors like Augustine or Saint Bernard—not to mention Italy's two most famous love poets, Dante and Petrarch. And Plato's doctrine of love as the desire for beauty had a peculiar attraction in *quattrocento* Florence.

The production of paintings, sculptures, books, and buildings were important parts of Florence's urban economy. Masaccio, Donatello, Brunelleschi, Ghiberti, Alberti: A visitor or citizen encountered their productions along every street like Orsanmichele and in every church or public building. What Plato and Ficino were saying was that these men were not just artisans, but exemplars of man's perennial urging toward a higher realm of the self, thanks to their love of beauty.

"Don't you see," the priestess Diotima tells Socrates, "that it's only in that kind of life, when someone sees beauty with the part [of the soul] that can see it, that he'll be able to give birth not just to images of virtue . . . but true virtue?" It is the lover of beauty "who has the chance of becoming beloved by the gods, and immortal—if any human being can become immortal."[14]

The theology of Saint Augustine or Saint Bernard made the ultimate goal of love, or *caritas*, the abnegation of the self, in order to be the servant of God. Ficino's Platonic theology, by contrast, resulted in an exaltation of the self. The attraction of physical beauty in the material world, as when we look at a person or a painting and say, "How beautiful!" turns out to be a powerful sign of the soul's yearning for divine perfection, fired by that perfection's palpable trace in the realm of appearances. And this is made possible, as Ficino explained in his most original work, the *Platonic Theology*, because the soul shares that same divine nature.

At this point, the theology of Ficino and that of Thomas Aquinas sound not so different. Thomistic man's proper place is at the center of creation,

---

*Ficino found further confirmation in Plato's *Phaedrus*, where Socrates says that the soul that has ɡlimpsed the Form of beauty in heaven naturally seeks it out on earth with the passionate frenzy of a ᴇr for his beloved, in a kind of "divine madness."

because he is the crucial mediating point between spirit and matter. Ficino's Platonic man occupies the same slot in the divine hierarchy. When the Book of Genesis tells us that we are made in the image of God, then we are to take it in a Platonic sense. Of all material creatures, we are the only ones who love God precisely because we are also spiritual beings like God. "At some point, therefore, our rational soul is able to become God, because with God inciting it, it naturally strives towards that goal"—in both the spiritual realm *and* the material one.[15]

This leads to a monumental conclusion: through the power of love we become fully conscious of our powers as spiritual beings. Suddenly we realize we have the power to shape our lives, our environment, our relations with others, with the same confidence and creative range as God Himself. "Therefore the mind in understanding conceives as many things in itself as God in understanding creates in this world," Ficino explains, "in speaking it utters them in the air; it writes them down on sheets [of paper] with a quill; in making images it figures them forth in the material of the world." Love's ascent, in short, teaches us how to become creators like God Himself.[16]

Ficino's Academy spread his Platonic gospel across Italy. Eager visitors to the house in Careggi included Piero de' Medici and his nephew Lorenzo the Magnificent; a throng of artists and poets and scholars; even (it appears) the Dominican friar Savonarola.[17] They all absorbed from Ficino the *Symposium*'s message that "poets and other makers of beautiful things" share the same desire to achieve virtue through their creative powers—and through their love of beauty, they draw themselves closer to God.

The message surfaces in the poetry of Lorenzo de' Medici himself:

> The soul's most holy bliss is to enjoy
> this good by means of longing, for desire
> proceeds from love and leads the soul to God.
> Love is the just reward of love that's loved.
> Love is what gives us everlasting peace.
> Love is true health, unfailing and complete.

And in the sonnets of another figure at the Medici court, Michelangelo:

> Love, when the soul quit God, made you be light
> And brilliancy, and me a steady eye;

So my great longing cannot fail to see
Him in what's mortal in you, to our hurt.
As heat from fire, likewise my admiration
Cannot be parted from eternal Beauty
Praising Him most like it who is its cause.

The Platonic Academy set off a courtly love poetry revival based on the models of Dante and Petrarch, but really inspired by Ficino's doctrine that love is the desire for beauty. Pseudo-Platonic dialogues discussing the nature of love, either profane or divine but preferably both, became steady bestsellers (as books like *How to Find the Love of Your Life* still are). All across Europe, poets from William Shakespeare to Pierre de Ronsard penned madrigals and sonnets to their Lady Love, which were actually testaments to a deeper love of the spirit. Meanwhile, painters like Titian used the rich pigments of the Renaissance palette to depict *Sacred and Profane Love*.

The best place to get a feel for Ficino's Platonism at full flood, however, is at Florence's Uffizi Gallery and Botticelli's twin masterpieces, *Spring* and *The Birth of Venus*. Both were inspired by love ballads from the pen of Angelo Poliziano, a close disciple of Ficino's and a major figure at his Academy:

Welcome to Spring
Who wishes a man to love,
And you, girls, in a ring
With those you're lovers of,
To make yourselves lovely for love
With roses and flowers in May.

The "girls in a ring" are in fact the Three Graces, allegorical figures from pagan mythology whom Ficino identified (following Plotinus) as symbolizing the circular movement of divine love, flowing ceaselessly from God to the soul and then back to heaven again; but also the triad, that ancient Pythagorean symbol of wholeness and perfection.* At the same time, the Graces were

---

*Ficino also identified this Pythagorean triad with the triad of Truth, Harmony, and Beauty in Plato's *Philebus*, plus Mercury, Apollo, and Venus in astrology, and even the Holy Trinity of Father, Son, and Holy Spirit. Confusing? From the Platonist point of view, the great advantage of allegory is that its meaning is never limited to a single proposition, as in Aristotle's logic. A symbol like the Graces can refer to all three triads or trinities at once, or more. "Whichever among these you as-identified with the pagan goddess of love Venus. She of course appears in both paintings: clothed in *Spring*, in the folds of classical drapery, but completely nude in the other as she emerges, newly born, from the sea—and the realm of the Forms.

Like the Graces and *Spring*, *The Birth of Venus* is arranged in a triad. On one side are the "passionate winds"—*zefiri lascivi*, Poliziano calls them—symbolizing the power of love at its carnal starting point, the passionate frenzy of Eros. On other side is the allegorical figure of Spring again, clothed, and looking very self-contained as she offers a cloak to the nude Venus. Physical profane love is transformed into chaste divine love, the endpoint of the Platonic creative ascent—just as the face of Botticelli's Venus dissolves into his depictions of the Virgin Mary.

Sexual desire carries the seed (literally) of its spiritual opposite; in a profound sense, they are indistinguishable. Through love we find the highest even in the lowest (as the Pseudo-Dionysius might say): perfection in imperfection; or harmony where others see discord. Ficino even claims that in the *Timaeus*, Plato locates Love at the very heart of the primeval Chaos from which cosmic order will emerge.[18] As inspired by Ficino, Botticelli's *Birth of Venus* blurs the frontier that divides the two sides of our nature, body and soul, in order to overcome their contradictions—and thus reconcile us with the unity of the cosmos.

Most people wouldn't think of the pagan goddess of love as a symbol of concord and balance. Certainly not the Romans, who saw only her frankly carnal nature, let alone Augustine or Neoplatonists of the Middle Ages. But in the 1400s, the poets and scholars at the Florentine Academy did—just as she and her allegorical entourage in Botticelli's painting symbolized the concord between ancient and modern thought. What Ficino had proved (or at least seemed to prove) was that there was no real clash between Christian and pagan systems of theology. In the end, they arose from the same source: the soul's love of beauty and perfection and its relentless aspiration for knowledge of God and therefore of ourselves.

Cyril Connolly once said that in every fat person was a thin person struggling to get out. For Ficino and his followers, inside every human body is a

---

sume," wrote Plotinus's disciple Proclus, "it is the same with the others, because all of them are in each other, and [all] are rooted in the One."

soul struggling to get out and realize its creative powers through the pursuit of the Eternal. The evidence is all around us. Everywhere we go on the globe we find churches, temples, holy sites, and tombs dedicated to one deity or another, along with sacred texts and artifacts. All express the same spiritual impulse and movement; all are products of the same desire to realize the highest truth.

It was a stunning revelation. Renaissance Platonism realized that it was this quest for spiritual perfection that bound together all the great religions and civilizations: Egypt, the Chaldeans and Babylonians, the Persians and Hebrews, the Greeks and Romans. All were suddenly revealed to be part of the same spiritual Big Push. All were revealed to be different aspects of the One.

The desire to trace the origins and contours of that Big Push overtook Ficino's Academy in its later years, especially after the arrival of Giovanni Pico della Mirandola. As intellectually gifted as he was aristocratic (he was actually Prince della Mirandola), Pico read not only Greek and Latin, but Hebrew and Arabic. Although only in his twenties, he had studied science and mathematics as well as literature and philosophy. He was as much at home with the medieval scholastics as with the wisdom of the ancients. Historians have labeled several scholars in the Renaissance as being "the last man to know everything," including Erasmus and Francis Bacon. Giovanni Pico is the true owner of the title.

His staggering range of interests and his inexhaustible scholarly energy were aimed at a single mission. This was to prove that all religions and philosophies, ancient and modern, pagan and Christian, actually formed *a single body of knowledge*. On the surface, Plato and Aristotle, Hebrew, Islamic, and Christian theologies, seemed hard to reconcile. But underneath them all, Pico argued, was a shared set of universal truths handed down over the centuries to certain great wise men, who then passed them along to their successors.

In this way, the essential message of Christianity had been with the pagans all along, "and it was with the human race from its beginning to the time when Christ appeared in the flesh; from whence the true religion, *which already existed*, was called Christianity."[19] Pico even drew up a final list of nine hundred theses that underpinned all philosophies and religions and doctrines, drawing from such diverse sources as the followers of Plato and Aristotle, but also from Thomas Aquinas and Duns Scotus, the Hebrew Kabbalah and Arab philosophers and Pythagoras—even the magical treatises of the mysterious ancient alchemist Hermes Trismegistus.

To modern eyes, the list veers from the esoteric ("What is called otherness in the *Parmenides* and supercelestial place in the *Phaedrus* is the same") to the wildly commonplace ("Friendship is a virtue"). The entries also reveal the heavy impact of Pythagorean formulae ("The proportion of reason to sensual passion is an octave"). Above all, they are a tribute to Plato, especially the notion of the soul as immortal and as "the source of motion and the governess of matter." For Pico, "the science of the soul is intermediate between natural and divine [knowledge]."[20]

In fact, Pico's goal was to dissolve any difference between theology and philosophy, science and literature, art and poetry. *All* knowledge was One, as aspects of the One: and human beings come uniquely equipped to unravel its final secrets.

And since all knowledge forms a whole, the corollary is never throw anything away. Every doctrine, no matter how esoteric or seemingly irrational or irrelevant, may hold yet another secret to understanding the rest. This was why Ficino translated Plotinus with an extensive commentary and broke off his work on Plato at Cosimo de' Medici's insistence in order to translate the secret works of Hermes Trismegistus.[21] It was also why Pico immersed himself in the Kabbalah and studied the ancient Orphic hymns in hopes that their harmonies might reveal special magical properties.

In truth as in love, what we want isn't always what we get—nor is it always where we expect to find it. To the Renaissance Platonist, the highest truths arrive with a sign: "Handle with Care." Christ and Moses clothed their revelation in allegories and parables; so did Plato (including the cave of the *Republic* and Atlantis in the *Timaeus*). "Divine subjects and the secret Mysteries must not be rashly divulged," Pico says. All "divine knowledge . . . must be covered with enigmatic veils and poetic dissimulation. . . ."[22] No one can know what other strange but powerful secrets might be buried in the most unlikely places, not by accident but by design.

It was a strange moment. The belief in the unity of all knowledge, and that throughout history the profoundest truths are the ones most heavily veiled, would lead the Renaissance mind down some dark passageways, including alchemy and black magic. In the age of Galileo, it led to a fascination with the Rosicrucians and the possibility that a secret brotherhood of the Rosy Cross controlled access to the world's final hidden truths.[23] Still later, the same impulse would lead researchers to pursue the "secrets" of the Freemasons and the Knights Templar, to hunt for the Lost Ark and the mysterious kingdom of Agartha in the bowels of the earth—or even UFOs.

If there was one Platonic staircase that led the soul from profane to divine love, there's another that leads from Pico's 900 *Theses* to *The Da Vinci Code*. In fact, scratch your average conspiracy theorist and you'll probably find a renegade Platonist underneath.

Still, modern conspiracy theories are geared to reinforce our sense of helplessness in the face of dark, powerful forces. By contrast, Pico's unity of knowledge, like Ficino's doctrine of Platonic love, exalted and celebrated the powers of man. Of all creatures natural or celestial, the human being has no fixed place in the Great Chain of Being. He alone is capable of occupying, according to his choice, any degree of life from the highest to the lowest.

"Thine own free will," Pico has God tell Adam in *Oration on the Dignity of Man* (the introduction to his 900 *Theses*), "shall ordain for thyself the limits of thy nature." The highest and most marvelous happiness for human beings is that they face no divinely imposed limits. "To [man] is granted the power to have whatever he chooses, to be whatever he wills." If he wants to be a sage or a garbageman, he is free to choose. However, if he chooses the life of intelligent understanding, "he will be an angel and a son of God" and be able to draw to himself the unity of all things—just as his own spirit is made one with God.[24]

Pico's is a heady vision: Doctor Faustus, indeed, without the Devil. And certainly the Renaissance Platonist vision of the unity of all knowledge stood in sharp contrast with the Aristotle of the medieval schoolmen, with his insistence on making divisions and distinctions and creating niggling little categories and compartments.

Yet ironically it was Ficino, Pico, and the Renaissance Platonists who saved Aristotle from the historical rubbish heap where his followers were leading him. Pico was a keen student of Aristotle; his emphasis on the power of free will sprang directly from reading the *Ethics*.[25] The Renaissance Platonist program recognized that Aristotle too was part of the One and that his insights had their place in the larger understanding of the cosmos.

In the end, it was Pico and his friends who gave Aristotle his significance in the life of the modern Western mind as the philosopher of nature, including human nature. That is how he appears in Raphael's *School of Athens*, that glorious visual summing up of the legacy of Greek philosophy—and the direct product of the ideas of Pico della Mirandola.[26]

Now when we enter the *Stanza della Segnatura* with the Florentine Platonists in mind, we immediately see that the entire theme of the painting is Pico's insistence that the philosophies of Plato and Aristotle formed a single harmonious whole and that the unity of all knowledge extends across the entire room, from philosophy and theology (represented by the fresco called the *Disputa*) to the arts and law.

In fact, Pico himself appears not once but twice in *The School of Athens*. On Plato's side he stands next to Pythagoras and looks directly at the viewer. He also stands with his back to the viewer on *Aristotle's* side, gazing with open admiration at the famed Peripatetic. A similar balancing harmonizing act carries over to the other figures in the painting, almost all of whom also appear in the catalog of great sages in Pico's *Oration on the Dignity of Man*.[27] The practical geometer Euclid is balanced by the mystical Pythagoras; Diogenes, the philosopher who celebrated owning nothing, is balanced by the pleasure-loving Epicurus.

Socrates, the creator of the *Republic's* ideal constitution, stands beside Plato; just as Solon, creator of Athens's real constitution, stands beside Aristotle. In a similar way, the astronomer Ptolemy stands opposite the Neoplatonist pagan priestess Hypatia, each reflecting the two aspects of the school of Alexandria.[28]

Each pairing, in fact, helps us to see Plato and Aristotle as Pico or any student of Ficino's would have seen them: as the twin "princes of philosophy," the unsurpassed masters of understanding the two halves of man's existence.

Plato holds a copy of his *Timaeus*, since Pico and his colleagues understood that Plato was superior to Aristotle in his understanding of metaphysics and of man as part of the divine order.[29] Aristotle, on the other side, holds his *Nicomachean Ethics*, the work that offered the key to understanding the principles of human virtue and happiness—the key to understanding man as a part of nature. Both stand under an architectural setting with three magnificent barrel vaults, suggesting the triad of perfection and the Trinity, since the unity of Plato and Aristotle, Pico wrote, prefigures the unity of God.[30]

At first glance, *The School of Athens* seems to sum up a heritage of time-

Giovanni Pico della Mirandola (facing the viewer, right), in Raphael's *School of Athens*. (To his lower right are Pythagoras and the Arab philosopher Avveröes). Pico is the only thinker to appear twice in the painting.

less wisdom. In reality, it reveals a daring new synthesis and heralds a new beginning for Western thinking. Giovanni Pico never completed his *Concord of Plato and Aristotle,* from which he claimed he would build "a new philosophy." However, he did leave his program for both Raphael's painting and his *900 Theses,* which expressed an attitude to knowledge best summed up by the modern physicist Niels Bohr, "We achieve clarity through breadth." For the Platonist, the Big Picture is always what counts. Our job is to figure out how all the small bits and fragments, even seeming opposites, actually fit together into a coherent whole.

Indeed, mention of the Big Picture leads our attention down the hall from Raphael's fresco to what in artistic as well as philosophical terms is the biggest picture of all: the Sistine Chapel.

> *What is this thing called love,*
> *[which] Through the eyes invades the heart,*
> *And seems to swell in the small space inside?*
> *And what if it burst out?*

. . .

Even as a boy, Michelangelo Buonarroti tells us, "I had a gift for beauty." Born in 1475, he grew up in the palace of Lorenzo the Magnificent, where he absorbed the ideas of Ficino's Academy and Platonist theology from the tutor of Lorenzo's sons, Angelo Poliziano. He may have met Giovanni Pico and heard him expound the reconciliation of Platonism and Christianity. Contemporaries all noted that Michelangelo's poetry was "full of Platonic conceptions"; so was his art.[31] In fact, if a single idea dominates Michelangelo's life and career, it was the notion that in moments of deep feeling and Platonic exaltation, the human mind can break through to God's perfection.

The Florentine Academy taught Michelangelo that the aim of all art was to re-create a preordained harmony, whose elements and proportions were laid down by God Himself. The best example was music. Ficino sang Orphic hymns, and Pico was fascinated by Pythagorean theories of mathematical harmony. Painting enjoyed a similar status thanks to the science of perspective.* Michelangelo turned sculpture into a similar pursuit of divine perfection. When he was a teenager, contemporaries considered his works the equal of the ancient Greeks and Romans. He told astonished friends that in his mind the perfect images he carved were already there, like Plato's Forms, embedded in the block of marble. They were only waiting for the hand of the artist to set them free.[32]

Michelangelo was a child of Florence in other ways. He was briefly a follower of Savonarola, as Machiavelli had been; and like Machiavelli, he was a true believer in the restored republic.[33] His earliest monumental work, the *David*, is a visual tribute to that older civic humanist philosophy of virtue and self-sacrifice for the sake of liberty.

But Michelangelo's hopes, like those of the author of *The Prince*, ended in disillusionment. When the Florentine republic fell in 1512, he wrote from Rome to tell his brother to stay inside, not speak or reveal his thoughts to anyone but God, "because the end of things is not known; just attend to your own affairs."[34]

This is just what Michelangelo did during his nearly decade-long stay in Rome, from 1505 to 1513. What he saw at the court of Pope Julius II only confirmed his gloomiest suspicions: "Virtue's what Heaven must despise . . .

---

*An idea that also inspired Leonardo da Vinci. See chapter 19.

seeing they would give us a dead tree from which to pluck our fruit." He had stormy dealings with a pope more interested in waging war with his neighbors and building the most grandiose church in Christendom (the new Saint Peter's) than in reforming the Church, and who appeared as often in a suit of armor as in papal vestments.

These were times, Michelangelo wrote, that would try the patience of Christ himself.

> *He should not come again into this province,*
> *Up to the very stars his blood would spread;*
> *Now that in Rome his skin is being sold;*
> *And they have closed the way to every goodness.*

> *Yet if High Heaven favors poverty,*
> *But other goals cut off our other life,*
> *What is there in our [inner] state that can restore us?*[35]

The answer is love. However, Michelangelo's perspective on love is far more turbulent and disturbing, almost self-defeating, than the tranquil version he learned in the garden of Lorenzo de' Medici's palace. It is underlined by a kind of anguish. Michelangelo constantly compares love to a burning fire that sears the consciousness and torments the body, but also scours away worldly corruption, so that the soul "like gold purged in a fire returns to God."

In other words, the creative ascent is not easy or carefully calibrated, as the scholars of Ficino's Academy imagined. It is filled with self-doubt and inner pain. But the process of suffering also makes us worthy of our spiritual perfection.

> *Only with fire can the smith bend the iron*
> *As he's conceived his beautiful work;*
> *And gold, except with fire, to its high mark*
> *No artisan can carry and refine.*
> *The phoenix cannot live again*
> *unless it first burns. . . .*
> *If by its nature [fire] goes up to Heaven,*
> *To its own element, and I'm converted*
> *Into fire, how can it be it will not take me?*[36]

Michelangelo began work on the Sistine Chapel ceiling in the spring of 1508. We know from his letters that the plan of the ceiling was largely his own.[37] By the time he finished four years later, he had transformed the pope's commission into his personal statement on the grand themes of the Platonism of his day—and into the artistic masterpiece of the Renaissance.

It is the perfect counterpart to *The School of Athens,* and Giovanni Pico would have been the perfect person to decipher the ceiling's rich complexity and its various veiled meanings. For instance, he would have immediately recognized why Michelangelo broke the ceiling down into three separate zones, each stacked above the other.

The lowest, running along the tops of the chapel's walls, are peopled with Old Testament figures who represent the human earthly realm. The second, with its enormous figures of prophets and sibyls, is the realm where the human mind first grasps the meaning of the Eternal through prophecy (which Plato compared with the "divine madness" of love) but also through the vision of physical beauty, symbolized by the nude so-called athletes arranged above each architectural bay.[38]

The third realm, the great spine of Michelangelo's plan, are the panels depicting the Book of Genesis, where the soul experiences God's presence directly. The entire work gives us a visual tour of what a disciple of Ficino would call *deificatio,* or the soul's return to God, the final consummation of spiritual enlightenment.

The Sistine ceiling contains no direct references to Christianity or Christ. Michelangelo the Platonist didn't feel the need for any, because his message is more universal. Instead all the scenes are from the Old Testament, which every Renaissance Platonist knew to be the ground zero of *docta religio,* the true religion shared by all peoples and faiths. In the same way, Michelangelo has paired each male biblical prophet with a female Roman pagan prophet, the sibyls who had prophesied the coming of a future Savior. This symbolizes the harmony of the religious revelation of the Hebrews not only with Christianity, but with the religion of the ancients.

It is only when we come to the central panels that we see that Michelangelo has moved Renaissance Platonism to a new level of consciousness. As art historian S. J. Freedberg observes, there is nothing like it anywhere in the writings of the age—perhaps not even in Plato's own works.[39]

The theme is the struggle of the human soul to escape its physical limitations of the body in order to realize its true freedom. The panels depict the central episodes from Genesis in a dynamic but abruptly edited sequence like a Stanley Kubrick movie, starting with creation and God's separation of light from darkness: a visualization of spiritual energy at its most divine and abstract. However, Michelangelo has arranged the sequence in reverse order. When we enter the chapel and look up at each panel, what we actually see is a chronicle of the soul's ascent from the realm of matter to that of pure spirit.

We start with the Drunkenness of Noah, where the body has completely taken over. All the same, just as in the *Symposium*, the ecstasy of inebriation paradoxically also hints at the spark for future transformation. Then comes the Great Flood, where physical catastrophe (like those engulfing Machiavelli's beloved Florence and the rest of Italy) stirs the human spirit to respond with courage and resolution.

Then comes man's recognition of the divine with the Sacrifice of Noah. As yet, however, this knowledge of the divine comes to us darkly and from a distance, thanks to the episode that comes next: the Expulsion from the Garden of Eden. Through Adam's Fall, humanity has lost touch with its spiritual side. Without that vital root, the world is no longer a garden of delights. Instead, it is "a dead tree from which to pluck our fruit," namely the fruit of virtue: a barren testing ground for man's free will.

What's missing is revealed in the central panel and the most famous, the Creation of Adam. It is also the most potent in terms of the Platonist tradition. Adam appears as the epitome of the classical ideal of male physical beauty—except that he is passive and inert, a dumb block of flesh waiting for the spark of the Holy Spirit, which Saint Augustine had identified as the finger of God. That divine finger now transmits the gift of life and spirit, reminding us of Pico's words in *Oration on the Dignity of Man:* "On man when he came to life the Father conferred the seeds of all kinds and the germs of every way of life."

By the act of creating Adam, God has transferred His own creative powers to man, "the mortal counterpart of God."[40] This is Michelangelo's secret message to his viewers: the secret of our own divine nature. We need only to recognize and unlock its potential to transform our lives and ourselves.

Plato taught that if you wish to be able to recognize God, Ficino wrote, "you must first learn to know yourself."[41] The same is true for Michelangelo. As Machiavelli noted, the world is a grim place, especially in 1512, where it

Creation of Adam, Sistine Chapel ceiling

seemed that every trace of freedom or liberty had been snuffed out. The slave "grows so much accustomed to his anguish that he would hardly ask again for freedom."

But the freedom *is* there, first revealed by love.

> *Love wakens, rouses, puts wings to feather*
> *So that the soul will soar*
> *And rise to its maker. . . .*

Michelangelo's ceiling was finished in 1512. The next year a church council officially endorsed Ficino's doctrine of the immortality of the soul. The world seemed on the verge of a final reconciliation of ancient philosophy and Christian theology, exactly what Raphael had made visible in his frescos in the *Stanze*.

Instead, a chain of events was about to abruptly change the direction of European thought once again—a chain that started virtually outside the *Stanze*'s doors.

Martin Luther (1463–94): He believed Satan himself had
introduced the study of Aristotle.

Eighteen

TWILIGHT OF THE SCHOLASTICS: THE REFORMATION AND THE DOOM OF ARISTOTLE

Compared to the study of theology, the whole of Aristotle is as darkness is to light.

—Martin Luther, 1517

"I'm not in a good place," Michelangelo wrote gloomily to a friend as the Sistine ceiling took shape, "and I'm no painter."[1] In those last weeks of 1510, Michelangelo would have risen every day before dawn, while the stars still shone in the darkness. As the sky turned a chilly gray, he would have made his way past the massive unfinished piers of the pope's basilica, Saint Peter's. Bramante's workmen would have appeared like shadows, as they yawned and stretched among the piles of masonry and coils of rope. Like Michelangelo, they were readying themselves for another day of back-crushing labor.

On his way to the Vatican Palace, Michelangelo might have caught sight of another man, a thickset young man with large flashing eyes and a firm, determined jaw. It was the kind of striking face Michelangelo might have used for one of his athletes, maybe for Adam himself. Then again, he might not have noticed him at all. The young man was in a monk's habit, blending in with the hundreds of other clerics, both lay and regular,* who wandered the winding streets of Rome.

The young monk was from the north, from Germany. He was in Rome on ecclesiastical business. While he was waiting for an audience with the head of his order, the Augustinians, he had decided to see the Eternal City's sights.

Unlike the modern tourist, he had no interest in seeing the Sistine Chapel or Raphael's *School of Athens* in the papal *Stanze*. Nor did he pay attention to the Forum or other monuments of the ancient Rome admired by the humanists. This monk had come to see the holy sites of medieval Rome, the City of Martyrs. There were the catacombs where the early Church had been born; the cemetery at San Sebastiano, where forty-six popes and eighty thousand martyrs were buried; and St. Peter's, where the relics of Christianity's two greatest saints, Peter and Paul, were laid.[2] The monk was twenty-seven years old, and no callow, inexperienced youth. Still, he was horrified by what he saw.

He had expected to find these holy sites surrounded with a hushed, hallowed atmosphere. Instead, the atmosphere was like a carnival, with priests saying Mass for weary, grimy pilgrims and their bawling children and then telling them to move on, with cries of, "Next! Next!" Other pilgrims pushed and shoved to get a glimpse of the severed arms of Saint Anne, mother of the Virgin Mary, or Jesus's footprint on a slab of marble, or one of thirty pieces of silver given to Judas Iscariot. One touch of the coin, it was said, was enough to spare a sinner 1,400 years in purgatory, the Church's vestibule between heaven and hell. That wasn't bad, although the monk knew that back home in the reliquary of Wittenberg Castle, a glimpse of a thorn from the crown of thorns and a branch from the burning bush could save a person 127,000 years of purgatorial torment, give or take a decade or two.[3]

The holy relic that drew the young monk most was Pilate's Staircase, the Scala Santa. It stood in a small chapel near Saint John Lateran. It consisted of twenty-eight white marble steps and was supposed to have been trod by Jesus when he was brought before Pontius Pilate. Constantine's mother, Saint Helen, had brought the staircase from Jerusalem to Rome in the fourth

---

* "Lay" meaning clergy like priests and bishops who dealt with the laity; "regular" meaning monks, nuns, and friars in holy orders.

century. Legend had it that the dark stains in the marble were drops of Christ's own blood.

Penitents stood in a long line to crawl up the Scala Santa on their knees. They were supposed to kiss each step on the way up, then at the top utter a short prayer. The reward for this feat, according to a recent papal decree, was a plenary indulgence—in effect a Get Out of Purgatory Free card.

Finally it was the young monk's turn. Grasping his rosary firmly in one hand and balancing himself with the other, he began his spiritual ascent—a very different one from Michelangelo or Ficino's.

Shoving off from his knees, the monk managed to climb the first step. He steadied himself and recited a short prayer:

> Holy Mother, pierce me then
> In my heart each wound anew
> Of my Savior crucified.

With a grunt he moved to the second step and repeated the same prayer. Then the third; and the fourth. It was easier than he had imagined. If only his parents were dead, he thought, so that he could use this miraculous staircase to save them from purgatory as well.[4]

He had just reached the last step, breathing heavily and perspiring under his monk's cowl, when suddenly he heard himself say, almost in a trance:

"*Who knows if any of this is true?*"

That terrible thought haunted him the rest of his stay in Rome and on the journey home to Germany. What if all the elaborate penances, pilgrimages, and viewing of relics—in effect the whole machinery of rituals and ceremonies that the Church classified under the heading "Penance and Good Works"—actually did nothing to save the human soul? He knew that certain reform-minded writers were dismissing the whole cult of relics and saints as a disgrace and a fraud. Still, he had gone to Rome hoping to feel spiritually cleansed. Instead, he came back feeling dirtier and more disgraced in the eyes of God than before.

Those feelings of inadequacy had haunted him almost from the moment he had become an Augustinian monk five years earlier. Who was he, miserable sinner that he was, to preach the word of God; to hear confessions and administer last rites; or even to touch the body and blood of Christ in saying the Holy Mass? Nothing had seemed to relieve that terrible burden and frightening responsibility.

Now, as he returned to Wittenberg to prepare lectures on the Bible and theology for his bored and restless students, his harrowing experiences in Rome made certain passages from Scripture leap off the page at him. One in particular left him transfixed, a passage from the letters of Saint Paul (Romans 1:17): "The just shall live by faith."

All at once, the powerful simplicity of the message struck home. All the pilgrimages and penances and vows and giving alms to the poor and climbing sacred stairs hadn't relieved his guilt, *because they didn't count.* It was faith, and faith alone, the confident resolute belief that Jesus Christ was his Redeemer, that made the righteous "live" through salvation and that finally lifted the veil of sin from the human soul.

"The just shall live by *faith.*" In other words, no relic, no person, no priest, not even the pope himself, could absolve anyone from sin, because such forgiveness was beyond the power of any mortal creature. Only God could do that, and only those who believed in Him with all their hearts would receive that absolution. In fact, there was no other kind of righteousness *except* through God.[5]

If that was true, then why had everyone else, including centuries of theologians, gotten it so wrong? How had the Church, after being founded on that rock of faith, gotten so far off track? Suddenly, Martin Luther thought he knew.

Sitting on his bookshelf were the works of Aristotle and his scholastic followers: William of Ockham, Duns Scotus, and Luther's own mentor Gabriel Biel. These were the vaunted intellectual giants of the medieval Church. He himself had taught their ideas for years, along with the works of Aristotle. Indeed, as Martin Luther would write later, "I have read [Aristotle] and studied him with more understanding than did Saint Thomas Aquinas or Duns Scotus."[6] However, by adopting Aristotle's view of man and nature, the Church's leading spokesmen had set that institution down the wrong path for centuries.

"It pains me to the heart," Luther wrote, "that this damnable arrogant pagan rascal has seduced and fooled so many of the best Christians with his misleading writings," especially the *Physics* and *Metaphysics* and *On the Soul.* It was time to shove these works aside and start over with Holy Scripture, and Holy Scripture alone. Time to clean house, intellectually and spiritually.

Gazing at the volumes on his shelf, "I cannot avoid believing," Luther mused, "that it was Satan himself who introduced the study of Aristotle."[7]

The scholarly output on Martin Luther and the Reformation fills entire libraries. The most recent popular "survey" of the period runs to some eight hundred pages.[8] So how does this extraordinary episode in the history of the West fit into the story of the clash between Plato and Aristotle?

The answer comes from Martin Luther himself. His first breach with the Church did *not* come with his famous *Ninety-five Theses*, which he posted on the Wittenberg church door on October 31, 1517. It came almost two months earlier, on September 4, when he published another set of theses, *Disputation Against Scholastic Theology*, which are less well-known but nearly as explosive.

They asserted that a Christianity founded on the spiritual power of God's grace—in effect Christianity in its Platonized form as received from Saint Augustine—and the view of law and nature derived from Aristotle could never be reconciled. "The whole Aristotelian ethic," Luther wrote, "is grace's worst enemy." And so as the tidal wave of Reformation overwhelmed the heart of Europe and changed its religious and cultural contours forever, it also swept Aristotle almost out of sight.

Plato's own legacy benefited from this shift in Western civilization's intellectual balance. But it was not its cause. If any single factor really doomed Aristotle as the Middle Ages had known him, and helped reformers like Martin Luther shove him to the sidelines, it was the invention of printing.

Of course, historians have told us at least since the eighteenth century that the printing press triggered a revolution in Western civilization, but not always why. The use of movable type to produce printed books transformed intellectual life not because it meant more copies of a book, but because it meant *identical* copies. As printing pioneers like Germany's Gutenberg and England's William Caxton soon realized, every page seven of a printed copy looks exactly like every other copy's page seven, without variation. This was something not possible even for the most careful and methodical scribe.[9]

Even if the printer or editor made a mistake on the first pass, his assistants could quickly correct it with a single shift of a piece of type—just one more reason why proofreaders are vital to the advance of civilization.* The process meant that every reader of a printed book could now read the same words or see the same image as every other reader; and that those words were as close as humanly possible to what the author had actually written. The same applied to dictionaries, maps, calendars, and other reference works and every translation of those works—as readers of Martin Luther's translation of the New Testament into German in 1522 were to find out.

It was like new sunlight breaking over the intellectual landscape. "Now all disciplines are restored," enthused the French writer François Rabelais, "the study of languages revived. . . . The whole world is full of learned men, of very erudite tutors, of very ample libraries; and it is my opinion that neither in the time of Plato, of Cicero, nor of Papinian, were there such facilities for study as we see now."[10] No wonder Rabelais saw printing as divinely inspired and saw it as the perfect antidote to the kind of highly imperfect education he had received from his scholastic masters at the University of Poitiers.

The printed book doomed the Aristotle of the medieval schoolmen. It ended his intellectual monopoly first of all because now authors appeared in print almost with the same relative ease as they appear online today. These included not only Plato but intriguing and hitherto remote figures like the poet Lucian; dramatists Terence and Sophocles; historians Plutarch and Tacitus and Josephus; and philosophers such as the Stoic Seneca and the Skeptic Sextus Empiricus.

In the preprint days, just trying to "read" Plato's *Republic* was a monumental undertaking. It might take a scholar to three or four different cities, as it did Ficino and Leonardo Bruni, and to a series of dank monastic libraries, in order to collate various incomplete manuscript versions. Then came the work of trying to decipher the original text buried beneath the omissions or finger faults of ignorant or careless scribes.

Now in the privacy of your own home, you had the text correct, complete, and whole—pure and uncorrupted, as Renaissance scholars liked to say. The era of having to rely on untrustworthy handwritten manuscripts, or some medieval glossator who spent a lifetime trying to make sense of an often muddled

---

*The most notorious early example is the so-called Wicked Bible, published by Robert Barker in London in 1631. In the Book of Exodus the typesetter made a fateful slip, so that the Seventh Commandment came out: "Thou shalt commit adultery."

or even counterfeit manuscript of Aristotle, was over. So was the age of the classroom commentator. The age of the *érudit*, the antiquarian, and the man of letters was about to begin.[11]

In the long term, the print revolution turned out to be a boon for Aristotle. His works could be studied by more readers than ever, in cleaned-up versions. Apocryphal works and even outright forgeries (like the fake Aristotelian *Theology*) were eliminated. But in the short term, it exposed the shortcomings of those who had relied on him as the ultimate authority on everything, especially in universities. Reformation scholars not only had more books, but had their time freed up to ponder, to cross-reference, and to set texts side by side. Thanks to printing, "contradictions became more visible, divergent traditions more difficult to reconcile"—and innovations faster to catch on.[12] The authority of Aristotle gave way to the authority of the printed word, including the Word of God.

The man who discovered the power behind that authority was not Gutenberg or Caxton or even Luther. It was Erasmus of Rotterdam. Later, some would say Erasmus "laid the egg that Luther hatched." This is not true. But Erasmus was the first to slay the scholastic giant—and he used the sword of Renaissance Platonism to do it.

Europe's most famous scholar was born in 1469, fourteen years after Gutenberg began producing his first printed Vulgate Bible. That book, as it happened, would be at the center of Erasmus's career as well as Luther's.

Erasmus grew up at a school at Steyn run by the Brethren of the Common Life, where his teachers steeped him in all the themes of the *devotio moderna* and Neoplatonic mystical piety. The focus on the inner emotions of belief, on the "life in Christ" as the highest expression of our spiritual essence and the highest form of wisdom, and on Holy Scripture as the primary authority on a devout life all became the guiding principles of his life and career.

The school's headmaster also gave him a passion for reading the ancient classics, especially Cicero.[13] In the 1480s, the only outlet for a boy with intellectual gifts but no connections (Erasmus was illegitimate) was the Church— even for a boy who was the illegitimate son of a priest. He entered the same order as Martin Luther, the Augustinians. But unlike Luther, Erasmus never felt any need to cleanse away an overwhelming sense of sin. Instead, his one wish always was to surround himself with good books and intelligent companions; to walk in a sunlit garden and discuss Cicero and the ancient poets; in short, to read, write, and dream.

All these were in short supply in the monastery at Steyn. When Erasmus got his first opportunity to escape and pursue studies abroad, he took it. He went first to the University of Paris, which he found was hardly better than his monastery, and then to England and Oxford, where he met the scholar who would change his life.

As a university, Oxford had not come very far from the days of Ockham and Roger Bacon; in fact, it had largely regressed. Few students or teachers were interested in Cicero or Erasmus's other literary heroes. There was, however, a new teacher at Magdalen College named John Colet, who had immersed himself in the humanism coming out of Italy and its Platonist themes. He and Erasmus found an instant harmony. In listening to Colet speak, Erasmus wrote later, he "seemed to be listening to Plato himself."[14]

This is not surprising. Colet was in regular contact with Marsilio Ficino, and he shared the same fascination as the Florentine for the parallels between Platonism and Christianity.[15] However, Colet picked up Ficino's *Platonic Theology* at the other, Christian end. He paid less attention to how Plato had foreshadowed the message of the Gospels than to how that message could and should be read in a bright Platonist light.

Reading it was part of the difficulty. Greek and Latin are what is called inflected languages, from the point of view of grammar. The ending of a word, and not (as in English or German) the word's position in the sentence, determines its meaning, even whether the word is the sentence's subject or object—or whether it is singular or plural. So changing just a single letter—for example, *-am* to *-ae* in Latin, or *-eiv* to *-ouv* in Greek—can turn the meaning of a sentence inside out.

That's precisely what centuries of ill-trained, inattentive, or just tired and bored monks and scribes had done to virtually every ancient text, including the Bible. As the first humanists in Italy discovered, recovering the original textual meaning required a combination of hard work and grammatical skill, ranging from collating as many copies as possible in order to learn which had the fewest mistakes, and where later copying errors had come from; to a fine-tuned sense of which word or grammatical form an author like Cicero or Plato might have used, in a given time and place—a medieval scribe's mistakes notwithstanding.

Over time Ficino, Colet, and their colleagues raised the art of recovering a corrupt text's lost meaning to a science, which they called philology. Cleaning up and clearing up the written works of antiquity became an Italian, and Florentine, specialty, as philology uncovered new or startling meanings in even the most familiar documents—as trained philologist Lorenzo Valla learned as papal secretary in 1440, when his rigorous examination of the so-called Donation of Constantine revealed it to be a forgery. It was bad news for the papacy but good news for Valla's integrity as a scholar—and for the growing reputation of philology as the latchkey for unlocking the truth.

For Colet, philology was only a means to understand one text in particular, the Bible. In his eyes, the New Testament revealed how faith in Christ was the sublime example of the soul's striving for a higher transcendent truth, and how that faith could lead the soul upward to redemption and union with God. Colet's sermons revealed to Erasmus for the first time a Neoplatonist message as old as Origen: that the path to salvation lay *inward* as a form of personal enlightenment rather than (or at least not exclusively) in *outward* rites and rituals.

It was also Colet who suggested to Erasmus that he fuse his two interests, the Bible and ancient literature, into one. He urged him to do for ancient Christian literature, including the New Testament, what Ficino had done for Plato: use the techniques of philology to produce a clean, definitive text free from copyists' errors and scholastic muddles, a "pure Scripture" that would show people what the Bible really said, not what tradition or the allegorists said it meant. By doing so, Colet urged, Erasmus could point others to the true spirit of Christianity and the true path to salvation.

To make this his life's work, Erasmus needed three things. He needed to learn Greek to read the New Testament—which, with immense difficulty and effort, he ended up having to teach himself. Second, he had to go to Italy, to study and absorb the emerging science of philology. This he did in 1506, stopping first at the University of Turin to receive a degree as doctor of theology, which licensed him to study and write on religious topics.[16]

The final thing Erasmus needed was a way to get his message out, to reveal the spiritual riches of the Bible and the Church Fathers to Western Christendom. He found that in the spring in 1507, when he arrived in Venice and walked into the print shop of the most able and profitable publisher in Italy, Aldus Manutius.

From the start, it was a perfect partnership. For the next decade and a half, we have to imagine Europe's most distinguished humanist doing almost all his writing in Aldus's workshop (and later that of Johann Froben in Basel), with the printing press clanking in the background. Erasmus would write out virtually everything from memory. Then he handed his manuscript to the printer, supervised the setting of the type, and finally corrected the pages as they came off the press. "Aldus kept me so busy," Erasmus remembered later, "I didn't have time to scratch my ears."

After a while, the Hollander got other eminent scholars to step in and do the correcting. Even Aldus Manutius himself took time from his busy publishing schedule to act as Erasmus's proofreader. "Why?" the astonished scholar asked him. "Because that way I can learn at the same time," Aldus replied.[17]

One by one, Erasmus's works poured out and were handed over to Venetian merchants, who loaded them aboard ships and pack mules to carry to every city in Europe. Aldus Manutius's Aldine Press made Erasmus the first writer to earn a living with his pen. This was no mean feat since his books were all written in Latin, which meant they could be read everywhere but only by a small minority.

The first was his *Adages*, a digest of quotations from classical Latin authors and Greek authors translated into Latin, an early Bartlett's *Quotations* which other scholars could use to perfect an elegant Latin style. The *Adages* did more than any other single book to introduce the insights of classical antiquity, including Plato, to a wide reading public—and to make Erasmus's reputation as the best scholar of his day.[18]

Then came an edition of Saint Jerome's letters; the *Enchiridion*, Erasmus's own guide to a Christian "purpose-driven life" (and heavily influenced by Pico's *Oration on the Dignity of Man*) and finally a translation of the New Testament in 1516. By exposing many of the errors of the old Latin Vulgate, Erasmus established a new appreciation for "pure Scripture" as the final authority on all things spiritual as well as many secular.

However, none of these compared with the success of the work that he wrote in 1509 after returning briefly to England, the satire that made him Christendom's biggest bestselling author: *In Praise of Folly*.

The book is an imaginary conversation with the goddess Moria (in Latin, Folly or Stupidity), in which she sings the praises of her devotees, who turn out to be members of the conventional medieval establishment. They include kings and popes and bishops and Erasmus's fellow monks, but above

Desiderius Erasmus (1483–1536): Plato and the printing press
turned him into the world's first bestselling author.

all, the university followers of Aristotle. Erasmus never goes after Aristotle directly, but for the rest—"realists, nominalists, Thomists, Albertists, Occamists and Scotists"—he accuses them of poisoning the true message of Christianity with "their syllogisms, major and minor, conclusions, corollaries, idiotic hypotheses, and further scholastic rubbish."

As Erasmus wrote, "The language of truth is always simple, says Seneca: well then, nothing is simpler or truer than Christ." However, the Aristotelians' formal logic and "torturous obscurities" had sullied that simplicity and truth, he asserted. "What, I ask you, has Christ to do with Aristotle, or the mysteries of eternal wisdom with subtle sophistry?"[19] The answer, Erasmus affirmed, was to get back to the original source of that faith, the Bible. The whole point of education should be learning the languages and skills needed for unlocking its message, especially a good grounding in Greek and Latin. Only then can the soul's desire for the highest wisdom finally be set free.

The idea of basing one's entire study on reading the Bible might strike us as rather narrow, but the fact was Erasmus had a strong case. It seems incredible today to realize that students in late medieval universities, which were dominated by the Church, learned almost nothing about religion. The traditional arts faculty ran everything, and it was no longer up to the standards of an Abelard or Aquinas. Most teachers were scarcely older than their teenage charges. They preferred to stick to rote memorization and to the traditional *trivium* of grammar, rhetoric, and logic, the last of which had come to mean memorizing the rules for conducting a formal dialectical disputation. No one ventured to discuss God or the soul or the Bible in class. With the Inquisition always watching, it was much too dangerous.[20]

As for philosophy, that subject largely came down to memorizing passages from Aristotle's *Physics* on the movement of the planets or parts of the soul. Much the same was true in medical schools (which is why even today a medical school graduate is referred to as a "physician"). Only the law schools presented some semblance of life and curiosity, which is why they would fuel the intellectual explosion in the last decades of the Reformation.*

Like the Church itself, by 1500 Europe's universities had become victims of their own success. They had become degree factories, and quality control suffered as a result. Just as there were priests who didn't know the Mass or drank or kept mistresses, so there were philosophy professors who invoked the name of Aristotle without having read a single one of his works, and theology professors who had never turned a page of the *Summa* or *The City of God*—or the letters of Saint Paul.[21]

Now, thanks to Erasmus's *In Praise of Folly*, a contempt for universities and their Aristotle-centered curriculum acquired intellectual chic. It has left its trace to this day, as when we talk about something being "trivial" (derived from *trivium*) or call someone a "dunce" (after the original "dunce," John Duns Scotus). When we turn to the popular literature and drama of the time, the scholar or university man cuts a very poor figure. Rabelais has Gargantua's university-trained tutor spend ten years teaching his charge to recite his grammar book backward. Shakespeare's Doctor Holofernes in *Love's Labour's Lost* is the typical pedant, whose mind is clouded by trivial obscurities or verbal quibbles in Latin. And when Shakespeare has Hamlet say, "There

---

*See chapter 20.

are more things in heaven and earth, Horatio, than are dreamt of in your philosophy," the philosophy he is referring to is Aristotle.[22]

Thanks to Erasmus, the new trend of the 1500s was away from universities and toward an entirely revolutionary idea: homeschooling. Printed books made it possible for a well-to-do merchant or country squire to teach his son (and sometimes his daughter) to be a classical scholar without leaving the house. Why bother going to Paris or Oxford to learn what the best minds had written, people began to realize, when your children could discover that for themselves on the shelves of your own library?

Erasmus's friends and disciples got into the act. Spain's Lluís Vives, England's Roger Ascham, and a host of others wrote bestselling treatises on how to immerse your children in "Christian learning" and the joys of ancient literature (which rarely included Aristotle). Erasmus even urged a friend to start his son on the classical languages at age two, so that the boy could greet his father when he came home with cries of, "Daddy! Daddy!" in Latin and Greek.[23]

The appeal involved a certain social snobbery as well. Since many university students came from lower-class backgrounds (ironically, like Erasmus himself) and drank and whored and gambled with the locals in their college dorms, the appeal of homeschooling was obvious to Europe's governing elites. Under the humanists' guidance, they hired tutors to train their sons in Latin, Greek, and (for the truly progressive) Hebrew—all in order to enrich their young minds with the riches of both antiquity and the Holy Bible and to make them part of an intellectual as well as social elite.

The humanist education that Erasmus and his friends invented wound up creating its own schools. One of the first was St. Paul's in London, founded by John Colet. Indeed, the program of classics-based humanities would enjoy a long history, almost as long as that of the medieval university—although eventually it took over there as well. Up through Victorian times, the educated gentleman was the man who could "read Plato with his feet on the fender," in Thomas Macaulay's phrase: in other words, read him in the original Greek without needing a dictionary. Elite schools like St. Paul's and Eton in England, or the Lycée Henri-IV in Paris, made generations of pupils grind their way through Virgil and Homer right down to World War I.

This steadfast devotion to Latin and Greek as the basis of a liberal education instead of science or math, however, did not start as willful blindness or upper-class bias.[24] It simply reflected the fact that in Erasmus's time, both languages were essential for reading the printed books of the day and for understanding Scripture as the first step toward reforming an intellectually bankrupt Church.

This had been Erasmus's goal from the start. Just as Aristotle and scholasticism obscured the soul's access to Christ's truth, he argued, so did the cult of saints and relics. In the mind of the Erasmians, the corruption of Aristotle's university was matched by the corruption of the Church and the deadwood of the arts faculty by the deadwood of the priesthood and monasteries. Both institutions were lost in the cave; both urgently needed new luminous guidance.

Erasmus was confident that where popes and bishops had failed, friends like Colet and Thomas More (whose house resembled Plato's Academy, Erasmus said, more than anyplace he ever visited) would use their learning to elucidate the Gospels' message instead of clouding it over. The example of Saint Socrates, as Erasmus once called him, would gently lead everyone to see that the soul's highest goal is wisdom and that the "philosophy of Christ" (*philosophia Christi*) is the highest form of wisdom there is.

Given the acuity of Erasmus's attacks on scholasticism and the Church in *In Praise of Folly* and elsewhere (at one point, he even has Pope Julius II being sent to hell), what is amazing is how little official disapproval he actually faced. In fact, far from treating him as a pariah, kings and popes competed to get him to come to stay at their courts. It wasn't just a symptom of Erasmus's celebrity. It was a sign that everyone knew something had to be done about reforming the Church.

In the end, Erasmus turned them all down. At the same time, his friend More became Henry VIII's lord chancellor, and another colleague, Guillaume Budé, became cultural adviser to France's king Francis I and helped to create the Collège de France.[25]

Oddly, it was in Spain that Erasmus's influence reached its height, under the leadership of the most unlikely of all Erasmians: Cardinal Cisneros, the head of the Spanish Inquisition. Spain had been the land of the Reconquista, of the original *cruzada* or crusade against all heretics, including Muslims and Jews. Its hero was Diego el Rodrigo, El Cid, and its instrument the Inquisition. Yet Cisneros was not at all threatened by Erasmus's call for a return to pure Scripture. In fact, it would inspire Cisneros to launch what would become the Manhattan Project of Christian humanism: a project so vast that it dwarfed the resources and achievements of Erasmus himself.

This was a printed edition of the entire Bible, Old and New Testaments, with the original Hebrew plus Greek, Aramaic, and Latin versions (including Erasmus's translation of the New Testament) set side by side, page by page, so that scholars everywhere could have a complete authoritative text of Scripture from Genesis to Apocalypse. Nothing like it had ever appeared before. It was the supreme achievement not only of Erasmian humanism, but of the new print culture. The Polyglot Bible seemed to promise a rebirth of understanding Christianity, just as the Renaissance had brought a rebirth of Plato and classical antiquity.

"The world is coming to its senses," Erasmus wrote, "as if awakening out of a deep sleep."[26] Work on the Polyglot's Old Testament was completed in 1517. That same year, Martin Luther broke out with his own revolt against Aristotle, one that would put the entire humanist program at risk.

"Here I stand, I can do no other."

In 1521, Martin Luther faced official condemnation from Rome for his heretical views not only on papal indulgences, but on salvation through faith alone and his belief that the papacy was in direct league with the devil. He was undaunted. He publicly burned a copy of the canon law in front of his students, saying that church law "made the pope a god on earth." Luther had also wanted to burn Aquinas's *Summa* and Duns Scotus, but none of his colleagues would lend him their copies.[27]

The battle was on. The key question was, who would back Luther in his onslaught against the status quo? Luther condemned the corruption of the Church; so had Erasmus. Luther attacked papal indulgences as a scandal and a blasphemy; so had Erasmus. Luther said the only way to get back to the truth of Christianity was through "pure Scripture"; so had Erasmus.

Luther said that Aristotle and the scholastic theology had polluted the Christian faith; so had Erasmus. Would Erasmus now step forward and endorse Luther as one of his own? Would he acknowledge that they were fighting on the same side and lend the tremendous weight of his reputation to the Lutheran cause?

Some hoped he might. "O Erasmus of Rotterdam," the artist Albrecht

Dürer, then working in Italy, wrote in his diary, "where will you be? Ride forth beside the Lord Christ, protect the truth, obtain the martyr's crown."[28] However, Erasmus had no intention of becoming a martyr. In the end, he preferred to work within the boundaries of the Church, not outside them. Despite their mutual antipathy toward the Aristotle of the scholastics, Luther's opposition ran far deeper. It hinged on an issue that had separated Boethius and Saint Augustine at the onset of the Middle Ages. It had at its heart the clash between Plato and Aristotle on free will.

It all went back to Aristotle's *Ethics* where he proposes that all moral action is about making the right choices, and choice is about *intention:* "Intention is the decisive factor in virtue and character"—a point Thomas Aquinas made a cornerstone of Catholic moral teaching. On the other side, Aristotle's teacher Plato argued that doing good versus evil was a matter of *knowledge versus ignorance:* in other words, the man who is ignorant of the good can no more choose good than one who is ignorant of algebra can solve a quadratic equation.

Saint Augustine extended that definition of ignorance to include ignorance of God. Truly knowing God, Augustine asserted, having that blind faith in Him that suffuses our lives and gains us salvation, is impossible for our corrupt human nature unless God acts to put it there. He, not us, determines our capacity for virtue, just as He determines our fate.

A grim conclusion—one that had troubled Boethius. His doubts about this denial of free will had led him to reassert Aristotle's point that the choices we make as rational beings are the causes of our right actions.* It was an attractive, not to say morally compelling, argument. From Abelard to Aquinas and Duns Scotus, the Church had come out more and more on Boethius's side. Avoiding sin, it insisted, requires an active act of will—like the drug addict who suddenly decides he won't go back to the needle. Such an act has merit in the eyes of God; by choosing to avoid sin and learning to do good, we have taken the first step toward changing from sinner into a righteous person.[29] This process not only makes us a good citizen, but lays the foundation of our salvation as a rational—perhaps even a calculated—process.

The word *calculation* applies here for many reasons. By the 1400s, the Church was regularly speaking of sinners as "debtors of Christ."[30] It was pre-

---

*See chapter 12.

pared to argue that Man's original sin was like a mortgage or credit card balance. Christ's sacrifice on the cross paid off some, if not most, of that debt. By adhering to the rules of orthodoxy, by following the outward forms and norms of the Catholic Church from pilgrimages and penance and attending Mass to special devices like papal indulgences (a sort of debt forgiveness), we could continue to pay off the balance until the day we died. Whatever was left, it was assumed, would be paid off in those long years in purgatory.

As a monk, Luther had once bought into the system. Now, sitting in his study in Wittenberg, surrounded by the texts that justified that approach to moral action, he saw it as systematic blasphemy. Instead, he swung back to Saint Augustine. Original sin is not a mortgage but a crushing, ineradicable stain that touches everything we do or say. Nothing less than God's personal grace will lift it from us. Nothing less will restore the power of the soul to will the good and choose good over evil. "A man without grace can will nothing but evil," he wrote—no matter how moral or upright he appears to others.[31]

Today, Luther would not be at all surprised or distressed to see bestsellers like *The God Delusion* or *The Atheist Manifesto*—or see that their authors base their claims on reason. Nothing would be more *natural*. Man by his nature despises God. In our hearts, Luther says, we despise God's commandments. "If it were possible, the will of every man would prefer a state of affairs where there was no law at all" and he was free to do whatever he wants.[32] Human beings think they want freedom; what they really want is license.

This is why, of all Aristotle's writings, the one Luther despised most was the one Raphael and the Renaissance had most celebrated: Aristotle's *Ethics*. Left to ourselves, we don't choose good, only lesser degrees of evil, like the heroin addict who switches to methadone. And reason, that supreme false god of the humanists, operates only to preserve the illusion that we are free and whole when we are not.[33]

Virtue for Luther is not a continuum. It was not possible, as the humanists fondly imagined, to progress from Aristotle's virtues to opening our heart and accepting God's grace. Instead, "To love God is to hate oneself." In the end, "we ought to want not so much what our will wants to want but just what God wants." This meant, among many other things, that Erasmus and Pico were wrong. There was not going to be a final reconciliation, with Socrates and Christ ending up sharing the same stage. There is no Big Push. There is only one decisive breakthrough, that of Christ. As Augustine explained in *The City of God*, His truth has set all the rest aside. The path of reason doesn't lead us toward the light of God, but only deeper into the cave: in fact, right to the gates of hell.

And in the larger picture, how could we ever compare our power with His power? If God foreordains all things, then nothing happens without His will, meaning there can be no free will in man or angel or in any creature. Receiving God's grace is the only real freedom that's left. Whatever happens, good, bad, or indifferent, "when He reveals His glory we shall all clearly see that He both was and is just!"

It was at this point that Erasmus finally roused himself to respond. Without the acknowledgment of man's free will, he replied to Luther, God's justice and mercy, and teaching of Scripture, would be without meaning. What would be the purpose of all those admonishments and parables of Christ, if everything happened according to God's predetermined necessity, "if good and evil were equally but tools of God, as the hatchet to the carpenter?" And what would happen if ordinary people, the multitude, came to this same conclusion—since the preservation of law and order depended on people believing that their choice of good over evil had some meaning?

Luther hit back hard. Erasmus's problem, Luther said, was that he refused to accept that the truth has consequences: "You do not think it matters what anyone believes anywhere, so long as the world is at peace." Instead, Erasmus wanted to treat the truths of Scripture as if they were human truths open to interpretation and revision, like the texts of his beloved pagan philosophers. However, "the Holy Spirit is no skeptic, and the things He has written in our hearts are not doubts or opinions, but assertions truer and more certain than sense and life itself."[34]

Indeed, intellectual and moral certainty was the hallmark of Luther's life and work. Certainty led him to scrap five of the seven sacraments, leaving only baptism and communion. It led him to throw out clerical celibacy and marry a former nun. It led him to turn against not only Aristotle and the scholastics, but that other pillar of Christian theology, the Pseudo-Dionysius: "Whoever he may have been, he shows hardly any signs of solid learning . . . being more a Platonist than a Christian."[35]

> Read Plato, Aristotle, and others of that tribe. They will, I admit, allure you, delight you. . . . But betake yourself from them to this sacred reading. Then, in spite of yourself, so deeply will it affect you, so

penetrate your heart, fix itself in your very marrow, that, compared with its deep impression, such vigor as the orators or philosophers have will nearly vanish.

The words are not Martin Luther, but John Calvin.[36] In 1536—the same year Erasmus died—Calvin published the ultimate fusion of "pure Scripture" with the theology of Saint Augustine, his *Institutes of the Christian Religion*. Calvin's single-mindedness in breaking with the Catholic Church exceeded even Luther's. His message turned the proposition that original sin guaranteed that man had no say in his own salvation into a full-fledged theory of predestination.

We are damned or saved from before our birth; man's powerlessness to affect his destiny by his own actions is complete. And as a refuge for that tiny minority who would be spared the torments of hell, John Calvin turned the Swiss city of Geneva into a bastion of piety and virtue (no cards, no dancing, all day Sunday at prayer) that rivaled Plato's *Republic* in its single-minded dedication to an ideal of spiritual perfection.

We've learned to be suspicious of certainty like this. It's the kind of dogmatic self-assurance that flies planes into buildings or herds dissidents and other "undesirables" into concentration camps. Luther says blood-chilling things about witches and Jews that remind us of another German leader four centuries later. These days we prefer Erasmus. Like that of the men and women of the Enlightenment who grew leery of Christian dogma after a century and a half of bloody religious wars, our distrust is born of hard experience.

Still, both Luther and Calvin display the power of Plato's *thymos* in action. It is the enemy of moderation—but also of hypocrisy and complacency. For Luther, the goal for every member of a church built on faith alone was that he or she "contemplate this one thing alone, that he may serve and benefit others in all he does, considering nothing except the need and the advantage of his neighbor."[37] In the same way, Calvin's Geneva, the original City on the Hill, drew thousands of grateful refugees to its gates. They weren't repelled by Calvin's rigid rules and religious services seven days a week; they were drawn to them. Indeed, for more than a century Geneva became the ideal model of a Christian commonwealth from the Scotland of John Knox to the Mayflower Compact.

For in the mind of its creators and admirers, the Reformation was not about creating something new but about recovering something lost, the true Church of Christ. Like philology itself, it was about restoring forgotten meanings, obscured by centuries of error and corruption. Above all, it was a re-dedication to first principles laid down by Scripture and Saint Augustine: the ideal of the Church as a community united around a fervent faith and an adherence to God's will as the true fount of spiritual freedom and wisdom. This freedom was the gift of God's grace, Augustine had said, which so "diffuses love through [our] hearts that the soul, being healed, does good not from fear of punishment but for love of justice"—the goal for all men that Plato had wanted from the start.[38]

Onsummato igitur mundo: per fabricam diuine solercie sex dierum. Creati eñ dispositi z ornati
tandẽ pfecti sunt celi z terra. Compleuit dʼ glosus opus suũ: z requienit die septimo ab operibⁱ
manuum suarũ: postq̃ cũctũ mundũ: z omnia que in eo sunt creasset: nõ quasi operando lassuſ:
sed nouam creaturam facere cessauit: cuius materia vel similitudo non precesserit. Opus enim propaga
tionis operari non desinit. Et dominus eidem diei benedixit: z sanctificauit illũ: vocauitq̃ ipsum Sabatũ
quod nomen hebraica lingua requiem significat. Eo q̃ in ipso cessauerat ab omi opere q̃d patrarat. Añ
z Judei eo die a laboribus proprijs vacare dignoscitur. Quem z ante leges certe gentes celebrem obser
uarunt. Jamq̃ ad calcem ventum est operum diuinorum. Illum ergo timeamus: amemus: veneremur.
Jn quo sunt omnia siue visibilia siue inuisibilia. Et a domino celi: domino bonor̃ omniũ. Cui data omis
potestas in celo z in terra. Et presentia bona: quatenus bona sint. Et veram eterne vite felicitatem quera
mus.

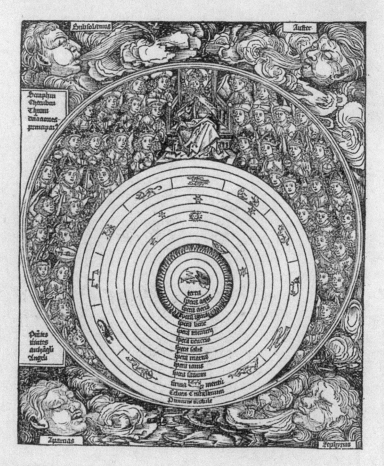

Medieval depiction of Aristotle's cosmos, with Earth firmly in the center

Nineteen

SECRETS OF THE HEAVENS: PLATO, GALILEO, AND THE NEW SCIENCE

It is the followers of Aristotle who have crowned him with authority, not he who usurped or appropriated it to himself.

—Galileo Galilei, 1632

Galileo's publisher once wrote that a picture is worth a thousand precepts.[1] Galileo's revolutionary experiments on falling bodies began with a simple ball. In order to see Plato's role in the birth of modern science, so will we.

I see a soccer ball lying in the grass and pick it up. I rub my hands over its bumpy black-and-white-checkered surface. I breathe the smell of grass and plastic. This is what Plato called sensory awareness, *eikasia* in Greek: the lowest form of human knowledge.[2]

I toss the ball into the air and kick it to a friend. She kicks it back, and soon we are running and passing it back and forth. A game begins to see who can keep the ball moving without stopping. We have entered the realm of *pistis*, the full recognition of objects and accepted beliefs and judgments

about them, like "This must be a ball" and "This must be a game"—or, in a
different context, "This must be money" and "This must be justice because
the judge and jury say it is."

As I run along, I spot another ball, a golf ball, also sitting in the grass. I
stop to examine it. It's smaller than my soccer ball. It isn't black and white like
the soccer ball; it exists to be hit with a club instead of a foot. Still, the two
balls have a lot in common, I realize, starting with their shape.

The game breaks off as I comb the meadow, looking for other similar
balls: baseballs, polo balls, beach balls. I go inside and start drawing diagrams
of balls, both as spheres and then as circles. What do these spheres all have in
common? Then I ask: What would the perfect sphere look like?

I pull out a ruler and compass. I begin tracing circles and measuring their
diameter and their circumference. I split them into sections, first on paper,
then in my mind. I am in Plato's realm of *dianoia*, the realm of geometry and
number.[3] I continue to draw and calculate and watch as the shapes dissolve
into lines, points, triangles, and parabolas. Finally, only the numbers are left.
I realize they express mathematical formulae that exist in perfect proportion
to each other, with each ratio (1:2, 1:3) leading constantly to a higher and
higher level of abstract order.

Then I have it. This order and proportion is everywhere, eternal, and
unchanging. A single unity governs all things. I cut my last links to the sensory material world and contemplate that unity of which my original soccer
ball is only a distant, dim shadow.

A voice at my shoulder tells me gently, "Now at last you are in the realm
of the real and the intelligible." I have achieved "the highest form of knowledge," the voice tells me, "and the vision of the Good." This is true knowledge, *epistēmē*: Plato's realm of the Forms.

The voice, of course, is that of Socrates from Book VI of Plato's *Republic*.[4]
My adventure with the soccer ball is in fact a retelling of the Allegory of the
Cave, describing a four-step ascent for truth that matches almost exactly the
ascent of love in the *Symposium*. Plato's allegory of man's upward climb from
the darkness of matter to the eternal light inspired the greatest minds of the
ancient world, including Plotinus. It touched Christian thinkers like the
Pseudo-Dionysius and Boethius and the greatest minds of the Renaissance
from Ficino and Michelangelo to Erasmus. It also lurks in the deepest recesses of modern science.

This may seem surprising. But the old idea that the rise of modern science involved a struggle between reason and religion is not merely wrong but misleading. It was really about the perpetual struggle between Plato and Aristotle. From the death of Nicolaus Copernicus in 1543 and Galileo's famous trial in 1633, until 1687, when Newton's *Principia Mathematica* first came off the press, Europe saw a steady transformation from a view of nature built around Aristotle to a new Platonized understanding that hit the Aristotelian schoolmen like a wrecking ball hitting a plate-glass window.

Physics and astronomy were the first battlefields in this clash, and the most famous. The fight began in the late 1500s in northeast Italy, where a gifted young mathematician would risk everything to prove that religion and science were not at odds. On the contrary, in his Platonic scheme of things, they were two views of the same Big Picture, like Ficino's divine and profane love.

Science and religion, he averred, were in fact emanations of the same truth.

Not many tourists go to the northeast Italian town of Padua today, except perhaps to see Giotto's famous frescoes in the Arena Chapel. However, for more than one hundred years after Giotto put away his brushes and closed his paint pots, Renaissance Padua was Europe's leading school of natural philosophy, or what today we call science.

The fiercely empirical spirit of Roger Bacon's Oxford and Ockhamist Paris had found a new home in the University of Padua. Like Bacon, Padua's teachers stressed the original principle of Aristotle's philosophy of nature: that knowledge is a process of discovery using the power of our senses. As one of Padua's most celebrated teachers put it, "All [knowledge] progresses from the known to the unknown."[5] The Paduan Aristotelians taught students that the scientist should never be afraid to venture into unfamiliar territory. He may not only discover something new, he can add new support for tried-and-true scientific principles—which, as far as Padua was concerned, meant Aristotle's principles.

All this sounds very modern.[6] So we aren't surprised to learn that one of Padua's distinguished alumni was Nicolaus Copernicus or that professors there were experimenting with rolling balls on inclined planes and swinging pendulums on horizontal crossbars. Nor are we amazed that the star of Padua's school of medicine was Andreas Vasalius, who led the first classes on human dissection since the ancient Greeks; or that in 1592, the university decided to hire a twenty-eight-year-old mathematician from Pisa named Galileo Galilei.[7]

Padua sounds like the perfect environment for a sharp, inquiring mind like Galileo's. But he was deeply unhappy there.[8] Why?

There are rows and rows of books on Galileo. There is even a book about Galileo's daughter. No one has yet written a bestseller about Galileo's father, but Vincenzo Galilei may hold the real key to understanding his more famous son.

Galilei worked as a court musician for the Medici in Florence in the 1560s and 1570s and published treatises on the theory of music. Glancing through the pages of his works, we see diagrams that remind us forcibly of diagrams of planetary movement in his son's works.[9] The reason is that Vincenzo Galilei was a mathematician as well as a musicologist. His goal was to return musical theory to its Pythagorean roots. The father, like the son, understood the power of number not as a way to count or measure, as Aristotelians did, but rather as Number, reason's window into the hidden order of nature.

Vincenzo must have demonstrated this to his son more than once, by picking up his lute and strumming a single note. Then he would put his son's finger in the exact midpoint of the string and strike it again. The note would rise exactly an octave. Vincenzo would move his finger again, and the note rose proportionately to the next octave, and so on.*

Pythagoras was the first to demonstrate that mathematical proportion was the essence of musical harmony. He also passed to his disciple Plato the notion that proportion was endowed with creative power. By cutting the string in half, we create two octaves where there was only one. In effect, we have doubled the string's musical output.[10]

So in music, so in life. Proportion in nature is not static but a dynamic progression, like the harmonies in music. Forms in music (like Bach partitas), as in nature and architecture, grow according to an orderly progression that is both pleasing to the senses and predictable to the mind. Mathematics reveals

---

*Vincenzo went further than this. Orthodox music theory stated that the ratio of 2:1 applied to strings that were tuned an octave apart as well. Vincenzo proved this was wrong by a series of experiments with weights tied to lute strings, which showed the ratio was actually 4:1. Scholar Stillman Drake argues that Vincenzo's son was living at home at the time, tutoring students in mathematics, and may have helped his father run the experiments.

that growth through exact but abstract formal relations. "Things are Number," Pythagoras is supposed to have said.[11] From Euclid's triangles and spheres to modern-day fractals, it's a concept loaded with significance.

We pick up our soccer ball again. This time we spin it on the end of our finger. The balancing point is the axis, the fixed unmoving line passing through its middle. Our senses tell us that the ball's axis is imaginary. Yet the axis is *there*, exerting its power over the ball. When we give the ball a spin, it rotates on its axis just as *every* sphere rotates on its axis, whether on paper or in reality.[12] In geometry, it is always the relationship between the parts, not the individual parts or balls, that matters.

Now, Euclidean geometry is a world of pure forms, but not Platonic Forms. Geometry's lines and points and circles, like the numbers in arithmetic, are still bound to empirical reality. This is why Plato gave it a ranking just below genuine knowledge, or *epistēmē*. But to other admirers, that is precisely its advantage. Plato himself could not resist making his five geometric solids the divine mind's basic building blocks for constructing the world.* Their proportionate progression in size and complexity revealed to Plato the harmonious structure of the cosmos. Later, as we've seen, Christian Platonists argued they revealed the workings of the mind of God.

Galileo was an eighteen-year-old medical student when he heard his first lecture on Euclid.[13] He never looked back. As a math teacher, he began studying the mechanics of motion; it was as a mathematician that he developed a lifelong interest in ballistics and fortifications, first at his *alma mater*, the University of Pisa, and then at Siena. It was as a math teacher that he came to Padua in 1592. It was also for love of mathematics that he left Padua eighteen years later.

Galileo had found that for all their belief in discovery and experiment, the Aristotelians at Padua held mathematics and geometry in very low regard. They looked at him the way a Princeton professor looks at a teacher of data processing at Dutchess County Community College: as a mere technician. To his disgust, Galileo's salary was barely one-fifth that of an equivalent professor of philosophy.[14] To the orthodox Aristotelian mind, mathematics was a useful but essentially abstract science, divorced from substantial reality.[15] Above all, it was detached from what Aristotle had defined as the real goal of science, which was understanding the final causes of things, from horses and

*See chapter 2.

soccer balls to the creation of the *polis* and the movement of the planets. Finding the final cause meant examining substances to discover why they existed and what their ultimate purpose was. This was an investigation for which mathematics could provide no help. As Aristotle's own critique of Pythagoras showed, it could end up being a positive distraction.[16]

Galileo's mind was moving in precisely the opposite direction. He was looking at ways in which mathematics could help to reveal preordained order in nature, open to empirical investigation. In the process, he was getting very different results from what the Aristotelians expected.

When Galileo arrived at Padua in 1592, he had already completed his experiments on falling bodies, including the one that is still his most famous. By dropping balls off a tall building, Galileo had demonstrated that heavier objects fell not at a faster rate than lighter ones, as Aristotle stated in the *Physics*, but at exactly the same rate—a rate that could also be expressed as a constant number.*

It was the kind of work that should have won praise from the experiment-minded, discovery-loving Aristotelians of Padua. To his dismay, however, their reaction was a great yawn. So someone throws a couple of balls off the top of a building, they said, both of which seem to land at the same time. Who cares? In their minds, the experiment said nothing about the underlying truth of Aristotle's physical theory, which had stood the test of time for centuries and been endorsed by greater minds than Galileo's—including the distinguished professors at Padua.

Galileo was furious. "Of all hatreds," he wrote, "there is none greater than that of ignorance against knowledge."[17] He knew that his experiments had shown that Aristotle was wrong twice—not only about whether two balls of different weights would hit the ground at different speeds, but also about the reason why they don't behave as Aristotle said they would. Aristotle had assumed that the motion of a falling body must have something to do with its substance or intrinsic qualities.[18] Its rate of descent would depend, for instance, on whether it was heavy or light (like a feather versus a cannonball), or made of natural substances that drew it more quickly down toward its

---

*Did he drop them off the Leaning Tower of Pisa, as legend claims? Historians used to scoff at the story. However, it came from a former student of Galileo who claimed to be present, and Galileo certainly was inclined to do spectacular experiments not just to impress his students, but to try to convince his fellow professors. We do know that in 1612, a professor of philosophy did drop balls off the Leaning Tower in order to prove Galileo *wrong*—with disappointing results.

home in the earth, or contained substances like the air in a balloon that kept it drawn upward toward the celestial spheres.

Galileo had shown, on the contrary, that the rate of descent of an object had nothing to do with its weight or what it was made of. Motion was a state, regardless of the object, and a uniform state for all objects. Aristotle had been wrong. And if he was wrong on small issues like falling bodies, then it was possible he was wrong on the bigger ones as well, like the movement of the heavenly bodies.

We don't know the exact date that Galileo first read Copernicus's *On the Revolutions of the Heavenly Spheres*.[19] We do know the proposition that the earth and other planets traveled around the sun rather than the other way around made a huge impression on him. It was made stronger in 1597, when he was given a copy of Johannes Kepler's first book endorsing the Copernican model. Galileo wrote to Kepler, thanking him and "congratulating myself on the good fortune of having found such a man as a companion in the exploration of truth." Galileo soon saw it was easier to explain phenomena like tides if you assumed the earth was not stationary, as Aristotle and Ptolemy had taught, but actually in motion.[20]

What really focused Galileo's attention on the heavens, however, was the sudden appearance of a supernova in the night sky in October 1604. Such a thing was not supposed to happen. According to Aristotle, no change should ever occur in the heavens. Everything existing in the celestial spheres, like the sky and the planets, was made from an immaculate and unalterable substance called the *quintessence*. The heavens were, as an Aristotelian philosopher says in one of Galileo's later dialogues, "ingenerable, incorruptible, inalterable, invariant, eternal"—indeed, as perfect and definitive as Aristotle's own works.[21]

Galileo's regard for Aristotle was already fading, thanks to his work on motion. The appearance of the supernova only confirmed his suspicion that the more he saw of the workings of nature, the more slipshod Aristotle's system seemed to be. He could recall the words of his father, Vincenzo, in a different context: "It appears to me that those who rely simply on the weight of authority to prove any assertion, without searching out the arguments to support it, act absurdly."[22] Now, Galileo decided, it was time to take the examination of nature to another level.

One of Galileo's close friends was Cardinal Paolo Sarpi, the official theologian of the Republic of Venice. One day in 1609, Sarpi told him that someone was trying to sell Venice a Dutch-made optical device that enabled men to see distant objects like ships at sea as if they were close up. It seemed a useful device for a seafaring nation like the Serene Republic. Sarpi wondered if Galileo thought that such a device might actually work and whether the Venetian Senate should buy it.

With his mathematician's understanding of optics, Galileo immediately realized that the device had to use two lenses, one in a concave shape and the other convex, in order to pass light and images from one to the other.[23] So he told Sarpi, Don't buy the thing yet. Give me a couple of weeks and I'll see what I can come up with. By the beginning of August 1609, he had made his own device, which he called in Italian an *ochiale* and which we call a telescope.

Galileo's telescope was only about as powerful as a normal pair of binoculars. But that was enough to describe ships in detail as they entered Venice's Grand Canal a full two hours before the sharpest-eyed sailor could spot them. It also allowed Galileo to turn his probing eye loose on the evening sky. The result was a series of astounding discoveries that tore the wheels off the entire Aristotelian and Ptolemaic system.

Galileo discovered that the moon was not a perfect unblemished geometric sphere, as Aristotle's cosmology demanded. It was rutted with craters and studded with mountains. He then turned his attention to Venus. He found that it was illuminated in a series of phases like the moon, suggesting that Venus must revolve around the sun as a fixed source of light.

He also found a series of smaller objects: the moons circling Jupiter. Aristotle's arguments about why there were only seven planets, one sun, and one moon in the sky, and why there could be no more and no fewer, were suddenly nonsense. The perfect system of the Aristotelian cosmos was anything *but,* and the way the Aristotelian mind had tried to understand the workings of nature turned out to be a mirage.

That's the way it looked to Galileo. In 1610, he quickly assembled his discoveries in a little book he titled the *Starry Messenger* and dedicated to the Grand Duke of Tuscany, Cosimo de' Medici. The problem was that no one believed him. From the start, Aristotelians dismissed what Galileo had seen through his telescope as an optical illusion. When Johannes Kepler saw the same things through *his* telescope, they said it was still an optical illusion. Even when Galileo gave them his telescope and offered to let them see the moon's craters for themselves, they refused to look. Aristotle had said that all celestial bodies were perfect. This meant they couldn't have any flaws. Therefore the moon's craters didn't exist, any more than the moons of Jupiter (or, as Galileo soon discovered, the moons of Saturn).

"They have shut their eyes to the light of truth. Faced by arguments like this," Galileo told Kepler, "I don't know whether to laugh or cry."[24] Still, Galileo refused to see that their objections had a strong empirical basis. The Aristotelians, who included professors of philosophy as well as several churchmen, were not idiots. They understood the principle of magnification. But how, they asked not unreasonably, could Galileo be magnifying objects that couldn't be seen with the unaided eye in the first place? It defied common sense. The academic establishment was furious with Galileo *not* because he was inquiring into things better left to theology, but because they thought he was a fraud.[25]

Indeed, this was the dirty little secret about the Copernican theory. None of it could be confirmed with direct evidence. Copernicus had come up with the notion that the earth must be going around the sun along with the other planets without making any new astronomical observations. He had simply found the idea in a book on the ancient Greek mathematician Aristarchus.* Again, the chief reason Copernicus did not publish his theory during his lifetime was not that he feared the disapproval of the Church—he was worried it was so contrary to our everyday experience, it would be laughed off the stage.[26] Nothing any astronomer had ever seen, not even Tycho Brahe's meticulous observations from his island observatory outside Copenhagen, confirmed any aspect of it. Brahe himself felt perfectly comfortable sticking to the old geocentric theory.

All Copernicus's theory had done was make the calculations of movements of the heavenly bodies easier. In fact, as Johannes Kepler demonstrated when he published his mathematical study of the elliptical orbits of the earth and other planets, it made them easier to the point of harmonious elegance.[27]

This was all the average Platonist needed to hear. He didn't care about "saving the appearances," as Aristotelians did—that is, making sure that everything we see and perceive has some explanation in our general theory. The Platonist knows appearances can deceive, because matter changes. Soccer balls come and go; they get run over or get stolen. However, the *geometry* describing their behavior, whether spinning on their axis or at rest, lasts for-

*See chapter 7.

ever. And what it says stands true not just for soccer balls, but for every sphere, real or imaginary, including the earth.

It was the math that mattered. And when the math yields a pattern of harmonious proportion, whether it's the golden section of the Greeks or the Sierpinski gasket and Mandelbrot set of modern fractal geometry, the Platonist knows, as Archimedes did many centuries before, that he is standing at the threshold of the truth.[28]

Thomas Taylor, the eighteenth-century mathematician and first person to translate the complete works of Plato into English, phrased it best: "Geometry enables its votary, like a bridge, to pass over the obscurity of material nature, as over some dark seas to the luminous regions of perfect reality."[29]

The Renaissance figure who grasped this point long before Galileo was Leonardo da Vinci. His voluminous notebooks reveal his peculiar fascination with observation and invention. This is his Aristotelian side. But his famous etching of Vitruvian Man reveals his more mystical, Platonic side. Leonardo was steeped in the Pythagorean formulae of harmonious proportion. He understood the creative power of the golden section. He provided the illustrations of Plato's five geometric solids for mathematician Fra Luca Pacioli's *Divine Proportion* in 1509, the first ever done using a three-dimensional perspective.[30]

The Vitruvian Man sprang from the same passion. Leonardo borrowed the Roman architect Vitruvius's belief that the parts of the human body all exist in exact proportion to one another, in order to construct a visual allegory of man's place in the cosmos.

Leonardo's man stands at the center of not one but two geometric figures, the square and the circle. Far from trying to combine the two, in other words "squaring the circle," Leonardo was content to show that the ratios derived from the golden section place the human being at the center of both geometric figures, depending on our perspective.[31] As with Ficino, Leonardo's man bridges the gap between infinity and matter, between divinity and mortality. But this time, it is mathematics and the science of proportion, not love, that enable us to see it and grasp our mediating role. No wonder Leonardo wrote in his *Treatise on Painting*, "Let no one ignorant of mathematics enter here"—almost exactly Plato's motto over the gate of the Academy.

Sixteenth-century astronomer and scientist Giordano Bruno was Galileo's older contemporary and chose to carry this fusion of Platonic theology and mathematics to the next level. His writings offered a direct parallel between geometry and Plato's theory of divine love and suggested that the revelations of the one would inspire the same mystical frenzy and creative vision of the other.

They evidently did for Bruno, who saw in mathematics a power others never imagined. For Bruno, the "dark seas" of material nature were not dead or inert. They teemed with spirits and demons, all waiting to be brought to life. These would then reveal nature's secrets to their mathematician master, just as Bruno was convinced they once had to the ancient Egyptians and the Pythagoreans.[32]

This conviction led Bruno to black magic and alchemy. His later works contain multiple geometric diagrams that are supposed to summon demons the way a finger on a button boots up a hard drive.[33] It is also why Bruno never doubted the truth of Copernicus's proposition that the earth moved. For Bruno, the earth was a living being.

The story of Bruno's dark, unstable genius and his Pythagorean magical math ends badly.* The Roman Inquisition sent him to be burned at the stake in 1600. They did so unwillingly. "You are more reluctant to pronounce this sentence," Bruno sneered at his inquisitors, "than I am to receive it." However, it was an object lesson for Galileo in how *not* to challenge traditional intellectual authority, especially concerning a Copernican theory that Bruno had upheld and which an Aristotle-dominated Catholic Church had denounced as contrary to orthodox faith.

In 1610, however, Galileo had little reason to worry. He was friends with the most powerful man in papal Rome, Cardinal Robert Bellarmine. The Jesuit order had tested his telescope and declared the mountains on the moon were genuine. By 1611, he even had the pope himself, Paul V, actively supporting his work and applauding his genius.

Of course, privately Galileo thought the condemnation of Copernicus was wrong. "The Bible tells us how to go to Heaven," he once quipped, "not how the heavens go." All the same, he made it clear he would not get dragged into a dispute over the Church's power to decide what was true in matters of fact (like the shape of the solar system) as opposed to matters of faith.[34]

Even after certain published remarks earned him an admonition in 1616

---

*Bruno's belief in Egyptian magical religion, which he shared with Ficino, would go on to become a key ingredient in Freemasonry.

to say no more about the Copernican theory, he accepted the ruling without demur. He also continued his research without letup. In his mind, this was no battle between religion and science. This was a battle between what he called "two chief world systems," one based on the traditional Aristotelian view of nature and the other new one confirmed by both the power of observation *and* Platonic mathematics.

Here Galileo also wanted to avoid the error of his colleague Johannes Kepler (1571–1630). For all his brilliant work, Kepler had insisted on making the five Platonic solids the basis for his model of the solar system, rendering it useless for further empirical research. It was a bizarre example of carrying the faith in the perfection of mathematics too far.[35] By contrast, Galileo understood that even a divinely ordered cosmos could not be perfect. There were craters on the moon and spots on the sun. Kepler himself had shown that the planetary orbits were not perfect circles as Aristotle and even Copernicus had assumed, but ellipses.

"There is no event in Nature," Galileo wrote, "such that it will be completely understood by theorists."[36] God's perfection was to be found in the numbers, not in the shapes or objects. Yet without real objects, the math can become an exercise in pure speculation or even hallucination, as Giordano Bruno's life revealed.

Galileo's science managed to fuse the Platonist's faith in mathematics with the Aristotelian faith in experience as the basis of discovery. All his work on mechanics, optics, and astronomy was deeply rooted in experiment and empirical research. When experience proved ambiguous or unreliable, however, Galileo realized then that mathematics must take over.

The universe, Galileo wrote, "is written in the language of mathematics, and its characters are triangles, circles, and other geometric figures, without which it is humanly impossible to understand a single world of it." Without mathematics, he concluded, "one wanders about in a dark labyrinth"—or what Plato might have called a cave.[37]

This was Galileo's most important contribution to the future of science. Galileo knew that if he could measure it mathematically, *then it must exist* even if he could not see it. This was whether one was talking about his own concept of velocity or, later, Newton's concept of gravity. His "mathematization of Nature" allowed scientists for the first time to anticipate discoveries and work out scientific theories, including Einstein's relativity three centuries later, long before the means of testing them existed.

Galileo had replaced a universe tied down to final causes that were inherent in things themselves with a universe infinitely open to possibility and change. This is still our universe, as when we speculate about the possibility of life on Mars or some distant planet. However, Galileo himself never doubted God's part in it, any more than Leonardo or Ficino did. As he put it in a fine Neoplatonic formulation, "Holy Scripture and Nature are both emanations from the divine Word." Like other Platonists, Galileo didn't have to see God to believe in Him. He only had to feel His perfection in His creation and stand aside in awe.

Others were not willing to accept the new paradigm.[38] They waged war on Galileo both in print and behind his back. What they couldn't do to Martin Luther, namely put him on trial in Rome, they were desperate to do to Galileo—and for many of the same reasons.

Lutheranism and Calvinism had pulled up the theological certainties built around Aristotle by the roots. Galileo was doing the same to Aristotle's physical sciences. Aristotle's defenders, churchmen and professors alike, saw themselves as trustees of a centuries-old orthodoxy. When Galileo dismissed them as ignorant blockheads and wrote, "If Aristotle had been such a man as they imagine, he would have been of intractable mind, obstinate spirit, and barbarous soul," they were bound to hit back with everything they had. [39]

It took them nearly fifteen years to get him in the end. They also had to overcome the biggest obstacle of all: the new pope, Urban VIII, who as Cardinal Maffeo Barberini had been Galileo's closest friend and one of his most enthusiastic supporters. It was Urban's election in 1623 that prompted Galileo to begin work on his magnum opus, not an erudite scientific treatise in Latin but a lively Platonic-style dialogue in everyday Italian, called *Dialogue Concerning the Two Chief World Systems*. It would finally prove to every reader why the Copernican heliocentric view was right and the old Aristotelian view wrong: all with—he hoped—the approval of the pope himself.

In the spring of 1632, the work was finally finished. Galileo was approaching seventy. He was in poor health, one of his beloved daughters had died, and he was experiencing problems with his eyesight that would eventually leave him all but blind. The *Dialogue*, however, was a smash hit.

Like Plato and his own father, Galileo preferred the dialogue form as a way to debate first principles, in this case scientific principles. The *Dialogue* takes place between a partisan of Copernicus and a partisan of Aristotle. Galileo also throws in a neutral observer who acts as the judge as to which has the better argument. However, Galileo gives the game away when he names Aristotle's advocate Simplicio (or Simpleton), and the odds are running against Aristotle from the first page.*

Over four fictional days of discussion and five hundred pages of text and diagrams, it is Aristotle versus Galileo head-on, as Simplicio's objections to Copernicus are demolished one by one. The men discuss celestial substances in light of the imperfections of the moon's craters and mountains; planetary motion and sunspots; and then finally, on the fourth day, ocean tides and how large recurrent shifts of the seas and oceans would be impossible if the earth were actually perfectly still.

More than any previous work, Galileo's *Dialogue* showed that if Copernicus wasn't right on every detail of the working of the solar system, Aristotle and Ptolemy were both very clearly wrong. The first printing sold out almost at once. Clerics and laymen alike sang its praises. One reader, the Dominican friar and militant Platonist visionary Tommaso Campanella, pronounced it the beginning of a new era.

However, not everyone bought the *Dialogue* for the same reasons. One of Galileo's friends, a papal official, was in a Roman bookshop when a Jesuit father came bursting in through the door. He wanted a copy of Galileo's latest book, he told the bookseller.

We're sold out, the man informed him. Trembling with rage, the Jesuit insisted. "I'll pay you ten *scudi* if you can get me a copy at once." The bookseller shrugged, and the cleric left in a fury.

Galileo's friend watched him go and turned to his companion. "The Jesuits," he said, "will persecute this book with the utmost bitterness." He was right.[40]

In the early morning hours of October 1, 1632, there was a knock at the door of Galileo's house in Florence. A sleepy servant swung open the door to reveal a man in black robes and a hooded cowl.

Galileo recognized him at once. He was the inquisitor of Florence. He had a summons for Galileo, he said, to present himself to the Holy Office in Rome within thirty days.

---

*There was also an ancient commentator on Aristotle named Simplicius, whose study of the *Physics* and *On the Heavens* were scholastic staples.

Galileo collapsed to the floor. His servants had to carry him to his bed. He knew that the summons meant that his enemies had finally turned his old friend the pope against him.

They had shown Urban VIII their copies of the *Dialogue*, with its clear support for Copernicus's heliocentric theory. He had waved away their suspicions. Then they had pulled out their ace in the hole. It was a copy of a papal memorandum from 1616 that summarized an injunction from then pope Paul V, explicitly ordering Galileo never to discuss Copernicus or his theories again.[41] Urban VIII was aghast. Galileo had never told him about the order. It seemed to him that Galileo had lied and deceived him and also defied the authority of the Holy See. What Cardinal Maffeo Barberini might have overlooked in an old friend, Pope Urban VIII could not. He immediately ordered Galileo to Rome.

Galileo argued for a delay, pleading "my great age, my many physical infirmities . . . the hazards of the journey." Couldn't the trial take place in Florence? Galileo probably knew the Florentine inquisitor would be on his side: the man had read the *Dialogue* and said he found nothing wrong with it.

The pope, however, was adamant. "He must come," he told Galileo's friends, "he can come by very easy stages, in a litter, with every comfort, but he really must be tried in person." Urban added, "May God forgive him for having been so deluded as to involve himself in these difficulties," because the pope never would.[42]

Galileo reached Rome in early November. He was still frightened, but he was (as the Florentine ambassador, who gave him lodging, noted) calm and collected. No one knew it, but Galileo had an ace of his own. He only needed the right moment to play it.

The trial of Galileo, the most famous in Inquisition history, did not begin until April 1633. Not a word was said about scientific theories. The charge of heresy rested entirely on the accusation that Galileo had disobeyed a papal order. The inquisitors presented their evidence against him, including copies of the *Dialogue* and the 1616 memorandum mentioning the papal injunction.

Then Galileo cleared his throat and began. He told the inquisitors he had no recollection of any such injunction. But there was more.

"In the month of February 1616," Galileo said, "Cardinal Bellarmine told me that since the opinion of Copernicus absolutely contradicted Holy Scripture, it could not be held or defended." However, he added, the cardinal conceded that "it might be taken hypothetically and made use of," as, for example, in research and writings such as his *Dialogue Concerning the Two Chief World Systems.*[43]

The inquisitors shifted uneasily in their seats. Could this be true? Bellarmine had been dead for nearly twelve years. Galileo then produced an affidavit Bellarmine had signed and sent him, stating that Galileo in no way had to abjure or do any penance for his previous support of Copernicus. The document acknowledged that he had been informed of the pope's declaration that a doctrine declaring the earth moved around the sun could not be held or defended. But there was no mention of any papal injunction against Galileo and no mention of future punishment if he failed to comply.

The inquisitors looked the letter over. They said, This is a copy.

I'll produce the original if you want, Galileo said. It's here in Rome. And eventually he did, signed in Bellarmine's own hand.[44] Far from ordering Galileo silenced, it gave him leeway to talk about Copernicus as much as he wanted as long as he did not assert that the heliocentric theory was *absolutely true*. Far from disobeying any papal injunction, it looked as though Galileo had been following the letter of the law, if not necessarily its spirit.

Galileo had won. The inquisitors were beaten.[45] The 1616 injunction was not signed, and some were beginning to suspect it might be a forgery. Not a single witness stepped forward to support the charges against Galileo, not even his worst enemies. All the other witnesses, including Bellarmine, were deceased.[46]

The Inquisition dithered for weeks. Finally it approached Galileo in private. Their prestige was at stake, said the inquisitors. Couldn't he admit to some wrongdoing so that they could find him guilty, with the understanding that he would be treated with full and complete leniency?

Galileo, confident that he had his enemies over a barrel, agreed. He publicly admitted that some portions of the *Dialogue* had gone too far in its espousal of Copernicus's theory. He then asked, with perhaps a slight wink to his judges, for leniency on account of his infirmity and advanced age. So it was with a sense of shock that he received, instead of some light penance, a sentence of indefinite imprisonment (although that was commuted within days to house arrest).

Galileo was devastated. As for the Catholic Church, it had wrought a public relations disaster. Three of the ten Inquisition judges refused to sign the sentence, which they knew to be a travesty of justice.[47] The archbishop of

Siena immediately offered to take Galileo into his residence on his own recognizance. A year later Galileo was finally allowed to return home, although he would spend the rest of his life living under supervision by agents of the Inquisition.

However, this did not stop him from finishing his final work on mechanics and physics, *Dialogues Concerning Two New Sciences* in 1638, four years before his death. Down to the end, Galileo protested that he was a better Aristotelian than his opponents because he believed in avoiding fallacies in reasoning, and because he believed "it is not possible that sensible experience is contrary to truth." All the same, his last work had to be printed not in Italy, but in Leyden in Calvinist Holland. Galileo himself never got to see a copy.[48]

For the Church, it was a bitter irony. It had condemned Galileo in order to prevent the Reformation's overthrow of Aristotle from spreading to the study of nature. Instead, Galileo's condemnation cemented the alliance between the new science and Protestantism. With the help of the printing press, Galileo and Copernicus took the intellectual bastions of Protestant Europe by storm. Mathematical mechanics set the new rules for scientific study, from astronomy and physics to chemistry and botany.[49]

Galileo had lost his fight; his new science had won the war. In John Milton's England, Galileo, "the Tuscan artist" with his "optic glass," passed into literature and legend:

> *Like the moon, whose Orb*
> *Through optic glass the Tuscan artist views*
> *At evening from the top of Fesolè,*
> *Or in Valdarno, to descry new lands,*
> *Rivers, or Mountains, in her spotty Globe.*[50]

This was perhaps the final irony. Galileo the obedient Roman Catholic became an overnight Protestant hero. He would be remembered as a champion not only of science, but of the principle of free inquiry versus papist tyranny, in Milton's words "a prisoner to the Inquisition for thinking in astronomy otherwise than the Franciscans and Dominicans licensed."[51]

It was easy to forget that it was the Church's favor that had enabled Galileo to rise so high in the first place, only to fall so far.

PHILOSOPHIÆ

NATURALIS

PRINCIPIA

MATHEMATICA·

Autore *JS. NEWTON*, *Trin. Coll. Cantab. Soc.* Matheseos
Professore *Lucasiano*, & Societatis Regalis Sodali.

IMPRIMATUR·
S. PEPYS, *Reg. Soc.* PRÆSES.
Julii 5. 1686.

LONDINI,

Jussu *Societatis Regiæ* ac Typis *Josephi Streater.* Prostat apud
plures Bibliopolas. *Anno* MDCLXXXVII.

Title page of Isaac Newton's *Principia Mathematica*, 1687

Twenty

GOD, KINGS, AND PHILOSOPHERS IN THE AGE OF GENIUS

In God's House (which is the universe) are many mansions.

—Isaac Newton

Where law ends, tyranny begins.

—John Locke

We talk a lot about rights in modern society. Some say too much. We have civil rights, human rights, legal rights, even animal rights. This way of talking, too, comes out of the struggle between Plato and Aristotle, but in a more complicated way than, say, the emergence of medieval logic or the Renaissance. This is because as European civilization advanced, the influence of Plato and Aristotle would reflect more and more in the spirit and less in the letter of people's thinking. It is also part and parcel of the age of new science Galileo had launched.

Galileo died in 1642. He was buried in Florence in the Church of Santa Croce, directly opposite the tomb of Michelangelo. This is only right, since together they had remade the Renaissance world in a distinctly Platonist frame.

Galileo's new science showed it was possible to think of that higher order not just in religious or artistic terms, as Michelangelo had, but in mathematical terms of the utmost precision. It was a precision that also explained how nature worked far better than Aristotle could. When a nineteen-year-old mathematical prodigy named Isaac Newton arrived at Cambridge University in 1661, Galileo's insight that mathematics could explain the workings of nature in terms of geometric mechanical motion had carried away the imagination of northern Europe.

What was true of planets and soccer balls, men realized, might also be true of plants, animals, and the formation of minerals. Mathematical mechanics might even explain the workings of the human body—as the English physician William Harvey discovered when he realized that the circulation of the blood followed the laws of hydraulics and that the human heart was nothing more than a mechanical pump.

Aristotle's science of final causes wasn't just dead. Except among a few diehard stragglers, it was as if it had never existed. What was left in people's minds was a universe that looked like one of those magnificent cathedral clocks we find in cities in Germany and Switzerland. Great descending weights run the clock hands as they turn on their axles; mechanical men blow horns and ring bells; doors open and saints appear. Mechanical angels circle and turn on grooved tracks, and mechanical cocks lift their wings to crow out the hour and half hour with daily precision.[1]

It all looked very impressive. It was also, as Galileo and Kepler had both shown, finely tuned and programmed. However, something was missing, what we might call the human factor. Where did humanity fit into all this? Where does a cosmos governed by impersonal mechanical laws leave us as rational creatures?

Harvey's fellow Englishman, Sir Francis Bacon, supplied one answer: It leaves us firmly in charge. As self-declared pundit of the new science, Bacon was delighted to see Aristotelian natural philosophy with its "contentiousness" (an odd complaint from a lawyer) and its fetish for words, not deeds (ditto), get swept away.[2] Now men could get down to the business of forcing Nature to reveal her secrets for our use, Bacon said. He liked to speak of putting Nature "on the rack" through constant experiment and verification, like a helpless prisoner being questioned in front of a judge and jury. "Nature exhibits herself more clearly," Bacon wrote, "through the trials and vexation of art than when left to herself."[3]

Across the English Channel, the biggest champion of the new mechanical worldview was René Descartes. Bacon was entirely ignorant of mathematics. Descartes was steeped in it. Reducing the operations of the universe to a series of lines, circles, numbers, and equations suited his reclusive personality. His most famous saying, "I think, therefore I am" (*cogito, ergo sum*), could be stated less succinctly but more accurately as "Because we are the only beings who do math, we rule."

For Descartes, the essence of mind is to think, and the essence of matter is to exist—and the two never meet. The physical world around us is governed by exact and necessary laws imposed by God, which we watch, analyze, and manipulate. Otherwise, nature never touches us at any point. "What is beyond geometry, is beyond us," as Blaise Pascal once put it—and therefore is of no interest to us. Descartes's worldview makes us spiders at the center of an enormous web not of our making. Or in his other famous formulation, we are the ghosts in the machine: souls in a world machine that operates inexorably and impersonally according to the laws of geometry and mechanics, while we operate the levers and spin the dials.

Before his death in 1650, Descartes had spread Galileo's fame up and down Europe, and with it the mechanical philosophy. In France and Holland, Cartesianism became virtually the official creed of scientists, mathematicians, and everyone else involved in the investigation of nature.[4] Descartes's books found eager readers in England, including the father of modern chemistry, Robert Boyle, and a shy, rather retiring teacher at Cambridge named Henry More.

More was very impressed by Descartes. Other modern philosophers, he wrote to a friend, "are mere shrimps and fumblers in comparison [with] him."[5] Yet the more he read, the more More had his doubts.

More couldn't help comparing Descartes's view of man and the universe with those of another author he revered, Marsilio Ficino. Descartes's dualism, his way of seeing the world as shaped by the action of the soul on matter, bore a superficial resemblance to Ficino's and also Plato's. However, while Ficino's message seemed full of life and hopeful possibility, Descartes's seemed positively gloomy. Matter in Descartes had become an inert oppressive presence, doing its job in a reliable robotlike way but surrounding and confronting us with its essential lifelessness everywhere we look—even in the eyes of our favorite pets.*

---

* Descartes completely rejected the idea that animals had mental states or consciousness like those of humans, including feeling love or suffering pain. He has been the bête noire of animal rights activists ever since.

Where do we find love and comfort in this comfortless, mechanical world? And above all, More wanted to know, *where is God?*

Descartes's answer was confident and pat. God was the omnipotent Legislator who has made everything and installed all the necessary rules that govern the universe, including the laws of mathematics, rather the way the manufacturer installs software on a new Android. Then God steps aside and lets His creation "do its thing." As part of the original installation, God has also put the idea of His existence into our minds.[6] But we can go for months or even years without clicking on that particular icon. And if we don't click on it, More realized, then we may never notice what's missing.

Descartes was no atheist. But More worried that his view of the world must inevitably *lead* to atheism. It was simply not possible that God would set up the cosmos and then walk away—and men should not be allowed to think so. In a universe in which everything has its place, He must still be somewhere.

But how to prove it? More and his friends, the so-called Cambridge Platonists, were stumped. Then in 1661 there arrived in their midst the young man who would, surprisingly enough, give them with the answer.

I say surprisingly, because Isaac Newton was hardly the person people would pick to be the cultural guru of his age. Everyone recognized that this son of a clergyman from northwestern England (born the same year Galileo died, in 1642) was an incredible math prodigy. He was twenty-seven when he took the prestigious Lucasian chair of mathematics at Cambridge. His predecessor willingly resigned in recognition of Newton's genius.[7]

The new Lucasian professor lectured to a largely empty classroom. The mathematical theories he expounded were so complicated, no student could follow him. Newton was also deeply secretive. He hid all his most important research from his colleagues and even friends. He invented integral calculus and used it for years in his own work, before finally, reluctantly, he was forced to let the rest of the world in on the secret.[8] And every minute Newton didn't spend working on optics, physics, astronomy (including inventing the reflecting telescope), some harmless alchemy, and other sidebars of his mathematical discipline, he spent furtively studying the Bible and church history.

After Newton's death in 1727, when he was the acknowledged scientific genius of his age, the dozens of folio notebooks he had filled with his biblical studies were discovered. People shook their heads. The last stages of a great mind sliding into senility, they concluded. Some even said they were the deluded products of mercury blood poisoning from Newton's years of chemical experiments.

The truth was that Newton's biblical research was central to his entire scientific career. They form the essential backdrop for his most famous work, the *Principia Mathematica*. For like a true son of Plato, Newton never lost sight of the Big Picture, including the problem that had so perplexed Henry More and the other Cambridge Platonists. Where do we find God in a material and mechanical universe?

Descartes's works had helped to push Newton's mind away from pure mathematics toward the problems of the new science like optics. Then in the late 1660s, Newton turned decisively against him. The "notion of bodies having, as it were, a complete, absolute, and independent reality in themselves," he decided, was not only misleading but dangerous. By separating body from mind and spirit, Descartes was denying the dependence of the material world on God's will and His providence. "A God without dominion, providence, and final causes," Newton later wrote, "is nothing else but Fate."[9]

By denying God, we deny our own spiritual freedom. We surrender ourselves to a world of pure material necessity. The intellectual tyranny that Newton had seen in the darkest chapters in the history of the medieval Church, he saw repeated in the tyranny of a godless, soulless science. He intended to correct that view and free men's minds for the future.

It was this goal that finally persuaded him to agree to publish his decades of research in physics, as *The Principles of Nature Mathematically Explained*, or the *Principia Mathematica*, in 1687—incidentally, the last major work of Western civilization written entirely in Latin. Most read it as the last word on Galileo's new science, as it set out the mathematical laws of nature that governed everything from the movement of the planets and comets to fluid mechanics and the lunar tides. From start to finish, however, Newton's own goal was to demonstrate the dependence of matter on God.[10]

He did this through his revolutionary concept of force. Nature as described in the *Principia* is a complex matrix of forces, from centripetal and centrifugal force, to magnetic force and inertial force (as in, "Bodies at rest tend to remain at rest"), to the most famous of all, the force of gravity. These

forces, Newton showed, exert a palpable and mathematically predictable influence on the behavior of all physical bodies. Yet they are entirely invisible
and beyond any purely physical or mechanical explanation.

Descartes's clockwork universe couldn't account for them. Newton's universe could. The *Principia* is the culmination of Galileo's insight that if you
can describe something mathematically, then it must exist. Newton never
tried to give an explanation for gravity. "To us," he wrote, "it is enough that
gravity does really exist, and act[s] according to the laws we have explained. . . ." All the same, "gravity must be caused by an agent acting according to certain laws."[11] The identity of that agent was self-evident to Newton. It
was God.

Nature's laws implies a lawgiver: it's an idea as old as the Bible or Plato's
Timaeus. However, Newton now carried this further by making the *physical*
nature of the cosmos itself proof of God's *spiritual* presence. "He is omnipres-
ent," Newton wrote. "In Him are all things contained and moved; yet neither
affects the other; God suffers nothing from the motion of bodies; bodies find
no resistance from the omnipotence of God." In other words, the rich diversity of nature, combined with its symmetry and regularity, reflects the will of
a benevolent God.[12]

Newton's God is a God who constantly watches over His creation. He
provides it with universally true general laws, then thoughtfully provides man
with the means to decipher them, namely reason. Newton also finally answered Henry More's question about where God Himself was in this meticulously ordered universe. He is *in between*. His spirit provides the space
through which all objects pass, from birds and trees to comets and stars in the
sky; and His infinitude is found in the infinity of the cosmos, stretching out
beyond our solar system into eternity. "He is not duration and space, but He
endures and is present. . . . He exists *always and everywhere*."[13]

The fact that the study of nature proved beyond refutation the existence
of a perfect and benevolent Creator was for Newton both exhilarating and
liberating. Men could now move forward with a new freedom, confident that
such a Supreme Being supervised and guided the complex workings of the
universe, including their own actions.

Others felt the same sense of freedom. The Royal Society of London for
Improving Natural Knowledge, to which Newton submitted his *Principia*,
had been moving down the same path since its foundation in 1660. Its members, which included churchmen as well as scientists like Robert Boyle, dis-

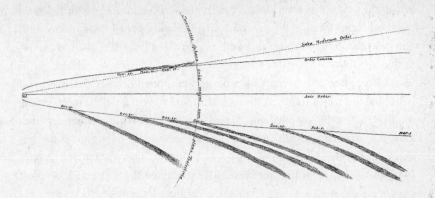

Newton's drawing of a comet. Where is God? He is *in between*.

coverer of the famous comet, embraced the *Principia*'s message with enthusiasm. Newton became an overnight hero and an icon of his age, as described by Alexander Pope in the epitaph for his tomb in Westminster Abbey:

> *Nature and Nature's laws lay*
> *hid in night:*
> *God said, "Let Newton be!"*
> *and all was Light.*

However, while Newton was putting the final touches on his *Principia Mathematica*, a crisis was brewing. There was a growing political force across the English Channel, a force that was as fearsomely modern as its roots were ancient. Some in England feared it. Others wanted to emulate it. Either way, the notion of a cosmic order built on the will of God was about to show a very different, more sinister face.

"Sire, it is time."

It was seven-fifteen in the morning. The man who uttered these words stood in the dim light of a single candle, which, like the flame in a church altar, burned in the king's bedchamber all night—as it did every night. He was the first valet of the king's bedchamber. His elegant clothes and hair were still slightly rumpled from sleeping at the foot of the king's bed, as the valet did every night. Behind him, servants lit a fire and opened the window shutters onto the gray morning, as a dull red glow rose over the gardens of Versailles.

The middle-aged, muscular but pudgy man rolled over in his bed. He sat patiently as servants removed his nightshirt and put on a richer, more ornate nightshirt. The door opened quietly and an elderly man and woman entered. The man was the king's doctor, who silently examined his patient as the servants rubbed the royal legs and arms back to life. The woman was Perette Dufour, the king's former wet nurse, who remained the first female to greet him every morning for more than half a century. Dufour had been the only person who could bear the pain of suckling the greedy royal infant, who by the time he was two years old had chewed off the nipples of all his other wet nurses.[14]

Dufour planted a kiss on her former charge as he sat upright and nodded to the valet. The bed curtains were still drawn. However, Louis-Dieudonné de Bourbon, King of the French and the Fourteenth of that name, was ready to receive visitors. The Sun King was about to shine.

The first to enter were the king's brother, the princes of the blood, the grand chamberlain, the four first gentlemen of the king's bedchamber, the grand master and masters of the king's robes, the four first valets of the royal bedchamber, and the first valet of the wardrobe. The chamberlain pulled aside the bed curtain to reveal, as if in a theater, the king in bed. Servants poured spirits of wine into a silver ewer so that Louis could wash his hands and then cross himself with holy water from another basin presented every morning by either the grand chamberlain or the first gentleman.[15]

Then one or the other presented Louis with his prayer book. The page was marked for the Office of the Holy Spirit. There were no clergymen present for the king's *grand levée*, and none who attended ex officio for the second or *petite levée* in another half hour, when the four secretaries of the dressing room, the two lectors of the chamber, the two majordomos and wardens of the royal plate, along with distinguished visitors, ambassadors, and other members of the French nobility, were allowed to see him be dressed and watch him choose his wig for the day.

The clergy were not excluded from the rest of the Sun King's daily routine. Louis regularly had a prayer service and then Mass later that morning, like clockwork, at ten o'clock.[16] The object of this daily ritual, however, was not the worship of God, but the worship of the king: a king who, in 1687, saw himself as omnipotent as any Roman emperor and sacrosanct as any pope.

For "all men are the image of God," one of Louis XIV's propagandists wrote, "but His true portrait is in the person of the sovereign; his authority represents His power; his majesty His *éclat;* his goodness His charity; his rigor His justice."[17]

The Sun King ruled a heliocentric universe as absolutely as the actual sun dominated Copernicus's and Galileo's solar system. He ran his kingdom with the mechanical clockwork precision of Descartes's cosmos. Like a caricature of Newton's God, he "governs all things, and knows all things that are or can be done." Every morning Louis rose like the sun, in a bedroom at the center of his magnificent palace at Versailles, which after twenty years was still under construction (one of the last rooms to be built, ironically, was the royal chapel). On every side for a quarter of a mile ran gardens with five thousand statues and five hundred elaborate fountains, while more than ten thousand servants, courtiers, and royal officials kept the palace in constant motion.

Then as now, Versailles overawed every visitor with its grandeur. Then as now, tourists were allowed to wander the grounds, gape at the statues and fountains, and even watch their king eat his dinner in public. As servants bore the gold and silver platters overflowing with meats and vegetables through the palace, every person was expected to bow and murmur reverently, "The food of the king." Then, surrounded by his family and dozens of courtiers, Louis XIV would consume four plates of soup, an entire pheasant, and a brace of partridge, followed by large slices of mutton and ham with garlic and gravy and a tray of hard-boiled eggs—all washed down with flagons of champagne.[18]

What the visitors were seeing was more than a prodigious appetite in action. They were witnessing how the richest and most populous kingdom in Europe had been made to revolve around a single man, in a ritual of obedience as solemn as the Last Supper. They were also watching the poverty of politics in 1600s' Europe.

The seventeenth century would be the great "century of genius" in science. It was the age of Galileo, Harvey, Boyle, and of course Newton. The political and social systems of Europe, however, seemed to have stalled out. Through his dark reading of Aristotle, Machiavelli had left behind a dilemma and a paradox.

Self-governing societies seemed doomed to be free but unstable. Because they existed in time, and were therefore subject to the vicissitudes of change and to men's passions, they would inevitably hit a wall.* Like ancient Rome and Renaissance Florence, they were doomed to fall into the hands of a despot in order to save society from mob rule. Freedom, in short, must eventually lead to unfreedom.

If this was true, Europeans asked, then why not start with unfreedom and be done with it? The solution seemed to be ceding all authority to a single absolute sovereign, who consciously modeled his power and glory after the ancient Roman emperors and their Neoplatonist propagandists.

What is usually called the Age of Absolutism in Europe in the 1600s was actually the age of Neoplatonist kingship. Louis XIV was not the only monarch who insisted that he was the living image of God, or that his authority must be as absolute and unquestioned as God's sovereignty over His creation. The portraits of the others cram the palaces and art galleries of western Europe: Philip III and Philip IV of Spain, Henry IV and Louis XIII of France, Victor Amadeus of Savoy, James I and Charles I of England. They appear dressed in the trappings of imperial glory. They are shown surrounded by clouds of angels and admiring courtiers and blessed by the gods of classical antiquity.

Like the Sun King, all of them turned their nation's printing presses and church pulpits into royalist propaganda machines. What was then "the mainstream media" routinely pointed to the monarch as an essential link in the Great Chain of Being, the center of a divinely preordained and fixed order. A king was more than just a political leader. Heaven had placed him on the throne not only to be obeyed, but to be loved and revered.

Louis XIV's favorite clergyman, Bishop Bossuet, proclaimed that a good subject must love his king "like the air which he breathes, like the light that fills his eyes, as much as his own life, indeed as more than his life." It was a commonplace that God had placed kings at the head of kingdoms, in the same way that He placed fathers at the head of the family: as loving, beneficent images of His own authority, against which there was no appeal because none was necessary. "Oh God," prayed another of Louis's panegyrists, "con-

---

*Venice, which managed to maintain its republican system of government uninterrupted through the centuries, was the exception, but the exception that seemed to prove the rule. Everyone agreed its case was unique, the product of its closed oligarchic politics and unusual social stability, which no other European state could emulate.

Equestrian statue of Louis XIV, Versailles palace. For John Locke,
the Sun King was at war with his own people.

serve for us this prince You have given us through Your love of us. . . . Cover
him with grace as he covers us with benefits. . . ."[19]

Aristotle and Plato would have dismissed this kind of obsequious language
as unworthy of free men. By the seventeenth century, however, it had become commonplace. It was also a lie.

Louis's propaganda machine disguised the sordid reality of the Sun King's
reign. The "benefits" that flowed to his subjects left nearly one in ten a homeless beggar, and as historian Pierre Goubert has noted, infant mortality was
running at 25 percent.[20] Even as Louis worried over which wig to wear, the
countryside where the majority of Frenchmen lived was, as the Venetian ambassador noted in 1660, "a sinkhole of indigence and misery."

Those who held government jobs or contracts, or attended the king at
court, grew rich. The rest starved or saw their incomes steadily shrink away.
France's nobility were immune from taxation; those who could least afford

taxes, the peasantry and small property holders in the towns, paid for every-thing from Europe's largest army and navy to the fountains and statues at Versailles. And those who refused to adhere to the king's formula of "one king, one kingdom, one faith," like the Protestant Huguenots, were perse-cuted, beaten, and eventually driven into exile by the tens of thousands.

In 1680, Europe's other kingdoms were scarcely better off. Yet to crowned heads everywhere, Louis XIV's absolutist ways seemed the last best hope for peace and stability. More than a century before, the Reformation had split Europe into two and even three warring religious camps, culminating in the catastrophe of the Thirty Years War. Civil wars, starvation, disease, and eco-nomic collapse had swept across the Continent, until the exhausted combat-ants made peace in 1648. Behind the trappings of loving authority and the reality of coercive power and chronic poverty, the message from Versailles was clear: Your only alternative is mob rule and apocalypse.

There were some, however, who were determined to set some limits on that awesome sovereignty and power.

Late one evening in August 1683, a man crouched in front of his fireplace with a pile of papers. As he fed pages into the fire, the flames would have lit up the rafters of the darkened room and the lean lines of his angular face. He was burning letters, memoranda, bills, published pamphlets, anything that might be incriminating. He knew he was being watched by spies. Although he had thrown them off his trail, at any moment he might be arrested for treason and join his co-conspirators in the Tower of London.

News of the arrest of the Earl of Essex, Lord William Russell, and Alger-non Sydney had reached him at his rooms at Christ Church College in Ox-ford. He had prudently left town for a friend's house in rural Somerset. Shortly afterward, the bishop of Oxford and the university's vice chancellor were or-dered to search his chambers. They had burned a pile of his books in the courtyard, the last such public burning in England. Other agents of the king began a massive search for anyone matching the description of John Locke.

Now Locke was destroying every trace of his associations and activities in the alleged plot against King Charles II—everything, that is, except a particu-lar manuscript. He took it with him as he left Somerset for the coast. The remaining papers Locke sent to a friend: "What you dislike," he wrote, "you may burn." He also provided details on settling his debts and directions for selling his clothes, books, and furniture in Oxford, including two silver candlesticks and his "linens, flannel shirts, waistcoats, [and] stockings." Locke also sent his friend a signed will, just in case the next stage of his plan went awry.[21]

A few days later, Locke turned up at one of the Channel ports. Money changed hands, and Locke slipped onto a boat bound for Holland. On September 7, 1683, he was in Rotterdam and free.

He would not return to England for another six years. By then his friends were dead, executed for their supposed complicity in the Rye House plot.* They had actually died for their part in the resistance to the growing tyranny in England and the spread of Louis XIV's Neoplatonist message across the English Channel.

Locke had traveled to France and Versailles. He had seen Louis XIV's *petite levée* and watched the elaborate rituals of absolute kingship, of total rule by one man. Locke's one goal in life was to make sure the same thing never happened in England. But whereas others tried to fight for freedom with guns or plots or revolutions, Locke would fight for it with ideas.

His weapon at hand was the manuscript under his arm. "Absolute monarchy," it read in part, "is inconsistent with Civil Society, and so can be no form of Civil Government at all." His book revealed why governments must serve the interests of everyone, rather than one person; and why one-man rule was the perversion, not the perfection, of nature—particularly the nature so brilliantly illuminated by his friend Isaac Newton.

It's not surprising that Newton and Locke were close, even intimate friends. As a Newton biographer noted, "Each recognized in the other an intellectual peer."[22] Both were keenly interested in the new science (Newton actually gave Locke a special gift copy of the *Principia*, which is today in Cambridge's Trinity College Library). Both were also keen readers of the Bible. Locke, in fact, told a biographer that he knew few men who equaled Newton in knowledge of both the Old and New Testaments.

And both were working on the same problem from different ends. This was figuring out how human beings fit into an infinite universe—and how we can salvage our freedom from the forces of blind necessity, in either the physical *or* the political realms.

---

*Whether a plot to kidnap Charles II was actually hatched at Rye House has been debated and redebated by historians ever since.

The answer they found was the nature of nature itself, as the product of a Beneficent Creator. Like Newton, behind nature and reason Locke always recognized the person and voice of God.[23] Newton's *Principia* revealed that the physical universe was governed by certain laws of nature, "a constant and regular connection in the ordinary course of things." That constancy reveals the will of an "all wise Agent," as Locke later wrote, "who has made them to be, and to operate as they do."[24] Locke's *Two Treatises of Government* revealed that the political universe is run the same way, through natural laws that guide men's behavior in the same sure way that they guide the movement of the planets.

In discussing this, Locke had found a kindred spirit in Aristotle. This was not the Aristotle of the schoolmen or the civic humanist of the Florentines, but the shrewd analyst of human nature in the *Ethics*.

In Book V, Aristotle noted that some laws are common to all people, whether Persians and Greeks, Egyptians or Babylonians. All agree that murder and theft are wrong; all agree that our word is our bond and that contracts must be kept. The origin of these universal rules for conduct and justice can't be written law, since all written law is based on them. So where did they come from? They come from our observation of nature, Aristotle said, and the experience of seeing what's fair and what's unfair in actual situations. From that experience, human beings extract a standard of justice that "has the same validity everywhere and does not depend on acceptance" by a particular people or government—but which is upheld by all of them and everywhere men institute fair and just laws.[25]

However different in other respects, Greeks and Persians, Egyptians and Nubians, Protestants and Catholics, Christians and Muslims, all enshrine these principles of natural justice in their laws. However, Aristotle insisted, the source of that justice is always the same: observation of the underlying order of nature.

Thomas Aquinas had noticed Aristotle's point and extended it. In his usual tidy way, Aquinas decided to divide man's encounter with the concept of law into a three-part hierarchy of importance.[26] Aquinas was a theologian, not a lawyer, so he put the actual legal codes of peoples and nations, including Roman law, at the bottom, while putting divine law, or *lex divina*, such as the Ten Commandments, at the top.

In between he put what he called the laws of nature, or *lex naturalis*. These included all the physical laws of nature (including motions of planets), moral principles like charity and self-preservation, and all those laws, including prohibitions against murder, incest, and theft, that all nations immediately see as just. Like divine law, this natural law reflects God's will. But instead of learning His will directly through the Bible and revelation, we learn this natural aspect of His will through our reason. Wherever men use their reason, Aquinas concluded, we will see them respect the laws of nature; and wherever we see the practice of *lex naturalis* in human affairs, then we know we are dealing with rational beings like ourselves.[27]

Then Aquinas was prepared to move on. But Aquinas also left an ambiguity for future generations to ponder. *Lex naturalis* could also be rendered as *jus naturale*; the Latin is unclear. Natural laws, in other words, could become "natural rights," meaning a legal claim we derive from nature and hold as individuals. But what kind of claim? And a claim against whom?

The answer the followers of Aquinas developed was that my natural rights are my claims against the community to protect and defend my person and those things essential to my well-being. These rights are mine by nature, "since all men are born free by nature," as the Dominican Francisco Suárez wrote in the late 1500s.[28] It was all too easy to see a close parallel between the way in which William of Ockham had borrowed from Aristotle's *Politics* to talk about the community retaining its sovereignty over those who exercise power in its name, like a pope or prince, and the sovereign natural rights of the individual drawn from the Thomist reading of Aristotle's *Ethics*.

Both powers are held as a matter of right, or *jus*. Both are temporarily transferred as a matter of convenience (to a prince or head of state in the community's case, to the laws of the state in the individual's case), to make it easier to protect and defend that power's original holders, the people and the individuals who make up "the people." In fact, by the 1500s some were concluding that perhaps there was even more overlap. Perhaps it was in order to protect those same natural rights that individuals banded together in the first place.

At this point, Aristotle could provide no more help. He had never bothered to ask why men set up city-states or governments. The fact that it was their nature to do so, as political animals (*zoon politikon*), did the trick. But Aquinas and his followers could help, and did.

In a pristine "state of nature," they decided, man was totally free but totally unsafe. He was prey not only to the elements and wild animals, but to his fellow man, for whom freedom was license to act not as *zoon politikon*, but as *homo lupus*. In Thomas Hobbes's famous formulation, life ends up being "nasty, brutish, and short."

To correct this, right reason dictates a solution. To avoid killing one another off, men make an agreement. They trade in their natural rights in exchange for *civil rights*, which are now recognized and protected by the community and those who wield authority in its name.

For example, the jurist Hugo Grotius (one of Locke's predecessors in this way of thinking) said this exchange involves a trade-off. What I *lose* from the point of total freedom, I *gain* by way of security and predictability.[29] Under the new arrangement, I won't be able to help myself to your pile of grain whenever I feel hungry, or your bank account. But I know you won't help yourself to mine, either; because if you do, the civil authority will punish you for it.

Steeped in the Latin of Roman law, Europe's jurists branded this agreement the *pactum societatis*. In their minds, it marked the birth of legitimate government. A couple of centuries later, Jean-Jacques Rousseau gave it a more famous name: the social contract. It's not based on a signed piece of paper or original physical act. Like the axis of Galileo's rotating earth, the social contract is imaginary, but it is still *there*, exerting its influence and power. Like any contract, it imposes obligations both on me *and* on my rulers. I am bound to obey the laws of the society in which I choose to dwell. The lawgivers, including a prince or king, are bound to respect my civil rights—or else.

Or else what? By 1600, that was the question every crowned head and magistrate felt entitled to ask. In a profound sense, it was *the* political question for Europe for the next two hundred years.

The problem was that many natural law theorists made breaking the contract too easy. It wasn't necessary for the ruler to threaten people's lives or seize their property; just being of the wrong religion, or not sufficiently committed to the right one, was enough. A generation of Catholic political writers, including Aquinas's followers, used the social contract to threaten Protestant rulers with overthrow and assassination. Protestants responded by arguing the same about Catholic kings.[30]

Two French kings in a row died from an assassin's dagger, while James I of England suffered a near miss in the Gunpowder Plot. His son Charles I did end up paying the ultimate price for supposedly breaking his covenant with his subjects; but as Englishmen learned, what was supposed to be a formula for liberty ended up being a formula for a decade of chaos and dictatorship.

No wonder many preferred the Louis XIV solution, to accept divinely ordained absolute rulership and be done with it. Others, like Locke's older contemporary Thomas Hobbes, decided that social contract theory needed drastic modification. In his grand theory of the state published in 1651, titled *Leviathan*, Hobbes insisted that the transfer of a people's self-sovereignty to a monarch and king did indeed take place but it was a onetime transaction. Once it was complete, there was no going back, ever. "For the Sovereign [must be] absolute . . . or else there is no Sovereignty at all."[31]

Hobbes's citizens realize that they must give up their natural liberty in order to protect them from themselves. They are like the alcoholic who hands the key to his liquor cabinet to a friend and says, "No matter what I say, don't give me back the key." He knows that unless someone stops him, he is a danger to himself and others.

Hobbes knew that some rights theorists, like the Calvinist Scot George Buchanan and the Spanish Dominican Juan Molina, still insisted that the alcoholic should get his key whenever he wants it—even at the price of civil war. Hobbes puts the blame squarely on Aristotle, who he said led men to connect liberty with democracy and goaded them into "loving tumults" and disorder, believing those were the way to secure liberty when they did just the opposite. Instead, Hobbes argued, nothing was safe unless we obey the sovereign; and "the Liberty of the subject, lyeth therefore only in those things, which in regulating their actions, the Sovereign hath permitted. . . ."[32]

Locke saw this line of argument as a complete perversion of the idea of natural rights. People aren't alcoholics; by and large, they are the same sober and hardworking people as Aristotle's householders in the *Politics*, who want to be left alone to live their lives. Instead, Locke insisted that the debate over natural rights return to its original framework of natural law. "The state of nature has a law of nature to govern it, which obliges everyone; and Reason, which is that law, teaches all mankind, who will but consult it."[33] Was it possible that God would devise such a system of natural laws and put man in the middle of them in order to create a nation of slaves? Locke said no.

John Locke was a doctor, not a lawyer. He was less interested in the legal aspect of the social contract than in its moral face. Locke saw at once that God must have constructed the framework of natural law for the same purpose that He devised Newton's universe: to set men free.

Therefore, that natural liberty was not something we surrender at all. Putting our trust in a beneficent God is one thing; trusting our liberty to a human ruler is quite another. Instead, we keep our liberty close and forever. It's ours to use even in civil society; and protection of that liberty is the final end of civil society.

This includes liberty of our person and our lives and those things that are extensions of ourselves, like our family and property. "Though the earth and inferior Creatures be common to all men," Locke wrote in his *Second Treatise*, "the labor that was mine, removing them out of that common state they were in, hath fixed my Property in them [which] no one has a Right to but [myself]." In fact, nowhere are we closer to God than when we create property from our own handiwork, just as man is the handiwork of his Lord God.[34]

Locke's natural liberty includes liberty of thought, since reason is another of God's gifts, including our thoughts about religion. This made Locke the first great advocate of religious toleration and author of three *Letters Concerning Toleration*, the second of which he sent to Newton for comment and approval.[35] Liberty included an equality before the law, since all men are equal before God; and it included a generosity of spirit and independence of mind that Aristotle had recognized as the hallmark of the virtuous man and which Locke saw would prevent a state of normal liberty from degenerating into a "state of license"—in other words, a perpetual riot.

All these liberties or rights are protected, not hindered, by the original social contract. Proper government is not a restraint on our natural liberty, as Hobbes and others thought. It is a net *increase*, since it provides a framework of security in which we can enjoy our civil liberties in ways not possible in the state of nature. It "is the one great reason of men putting themselves into Society, and quitting the State of Nature."[36]

With it, however, come certain duties. One is the duty to use our reason as God's gift; another is to protect our liberty and the liberty of others. The most important, however, is the duty of the sovereign to respect that liberty: and when he doesn't, when "he that in a State of Society would take away the Freedom that belongs to those of that Society," and pretends to be our master rather than our servant, then it is *he*, not us, who is the real rebel against society.[37]

Locke's conclusion was startling, not to say world shattering. A monarch like Louis XIV, or any of his would-be imitators, in effect is at war with his subjects.* When that happens, Locke asserted, then lawful government is at an end. We are all thrown back into the original state of nature. "Where the

---

*Something Louis's wet nurses might have agreed with.

government is dissolved," Locke explained, "the people are at liberty to provide for themselves, by erecting a new legislative" body to act in their name.[38] The social contract starts over from scratch. Government by popular consent is not just a good idea, as it was for Aristotle and Ockham. For Locke, it is an inescapable law of nature. It is what separates a society of free men from a society of slaves.

To others like his late friend Algernon Sidney, that "legislative body" representing the people was England's Parliament, and always had been.[39] To Locke, it really didn't matter. The issue was not historical precedent, but natural right. The real power was power invested in the people, now and forever. It could not be taken away by any earthly man or institution, including Parliament itself.

This was a truly radical idea. It was too radical for an England weary of a century of tumults and intrigues. In 1688, the English replaced their monarch James II and brought another, James's daughter Mary and her husband, William, from Holland. Locke returned to England with them in the royal yacht, but not in triumph. The arguments Parliament chose to justify its removal of one king and replacing him with another implicitly rejected Locke's populist appeal and substituted the more conservative historical one of his dead friend Sidney.[40]

John Locke, former fugitive and would-be revolutionary, died in 1704. His last work was a series of paraphrases of the sayings of Saint Paul, which he sent to his friend Isaac Newton. No man had labored more to reconcile the God of the New Testament with the laws of nature expounded by Aristotle and Aquinas. "He that shall collect all the moral rules of the philosophers," he once wrote, "and compare them with those contained in the New Testament, will find them to come short of the morality delivered by our Savior, and taught by his apostles; a college made up, for the most part, of ignorant but inspired fishermen."[41] Yet for other reasons no one's influence would be more important in the secular age to follow: Locke's belief that a government of the people, by the people, and even as for the people is a matter of natural law and right would take root across the Atlantic in the fertile soil of the New World.

Twenty-one

ARISTOTLE IN A PERIWIG: THE CULTURE OF THE ENLIGHTENMENT

Commerce [is] the eternal link between men.

—Voltaire

It is not from the benevolence of the butcher, the brewer, or the baker,
that we expect our dinner but from their regard to their own interest.

—Adam Smith

The eighteenth century is famously the age of wigs and salons, of wits and *philosophes*, of experimental science and the first turning of the wheels of the Industrial Revolution—and the transatlantic slave trade. In England, the era dubbed itself the Augustan Age. On the other side of Europe, Immanuel Kant coined another term: the Age of Enlightenment.

They might just as well have called it the Age of Locke. No thinker since Socrates dominated the minds of his immediate successors as John Locke did. His ideas were the flammable fuel of the Enlightenment, and sent it soaring to new intellectual heights. But this was not Locke the political theorist: his *Two Treatises of Government* were less read than used to be thought.[1] The Locke who inspired the eighteenth century was the philosopher who wired

Aristotle's most important insight, that all knowledge comes through experience, into the modern Western mind.

Locke's *An Essay Concerning Human Understanding*, written in 1690 after the Glorious Revolution, decisively moved the Enlightenment in Aristotle's direction.* This was Aristotle the father of empirical science, the advocate of rational argument reinforced by the evidence of the senses. It was Aristotle shorn of substances, essences, categories, and final causes and selectively edited.[2] Apart from three or four texts—and only certain key passages of those—the rest of his work was left to gather dust.

However, those texts were enough. Virtually every eighteenth-century artistic endeavor from poetry to music and painting was governed by rules drawn from Aristotle's *Poetics* and Book II of the *Rhetoric* (Locke's personal favorite).[†] Politics and moral thinking—and the Enlightenment was *the* century of great moral debates—were also dominated by the problem of how to reconcile the social virtues described in Aristotle's *Ethics* with the political processes set forth in his *Politics*. The result was Adam Smith's *Wealth of Nations*, not to mention the American Constitution.

Impressive for a philosopher who had been dead more than two thousand years and who had nearly been consigned to history's dustbin during the Reformation. All the same, John Locke said that the place to start the study of how men behave was Aristotle.[3] With a handful of exceptions, the Enlightenment followed his advice.

On the other hand, it entertained no illusions about Aristotle's limitations. A century and a half of humanist scholarship had given Europeans a far better understanding of both Plato and Aristotle in historical context than was possible for someone like Erasmus. The eighteenth-century mind had thoroughly probed the political economy of the ancient Greek *polis*. It understood as Machiavelli never could why the ancient world failed to sustain its ideals of citizenship.

It also realized how much ancient Rome had owed to Greece in terms of thought and culture. Enlightenment historians like Edward Gibbon and phi-

---

*Including, some would argue, in Aristotle's direction on slavery. Modern critics like to point to Locke's Constitution of Carolina, which upholds chattel slavery in that colony, and passages in the *Second Treatise of Government* that deny the slave the same natural rights as free men, as proof of his hypocrisy on this issue. How fair it is to condemn an author's views based on a standard that he, in a very different time and place, was the first to conceive, seems a matter for debate.

†See chapter 23.

losophers like David Hume understood how Christianity had evolved as the fusion of Judaism and Neoplatonism; how much Christian Neoplatonism and Plotinus's pagan version overlapped; and how ancient Stoics, Epicureans, and Skeptics offered philosophical insights as powerful and relevant as the Big Three: Socrates, Plato, and Aristotle.

Finally, the Enlightenment understood the enormous historical and cultural distance that separated it from the "ancients"—thanks in part to the rise of Christianity. The big loser in all this, however, was not Aristotle but Plato. His *Republic*—later so much admired by the Romantics—was the one work of political philosophy the Enlightenment most despised. Adam Smith's teacher Francis Hutcheson pronounced its theory of politics unworkable; Smith's friend David Hume referred to the book's "illusory and visionary rantings." On the other side of the Atlantic, John Adams said there were only two things he ever learned from reading Plato, and one of them was that sneezing will cure hiccups.[4]

Thomas Jefferson was even more excoriating. He once confessed in a letter to Adams that he had been rereading the *Republic*. "I laid it down often to ask myself how it could have been that the world should have so long consented to give reputation to such nonsense as this?" Jefferson had to conclude that Plato had always been a fraud, "a dealer in mysticisms incomprehensible to the human mind," which had been allowed to inject "an impenetrable darkness" into Western culture. "O Plato!" Voltaire exclaimed. "You have done more harm than you know."[5]

Why did the Enlightenment dislike Plato so much? Because his worldview directly contradicted the view of reality and human nature the Enlightenment derived from John Locke, and ultimately from Aristotle.*

That view was, first, that *man is an individual*, an individual born with a natural sociability (an updated version of Aristotle's *zoon politikon*) but also a desire to protect his own natural rights and his own self-interest. "It is love of self," Voltaire would write, "that encourages love of others." That self-interest was derived from nature, "which warns us to respect [the self-interest] of others."[6] This was one reason the Enlightenment, like Aristotle, so strongly opposed the *Republic*'s formula for communism. The abolition of private

---

*In fact, the only Greek philosopher Jefferson mentions as an influence on his Declaration of Independence is Aristotle.

property was not only contrary to natural right, it would also ensure that the bonds that connected men to each other would be founded not on mutual respect and friendship, but on envy or even hate. "Nothing can be conceived more destructive of human happiness, more infallibly contrived to transform men and women into Brutes, Yahoos, or Daemons," John Adams wrote, than community of property.[7]

Second, *the key to happiness is understanding how the real world works.* This idea stood in contrast to Plato-inspired utopian dreams, including John Calvin's Geneva (a favorite target in the Enlightenment). Our highest ideals are not reflections of some transcendent reality, Enlightenment thinkers argued, or some higher truth. They are just that, ideals: insubstantial playthings of the mind that can deceive as often as they can inspire. This is what led Jefferson to dismiss the "dreams of Plato" and dub Plato's ideal of a Philosopher Ruler "whimsical" and "puerile."

Third, *the only way to understand that world is through observation and analysis of our experience,* not inward self-reflection. In the words of the Scottish thinker Thomas Reid, "Settled truth can be attained by observation." Reid's disciple John Witherspoon, who deeply influenced the American Founding Fathers, explained that we know things "by tracing facts *upwards* rather than reasoning *downwards.*"[8] Indeed, "how can we reason" at all, the poet Alexander Pope asked in his *An Essay on Man*, "except from what we know," meaning from our five senses? Indeed, the formal name of Thomas Reid's philosophy, Common Sense Realism, sums up the Aristotelian stamp on the age.

Nearly every one of these principles flowed directly from the most influential book of the age, Locke's *An Essay Concerning Human Understanding.* Completed in 1686 while he was still in exile in Holland but not published until 1690, the work was a full frontal assault on the theory of knowledge stretching back to Plato, that human beings come into the world with the most valuable things they know already programmed in their minds. Mathematical truths, the rules of logic, the existence of God: All we had to do, René Descartes and other Plato-influenced thinkers had argued, was reflect deeply in order to bring them into our consciousness.[9]

Locke argued that we are not born with any innate ideas or knowledge about anything. Everything we know, we have to learn from outside ourselves. The mind is (in Locke's most famous metaphor) a tabula rasa, a blank slate on which our experiences are written by our sense perception of the world. Perception of the world, Locke wrote, is "the first step and degree towards knowledge, and the inlet of all the materials of it."[10]

What Plato had treated as the basest form of knowledge, our sensory grasp of objects, or *eikasia*, Locke now argued was the *only* path to knowledge.* What we see (or touch or hear or smell) is what we get, and the only thing we get. The rest, in a very formal sense, is up to us.

Because what we sense are either the primary qualities of objects themselves, like their size, volume, mass, velocity, length, and width; or their secondary qualities, like taste, loudness, and color. We then have to figure out how they all fit together. Our reason, Locke said, sorts the disparate sense impressions into coherent patterns on the tabula rasa, which in turn become our ideas: the one true objects of knowledge.

This was a radical step.[11] When we say, "This is a cow and this is beef stew," or, "That's a star, but that is a planet," Locke insisted we are actually saying "it is my impression that this jumble of qualities must be *x*"—nothing more and nothing less. So how do we know that what we think and say about the world is actually true? By drawing on our past experience, Locke says, and comparing our notes with others. We say, "Did you see what I saw?" or, "Looks like a cow to me. Do you agree?" When everything fits together—our own perception and judgment and the perception and judgment of others—we can be reasonably certain that we are on the right track.

"Reasonable" is the operative word for Locke. We can never be *completely* certain that our idea of reality, and how things really are, exactly fit. All we know is that our perceptions lead us to think so because of their "conformity with our own experience, or the testimony of others' experience."[12]

Someone might ask Locke how we know there really *are* cows and planets out there. How can we be sure we're not just living an endless dream (or a nightmare, as in the movie *The Matrix*)? As a professing Christian, it would have been easy for Locke to respond: Would a beneficent Creator, infinite in power, goodness, and wisdom, leave men so confused and uncertain as to not know what's real and what's not?[†]

---

*Although the Enlightenment did award the original credit for this insight to Aristotle. The Frenchman Nicolas de Condorcet praised Arisotle as the first thinker to realize that "even our most abstract ideas, the most purely intellectual as it were, owe their origin to sensation."

†This is what his most famous opponent, Bishop Berkeley (1685–1753), would do.

Locke did not. He was content to assume that our mind's picture of the world represents that world, because he knew that the assumption *works*. When I try to lift a 250-pound boulder with a fork instead of a forklift, I soon discover whether my ideas conform to reality or not. I'm free to doubt whether the cow I see is really there. When she gives me a quart of milk, however, my doubts are over—or should be.

In other words, we know we can trust our ideas when they bear practical fruit. Locke puts us firmly in the real world, just as Aristotle did. He had no patience with metaphysical speculations of the Neoplatonist kind. "You and I," Locke once wrote to a philosopher friend, "have had enough of that fiddling."[13]

This marked an irrevocable shift in Western thinking. The old celestial spheres and hierarchies left over from the Middle Ages had already been done in by Newton's infinite universe with its mathematical laws. As the eighteenth century wore on and Locke's influence grew, the rest of the traditional Neoplatonist frame fell away as well. The World Soul and its divine emanations dissipated into thin air. So did the Great Chain of Being. What was left was a world of "real time" and absolute spatial dimensions. It was a world without angels or demons or ideal Forms; a world with no unseen forces except those we can measure and calculate, predict and control.

Later, some regretted this loss of belief in the supernatural.[14] Enlightenment men and women judged it a net gain. They gave up looking to angels for guidance—but they also gave up looking for witches to punish. Instead of waiting for divine radiance to transform their inner selves, they confidently relied on their reason and their five senses in order to explore their world— and to discover the laws of nature. Alexander Pope put it in verse:

> *Take Nature's path, and mad Opinions leave;*
> *All States can reach it, and all heads conceive;*
> *Obvious her goods, in no extreme they dwell;*
> *There needs but thinking right, and meaning well.*[15]

What that exploration of the world revealed to the Enlightenment (since by 1780 it included not only America and Asia but the Pacific and Australia) was a systematic natural order governing not only the physical world, but the social and political realms as well. Just as Newton had applied observation and analysis to reveal the laws of the world system, so the eighteenth century applied itself to find the laws that would allow our social and political systems to run at their optimal level.[16]

No one assumed that the answers would be as precise or mathematical as Newton's had been. The social scientist's passion for number crunching would come later. In the end, what the Enlightenment wanted was knowledge it could work with; the knowledge it needed on Locke's terms, in order to be happy. "What is that which moves desire?" Locke wrote. "I answer, happiness, and that alone."[17] "The pursuit of happiness" became not just an American but the main Enlightenment enterprise for nearly one hundred years after Locke's death.

John Locke had been a Protestant Dissenter and a Puritan at heart. His definition of happiness included a heavy dose of man's duties to God. The eighteenth century was less particular. It found it easy to equate happiness with pleasure, although it never forgot that the latter included the pleasures of the mind. And when the Enlightenment wanted pleasure, it knew just where to look for it.

That was the city.

The spirit of Aristotle had always found a congenial home in large urban environments. The same was true in the eighteenth century. By 1700, Europe had a dozen with populations exceeding one hundred thousand or more. They were commercial cities with bustling streets and shops, plenty of foreign visitors and merchants, and a thriving business center. London, Paris, Amsterdam, Hamburg, Edinburgh, Bordeaux, Venice, and Antwerp marked the confluence of trade, taste, and enlightenment. They were the centers of Europe's new affluent lifestyle and the first consumer culture.

After the grim years of the Thirty Years War and Louis XIV, Europe's economy was thriving again. The age of plagues and famines was finally, definitively over. Long, harsh winters like that of 1708, when the wines of Burgundy froze in their bottles, faded as a bout of global warming swept over Europe. Meanwhile, ships bearing goods from remote parts of the globe, including China, India, and South America, filled Europe's ports and harbors.

Goods that had once been unattainable luxuries for the privileged few were becoming the standard possessions of Europe's businessmen, lawyers, doctors, and prosperous shopkeepers. Their homes filled with porcelain from China and Japan, rugs from Persia and Turkey, and overstuffed furniture made from mahogany and brazilwood and teak. Their tables offered delicacies like chocolate from America and tea from Asia. Their closets overflowed with garments made from imported linen, cotton, and damask silk.

Here was truly an "embarrassment of riches"—embarrassing, that is, from a traditional Christian moral perspective, which for centuries had taught that money was the root of all evil. Instead, as Europeans poured themselves a cup of tea from a pot made from Mexican or Bavarian silver, stirred in a lump of sugar from the West Indies, and sat back in their plush armchairs, they felt compelled to conclude that wealth not only made life more comfortable, it also made people better.

Today, we have long been conditioned to believe the opposite—not by Christianity, but by nineteenth-century Romanticism. The Romantics, however, were the stepchildren of Plato. It was Aristotle who first made private property the basis of the good life and the independent householder the basis of the free *polis*.[18] The world of the Enlightenment took him firmly at his word.

Aristotle thought of this property mostly in terms of land. Earlier thinkers who copied his analysis of freedom, including Machiavelli, had done the same. Now, in the new urban environment of 1700s Europe, it made sense to switch from talking about freehold land as the basis of men's virtue and freedom to appreciating more commercial forms of property like ships, warehouses, stocks and bonds, and merchandise and commodities of all kinds.

A sterner generation had seen the businessman as a prevaricating poltroon. The Enlightenment came to appreciate how doing business required important moral virtues: foresight, prudence, and frugality in saving in order to build capital and pay workers.[19] Even more important, the exchange of goods also made both seller and customer more aware of the needs of others and more eager to work together in order to achieve a win-win result. Commerce not only made it possible to buy the good things in life, it also shaped a human personality geared to appreciate those good things and to recognize their value to others.

This raises an important issue. If men really were improving, we ask, then why did they tolerate the African slave trade, which dramatically increased in volume in the eighteenth century? And wasn't all that affluence that the Enlightenment celebrated the fruits of slave labor in the sugarcane fields of the

Jean-Antoine Watteau, *L'Enseigne de Gersaint* (Gersaint's Shop Sign; 1720). Do commerce and capitalism make people better? Aristotle inspired the Enlightenment to say yes.

Caribbean, the tobacco and cotton plantations of Virginia and the Carolinas, and the coffee farms of Brazil? Those are the questions critics would ask.

In answering the critics then and later,* the Enlightenment stood on firm ground. It knew the overwhelming bulk of Europe's growing affluence sprang from inter-European trade, not from its slaveholding colonies; indeed, those countries most dependent on those slave-holding colonies, Spain and Portu-

---

*One was the artist William Blake, who in 1793 engraved a set of drawings revealing the aftermath of a slave revolt in Surinam with its brutal reprisals, which fed his distaste and despair for modern civilization.

gal, showed the slowest rates of growth. Some of the important beneficiaries of that affluence, like Austria and Germany, had no colonies at all. And money from the slave trade played almost no part in the economic develop- ment of countries like France and Britain, compared to other sources of capital.[20]

Nor did slave labor play any part in what were the real drivers of Enlightenment Europe's economic takeoff, commerce and manufacturing. The reason wasn't moral but (as we might guess) practical: to a man counting his costs, unwilling labor was expensive compared to the willing kind. As Adam Smith pointed out in his *Wealth of Nations*, "the experience of all agents and nations . . . [is] that the work done by freemen comes cheaper in the end than that performed by slaves." The reason is "the slave consults his own ease by making the land produce as little as possible," while the free worker has a self-interested stake in making it more productive, or any other trade he is engaged in, even at the most menial level—and production was at the heart and soul of the new capitalist order.[21]

Far from depending on slave labor and the slave trade, the age of commerce signaled their doom, just as the factory foretold the demise of the plantation. And it was Enlightenment Europe, and no one else, that did end slavery around the world. Adam Smith's teacher Francis Hutcheson was the first Western philosopher to be an outspoken opponent of slavery, declaring, "Nothing can change a rational creature into a piece of goods void of all rights." Slavery itself became illegal in Britain in 1772. The first bill to end the slave trade was introduced into Parliament in 1791 and finally passed in 1807. The French took the step of ending slavery altogether in 1789; and although Britain didn't abolish slavery in its colonies until 1833, by then it existed largely as a holdover from an obsolescent past rather than a mainstay of Britain's economy.

In short, Aristotle had been right all along. Freedom and slavery were indeed mutually excusive states—although being a fourth-century-BCE Greek, he drew the boundary between them differently than we would today or in Enlightenment Europe. Because the truth was, with the new economic order, a new moral perspective was taking shape. The Enlightenment term for it was "politeness."

The term was coined by a John Locke pupil, the third Earl of Shaftesbury, in one of the most influential books of the early Enlightenment, his *Characteristics* (1711). It came from the word *to polish*, and Shaftesbury used it to describe the cumulative effect regular social interaction with others has on refining our personalities and smoothing out our basic manners. "We polish one another," Shaftesbury wrote, "and rub off our corners and rough sides by a sort of amicable collision"[22] and we learn to act less like boors and more like ladies and gentlemen.

No place generated more of these polishing collisions than commercial and urban society, out of which emerged the kind of person we see in the portraits of Watteau, Joshua Reynolds, and Élisabeth Vigée-Lebrun. Evolved, sophisticated, in a word *polite*—the kind of person ready to appreciate the finer things in life and work with others in order to acquire them.

Since Locke had been Shaftesbury's personal tutor, we can even put the politeness issue in Locke's terms. When we do a business deal in Rio de Janeiro or Calcutta, read a newspaper detailing market trends in Frankfurt or St. Petersburg, window-shop on Oxford Street or on the rue St.-Honoré, share a table with a stranger at a coffeehouse, or split a cab with a traveler on the way to the airport, we are steadily adding to our stock of experience of the world, which in turn gives us a better idea of how the world works and what our own priorities need to be. This forces us to be more practical and pragmatic. We grow more concerned with producing a beneficial result than standing on outdated or dogmatic principles.

Far from creating a poltroon, the eighteenth century saw the world of commerce creating a person who might have stepped out from the pages of Aristotle's *Ethics*. This was someone intellectually alert and morally centered, regardful of others by habit and therefore not inclined to extremes of behavior. His income gives him leisure to enjoy the finer things in life that the man working his sixty acres from dawn until twilight never could. He knows how to be moderate in his tastes, and (to put it in Aristotle's exact words) "since he takes few things seriously, he is not excitable." He accepts good and bad fortune as it comes, "because he estimates himself at his true worth."[23]

Above all, he is inclined to be tolerant of others, whether they are Christians or Muslims or Jews—if only to avoid missing a good business deal. This had been important to Locke as well. He despised religious bigotry as much as he despised metaphysics. Locke's reasonable man knows the limits of his own knowledge. He holds his opinion, especially on controversial subjects like religion, with a certain tentativeness born of respect for the unverifiable and the unknown.[24] When he is confronted by an opposite opinion, his first instinct is not to burn someone at the stake or tie him to the rack, but to listen with a little charity and forbearance—even when he is convinced that person is wrong.

Taken together, these traits formed the virtues of a new urban type: the men and women of a polite and commercial age. The French will describe them as *bourgeois*; in German, they are *bürgerlich*; in English, the middle class. Later, the bourgeoisie will become figures of fun and contempt. They are mocked in *Madame Bovary* (not to mention *Desperate Housewives*) and excoriated in Marx's *Das Kapital*. The Enlightenment, however, saw in middle-class man an up-to-date reflection of Aristotle's political animal: a being designed by nature to work peaceably and constructively with others on the basis of free will—and to make a little money while he did it.

Middle-class man scores low on Plato's *thymos* meter. Some would say low on the testosterone meter as well. He is no Martin Luther. Still, he is probably a more congenial neighbor, and he was to be the essential building block for what the eighteenth century treasured most after two centuries of religious war and upheaval: a little peace and quiet.

No place seemed to exhibit the virtues of "a polite and commercial people" more than Locke's England, and no one appreciated those virtues more than the French writer Voltaire. Born in 1694 with the most sophisticated mind of his age, he had grown up watching the dismal last years of Louis XIV's reign. He had seen its pride and glory fizzle out in military defeat, famine, and bankruptcy. When the Sun King died in 1715, the crowds spat on his funeral cortege.

Voltaire came to believe that the enlightened future lay with England, the land of Newton, Locke, and men of business. His trip to England in 1726 confirmed his view that "commerce, which has enriched English citizens, has [also] helped to make them free."[25]

Voltaire came back singing the praises of making money instead of war. He praised the Quaker businessmen he met who quietly went about their business but "never bow to anyone, having nothing in their hearts but charity and respect for the laws."[26] He pointed out that the Quakers had once been wild religious fanatics (hence the name, from their convulsions when in the grip of the Holy Spirit), but by devoting themselves to business, they had learned to be at peace with their neighbors; and by enriching themselves, they had also enriched their nation.

In addition, "a commercial nation is always very alive to its interests and neglects none of the knowledge that can be useful in its business," including science. So it was not surprising to him that the land of merchants and Lloyd's of London was also the land of Newton and Locke.

Voltaire's extravagant praise of Locke ("never, perhaps, has a wiser, more methodical mind existed than Mr Locke") pales in comparison with his praise of Newton. Here was a genius, Voltaire wrote, "the like of which has scarcely appeared in ten centuries."[27] Isaac Newton had demonstrated to Voltaire's satisfaction that human reason alone can discover the true inner workings of nature and the universe. Indeed, the human mind could achieve almost any goal it set for itself, as long as it remained grounded in experience and truth.

Newton's greatest fortune, however, was to be born in a free and tolerant country "at a time when, scholastic extravagances being banished, reason alone was cultivated and society could only be his pupil and not his enemy." Voltaire was well aware of Shaftesbury's dictum that "all politeness is owing to liberty." If commerce and property were the fruits (as well as the causes) of modern liberty, so were science and the arts. Galileo had spent his last days under house arrest; Descartes died in exile in Sweden. The most noble-born Englishmen had vied to be pallbearers of Newton's bier. Voltaire noted that the English reserved tombs at Westminster Abbey not just for their kings, but for great poets like Chaucer, Edmund Spenser, and Ben Jonson.[28]

Voltaire urged his fellow Frenchmen to consider "which the more useful to a nation, a well-powdered nobleman who knows at exactly what time the king gets up and goes to bed . . . or a businessman who enriches his country, issues orders from his office in Surat or Cairo, and contributes to the well-being of the world."[29] What led Alexis de Tocqueville to praise America as a cultural and political model, Voltaire did one hundred years earlier with England. I have seen the future in England, he said in effect, and it works.

The burning question was whether the past would allow that to happen.

After all, not everything was politeness and sophistication in the eighteenth-century metropolis. In most places, the old medieval core of the city still stood, dark and rotting. A visitor to eighteenth-century Hamburg said the city's most characteristic smell was that of an open sewer. Most would have said the same about the poorest areas of London.

Still, the point was the people began to *notice* that things smelled, that their streets were dirty and their alleyways unhealthy. They were demanding things like working plumbing, streetlights (starting in London in 1694), and urban renewal projects that would create a physical environment to match a new "polite and commercial" culture.[30] The transformation of Europe's cultural frame demanded a material transformation, as well.

The most famous of these urban renewal projects still looks pretty much as it did when it was completed in 1775: the New Town in Scotland's Edinburgh. Its gardens, squares, and gracious town houses were consciously designed to be the setting for a refined urban community. It was not just aristocrats who bought houses there, it was businessmen and lawyers, shopkeepers and master artisans. For Edinburgh was also one of Britain's fastest-growing commercial centers, which in turn spawned a lively arts scene. Its university drew some of the most open and enlightened minds in Europe and students from every class of society. As much as London or Paris, and certainly more than Berlin or Madrid, Edinburgh was the epicenter of Aristotle's Enlightenment.

Small wonder, then, that it dubbed itself the Athens of the North. On any given day, you could find philosopher David Hume exchanging a glass of port with historian William Robertson, or scientist James Hutton speaking at the prestigious Oyster Club on his startling theory of the geological evolution of the earth (it's the one we still hold today). One could also find Professor Adam Smith hurriedly alighting from the daily coach from Glasgow where he taught to attend a meeting of the Select Society, Edinburgh's most influential circle of literati, scientists, and enlightened clergymen.

And all the while, hanging over them was the shadow of the Scottish Highlands.

For the purple-gray mountains that rose up to the north of Edinburgh were inhabited by fearsome men in kilts: beings who seemed more like beasts than men. In the early 1700s, the Highlands were a law unto themselves, where scattered clans lived a life almost unchanged since the days of Braveheart William Wallace. It was a world by Enlightenment standards of boundless superstition and unrelieved poverty—and mindless violence.

In 1745, during the revolt of Bonnie Prince Charlie, those Highland clans suddenly swept down on Edinburgh and Glasgow. The clansmen with their bagpipes, claymores, and incomprehensible Gaelic held the terrified citizens for ransom and then marched to within two hundred miles of London before they were finally defeated. The revolt of the clans was followed by a savage repression, traces of which are still visible in the barren, unpopulated landscape of the Scottish Highlands.

Still, the 1745 revolt left behind a sobering question for the Enlightenment to ponder. Why do some societies like England and France and cities like Edinburgh become polite and commercial, while so many others do not—even when they are right next door?

Unlocking that mystery became the next great goal for the Enlightenment, and the Scottish Enlightenment in particular. It was an Edinburgh judge, jurist, and student of natural law, Lord Kames, who first pointed the way. In his library, he had gathered material about societies ranging from the Americas to the Hottentots of the South African Cape; China and Persia and India; and the Greeks and Romans of the ancient world. Here was data that could be used to create the first true comparative anthropology, something Aristotle had set out to do with his *Politics* but with far more limited materials: namely, a genuine science of the human community.

Kames was the first on this track, with his *Historical Law Tracts*, published in 1761. He soon had company, including William Robertson, David Hume, and most famously Adam Smith. Their goal was a science of man akin to Newton's natural science, in which the empirical data would be assembled and analyzed in order to construct a theoretical model that explained how all the parts fit together—not simply at any given moment, but as human society changes over time.[31] Because unlike the universe, human communities and the laws governing them *do* change over time; and, the Scottish enlightened mind concluded, they change for the better.

The result was the first full-blown theory of human progress. It divided human history into four distinct stages of growth, based on how human beings make their living (what later Marx would call "the means of production"). "Hunting and fishing," Lord Kames wrote, "were the original occupations of man," when the notion of human society hardly existed. The second stage of human evolution came when humans learned to follow animal herds and later domesticate them. This pastoral nomadic stage was the world of Scottish Highlanders as well as the Laplanders of northern Europe and historically the Germanic tribes who had invaded the Roman Empire.

The pastoral nomadic society is built around the extended family ties of tribe and clan. "If that may be called a society," Kames added, perhaps with a uneasy glance toward the Highlands outside his window, "which hath scarce any other than a local connection" and lacks any awareness of a larger world outside itself.[32]

Instead, for Kames "the true spirit of society" was one that Aristotle would recognize. It "consists of mutual benefits and making the industry of individuals profitable to themselves as well as others." This must wait until the third stage, the agrarian stage, when the need to bring in an annual harvest "connects individuals in an intimate society of support." The community ceases to be mobile and becomes fixed in the village, farm, and field. New crafts arise—plowman, blacksmith, carpenter—and new relationships: lord and tenant, master and slave.

This was the medieval Europe of the Domesday Book and the Crusades—but also the Magna Carta. Civil society in its agrarian stage supplies new forms of cooperation, but also new conflicts. With it comes the first sense of natural right as well, Aquinas's and Locke's individual claims and obligations, which in Lord Kames's words, "earlier custom cannot control." Resolving them requires for the first time written law and permanent government. The law code, the circuit judge, and the royal palace gradually replace the patriarch of the clan or elders of the tribe. For those who depend on their authority, this is a marked advance. However, they owe this advance not to the benevolent character of their rulers or divine sanction, as rulers themselves try to pretend, but to the changing nature of society itself. "In every society," Kames concluded, "the advances of government toward perfection are strictly proportioned to the advance of society" toward mutual cooperation and improvement. The better we all get along, in other words, the more benign our rulers can afford to be.

However, the progress of civil society is still not done. There is a fourth, commercial stage to come: the world of the businessman and tradesman. The scene of the action shifts from the village to the town and seaport, from farming and cultivating the land to trade and cultivating the exchange of goods and services. A new kind of community springs up, the polished urban world Voltaire and Shaftesbury praised. It is a community with a new complexity, but also with a new unprecedented dynamism.

Commercial society, wrote Kames's friend William Robertson, is "a society of human beings bound together by one of the strongest of all ties, the desire of supplying their mutual wants." Cleric as well as historian, and famed provost of the University of Edinburgh, Robertson is not as well known a name as Adam Smith or even David Hume.

Yet Robertson's crucial contribution was overlaying Kames's dynamic four-stage theory onto the history of Europe. The result was something of a surprise, especially to those writers like Voltaire used to celebrating the Renaissance as the "rebirth of letters" and the start of the modern spirit. What Robertson discovered was that the crucial start of Europe's commercial stage came in the Middle Ages, that despised epoch that Voltaire, Shaftesbury, and many others dismissed as an age of Gothic barbarism. (That term, "Gothic," would stick for describing its architecture.) The reason was the Middle Ages had also witnessed a brisk revival of trade, especially after the Crusades, which brought a spirit of freedom and independence to its cities that gradually spread across western Europe. "A great body of the people were released from servitude," Robertson wrote. "Towns became so many little republics, governed by known and equal laws, and liberty was deemed such an essential and characteristic part in the constitution" that any escaped slave living there a year and a day was instantly declared free.[33] In short, what had made the Florence of 1402 free wasn't Divine Providence or even its laws, but how it made its money through trade and industry—which in turn made men change the laws to accommodate their new sense of freedom.

It was a pathbreaking way of seeing man's freedom, not as a divine gift but as a product of society itself. Not only did commerce and liberty go together, but they gave history an entirely new, hopeful direction. For Polybius, Saint Augustine, and the other heirs of Plato, human history had been an inevitable downward slide. Now thanks to Kames and Robertson, it turned into a steady upward climb. Robertson conceded some places in Europe had felt the progress of change more quickly than others, as in the Italy of Leonardo and Michelangelo and the Low Countries of Erasmus. Others never did, like the mountainous Balkan regions and the Highlands of Scotland.

Nonetheless, "as soon as the commercial spirit gains an ascendant in any society," Robertson declared, "we discover a new genius" in its government, its dealings with others, and its entire outlook on life.[34]

"The mind acquires new vigor [and] enlarges its powers and faculties," he noted, just as it "softens and polishes the manners of men." It was commerce that prepared cities like Florence to rediscover the value of political freedom, and it was commerce that encouraged them to raise the fine arts to a new, more refined level.

Robertson noted moreover that the commercial stage was also when European science came into its own, as men became systemically dissatisfied with a theological explanation of nature and demanded a more precise and empirical frame in order to get things done. Hence, it was little wonder that commercially minded Venice became Galileo's most reliable patron, or that the maritime trading nations England and Holland became home to the finest scientific minds of the age, from Newton and Descartes to Locke and Leeuwenhoek, the inventor of the microscope.

In sum, the growth of commerce triggered a sense of personal independence in people—it gave men and women the confidence to make up their own minds and resolve conflicts on their own, without the need of awe-inspiring kings or emperors—or witch doctors and priests. In commercial society, men no longer have to be terrified into obedience or being moral. The Golden Rule of morality as Aristotle originally formulated it in his *Ethics*, that "we should behave toward our friends as we would wish them to behave toward us," becomes internalized and a mainspring of action. We cooperate—out of self-interest, of course, but we cooperate nonetheless. Our pocketbooks, but also society, benefit from our newfound liberty.

Taken all together, William Robertson concluded, a community of free and active individuals takes shape, in which "*industry, knowledge,* and *humanity* are linked together by an indissoluble chain." This was the Europe emerging in his own time. There was no reason to assume its polished and enlightened progress was not the face of its future, and the growth of liberty as well.

"Liberty" is the key word. For Locke, man's freedom was innate and inborn, unalienable in the proper sense, meaning never to be given away, even voluntarily. But the Enlightenment saw that liberty is also the result of a dynamic process, as well as a birthright. Indeed, this idea of the steady dynamic progress or evolution of civil society was the Scottish Enlightenment's weightiest discovery. It soon found enthusiastic adherents in England and France, then across the Continent and the British Empire, including in America. Even its later critics like Jean-Jacques Rousseau never questioned the empirical process it described, only the values assigned to it.* In its broad strokes, it remains the Western view of history to this day.

Yet in many respects, it is only an extension of Aristotle's insight that the essence of life is the potential for growth. This turns out to apply to society as well as the individual, and includes the growth of political institutions. And

*See chapter 22.

here the eighteenth century reached its most shattering discovery, that the Greek *polis*, with its ancient ideal of liberty, was no liberty at all. The Enlightenment thoroughly studied its physical remains in Athens and Rome and Sparta. It read the histories of the ancient world with a new critical eye and began conducting the first archaeological excavations in places like Pompeii and Herculaneum. What it found were societies that were, in modern terms, repressive (as in the fate of Socrates), superstitious (all those temples dedicated to nonexistent gods), materially poor, and incredibly violent. The ancients "were extremely fond of liberty," David Hume remarked, "but they did not understand it very well." Above all, it noted that the Greeks and Romans had never developed a full-fledged notion of individual right. Their notion of politics consisted largely of massacres of one city's faction by another, just as their notion of morality had encompassed infanticide and vendetta murder.[35] With a sense of shock mingled with self-satisfaction, the Enlightenment had to conclude that the average Athenian or Spartan had more in common with Highland clansmen or Carpathian shepherds or Bedouin tribesmen than they did with the modern civilized citizen of London or Paris or Edinburgh.

The Romans were even worse. For all their vaunted discipline, valor, and rule of law, they plundered their conquered provinces with brutal rapacity and degraded their inhabitants so that "they lost not only the habit but even the capacity of deciding for themselves, or of acting from the impulse of their own minds." The Roman Empire, Robertson concluded, "degraded and debased the human species," sowing the seeds of its own destruction—a point Edward Gibbon would later extend in his *Decline and Fall of the Roman Empire.*[*][36]

Because only the men (and eventually women) of commercial society are truly ready, intellectually and materially, to be entrusted with true liberty—"modern" liberty in the Enlightenment formulation—in which government leaves as much decision making in the hands of individuals as possible to enable them to live their lives as they, not others, see fit.

Compared with the ancients, medieval man had felt like a dwarf standing on the shoulders of giants. Erasmus and the Renaissance mind felt much the

---

*The heart of the problem, as the French philosopher Montesquieu explained, was that even the greatest ancient cities, like Rome and Alexandria, still lived in a world that was overwhelmingly rural, and that denigrated the value of commerce and "the lucrative arts" as unworthy of free men. Montesquieu noted Plato's dictum in the *Laws* that no citizen shall ever be allowed to engage in business or trade.

same. Now, thanks to the Enlightenment, Western civilization felt free to lay aside the burden of the ancient past and keep its eyes on the road ahead.[37]

But where were they headed? And above all, what was the driving engine behind all this progressive change?

It was yet another Scot, David Hume, who supplied the answer. Born in 1711, Hume lived in Edinburgh and eventually bought a house in the New Town. In his lifetime, Hume wore many hats. He was a philosopher, historian, literary critic, and social scientist. His most important contribution was to focus on the single principle that centuries of moralists starting with Plato had condemned, but which Hume showed actually kept civil society dynamic and expanding.

This was the power of self-interest. Hume was careful to distinguish it from mere selfishness. Self-interest was instead the passionate desire to improve our material circumstances that beats in every human heart and fills every human mind, even in the most barbarous and primitive societies. As Kames put it, "Men thirst after opulence." That thirst, Hume realized, was the driving engine of social and economic change.

In the early stages of society's evolution, people can't afford the untrammeled operations of that passion. The needs of the individual must yield to the imperatives of the group, such as the need to share the spoils of the hunt or the meager bounty of the harvest. In commercial society, however, self-interest can find a range of constructive outlets. Instead of enriching ourselves by robbing our neighbors at swordpoint, we open a store or bank. Instead of seeing the stranger from a foreign land as a potential enemy, we see him as a potential customer. Instead of representing a threat to the safety of the group, self-interest becomes a force for constructive cooperation with others, in order to get the things we want and achieve the results we dream of.

Commerce, Hume wrote, "rouses men from their indolence" and "raises in them a desire for a more splendid way of life than what their ancestors enjoyed." Indeed, the more the power of self-interest is unleashed in commercial society, Hume concluded, the faster society progresses. That power is the secret of the progress of man and the wealth of nations.[38]

That, of course, is the title of the most famous work to come out of the Enlightenment, one directly inspired by Hume and nearly the only one still deemed relevant today. Adam Smith's *An Inquiry into the Nature and Causes of the Wealth of Nations* is a great compendium, a kind of Enlightenment *Summa*, of three decades of research and thinking on the science of man.

Smith knew and worked alongside Kames and Hume and Robertson; he had combed through the works of his French counterparts like Montesquieu and Voltaire. His own lectures at the University of Glasgow laid out a four-stage theory of society very similar to Kames's.

Today we tend to think of *Wealth of Nations* as a work on economics. It is in fact a treatise on the history of civil society and on the driving principles that give commercial society its dynamism and affluence. People usually identify that driving engine as the division of labor. In truth, the division itself springs from Hume's power of self-interest, the desire of some (but not everyone) to so dramatically improve their lives materially that they focus entirely on that skill or trade that brings the greatest return. This in turn generates a surplus so abundant, so far in excess of that possible in other previous stages of society, that these entrepreneurs enrich not only themselves, but the rest of society—even the politicians and intellectuals who scorn the business class on whom their own prosperity ultimately rests.

Smith tells us not everyone can be Steve Jobs or Dave Thomas or Richard Branson. But under capitalism, not everyone has to. A handful of such persons will be sufficient, provided their creativity and egos are given plenty of room, which is precisely what the free marketplace does.

Smith had to agree with Hume: commerce and self-interest feed on each other. The more freedom we give to both, as happened in western Europe after the Middle Ages, the faster society grows and improves. Free markets free men's minds, their bodies (Smith delighted in pointing out that slavery was not only unjust but less profitable than free labor), and their individual spirits, even as they fill their pocketbooks with the fruits of natural liberty unleashed.

"All systems of preference or of restraint, therefore, being completely taken away," Smith wrote, "the obvious and simple system of natural liberty establishes itself of its own accord. Every man, as long as he does not violate the laws of justice, is left perfectly free to pursue his own interest his own way." The result is "so great a quantity of everything is produced, that there is enough to gratify the slothful and oppressive profusion of the great, and at the same time abundantly to supply the wants" of even the poorest and most despised member of society, to a degree that would boggle the minds of even the rulers of a barbarous society.[39]

Smith recognized that not everything would be sunny in a society geared around the unleashing of self-interest and economic growth, what we call capitalism. Some people would inevitably be left out of society's benefits—not its material ones (what welfare recipient doesn't own both a TV and a cell phone?), but its cultural ones, as the grind of making a living deprives them of leisure and opportunity for enrichment of the spirit. Preventing this kind of "mental mutilation," Smith wrote, deserved "the most serious attention of the government."[40]

Hume, too, worried that commercial society's increasing reliance on the need for credit, coupled with a mounting national debt, would require massive tax hikes that might eventually consume everything in sight. "Either the nation must destroy public credit," he wrote toward the end of his life, "or public credit must destroy the nation." And as Scotsmen who could remember when armed Highlanders had roamed the streets of Edinburgh, Smith and Hume sensed the fragility of civilization in the face of barbarism, in ways some of their successors and admirers did and do not.

Still, on the whole there was every reason to be hopeful. Commercial society would grow, and social and political institutions would grow with them. The system of modern liberty unleashed by capitalism would succeed in freeing men from tyranny, just as it freed them from material want. The American Revolution and then the Declaration of Independence in 1776 (ironically, the same year Smith's *Wealth of Nations* appeared), which Smith and Hume both applauded,* seemed to prove their point. Everywhere, it seemed, the empirical hopeful spirit of Aristotle's Enlightenment was winning out.

Yet at that same moment, the new disciples of Plato were plotting their revenge.

---

*"I am an American in principles," Hume told Benjamin Franklin in 1775, "and wish we would let [them] alone to govern or misgovern themselves as they think proper."

Jean-Jacques Rousseau (1712–78): He turned Plato's *Republic* into a program
for cultural renewal and political revolution.

Twenty-two

STARTING OVER: PLATO, ROUSSEAU, AND REVOLUTION

You must make your choice between the individual and the citizen, you cannot be both.

—Jean-Jacques Rousseau, 1762

O Liberty, what crimes are commited in your name!

—Madame Roland, 1793

"I enter with secret horror this vast desert of the social world."[1]

With downcast face, a pale young man with intense, troubled eyes, walked the streets of Paris toward his rooming house. It was 1742, and the city around him teemed with a sense of discovery and excitement. Paris was home to brilliant artists and writers, elegant salons, and an emergent political culture, led by men like Voltaire and the Baron de Montesquieu, that after the disasters of the Louis XIV years hoped to rebuild France on the principles of modern liberty that they had seen in Locke's and Shaftesbury's England.

It was the heyday of the rococo, and Parisian galleries sparkled with the works of Watteau, François LeMoyne, and François Boucher. Shopwindows offered goods imported from four continents. Restaurants and cafés served delicacies to their sophisticated clientele. France's finest architects like

Jacques-Ange Gabriel vied to build opulent *maisons* for kings, aristocrats, and
government officials. Here was commercial society at its most prosperous and
refined.*

It all meant nothing to the young man—or rather everything. A carriage
with laughing young people, elegant in their powdered wigs and silken
dresses, suddenly rolled past. He stared with burning eyes. He would have
given anything to have been with them, but it was not to be.

He sighed and looked up. He had reached his run-down hotel near the
Sorbonne on Paris's Left Bank. Long ago, these narrow streets had seen the
darting figure of Peter Abelard and the lumbering form of Thomas Aquinas.
Now they were plunged in a dank darkness, and a dismal stony silence greeted
him as he opened his rooming house gate.

He mounted the mold-covered stairs, each creaking under his weight.
The fact that the rooming house he had chosen since coming to Paris had
once been occupied by writers like himself who had gone on to greater things
did nothing to relieve his disappointment and despair.

He entered his tiny dingy room and slammed shut the door. From the
leather case under his arm, sheets of music leaked out. They spread across the
floor, the title page uppermost. "A *Dissertation on Modern Music*, by Jean-
Jacques Rousseau."

He was ruined, Rousseau told himself. He had come to Paris in hope of
being recognized as a musical genius. He was already thirty years old but
looked and acted younger than his age. Born in Geneva, Switzerland, he had
grown up with a charming but irresponsible watchmaker of a father who
abandoned him at ten, leaving him to be passed from one unwilling relative
to another. (His mother had died giving him birth.) Jean-Jacques didn't lack
for brains or good looks or charm. A warm, passionate talker, he was the kind
of sensitive young man whom older women regularly fall in love with—and
vice versa. One of them, a Madame de Warens, had been his protector and
lover, almost his substitute mother, for nearly a decade. From Geneva he had
wandered through the Savoy to Venice, the city of Vivaldi and Casanova,
dreaming of love and fame—especially literary fame.

From his early twenties, Rousseau had tried his hand at poetry and drama
and music (including a drama he titled, with no sense of irony, *Narcissus*).

---

*Visitors to Paris can still stay in Gabriel's most famous masterpiece, the Hôtel de Crillon on the
Place de la Concorde.

No one paid much attention. For all his efforts, all he had to show was a certificate from the French Academy of Sciences blandly thanking him for a new form of musical notation he had invented.[2]

He returned home crushed by their polite indifference. "I was thirty years old," he would write later. "I was on the streets of Paris, where one does not live for nothing." As his savings dwindled, he took whatever odd jobs he could find, including copying sheet music—the most menial level of a musician's life. He managed to find a publisher for his treatise on musical notation, but no one wanted to read it any more than they wanted to hear his operas or plays.[3] "I gave up all hopes of advancement and fame," he wrote later in his *Confessions.* Survival in the most cosmopolitan city in Europe had become his sole priority. For the next few years, he earned a meager income as an obscure literary hack.

Then one day in 1749 he set out for a solitary walk in the gardens around the castle at Vincennes. On the way, an article in the newspaper *Mercure de France* caught his attention. It was on an essay contest being sponsored by the Academy of Dijon on the topic "Has the restoration of the sciences and arts tended to purify morals?" The term *restoration* is striking. The standard view of the time, shared by Voltaire, Shaftesbury, and others, was that the end of the ancient world had meant an end to the polite arts and sciences in Europe, which required the Renaissance to restore them to their proper place.

Rousseau, at least, understood at once what was meant. Had the growth of polite society, the fruit of commerce and progress, made men and women more moral, as leading Enlightenment voices were claiming, or not? Just as suddenly, Rousseau had the answer. No, it hasn't made human beings better, it has actually made them *worse.* Far from making people love virtue, commercial society had filled their heads with a love of luxury and vice. Far from making them respect and help their neighbors, it had unleashed an ugly selfishness—including, he realized, in himself. And instead of drawing people together, it had driven them apart, producing "only a frightful solitude" in which each person was a stranger to every other, "for no man dares to be himself."[4]

Rousseau rushed home. He feverishly composed an essay on the subject, which he later published as *A Discourse on the Moral Effects of the Arts and Sciences.* Thanks to progress, it read, "a vile and deceiving uniformity reigns in our morals, and all minds seem to have been cast in the same mold: constantly politeness demands, propriety commands; constantly one follows custom, never one's own genius." Economic and social improvement may have brought with them luxury and ease, but also "a train of vices: no more sincere friendships; no more real esteem; no more well-founded trust."[5]

Instead, Rousseau wrote, "we have Physicists, Geometricians, Chemists, Astronomers, Poets, Musicians, Painters; we no longer have citizens" of the kind who once made Rome and Greece the pride of humanity, including his particular hero, Socrates. Socrates, "the wisest man in Athens," had also realized that the sophisticates of his home city were ignorant of the real human virtues.[6]

This was no coincidence. Even as "the conveniences of life increase," his *Discourse* read, "the arts improve, and luxury spreads, true courage is enervated, the military virtues vanish." Indeed, "the study of the sciences is much more apt to soften and effeminate men's courage than to strengthen and animate it."

Far better, Rousseau rhapsodized, to live like the ancient Spartans, who fought and died for their country and banned all trade and artistic production; or even like the nomadic Germanic tribes. The Romans had branded them ignorant barbarians, yet they managed to topple the greatest empire in history "with no other treasures than their bravery and their poverty." For the sake of humanity, Rousseau prayed to God at the end of his *Discourse*, "deliver us from the Enlightenment and the fatal Arts of our forefathers, and restore us to ignorance, innocence and poverty!"[7]

It was a strange manifesto to appear in 1750, just two years after Montesquieu's *Spirit of the Laws* and fully a quarter century before Smith's *Wealth of Nations*. Rousseau sent a copy to Voltaire. The great man wrote back, saying he found the thesis interesting. "Unfortunately," he added with a scornful smirk, "after sixty years I have lost the habit of walking on all fours." Still, it says something about the temper of the age that Rousseau's essay took first prize at Dijon. His friend Denis Diderot, who like Voltaire had his doubts about the thesis, told Rousseau that when the *Discourse* appeared in print, "it has gone up like a rocket; such a success has never been seen before."[8]

Rousseau had finally won the fame he craved: ironically, by savaging the character of the very society that now wholeheartedly embraced him. Some scoffed at him as the "new Diogenes"; and indeed like Diogenes, Rousseau discovered that the more he abused people, the more they sought his company.

Yet Rousseau's success was far more significant. It involved nothing less than a revolution in how people think about modernity and civilization. Rousseau would overthrow nearly every tenet of the Enlightenment by self-consciously drawing on the one book it most despised: Plato's *Republic*.

David Hume dismissed the *Republic* as "visionary ranting." Rousseau, by contrast proudly pronounced it the first book on education ever written.[9] Indeed, almost everything Rousseau wrote or thought after 1750 until his death in 1778 reflected one or another aspect of Plato's works.

This was not the mystical Plato of the Neoplatonists (even though he seems to have read the dialogues in Marsilio Ficino's venerable translations) or Plato the sacred geometer of the neo-Pythagoreans.[10] This was Plato in the raw, the unflinching moral absolutist who denounced the corruption of his native Athens and admired the austere warriors of Sparta. It was Plato the would-be Philosopher Ruler who wanted to banish the arts and private property and train children from birth in the art of nature instead; whom Rousseau saw as the man who could teach Western civilization how to start over, and thus save itself.

Unlike Shaftesbury or Adam Smith or even Thomas Jefferson, Rousseau comes to the intellectual table as the student of no one. He was almost entirely self-taught. As a lonely boy he turned to books—including Plato—as a source of inspiration and to feed his own prejudices rather than to deepen his understanding. In this way, he may be the first modern reader. Certainly he was more a journalist, albeit a brilliant one, than a genuine philosopher. He has a gift for eye-opening overstatement and for hammering his Enlightenment opponents—the "sellers of smoke to the highest bidder," as he called them—at their strongest points, in ways that expose their unexpected vulnerability. All the same, the main thrust of his Platonic critique of his age boils down to two simple propositions.

The first is that capitalism brings out the worst, not the best, in us. The belief that commerce and the pursuit of money corrupts good morals permeated Plato's *Laws* as well as his *Republic*. The French *philosophe* Montesquieu had dubbed it "the Platonic complaint," and Rousseau makes it very much his own.[11] In 1755, he published his second essay for the Dijon prize, titled *Discourse on the Origin and Basis of Inequality Among Men*. Almost a century before Karl Marx, it excoriates capitalism as the source of all man's corruption, greed, and mindless materialism and denounces the establishment of private property as one of the great tragedies of history.

Contrary to Locke, Rousseau believed that property was not a natural right, but a cruel afterthought. Man is everywhere born free, as Rousseau puts it in his most famous phrase, and is everywhere in chains. Why? Because of the invention of property. "How many crimes, wars, murders," Rousseau complained, "how much misery and horror the human race would have been spared" if the institution had never been invented.[12]

Rousseau's *Discourse on Inequality* stood John Locke and the Scots on their heads. Primitive and pastoral nomadic man, even man in the state of nature (sometimes misleadingly called Rousseau's "noble savage"), turns out to be far happier than his civilized counterpart. "Nothing is more peaceable than man in his natural state," he wrote. "Placed at an equal distance from the stupidity of animals and the fatal enlightenment of civilized man . . . he is restrained by natural pity from doing harm to anyone, even after receiving harm himself." He mischievously even quoted Locke to prove his point: "Where there is no property, there is no injury"—and therefore no injustice.[13]

Did Rousseau believe his idyllic picture of primitive man had any basis in reality? Certainly he could, and did, recite pages of research about tribal societies in America and Africa to bolster his point. But in the final analysis Rousseau wanted to use his noble savage, whose "ignorance of vice prevents him from doing evil," to act as a kind of Platonic ideal: a model of human perfection who sets the shortcomings of modern man in sharp relief.

In Rousseau's world, natural man is strong, virile, and altruistic, in addition to being fully in touch with his own feelings. Civilized man turns out to be weak, effeminate, greedy, and self-interested to the point of cold cunning. Like the stereotypical New Yorker, he is incessantly asking: "So what's in it for me?" If natural man is Tarzan mixed with *Dances with Wolves*, civilized man is Ebenezer Scrooge, Simon Legree, and *Wall Street*'s Gordon Gekko rolled into one (indeed, Charles Dickens's moral outlook as well as Oliver Stone's owes a great deal to Rousseau).

The Scottish Enlightenment, of course, made this passion for self-interest, whatever its faults, the driving engine of progress and improvement. For Rousseau, by contrast, it is the engine of man's downfall. It makes a wasteland of his primeval Garden of Eden. Like the modern green activist, Rousseau saw the destruction of the environment and the pursuit of profit going hand in hand. Thanks to man's greed, "vast forests were transformed into pleasant fields which had to be watered with the sweat of men," and slavery and misery sprouted up among the crops.*

"It is [the invention of] iron and wheat," Rousseau wrote, "which first civilized men and ruined the human race" (he had already lambasted the invention of the printing press in his first *Discourse*) and enabled "a few ambitious men" to subject the rest of the human race "to labor, servitude, and misery."[14] Working for a living becomes man's greatest curse, symbolized by the daily drudgery of the "nine to five" routine: the bleak cave of capitalism.

Because in Rousseau's world just as in Plato's, the less we have, including material possessions and new technology, the healthier, stronger, and more moral we are. And the less we think about our own selfish needs and wants, and the more we think about the needs of others and the group, the more our inner humanity and innate virtue will come out.

That led to Rousseau's second insight. If men are to be happy, love of self must be replaced by the love of community. Here he came down firmly on the side of ancient versus modern liberty and on the side of the ancient Greeks and Romans, who assume the proportions of a race of superheroes in his mind.[15] "What prevents us from being the kind of men they were?" he asked. "The passions of self interest," which, "along with an indifference to the welfare of others," have been set loose by a corrupt modern society. Replace them with the right kinds of laws and institutions, Rousseau believed— those of an earlier, simpler age—and we might become our own race of superheroes.

Still, critics like Voltaire had a point. Even if Rousseau was right and men really were stronger and happier in earlier times and under more primitive conditions, did he truly think we could turn back the clock? Yes, we can, Rousseau affirmed, thanks to the most powerful tool modern man has to shape the kind of society he wants. This is compulsory education.

Rousseau's own treatise on education, a series of letters addressed to an imaginary new parent named Émile, did not appear until he was fifty. But in a profound sense, the theme was already present in his other work, as was his debt to Plato's *Republic*. It was not laws or constitutions alone that held the

---

*This was of course literally true in the Americas, where growing and processing sugarcane employed an African slave labor force that dwarfed anything from the ancient world.

ancient free *polis* together, Rousseau asserted. It was a passionate commitment to an ideal of unity, which all the children of ancient Athens, Sparta, and republican Rome were compelled to learn and absorb from birth: "with their mother's milk," as Rousseau liked to say.

By a similar reform of education, the *Émile* argues, we can craft the same kinds of citizens. They will not grow up to be the well-fed, prosperous individuals of commercial society. Instead, they will live to become lovers of virtue and passionate defenders of liberty. Instead of saying, "What's in it for me?" they will constantly ask, "What can I do for others?" They will become impervious to the corruptions and temptations that come with adulthood. Like an army of little Socrateses, they will learn to obey the "inner voice" of conscience instead.

Rousseau's other educational doctrines (he thought book learning and the study of math and science largely a waste of time) don't bear much scrutiny today. However, his belief that through education we can insulate children from the bad influences of the society around them, and retard adverse social processes, left a deep imprint on Western pedagogy. Anyone who's been forced to take sex education or antidrug or anti–drunk driving classes in school, or participate in a Let's Recycle bottle drive, has experienced the Rousseau formula firsthand.

Rousseau's own agenda, however, was far more ambitious. He foresaw the day societies would have an entire compulsory education system like that drawn up by Plato in the *Republic*, in which every citizen will learn how to dedicate himself or herself to a life of virtue, meaning a devotion to the freedom of his or her nation, from the day he or she draws a first breath: "The newly born infant, upon first opening his eyes, must gaze upon the fatherland, and until his dying day should behold nothing else." For this reason, Rousseau's political works are hymns of praise to Plato's favorite Greek city-state, ancient Sparta.

For Plato, Sparta's constitution came the closest in reality to his own political ideal, that of a "total community," as he puts it in the *Laws*, in which "everybody feels pleasure and pain at the same things, so that they all praise and blame with complete unanimity." It is also the one most able to hold corruption in check, by banishing its primary source: individuality. In war and in peace, Plato argued, no citizen should "get in the habit of acting alone and independently" and instead must obey his leaders "even in tiny details, just as they did in Sparta."[16]

Likewise for Rousseau, Spartan man is the one closest to primitive man in his mental and physical toughness[17] and in his ignorance of corrupting civilized comforts, including self-pity. In *Émile,* he tells the story of the Spartan mother who learned that her five sons had all been killed in battle. Don't worry about that, she says. Did Sparta win? Rousseau concludes that Plato only taught posterity how to cultivate virtue. The Spartans showed us how it's actually done.[18]

For the rest of the Enlightenment, Sparta had come to symbolize "ancient" liberty at its most barbaric and brutish.[19] A casual observer of a movie like *300*, with its blood-drenched picture of Spartan warriors at the battle of Thermopylae, has to agree. But Rousseau would see something else. He would see a people dedicated to defending their freedom regardless of the personal cost; a nation trained not only for a life of self-sacrifice, but also for single-minded victory over tyranny and evil. The result was a dedication to virtue that could conquer every enemy or obstacle. It is the true victory of mind over matter—just what Plato's idealism was all about.

Indeed, what repelled the rest of the Enlightenment about Sparta, its crude anti-intellectualism and its closed nature, was precisely what appealed to Rousseau most. Here was a society in which man's natural instinct for self-love was ruthlessly and categorically suppressed. In its place sprang up a passionate love of community, including an instinctive hostility toward outsiders. "Every patriot hates foreigners," Rousseau wrote with relish. "They are nothing in his eyes. . . . Abroad, the Spartan was selfish, grasping, and unjust, but unselfishness, justice, and harmony ruled within his walls." Indeed, as Plato pointed out, of all ancient cities Sparta had no need of walls, because the other Greek cities knew that war against the Spartans meant instant defeat. [20]

Therefore, the goal for all education must be to give the nation walls of muscle and steel (as Plato might put it) rather than stone: a citizenry focused entirely on preserving the social contract in its original form. Rousseau composed his version of *The Social Contract* in 1761. It is still probably the most widely read of his works, but it is also the easiest to misunderstand.

Like John Locke, Rousseau saw the social contract as a mandate for overthrowing any tyranny that violates its terms. However, its character could not be more different. Instead of securing individual rights, Rousseau's contract creates a community bound to a collective will and destiny, which he termed the General Will. Under its shelter each citizen receives his share of personal liberty, but also public obligations. Because we are human beings, the conflict between our individual will and the General Will becomes inevitable. In Rousseau's case, however, it is the *individual*, not the community, who must give way. He must learn that this General Will is actually his true, better self. This in turn requires a compulsory training, so that obeying the General Will becomes the leading passion in our lives.

The Enlightenment rested its entire worldview on Locke's updating of Abelard's dictum (ultimately derived from Aristotle) that we must understand in order to believe. Rousseau told eighteenth-century Europe that it had its priorities backward. It is not our reason or our understanding that allows us to change the world, but our *passions*, our emotional commitment to an idea or cause. Building for the future therefore must be about cultivating the passions and the feelings, not the mind, so that we can embrace the life of virtue (literally) body and soul.

I feel, therefore I am. Here Rousseau parted ways with Plato—and pointed the way to the Romantics. The orthodox Platonist, after all, is bound to believe that the source of all virtue is knowledge and reason. Rousseau, by contrast, saw reason and virtue as locked in permanent conflict. If we are to be free and pure in heart, our reason will have to take the backseat: "The mind is a Sophist who leads virtue to the scaffold."[21] It is that "inner voice," which for Rousseau meant the conditioned conscience, that must take charge.

This is not to say that Rousseau ignored the utility of reason. Reason will show us how to replace the corrupt old order with a new virtuous one; it allows us to act as a Platonic statesman,[22] drawing up political blueprints for the future with almost mathematical exactitude. Rousseau even compared the problem of how to make men obey the law with squaring the circle in geometry: a Platonic conceit if ever there was one.[23]

So when a Polish nobleman asked him to draw up a model constitution for a future independent Poland, Rousseau was pleased to oblige. It was his chance to play Philosopher Ruler, and he made the most of it. The constitution he drew up could not be more different than the one James Madison would draw up for the fledgling United States (which was influenced, as we know, by his reading of David Hume). Instead of limiting the power of government, Rousseau's extends it in every possible direction. In fact, it reads a lot like the first three books of Plato's *Republic*—which is hardly a coincidence. Children must be trained to love their fatherland and its liberty "with their mother's milk."* Education must be compulsory and include military training from an early age, since in a true republic every citizen must be a soldier, trained to fight and die for the nation. There must also be constant rounds of civic festivals and public rituals to make people proud of their country and its customs, and in which participation is compulsory.

It is here that Rousseau saw religion as important. A truly civic-minded religion is not about moral teaching—the State will take care of that—or private consolation. Its role instead is to offer a set of rituals and dogmas that teach people that the best way to worship God is to worship the community: nothing more and nothing less. Modern mass politics, with its self-conscious public rituals, from the French Revolution's Cult of the Supreme Being to Hitler's Nuremberg rallies, had been born—and with it its leading rationale. For "everything that destroys social unity is worthless," Rousseau declared, "and all institutions that set men at odds with himself are worthless"—including the belief in God. One of the secrets of Sparta's success, Rousseau tells us, is that it never left its citizens any free time of their own. We can be either individuals or citizens, but not both.[24]

And like the ancient Spartans, Rousseau's Poles must be trained to dislike foreigners and not engage in trade with them. "Cause money to be an object of contempt, and if possible, useless besides," he wrote, along with all forms of luxury and "womanly adornment." Teach people to tend their fields and not bother their heads with anything else. There will be no need to abolish private property as Plato's *Republic* did, because if the citizens' passions are properly conditioned, it will be unnecessary. As a result, the Poles may be poor and cut off from the rest of the world. "You will live, however, in an atmosphere of true abundance, of justice, and of freedom," with happy hands and hearts and minds, which are the foundations "of a strong state and a prosperous people."[25]

Strength through joy; work makes you free. It is Rousseau who first points the way toward those chilling formulations. Today we are only too aware of where this story ends. But it is important to realize that those who read

---

*Rousseau was a strong advocate of maternal breast-feeding as more natural and healthier for children. He blamed its decline (since his ancient Greek and Roman heroes were all breast-fed by their mothers as a matter of course) on the modern woman's devotion to dresses with plunging necklines: yet another example of commercial society's "corruption," in this case ruining the virtues of motherhood. "When mothers deign to nurse their own children," he wrote, "there will be a reform in morals; natural feeling will revive in every heart; there will be no lack of citizens for the state."

him in the three decades before the French Revolution did not. They saw only a refreshing new political vision, a way to think about man's progress apart from the materialistic values of commercial society—in short, a vision of humanity freed from the ever-expanding "getting and spending" that the neo-Aristotelians of the Enlightenment had seemed to forecast for Europe's future.

Indeed, the admiration for Rousseau started at the top of the intellectual pyramid. Immanuel Kant was the most respected philosopher in Germany. Yet in forty years, Kant interrupted his daily postluncheon walk only once, when his copy of Rousseau's *Émile* arrived. His austere office had no picture or decoration—except for a portrait of Rousseau.

"What Kant prized in Rousseau," writes historian Ernst Cassirer, "was the fact that he had distinguished more clearly than others between the mask that man wears [in commercial society] and his actual visage."[26] Kant, of course, realized that Rousseau's picture of the noble savage was an ideal construct: "This wish for a return to an age of simplicity and innocence," Kant concluded, "is futile." We are what we are, as modern human beings.[27]

But Kant did agree with Rousseau that the growth of civilization adds nothing to man's moral makeup; instead, it usually ends up becoming a distraction from our moral duty. So the task ahead lies in creating institutions that will reflect our true moral nature, the voice of conscience that recognizes certain moral actions as an urgent duty without room for reflection or compromise.

Kant termed that voice *the categorical imperative*. It is really a more sophisticated version of Rousseau's "inner voice," which ultimately answers the call of the General Will.[28] Kant's goal, however, was far grander and more utopian. He did not want to throw out enlightenment or commercial society or progress; instead, they should be fused together with our higher moral nature to create a brand-new stage of civil society, that of a single cosmopolitan culture and a single world government. Kant summed up the goal of this world government in the title of his tract *Perpetual Peace*, published in 1795; in which no nation may breach the peace of another and whose guarantor is Nature herself, as a reflection of divine providence, whose aim "is to produce a harmony among men, against their will and indeed through their discord."[29]

Unfortunately, until then, Kant wrote, "human nature must suffer the cruelest hardships under the guise of external well-being." No wonder Rousseau preferred man's savage state, Kant observed, so long as this last stage to which the human race must climb is not attained.[30] Over Kant's reading of Rousseau flutters the flag of the United Nations, but also the first pages of Georg Friedrich Hegel's *Philosophy of Right* and Auguste Comte's *Positive Philosophy*, not to mention Marx's *Das Kapital*. With the fusion of Kant and Rousseau, the European mind was on the brink of a new way of visualizing the direction and purpose of civil society: toward the abolition of the self-interested individual, instead of his ultimate triumph.

Rousseau's influence cut in many, sometimes unexpected, directions. In France itself, after his death in 1778, intellectuals by and large fell in line with his political evangelism. Many, like the Count de Mirabeau, Jean-Paul Marat, Maxmilien Robespierre, and Louis-Antoine de Saint-Just, would become leading prophets of the French Revolution.[31] Others resisted, especially ordinary people. Perhaps they sensed that like many reformers, Rousseau loved humanity more than he liked human beings and that if his plans for their happiness and welfare were really implemented, they might have the opposite result.

Above all, they were shocked by his complete deprecation of Christianity and his clear insistence that God, Christ, and Church played no part in helping men and women to be moral and free. As a result, Rousseau had his house stoned and his windows broken and found himself assaulted in the street. His native city of Geneva turned against him and revoked his citizenship. Still, the man who said, "It is easier to force people to do good than to induce them to do it out of their own free will," couldn't have been surprised if *le peuple* took a dislike to him.[32]

A far bigger surprise was how young middle-class readers turned to his books with an enthusiasm bordering on hysteria, both men and particularly women. Rousseau himself had a strong dislike of educated women.[33] He blamed them for most of the corruption of contemporary society; their place was in the kitchen and in the nursery, not shopping or organizing salons or reading books. Yet they read Rousseau in droves, especially his blockbuster novel published in 1761, *The New Heloise* (*La Nouvelle Héloïse*).

As its title implies, it is a modern retelling of the story of Abelard and Héloïse, involving the passionate love of a tutor for his underage female student in defiance of all social convention. Page follows page of sighing, longing prose and weepy outbursts of frustration interspersed with complaints about being misunderstood by adults and society. *The New Heloise* is like an extended episode of *Gossip Girl*. It is in fact the direct ancestor of the Harlequin romance, and spawned a host of imitators. More than any single work, *The New Heloise* made "I feel, therefore I am" the unspoken motto of adolescence, right down to today.

That seems a strange achievement for a man who claimed to worship the stoic warriors of ancient Sparta and Rome. However, as he disclosed in his autobiography, *The Confessions*, Rousseau's secret was to reveal at length how unhappy everyone is under the stressful conditions of modern society because they aren't allowed to get in touch with their true "inner voice." Then as now, this discovery guaranteed a huge teen readership.[34]

A typical example was Jeanne-Marie Phlipon. She was a Paris native, and first read *The New Heloise* in 1772 at age eighteen. It had a powerful impact. "Rousseau became the interpreter of feeling and ideas I had before then," she remembered later, "but he alone could explain to my satisfaction."[35]

Hitherto she had been an admirer of Voltaire. She quickly dropped him for Rousseau. She immediately read his political works, including *The Social Contract*. Jeanne-Marie fantasized about becoming a heroic Spartan mother, exhorting her husband and children to great deeds in defense of freedom and liberty. She scorned the social niceties of her middle-class life as petty and artificial. "Let France awaken and come to life!" she would write. "Let man recapture his rights, let justice commence his reign, and from one end of the kingdom to the other let one universal cry be heard—*Long live the people and death to tyrants!*"[36]

In 1780, she married Jean-Marie Roland de la Platière and found a Rousseauian soul mate. As Monsieur and Madame Roland, they dreamed of a society in which men and women would finally be in touch with their inner selves and free from the grip of corrupt institutions like the Catholic Church and the monarchy—a society in which all Frenchmen would live in the bright clear air of freedom.

They had plenty of company. In the decade after Rousseau's death, his works inspired an entire generation to purify and simplify their lives by getting in touch with their feelings and coming together to battle corruption and injustice. Young men gave up wearing powdered wigs; young women donned loose-fitting, flowing dresses that made them look like classical Greek and Roman statues. Meanwhile, the most talented painter of the era, Jacques-Louis David (1748–1825), translated Rousseau's ideas into a more permanent visual form.

David's three most famous canvases were, and still are, masterpieces of political propaganda. Painted in the heady days before the French Revolution, between 1785 and 1788, they self-consciously express the principle drawn from the third book of Plato's *Republic* and Rousseau's *Considerations on the Government of Poland:* that if art is to exist in a free society, it must serve the public good by promoting virtue.

There is *The Death of Socrates,* completed in the fall of 1787. Rousseau had strongly identified with Socrates, the wise man and seer who endures persecution but whose vision lives on after his death.[37] While his followers weep and cannot bear to watch him die, Socrates stoically takes his cup of hemlock and points upward, toward a better world to come. In Rousseau's terms, this will be not an afterlife, but a new political and social order founded on the great teacher's words.

The second, *The Lictors Bringing Brutus the Bodies of His Sons,* encapsulates Rousseau's theme of heroic self-sacrifice for the sake of the community. Brutus the republican Roman statesman has sentenced his own sons to death for treason. The return of their bodies to his house for burial prompts typical tears and fainting from the womenfolk, but Brutus sits unmoved beside a statue of the goddess Roma. Like Abraham with Isaac, Brutus chooses to sacrifice his offspring to his deity, in this case civic freedom.

The third and most famous, *The Oath of the Horatii,* caused a sensation the instant it was unveiled in 1784. It shows three brothers swearing an oath to defend the Roman republic. Their outstretched arms form an angle of energy like the spoke of a rotating wheel, as their father raises their swords toward heaven with a gesture of benediction. As an icon of ancient virtue and the power of men who unite to face their destiny, the image became indelibly fixed on the French national imagination. The crowds that came to see *The Oath of the Horatii* strew a carpet of flowers at its feet. [38]

Meanwhile, the admiration of Rousseau himself took on cult proportions. After his death in 1778, his house in Ermenonville, where he had retired by the side of a lake to escape the corruptions of modern life, became a shrine to thousands of dedicated pilgrims—"half of France," according to one astonished observer. The pilgrims included Jacques-Louis David, the Rolands (of course), and a host of young foreign intellectuals, including the future Madame de Staël.

There was also a fair, rather willowy woman with elegant clothes and a

Jacques-Louis David, *The Oath of the Horatii* (later-nineteenth-century engraving)

German accent. She, too, was a devoted reader of Rousseau's works and came to Ermenonville with her two beautifully dressed children in the spring of 1780 to show them the grave of the great man.

That day, the boy and girl wandered around the lake under the watchful eye of their nursemaid. They may have thrown stones in the water, until their mother called them back. It was time to leave for home, back to Versailles, where her husband was waiting.

The woman was the queen of France, Marie Antoinette. She and her husband, King Louis XVI, boasted proudly that their son the dauphin had been raised on the "natural" principles laid down in Rousseau's *Émile.**
Marie Antoinette was so much a fan that she had helped to establish a subscription fund for publishing Rousseau's forgotten musical works (another subscriber was Benjamin Franklin).[39]

Rousseau taught his disciples that the time for talk was over; it was time

---

*The queen also had a farm built on the grounds of Versailles, where she could practice the simple rustic virtues of milking cows and growing vegetables. Known as *le Hameau*, or the Hamlet, it still stands today.

for action. Don't accept the world for the corrupt, wicked, exploitative society that it is. Change it into something better, Rousseau had said, by returning humanity to its natural liberty. The royal couple had already shown their support for liberty by backing the American colonists against Britain in the War of Independence. Like so many in the 1780s, the royal couple hoped that by embracing Rousseau's principles, they could help to do the same for France.

They did, but not in the way they thought.

"There will be either a violent crisis which may overthrow the throne, and give us another form of government," Madame Roland had predicted, "or there will be a state of lethargy similar to death."[40]

In the winter of 1788, the king's superintendent of finance was sitting at his desk. On it was a sheet of paper with rows of complicated figures. Not good news, he told himself. In fact, the more he looked them over, the more the ball of anxiety in his stomach turned to ice. He was Étienne-Charles de Loménie de Brienne, Archbishop of Sens and a member of the French Academy—and a friend of Voltaire. Brienne represented France's old regime at its most intelligent and progressive. But even he could see no way out of the catastrophe that loomed ahead.

In his hand was the balance sheet for France's annual expenditure and revenues. It was the first annual budget the French monarchy ever prepared—and the last. Brienne's numbers showed an annual expenditure of 629 million livres (the French equivalent of pounds); they also showed the annual income from all taxes and sources at just over 500 million livres. The shortfall of 129 million livres, he noted with a grimace, was almost equal to France's entire budget for the army and navy.[41]

But that was not all. Louis XVI's war in support for the American rebels had turned the French Crown's annual debt into an ocean of red ink. The current debt service alone was costing the French Crown 318 million livres. Brienne made a rapid calculation. That meant more than 50 percent of royal income. There was no way to make up that difference, especially when the richest sections of French society, the aristocracy and the Church, still paid no taxes at all.[42]

David Hume had once said that either a nation must destroy its debt, or the debt would destroy the nation. France was about to put his prediction to the test.

Indulging the Rousseauian impulse to support natural liberty in America had doomed Brienne's predecessor, Jacques Calonne. Already the Swiss banker friends of the regime had begun to say they could loan the Crown no more money. Their refusal had cost Calonne his job. Now it was Brienne's turn. On August 25, 1788, he, too, was forced to step down—but not before he wrung from the king a promise to summon an Estates General, the first in 170 years, to address the debt crisis.

Meeting in the spring of 1789, it did far more than that. When Louis XVI refused to agree to sweeping political and fiscal reforms, the members of its Third Estate—merchants, doctors, town notables, and lawyers—met separately to swear an oath never to adjourn until France's long-standing problems were solved, dubbing themselves a National Assembly. When the government tried to arrest them in mid-July, Paris rose up and on July 14 seized the Bastille. Revolution had come to France. The moment the Rolands and their Rousseauian friends had prayed for had finally arrived.

Many, including a few in the government itself, still hoped to bring reform to France along the lines of the American and British constitutions. They failed to realize that the political systems of those countries succeeded by adopting not Rousseau's principles, but the enlightened Aristotle's. Individual liberty and property were safeguarded, not threatened, as matters of natural right. A separation of powers allowed their constitutions to articulate, not flatten, existing social and sectional differences.

For the French, however, the temptation to act like Platonic legislators was too much. What started as an effort to deal with a fiscal crisis ended up becoming a program for remaking the nation according to the Rousseauian ideal of justice and virtue. "We are an assembly of philosophers," gushed one member of the new national assembly in 1792, "engaged on preparing the happiness of the world."[43]

As the political ferment in Paris grew headier and more militant, the Rolands' house in the rue Guénégaud became the staging ground for many of these self-appointed Philosopher Rulers. Like the fraternal brothers in David's *Oath of the Horatii*, they saw themselves standing united in order to serve the General Will—and change the direction of human history.

Rousseau had averred that the man who dares to bring true liberty and equality to a people "must feel that he is capable of changing, so to speak, human nature. . . .The lawgiver's great soul is the true miracle that must vindicate his mission."[44] The Rolands' friend Maximilien Robespierre believed he was such a man. For a time he convinced others as well (Jacques-Louis David served as his de facto minister of propaganda). Robespierre's goal was to banish tyranny and injustice not just from France, but from the planet. There was no room for compromise or second thoughts. In his grandiose vision, any resistance to the revolutionary regime sprang not from reasonable doubts about whether men could be made good by legislation alone, but from resistance to the idea of virtue itself.

It's worth remembering that Platonism lends itself to conspiracy theories.* The belief that appearances deceive easily grows into the conviction that they deceive for a reason: that hidden manipulators want to keep us in the cave and want, literally, to keep us in the dark. Rousseau himself suffered from a lifelong fear that enemies were constantly working to undercut his success—the same people who were working to keep the world corrupt and unjust. Robespierre believed the same thing. When the National Assembly abolished the monarchy in 1792 and the rest of Europe turned to put Louis XVI back on his throne, Robespierre's utopian hopes became fused with Rousseau's paranoid style. The result would be the Reign of Terror.

"Citizens, the nation is in danger," Robespierre proclaimed. "Domestic enemies more fearsome than foreign armies, are secretly plotting its ruin. . . ."[45] In the steamy summer of 1793, Robespierre and his allies warmly embraced the term *terreur*. If people weren't willing to sacrifice themselves for the general will, then they would be terrorized into doing it. Sometimes, as Rousseau had warned, men must be forced to be free.

Not being *for* the revolution was as evil as being against it. "You must punish not merely the traitors," Robespierre's ally Louis-Antoine Saint-Just (another Rousseau devotee) proclaimed, "but even those who are merely indifferent," since that indifference sprang from a love of self that was the source of all evil—and doom for any radical transformation of modern society.[46]

By 1793 most of the Revolution's real opponents, the royalists, had long since fled abroad. So had most of its moderate voices, like the Marquis de Lafayette. All that were left to punish were those insufficiently committed to the new order and to obeying the General Will. Thousands would pay with their lives for that "indifference."

As the guillotine claimed its victims, increasingly whatever was not for-

*See chapter 17.

bidden was made compulsory. Wage and price controls were imposed; universal conscription sent tens of thousands of unwilling Frenchmen into the army to fight the monarchies of Europe. Churches were closed and Christianity banned, along with the traditional calendar, saints' days, and seven-day week. Saint-Just spoke of taking children away from their parents at age five and training them, like ancient Spartans, to become workers or soldiers. For the first time in European history, the word *communisme* floated in the air.[47]

Robespierre is the first true modern dictator: the man who rules not as the living image of God, as the kings of old had, but as the living image of the will of the people. His virtue becomes unassailable, since it is identical with that General Will; just as he can have no flaws—Robespierre's nickname was "the Incorruptible"—so can he have no opponents or rivals. And among Robespierre's earliest victims were his fellow Rousseauians Monsieur and Madame Roland.

They had begun to have doubts about where their former protégé was leading the Revolution. In the France of the Reign of Terror, the price of doubt was death. The husband chose suicide. The wife, who had shed tears when she first read *The New Heloise,* did not. She mounted the scaffold on November 8, 1793. Her fellow Rousseau enthusiast Marie Antoinette had gone to the guillotine a few weeks before. Madame Roland's final plea, "O liberty! O liberty! what crimes have been committed in your name," marked her belated realization that the utopian path to man's freedom had opened the door to its opposite.[48]

This was why, three years before, on the other side of the English Channel, the statesman Edmund Burke had dubbed Rousseau "the insane Socrates" of the French Revolution. Even before the Reign of Terror, Burke saw in revolutionary France a tragic playing out of the Platonist temptation to perfect society through reason alone while ignoring human nature as Aristotle and the Enlightenment had defined it, in order to make us into something better.

"In the groves of *their* Academy," Burke wrote, "at the end of every vista, you see nothing but the gallows."[49] Sadly, it was not the last would-be modern Platonic republic to be adorned in this way.

Caspar David Friedrich (1775–1840), *Morning Light*

Twenty-three

"FEELING IS ALL": THE TRIUMPH OF THE ROMANTICS

One power alone makes a poet: Imagination, the Divine Vision.
—William Blake

A poet participates in the eternal, the infinite, and the one. . . . Plato was essentially a poet.
—Percy Bysshe Shelley

On October 11, 1794, Rousseau's remains were interred at the Panthéon in Paris, formerly the Church of St. Geneviève. The crowds cheered and the poets sang:

> *To the immortal Rousseau the French people shall excel*
> *one other in rendering homage to this man,*
> *to whose wisdom illustrious liberty bears witness*
> *and who shall be immortal in memory's temple.*[1]

Some weeks earlier on July 28, that same crowd had cheered as a horse-drawn cart slowly wound its way through the streets, bearing four men to the guillotine.

The oldest, Georges Couthon, lay in the straw at the bottom of the cart, his body smeared with manure. The man beside him had been so badly beaten at his arrest that one eye was dangling from its socket. A third, a young man with open shirt and a pale, almost angelic face, stood with his arms tied behind him. A fourth sat with hair askew and a great bandage wrapped around his face. He watched stone-faced as the crowd danced and sang, while women and children spat into the cart. "Go down to hell with all the curses of mothers and wives!"

Since the previous summer, the Reign of Terror had claimed some seventeen thousand victims by firing squad or the guillotine.[2] On this day, the guillotine's body count would be more than eighty. But this time those going to their death were the Terror's own architects. Like its later imitators in Russia and Iran, the French Revolution proved best at devouring its own children.

The sea of humanity parted to let the cart enter the Place de la Concorde—exactly where Louis XVI had been executed in 1793, and Marie Antoinette and Madame Roland a year later. Guards roughly shoved the prisoners out. One by one they staggered up the scaffold steps. Couthon, former interrogator in chief of the Committee of Public Safety and a deformed cripple, had to be dragged out and his head inserted sideways through the guillotine's wooden block. The cherubic-faced Louis-Antoine Saint-Just, popularly known as the Angel of Death, was next. He had dreamed of turning France into Rousseau's Sparta. Instead, he wound up one more headless victim of a utopian vision turned blood-soaked nightmare.

The last prisoner to die was "the Incorruptible" himself, Maximilien Robespierre. Thirty-six years old, the most powerful man in France had become the most hated by virtue of his thirst for blood. Before his arrest, he had tried to commit suicide with a pistol but succeeded only in shattering his jaw. Now, as the executioner yanked away Robespierre's bandage, the jaw was pulled from its socket. The Incorruptible let out a scream of surprise and pain that filled the crowded square with a sound more animal than human.

The crowd roared as the blade rose and fell for the last time. When Robespierre's head was held up to the mob's cheers, "it presented the most horrendous spectacle imaginable, a monstrous, inhuman face"—the final ghostly face of Rousseau's Republic of Virtue.[3]

Far away on the other side of the English Channel, another man was walking the serene hills of rural Somerset. It was a bright and warm, sunlit day. Clouds flew along the wind and washed the trees in shadows. Larks sang in the meadow below as insects buzzed past his head. As the man stopped and sat in the shade of trees to contemplate the scene, thoughts ran through his mind, which he recorded in a poem:

> To her fair works did Nature link
> The human soul that through me ran;
> And much it grieved my heart to think
> What Man has made of Man.

Although he was English, William Wordsworth had been a keen supporter of the French Revolution. In 1791, he had gone to France to see what all the excitement was about. He had fallen in with a revolutionary army officer named Beaupuy who had set Wordsworth to reading Rousseau. They had discussed the author of the *Discourse on Inequality* at length as they walked the shady banks of the Loire River in Orléans. One day they passed a homeless girl, her figure wasted with starvation. Beaupuy pointed. "*That*," he said, "is what we're fighting for!"[4]

That was what Wordsworth wanted to fight for as well. When he moved to Paris in October 1792, he had the chance to see the Revolution in full vigor. The crowds and the excitement were everywhere; the sense of founding a greater future for man was palpable. "My heart was all / Given to the people, and my love was theirs," he remembered later. "Bliss was it in that dawn to be alive, but to be young was very heaven!"[5]

Wordsworth even hoped to establish a friendship with the Rolands and their circle of fervent Rousseauians. It was just as well he didn't. When the Reign of Terror came, Wordsworth escaped arrest by a miracle and returned to England in December a sadder but wiser man.

He had left with no faith in his own government and still less in the society he saw taking shape around him. It was an England of factories and smokestacks, of hard-faced merchants and manufacturers with bulging pocketbooks and factory workers with blackened faces, dull eyes, and sunken cheeks: the dark underside of commercial society. He had hoped to bring to England the same sweeping hopes for liberation he had experienced in France. Then the gruesome course of the Reign of Terror—soon to be followed by the cynical corruption of the Directory and the dictatorship of Napoleon in 1798—killed Wordsworth's love affair with revolution. It did the same for many other intellectuals in Germany (Beethoven and the poet Hölderlin), in Spain (the painter Francisco Goya), and in America, where the ranks of the disillusioned included Thomas Jefferson.

The French Revolution was the first God That Failed.* But the liberal disillusionment with communism in the 1950s was nothing like the unprecedented, and hence more devastating, brutal exposure by the Reign of Terror of what painter J.M.W. Turner called "the fallacies of hope," the emptiness of Rousseau's utopian vision. The crucial question became, What would take its place?

For Wordsworth, the answer came in those long walks, and later in the cottage he shared with his sister Dorothy in the beauties of the Lake District.

> For I have learned
> To look on Nature, not as in the hour
> Of thoughtless youth; but hearing oftentimes
> The still, sad music of humanity . . .
> And I have felt
> A presence that disturbs me with the joy
> Of elevated thoughts; a sense sublime
> Of something far more deeply interfused,
> Whose dwelling is the light of setting suns,
> And the round ocean and the living air,
> And the blue sky, and in the mind of man . . .

(*Tintern Abbey*, 1798)

In the end, what replaced the spirit of revolution was the spirit of Romanticism. The Romantic, a term that the Enlightenment had associated with the picturesque and/or merely foolish (which still lives on when we talk about someone as an incurable romantic), assumed after 1800 a powerful cultural force—so powerful that it persists, almost unrecognized, as the foundation of

---

*This was the title of the collection of essays by ex-Communists, including Stephen Spender and Arthur Koestler, published in 1949.

popular Western culture today. At its center was Nature with a capital N. Faith in the rights of man yielded to a faith in Nature—"the nurse, the guide," Wordsworth wrote, "the guardian of my heart and soul of all my moral being." The German poet Hölderlin said the same: "Boldly forget what you have inherited and won—all laws and customs—and like new born babes lift up your eyes to godlike nature."[6]

This belief in an eternal and beneficent Nature bore a striking resemblance to the belief in Christianity it replaced, and not by accident. After 1725, orthodox Christian belief faded from the intellectual scene, as the Enlightenment drove out the last remnants of medieval Neoplatonism. By a strange twist of irony, opponents of Enlightenment like Rousseau and Wordsworth would rediscover in Nature what Neoplatonists had found in the God of revelation: the radiant presence of a transcendent moral order, of an Absolute ready to guide humanity to illumination (artists like Goethe and Turner became as obsessed with the study of light as they were with the study of clouds and mountains) and ultimate knowledge.

The Romantics' worship of Nature turned what the Enlightenment had celebrated as man's power of *outer* observation into a form of *inner* contemplation. " 'Beauty is truth, truth beauty,' " John Keats would write, "—that is all Ye know on earth, and all ye need to know." Man's senses, which Plato treated as the source of error and Locke the source of useful knowledge, were transformed by Romantic artists and poets into the source of divine truth. In one dramatic stroke, the nineteenth century discovered in the sensate world of forest, hills, waterfall, and pasture, as well as in sex and opium, the knowledge of the Good and the One.

The Romantics, both progressives and conservatives (and there *were* politically conservative Romantics, like Samuel Taylor Coleridge and the French poet Chateaubriand), still stuck to Rousseau's critique of capitalism. Commercial society was still soulless, hard, and unjust. The war with Aristotle's Enlightenment was just as intense, and its celebration of a self-centered artificiality still offended as a betrayal of the innocence and promise of Rousseau's natural man. As German poet Friedrich Schiller put it, in modern society "the essential bond of human nature has been torn apart, and a ruinous conflict [has] set its harmonious powers at variance."[7]

Far back in 1778, Rousseau's friend Denis Diderot actually set up the debate in terms of Plato's cave:

Do you wish to know in brief the tale of almost all our woe? There once existed a natural man; there has been introduced within this man an artificial man and there has arisen in the cave a civil war which lasts throughout life.[8]

The Romantics yearned for a way to end this war in the cave. They wanted some way in which our Aristotelian instinct to engage our reason in the material world and our Platonic desire to realize our spiritual inner nature could be, if not finally reconciled, at least overcome. Of course, this wasn't going to be easy. As we've seen, the creative drive of Western civilization had arisen not from a reconciliation of the two halves but from a constant alert tension between them. But that didn't stop the Romantics from trying.

Still, for the first time Western man was aware of the conflict. The hope for working out some final synthesis—a way of living in the modern world without being devoured by it—charts the course of the rest of European and Western culture, even down to today.

And it starts with a man walking alone in a forest.

> One impulse from a vernal wood
> May teach you more of man,
> Of moral evil and of good,
> Than all the sages can.

Wordsworth's belief that nature embodied a genuine transcendent moral law—in Plato's terms, the Good in Itself—came to him slowly beginning around 1793. Naturally he didn't come up with it entirely by himself. It had antecedents in various other poets and thinkers, especially in England. But Wordsworth was by far its most articulate spokesman, and by 1798 he had a full-fledged creed to be communicated to others.

"O glide, fair stream! forever so, / Thy quiet soul on all bestowing, / Till all our minds for ever flow / As thy deep waters now are flowing."[9] The idea that nature's creatures, plants, and even its rivers and mountains embody an unselfishness, a wisdom and an intensity of life, shared with those human beings who live closest to nature, may seem naïve. But not if we are members of Greenpeace—or followers of Plotinus. The Romantics' fascination with nature led them to rediscover the Great Chain of Being and Plotinus's World Soul with passionate excitement.

> Wisdom and Spirit of the Universe!
> Thou Soul, that art the Eternity of thought!
> That givest to forms and images a breath
> And everlasting motion! . . .

(The Prelude, 1798)

The difference was that the Romantics saw the One of creation less as a rational hierarchy than as a powerful feeling of connectedness and serenity that at times seems entirely Zen. To quote William Blake:

> To see the world in a grain of Sand
> And a Heaven in a wild flower
> Hold Infinity in the palm of your hand
> And Eternity in an hour.

Except the origins were not Zen at all, but the writings of Rousseau. Back in the early summer of 1765, Rousseau had fled from his enemies, both imaginary and real, to a tiny house on an island on Lake Bienne in the Swiss Alps. There he had an experience so intense that it changed his life.

Sitting and listening to the rhythmic flux and reflux of the waves outside his window, he found he became completely at one with nature. As he described it later, all pain from the past and fears for the future faded away, leaving nothing except an intense awareness of nature's permanence and of Being in Itself. "I realized," he wrote in his description of the experience in *Reveries of the Solitary Walker*, "that our existence is nothing but a succession of moments perceived through the senses." In the solitude of nature, "my soul, exalted by these sublime contemplations, rose into the presence of the Divinity."[10]

At the time it was a revolutionary, even subversive, concept—more subversive than his attack on capitalism or his version of the social contract. The philosophers of the Enlightenment had built their understanding of human identity on the premise that man was, to paraphrase Aristotle, a social animal.[11] We instinctively hate being alone and crave interaction with others, they taught. Locke's theory of knowledge had the same thrust. Verifying the truth of our own ideas requires constantly comparing them with the experience and judgment of others.

And the best place to get this kind of knowledge through interaction, said Montesquieu, Hume, and others, was in commercial society. It was when you allowed people to go off on their own, to become isolated and brood over their own thoughts—the solitary hermit in his cave, the monk in his cell, or (one could add) Rousseau in his cottage—that they start confusing fantasy with reality and end up getting us all in trouble.

Rousseau reversed the Enlightenment formula. *Solitary* man is best. Mingling with others brings out our competitive urges and our false self-regard, which (as the *Discourse on Inequality* explained) inspires all the corruptions of commercial society. For Rousseau, the final cure had to come through the social contract and submitting to the General Will. Until then, however, nature in all its silent vastness would do. Starting two decades after Rousseau's death, the Romantics were delighted to take him up on his offer.

The remote cottage on the heath; the lonely walk through the mountains, often for hours; the serene contemplation of a rainbow or a sunset across the waves of the sea: These became the characteristic setting for Romantic writers, poets, and painters and all those who wished to participate in this new form of inner enlightenment through nature—an enlightenment so analogous to the experience of knowing Plato's Good in Itself that it seems superfluous to point it out.

> The immeasurable height
> Of woods decaying, never to be decay'd,
> The stationary blasts of water-falls . . .
> The unfetter'd clouds, and region of the Heavens;
> Tumult and peace, the darkness and the light
> Were all like workings of one mind, the features
> Of the same face, blossoms upon one tree,
> Characters of the great Apocalypse,
> The types and symbols of Eternity,
> Of first, and last, and midst, and without end.

> (*The Prelude*, Book VI)

Of course, there was also a darker side to this worship of nature, as Percy Shelley liked to point out:

Swiftly walk o'er the western wave,
Spirit of Night!
Out of the misty eastern cave,
Where, all the long and lone daylight,
Thou wovest dreams of joy and fear,
Which make thee terrible and dear,
Swift be thy flight!

Wrap thy form in a mantle gray,
Star-inwrought!
Blind with thine hair the eyes of Day,
Kiss her until she be wearied out;
Then wander o'er city, and sea, and land,
Touching all with thine opiate wand—
Come, long-sought!

("To Night")

Ironically, this darker side owed its start to Rousseau's great rival Edmund Burke. In 1757, fresh from college, the young Burke had penned *A Philosophical Enquiry into the Origin of Our Ideas of the Sublime and Beautiful*. The notion of the sublime (literally the feeling of being raised up to a higher level) came from a Hellenistic philosopher and Plato admirer named Longinus, who defined it as a sense of grandeur and awe inspired by a work of art so beautiful that we feel ourselves in the presence of the divine.[12]

The Renaissance Neoplatonists deeply admired Longinus and swept him up in their belief that art had the power to convey divine truth. With a single decisive stroke, Burke detached Longinus's sublime from the standard classical ideal of beauty. The real source of our experience of the sublime, the youthful Burke argued, was our most intense feelings; and of these the most important were fear of pain and danger, especially from a nature beyond human scale and beyond man's control.

These included the awe-inspiring mountains and vertiginous valleys of the Alps; the destructive power of cataracts and avalanches and storms at sea; the deathlike "solitude and silence" of night; and "the roaring of animals" like lions and tigers (the big cats were soon to become the Romantics' archetypes of Nature at her freest and most untamed).[13]

Hence the statesman who warned the world about the danger of Rousseau's politics became ironically one of the prophets of the Rousseauian worship of nature. Burke's formula found its way into the poems and paintings of the early Romantics, as well as their novels, from Horace Walpole's *Castle of Otranto* to Mary Shelley's *Frankenstein*. They still live on in their modern cinematic offspring, the horror movie.

But they also pointed to another powerful lesson to be drawn from the contemplation of Nature's dark side: the puniness of man and man's efforts in the face of her destructive power.

> *Blow, winds, and crack your cheeks! Rage! Blow!*
> *You cataracts and hurricanoes, spout*
> *Till you have drench'd our steeples, drown'd the cocks!*
> *You sulphurous and thought-executing fires,*
> *Vaunt-couriers to oak-cleaving thunderbolts,*
> *Singe my white head!*
> *And thou, all-shaking thunder,*
> *Strike flat the thick rotundity o' the world!*

We see it in a painting like Caspar David Friedrich's *Wreck of the Hope*, in which a ship trapped between icebergs is crushed and overwhelmed with the same lack of concern and pity as a child crushing a beetle. We also see it in the terrifying lightning-slashed landscapes of George Stubbs, and above all in the canvases of J.M.W. Turner, England's greatest painter and greatest observer of the violent, hostile moods of nature as the Absolute.

His pictures give us typhoons, snowstorms, and avalanches in vivid colors and light. Luminescent arcs of blue and green sweep the scene or drench the landscape with shimmering golds and bloodred scarlets. Turner's nature is so immense and impersonal that it becomes abstracted from its normal visual appearance. In fact, Turner is the inventor of Abstract painting nearly one hundred years before the term was coined.*

In Turner's paintings human beings appear as tiny insignificant dots. They and their pitiful works are swallowed up in great spiraling vortices of disaster. "Hope, fallacious hope," Turner wrote, "where is thy market now?"

---

*Needless to say, his contemporaries weren't taken with the result. His submissions to the Royal Academy's annual exhibits toward the end of his life became known as "Mr. Turner's little jokes."

J.M.W. Turner (1775–1851), *Snow Storm: Steam-Boat off a Harbour's Mouth*

The pessimism that arose from the failure of the French Revolution soon found a new home in a Romantic pessimism about man's fate when face-to-face with nature. If Plato is the original pioneer of pessimism—a belief that man's greatest achievements must inevitably be overwhelmed by the forces of corruption and decay and, like Atlantis, subside back into the timeless sea—then nineteenth-century Romanticism is its messenger into the modern era.

Some were crushed by this lack of hope. Suicide became an occupational hazard for young Romantics. The writer Schopenhauer even recommended it to his readers. Others like Turner and Francisco Goya were inspired by their pessimism. Still others like Lord Byron positively embraced it. "Let me be," his *Childe Harold* tells the dark storm, "a sharer in thy fierce and far delight, a portion of the tempest and of thee." Just as the Romantics became fascinated by storms and lightning (and by the famous scene on the heath in act III of Shakespeare's *King Lear* quoted above), so the Byronic impulse produced another stock character from the Romantic inventory: the solitary hero who rides off to death with a smile and cheerfully accepts his doom.

The land of honorable death
Is here . . .
A soldier's grave, for thee the best:
Then look around, and choose thy ground,
And take thy rest.

What separates Byron's hero from Rousseau's is that while the latter rides the storm and risks death for others, the former risks it only to gratify himself. He is the emblematic *anti*hero. His real battle is not against corruption or enemies or even conventional values, as in Byron's *Don Juan*. It is against the Absolute itself, as he dares to pit his own will against the Immense All. It may be disturbing, even outrageous: but it is also heroic. As in the westerns of Sergio Leone, however much we regret the hero's three-day beard, his cynicism, and his ruthless brutality, we have to admire his single-minded yet casual defiance of fate. Middle-class man seems to shrink to triviality beside the Man with No Name.

No wonder, then, that despite their best democratic instincts, the Romantics became fascinated by Napoleon, and still more by the figure of Lucifer. The line from Milton, "better to reign in hell than serve in heaven," became a catchphrase for Romanticism's Byronic mood, even as Mephistopheles serves as alter ego for the age's greatest hero, Goethe's Faust.

And so I turn to the abyss
Of necromancy, try if art
Can voice or power of spirits start,
To do me service and reveal
The things of Nature's secret seal.[14]

Doctor Faust's insatiable desire for absolute knowledge to the point of selling his soul to the Devil will make him emblematic of Romantic striving for the ultimate thrill, a willingness to break all conventional rules, even to the brink of nihilistic self-destruction. As Mephistopheles says, "All that exists, deserves to be destroyed." It is a sentiment that became Karl Marx's favorite quotation and it animates all the works of Friedrich Nietzsche.

Faust's author, Johann Wolfgang von Goethe, saw where all this was going. He had lived through the French Revolution and Napoleon's conquest of Germany. He tried to head things off with his famous pronouncement "Classicism is health, Romanticism disease." No doubt he was thinking of Romanticism's brooding pessimism, the craving for intensity of experience, however immoral or bizarre, which in his mind stood in such contrast with the timeless serene stability of Greek and Roman art. Indeed, Goethe's remark set off a debate about the meaning of classic and Romantic in the arts that has kept critics and historians occupied ever since.[15] Yet it is also profoundly misleading.

The real split is, again, between the legacy of Plato and Aristotle. Because all the rules that Romantic artists and poets yearned to shatter, the conventional neoclassical rules that governed every art in eighteenth-century Europe from painting and opera to architecture and poetry, actually stemmed from a single source: Aristotle's *Poetics*.

Aristotle wrote very little about painting or music and nothing about architecture, and he left behind a *Poetics* that was woefully incomplete. Still, he also gave us a chest of analytic tools for understanding poetry and art to which critics have helped themselves ever since.[16] Nearly everyone who talked about art from Roman times on drew one crucial lesson out of Aristotle: that the basis of the best art was based on an imitation of nature, or *mimesis*. In short, what Plato had said was the artist's biggest sin—that his work is a mere copy of material reality, which is itself a copy of the Forms Aristotle made his leading virtue.[17]

Imitation was, Aristotle said, natural to human beings and a constant source of pleasure.[18] To create a painting of clouds that actually look like clouds and trees that look like trees, or to craft a dramatic scene of horror (as in *Oedipus Rex*) or a happy scene such as a family reunion that vividly captures real-life emotions, is what connects an artist's or poet's work to his audience. Aristotle called the experience *katharsis*, which was the most important benchmark of artistic skill. This meant that an Aristotle-influenced art was above all a spectator-driven art. Whether he was painting a picture or cutting statues, writing a poem or composing a drama, Aristotle's artist aimed at presenting a picture of "nature as it is, or ought to be" that would move an audience in much the same way Aristotle wanted his public speaker to do.[19] Eventually, the rules of the *Poetics* became a subgroup of the *Rhetoric*, since both rested on the same principle. Above all, every poet or artist (like the orator) needed an inspiring message to communicate to his audience, so that their emotions can be moved by virtue and away from vice.

The Roman poet Horace summed up this Aristotle-based approach with a simple maxim, *Ut pictura poesis*, which we can translate as Every picture should tell a story. Every poem or story should therefore paint a verbal picture, which will be, Horace added, *dulce et utile*, or "both beautiful and useful," meaning morally uplifting.[20] For nearly three hundred years, from the High Renaissance until Jacques-Louis David, the fine arts in Europe followed Horace's advice. It was the foundation of all so-called academic art (named after Raphael's academy, not Plato's), while Aristotle's insistence that the most beautiful art imitated nature "as it is, or ought to be," became a fundamental axiom of neoclassicism.[21] "Nature as it ought to be" turned into imitation of the most ideal—which after the Renaissance clearly meant the Greeks and Romans.

Since the ancients had notably executed the most perfect human forms, the most harmonious architectural proportions, and the most stirring poems and dramas, they were obviously the ones to imitate. Nature herself, with her occasional warts and farts and sagging breasts, and clouds when there should be sunlight, and cowardice where there should be heroism, could wait.

She waited for three centuries, while art students spent their time examining ancient statues and buildings and writers practiced writing verse like Pindar and Horace and Virgil. The guru of eighteenth-century neoclassicism, J. J. Winckelmann, was succinct: "The only way for us to become great . . . is [by] the imitation of the Ancients."[22] Critics like Winckelmann drew a firm line between creative imitation and mere copying. All the same, art on these terms inevitably turned into a relentless training on how to reproduce the techniques of the Greeks and Romans and not much more. The result was office buildings done up as Greek temples; statues of scientists (including Isaac Newton) and statesmen like Napoleon and George Washington dressed in Roman togas; plays meticulously written in classical meter and adhering rigidly to Aristotle's three unities;* and paintings in which every figure was painstakingly derived from some Roman sarcophagus or Hellenistic statue.

In the hands of a master like Jacques-Louis David, the results could be breathtaking. However, the academic approach also served as an excuse for the pedantic and second-rate—as anyone who looks at the paintings of Joshua Reynolds or Raphael Mengs, or reads the dramas of Voltaire, soon realizes.

To the Romantics, it became apparent something was missing. It took

---

*These were unity of action (the plot should form an organic whole with no loose ends), unity of time (the plot should, if possible, take place in a single day), and unity of place (no sudden shifts of location), according to sixteenth-century interpreters of the *Poetics*.

some time, but they eventually found it, perhaps not surprisingly, in the pages of Plato.

The source was Plato's dialogue *Ion*, and Percy Bysshe Shelley was the first to stumble on it one afternoon in Pisa, in the early winter of 1821. Not yet thirty, Shelley had seen plenty of tumult in his short life. He had been expelled from Oxford for writing a pamphlet advocating atheism. He had then quarreled with his father and eloped with a sixteen-year-old waitress. When the marriage collapsed, Shelley had run away with the daughter of Mary Wollstonecraft, the feminist writer. This daughter, also named Mary, would write one of the classic Romantic expositions of the dark side of nature, *Frankenstein*.

In 1818, Shelley had moved from England to Italy in order to escape from what he saw as modern society at its most corrupt and commercial. So had several of his friends. Renaissance Pisa, once the hometown of Galileo, was now a refuge for English Romantic poets: "a nest of singing birds," as one of them called it. Lord Byron lived just down the road in a large country house. Shelley himself, however, preferred to live in town, in rooms that he and Mary had filled with cheap furniture, plants, and books.

One of those books, the dialogues of Plato, was in his hands now. Outside, the weather had turned chilly. Inside, however, a fire burned in the grate, and with greenery filling every window, "the sunny winter," he told a friend, "is turned into spring."[23] Shelley was as fascinated by ancient Greece as he was contemptuous of his own society. He had used Greek myth for the setting of his most famous poem, *Prometheus Unbound*, and had done a translation of Plato's *Symposium*.[24] However, it was turning the pages of another Plato dialogue, the little-known *Ion*, that changed his view of his poetic art—and reoriented the direction of nineteenth-century Romanticism.

Shelley had his finger on the specific passage and read it again. It was where Socrates praises the art of poetry as "a power divine," in which the inspiration of the Muse is passed not just to the poet, but to his audience as well. "For a poet is a light and winged thing," Socrates says, "and holy, and never able to compose until he has become inspired, and is beside himself, and reason is no longer in him." His works "are not of man or human workmanship, but are divine and from the gods." Indeed, so long as the poet has this divine power, "it is God himself who speaks, and through [the poet] is conversing with us."[25]

This, Shelley realized, was precisely what had been missing from the old academic canon of art that he and his friends despised. It was the role of inspiration, and the Plato-derived idea that the true poet and artist is someone with an inner vision imbued with divine truth. Shelley had encountered some of that notion already in the *Symposium* and *Phaedrus*, as had the Renaissance. William Blake expressed something very similar when he said, "One power alone makes a poet, Imagination, the divine Vision." Immanuel Kant had chimed in: "Where an author owes a product to his genius, he does not know how the *ideas* for it have entered his head" because they clearly come through an inspiration beyond calculated rational judgment.[26]

Shelley also knew William Wordsworth's definition of poetry as "the spontaneous overflow of feelings" aroused by our unmediated encounter with nature.[27] What Shelley saw in the *Ion* was the outline of a far more powerful idea. Great poetry is not just an expression of an unfettered imagination or feelings, but "the center and circumference of knowledge" itself. The poet was the living intermediary between mankind and the eternal Forms of Plato.

Shelley dashed to his desk and began writing. What came out was his *A Defence of Poetry*, a full-fledged rewriting of the history of the West with the poet and artist at its center. Little read today, it in fact set the forward trajectory of the arts in the West for the next two centuries. Shelley's poet is the inspired genius whose contact with the Eternal via imagination reflects a higher timeless reality more accurately and incisively than does Nature herself. "A poet," Shelley wrote, "participates in the Eternal, the Infinite, and the One," while his works "[are] the very image of life expressed in its eternal truth."[28]

Shelley's definition of poetry included much more than writing verse. Like the Greek *poesis*, meaning "creation," it included *all* forms of art, everywhere and at all times in history. What words and meter, allegory and simile, are for the poet, paint and canvas are for the painter, notes for the composer, and marble for the sculptor and architect. They are the means of reflecting a higher reality, of "redeeming from decay the visitations of the divinity in man." Art in this sense transmutes all it touches and immortalizes everything it encompasses. Poetry, he wrote in a famous passage, "lifts the veil from the hidden beauty of the world and makes familiar objects be as if they were not familiar," but rather beautiful emanations from the Godhead, "clothed in its Elysian light."[29]

"Poetry is not like reasoning" or logic, Shelley argued. It springs from a realm of intuitive feeling "beyond the control of the active powers of the mind."[30] And in a world that has systematically lost touch with its true inner self like the materialist commercial society of the nineteenth century, with its "satanic mills" (Blake's phrase) and Wedgewood porcelain factories, those who can rediscover that intimate connection with the divine once known to Plato and the Greeks will enjoy a special status and social value.

"The poet, as he is the author to others of the highest wisdom, pleasure, virtue, and glory," is therefore "the happiest, the best, the wisest, and the most illustrious of men."[31] His outward circumstances may not reflect it (Shelley's own health was bad, several of his children died early, and his wife, Harriet, ended her life in suicide), but as with Socrates, his special gift of insight imbues him with an inner felicity that those who stand outside the arts—mere businessmen and soldiers and politicians—can never hope to achieve. The poet handles the True and the Beautiful and the Good firsthand; and through their works, others are able to enjoy some connection with that eternal wisdom.

By his works, Shelley was saying, ye shall know him—meaning the poet and artist. And through the power of art, human beings might still find a redemption that the decline of Christianity (and Shelley despised organized religion almost as much as he despised capitalism and parliamentary government), or the failure of revolution in 1789, still denied them.

The redemptive power of art. Others in the Romantic movement shared the same vision, especially in Germany, where under the influence of Immanuel Kant they had come to see the creative imagination as an essential bridge between man's objective analytic reason—in short, his Aristotelian side—and his subjective judgment.[32] The poet Friedrich Schiller, for example, had foreseen a future society in which art would be the very center of education. His 1794–95 *Letters on the Aesthetic Education of Man* took their motto from Rousseau: "If reason makes the man, it is the emotions which lead him"—while the key to training the emotions is art.

Through the experience of art, Schiller argued, the child can share in the same awareness of grace and beauty as the great artist. By showing us how directly in Aristotle's terms matter and form become one, art resolves the modern conflict between our natural self and the self fashioned by reason. Diderot's civil war in the cave is suddenly over; man is restored to himself.

Until he achieves that harmony, Schiller insisted, man can never be truly free. But once he has, a glorious new era for humanity will emerge, forged by imagination and beauty.[33]

Shelley, however, decided to take this magnificent vision a stage further. The poet's ability to dream the impossible dream yet make it reality through his work applies not only to the arts, but to *every* form of human creation. Shelley's poets included "not only the authors of language, and of music, or the dance, or architecture, and statuary, or painting; they are the institutors of law, and the founders of civil society and the inventors of the arts of life." Pythagoras, Plato, Francis Bacon, and Isaac Newton; Moses, Jesus Christ, and Luther: All share for Shelley the same transformative power of imagination as Homer, Michelangelo, Shakespeare, and Dante (by comparison, Locke, Hume, and Voltaire come out looking very much second best). For Shelley, there is no distinction between the poet and other great agents on the world stage, in politics, religion, or other forms of life. Everywhere and at all times in history, they express the same spiritual truth and power, "the influence which is moved not, but moves."[34]

If all great men are poets, then are all poets great men? Aristotle's logic would say no, but Shelley enthusiastically proclaimed yes. This is what led him at the conclusion of the *Defence of Poetry* to dub his poets "the unacknowledged legislators of the world." They are in fact Plato's Philosopher Rulers in the flesh, for a world desperately needing the emanations of their genius.

That may seem far-fetched (except to poets), but the important word for Shelley is "unacknowledged." Whether a society knows it or not, its artists are the advance guard of the human spirit (*avant-garde* was coming into vogue in the 1820s as an artistic rather than military term). They are able to see farther, grasp with deeper insight, reconcile the conflicts in the human soul more fully, and then chart a course forward that the rest of humanity later only dimly and imperfectly follows. Schopenhauer put it differently but more vividly: "Talent is like the marksman who hits a target which others cannot reach; genius is the marksman who hits a target others cannot even see."[35]

As Socrates had warned in the *Republic*, such cultural sharp shooters are bound to be scorned and resented by their duller neighbors. Their personal lives will probably be a mess, as Shelley's and Byron's and Coleridge's were, with plenty of disorder and loose ends (all those mistresses, unpaid bills, illegitimate children, and addictive drugs). Dazzled as they are by the light of higher truth, not a few will appear insane. Nonetheless, for Shelley and his generation, they are now the true makers of history and civilization. The rest, including the Enlightenment's middle-class man, merely sponge off their imaginative creations, from the Parthenon and the *Republic* to the Sistine Chapel ceiling and the *Principia*. The picture is vividly summed up by Friedrich Nietzsche's later image of civilization as essentially a history of geniuses, in which "one giant calls to another across the desert intervals of time and, undisturbed by the chattering dwarfs who creep about beneath them."[36]

But what if one day the giant decided to reach down to those chattering dwarfs? What if the poet, having captured the light of truth in his imagination, turned back like Socrates or the god Prometheus (*the* crucial Greek myth for Shelley) and went down into the cave to share his fire from heaven with the masses?

The effect would be, to use a metaphor the Romantics loved, electric. "A great and free development of the national will," Shelley predicted, would be the result, "as if from a new birth."[37] This, Shelley decided, had been the problem with political revolutions like France in 1789. They had been put together not by men of artistic genius, but by lawyers like Georges Danton and Robespierre, who for all their rhetoric about virtue and freedom were no different from their predecessors—or in Shelley's mind, the British politicians of his own day. Their imaginations were just as limited, their thirst for material power just as insatiable, their reliance on brute force to resolve conflicts (Shelley was a vegetarian and pacifist) just as oppressive.

What was needed instead was a revolution led by poets and artists like Shelley and his friends. Then, he believed, humanity would achieve the future Kant had foreseen, a world of perpetual peace and harmony. Mankind would witness the overthrow of intellectual as well as political tyranny and the establishment of the rights of man and—with a nod to Mary Wollstonecraft—the rights of woman. The dream that had haunted the Platonic imagination since Saint Augustine, of an Eternal City united by love and equality and justice, would be realized, with the poets (as opposed to God or the theologians) leading the way.

Shelley himself never got the chance. On July 8, 1822, Shelley and a friend boarded his sailboat, the *Don Juan* (Shelley chose the name as a tribute to Byron's most famous amoral hero), and set out from the port of Leghorn under a lead gray sky with thunder and rain threatening. The *Don Juan* was never seen again.[38] Eleven days later, the two men's bodies washed up on the beach between Viareggio and Massa. Mary Shelley and a small knot of friends, including Byron, pulled Shelley's putrified corpse up from the temporary grave where Italian authorities had buried it and placed it on a funeral pyre along the beach.

As the flames slowly caught and the smoke rose over the heartbroken circle, Byron threw off his clothes and leaped into the sea. He swam over to his own boat, the *Bolivar*. Already an outrageous plan was taking shape in his mind, of which a poem published the year before offered a clue:

> *The isles of Greece! the isles of Greece!*
> *Where burning Sappho loved and sung,*
> *Where grew the arts of war and peace,*
> *Where Delos rose, and Phoebus sprung! . . .*
> *I dreamed that Greece might still be free;*
> *For standing on the Persians' grave,*
> *I could not deem myself a slave.*

That previous April, the word had spread through the English colony in Pisa: "Greece has declared its freedom!"[39] Since the fall of Constantinople nearly four centuries earlier, Greece had labored under the domination of the Ottoman Empire. In the spring of 1821, Greek guerrillas rose up in arms against their Turkish masters. The revolt became an instant Romantic cause célèbre. The prospect that the original home of democracy, the land of the Parthenon and Homer and Plato's Academy, might once again gain its liberty prompted men and women across Europe to open their pocketbooks in support. Committees were formed, funds raised, arms and ammunition purchased. Shelley himself had talked of going to join the Greek rebels, but he never made an effort to leave his Pisa apartment.

Byron, on the other hand, did. On December 29, 1823, he set sail from Italy with a small ship packed with livestock, four horses, medicine for an army of one thousand men, and chests full of gold coin and forty thousand British pounds in bills of exchange. He headed for the port town of Missolonghi, headquarters of the Greek insurgent government.[40] Arriving on January 4, he expected to find a setting of sunlit temples and an army of modern-day Homeric heroes waiting to be led in the fight for their freedom and the rebirth of European culture from its ancient roots.

Instead he found a miserable fishing hamlet, its streets running with stale fish offal and human excrement. A cold rain fell incessantly and the Greek rebel leaders quarreled and schemed for power—much like politicians everywhere. Missolonghi was also a cesspool of disease, and in mid-February, Byron was struck down with a violent fever.

For two months the poet shivered in the filthy sheets of his bed, passing in and out of consciousness while ignorant doctors applied leeches and bled him so profusely that his immune system collapsed. On April 19, 1824, Byron closed his eyes for the last time. He was just thirty-six. The first experiment in a revolution led by poets had ended in misery and squalor.

It was only a foretaste of what was about to come.

Georg Friedrich Hegel (1770–1831): He taught his disciples that
the modern state would save us all from ourselves.

Twenty-four

VICTORIAN CROSSROADS: HEGEL, MARX, AND MILL

Change in any society begins with class strife.
—Plato, *Republic*, Book VIII

The proletarians have nothing to lose but their chains. They have a world to win.
—Karl Marx

The sole end for which mankind are warranted, individually or collectively, in interfering with the liberty of action of any of their number is self-protection.
—John Stuart Mill

One by one, the trees came down—"as though of their own accord," as Alexis de Tocqueville, an eyewitness, put it. The lofty oaks and poplars that lined Paris's boulevards fell under the blows of hundreds of axes, while teams of men and women grimly wrestled them into the roadway. Others were pulling up paving stones.

The populace of Paris "went about their business silently, regularly, and hurriedly," Tocqueville wrote while watching the work of destruction from his window.[1] By morning on February 24, 1848, there were more than fifteen hundred barricades blockading the city's streets, made from four thousand felled trees and (it was estimated later) one million paving stones. No one gave Paris's working people orders; no one had given them an agenda. They were, however, in full revolt against the monarchy of King Louis-Philippe, whose troops had made the mistake of firing on protesting crowds the day before, killing forty. By the afternoon of February 24, Louis-Philippe realized he had no choice but to flee the city and abdicate in favor of his son.

Great crowds had gathered at Paris's city hall, the Hôtel de Ville. At their head was a tall willowy man with a stentorian voice and dramatic gestures. He was Alphonse Lamartine, France's most popular poet and a leading political radical. On the steps of the Hôtel de Ville, Lamartine proclaimed the end of the monarchy and the establishment of the French Second Republic, with the 1792 tricolor as its flag. The new republican government promised workers a national living wage, the right to organize unions, and universal male suffrage—a step even Robespierre had shied away from. "We are making together the sublimest of poems," Lamartine told the cheering crowd.[2]

The revolution of the poets Percy Shelley had prophesied had begun.

It did not stay in France very long. By March, the revolutionary fervor spread to Germany and Austria. In Berlin, crowds forced the king of Prussia to grant a new constitution; in Vienna, they clashed with troops and compelled Prince Metternich, chief architect of the conservative European order since the defeat of Napoleon, to resign and flee. In Rome, the pope was expelled and a new Roman republic was proclaimed. The Venetian republic was restored in the city of gondolas and canals. Very suddenly, liberty and the rights of man swept Europe with (compared to the original French Revolution) hardly any shots being fired. As historian Alan Taylor later put it, heaven and earth never seemed closer than in 1848; or man's redemption by a great moral ideal more fully within reach.[3]

Then the poetry and music died. To the shock of Lamartine and his middle-class allies, the new French national assembly elected on the democratic principle of one man, one vote, turned out to be more conservative than its royalist predecessor. Millions of peasants and small-town shopkeepers were determined to keep their hard-won property against any radical threat and to rein in the demands of Paris's workers for higher taxes on the haves and "the right to work" at government expense for the have-nots.

Across the rest of Europe, Germans, Czechs, Poles, Hungarians, Italians, Ukrainians, and Serbs quarreled over the borders and ethnic makeup of their newly liberated nations. Eventually, troops had to be called in and the barricades knocked down. The old crowned heads, including the pope, gradually restored their power. Even Metternich eventually returned to Vienna, deftly stepping from his carriage with imperial éclat.

In France, the last stand of the poets came in the last days of June. Alphonse de Lamartine was an unabashed admirer of the French Revolution of 1789. He had written a book about it, praising the Rolands and their fellow Rousseauians.* However, when he and his colleagues refused to give in to the workers' demands for the right to work, they found themselves besieged and cut off by barricades just as Louis-Philippe had been. They had to call on the rest of France to help put down the revolt. The rest of France (still smarting from memories of the Reign of Terror) was all too happy to help.

The fighting lasted for four days, from June 24 to 28. More than fifteen thousand Paris workers desperately fought street to street, house to house, against infantry armed with muskets and cannon. There was no quarter on either side. The archbishop of Paris stepped into the firing line to stop the slaughter. He was killed by a stray bullet. More than four thousand Parisians died in the fighting, many of them unarmed. Another twelve thousand were thrown into prison. Three thousand of those were summarily shipped to France's colony in Algeria.[4]

The revolution of the poets had ended in a bloodbath. The Second Republic had been saved—but by shooting down the working poor, whom it claimed to protect. A chastened Lamartine did stand for president in the election that December. He came in dead last. The winner was the great Napoleon's nephew, Louis Napoleon, who would soon overturn the Second Republic and crown himself Napoleon III, emperor of France.

The promise of liberty and democracy in 1848 had not drawn people together, it had driven them apart. Alexis de Tocqueville became convinced the June Days were not a political struggle at all, but "a sort of slave war . . . the revolt of one whole section of the population against the other." A German observer called it "the first great battle between the two classes that split modern society."[5]

Unlike Tocqueville, he had not witnessed the bitter fight. He had visited Paris in March as a reporter for a local German newspaper. Thickset and hirsute, with a greasy beard and an untidy mane of salt-and-pepper hair, he had watched the crowds' excitement and sense of exaltation in the early weeks of the 1848 revolution, and their belief that the establishment of a re-

*This was *L'Histoire de la Gironde*, published in 1832.

public meant the nation's poorest and neediest would finally be free. He returned to Germany to see the same expectation sweep workers, students, and the peasantry of that country. He spoke to open-air meetings in support of revolution and a workers' democracy.

Then, as in France, the middle class in Germany and Austria closed ranks with the aristocrats and monarchs against the radicals. The poets and intellectuals left the working poor to their fate—including the firing squad.

For the young reporter, the events in Paris in June were the final straw. He was done listening to talk about the rights of man and liberty. And he perceived in the Paris workers' desperate struggle the outline of a larger, more decisive conflict to come.

"The Paris workers were *overwhelmed* by superior force," he wrote in the pages of the *Neue Rheinische Zeitung*, "but not *subdued*. They have been *defeated*, but their enemies have been *vanquished*." His pen dripping with rage and sarcasm, he went on: "The momentary triumph of brute force has been purchased with the destruction of all the delusions and illusions" of the poets and their middle-class allies. Above all, it marked "the division of the French nation into two classes, the nation of owners and the nation of workers."

"The victory of the people is more certain than ever," the headline of his article bellowed. *"The second act of the French Revolution* is only the beginning of the European tragedy"—and the inevitable victory of the working class, or what he called *the proletariat*.[6] Then he signed the article with the byline *Karl Marx*.

But how would this proletariat win? Marx already had the battle plan, written with his friend Friedrich Engels. It was titled *The Manifesto of the Communist Party*, penned between December 1847 and February 1848. At the time, their Communist "party" consisted of exactly two people, Marx and Engels. However, Marx was confident that once the workers of Europe realized that their struggle was not against kings or despots, but against commercial society itself and its keystone, private property, they would rise up in such numbers and with such a fury that no one could stand in their way.

In 1848, Europe was emerging as a world of factories and mines, railroads and slums. Modern ideals of national sovereignty and majority rule were becoming common political coin, while modern science was poised for the next round of breakthroughs: four years earlier, Charles Darwin wrote out the 230-page outline for his *On the Origin of Species*.

In the shadow of 1848 the next great battle between Aristotle and Plato was about to begin anew. "There is a specter haunting Europe," the *Communist Manifesto* began, "the specter of Communism." In truth it was the specter of Book VIII of Plato's *Republic*. Those pages first spawned the idea of history as class struggle, a perpetual battle that Aristotle and his many followers over the centuries had sought to defuse but which Marx now yearned for—because, he dared to believe, it would create a new community more radiant and perfect than anything dreamed of by the Romantics or Plato and his Philosopher Rulers.

Marx was more of a Romantic than he cared to admit. He was born in 1818, the year Mary Shelley published *Frankenstein*. In college, he dreamed of becoming a poet. His earliest extant work is a verse tragedy, titled *Oulanem*, which Marx hoped might become the next *Faust*.[7] He also had a Byronic fascination with suicide pacts and pacts with the devil and enjoyed quoting the line from *Faust*'s Mephistopheles, "Everything that exists deserves to perish"—especially the middle-class capitalist society into which he had been born.

Like Rousseau and the Romantics, he saw that society as selfishness run amok. Surely, he agreed with Shelley and others, man was meant for something more than a kind of perpetual Wal-Mart shopping spree, with everyone intent on buying the material goods they think will make them happy, but indifferent to the fate of everyone else—while ready to use their shopping cart on anyone who gets in their way.

Marx believed that an event even more terrible and final than the French Revolution or the June Days would be needed to break the spell cast by commercial society. The man who helped Marx reach this conclusion was a figure he never met and whom he later bitterly repudiated: Georg Friedrich Hegel. But he was Kant's rival and heir and the most consequential German thinker in half a century.

For forty years, from 1795 until his death in 1831, Hegel taught first at the University of Jena and then in Berlin. A remote, even glacial figure, he was the German Sphinx—but also the first truly global philosopher. From America to Russia, Hegel was as controversial as he was influential. Schopenhauer attacked him as a "flat-headed, insipid, nauseating, illiterate charlatan." A century later, Karl Popper called his writings a "despicable perversion of everything that is decent."[8] Nonetheless, he dominated the continental academic mind like no one since Descartes. Marx, Schopenhauer, Nietzsche, Kierkegaard, Freud, Bergson, Sartre, Claude Lévi-Strauss, Michel Foucault, Jacques Derrida: All of them carry, to one degree or another, the mark of Hegel, if only in some cases as a symbol of everything they detested.

His written works, like *The Phenomenology of Mind*, are monuments of intellectual synthesis. But the real secret of Hegel's success was his skill in fusing the moral fervor of Rousseau with the rigorous philosophizing of Plato, all expressed in a dense, almost incomprehensible, prose. If Hegel didn't always know what he was talking about (as when he discussed planetary orbits[9] or economics), he certainly *sounded* as though he did—and sounded as though he were also saying something new and profound. In fact, it was a shrewd reshuffling of a worn-out Neoplatonist metaphysics, cast as universal history.

"Let us begin," Rousseau wrote at the start of his *Discourse on Inequality*, "by setting aside all the facts." This is precisely what Hegel does in his *Philosophy of History* and his *Philosophy of Right*, his most influential works. His subject was the history of civil society made famous by Scots like Adam Smith, or what the nineteenth century called "universal history." Like Plato, Hegel was interested not in what happened, but *why*. Unless you could give a reason why something happened, Hegel argued, then it was of no interest: certainly not to the philosopher. Because then it had no significance in the story that Hegel really wanted to expound: the march of Absolute Reason toward perfection.

Another term for Absolute Reason was Idea, or Spirit: for Hegel, they are all the same.[10] Like Plato's Ideas or Forms, Hegel's are more real than the material world they direct or reflect.* For Plato Ideas exist prior to material reality. For Hegel they emerge as part of material reality over time, like an image painted on the spokes of a wheel that becomes visible only when the wheel is in motion. The painter in this case is God or Providence, who has decided to make human history "the unfolding of Spirit in time," until Spirit, Nature, and History are One. Once man knows this, Hegel proclaimed, he will finally achieve his freedom.[11]

---

*Hegel was helped here by the fact that in written German, every noun begins with a capital letter. A table is a Table; a sandwich a Sandwich; and likewise history is History and ideas Ideas—suggesting a realm of disembodied yet potent universals that someone with a Platonist bent is bound to find irresistible.

That unfolding is not a simple linear progression by stages, as the Enlightenment had thought. For Hegel, history moves according to a three-step process. There is first the *thesis*, embodied in concrete events and persons. Then, comes the *antithesis*, the negation of the thesis arising from its own contradictions. Then finally, comes the *synthesis*, which reconciles the truths common to both, arriving at a new level of understanding—and a new stage in the advance of Absolute Spirit.

The term for Hegel's three-step logical development is the dialectic, after Plato's method of arriving at truth. Later, some would say Hegel borrowed the concept from Kant, others from the German philosopher Johann Fichte.[12] But we can see where it really came from: Plotinus and Neoplatonism, where the same three-step movement—procession, retrocession, and then merger with the One—leads the initiate up the Chain of Being to the World Spirit.*

Plotinus's World Spirit, the final cause of everything, becomes Hegel's Absolute Spirit or Idea—which, Hegel insisted, requires the dimensions of time and space in order to realize its concrete perfection. For example, men have automobiles which allow them to travel where they want and enjoy a greater independence and mobility: the very embodiment of Freedom. Then, the influx of more and more automobiles causes traffic jams and gridlock in city streets: the antithesis of mobility and Freedom. So then come stop signs and traffic laws, the perfect synthesis allowing people to get where they are going but also preventing our desire to get where we want from degenerating into anarchy.

In this sense, the stop sign, which at first glance places a limit on our freedom, actually (or objectively, in Hegel's terms) *protects* our freedom, even extends it. In effect, this becomes Hegel's account of modern history as well. The Middle Ages had been a period of moral clarity and spiritual uplift, but at the price of a narrow, cramped view of man and a tyrannical Church.[13] The Renaissance broke the shackles of the first, the Reformation of the second. Out of both arose modern commercial society with its individual economic and political freedoms, from Venice and Florence to London and Paris.

Thus far, Hegel's history sounds a good deal like Adam Smith's. It turns out, however, that Rousseau had it right all along. Instead of making human

---

* Its ultimate source may again be Pythagoras, where one or the Unlimited (what Hegel called the *Subject*) produces its opposite, two or the Limit (Hegel's *Object*), which then come together to form three, the triad, from which all other forms and numbers arise.

beings happier, commercial society only makes them feel alone and resentful—or to use a term Hegelians would make famous, alienated. We find ourselves in capitalist society like visitors at a banquet. We see the piles of food, magnificent wines, and exotic delicacies: we hardly know where to start. But just as we get close to the buffet table, other people cut in front of us. They already have plates, glasses, and cutlery. Where did they get them? we wonder.

Then we see people sitting and gorging themselves while we are still waiting in line for our first scoop. When we do finally get to the table, we find all the best food is gone and the serving plates licked clean. "You arrived too late," someone says; or, "It's your own fault. You should have cut in line like the rest of us." We go home hungry and resentful. When a friend asks us how we liked the banquet—or living in a capitalist society—we answer, "There's got to be a better way."

There is, Hegel argued. What we need, he says, is someone who will make us feel welcome and show us where the plates and glasses are; who makes sure that the other diners respect our place in line and allow us to get our turn at the pasta salad, creamed salmon, and lobster thermidor; and, finally, who makes sure that we, too, have a place to sit to enjoy our share of the bounty.

That someone, Hegel declared, is the State. Its development as an autonomous actor in history is in fact the next and final stage of freedom *beyond* commercial society. It smooths out all the problems of capitalism, with its "atomistic principle which insists upon the sway of individual wills" but ends up making men feel powerless.[14] What Rousseau and Romantic nationalists had seen in the *idea* of the Nation, a community shaped by laws, customs, and traditions into "one single being," or General Will, they can now achieve *concretely* through the actions of the State. Under its aegis, teams of bureaucrats become a virtual cadre of Philosopher Rulers who bring order and justice to a needy world. As in Plato's *Republic*, justice is the source of freedom, not the other way around.[15]

Hegel is the true godfather of the nanny state, or welfare state—with Plato standing beside him at the baptismal font. Unemployment insurance, health and safety regulations, minimum wage laws and aid to dependent children, the income tax and federal deposit insurance: All these become justified as the State acting to protect us from ourselves, because the State is our Better and Higher Self. As Hegel wrote, "The Government, regarded as an organic totality," is the concrete embodiment of "the indwelling Spirit and the history of the Nation." It is, he concluded, "the Spirit of the People itself."[16]

Once men realize this, they will realize that government, like the stop sign, exists to preserve freedom, not—as Locke and others feared—to restrict it. Modern liberty as the Enlightenment conceived it suddenly seems not so desirable after all. It seems a barren, rather empty place, like waiting endlessly in line at the banquet, compared with the comfort and security of the State's constantly outstretched arms.

"Society and the State are the very conditions in which Freedom is realized."[17] Indeed, in time humanity will discover that obeying the laws of the State is the only *true* freedom, since it is the only one that connects us to "the self-realization of Reason" and the larger process of history itself—and thus gives us final absolution from Diderot's civil war in the cave.

However, all this comes at a price.

The dialectical movement of history is not smooth and seamless. It is a bumpy and choppy ride, with lots of turmoil—not to mention bloodshed. The conquests of Alexander, the fall of Rome, the Crusades, the Inquisition, are all for Hegel cruel but necessary steps on reason's path to perfection. When Hegel's theses and antitheses collide, they tend to collide on the battlefield, in bitter, violent street clashes, in torture chambers and prison cells, and in revolutions.

Plato had made constant revolutions the dynamic of man's life in society, and so does Hegel. Synthesis appears only after a *crisis*—another word Hegel made famous—and history on Hegel's terms is a series of crises. Indeed, "periods of happiness in history" are, in Hegel's words, "empty pages." They contribute nothing to mankind's advance. During peacetime, he wrote, "civil life becomes more extended, every sphere is hedged in . . . and at last all men stagnate." Men are better off, Hegel decided, when they are forced to face danger and uncertainty, forced to rise to the occasion. "Let insecurity finally come in the form of Hussars with glistening sabers, and show its earnest activity!"[18]

It may be easy to be philosophical about bloodshed, war, and death from behind a desk or in front of a blackboard. Still, the legend is that Hegel wrote *The Phenomenology of Mind* to the sound of gunfire from Napoleon's victory at Jena, where Hegel was a professor. Hegel welcomed the advent of

Napoleon—"this great soul, this extraordinary man"—as signaling the next great stage in history, the emergence of a World State, even though it meant the end of thousands of lives and the defeat of his own country, Prussia.*

Hegel never lived to see the events of 1848, but Marx did. They shattered whatever remaining doubts he still had that Hegel's nation-state was "the Spirit of the People." Instead, he would strip Hegel's Platonizing vision of history to its bare steel skeleton and recast it as the specter of global apocalypse.

On August 24, 1849, Karl Marx arrived in London after being expelled from Prussia for his activities in the revolution the previous year. He was thirty-one years old. Except for a couple of brief visits to the Continent, England would be his home and refuge for the rest of his life.

For thirty-four years, he marched down almost daily to the British Museum to conduct research and gather material for his socialist writings. The weightiest, On Capital, or Das Kapital, remained unfinished at his death. During those thirty-four years, he never bothered to ask why in England, the land of Locke, Burke, and Adam Smith, he was left alone to work, while in Germany and on the Continent he was always subject to the threat of arrest. Instead, his entire focus was on how to "annihilate" (one of his favorite words) societies like Britain and how to use Hegel to do it.

Even after he broke with his former master, Marx was convinced that Hegel's dialectic was "the key to human understanding." However, Hegel hadn't gone far enough. The real scene of the action, he had concluded even before 1848, was not politics but the evolution of civil society described by Hume, Adam Smith, and their disciples. The course of history is made not by phantom Ideas or Absolute Reason, but by how men earn their material living (hence the Marxist term *dialectical materialism*) and how that, rather than some abstract dream of freedom, determined the character of their societies.

Yes, the Middle Ages had been replaced by the Renaissance and Reformation. However, this was because the urban merchants of cities like Florence

*The eventual collapse of Napoleon's empire left Hegel unfazed; he simply switched his loyalties back to Prussia and ended his days extolling its monarch, Frederick William III, as the new "world historical individual." That particular king proved a disappointment. However, Hegelians and their offspring continued to look for such a figure, the charismatic embodiment of "substantive rationality and immediate actuality," from Mussolini and Hitler to Fidel Castro and Hugo Chávez.

and Nuremberg had ripped apart the bonds of an agrarian feudalist economy in order to reap the full measure of their trading profits. And yes, traditional feudal monarchies had given way to constitutional government, from England in 1689 to France a century later—but only because the rising bourgeoisie had won over the workers and peasants from their feudal masters with fine phrases about liberty and the rights of man.

Instead of being the voice of freedom, liberalism, like Hegel's nationalism, was only the voice of a greedy bourgeoisie, "a few vulgar and self-educated upstarts transformed into eminent cotton spinners [and] sausage makers." They disguised their greed for profit under a cloak of natural right, including the right to private property. This disguise was not deliberate, or at least not entirely so. It was the inevitable result of living in a world that *could not confront its own contradictions*; that must hide the material struggle for dominance and exploitation under a cloak of high ideals, hiding it even from the exploiters themselves. Marx's term for this disguise was *ideology*. Friedrich Engels coined a phrase that sums it up better: false *consciousness*.[19]

False consciousness is the Marxist version of the cave. It is that shadowy realm of falsehood and deceit by which the bourgeoisie maintain their power by pretending that it is founded in nature (as Aristotle would say) when in fact it is a rigged game. False consciousness comforts the ignorant and assuages the guilt of the guilty. It helps to keep reality at arm's length.

The Middle Ages had its version of false consciousness, namely Christianity: hence Marx's famous aphorism that "religion is the opiate of the masses."* Capitalism has its version, too. This is the supposedly scientific worldview of Locke and the Enlightenment, which pretends that the pursuit of self-interest was natural and inevitable. However, the reign of "ideology" will come to an end when the final victors of history, the proletariat, come to power.

The powerless shall indeed inherit the earth, because, as Hegel taught, each stage of history produces its antithesis, and thus its ultimate doom. The ancient world had produced the slaves, Jews, and cultural outcasts who became the backbone of Christianity and thus destroyed the Roman Empire. The Middle Ages produced the bourgeois merchant class, on whose money kings and barons and the Church became totally dependent even though

---

*The phrase, in fact, was not his but the poet Heinrich Heine's. Nor was "From each according to his abilities, to each according to his needs" (Louis Blanc) or "The proletariat have nothing to lose but their chains" (Jean-Paul Marat) or "Workers of the world, unite!" (Karl Schapper). And it was Blanc, a French Socialist, who first coined the phrase *dictatorship of the proletariat*.

they treated it with contempt. Here—however briefly—Marx's vision of history overlaps with William Robertson's, and Adam Smith's.

Now in 1860, Europe's industrial bourgeoisie were in turn breeding a viper in their nest, their workers. For without them, the machines wouldn't run, the wheatfields wouldn't be harvested, the cotton mills and coal mines would fall silent. When the proletariat realized their latent power (and the job of Marxist intellectuals is to make them aware of it), they will rise up in a revolt that will set the June Days in the quiet shade.

It will be "the day of Judgement," Marx wrote, "when the reflection of burning cities are seen in the heavens . . . to the accompaniment of thundering cannon . . . and inflamed masses scream . . . and self-interest is hanged on the lamppost."[20] The June Days were always Marx's touchstone for understanding class relations and the historical role for the proletariat. He never doubted for a moment that communism meant revolution, and a violent one at that. "When our turn comes," he told the Prussian assembly in 1849, "we will not disguise our *terrorism*"—and over time Marx's followers, from Russia to North Korea, have generally adhered to his advice.[21]

Still, the proletariat itself remained for Marx an abstraction, nothing more. He knew nothing about the working poor and never set foot in a factory. His entire picture of their lives was drawn from Engels's book *The Condition of the Working Class in England*, published in 1844, even though much of its data was dated and even faked.[22] Marx detested socialists who did come from working-class backgrounds, precisely because they tended to oppose violence and looked for a way for labor and capital to cooperate. He drove one, Wilhelm Weitling, out of the Communist International; another, Ferdinand Lasalle, he denounced as that "Jewish nigger" and did everything he could to cripple Lasalle's efforts at creating an antirevolutionary socialist movement.[23]

It is often said that Marx's materialism turned Hegel upside down. Marx himself said it. In fact, both were fixated by the same abstraction, History: meaning that the future has a fixed and inevitable destiny. Marx's concept of history comes straight out of Book VIII of the *Republic*. It is history as class struggle pure and simple, a ruthless cycle of "war and hatred" without end.

Except that Marx's class struggle *does* come to an end. "History is the judge," Marx once said, "the proletariat is its executioner." When the smoke clears and the rubble finally subsides, the proletariat will find itself in charge—freeing man for now and forever.

Since economic production no longer requires exploitation of one class by another, the driving dialectic of history, class struggle, also comes to a halt. At a stroke all contradictions are finally resolved, just as the Romantics had always envisioned. Subject and Object; freedom and necessity; our natural self and social self; even (with the death of false consciousness) reality and appearance, become one.

The State withers away—meaning Hegel's nanny state—since it is no longer needed. Everyone finds an equal place at the banquet to which everyone has willingly contributed: from each according to his ability, to each according to his need. "Man, at last the master of his own form of social organization," Engels wrote, "becomes at the same time the lord over nature, his own master—free."[24]

Human beings will finally become whole and complete. They will, in Marx's phrase, "work in the morning, fish in the afternoon, and write poetry in the evening." For all his rage, Marx the dialectical materialist turns out to be a man as obsessed with spiritual enlightenment as the poet Shelley or Saint Augustine. To Socrates, it was "this condition of the soul we call Wisdom." Marx called it "the kingdom of freedom." It will come, he once wrote, only when men are finally freed from their material limitations, or the kingdom of necessity. "The kingdom of freedom actually begins only where drudgery, enforced by hardship and by external purposes, ends. . . . It lies beyond the sphere of proper material production."[25]

By chance, at the same time that Marx was sitting in the British Museum dreaming his dream of man freed from material necessity, another man on the other side of London was pondering the same problem. He occupied a tidy office in India House in Kensington. Decades before, he had been England's most astonishing boy genius. Now fifty years old, slight of build and balding, he was the living heir to the assumptions of the Scottish Enlightenment. He would take up the question of human freedom from the opposite end of Marx's perspective—one might say from the Aristotelian end.

His name was John Stuart Mill.

He had learned Greek at age three. When he was seven he was reading Plato's dialogues in the original and poring over Hume and Gibbon. At eleven he was the master of Newton's *Principia* and Aristotle's logic.[26] By the time John Stuart Mill was sixteen, he was writing his own textbook on economics.

All this was due to his father, James Mill. When John was born in 1806 (the year Hegel was listening to Napoleon's guns at Jena), the elder Mill decided to raise his son according to the Lockean behaviorist principles of his mentor, Jeremy Bentham. He was determined to turn this particular tabula rasa into the next generation's spokesman for the philosophy he and Bentham had developed, called Utilitarianism.

The logic of Mill's Utilitarianism was Locke and Hume undiluted by any human sentiment. All human action flows from perceived self-interest, and all knowledge is derived from sensory experience, of which the most direct and important are pain and pleasure.[27] Therefore, Jeremy Bentham concluded, logically the best way to get people to behave morally is to maximize the pain they suffer when doing bad and maximize the pleasure from doing good, especially the public good, which the Utilitarians defined as "the greatest good for the greatest number."

James Mill applied much the same calculus to homeschooling his son. The short-term pain a five-year-old might suffer from spending long hours studying Greek verbs and drawing diagrams of ellipses instead of playing with toys or friends would be outweighed by the long-term benefit of having a finely trained mind ready to work for the greater happiness of mankind. The plan succeeded beyond James Mill's hopes. The more knowledge little John absorbed, the more his father piled on the books. When the boy had absorbed all he could, James Mill set him to work teaching his brothers and sisters (while sending him to bed without supper if they failed their lessons) and editing Bentham's legal writings. By 1826, twenty-year-old John Stuart Mill had become a miniature clone of his father, including mirroring his political and philosophical beliefs.[28]

Then, perhaps inevitably, the mirror cracked. John Stuart Mill had convinced himself that his entire goal in life was to be a progressive reformer like his father. Then one day he asked himself a vital question:

> Suppose that all your objects in life were realized, that all the changes in institutions and opinions which you are looking forward to, could be effected at this very instant, would this bring a great joy and happiness to you? And an irrepressible self-consciousness distinctly answered, "No!"

It was, he remembered later in his *Autobiography*, as if he had woken up from a dream. It instantly plunged him into a deep depression: "I seemed to have nothing left to live for." Everything he had learned and done had been to please others, including his father. What he now realized was that there had been nothing left for himself.[29]

The depression lasted for two years. What pulled him out was the one thing that his father and Bentham had most despised: Romantic poetry at its most "useless," especially Wordsworth and Samuel Taylor Coleridge. Later, Mill called reading Wordsworth for the first time one of the great events of his life.[30] He discovered through the Romantics what had been missing from the Utilitarian calculus, namely the actual experience of life.

He had learned that for most human beings, "experience" is not a philosophical abstraction or passive absorption of information. It is an active engagement with the world, a constantly changing encounter with empirical reality, including the lives and dreams of others. Mill discovered that a walk through the mountains or down a London street or playing a game of cricket (which his father never allowed him to do), riding to hounds or playing softball on weekends or running for a simple political office like alderman or sheriff, opens a door to personal growth and self-fulfillment, as well as to physical and mental health, that no amount of time buried in books can duplicate.

> *Thanks to the human heart by which we live,*
> *Thanks to its tenderness, its joys, and fears,*
> *To me the meanest flower that blows can give*
> *Thoughts that do often lie too deep for tears.*

Mill's encounter with the Romantics, and then other minds outside his father's circle, forced him to revise Utilitarianism. He never gave up the idea that utility—that is, the greatest good for the greatest number—should remain an important guide to public policy. But it cannot be the *only* guide. He learned from Thomas Macaulay's famous critical review of his father's *Essay on Government* that trying to construct a political vision from purely deductive principles is a guaranteed failure, because it ignores the complexities of real life. If Bentham and his father had led an enlightened Aristotle down a Platonist dead end, Mill's goal was to lead their Aristotle back out again.

To start with, he learned from Coleridge (who was an avowed Burkean conservative as well as a poet) that the social world around us is not just the result of wrongheaded thinking or systematic injustice, as his father and Jeremy Bentham believed. It reflects a complex organic historical development and consists of institutions that give meaning and purpose to the lives of ordinary people, however pointless they may seem to the ivory tower philosopher. Social reality has a hidden purpose, Coleridge taught—a purpose that, like Nature herself, we tamper with at our peril.[31]

Then Coleridge and Macaulay both showed him that the first task of an intellectual is not to trash and overturn existing institutions of his society, as both Bentham and Marx tried to do. It is to understand first of all how and why they came about. By doing so, we can discover certain basic principles of human nature to serve as the basis of thoughtful reform instead of headlong revolution.[32] And from the French philosopher Auguste Comte, Mill learned that once we have discovered those principles, it might be possible to construct a science of man (which Comte called *sociology*) that will be as certain and universally applicable as Newton's *Principia*.

This became Mill's new ambition, one worthy of his tremendous brainpower and learning acquired at such a personal cost. It was to do for the modern age what Aristotle (that "judicious utilitarian," as Mill called him) had done for the ancient and medieval worlds: bring together our understanding of man and our understanding of nature into a single overarching system. Mill even devised his own system of logic to serve as its framework.* However, Mill wanted his new system to take into account two realities that the historical Aristotle would have missed. The first was the reality of man's material historical development, as Smith and Hume (and Hegel and Comte) had acknowledged.[33] The other was the overriding importance of individual freedom.

This was, of course, something Hegel had *not* acknowledged (or Comte, for that matter). Like Marx, Hegel built his philosophy entirely around proving that man's happiness depended on reaching the final stage of community,

---

*Called *A System of Logic,* it tried to argue that all correct inference flows from induction—that is, from sensory experience. Even the classic example of deductive reasoning, "All men are mortal; Socrates is a man; therefore Socrates is mortal," derives its truth, Mill argued, from our noticing that individuals we know die, which leads us to conclude that eventually all men will die, including Socrates. Modern logicians are not so easily convinced. However, *A System of Logic* was an instant bestseller when it was published in 1843, and copies appeared in virtually every bookshop in London: proof of what a literate public really looks like.

either the nation-state or the classless society. Indeed, Hegel had no interest in unleashing the power of the individual unless he happened to be a "world-historical individual" like Alexander or Napoleon.

The Romantics, however, did. What Mill ultimately did was to steal their clothes while they were out bathing with the Infinite. The amount of individuality in a society, he would write, "has generally been proportional to the amount of genius, mental vigor, and moral courage it contained."[34] One could in fact sum up Mill's final vision of the free society as "Every individual his own genius." However, Mill had also reversed the Romantics' formula. He was determined to show that free market capitalism was not the enemy but the savior of the free creative individual.

Mill never completed his great plan for what he termed "an Exact Science of Human Nature." However, the works he did leave before his death in 1873 on logic and political economy, plus *On Liberty* (1859), *Considerations on Representative Government* (1861), and *Utilitarianism* (1863), stirred British intellectual life as no other author had. Mill is the direct progenitor of British liberalism, not to mention modern libertarianism. Indeed, later eminent Victorians like Arthur Balfour and Leslie Stephen explicitly compared his impact on the British intellect to that of Aristotle in the Middle Ages.[35] When young men at Cambridge or Oxford in the 1870s or 1880s discussed any question on politics or economics or metaphysics, the cry would inevitably come up: "Read your Mill!"

Of all his works, the one that lives on today is the shortest, *On Liberty*, which he wrote with his wife, Harriet Taylor, and published in 1859. It has enshrined Mill's interest, even obsession, with protecting the freedom of the individual to do what he or she desires (Mill was a keen supporter of votes for women) without interference except to protect public safety. It is the *Nicomachean Ethics* of today's libertarians.

It also set Mill in direct opposition to Hegel and Marx. "Mankind are greater gainers," its introduction reads, "by suffering each other to live as seems good to themselves than by compelling each to live as seems good to the rest."[36] It is hard to imagine any sentence more at odds with Hegel's *Philosophy of Right* or Marx's *Grundrisse*.

At the time, *On Liberty* had another important purpose. It spelled the definitive end of the teleology—or the idea that everything that happens serves some greater higher *telos*, or purpose—that both Plato and Aristotle (not to mention Saint Augustine and Hegel) had used to describe human nature and human affairs. In the *Politics*, Aristotle did see individual house-holders as the foundation of a free society, but he still believed that human nature itself was directed toward a single *telos*.* Mill responded that we are here to fulfill not one final single end, but *many ends*—as many as there are individual human beings.

For Mill, it is the healthy diversity of purposes and destinies that makes for a happy society and a truly free society. The purpose behind individual liberty is *not* allowing people to do whatever they want, it is allowing people to do what his father had never permitted him: to discover in their own way what truly fulfills them. This, Mill argued, is the essence of true freedom.[37]

This was also the great key to Western civilization and its history, Mill argued: the increasing empowerment of the individual. "What has made the European family of nations an improving, instead of stationary, portion of mankind?" Mill asked. Not any innate superiority, but "their remarkable diversity of character and culture." This diversity has created a "plurality of paths for its progressive and many-sided development," from the various Greek city-states to modern nations: indeed the more the better.[38] For Mill, uniformity is the enemy of progress, because it becomes the enemy of individuality and personal choice.

This is true for capitalism as well. Mill agreed with his father and Bentham that the free market has an optimal economic utility, because it provides the most goods of the highest quality at the lowest price. However, the secret to keeping those who attend capitalism's banquet happy is not just keeping the price of a ticket low or providing more food; it also means allowing attendees to choose when they are going to eat, and which dishes. The free market works best at sorting out these individual preferences, something that (as anyone who visited a department store in East Germany or the Soviet Union realized) government does very poorly.†

In doing so, the market also serves a *cultural* utility. Far from generating chaos, the result of diverse choices is a division of labor that benefits everyone. As Mill states, "The only unfailing and permanent source of improvement is liberty," and his *Principles of Political Economy* made it clear that free market capitalism's chief virtue was that it made sure there were "as many

---

*See chapter 4.
†Explaining why fell to a coterie of Mill followers on the Continent, the so-called Austrian school of economists. See chapter 29.

possible centers for improvement as there were individuals."[39] For Mill, uniformity is the enemy of progress. Diversity is the regular source of growth and renewal, whether one is talking about the Manchester cotton mills or Silicon Valley.

In the same way, Mill believed, representative government on the British or American model worked best because it encouraged individuals to stand up for their rights, thus encouraging an energetic self-reliance.[40] The most famous example of how individual freedom works to achieve public goods is found in *On Liberty*'s discussion of freedom of thought.

Allowing men and women to say what they believe, Mill argues, and publish what they think is true promotes the spread of new discoveries and truths while pushing out the false and misleading. This is what is sometimes referred to (somewhat misleadingly) as "the marketplace of ideas." Mill's analysis owed less to economics than it did to the Romantics. Freedom of speech adds to the creative intensity of life. The free exchange of ideas will prevent a culture from growing stale and rigid. Even debates about issues that seem entirely settled, like whether the earth is flat or if the Holocaust happened, can serve this purpose of wakening us from "the deep slumber of decided opinion." It is a fact, Mill argues, that "the fatal tendency of mankind to leave off thinking about a thing when it is no longer doubtful is the cause of half their errors."[41]

The other half, he implies, is the result of dogmatism and the freezing up of society against its lone voices of dissent. Socrates, Jesus, Martin Luther, Galileo: Shelley had treated them as great poets, whose insights illuminated eternal truths. The value of these figures for Mill is as history's great *dissenters*, the unpopularity of whose opinions serves as a benchmark for society's next advance. That society which opens a space for individual dissent, and actively debates its own most basic tenets and truths, is for Mill the one that lives and breathes and grows. The one that doesn't stagnates and dies.

"A people, it appears, may be progressive for a certain length of time, and then stop. When does it stop? When it ceases to possess individuality." This is what happened to Egypt and China, Mill affirms. It hadn't happened to Europe—yet.[42] But could it? In 1859, Mill saw two dangers on the horizon.

The first was the expansion of democracy. This was a paradox for someone who, on the political front, was one of democracy's biggest champions—including votes for women. However, Mill sensed in the sheer bulk of mass democratic society a new and unforeseen kind of tyranny, "the tyranny of the majority." The individual will feel a pressure to agree with a consensus shared by millions and millions of people whose views have assumed equal cultural value; the validity of a point of view will simply be that everyone else holds it. Those outside the consensus, Mill believed, will become outcasts—even viewed as a threat.

Middle-class man would be replaced by mass man, Mill feared, the compulsive conformist who "practices a social tyranny more formidable than many kinds of political tyranny."[43] This was long before anyone had thought of television. Today, it's a nightmare that still haunts many intellectuals: the fear of being buried alive in a society that plays video games in the morning, shops at Wal-Mart in the afternoon, and watches *Keeping Up with the Kardashians* in the evening.

Some see this fear, like Mill's, as a thinly disguised elitism. Others have pointed out that the dangers lie very much the other way: that the complete indulgence of individual preference to the point of what Mill approvingly called "eccentricity" opens the door to no cultural or moral standards at all— as anyone browsing the Internet soon realizes.* Still, no one wants to live in a world in which individual creativity has been reduced to designing our own vanity plates. Mill's fears about what a truly democratic culture might look like poses a nagging problem for the Aristotelian calculus. It hangs over *On Liberty* as much as it does over Matthew Arnold's *Culture and Anarchy* (virtually a point-by-point refutation of the first chapter of *On Liberty*) and, much later, David Riesman's *The Lonely Crowd*.

The other danger Mill sensed was the growth of socialism, specifically Marxist communism. Again, this was paradoxical from someone who came to describe himself as a socialist and saw relieving poverty as a social imperative. Mill's later writings strongly reflect the view that an entirely market-driven system must eventually give way to one that shares more of the fruits of prosperity with others.

All the same, the touchstone of Mill's version of socialism remained individual choice. As Nicholas Capaldi has argued, Mill's socialism is one in which formal class distinctions disappear and everyone becomes an autono-

---

*One of those was Thomas Macaulay, who felt Mill's worries about excessive conformity in modern democratic society were misplaced compared with the threat of a collapse of any intellectual standard. "He is really crying 'fire,' " Macaulay wrote in his journal, "in Noah's flood."

mous entrepreneur. Mill never accepted the Rousseauian notion of a general will to which the individual must submit. On Mill's terms, redistribution of income and resources must be voluntary, rather like a farmer's co-op or a start-up software company in which employer and employees agree to share the profits.[44]

This was precisely the kind of socialism Karl Marx most detested. By the same token, Marx's version was the one that Mill most feared. He watched the founding of the first Communist International, spoke to some of the English delegates who attended, and did not like what he heard. Marx, like Hegel, believed crisis and revolution were history's path to freedom. Mill believed history showed they were the path to slavery. The idea of the proletariat seizing the means of production was "obviously chimerical," he wrote, and would only plunge humanity into the brutal state of nature envisaged by Thomas Hobbes.

From it would emerge a society far worse than its bourgeois successor, he warned. If the compression of individuality by the majority was already becoming a problem, "it would probably be much greater under Communism. . . ."[45] Man's progress would be stifled; the wellsprings of creativity would dry up; and society would be reduced to "a multitude of well-cared-for slaves, rather than a nation of free and independent men. . . ." If, therefore, Mill concluded, "the choice had to be made between Communism with all its chances [of failure], and the present state of society with all its sufferings and injustices . . . Communism would be as dust in the balance."[46]

After 1870, however, that was the choice men—or at least intellectuals— were increasingly called to make. Mill had stated (echoing David Hume) that the story of history is the struggle between liberty and authority. Are human beings happiest when they are left alone or when they submit to an order greater than themselves?[47] As the nineteenth century wore on, the heirs to Aristotle and the Enlightenment became the staunchest defenders of liberty, while the partisans of Plato were increasingly attracted to the authority side of the barricades.

This is the origin of the famous split between classical liberalism and its modern paternalist and statist cousin, progressivism. It was already happening in Mill's own country. Shortly after his death, the so-called British Idealists would use Hegel to fashion a distinctly Anglophone theory of the welfare state.[48] On the other side, Herbert Spencer would mount a countertheory in

The Man Versus the State that made far more concessions to laissez-faire economics than Mill the on-again, off-again socialist could ever have endorsed.

In Spencer's case, at least, another factor had entered the arena—one that had dazzled Karl Marx almost as much as it did Spencer. It was a book by Charles Darwin called *On the Origin of Species,* and it would open a brand-new front in the perennial battle between Plato and Aristotle, this time in natural science.

PLATE II

LONDON: EDWARD ARNOLD.

"If [the] individual cannot propagate he has no issue—so with species." Charles Darwin (1809–82)

Twenty-five

THE SCALE OF NATURE: DARWIN, EVOLUTION, AND ARISTOTLE'S GOD

The fundamental principles of all nature are change and motion; he who does not recognize this truth does not recognize nature herself.
—Aristotle, *Physics*, Book III, Chapter 1

All nature exists in a state of perpetual improvement.
—Erasmus Darwin, *Zoonomia* (1794–96)

That night they made camp.

They pulled their *lancha* up on the beach and started their campfire, the smoke rising in the twilight while vampire bats circled in the trees overhead. It was their third day out from San Fernando as they paddled along the sluggish Apure River. The brown water was sometimes so shallow that the *lancha* would get stuck on a sandbar and the natives would have to get out and push it off. All around them was the forest: a thick green canopy that hung over the river, while monkeys screamed and strange birds called from the branches of cedar, mahogany, mimosa, and brazilwood.[1]

The *gringo* had samples of all of them in his bag, along with herbs, fruits, bugs, and butterflies. There were also rocks and mineral samples, together with his three constant companions: his notebook, his compass, and his sextant, which he used to chart their course until he reached his final goal.

It had been a strenuous day, and they slept a deep, dreamless sleep. In the morning the *gringo* set off again on foot, observing and writing in his notebook. After a few hours he circled back to camp, where he caught a whiff of breakfast being cooked on the campfire. Before the full steaming heat of the day set in and the inevitable armies of mosquitoes descended ("persons who have not navigated the great rivers of equinoctial America," he would later write, "can scarcely conceive how the multitude of these little animals can render vast regions almost uninhabitable"),[2] he decided to wander along the shore to the sandbar where the day before they had caught a glimpse of sleeping crocodiles.

An insect buzzed over his head, and he brushed it away. He had stopped to examine an interesting agglomeration of mica embedded in the sand when he realized he was standing on the footprint of a jaguar. It was a fresh footprint.

He rose slowly and glanced to his right. There in the foliage, under the shade of a ceiba tree, was a large adult jaguar. He had once seen a tiger in the Frankfurt Zoo, but this was no zoo. When the jaguar turned its luminescent green eyes in his direction, he felt the blood drain from his face and his heart pound in his chest.

He forced himself to remember the advice the Indians had given him about an encounter like this: Don't run; don't show any fear. I must turn and then calmly, deliberately retrace my steps. Do nothing to startle the jaguar, or that might be the last thing I ever do.

Step by gingerly step, the *gringo* moved back toward camp. A monkey screamed overhead, startling him. "How often was I tempted to look back in order to assure myself that I was not pursued!" he remembered later.[3] Finally, after fifty yards or so, he did turn back. The jaguar was still there, motionless, but its attention was on a herd of capybaras crossing the river farther downstream. Its mind was on breakfast, and suddenly so was the *gringo*'s.

He arrived back at camp and breathlessly told his story to the natives and his assistant, a French doctor named Aimé Bonpland. The men laughed and shook their heads.

"Why do you do it, Señor Humboldt?" one of the natives later asked him. "How is it possible to believe that you have left your own country to come to this river to be devoured by mosquitoes, and measure lands you do not own?"[4]

Why? Alexander von Humboldt only smiled in reply. It was a question he had heard often during his days in Brazil. If he had wanted to formulate a short but complete answer, he would have said: I am here to read the Book of Nature.[5] I am here to see it in all its forms, colors, and powers; to hear it in the cries of the sapajous, the moans of the alouatta apes, the cries of the curassow, the parraka; to study it in the trees and plants and the myriad butterflies and mosquitoes: and yes, even in the eyes of the jaguar. I am here to trace that great underlying harmony that pulls all of God's creation, including its plants and animals and rivers and mountains and unseen magnetic currents and the distant stars and planets, into one single cosmos. For Alexander von Humboldt, the friend of Goethe and Schiller, feeling that overarching harmony was the very essence of the sublime.[6]

The next day, they reached their goal. The brackish waters of the Apure rounded a tree-lined bend and Humboldt found himself gazing across a vast expanse of water. Under a heavy leaden sky, wind stirred the distant trees. A strong current suddenly seized their boat as whitecap waves washed up to the gunwales of the *lancha*. The natives grabbed their paddles to help steady the boat. They were in the flow of the mighty Orinoco River.

Over the next several days, Humboldt would watch natives hunting monkeys with blowguns and would test the voltage of electric eels.[7] He would make a series of readings of the earth's electromagnetic field, which in the next decade would become the basis of a new scientific law.* He would also chart the exact geographic position where the Orinoco flowed into the headwaters of the Amazon River, thus forcing every map around the world to be changed.

When after three years in Latin America he finally returned to Europe in the summer of 1804, he wrote an account of his journeys called *Personal Narrative of a Journey to the Equinoctial Regions of the New Continent*. It would inspire a new generation of naturalists and botanists and zoologists, and one English teenager in particular. He was a medical student at the University of Edinburgh and the son of a wealthy doctor. His father had decided young Charles would make a better clergyman instead and had sent him to Cambridge. There, in his last year, he read Humboldt's book and became enchanted by its picture of rain forests and tropical sunsets and strange plants

---

*This was the law of decreasing magnetic intensity, a band that circles the globe roughly in the vicinity of the equator.

and beasts. "It stirred up in me a burning zeal," Charles Darwin remembered, "to add even the most humble contribution, to the noble structure of Natural Science."[8]

Darwin's contribution would be far from humble and would reach far beyond natural science. It would change forever the way we thought not only about the natural world, but about our own social universe—even the meaning of human life. Darwin took his original inspiration from Humboldt's dream of uncovering the hidden interrelations that bound all nature, both living and nonliving, into one constantly changing system. The German naturalist was "like another sun," Darwin would tell a friend in 1831, "who illumines everything I behold."[9] That spring he himself reached Brazil, on his own voyage with a small navy surveying vessel called HMS *Beagle*.

There Darwin realized that the light from Humboldt's work was only the reflection of another, more distant luminous influence. This had been a man walking on a sunlit beach on the isle of Lesbos many centuries before, who stooped to pick up a tiny mollusk and wondered what was inside.

The eighteenth century had seen an enormous flourishing of the physical sciences, especially physics and astronomy. Pierre-Simon Laplace and Leonhard Euler raised Newton's mechanics to a level of exquisite mathematical precision, like a finely made Swiss watch. Astronomers like Frederick William Herschel made almost daily discoveries with their new advanced telescopes, which both expanded and confirmed Newton's picture of the universe and his theory of universal gravitation.

The natural sciences, however, hung back. Zoology, botany, and "natural history" (what we call biology) was still stuck at the starting line of Aristotle's definition of science, that of classification. Their classifications according to species and genus had become very sophisticated, thanks to the great Swedish biologist Carl Linnaeus (1707–78). It's the basic system we still use. Thanks to hundreds of naturalists who collected biological specimens for zoos and botanical gardens and medical researchers, there was plenty of observation and description of the world's life forms, or what Linnaeus had dubbed "the system of nature." Still, no one had yet found a satisfactory structure for explaining how everything fit together—certainly nothing remotely close to what Newton had done for the physical sciences.

With the expansion of Europeans to every part of the globe, from Latin

America to the South Pacific, the sheer variety of plants and animals they found was astounding. Humboldt alone brought back no less than sixty thousand botanical specimens from his Latin American trip; more than one in ten were completely unknown to European researchers.[10] The new discoveries forced botanists and zoologists to toss out the old ways of thinking about their disciplines—including Descartes's mechanics and Aristotle's vital principles, which had somehow hung on into the 1600s—without offering a clue as to how to construct a sure new way.

The ongoing study of physiology and anatomy did yield a lot of useful information about function and organic structure, especially within related species. But there was nothing that helped to relate botany to zoology the way physics was now intimately related to astronomy; in fact, physiology was considered part of physics.[11] Certainly there was nothing that passed that ultimate test of an exact Newtonian science, the power of prediction. John Michell had predicted the existence of binary star systems three decades before Herschel found one with his telescope in 1796.[12] But who had ever been able to predict the existence of a new marine animal or mammal, let alone explain what caused them to come into existence?

In 1800, the life sciences seemed doomed to be a science of observation and description only. They offered no explanatory power and no possibility of arriving at precise laws to explain why embryos become one animal instead of another; or how vertebrates are related to invertebrates or horses to pigeons—let alone elephants to elephant grass. John Locke had even concluded it was impossible. The study of living nature, he decided, could never be raised to the level of genuine knowledge like Newton's *Principia*, because it offered no route to mathematical certainty.[13]

It had been Alexander von Humboldt's mission to change that mind-set. Before he died in 1859, Humboldt's great gift to his fellow naturalists was to tell them that what their work lacked in deductive Euclidean precision was more than made up for in buzzing, blooming real life. What they were observing and classifying weren't just birds or plants or mineral samples. They were students of empirical reality in all its vivid richness and diversity. Beneath this seemingly infinite variety lurked clues of a vast underlying interlocking system.

Why was Humboldt so confident the secret of the system could be cracked? Because man was part of that system of nature himself. He carried its laws not only in the makeup of his mind but in his heart and feelings.

Humboldt's Romanticism was expressed not through poetry or a paintbrush, but with a notebook, compass, and specimen jar. "A book on nature," he wrote, "should produce the impressions that she herself elicits . . . in a vivid language that will stimulate and elicit feelings," including a sense of the sublime.[14] Wordsworth had said, "When we dissect we murder." Humboldt replied: When we dissect we discover a living part of ourselves.

But where to start? Curiously enough, there was a clue on the very island where Humboldt did some of his most exacting research and where a statue to Humboldt still stands in its capital city. This was the island of Cuba, where three hundred years earlier a man in a drab brown friar's cowl had forced the West to confront the way it thought about human nature, reason, and the history of mankind.

Born around 1474, Fray Bartolomé de Las Casas had two lives. The first was as a Spanish planter on a freshly conquered Cuba, where he received a royal grant of land tenure (*encomienda*) in 1513. Las Casas proceeded to rule over his Indian serfs with a brutality that was not unusual in the early years of the Spanish conquest of the New World but was unusual for a man of the Church—in fact, a Dominican friar.

All that ended one Sunday in 1514, when a fellow Dominican priest refused to give Las Casas communion because of his sadistic treatment of his Indians. The refusal plunged Las Casas into a severe emotional crisis, after which he gave up his *encomienda* and began his second life: as the devoted protector of the Indians in Cuba, dedicated to altering their servile status under the Spanish Empire.

That empire had grown with astonishing speed. In 1519–21 Hernán Cortés and a handful of men had conquered the Aztecs, destroying their great cities and toppling their temples. Francisco Pizarro and an even smaller band of conquistadors did the same to the Incas, while Spanish settlers overran the islands of the Caribbean. Less than thirty years after the death of Columbus, Europeans had spread devastation and disease across the southern lands of the New World, reducing the native population to barely a fraction of its pre-conquest size: perhaps 1.5 million died in Mexico alone.[15] The Spanish Crown had introduced the *encomienda* system to keep the remainder working as virtual slaves, and to extract the wealth from lands that reached from the southern tip of South America to California and New Mexico.

The process of building this vast empire and extracting its wealth, however, had left a nagging doubt. By 1550, the Spanish were asking themselves a classic Platonic question: Our empire might be great, but is it *just*? Spain's canon lawyers framed the issue slightly differently. By what right did the king of Spain claim sovereign rule over a people and land more than three thousand miles away?

The issue was considered so grave and pressing that a church council was called to resolve it, at Valladolid in 1550. With King Charles V himself presiding, Spanish churchmen assembled to hear a debate on the moral and legal status of the New World's indigenous peoples. Arguing the Crown's case was Juan de Sepúlveda, brilliant canon lawyer, humanist, and "one of the best trained minds of his time."[16] Traveling across the Atlantic to argue the other side was Las Casas.

He was now seventy-five, but still sharp and vigorous. He was the acknowledged champion of the belief that native Americans not only were capable of being baptized and received into the Church (many clergymen argued otherwise), but had deserved the same rights as Spaniards—including the right to govern themselves without Spanish rule. He had forced an end to the *encomienda* system in 1542. Now he aimed to dissolve the Spanish Empire itself.

Sepúlveda rose to speak first. The centerpiece of his argument was drawn from Aristotle's assertion in Book I of the *Politics* that some peoples are slaves by nature because they lack the reason needed to live in society and thus require a master to supply it.* The Indians of the New World, Sepúlveda insisted, were such a people. Their heathen religion and customs such as human sacrifice, cannibalism, and incest (the Inca emperors married their sisters to perpetuate their royal lineage) marked them as barbarians whom God "has willed to lack reason" and therefore doomed to perpetual servility.

"How can we doubt," Sepúlveda said, "that these people, so uncivilized, so barbaric, so contaminated with so many sins and obscenities," are "as children to adults" and unfit to govern themselves? Therefore, conquest and rule by a civilized nation like Spain was not only just but actually for their own good: a classic argument for imperialism, then and later.[17]

---

*The interpretation of the crucial passage (in chapter 5, 1245a21–1245b32) is ambiguous. Some modern scholars like R. Schlaifer in *Theories of Slavery from Homer to Aristotle* insist that "Aristotle in no place clearly indicates how a true slave may be known from a free man." Sepúlveda (who had published a translation of the *Politics* in 1548) believed otherwise. For obvious reasons, many Spaniards were ready to accept the authority of Sepúlveda's Aristotle against any other reading.

Whatever is, must be right. Sepúlveda's arguments were an example of how Aristotle could be applied to justify a status quo, regardless of its obvious shortcomings. Las Casas, however, threw Aristotle right back at him, together with an appeal to natural law that he borrowed from the most famous member of his order: Saint Thomas Aquinas.[18]

Las Casas pointed out that far from being natural slaves, the natives before the conquest showed every one of the characteristics that Aristotle defined as the basis of the good life. They had lived in large cities; they had a regular system of government that conformed to the norms of natural law; they had an established language and religion and laws of marriage; they even (contrary to Sepúlveda's assertions) had a sense of private property. They also had a sophisticated grasp of mathematics—that classic measure of rationality—and astronomy, and had built monuments that were the equal of the Pyramids of Egypt.[19]

But then Las Casas went further. He knew he could not refute every instance of human sacrifice or cannibalism that had so shocked the Spanish conscience (compared with, say, burning people at the stake). So he showed that these actions *were rational in the cultural context in which they had taken place*. For example, since life is man's most valuable possession, the fact that the Indians practiced mass human sacrifice showed a veneration for the divine far beyond any felt by ancient Greeks and Romans.[20] Likewise, Spanish women could learn something, he suggested, from the devotion Aztec women showed to the education and welfare of their children, even though its content was very different. In their own time and place, then, the native Americans clearly met Aristotle's criteria of rational human beings capable of virtue. Therefore they deserved to be left alone to govern themselves—and certainly not to be treated as slaves.

The Valladolid council adjourned without reaching a final decision. Perhaps not surprising, Spanish rule went on as before. But Las Casas's arguments marked a turning point in the evolution of the Western mind.

It was a new way of seeing others who are culturally different: not as irrational or savage creatures deserving contempt or conquest, but as people like ourselves dealing with universal needs and desires in their own way. "All the peoples of the world are one," was Las Casas's final pronouncement, meaning they all share one nature. That nature rested on man's reason, the one characteristic that all human beings share regardless of where they live. Underneath the wide diversity of societies, from the most primitive to the most advanced, was a single common human nature addressing the same problems in the same way but with different results, because of differences in the physical and cultural environment.

"Thus mankind is one," Las Casas had told the king and his bishops, "and no one is born [superior and] enlightened." From this it follows, he explained, that "the law of nations and natural law apply to Christian and Gentile alike, and to all people of any sect, law, condition, or color without any distinction whatsoever."[21]

All mankind is one. It took a long time for this revolutionary argument, with its inheritance from Aristotle and Thomist doctrine, to gain firm purchase in the West. In the age of Atlantic empire and the Middle Passage, when shiploads of black Africans were being sent to the Americas, Europeans' instincts and self-interest ran very much the other way. Nonetheless, the nagging doubt that had triggered the Valladolid debate in the first place remained. By what right did one race of men enslave another race, Europeans continued to ask (if only in whispers), when they shared the same rational nature?

The ultimate answer was, none. Interestingly, the final, decisive piece to the puzzle was supplied by Rousseau. Everywhere men are born free, he had written, yet are everywhere in chains. That meant that *no one* was destined to wear chains, whether they were white Europeans or black Africans, the archetypal "noble savage." The same men who led the Reign of Terror abolished slavery in France. In England, opposition to the slave trade became one of the hallmarks of English Romanticism. Both Turner and Blake were sickened by it and used their artistic skill to portray its horrors. Writers like Shelley, Coleridge, and Wordsworth joined forces with Christian evangelist William Wilberforce to get it outlawed.

Alexander von Humboldt stood foursquare with them, for the same reasons. He wrote: "We maintain the unity of the human species [and] at the same time repel the depressing assumption of superior and inferior races of men. . . . All are in like degree designed for freedom."[22] Designed, that is, by Nature herself: a point that brought together all the different strands of thinking about cultural difference. Now it turned out our physical and moral makeup is only one aspect of a larger creative system.

Las Casas and the Thomists had pointed out that nature was the physical frame where over time man reveals his fundamental rationality. He does this first of all through his contemplation *of* nature, which leads him to infer the

existence of a divine Creator, or what the Enlightenment called "natural religion." He does it secondly through his actions *in* nature: his reshaping of his
physical environment to suit his own needs and desires, including his natural
desire to live with others: what the Enlightenment had dubbed "the progress
of civil society."

In the end, all these developments flow from the same source, man's reason as a work in progress. "All men are equally made in the image of God
with a mind and reason," as Cardinal Bellarmine had said; which was epitomized by that supreme act of reason conquering nature, the acquisition of
property. It also reflected the basic point Thomas Aquinas had extracted from
Aristotle some six centuries earlier. Man is above nature but *also part of it*: he
is subject to the same laws, both morally and physically. But do things work
the other way? If it is part of man's nature to change things for the better, then
perhaps it is true, at least to some degree, of Nature herself.

Probably the first person to seize this insight was Erasmus Darwin, born
in Derby in England in 1731. He took his first name from the sixteenth century's most famous humanist and gave his surname to the nineteenth century's most famous scientist. Unlike his future grandson, however, Erasmus
Darwin was a portly, boisterous extrovert. A doctor by training, he took almost
as much relish in man's achievements in science and technology—the indus-
trialist Matthew Boulton was one of his closest friends—as he despised organized Christianity and the institution of slavery. Dr. Erasmus Darwin saw
man's place in physical nature as something to be celebrated rather than
glossed over. The human life cycle from helpless childhood to rational man-
hood; the spread of cultivated fields, great cities, and productive machines
across the landscape: All reflected a dynamic system of improvement embedded in Nature herself, as well as society, which he dubbed *evolution*.

Evolution is a true Aristotelian concept, even if the term is not.[23] Aristotle
had argued that all change in nature was the prelude to completion, even
fulfillment. Aristotle, however, was thinking of the development of individuals *within* a species, like our old friend Rover the Lab retriever, whose growth
over time reflects the transformation of potentiality into actuality. Aristotle
spurned any notion that species themselves changed over time, any more
than did the planets in the heavens.

Erasmus Darwin was the first thinker to use the concept of evolution to
describe nature as a whole.[24] Everywhere he looked in 1700s England and
Europe, the good doctor saw a ceaseless, ever-expanding process of birth,

growth, and death in which every species—including man—expresses the potential for unlimited growth and improvement.

> *The heady prospect made him burst into poetry:*
> *Shout round the globe, how Reproduction strives*
> *With vanquish'd Death—and Happiness survives;*
> *How Life increasing peoples every clime,*
> *And young renascent Nature conquers Time.*[25]

But exactly how did this renascent Nature end up producing all this Happiness? What is the engine (as his friend Matthew Boulton might have said) that powered its growth and improvement? In the case of the progress of civil society, it was man's reason. Man's mind led him to constantly improve his physical environment, whether one is talking about the steam engine or the Parthenon—or the temples at Taxlala and Machu Picchu, Las Casas would add, and the Iroquois's wigwam and the Eskimo's igloo. Indeed, it was that same invincible reason that led men to see the processes of nature as a whole.[26]

So what is it that triggered Nature to do the same? That was the question Erasmus Darwin and his great French rival, Jean-Baptiste Lamarck, could not answer. They left it to Darwin's grandson to find it in the same place where Alexander von Humboldt had first plunged into the Book of Nature: in the lush jungles of South America.

"I was a born naturalist," Charles Darwin said later. If so, none of his family or teachers noticed it. They saw instead a rather dull and lazy boy. "I was considered by all my masters and by my father," he admitted in his *Autobiography*, "very ordinary, rather below the common standard in intellect." He did badly at Greek and Latin, the bread and butter of education in his day. Whatever he learned of Virgil or Homer "was forgotten in forty-eight hours." One day his despairing father said, "You care for nothing but shooting, dogs, and rat-catching, and you will be a disgrace to yourself and your family."[27]

What Charles Darwin really enjoyed were long walks alone or with friends, sometimes covering thirty miles in a single day. On the way, he collected odd bits of minerals and strange-looking bugs (his sister convinced him it was wrong to kill insects for the sake of collecting, so he gave it up) and became particularly absorbed in watching birds, making precise notes about their songs and plumage.

Although he earnestly studied chemistry—at school his nickname was "Gas"—and found Euclid's geometry a stimulating read, Darwin saw nothing in the science of his day to attract his passion. When his father sent him to medical school at Edinburgh, he found the subjects as uninspiring as the professors were dull. He read his grandfather's *Zoonomia*, which anticipates so much of Charles Darwin's later thinking, with admiration. But on a second reading, "I was much disappointed; the proportion of speculation being so large to the facts given."

It wasn't until he arrived at Cambridge, ostensibly to study theology, that Darwin found two books that would change the direction of his mind and the focus of his life. One was Humboldt's *Personal Narrative*. The other was a book by Herschel, wordily titled *Preliminary Discourse on the Study of Natural Philosophy*. It powerfully suggested that the natural sciences could still gain what everyone said they lacked most, namely a systematic basis for certainty.

Herschel was an astronomer and physicist. He was the son of an even more famous astronomer. Picking up his book, Darwin must have expected him to treat mathematical laws as the be-all and end-all of true science. But surprisingly enough, Herschel didn't. The face that appeared on the book's title page was not that of Newton but that of Sir Francis Bacon; and the entire book was about the power of observation and practical experiment to generate a provisional explanation, or *hypothesis*, which, once we add more observations to either confirm or deny our hypothesis, gradually solidifies into a general law. That law, Herschel admitted, might not be mathematically precise—or at least not at first. But once it's tested by time and dint of example, it can be enough to explain what's going on.

The key was finding a provisional link between cause and effect. "I gave both the dog and the cat some vitamin D," the experimental scientist says to himself, "and both their skin rashes went away." This discovery leads him to make a hypothesis: Whenever an animal with a skin rash is given this amount of vitamin D, it will be cured. He will be able to reexamine old cases—"I saw a dog the other day eat some broccoli and its skin rash disappeared, so broccoli must contain vitamin D"—and open the way to considering new ones. When he gives vitamin D to his spouse and her skin rash actually gets worse, he doesn't throw up his hands in despair. He wonders why vitamin D works for animals but not for humans and launches his research on a new line of investigation.

Reasoning in science, like reasoning in real life, is a process. It is, as Herschel showed, an *inductive* process. His book had a big impact on John Stuart Mill, who recast his system of logic to accommodate Herschel's inductive, observational theory of science. It also had an impact on Darwin the would-be naturalist. Herschel made him realize that Humboldt's travels in South America that had fired his imagination so much were about more than breathtaking vistas, exotic animals, and romantic tropical sunsets. Herschel had shown how a system of classification like Humboldt's natural history could be turned into a framework for grasping the causal laws of nature that governed its operations.

Another scientist, William Whewell, offered an additional perspective. Induction, the patient gathering of data and the teasing out of causal factors, was clearly important to scientific research. However, the big breakthroughs, Whewell argued, required the more powerful force of the imagination. It was these inspired intuitive leaps, akin to those of a great painter or writer, that allowed "a genius of a Discoverer" like Galileo or Newton to suddenly sort our ordinary perceptions of things into an extraordinary and meaningful pattern—including our perception of living nature.[28]

It's not clear whether Charles Darwin dared to think of himself in those terms, as a biological Michelangelo. But when he set sail in HMS *Beagle* on December 27, 1831, all these elements—the idea of the scientist as imaginative genius, Aristotle's view of nature as change and process, and Humboldt's Romantic vision of biological nature and humanity as one—were about to come together in a great shattering climax.

The trip itself was *anti*climax. It turned out that Charles Darwin, who had not been to sea before, suffered from torments of seasickness. "I loathe, I abhor the sea and all ships which sail in it," he wrote to his sister, "I hate every wave of the ocean." The *Beagle*'s captain was all too happy to leave his miserable passenger on land for three or even six weeks at a time, while the *Beagle* completed her work of drawing up hydrographic charts on the South American coast. Darwin would spend almost four-fifths of the five-year voyage on land, gathering specimens, walking, watching, and thinking.[29]

That suited Darwin. Humboldt's vivid descriptive prose had not prepared him for the lush scenery of green-carpeted mountains and volcanoes and hundreds of insects and birds of species he had never known before. It was like "giving a blind man eyes," he wrote in his journal. "He is overwhelmed with what he sees and cannot justly comprehend it. Such are my feelings and such may they remain."[30] Darwin watched the flights of strange butterflies, examined volcanic outcroppings, and dislodged fossils from sedimentary rock. He met the natives of Tierra del Fuego, who had never seen white men and whose fierce appearance and bizarre folkways put his belief in the unity of mankind to a severe test.[31]

He saw the same giant sea turtles Humboldt had seen on the islands of the Galápagos (turtles so large, he noted, that a team of six men could barely lift them), and the strange lizards, each more than two or three feet long, which dotted the black lava rocks like "imps of darkness." He also estimated there were at least twenty-eight species of land birds, almost all previously un-known, that lived in the Galápagos and nowhere else on the planet—a point that would figure prominently later in his theory of evolution.[32]

At the time, however, it was the geology of the places he visited that inter-ested him most. He noted the long, slow transformations of the landscape due to volcanic activity and sedimentation, and shifts in the earth's surface, all of which confirmed geologist Charles Lyell's theory that the history of the earth was one of constant change and gradual upheaval. Darwin thought about devoting his time to writing a book on geology when he returned to England in 1836. A book on biology was far from his mind—certainly not a pathbreaking work like *Origin of Species*.[33] However, what he had seen of birds and butterflies, tortoises and fossils, did puzzle him enough to start him leafing through his notebooks as he prepared the natural history volume for the official account of the *Beagle*'s voyage. Darwin began by asking himself the classic Platonic question that every great thinker asks: *Why?*

"Why is life short?" He wrote. "Why does [the] individual die?" Then he asked himself: Why do so few of so many individuals of animals or plants survive, yet just enough to perpetuate their species? Why do offspring re-semble their parents, yet with enough differences to be distinct? Most cru-cially, why are some species so different from others, like tortoises and finches, yet so similar to still others? And finally, why do some species perpetuate themselves while others die off? "If [the] individual cannot propagate he has no issue—so with species."[34] How did nature make that ultimate selection?

Then very suddenly, in the spring or early summer of 1837, Darwin had the answer. His comments on the data in his notebooks show a new confidence and a sense of direction. He realized it meant chucking the idea that life on earth began at an act of deliberate creation such as the one described in the Bible—or in Plato's *Timaeus*. If that had been so, then men would not have been born with nipples (a puzzle that particularly fascinated Darwin). Unlike those of women, male nipples serve no possible purpose foreseen in the mind of a Creator. Instead, they must be a trace of a *prior* state when they were of use, Darwin decided, which had since disappeared from the human species. "So with useless wings under elytra of beetles. Born from beetles with wings, and modified": modified not by a Creator, but by the passing of generations, which bring with them a constant, inexorable process of change.[35]

What Darwin had discovered was a way of seeing nature as an endless chain of mutability of species, reaching back through time to the very origins of life. On one side, Darwin's theory was a leap into an unknown future; on the other, it was also a sharp glance backward. It revealed that Aristotle's notion of a "scale of nature," a continuous ladder made up of living things leading from the lowest to the highest order, was not so wrong after all—nor was Darwin's grandfather's picture of propagation as a process of self-renewing improvement and perfection.[36]

The problem with Aristotle, whom Darwin described as "one of the greatest, if not the greatest, observers who ever lived," was that he had assumed that the species that made up this scale of nature, from the lowest plants to man himself, were fixed because the changes within species come so imperceptibly slowly, just like the geology of the earth.[37] In fact, as fossils showed, species change all the time in the sense that some die off while others carry on. Even among those that carry on, individuals vary—a variation they are poised to pass to their offspring.

Each individual man or dog or mosquito, then, has the potential to alter the species or, *given enough time to perpetuate enough variations*, launch a new species itself. In short, the scale of nature is actually geared away from fixity of species, as Aristotle had wrongly assumed, and toward ceaseless variation. And what was true for one species, Darwin decided, must be true for entire classes of mammals and vertebrates and the entire range of living animals.

As he pored over his notes and other examples from other naturalists, Darwin saw the same history being replayed again and again. Enough of one species survive to propagate the species, while others of another do not—while still others manage to branch off to generate entirely new species. Very suddenly, the phenomenon of shared characteristics also made sense: as the trace of a common ancestor, some of whose offspring lived to carry forward the variations (like men with nipples and bugs with wings) while the rest faded away.

Thus the similarities between lizards and crocodiles; jaguars and tigers; men and the higher primates—between mammals of every description. Indeed, all life, he wrote in his notebook, "animals, our fellow brethren in pain, disease, death, suffering, and famine—our slaves in the most laborious works, our companions in our amusements—they may partake our origin in one common ancestor—we may be all melted together." The reason all mankind is one, in short, is that all *nature* is one.[38] Darwin had answered the *why* of evolution—at least in his own mind. The *how* came to him a year later in 1838, when he was reading a book by clergyman, amateur scientist, and economist Thomas Malthus titled *An Essay on the Principle of Population*, for "amusement," Darwin said—meaning not as part of his own research. Malthus had written on the higher mathematics of the progress of civil society, or what Malthus feared might be its inevitable *lack* of progress. His twin starting points were that man's ability to reproduce himself expands at a geometric rate, while his ability to feed himself from cultivatable land can grow at only an arithmetical rate. At some point those two lines must intersect, at the expense of everyone's need to eat.

Suppose my wife and I own a farm, Malthus was saying. Our children have their children, who in turn have theirs. We all set to work to bring more land under cultivation to feed an ever-growing number of mouths. The more they eat, the longer our children and grandchildren live, the more they prosper, and the more they multiply. Eventually, their numbers grow so fast that no matter how much land we put under the plow, there's never enough to feed everyone. Starvation sets in; the new offspring die, as do the old; the fields fall fallow. Prosperity is at an end.

Erasmus Darwin and his fellow optimists were wrong, Malthus argued. The power of propagating the species is the enemy, not the friend, of progress. Civil society will be doomed unless it finds decent ways to restrain our natural tendency to have more and more children. Otherwise, Malthus warned, we are doomed to a constant "struggle for existence" that will pit rich against poor, haves against have-nots, in ruthless competition for ever scarcer resources. If history is class struggle, Malthus suggested, it is because biology by the numbers makes it so.[39]

The title of *An Essay on the Principle of Population* referred to human populations. But it occurred to Darwin that its strictures might also apply to other kinds of populations. Malthus believed men multiplied faster than food. If that were also true of animals or even plants, then they too must compete to survive. "It at once struck me," Darwin remembered, "that under these circumstances favorable variations would tend to be preserved, and unfavorable ones to be destroyed."

"Tend" was the key word. Not every weak link dies out, nor do all those favorably fitted to circumstance flourish. However, enough do to form a new species—and to launch nature's tendency to endless variation in a new direction. "Here then I had at last got a theory by which to work," Darwin wrote in his *Autobiography*.[40] He finally had his *how*, which he called *natural selection*.* His disciple Herbert Spencer coined a more portentous phrase for it, *survival of the fittest*, although survival of the adaptable would have been more accurate. Those who can adapt to the current environment, whether we're talking turtles or wheatgrass or people, live to propagate and continue the species. Those who can't, won't.

Natural selection became one of the most contentious parts of Darwin's theory of evolution, in part because of its source.[41] However, Darwin's unexpected move was not in relying on Malthus's law of population; it was in turning it from a barrier to progress into progress's driving engine. Natural selection at long last solved the problem of what was the underlying structure of all natural history—indeed of life. For Darwin, the process *is* the structure. He had turned nature's most obvious characteristic, its propensity for change, into its greatest virtue.

That was still not the most controversial part of Darwin's theory of evolution, and he knew it. It took him four years to write any of it down. In 1842, he wrote a draft of thirty-five pages in pencil; in 1844, he expanded it to two hundred. He showed it to no one. He set aside some money and some instructions for his wife on publishing it if he died (he was only thirty-five). It was not until 1858—when his friends Charles Lyell and Joseph Dalton

---

*The word *evolution*, by the way, never appears in any of his notebooks or preliminary sketches for *Origin of Species* or in its first printed edition.

Hooker arranged for a paper by Darwin to be read to the Linnean Society in London at the same session as a paper by Alfred Russel Wallace, who proposed almost the exact same theory of evolution—drawn from a similar trip to South America and from the same sources, including Malthus—that Darwin's hand was finally forced.[42] A year later, he published *On the Origin of Species*. The debate and controversy have not died down since.

What made Darwin so reluctant to reveal his theory in public, and why did it win almost as many opponents, both in and outside the life sciences, as it did adherents? Certainly Darwin, who was a religious agnostic, knew it spelled the doom of the age-old creation story of the Book of Genesis. In fact, to this day the conflict over evolution is defined as a clash between Darwinists and so-called Creationists. Yet the history of geology has exposed the intellectual inadequacies of the seven-day creation story far more decisively than evolution has, and before Darwin arrived on the scene. His own theory depended on it. Yet it is Darwin, not Charles Lyell, who is the recurrent object of wrath and loathing.

Is it because Darwin proposed that human beings were descended from higher primates? That claim, which Darwin developed in *The Descent of Man* in 1871, certainly raised plenty of ire at the time and since—and not just among dyed-in-the-cloth evangelicals. The entire foundation of Romantic liberalism, not to mention the Thomist position of Las Casas and others, was that man is part of nature but also *above* nature, because of the spiritual essence of his soul.

No such immanent divine spark survives Darwin's evolutionary logic. In fact, Darwin made a joke of it back in 1838 in his notebook: "If all men were dead, then monkeys make men, men make angels." Man thinks himself a great work, he wrote, worthy of being created by a deity. "More humble and I believe true to consider him created from animals."[43]

This was a position more extreme than anything eighteenth-century Deists like Voltaire or Thomas Jefferson might have assumed. It also gets us closer to the truth about the opposition to Darwin: not because of what evolution says about *men*, but because of what it says about God. The traditional Western notion of God as Supreme Creator rested not only on Genesis but on Plato's *Timaeus*, implying that the cosmos is a deliberate copy of divine perfection. This is especially true of man, who, as Christianity had argued from its start, had been made in God's image—with all the force that Plato's theory of Forms could give that statement.

Now Darwin was implying that we are not the copy of anything perfect or divine. We are just one more set of beasts roaming the planet equipped with our natural reason as our only distinguishing mark. This didn't just topple the foundation of Christian moral teaching and metaphysics; it meant that one entire half of the traditional Western worldview, the Platonist half, had to come crashing down from heaven to earth.

Darwin knew what he had done by overthrowing the notion that Nature's God creates according to a model of foreordained perfection. "But how much more simple and sublime [a] power," he wrote in his notebook, "let attraction act according to certain law, such are inevitable consequences— let animals be created, then by the fixed laws of generation, such will be their successors." Darwin's God (assuming he had one) may not look like Plato's or Saint Paul's very much, but it does bear a family resemblance to Aristotle's.[44]

Aristotle had been as obsessed with perfection as his great teacher—witness his views on astronomy. But he was also willing to shrug and say: Look, if it exists, there must be a reason. In Aristotle's mind, viewing the world as a copy of anything—even the mind of God—gets us nowhere. It is arguable whether Aristotle even had a conception of a God, but he did have a Prime Mover without whom nothing else moves.

Aristotle also said that if something exists, then it *must* change, including the cosmos itself. Only the Prime Mover does not. Only He is unmoved, eternal, and perfect. The rest of reality is bound to the laws of nature: doomed, in other words, to various states of *im*perfection. That's what makes it reality. And if evolutionary change is the rule for the rest of the cosmos, then why not for man himself?

Aristotle's God is not a caring god. His nature is pure actuality (*energeia*) and excludes all possibility of Him worrying about the creatures of the cosmos, let alone desiring any outcome. However, without Him the potential dynamism of matter would remain untapped. Wrapped in eternal self-contemplation, He summons up by His mere presence the latent powers of nature. God does not go out to the world, but the world cannot help reaching out to Him.[45]

Even though Darwin pulled down the Judeo-Christian Neoplatonist framework of nature—not just Genesis but the *Timaeus*—we are still left with some firm metaphysical ground. A new way of understanding the universe appears. It is one closer to Aristotle's, of a constantly changing but rational order embedded in eternity without beginning or end on any meaningful scale we can recognize, but of which we have no choice except to be part.

There may be no Genesis or redemption. But when we examine the 1-billion-year remnant of rock shale or a 1.2-million-year-old Neanderthal skull, when we watch a butterfly emerge from its chrysalis or witness a supernova, we can say with Aristotle, "That is God thinking."

Twenty-six

UNSEEN WORLDS: PHYSICS, RELATIVITY, AND THE NEW WORLD PICTURE

The true Logic of this world is the Calculus of Probabilities. This branch of Math., which is generally thought to favour gambling, dicing, and wagering, and therefore [to be] highly immoral, is the only "Mathematics for Practical Men."

—James Clerk Maxwell, c. 1859

Such an interpretation of the properties of matter appeared as a realization, even surpassing the dreams of the Pythagoreans, of the ancient ideal of reducing the formulation of the laws of nature to considerations of pure numbers.

—Niels Bohr, Nobel Prize speech, 1921

After completing his manuscript of *Das Kapital,* Karl Marx could lay down his pen with no inkling that his universe was about to collapse.

Not his political and social universe: that was precisely what he was hoping and planning for. The wave of upheaval, crisis, revolution, and war that engulfed Europe in the century after 1867 would have been his element. Even the two world wars coming in the next century would only have fed Marx's appetite for apocalyptic destruction.

Instead, it was his *physical* universe that would was about to be overturned. It started with his own desk.

As Marx rubbed his fingers along its surface, he would have felt its rough

wooden grain and its hard solidity—like the solidity of the other dark mahogany Victorian furniture scattered around the room. Rising to his feet, he
would have heard the floorboards creak beneath him. He would have glanced
at the pictures on the wall and the books on the shelf, and smelled the boiled
potatoes as his wife made supper in the kitchen.

Outside Marx could see people passing by, and carts and horses. In the
distance would come the sound of a train driving along its iron tracks with
powerful clockwork precision—driven by the same physical laws that powered the factories and foundries of Europe, that governed the growth and
movement of the birds and animals and plants Darwin had described (Marx
was a keen admirer of Darwin, whose laws of natural selection had a strong
impact on his own thinking), and that brought out the moon and stars overhead when darkness fell.

Or so it seemed.

Every day everything Marx saw confirmed what he, and virtually everyone
in mid-Victorian Europe, believed: that they lived in a solidly material world,
securely made up of things and persons and events known through the experience of our senses. He had even called his theory of history dialectical *materialism*, on the grounds that it was matter that mattered, and physical
matter—not ideas or spiritual or unseen entities—that was the only touchstone of reality and truth.

This was Newton's world as well. His mathematical laws of motion and
gravity, which defined all physical cause and effect, were themselves defined
by the immutable absolute dimensions of space and time. Matter, Newton
wrote, was "solid, massy, hard, impenetrable . . . no ordinary power being
able to divide what God Himself made one in the first creation."[1]

For the next two hundred years, even religious thinkers and theologians
came to accept those material laws as the final fruit of science, and the final
ground rules of all common sense. David Hume and Immanuel Kant doubted
we could ever really get to know that material reality, what Kant called the
thing-in-itself, directly. They were resigned to the fact that it could only be
known through perception, what others would call sense data. But no one
since Bishop Berkeley doubted that this material reality was actually there.
And no one since Newton, not even Marx, ever doubted that it was governed
by the laws set forth in his *Principia*.

Yet in 1867, Scottish physicist James Clerk Maxwell was completing a series of computations that would start the process of throwing this entire New-

tonian universe and its most basic assumptions, including the nature of matter, into upheaval. Everything defined as "the real world" since Aristotle was about to be rocked on its foundations—with Plato and especially Pythagoras looking more right than wrong.

Maxwell grew up near Dumfries, in southwestern Scotland, in a family of down-at-heels but well-to-do eccentrics. It was said his grandfather once saved himself from drowning in India by floating down river on his bagpipes, then chased away marauding tigers at night by playing away at the pipes until he was rescued.[2] His grandson loved puns and puzzles as well as geometry and mechanics; and after graduating from Cambridge in 1854 and teaching for a time at the University of Aberdeen, he withdrew to his family's run-down estate to take on one of the major scientific puzzles of the age; whether light was a wave or a particle.

Ever since Newton's study of optics disclosed the existence of the spectrum, speculation on the question had raged. Maxwell's research led him to conclude finally that it was a wave, and from there he went on to tackle two other phenomena that had fascinated the eighteenth century: electricity and magnetism. Maxwell was the first to demonstrate that both in fact formed a single field and obeyed the same laws, which he set forth in four simple but epoch-making mathematical equations. Using those equations, he was even able to compute the actual speed of light at 186,000 miles per second—that is, fast enough to circle the earth seven times in a single stroke.[3]

All this would have been enough to win him scientific immortality, but Maxwell pushed further. He began arguing that light itself was an electromagnetic wave and that its visible spectrum, from red to violet, was only a small portion of a much bigger field of *invisible* electromagnetic radiations. These ranged from very long ones, which came to be called radio waves (the existence of which Heinrich Hertz confirmed twenty years later, in 1888), and very short ones, namely X-rays (later discovered by another German, Wilhelm Röntgen, in 1895).[4]

In short, here was an entire range of scientific phenomena invisible to the senses but obeying exact mathematical laws. Indeed, Maxwell's theory of electrodynamics was not unlike Newton's theory of gravity, but with a crucial difference. These laws existed not as equations on a chalkboard but as statistics in a table. Maxwell showed this when he took his theory to the study of gases and heat, and a theory propounded by Rudolf Clausius that heat was actually the result of kinetic motion of tiny bodies or atoms inside those gases. Maxwell postulated that the laws governing their motion could only be uncovered using statistical probability. Here he was thinking about the famed Gaussian bell curve, named after mathematician Carl Friedrich Gauss (1777–1855), which showed how serial observations or measurements—like the heights of a cluster of trees and speeds of a street full of cars—tend to bunch up around a standard distribution, with a few being very tall (or very fast) and a few very short (or very slow), and the rest grouped somewhere around the middle.

It was an astonishing idea. Since Aristotle had first stated that "the *fact* is the starting point" of all knowledge, it had been assumed that exactitude was the sine qua non of all scientific truth. We want to know how *this* planet or comet travels through space, and exactly at what speed; we want to know at exactly what temperature *this* bar of iron reaches its melting point, and under what specific conditions. The whole advantage of applying mathematics to the study of chemistry or astronomy is that it enhanced that sense of exactitude—even put the final seal on it.

On the other hand, with his belief that statistics was "the mathematics of practical men," Maxwell would have relished the example of horse racing.[5] Of course, no one can say whether a particular horse will actually win a particular race on a particular day, even given the competing field. But someone knowledgeable about horses, and the field, can give you odds on your horse's chances based on its probability of coming in win, place, or show.

Still, that's gambling, not science. But suppose you are running a thousand horses, all the same age and from the same bloodline and all raised on the same farm and fed the same diet—and that you have the same information about every horse in the field and its thousand siblings. You run them all in a series of races and plot the results on Gauss's curve. Then it's possible to learn a lot, not just about which bloodlines are likely to win and which to lose, but also about horses in general and how to raise a winner—as well as about the nature of the horse race itself. In fact, it may be possible to project the winning order of an entire field without mentioning a single particular horse—and without running a race at all.

Maxwell was proposing to use statistical models to study phenomena, like atoms in a gas, where it wasn't empirically possible to get an exact count; they pose the same problem as when we shake a box full of marbles and try to observe each marble's speed and direction. Likewise, it could come in handy in studying things that won't give us any useful sensory information, like the unseen world of the electromagnetic spectrum—or later, the atom.

Maxwell used it in 1857 first to analyze the rings of Saturn. Although he couldn't describe the motion or behavior of every particle that made up the rings, he could set up a description using his statistical model, showing that certain sizes of particles would end up in the different classes of orbits, and what their probable speeds might be.[6] When he moved on to gases, the results were even more amazing. But when it came to studying light waves, Maxwell found that he had struck a conceptual reef. The question was, what do the waves move through? Without a fixed frame of reference for computing speed and distance, Maxwell's theory looked incomplete. Some proposed "ether," an "elastic solid" that provided the medium through which light could travel the way a lake provides the medium for waves from a speedboat or a dropped pebble. Surely if light moves, they argued, it must move through *something*. Once again, the materialist faith that all things must occupy some physical space—even light—remained unshakable.[7]

So Maxwell's breakthrough in the study and nature of light went nowhere for almost thirty years. Meanwhile, his insights into the explanatory power of statistics were about to be turned into an epoch-making theory about the very nature of matter, by an intense, rather alarming young man with a thick black beard named Ludwig Boltzmann.

If Maxwell was the Da Vinci of nineteenth-century physics—introspective, insatiably curious, playful to the point of whimsy, and relishing the role of mysterious polymath—Boltzmann was its Michelangelo. Born the son of an Austrian civil servant in 1844, he was intense, physically imposing, moody, and explosive. His family had no intellectual pretensions; he showed no great aptitude for intellectual subjects, let alone physics or mathematics, until he met Josef Stefan at the University of Vienna in the early 1860s. Stefan was a physicist, and a good one: he was up for the directorship of the Institute of Physics previously held by Christian Doppler, discoverer of the Doppler effect. In 1866, Stefan beat out his competitor, another brilliant Austrian, the twenty-four-year-old Ernst Mach.

Stefan took an immediate liking to the clever but awkward Boltzmann. He gave him articles by Maxwell and an English grammar and dictionary to help him read them; Stefan was one of the few scientists in central Europe

who understood how revolutionary Maxwell's theory of an invisible electromagnetic field really was. But above all, Stefan was a believer in the theory of
the atom, and he passed belief in its existence on to his young disciple with
the passion of an act of conversion.

The idea of atoms, and their free motion in space, went back before Plato
and Aristotle, of course, to the Eleatic philosophers Democritus and Leucippus, and then forward to their Roman admirer Lucretius (c.100–c. 55 BCE).
For almost two thousand years, the idea that reality might be made of innumerable tiny unseen bodies that combined and recombined to form physical
objects had seemed ludicrous, especially given the huge prestige of Aristotle's
own physics. Atomism also carried the taint of atheism, since it seemed to
deny the existence of spiritual substances, including the soul—although
Newton found himself occasionally drawn to the theory. Still, for centuries
atomism seemed the last extremity of godless materialism—a strange irony,
given its later fate.[8]

Then in the mid-nineteenth century, it experienced a sudden resurgence,
when the idea of the atom proved useful for isolating and studying the behavior of gases under different conditions and at different temperatures. Rudolf
Clausius, for one, realized that heat is the result of motion, and that what is
in motion could best be explained as tiny, as-yet-unseen molecules or atoms.
Still, for believers like Stefan and his friend Josef Loschmidt, atoms remained
an unproven hypothesis, nothing more.

Maxwell's theory of the electromagnetic field, however, gave them new
hope. Atoms were invisible—but so was Maxwell's electromagnetism. Maxwell's electromagnetism explained certain phenomena by simplifying the
mathematics; so did atomic theory. But it was thirty-year-old Boltzmann who
saw that Maxwell's work on statistical probability opened a whole new horizon for understanding the nature of the atom—and with it perhaps the fate of
civilization itself. "Was it a God who wrote these signs?" he once exclaimed,
while teaching Maxwell's theories to his students, and meant it.[9]

What Boltzmann did was connect Maxwell's electromagnetism and Clausius's atom directly to the hottest new issue in nineteenth-century physics,
thermodynamics. In 1850, Clausius had discovered its second and latest law:
For all the available energy in a system—the crankshaft of a moving train, the
steam in a boiler, water flowing down a mill race or over a dam, a comet
sweeping across the sky—some energy is lost and becomes unavailable. Over
time, Clausius argued, the unavailable energy will tend to increase, as avail-

able energy gets lost—as when a spinning propeller gradually slows down or (on the issue of heat transfer) when very cold milk is poured into a very hot drink, and both tend to approach room temperature and become tepid.

Clausius dubbed this unavailable lost energy *entropy*: and his famous second law stated that entropy is always increasing. To some, the idea was shocking. It suggested that all systems eventually run down, including (inevitably) the universe. To more lively imaginations in the later nineteenth century, the law of entropy seemed a signal of eventual doom—not only for the physical world but for civilization itself.*[10]

Boltzmann, however, was able to give the law of entropy a more hopeful thrust, thanks to the laws of probability and the properties of the atom. Clausius and his colleagues were still thinking of heat as a fluid, a material that transferred from one place to another like water in a bath—which through entropy goes down the drain and is lost forever. But if heat was actually the random motion of atoms within a given system, then entropy was simply a measure of atoms reaching a disordered state after a more ordered one.[11]

Imagine a deck of cards, arranged by suit and rank down to the last card— a highly ordered state. We shuffle the deck and find that some cards are now out of order, but others are still in their original sequence. We shuffle a second, even a third time: the number of hearts or diamonds still in sequence steadily diminishes. Finally we have a deck in which the distribution almost seems random: the final stage of entropy.[12]

But Boltzmann pointed out that nothing says the process of shuffling the deck *has* to result in growing disorder. It is possible, but not probable, that hundreds or even thousands of reshufflings might restore the original sequence. In short, over time entropy tends to grow—but it is not inevitable. Disorderly states are more probable than orderly ones: but not every orderly state will necessarily run down and dissolve into chaos. Ordered systems will take shape, and retain their shape, in certain places—in the solar system, in the human body, even in society—even as disorder takes over in others, by a formula Boltzmann drew up:

$$S = K \log W$$

S, entropy, is proportional to the logarithm of W, the probability of a given state.[13]

---

*One such was American historian Henry Adams. A picture of inevitable entropy and decline pervades his autobiography, *The Education of Henry Adams* (1907).

But Boltzmann's theory was also saying something else, almost equally profound: the probability of any state increases as its energy decreases. Low-energy states are therefore more probable—while usable energy (like our train crankshaft, or water flowing over a dam) is energy in disequilibrium—and that includes electricity. Boltzmann's statistical mechanics had suddenly opened the door to a new understanding of how electricity acts and flows from positive to negative—i.e., from high-energy states to low-energy ones—and how atoms directly affect the unseen properties of matter, from electrical conductivity to the vicosity of fluids.

A whole new world was opening up, not only for physics but for chemistry, as well—even perhaps biology—that is, if atoms exist.[14]

Others had their severe doubts. One was Boltzmann's fellow countryman, Ernst Mach, his former mentor's rival and now holder of a prestigious chair of experimental physics at the University of Prague.* Mach's entire approach to science was that the only legitimate starting point for the investigation of nature had to be the classic one defined by the eighteenth-century empiricists: sense perception. "The aim of science," Mach wrote, "is to obtain connections among phenomena" within that field of experience—and then describe them in the shortest and most economical way possible as scientific laws.[15]

Boltzmann's theorem flunked on both counts. No one had ever seen an atom. The theory of entropy worked just fine without them—and without Boltzmann's elaborate statistical mechanics. Portraying heat as atomic motion seemed equally absurd; but nothing offended Mach and his empirically minded colleague Henri Poincaré at the University of Paris than Boltzmann's introducing entities (i.e., atoms) whose existence could not be independently judged, solely on the grounds that they made the calculations clearer and more elegant.

Where was the clear picture of reality? Mach wanted to know. Where were the facts? Stick to the verifiable facts, he told Boltzmann and everyone else, and leave these speculations to the metaphysicians. It's a line John Locke himself might have taken—and one rooted in the firm confident faith in Newton's universe.

---

*Mach's most lasting contribution to physics was revealing what happens when a bullet or shell approaches the sound barrier and pushes a compression of air in front of it. Mach had taken photographs of the shadows of these invisible shock waves. His formula for measuring the speed of sound still carries his name—which is why we still talk about a jet plane traveling at Mach 1 or Mach 2.

Boltzmann was devastated. With prestigious intellectual gatekeepers like Mach (who moved on to the University of Vienna in 1895) and Poincaré standing in his way, his theory of a vast and important unseen world of atoms determining the basic processes of nature, remained just a theory and an unproven one.

At Vienna, meanwhile, Mach's reputation as a philosopher of science would only grow. He drew to his classes and seminars three distinguished figures: the economist Otto Neurath, physicist Philipp Frank, and mathematician Hans Hahn—the core of what would become the famed Vienna Circle. They were delighted with Mach's way of describing scientific laws as pictorial summaries of experimental facts or events, which we put together in order to make complex sense data comprehensible in terms of ordinary experience.

Neurath, Frank, and Hahn were joined by other intellectual luminaries like Moritz Schlick and Rudolf Carnap to found an informal school of philosophy of science called Logical Positivism or Logical Empiricism. It would be the dominant school for scientists, thinkers, and mathematicians in eastern Europe for nearly half a century. Besides Vienna and Graz, its strongholds included Prague, Cracow, Budapest, and Lemberg (Lvov in Ukraine), with outposts as far away as Oxford, Chicago, and the University of Uppsala. At their first international meeting in Prague, they proudly drew up a list of their heroes from philosophy's past.

It was an impressive list. Auguste Comte, John Stuart Mill, David Hume, and the philosophers of the Enlightenment were joined by Epicurus, Jeremy Bentham, the physicist Albert Einstein, and the master of the logic of mathematics Bertrand Russell, as well as Mach and Poincaré. But one figure clearly held pride of place in their intellectual pantheon, namely Aristotle.[16]

And no wonder. Aristotle was the founder not only of the logic to which they looked for their framework of truth, but also of the idea of science as a unified system based on human experience. Their ultimate goal, as one of them later put it, was to free the European mind from fuzzy metaphysics and dogma and to return "in some measure to the classical goal of philosophy as defined by Aristotle," which was a way both of understanding nature and of living in the world.[17]

In this, their chief foe was not the Catholic Church (many, like Mach, were raised and educated as Catholics) or Boltzmann—in the early days, they hardly gave him a thought. Rather, it was Georg Friedrich Hegel. In Hegel's view, the laws of science were just one part of the unfolding of the great chain of dialectic, which would eventually integrate everything under the sun, from physics and biology and the output of industry to the meaning of the individual and the family and the State—into the ultimate objective reality of the Absolute.

But underlying the Hegelian formulation of science, of course, was the great unspoken presence of Plato and his metaphysics.* For Hegel, the world of sense data—what he loftily dubbed subjectivity—is simply Plato's original realm of the cave and the source of all unclear thinking. It confuses what is concrete (this is *my* bicycle, *my* spouse, *my* plans and dreams for the future) with what is real. Objectivity, the basis of all certain knowledge, can arise only when the individual disappears from view. This is true whether one is talking about the laws of physics and statistics, or about the laws of social and political progress. By thinking big and objectively, the Hegelian realizes how small and insignificant he—or at least most other people—must be.

The metaphysical dogmas of Hegel were a dominant influence in the universities of the new German Empire, especially the University of Berlin, but they offended Mach and the Logical Empiricists. They wanted to lay out a more flexible, empirically based approach to science. Science should deal with perceptible individual facts and events, they argued, and nothing else. Our mind's job is to match our words and mental images to those facts and nothing else.

In short, Mach's answer to Hegel was like Sergeant Friday's: "The facts, ma'am, just the facts." One of his disciples later put it almost the same way: "Something is real if it is a part of the system of symbols that denotes the world of facts."[18] All the rest, the whole weighty fabric of metaphysics from Plato to Hegel, needed to be shoved aside so that men could think clearly and accurately—and finally be free.

The Logical Positivists' goal, to free the European mind from the yoke of Hegel, might have been admirable. But in the process, their principal victim was Boltzmann.

Henri Poincaré wrote a devastating attack on his kinetic theory of atoms, arguing that in any closed system, Boltzmann's atoms, by his own formulation, must eventually return to their original condition, thus contradicting the

---

*See chapter 24.

law of entropy. (He conveniently ignored the fact that if everything is made up of atoms, there is no such thing as a closed system.)[19]

Poincaré's blast seemed the last word on the subject. Boltzmann's bitterness grew, not only toward Mach and the scientific establishment but toward another rising physicist named Max Planck, who was using the same probability theory to study the release of energy—except by explicitly rejecting Boltzmann's atoms and replacing them with electromagnetic waves.

With the new century, Boltzmann seemed a forgotten, failed figure. In late 1905 he wrote to a friend, "I have reached 62 years of age and I have gained no peace of mind."[20] He spent that Christmas and New Year bedridden. In May 1906 the university decided he was too ill to teach any longer—the future of physics was passing into other hands. Then came news that his old antagonist Poincaré had been made president of the French Academy of Sciences. In a fit of despair, Boltzmann took his own life.

The University of Vienna, according to newspaper reports, plunged into "active mourning."[21] Ernst Mach made some brief remarks of regret about the death of the man whose theories he had done most to discredit, suggesting that perhaps Boltzmann's nerves weren't strong enough for the rough-and-tumble of classroom and laboratory. For others, however, the sense of grief would grow—not least because Boltzmann died at the very moment when his atomic theory was about to win, and when Mach himself would be denounced as a "false prophet" by the same physicist who had earlier rejected Boltzmann's theory, Max Planck.

The truly pivotal moment, however, had come even before that, when an obscure twenty-one-year employee at the Swiss Patent Office in Geneva merged Boltzmann's theory with the next giant step in the demolition of Newton's cosmos, relativity.

His name was Albert Einstein. Born in Ulm in Germany in 1879 to Jewish parents, he had been a brilliant if underachieving student at the Zurich Polytechnic and, after marrying and having a child, decided a civil servant's job and salary at the Swiss Patent Office suited his future well. Einstein, however, was one of those students who learn more outside the classroom than in it, and even at the Polytechnic, he had been fascinated by a series of experiments at the University of Berlin conducted by an American physicist, Albert Michelson, and their rather unexpected results.

Michelson was a meticulous, conscientious man and a former science instructor at the U.S. Naval Academy in Annapolis. He had come to Berlin to work on a new kind of interferometer, a device made up of reflecting mirrors for measuring the speed of light. His had a longer optical path-length. This, he reasoned, would allow scientists to detect variations in light's velocity with more precision than ever.

It was a classic experiment in optics, Isaac Newton's original home turf. It seemed innocent enough—except that no matter how Michelson moved his apparatus and no matter in what direction, when he flicked on the light and measured the light speed, he always came up with the same result: 186,000 miles per second.

Michelson couldn't believe it. According to Newton's *Principia*, this shouldn't happen. It was light's duty to change speed according to how it was made to travel. Clearly something was wrong with his interferometer. Michelson went home to America deeply disappointed.

He repeated the experiment in Chicago a year later with a chemist friend, Edward Morley. It showed the same result. No matter what they did or what deflection angle they used, the speed of light was always the same.

Albert Michelson went on to found the American Physical Society. He was the first American to win a Nobel Prize in physics (1907). However, until his death in 1931, he considered his most famous experiment a failure. He could not believe that the problem was not his device or his skill as a scientist but Newton's laws about space and time.[22]

Einstein thought otherwise. Even as a student, he had wondered whether Newton's most fundamental assumption—that space and time form an exact and immovable grid in which all physical events, like light traveling from one point to the next, take place—was really true. As a teenager, Einstein had once wondered, "What would the world look like if I rode a beam of light?" Around 1900, he began to work out the details and discovered that if somehow he did ride a light beam, he would cut himself off from the passage of time.[23]

An interstellar horse race demonstrates Einstein's point. Suppose the horses come out of the gate at the exact moment the course clock strikes noon. The horse I'm riding is traveling at the speed of light. In one second I move 186,000 miles; but so does the light beam carrying the image of the clock hands reaching twelve. When I look back, *to me* the clock hands have not changed; time is frozen. For the other riders, however, the clock is mov-

What if a horse and rider could race at the speed of light?

ing on and the chimes are sounding: for them, the time on the clock seems "normal."

But *normal* now has no meaning—or rather, it has a provisional or relative one. The faster we approach the speed of light (and at half the speed of light, when my watch says three and a half minutes past noon, the course clock will appear to be a few seconds slower), the more we find ourselves in our own little world of experience of space as well as time. This is because the faster I go, the longer the light bearing visual images of the course will take to reach me, making them appear elongated and distorted. By the same token, those observers at the starting point will experience time as slower than the racer; and the dimensions of their space will be normal *for them* but different from mine.

Objectivity, the Newtonian view, the God's-eye view of space and time—all had been crushed. Subjectivity—what we see and experience from our own vantage point—had won. What's left in common is the ability to share information about different perspectives. In fact, what's usually called the theory of relativity (a term Einstein never used) should really be called the theory of perspective.[24] For thanks to Einstein, what the Renaissance artists had used to represent reality had now *become* reality—a way to measure seeing from a particular point of view.

What Einstein had really done, however, was to show that science was less about describing objective *facts*, as the Logical Positivists were claiming, than about measuring subjective *observations*. We can say "measure" because, thanks to Ludwig Boltzmann, the data drawn from our subjective observations still retain the power of mathematical prediction.

Einstein had never even heard of Boltzmann from his teachers at the Polytechnic (or of Maxwell, for that matter) and began reading his works, especially his *Lectures on Gas Theory*, on his own. "Boltzmann is quite magnificent," he wrote to the young woman who would become his wife. "I am completely persuaded by the correctness of the principles of the theory, that the question is really about the movement of [atoms] according to certain conditions."[25]

But he was equally persuaded by the idea that statistical probability had the power to illuminate certain otherwise-invisible features of nature that included the electromagnetic spectrum as studied by Max Planck. Planck had borrowed from Boltzmann the idea of dividing the energy of an electromagnetic wave into smaller units in order to give a theoretical deviation of the spectrum of radiation flowing out from an object. It was an elegant way of proceeding, as Boltzmann himself had shown in writing about gases. Boltzmann had even coined a term for these smaller bits, *quanta*, a German word meaning "quantity."

They behaved beautifully as statistical units. But did these smaller units or lumps, which Planck's formulae described, really exist? Planck was stumped. And since he had rejected the rest of Boltzmann's theory of atoms, he was permanently stumped: that is, until Albert Einstein picked up Planck's latest work and began reading it with Boltzmann's atoms in mind.

The paper Einstein subsequently wrote showed that treating every "quantum" of radiation energy as a physically independent entity produced formulae for the energy and entropy of a volume of radiation that matched exactly the derivation of those quantities in terms of traditional thermodynamics. In other words, just as a physical gas was made up of individual atoms, so the "gas" of electromagnetic radiation was made up of individual and distinct particles whose presence remained invisible but whose behavior was mathematically predictable.

This was no mere mathematical stunt. Quanta really were atoms of energy—and were the constituent parts that made up the light spectrum. Instead of a wave of energy, as Maxwell and others had conceived it, light was a stream of quanta (or photons) traveling at an incredible speed past other atoms—which incidentally is why the speed of light is constant, no matter what medium it passes through, as Michelson's experiments had shown.

Indeed, light turned out to be the *only* constant. Everything else, even time (as the relativity theory showed) and space and the objects that occupy it, are subject to the laws of the quanta—and the atoms that make it up.

But what *is* the relationship between the quantum and the atom? That would be the next step in uncovering the nature of the unseen world. And it would come at the hands of Danish physicist Niels Bohr, on the eve of the great cataclysm that would engulf Europe: World War I.

Contrary to historians, what really divided Europe in the years before 1914 was not nationalism or alliances or imperial ambitions for a "place in the sun." It was a rift in Europe's cultural crust separating the major portion of German-speaking Europe from its neighbors. Inside the rift, Hegel's Plato-influenced German idealism ruled, above all the notion that ultimate reality is found not in the vicissitudes of empirical experience but in the realm of the Absolute, of mind and spirit.[26]

Outside the Hegel Line and across the rest of Europe, various schools of thought and lines of inquiry competed for attention. They included Catholics and Protestants; John Stuart Mill–style liberals and Burkean conservatives; Logical Positivists and Social Darwinists; Enlightenment Deists and out-and-out atheists. But most looked to Aristotle and his intellectual offspring, including Aquinas and John Locke, as their original progenitors, if not their actual inspiration. They argued passionately among themselves in university lecture halls, academic journals, political discussion groups, writers' and artists' studios, even newspapers and secondary-school common rooms. Over time, however, they generally found themselves resisting the aggressive thrust of Hegel's idealism, or being engulfed by it—and by the disciples of Hegel's unacknowledged bastard heir, Karl Marx. For after 1848, Hegelianism—like Absolute Spirit itself—seemed destined to sweep everything before it.

It's not hard to describe the Hegel Line on a map. To the east, it separated Germany from the Austro-Hungarian Empire and its twin capitals, Vienna and Prague—the home not only of Logical Positivism but of the first glimmerings of Mendelian genetics. To the west, it ran roughly along the border between Germany and France, although later in the twentieth century Paris would become one of Hegelianism's most important outposts. To the north, Great Britain was largely sheltered from its influence by its own long empiri-

cal tradition, as well as by the rise of Darwinism. Even so, important outcroppings appeared at Cambridge and Oxford in the 1880s. In the United States
they came as early as the 1850s, where American Transcendentalists like
Ralph Waldo Emerson came to worship at the temple of *The Phenomenology
of Spirit.*[27]

Farther north, Scandinavians by and large resisted the spread of Hegelianism. The existentialist philosopher Søren Kierkegaard made it his principal
target. To the south, however, the Hegel Line thrust deep into Italy, where
Benedetto Croce (1867–1941) made his version of Hegel's science of history
a virtual orthodoxy; he became as much the intellectual dictator of Italy as
Hegel had been of Germany.[28] At the farther ends of Europe, in Spain and
Russia, it is hard to find a serious thinker in the later nineteenth century who
wasn't influenced by the philosopher from Jena.[29]

What made Hegel so irresistibly appealing? First of all, his totality as a
thinker. His theories didn't just draw together science, art, history, and philosophy into a consistent (if not always coherent) whole. His vision of totality
also embraced, and subsumed, the individual. As with Plato, Hegel taught
that the key to human happiness was belonging to an entity larger than ourselves. For Hegel and the Hegelian, the desire of each person to lead his or
her life as he or she pleases—the Lockean individual of the Enlightenment—
was as morally absurd as it was physically impossible. We are all inevitably
parts of larger and larger wholes, Hegel explained, both organically (the individual and his family belong to a village or town; that local community is part
of the nation; and so on) *and* over time, as all things become integrated into
the ultimate reality of the Absolute—including the State.[30]

What the Catholic Church had been for Saint Augustine, the modern
political state became for Hegel and the Hegelians: the universal community
of the future. The crucial difference was that Augustine's community was
bound together by belief in a supreme power greater than itself. In sharp
contrast, Hegel's State is held together by its belief *in* itself, and the certainty
that in the long run it can do no wrong. "The State is the reality of the moral
idea," he wrote in *The Philosophy of Right,* "which thinks and knows itself,
and fulfills what it knows."[31]

Marx had substituted the word *class* for *the State,* but the effect was same.
Both for Marx and for Hegel, the illusory freedoms set forth by Locke and the
Enlightenment were doomed to disappear. History and the future belonged
to newer, stronger forces, and Hegel's legacy was to prepare the way for it.

Marx had seen the future arise from the proletariat. For Hegel himself, it had risen up from the squabbling principalities of Germany and central Europe, the trash heap left behind by the decay and collapse of the medieval Holy Roman Empire, the disasters of the Reformation, and Napoleon's conquests. He had concluded that the full development of the Absolute in history, including the State, belonged to the German race. "The German spirit is the spirit of the new world," he wrote. "Its aim is the realization of absolute Truth as the unlimited self-determination of freedom," meaning freedom *not* in the Anglo-American sense of rights and natural law but in the sense of belonging to a greater, more real whole.[32]

At the University of Berlin, Prussia's capital, first Hegel and then his disciples held forth to generations of students on the inevitable triumph of the German spirit in History, and on the kingdom of Prussia as the state that most embodied that idea.[33] The nickname for the Berlin faculty became "The First Guards Regiment of Learning." Other German universities, like Freiburg and Heidelberg and Leipzig, also played their part in the march of German nationalism. It would be a gross error to imagine that every German scholar or thinker in 1860 was an Hegelian.* All the same, Hegel's Berlin became the epicenter of a series of seismic tremors, both intellectual and political, that would remake the map of Europe. They would erupt first to the east, along the German-Austrian border at Königgrätz in 1866, where the Prussian army decisively defeated the Austrian forces in a driving rainstorm.

The battle of Königgrätz decided not only who would dominate Germany but the intellectual future of continental Europe. First the Saxons saw the writing on the wall and became a Prussian ally. The other German states, like Bavaria and Hanover, soon followed. Four years later Kaiser Wilhelm I, his first minister Otto von Bismarck, and the Prussian army would repeat their triumph, this time over the French in the Franco-Prussian War. In 1871, a united German state and empire had emerged that was poised to become the colossus of Europe and the fulfillment of Hegel's dream.

Germany would soon pass both Britain and France as a producer of iron and steel and coal. Its scientists pioneered the industrial development of drugs, synthetic dyes, and chemicals, while its universities became major centers of research and learning (the chief reason Albert Michelson came to

---

*A good example is Max Weber, who constructed an entire sociology uncontaminated by Hegelian ideas and who proved resistant to their instinctive allegiance to an extreme German nationalism. The influence of Nietzsche, however, proved more challenging. See chapter 28.

Berlin in 1881). Its finest minds became cultural legends, from Goethe and Beethoven to Kant, Leibniz, and Hegel himself. To be German (or barring that, at least of Germanic racial stock) was to be in some degree a participant in Western civilization at its highest trajectory.

Meanwhile, the efficiency of Germany's Hegelian-inspired government bureaucracy became the envy of Europe. Its offer of unemployment insurance to workers in 1881 forced virtually every other country to take the first tentative steps to creating the modern welfare state. At the same time, its disciplined and invincible army became an inspiration to military gurus around the world—while its navy aspired to be a global presence as powerful as that of Britain's Royal Navy.[34]

By 1880, British statesman Benjamin Disraeli pronounced "the German revolution" a greater event than the French Revolution of the previous century.[35] Rousseau's revolution, after all, had ended in terror and blood. Hegel's revolution in Germany, by contrast, seemed on the brink of universal fulfillment. History—and the march of the Absolute—were clearly on the Germans' side.[36]

By 1905, that march had advanced far enough to alarm those on the other side of the Hegel Line, especially in the West. France and Britain had made common cause and in 1904 signed an Entente Cordiale, while France brought along its traditional ally, Russia, to make a third at the table. Emperor Franz Josef of Austria and his entourage sensed where their geopolitical and strategic future lay and signed a similar alliance with Germany, as did the newly unified Italy.

Other parts of the Austro-Hungarian Empire, including its universities, were not so sure. Indeed, the hostility on the part of Ernst Mach and the Logical Positivists to the systems of Hegel was at least in part a declaration of independence against the encroaching monolith of imperial Germany—a declaration of cultural and intellectual independence as loud and clear as the American declaration of political independence in 1776.*[37]

Something similar was happening in the new atomic physics. In 1910, Denmark stood well above the Hegel Line. So it's not surprising that when

---

*Why was Austria so immune to Hegel? One reason was that Kant, Hegel, and Fichte were all for a time on the Catholic Church's Index of Prohibited Books. By the time they came off, Austrian schools and universities had found other intellectual mentors, including the Catholic philosopher Franz Bretano and (thanks to the German translation by T. Gomperz) John Stuart Mill.

Niels Bohr decided to study physics, he turned first not to study in neighboring Germany but with J. J. Thomson at Cambridge, and then Ernest Rutherford at the University of Manchester, who was the best experimental physicist in the world. Like Einstein, Rutherford was a convert to the atom, and in 1911, he proposed a definitive model of how its tiny world worked. Rutherford based it on the model of the solar system, with a heavy central core or nucleus akin to the sun at its center, and electrically charged particles or electrons circling the nucleus like the planets.

It was brilliant, it worked mathematically, and it had the advantage of appealing to what had become by 1900 a robust commonsense image—the heliocentric cosmos of Copernicus and Galileo. But Bohr saw at once that there was a problem. All systems run down, even the solar system eventually—that was the lesson of entropy. What keeps the electrons in their orbits? If they really are like little planets, they must wind up falling into the nucleus. Something else must keep them from losing energy—some new undiscovered principle that limits the energy every electron gives out to a fixed value so it doesn't drain away.

Bohr found it in Planck's quanta. As long as the electron in a hydrogen atom, for example, stays in a single orbit, it emits no energy. When it jumps from one orbit to another, it emits a quantum of energy—and the energy difference between the two orbits is released as a tiny burst of light. That light is reflected, Bohr discovered, in the spectrum that each element generates not as a continuous range but as discrete bright lines that define that element. Hydrogen, for instance, releases three lines, one red, one blue-green, and one blue. Each is the visible trace of a release of energy as the electron jumps from orbit to orbit.

Bohr published his paper "On the Constitution of Atoms and Molecules" in 1913. As the prospect of war hovered over Europe, an even greater event broke over Western civilization: the overthrow of Newton's universe, and the overthrow of matter.

Bohr's paper revealed the precise mathematical workings of an unseen world that underlies everything, and whose only visible trace is a series of spectral lines like a footprint. Matter—the primary building block of nature for every scientist since Aristotle—turned out to be nothing but packets of energy.

At the center of the action is the movement of electrons. When electrons

remain tied to their atomic nuclei, they generate stability—the apparent solidity of objects, which are actually atoms in a low-energy state. When they
jump from their ground state to the next energy level, they create the phenomenon known as electricity. When they do, however, the energy released
can trigger the electrons of other atoms to do the same. If they get the right
boost of quantum energy (defined as the resonant frequency multiplied by
something called Planck's constant), electrons respond to each other like
tones on a musical scale. They can even bind atoms together to form molecules, the building blocks of chemistry. In short, the mechanics of the quantum revealed not only the nature of electricity but also the atomic nature of
the chemical bond.[38]

A new scientific future was exposed in the unseen but mathematically
precise, even harmonious, workings of the atom. Instead of the music of the
spheres, Bohr now offered the music of the quantum: no wonder he felt free
to invoke Pythagoras in his 1922 Nobel Prize speech. Number now defined
the parameters of a new reality, the reality of the *field*: a range of probabilities
about where electrons will be at any given time, subject to the laws of relativity and the quantum—and the speed of light, the one remaining constant. As
Einstein put it: "There is no place in this new physics both for the field and
matter, for the field is the only reality."

It wasn't just Newton's mechanics and Aristotle's matter that had been
exposed as illusions. So were the dominant political ideologies of the age.
Everyone, including Marx and his followers, assumed that power derived
from controlling the biggest material resources, from territories and colonies
to gold mines, oil wells, armies, and navies. The future would belong to those
institutions able to muster and control those vast physical assets and deploy
their power. And the bigger the institutions—empires, nations, corporations—
the bigger the power they would wield. In politics as in sex, men at the dawn
of the twentieth century said, size is destiny.

Yet now the greatest power of all turned out to be not immensely large but
infinitesimally, even invisibly, small. It lay in the unseen heart of the atom, its
nucleus: a power Einstein defined precisely as mass times the speed of light
squared or $E=MC^2$. "Assuming that it were possible to effect that immense
release," Einstein told a biographer in 1921, "we should merely find ourselves in an age compared to which our coal-black present would seem
golden."[39]

Thirty years after Einstein's word and Bohrs's pathbreaking paper, a group of scientists and engineers would gather in the New Mexico desert to put that prediction to the test. The place was Los Alamos: the test would be the first atomic bomb. The power of the unseen world had finally, definitely overthrown the visible one. It came as the latest battle between Plato and Aristotle had reached its climax—and putting Western civilization to its severest test yet.

Friedrich Nietzsche (1844–1900): "Everything about Socrates is wrong."

Twenty-seven

TRIUMPH OF THE WILL: NIETZSCHE AND THE DEATH OF REASON

Men must become better and more evil.
　　　　　　　　—Friedrich Nietzsche, *Thus Spoke Zarathustra*

Whatever their differences, Plato and Aristotle did agree on one thing: the importance of reason in human affairs.

In Plato's case, the path of reason was more speculative and inward-turning, based on a search for timeless a priori principles. Aristotle celebrated a more practical version of reason, embedded in the rules of logic and science — and in empirical experience. But both assumed that distinguishing truth from falsehood was man's most important mission, and that his mind was the surest guide for doing it.

For more than two thousand years, their successors embraced the same idea. Christianity tended to see human reason in more Platonic terms, as a reflection of the mind of God. Following Aristotle, the Enlightenment treated it as a powerful ordering mechanism, not only generating scientific knowledge but also enabling us to grasp the basic forces governing our own history—a point with which both Hegel and Marx would have completely agreed.

But none ever doubted that reason was the essential core of human identity. Even the Romantics, with their celebration of feelings and emotions, were chasing after a richer synthesis of our spiritual and rational natures, not the permanent overthrow of the latter.

Then very suddenly in the 1880s, new ideologies sprang up in Germany and France arguing for just that. Their proponents asserted that it wasn't what we know that makes us powerful, but what we believe—even if it's a lie. Instead of knowing and analyzing reality, they proclaimed, man's mission is to transform it in ways no previous generation could ever have imagined.

"Other people have saints; the Greeks had sages."

The man who penned this aphorism in 1872, and the first exponent of the new irrationalism, was an obscure professor of classical philosophy at the University of Basel named Friedrich Nietzsche. His classes were empty. Other professors, especially the philosophers, urged students to stay away.[1] They had been outraged by the book on Greek drama he had published the year before, *The Birth of Tragedy Out of the Spirit of Music*. However, Nietzsche's handful of lectures about the earliest Greek thinkers—Thales, Anaximander, Anaxagoras, Parmenides, Democritus, and Nietzsche's particular favorite, Heraclitus—reveals a good deal more about Nietzsche than does his more widely read book on tragedy and Apollinian and Dionysian man, and far more about Nietzsche's place in what would happen next.

The pre-Socratics were a strange subject for serious lectures. After twenty-five hundred years, the written works of these earliest Greek thinkers had almost vanished. About all that survived were fragments quoted by Plato and Aristotle, largely in order to refute them. However, enough survived to allow scholars to get a broad idea of their theories: Parmenides's belief in the unity of Being, for example, and Democritus's atomism.[*]

The question the pre-Socratics had rallied around was: What is reality? As we saw, Socrates had changed the key philosophical question to: How should

I live? All the same, the pre-Socratics' answers to the first, Nietzsche suggested, already implied the second. It's just that their approach took them in a sharply different direction from Socrates's: one that put a premium on man's place *in* the world, instead of *above* or *apart* from it, which to Plato and Aristotle was the consequence of his possessing reason.

Now Nietzsche proclaimed that Plato and Aristotle had been wrong all along. The pre-Socratics were the real geniuses of Greek civilization. When their works were lost, he believed, "indescribable riches were lost to us." However, enough remained to show they understood reality had little to do with the mind, and a lot to do with being in the here and now.[2]

For Nietzsche, the most important of the pre-Socratics was Heraclitus. "Heraclitus's regal possession is his extraordinary power to think intuitively" rather than through the mediation of formal categories, or "the rope ladder of logic." Heraclitus denied any separation of mind and matter, body and spirit; "he altogether denied Being"—that obsession of Greek philosophers after Parmenides, including Socrates and Plato. Heraclitus was the first to realize that "good and bad are identical" in the constant flux that is existence.

Of course, the consequences of Heraclitus's most famous saying, "All things change," or *Panta rhei*, can appear paralyzing to the human mind. It means nothing is permanent, even from moment to moment. Nietzsche likened it to a mental earthquake. But the impermanence of everything, including the universe, should be a formula for serenity rather than despair. "It takes great strength" to realize that we are destined to ride the hurricane of change alone and to accept the ceaseless fluctuation of everything we see or touch or hold dear. However, when we do, we will be prepared to see life as a whole, including ourselves.[3]

"Let the wheel of time roll where it will," Nietzsche affirms, "it can never escape truth." Nor, will we. Modern man will realize that mind and body, good and evil, Being and Becoming, the Many and the One, are all false choices. "They are but the flash and spark of drawn swords, the quick radiance of victory in the struggle of opposites," without end or beginning. This is why, Nietzsche concludes, "the world forever needs Heraclitus." The greatest of pre-Socratic thinkers raised the curtain on history's greatest secret, the bleak truth behind the Delphic motto "Know thyself."[4]

Ride the hurricane. It is not hard to hear in all this the voice of Romanticism recast as a reading of early Greek philosophy. It appears also in

Nietzsche's other great influential work, the *Birth of Tragedy* (1872), his celebration of the Greek god Dionysus as the presiding spirit of spontaneity and creative insight, versus Apollo as the symbol of bloodless reason. It certainly had a Byronic ring, as does his evocation of genius as the life force of civilization, with "each giant calling to his brother through the desolate intervals of time"—a line he might have stolen from Percy Shelley but that in fact comes from Schopenhauer.[5]

Yet Nietzsche's project became far more radical. It involved a wholesale tearing down of every familiar landmark of Western thought, starting with its first philosopher-martyr, Socrates. "Everything about Socrates is wrong," he would write.[6] Nietzsche saw him not just as some dead figure out of the pages of a philosophy text, but as a living, baneful presence in the modern world, to be argued with, refuted, and ultimately overthrown. He devoted his life to purging Socrates's influence on Western man, compared to whom Plato and Aristotle were minor cast characters.

Why Socrates?[7] Because, Nietzsche charged, it was Socrates who first elevated the importance of reason over instinct. It was Socrates who first made men look to the heavens for truth and happiness instead of being content to ride the ceaseless flux.

It was also Socrates who introduced that shoddiest and most misleading of all false *daemons*, the voice of conscience, which convinces us we need to feel guilty about what actually makes us feel good. For Nietzsche, Socrates is the original father of Western decadence, an issue that consumed him until Nietzsche finally went mad. Nietzsche concluded that Socrates's enemies might have been right. "Could Socrates have been the corrupter of youth after all?" he asked bitterly. "Did he deserve that cup of hemlock?"[8] Nietzsche answered with an enthusiastic "Yes!"

Then came Plato, who only completed what Socrates had started. Plato taught Western culture to think of reason, self-denial, and the realm of spirit as good and spontaneity, pleasure, music and art ("Plato is the greatest enemy of art Europe has ever known"), and the world of the senses as bad. Plato's works mark the birth of good and evil that Christianity would go on to inherit—and with it the death of freedom.[9]

The result was that Western man was divided against himself. The free, spontaneous spirit of Dionysian man and pre-Socratic Greek civilization, which inspired its finest music, art, poetry, and drama, was steadily crushed out under the cold, calculating gaze of Plato and his cultural offspring, Apollonian man.* "The dying Socrates became the new ideal," along with the theoretical man, who thinks rather than feels and who prefers martyrdom (as the early Christians did) to resistance. Aristotle followed this up by reifying reason into science, forcing the natural world to bend to the mind's instinct for system and order; while "virtue" (meaning obeying the law and getting along with others) became the focus of social and political life.

From there, the story of the West goes quickly downhill. At the edge of the Roman world, an obscure Jewish priestly caste turned Plato's ascetic formula into the ethical outlook of an entire society called Christianity. "Christianity," Nietzsche snorted, "is Platonism for the masses"—a sentence Origen himself might have uttered, but in a very different tone. The Christian Middle Ages relegated all human spontaneity and vitality to the cultural margins, like the vagabond troubadours. Except for a short burst of freedom in the Renaissance of Michelangelo and Leonardo, the Enlightenment and the modern age remained trapped in Plato's icy grip.

"The tempo of life slowed down, dialectics [took the] place of instinct, seriousness [was] imprinted on faces and gestures." Men became obsessed with making themselves useful through science and commerce; a de-Christianized conscience became a weak-willed sink of pity open to every humanitarian cause. Then came "the advent of democracy; international courts instead of war; equal rights for women . . . whatever symptoms of declining life there are." Nietzsche did not hesitate to throw in Hegel (with his obsession with ideas as the only reality) and Marx as two more sorry specimens from the same decadent cesspool.[10]

Instead of a history of progress, for Nietzsche the history of the West since Plato has been a history of decadence and diminishing vitality, "an age of exhaustion, of [growing] evening and twilight." If Western man is to save himself from the final darkness, Nietzsche predicted, he will have to recapture that clean sense of drive and energy of the pre-Socratic age: what Nietzsche dubbed the will to power.

The early Greeks, the Homeric heroes and Heraclitean sages, had it. The German barbarian tribes, those "blond beasts" who destroyed a previous dec-

---

*Nietzsche certainly knew that Raphael had depicted Apollo as the patron god of Plato and his companions in The School of Athens.

adent exhausted civilization, the Roman Empire, had it. The Japanese samu-
rai, Genghis Khan, the medieval freebooting knight, the Renaissance
condottiere: All had led "a disgusting procession of murder, arson, rape, and
torture" but emerge "exhilarated and undisturbed of soul." This is because
they possess that will to power, that spark of vitality that in history is "the
privilege of the strong" and is embodied in "war, adventure, hunting, dancing, war games, and in general all that involves vigorous, free, joyful activity";[11] and in them, as it does not in modern man, it remained undimmed
and unchecked.

Did Nietzsche really believe that the last best hope for humankind would
be bands of these violent warriors, the moral equivalent of today's Hell's Angels or Crips and Bloods? Yes, he did, because he saw in them the true dynamic of historical change. Nietzsche's analysis was able to go far beyond
Rousseau's admiration for the "noble savage," thanks in large part (ironically)
to Hegel. Historical progress for Hegel is thoroughly blood soaked; so is it for
Nietzsche. The founders of all great civilizations are "men of prey," Nietzsche
asserted, men "still in possession of unbroken strength of will and lust for
power, [who] hurled themselves on weaker, more civilized, more peaceful
races"—those who, like the modern West, had been made more peaceful
because their inner vitality had died out.

So in the final analysis, Nietzsche's version of "the cunning of history"
looks a lot like Hegel's and Plato's, except in reverse. The so-called winners in
history, like modern Europe, turn out to be its biggest losers and vice versa.
To most readers (and very few people read Nietzsche's book until after his
death), this must have seemed an absurd paradox. In 1881, when Nietzsche
wrote the bulk of his most renowned work, *Thus Spoke Zarathustra*, European civilization never seemed more powerful or permanent. Its factories
belched forth goods that traveled by rail and from seaports to every corner of
the globe. Its colonial empires ruled three-quarters of the earth's inhabited
surface. Its science, literature, music, and philosophy set the standard of high
human achievement. It breathed the spirit of Progress from every angle. Yet
Nietzsche sensed that it had reached a tipping point, not in its outer strength
but inside its head. He believed the instrument of its destruction would be
the very thing that gave Victorian Europe its great sense of pride: its reliance
on science.

The new scientific outlook of Darwin's evolution and Ernst Mach's physics had demonstrated to all concerned that there was no heaven above, only

an open, empty sky.* "Metaphysical reality" was a self-contradiction.[12] Science had left Western man standing alone on an empty train platform, with all the emotional and intellectual baggage left by a Christianity that had been based on a myth and had absorbed a lie: Plato's assertion that man had a "higher" rational self, when all it was was his own fear of life.

It was a shattering revelation. Nietzsche summed it up by the phrase "God is dead." At almost the same time, the characters in Fyodor Dostoyevsky's novels were pointing out that if God was truly dead, then everything is permitted. Dostoyevsky wrote these words with something approaching despair. Nietzsche says it with the shuddering glee of a man singing under the bracing spray of an ice-cold shower.

"What does not destroy us," he was fond of saying, "makes us stronger," including the death of God and Socratic reason. *Now* was the time for European man to recover his vital roots, he proclaimed. *Now* was the time for Europeans to become once again a race of Dionysian "free spirits."

Nietzsche had seen the evolution of Greek culture as a battle between vital Dionysian man and rational Apollinian man. By the time he wrote *On the Genealogy of Morals* in 1887, he was seeing it as the battle between Plato and his pre-Socratic predecessors.[13] Plato had won, or so it seemed. Now with the death of God, the West has a chance to replay the match. The result would be an intellectual revolution more sweeping than any in history, a "transvaluation of all values," as Nietzsche put it, in which Western man would finally realize that asceticism, self-sacrifice, humility, industry, and pity are actually *evil* because they are the enemies of human vitality. Joyous spontaneity and the will to power, on the other hand, the desire to rule and dominate and plunge headlong into the great adventure of the endless flux, would be revealed to be *good* because they express the sources (if not necessarily the fruits) of vitality and life.

When we realize this, Nietzsche predicted, a new dawn will break for mankind. We will find ourselves in a world "beyond good and evil," as the title of one of his books states. It will be an immeasurably new experience, but also immensely old. Men† will find themselves once more at the point at

---

*Nietzsche did not live long enough to see Einstein's theory of relativity, but it would have added to his sense of morbid excitement.

†Here Nietzsche was not thinking of man in a generic sense. Like his master Schopenhauer, he had a low opinion of women. Schopenhauer called them long on hair and short on ideas. Nietzsche said their job was "to wait upon the warriors at the feast." He certainly considered the rise of the women's suffrage movement one of the key indicators of Western decadence.

which Heraclitus had begun the great Western adventure. This came as no surprise to Nietzsche. All history turns out to be an endless repetitive cycle, in which every event and every thing—"*this* bird, *this* sun, *this* snake," as Zarathustra says—is played out the same way again and again.[14]

Thus Spoke Zarathustra is a parable of the end of modern civilization. The main character, the prophet Zarathustra, has entirely reconciled himself to this bleak reality and the fact that in a world of eternal recurrence, the only choices that matter are the ones we make for ourselves. This realization transforms him into a new kind of human being, the new man, the *Übermensch*, or Overman. He is a being beyond good and evil, because "the greatest evil is necessary for the Overman."[15] He is a being freed at last from Plato and Aristotle and the chains of Western rationalism. He is a being suffused with the will to power.

"My hour is come," he tells the sun, "this is *my* morning, *my* day is breaking; rise now, rise, thou great noon!"

> *Thus spake Zarathustra, and he left his cave, glowing and strong as a morning sun that comes out of dark mountains.*[16]

By the time the fourth and last part of *Zarathustra* was published in 1892, Nietzsche had gone hopelessly insane. The prophet of the overthrow of reason had gotten his wish. Two years earlier, a book published in Paris, *Time and Free Will*, had launched an attack on the temple of rationality from a very different direction.

Nietzsche's turn back to the pre-Socratics ends in a cave. Henri Bergson's begins with a race.

It's the most famous imaginary race in history, between the great Greek hero Achilles and a tortoise. The pre-Socratic thinker Zeno, a follower of Parmenides, dreamed it up as a way to prove that motion, and change, is impossible.

Achilles and the tortoise are set to run a race around a stadium track. Achilles generously gives the tortoise a head start. The starter says, "Go!" and the race is on. However, Achilles is doomed to lose even before he leaves the starting block.

Why? Because, Zeno says, by the time Achilles gets to point A, where the tortoise started, the tortoise will have already moved ahead to point B. When Achilles reaches B, the tortoise has crawled to C; when Achilles finally reaches C, the tortoise is already at point D.

And so on. Common sense says Achilles must win the race. However, reason and the diagram show that no matter what Achilles does to catch up, he can't reach the point where the tortoise was before the tortoise will have moved to a point ahead of him. The race is over before it begins.

Zeno's race is a famous example of a logical paradox. Zeno used it to show that there was no such thing as a *state* of motion; change isn't something that happens *to* objects (like Achilles running on the track or an arrow in flight) because all we can know are objects in the moment, here and now. It is being there that counts, while the journey itself—like the race—is meaningless.

Aristotle in Book VI of the *Physics* replied to Zeno's paradox by pointing out that while space may be theoretically divisible into infinitesimally small segments, time and motion are not. In real life, motion takes place over finite distances in finite amounts of time. Achilles will win because he is running from A to B at a faster speed than the tortoise; the points don't enter the picture unless he happens to stop at one of them. "Everything that is in motion is in motion [over] a period of time," Aristotle sniffed, unless it is at rest—and vice versa.[17]

Aristotle dismissed Zeno's paradox without answering it. Although philosophers over the centuries pondered the problem Zeno raised, few considered it important enough to overturn our commonsense understanding of how time, distance, and space interact. No one, that is, until a young teacher in the French town of Clermont-Ferrand decided Zeno might have had a point.

The year was 1886, and Henri Bergson was out for his customary afternoon walk after teaching his students at the high school about the pre-Socratics and Zeno's race.* Suddenly, he tells us, it occurred to him that Aristotle and all thinkers after him had approached the entire question of time from the wrong end. In trying to refute Zeno, they had always treated time as a measure of *motion*, especially over physical distance, as in a race or with the speed of light. They had failed to see time as Zeno and the pre-Socratics had, Bergson believed, as a dimension of human consciousness.[18]

---

*Yes, there actually was a time when high school students (at least in France) studied Greek philosophy.

This aspect Bergson dubbed *duration*. The experience of duration forms the backbone of what Bergson asserted had to be an entirely new way of thinking about human existence. This experience has nothing to do with our ordinary consciousness or the intellect. It is a feeling grasped in an introspective, imaginative leap of intuition—like a diver plunging over a waterfall.

Bergson's rational mind, the intellect, sees life only like a movie on reel-to-reel tape. It watches a series of discrete episodes that roll along like a film of Zeno's race and are then tossed into a box titled "My Life as My Mind Saw It." Intuition works like a compact disc in which the digital bits instantly assemble and form one continuous whole. "Intuition is knowledge at a distance," meaning it contains both past and present and simultaneously looks ahead to the future.[19]

That whole constitutes *memory*, for Bergson an entirely separate level of human consciousness from that of reason.[20] Instead of slicing things up as the Aristotelian intellect does, memory pulls them together into a meaningful pattern. Sometimes by mistake, as when we remember meeting the love of our life in Boston when it was actually Paris. In every case, however, it is the larger significance of an event or place or person that shines through the clouds of memory. At that moment, Bergson averred, we experience time at its most fully and intuitively real, at "the intersection of mind and matter."[21]

Intuition returns us to our original starting point as living beings, what Bergson dubbed the *élan vital* (vital force). It is the trace of our animal instincts that have persisted through the evolutionary winnowing. Bergson was a committed Darwinian. His work is unimaginable without *Origin of Species* or Heraclitus, whose philosophy of ceaseless change fascinated Bergson as much as it enthralled Nietzsche. At the same time, the Frenchman saw evolution as a spiritual as well as material process. He evoked an image of evolution as the upward march of the *élan vital*, "gushing out unceasingly . . . from an immense reservoir of life" until it evolved into human consciousness.

"The life of the body," Bergson says, "[is] on the road that leads to the life of the spirit." These are words Ficino might have written, or Plotinus.[22] Except that in Bergson, the Great Chain of Being has become modernized and personalized. It is more of a Great Escalator of Consciousness, like the *ascenseur* in the Eiffel Tower. Whatever leads our intellect toward the contemplation of matter, including the physical sciences, pushes us back down toward the ground where we started. Whatever presses the button of our intuition, however, steadily lifts us up to survey and experience the whole of life—including our lives with others. Ultimately it leads us to our Creator.

Even though the Church put Bergson's books on the Index, it is easy to see why French neo-Thomists and Catholics like Charles Péguy found in Bergson a line of reasoning that would reconcile modern science, including Darwin, with traditional religious belief. (At the end of his life, Bergson became a Catholic in all but name.)[23] They would also turn Bergson's vitalist philosophy into a formula for national regeneration, La Réveille Nationale, that galvanized France's conservative youth on the eve of World War I—and probably saved France from ultimate defeat.

It's more amazing that some readers found a similar parallel between Bergson and Marxism, yet that is exactly what Bergson's fellow Frenchman Georges Sorel did. It was Sorel, one of the twentieth century's most original (if perverse) minds and the intellectual master not only of Lenin but of Benito Mussolini, who would turn Bergson's *élan vital* into the hammer of totalitarianism.

Sorel was born in Cherbourg in 1847, and was an avowed Marxist when he attended Bergson's classes at the École Polytechnique. There he realized that the transformation of consciousness Bergson was proposing described the true goal of Marx's dictatorship of the proletariat and classless society. Marxism aimed to establish more than just an egalitarian version of capitalism, Sorel realized. It was to be a kingdom of freedom, as Marx had said, a great spiritual unburdening that would lift humanity to a new level of conscious experience.*

But how to get there? To put it crudely, Sorel threw Bergson and Marx together in the test tube, and out came a Gallic version of Nietzsche. Before the new egalitarian society can be built, Sorel decided, the old one must be torn down—destroyed utterly. That meant more than just overthrowing the bourgeoisie. It meant crushing out the false scientific rationality of the Enlightenment, which (Sorel agreed with Nietzsche) were actually an invitation to decadence.[24] True revolution meant reviving the bold heroic spirit in the age of engineers and machines. True revolution meant above all unleashing a cleansing, leveling violence, a violence "without hatred and without the spirit of revenge," which will tap into the deep resources of man's *élan vital* and sweep everything before it.

*See chapter 24.

Sorel admired Darwin; so did Karl Marx. They were bound to admire a science that reduced everything to a struggle for material existence. Some Victorians were shocked by Darwin's less than sunny picture of nature as "red in tooth and claw," as the poet Tennyson put it. Sorel reveled in it and tied his politics of violence to an existential Darwinian process that would crush out the weak and unfit and leave the future to the strong.

For Nietzsche, that vehicle for creative destruction had been his barbarians suffused with will to power, the "blond beasts."[25] For Sorel, it was the proletariat, working men and women who, when turned loose on the street by a general strike, would with their calloused hands pull down the bourgeoisie from their pampered perch. One of his favorite fantasies is of workers using their hammers and crowbars to batter down the walls of the Palais Bourbon, the seat of the French government—and crushing the corrupt ministers inside it.

By Sorel's reckoning, the mistake conventional Marxists made was to assume that this proletarian revolution could be set off by appeals to the working class's reason: "You will control the means of production," "You have nothing to lose but your chains," and so on. What was really needed, Sorel said, was something closer "to the fluid nature of reality": a direct appeal to their most basic instincts, which are the real mainsprings of human action.

"It has been stated that the Socialist war could not be decided in one single battle," Sorel wrote.[26] However, history had shown that a great belief or expectation of liberation in the future—however irrational—can inspire men to flights of heroism even in the face of impossible odds. Three hundred Spartans held off a Persian army in the hundreds of thousands at Thermopylae in order to save Greece from foreign tyranny. Early Christians believed that the return of Christ would cast the pagan world into oblivion, and they gladly fed themselves to the lions to make it happen. Martin Luther summoned the German people to crush the Antichrist and the Catholic Church and set off the Reformation. So why couldn't mobilizing a similar vision of impending apocalypse that will create a new world order set the working masses at the throats of the bourgeoisie?

Sorel's term for this kind of vision is *myth*, with all that word's Platonic associations. Plato had made it clear in the *Republic* that no society, no matter how just its laws, can keep the majority of its citizens honest without resorting to some salutary beliefs or myths, which, even if they are literally false, encourage social solidarity and obedience to the rulers. Plato called these myths *the noble lie.* Josef Goebbels coined a more cynical term, *the big lie.* It will be the essence of mass politics in the ideological age. "It is not necessary that men move mountains," Sorel's disciple Benito Mussolini liked to put it, "only that other men *believe* they moved them."

Indeed, without realizing it, Georges Sorel had defined the contours of totalitarian politics in the twentieth century. Violence equals *élan vital* in action. Myth equals the power to shape reality through mass propaganda. Apocalypse, including the massacre of millions, becomes a cleansing social vision. In the Romantic era, the translation of vision and instinct into action had produced great works of art. In the twentieth century, Sorel believed, it will produce great works of *violence.*

All that was needed was a crisis to set it off. It came in August 1914, as Europe was plunged into its first general war in one hundred years. Heraclitus had made war the father of all things.[27] Nietzsche added that war makes sacred every cause. Bergson had talked about the *élan vital* as a great cavalry charge: "one immense army galloping beside and before and behind each of us in an overwhelming charge able to beat down every resistance and clear the most formidable obstacles, perhaps even death."[28] A generation of French disciples of Bergson, including Charles Péguy, went off in 1914 to fight and die by the millions. A generation of German disciples of Nietzsche went into battle with copies of *Thus Spoke Zarathustra* in their backpacks, with the same result. It was left to Sorel's disciples, and Marx's, to finish what they had started.

World War I killed off nations, empires including Russia's, and fifteen million people. It left in its wake an intellectual climate that celebrated the forces of unreason, violence, and primitive myth—in books, novels, art, music, and politics. In fact, a postwar generation would teach Europe to think about politics as an art in which great leaders of genius, like great artists, could weld men together and magically create new, higher forms of community, akin to the imagined utopias of earlier ages.

Plato's *Republic* would at last be realized—not through the power of reason or virtue but by propaganda and violence.

It was after midnight. The train pulled into the rather shabby pink-granite-and-stucco station and sat sighing beside the platform after its long journey—nearly three thousand miles from the Swiss frontier. A short man wearing a goatee and a fur hat disembarked. Two other men followed him. One, rather heavyset, also wore a goatee; the other, also large and burly, had a thick mustache and dark, watching eyes. A small crowd had gathered to salute them. Many had tears running down their cheeks.[29]

The trio said nothing. They made their way under a newly painted sign that read: PETROGRAD. They passed without speaking into the station and turned toward a set of double doors. It was a large, gilt-ceilinged room filled with other comrades, some they hadn't seen for years; others wore military uniforms. At their head stood a demure bearded man with eager, watery eyes and carrying an enormous bouquet of roses.

He began to speak in a quavering voice. "Comrade Lenin," he said, "in the name of the Petrograd Soviet and of the whole revolution, I welcome you to Russia."

As the man spoke, Vladimir Ilyich Lenin paid no attention—just as he ignored the bundle of roses that was thrust into his arms. He glanced impatiently around the room. He was returning to Russia after nearly a decade and a half in exile. It was April 16, 1917. His moment had come to complete the mission he had set for himself more than twenty years before. Together with the two men behind him, Lev Kamenev and Josef Stalin, he did not intend to fail.

Lenin waited until Nikoloz Chkheidze, the Menshevik head of the Petrograd Soviet, finished his short speech. Then he pulled off his fur cap, glanced with gleaming eyes around the room, and spoke:

"Dear comrades, soldiers, sailors, and workers, I am happy to greet in you the victorious Russian revolution. . . . Not today, but tomorrow, any day, may see the general collapse of European capitalism. The Russian evolution you have accomplished has dealt it the first blow and has opened a new epoch. . . . Long live the International Socialist Revoluion!"[30]

Lenin's arrival at the Finland Station signaled the start of the Communist revolution in Russia, one of the great catastrophic events in history. Lenin's list of class enemies did not consist just of the czar and the Orthodox Church and Russia's aristocracy and bourgeoisie.* It also included the exponents of Logical Positivism, all who cast doubt on the idea that the only genuine science was Marxism. Lenin had written an entire book on the subject titled *Materialism and Empirio-Criticism.*

---

*And eventually the Mensheviks. Chkheidze mistakenly believed the Communist revolution would bring freedom to his native Georgia. Instead, he would narrowly escape execution and die in exile in Paris in 1926.

Marxism, Lenin said, was "a solid block of steel" from which you cannot change a single component without "abandoning objective truth, without falling into the arms of the bourgeois-reactionary falsehood." If the followers of Ernst Mach, including Albert Einstein, weren't willing to see that the solution to the world's perplexities was applying the laws of dialectical materialism, then they should be on notice that they were part of the problem.[31]

Europe had seen revolutions come and go. But with Lenin something new had come to roost. The price of revolution was now ideological, as well as political, conformity. The French Revolution had seen its enemies as aristocrat and the Church. The Russian Revolution extended that standard to include intellectuals, teachers, writers, artists—anyone who refused to comply with what would come to be called "the party line"—the official Communist Party credo on any subject from politics and education to art and architecture.

It was Lenin's declaration of a new front in the class war: a war on free intellectual inquiry. It was a chilling foretaste of what was to come, not just in Soviet Russia but across Europe over the next decades.

What is striking about the politics of both left and right in the interwar years is how unabashed they were about their own extremism. They despised middle-class democracy as much as they did capitalism; they blamed both for the catastrophe of 1914–18. Christianity, the Enlightenment, liberalism, Victorian values and mores—all were to be swept away. A new vitalist elite would generate what Sorel called an "artificial world of order" made up of avant-garde books, music, films, and paintings on the one side and heroes, mass rallies, and war machines on the other. Mussolini himself would find eager allies among Italy's Futurists, while Hitler would recruit many of the figures of avant-garde German cinema, including Leni Riefenstahl and the wife of *Metropolis*'s Fritz Lang.

Elsewhere, artists and writers willing to toe "the party line" would find a similar ally in Stalin's Communist Party. They included Pablo Picasso, Diego Rivera, Frida Kahlo, Tristan Tzara, Louis Aragon, George Grosz, Pablo Neruda, Ernest Hemingway, Bertolt Brecht, Ben Shahn, Langston Hughes, Aimé Césaire, Malcolm Cowley, J. D. Bernal, Stephen Spender, and Jessica Mitford. On the fascist side, the list is shorter but equally dismal: Emil Nolde, Louis-Ferdinand Céline, Carl Schmitt, Pierre Teilhard de Chardin, Pierre Drieu La Rochelle, Hendrik de Man and his nephew, later founder of Deconstructionism Paul de Man, William Butler Yeats, Thierry Maulnier,

Lázló Moholy-Nagy, Philip Johnson, and Günter Grass rounded out the list. The traditional idea, so dear to the Romantics and dating back to Plato's portrayal of Socrates, that intellectuals are the natural foes of tyranny proved fatally flawed.

Indeed, from Lenin's arrival at the Finland Station until the Munich conference in 1938, the forces of illiberalism seemed to sweep everything before them. The Hegel Line was morphing into the Nietzsche Line, as the philosopher of nihilism displaced the philosopher of the Absolute as Germany's most potent original thinker. Sociologist Georg Simmel even pronounced Nietzsche's philosophy as important a revolution in thinking as Copernicus's theory of the solar system.[32] Yet its impact ran in the opposite direction. The disillusioned author of the Weimar Constitution, Max Weber, complained that Nietzsche had killed the Western faith in science and with it sealed the doom of democracy.[33]

Then Martin Heidegger at the University of Freiburg did Nietzsche one better. He claimed to find in Heraclitus and the pre-Socratics a doctrine about existence "not for every man but only for the strong": a radiant truth reserved for those who were willing to throw themselves without hesitation into the ceaseless flux of Being.[34] Heidegger's message would carry his students directly into the heart of Hitler's Nazi revolution.

Meanwhile in Italy, a young socialist agitator named Benito Mussolini had read Sorel's *Reflections on Violence* and translated its political program into the creed of fascism.[35] Hegelians like Benedetto Croce and Giovanni Gentile quickly shifted allegiances and hailed fascism as the next great stage in human history.[36] In France, every thinker or writer wanting to make a name for himself crowded either to the extreme left with Marx, Lenin, and Sorel or to the extreme right and its heady brew of Nietzsche, Heidegger—and Sorel.

In England, occasional exponents of the new irrationalism were also popping up, like Wyndham Lewis, the founder of Vorticism, and Oswald Mosley; while Marxist communism found passionate support in a generation of university students. But most intelligent men and women watched what was happening on the Continent with deep foreboding.

> *Things fall apart; the centre cannot hold;*
> *Mere anarchy is loosed upon the world, . . .*
> *The best lack all conviction, while the worst*
> *Are full of passionate intensity.*

Martin Heidegger (1889–1976): He saw Nietzsche's will to power reflected in what he called "the inner truth and greatness of National Socialism."

By 1932, as depression swept the industrial world, those words by William Butler Yeats seemed watchwords of an even more terrible catastrophe to come.

Three years earlier, the Logical Positivists held their first international conference in Prague. Although they now called themselves the Vienna Circle, the meeting was the first of a series that would draw attendees from around the Western world. Many came from the countries of eastern Europe, recently made free and independent in the aftermath of World War I. From Vienna there were Hahn, Frank, Moritz Schlick, and Herbert Feigl; Prague's contingent was led by Rudolf Carnap, professor of natural philosophy. From Poland came the logicians Alfred Tarski, Jan Łukasiewicz, and Stanisław Leśniewski; from England, the philosopher A. J. Ayer; from America, W.V.O. Quine and Charles W. Morris. There was even a contingent from Berlin led by Hans Reichenbach and Carl Hempel.[37]

By 1929, Logical Positivism's proponents had reconciled themselves to the new physics, including relativity, while still holding out hope that their belief in the power of reason and science could still set the human mind free from ignorance and dogma. Reinforcing that view was the new book on logic by their fellow Viennese, Ludwig Wittgenstein, which asserted that "a proposition can be true or false only in virtue of being a picture of reality."[38] Logic, Wittgenstein had concluded, forms the essential frame for our picture, within which we group observations into true statements, including scientific observation.

Wittgenstein's *Tractatus Logico-Philosopicus* (to give the book its full ponderous Latin title) had at last brought together the two halves of Aristotle's living legacy—his logic and his empirical science—and shown that they are inseparable, indeed that they define our world. Because "what we cannot speak about," Wittgenstein wrote in the *Tractatus*'s last sentence, meaning what can't be verified by empirical observation, "we must pass over in silence." Three thousand years of fuzzy thinking and foggy logic, from Parmenides's problem of Being to Hegel's dialectic and Nietzsche's Eternal Recurrence, had been neatly broomed away.

But it was too late. The scholars who met in Prague saw themselves as exponents of a Western tradition of science and rational thought and the heralds of a new era of intellectual freedom. Their opponents, however, were closing in from both east and west. Teaching human beings to think clearly was no longer enough.

In 1932, Adolf Hitler swept into power. As rector of the University of Freiburg, Martin Heidegger would dismiss all Jewish faculty, and in his rector's address in May 1933, he urged his students to throw themselves into the great adventure of National Socialism: "Our nation realizes its own fate by risking its history in the arena of world power in which all human existence is affected and by continually fighting for its own spiritual world . . . and no one will prevent us from doing that." At the end, Heidegger quoted Plato's *Theaetetus*, "All greatness stands firm in the storm," raised his arm with a "Heil Hitler!" and stepped down to thunderous applause.[38]

In 1934, Left and Right clashed in the streets of Paris as French politics settled into a simmering hatred and resentment that would paralyze Europe's biggest democracy in the face of a rising Nazi Germany. "The only way to love France today," poet Pierre Drieu La Rochelle wrote, "is to hate it in its present form." Both Fascism and Communism found a new congenial home in the country of Voltaire—but also of Rousseau and Robespierre. Meanwhile, democracy in Poland and Austria was submerged under authoritarian dictatorships. In 1936, Moritz Schlick was murdered in his class at the University of Vienna by a demented student while civil war broke out in Spain. Two years later, Austria was absorbed into the Third Reich. A year after that in 1939, German tanks rolled into Prague and then into Poland.

Men of intellect and science, and not only Jews, fled. Einstein, Freud, Carnap, and the surviving members of the Vienna Circle; philosophers Ernst Cassirer and Walter Benjamin; conductors Otto Klemperer, Arturo Toscanini, and Bruno Walter; physicists Enrico Fermi and Leó Szilárd: These are only the best known. A curtain of intellectual darkness had descended across the heart of Europe.

What would lift it? The answer came from many thousands of miles away, from a place that hitherto had played a fairly marginal role in the cultural history of the West. However, it would soon pour out its resources of mind and matter like a sheet of revivifying water across a parched and embattled landscape.

Twenty-eight

COMMON SENSE NATION:
PLATO, ARISTOTLE, AND
AMERICAN EXCEPTIONALISM

America, though but a child of yesterday, has already given hopeful
proofs of genius . . . which arouse the best of feelings of man, which
call him into action, which substantiate his freedom, and conduct him
to happiness . . .
—Thomas Jefferson, *Notes on the State of Virginia* (1781)

The whole function of philosophy ought to be to find out what definite
difference it will make to you or me, at definite instants of our life, if
this world-formula or that world-formula be the true one.
—William James, *Pragmatism* (1907)

"I think that in no country in the civilized world is less attention paid to philosophy than in the United States."

When Alexis de Tocqueville published this sentence in his *Democracy in America*, it was the heyday of Hegel, August Comte, Victor Cousin, and half a dozen leading lights of classical liberalism in both Scotland and England, including Tocqueville's twenty-five-year-old friend John Stuart Mill. Compared to the heady debates being waged in lecture halls, periodicals, and bookstalls, intellectual life in the young republic must have seemed very placid—and far removed from that great tradition reaching back to Plato and Aristotle.

Yet America was Aristotle's offspring in more ways than one. Born in the age of Sir Francis Bacon, it grew under the double engines of commerce and slavery in the era of John Locke and achieved independence under the tutelage of the Enlightenment. The most famous saying from America's most important constitutional architect, James Madison—"If men were angels, no government would be necessary"—is a sentiment torn from the pages of Aristotle and Machiavelli if ever there was one.

Tocqueville himself noted that "Americans are more addicted to practical than to theoretical science," and that "they mistrust systems" of the usual Platonic-Hegelian pattern. "They adhere closely to facts, and study facts with their own senses." In fact, Tocqueville concluded that they had invented their own philosophical method without realizing it, one that "accepts tradition only as a means of information and existing facts only as a lesson to be used in doing otherwise, and doing better." In short, a bias toward progress was built into the American character, along with a love of liberty both political and personal, in which the American "is a subject in all that concerns the duties of citizens" in a self-governing republic, but "is free, and responsible to God alone, for all that concerns himself."[1]

On one side, "I know of no country," Tocqueville wrote, "where the love of money has taken stronger hold on the attention of men," but on the other, none where reverence for religion was so widely and evenly spread. In America "liberty regards religion as its companion in all its battles and triumphs—as the cradle of its infancy, and the divine source of its claims." Indeed, "it considers religion as the safeguard of morality, and morality as the best security of law, and the surest pledge of the duration of freedom."[2] Certainly since 1789, the relations between liberty and religion in Tocqueville's own country had been very different. Yet on nearly every issue that seemed to split Europeans apart—democracy versus aristocracy, religion versus science, commerce versus established tradition—Americans seemed to have struck a harmonious balance.*

For America was born under the shelter of Plato's legacy as well. From the moment the first Pilgrims alighted at Plymouth Rock, it was the stepchild of the Reformation and became home to a peculiarly fervent evangelical Christianity. The utopian hope of making America a "shining city on the hill" and one nation under God—a historically grounded version of Augustine's Heav-

---

*The exception, of course, was slavery. But even here, Tocqueville noted, the clash was between two competing visions of liberty rather than between opposed political ideologies or conflicting classes.

enly City—has supplied as much drive and energy to America's development as its more practical Aristotelian side.[3]

But at its core was that practical desire "to tend to results without being bound to means," said Tocqueville, "and to aim at the substance through the form." Although the Frenchman noted that Americans had no philosophical school of their own, they certainly had a philosophical method—one that a pair of American thinkers in Gilded Age Boston would sum up as Pragmatism. Often abused, and just as often misunderstood, the Pragmatism of William James and Charles Sanders Peirce was in fact an attempt to capture that peculiar balance that is the heart of what is called American exceptionalism—and that forty years later would be summoned forth to save the rest of Western civilization.

This, indeed, is what makes America so striking. More than any other Western nation, its history has been characterized by a dynamic, if often unstable, balance between these two conflicting legacies. That balance lies at the core of the American "genius" for high-minded purposeful action that Jefferson noted; that caught the attention of Alexis de Tocqueville some fifty years later, when he pronounced America "a land of wonder"; and that has dazzled, puzzled, and exasperated foreign observers ever since.

Balance was of course the leading hallmark of the American Constitution itself—and the goal of all self-governing polities since Aristotle.

It's worth recalling the sharp contrast between Aristotle's view of governance and the one embodied by the Platonic tradition. The focus was not on the One (or the Absolute) but on the One balanced by the Few and the Many. There is no Philosopher Ruler or king standing in the image of God's plenitude of power. He is sent packing to the realm of the perfect Forms—and out of the realm of reality.

What rules instead are concrete constitutional arrangements based on real-life experience, distilled into a code of laws. Politics is above all a real-time partnership, requiring people's participation more than obedience, one in which the good life is found in living the process, not necessarily in the final result.

It was this view of constitutional "mixed" government that the Founding Fathers inherited from their Florentine and British forebears.[4] Achieving that classic balance between the One, the Few, and the Many, however, had al-

William James (1842–1910). "There is absolutely nothing new in the pragmatic method," he wrote. "Socrates was an adept at it. Aristotle used it methodically."

ways implied the goal of *stability*. If the mixture was allowed to change in any way, then Polybius's and Machiavelli's cycle of decay and doom would kick in—and change was the one thing Western man could not avoid. Even in the age of Enlightenment, men like John Adams sensed that liberty, no matter how desirable, was still fated not to last.[5]

The genius of the Constitution's chief author, James Madison, was to conceive of this constitutional balance as *dynamic*, not static. In Madison's vision, the legislative, executive, and judicial branches of American government would have their powers separated out, so that instead of cooperating they would be locked in permanent but dynamic competition. No group of cunning and unscrupulous men could seize control of one branch to dominate the others, as the Medici had in Florence (and as, many Americans felt, King

George's ministers had taken control of the Parliament in Britain), because other groups of cunning and unscrupulous men would naturally use the other branches to fight back.

It was in its way, a breathtaking proposition. But "ambition must be made to counteract ambition," Madison wrote. In this way, "through supplying opposite and rival interests," the separation of powers in the federal Constitution would "supply the defect of better motives"—a phrase that landed him in trouble with those, like John Adams, who preferred a more high-minded approach to republican government.[6] Indeed, it still provokes some resentment from those who believe that government, even in a free society, still has some Platonic duty to cultivate the virtues of its citizens.[7] Madison, however, was an admirer of David Hume as well as Aristotle. He understood better than some other Founding Fathers the tenacity of self-interest—and the lack in real life of enough better motives to go around.

In what David Hume had called the "perpetual intestine struggle between Liberty and Authority," Madison had concluded that the best way to preserve liberty in a modern society like America was to hobble authority through what he called countervailing interests. We have another term for it: gridlock. Through gridlock, Madison predicted, "the private interest of every individual may be a sentinel over the public rights. . . ." In this way, he wrote, it will be "very difficult, either by intrigue, prejudice, or passion, to hurry . . . any measures against the public interest." Except the "he" in this case wasn't Madison, but Hume himself.[8]

Madison saw the same healthy gridlock emerging in the looming battles between the federal government and the separate states, as well as between the new states and the old. In fact, in Madison's mind, the more the better. As settlers began moving beyond the Appalachians to the Mississippi and Great Lakes, and new states like Kentucky and Tennessee and Ohio came into the Union, the growing diversity of sectional interests would work in favor of everyone. "The society will be broken into so many parts, interests, and classes of citizens," Madison explained in The Federalist Papers, "that the rights of individuals, of the minority, will be in little danger from interested combinations of the majority."[9]

At the stroke of their pens, Madison and the Constitutional Convention of 1787 had at last devised a system that overcame the oldest objection of all to free government, that it could work only on a scale the size of Aristotle's Greek polis, perhaps five thousand people in all. The United States was now designed in such a way that the larger it grew, the freer it became. Democracy was finally able to embrace diversity and conflict instead of shunning it. What Rousseau feared as modern liberty's greatest weakness, its reliance on self-interest, turned out to be its hidden strength. And Plato's shame, the relentless pace of temporal change, was revealed to be Aristotle's glory.

For if the statesmen of the early American Republic anticipated the perpetual clash of interests *within* the halls of government, they expected just the opposite outside. The ruling American public ethos promised a more coordinated meshing of men's private desires and their public obligations, in the dynamic balance between the American instinct for individualism and the impulse for voluntary associations. It struck John Stuart Mill's friend Alexis de Tocqueville when he first visited the United States in 1831. Tocqueville saw how America offered strange proof of how Aristotle's *zoon politikon*, left to his or *her* own devices (he noted that the social freedom of American women was one of the glues of American culture), could create a sense of virtuous community purpose equal to anything Plato wanted to cultivate.

"Americans make associations to give entertainments," Tocqueville wrote in *Democracy in America*, "to found seminaries, to build inns, to construct churches, to diffuse books," to create hospitals, schools, and prisons, and to send missionaries to the tropics. Americans had learned that in a democracy, "individuals are powerless, if they do not learn voluntarily to help one another."[10] However, once they join together, "from that moment they are no longer isolated men, but a power seen from afar, whose actions serve for an example, and whose language is listened to." One such voluntary national movement, the temperance movement, would bring about the Eighteenth Amendment. Another, the abolition movement, would trigger the Civil War and end slavery in the United States.[11]

Tocqueville saw that some in Europe like Hegel argued that the way to help the individual overcome a sense of powerlessness in modern society was to increase the powers of government. Tocqueville believed this was a mistake. Such a move would destroy the motivation for volunteerism and the impulse for drawing together for a common purpose. "If men are to remain civilized," he concluded, "or to become so, the art of associating together must grow and improve in the same ratio in which the equality of conditions is increased."[12]

Certainly nothing displayed the power of this "art of associating" better than American business. "Today it is Americans who carry to their shores nine-tenths of the products of Europe," Tocqueville wrote in 1832. "American ships fill the docks of Le Havre and Liverpool, while the number of English vessels in New York harbor is comparatively small." Already by 1800 the United States had more business corporations than all of Europe put together. In short, American business was business almost before its founding.[13]

For Tocqueville and other foreign observers, American business embodied an energy that pulled down barriers social as well as geographic, as commerce and industry spread from New England across the Northeast; wealth was "circulating with inconceivable rapidity, and experience shows that it is rare to find two succeeding generations in the full enjoyment of it." Business was the new republic's most valuable renewable resource: indeed, "Americans put something heroic into their way of trading" that Tocqueville found fascinating and that he saw as in deep contrast to the slaveholding society of the South, where slavery "enervates the powers of the mind and benumbs the activity of master and slave alike."[14]

Tocqueville was struck by another important balance Americans had achieved, between the push for material progress and enlightenment and their evangelical Protestant roots. Never had Tocqueville seen a country in which religion was less apparent in outward forms. Still, it was all-pervasive, "presenting distinct, simple, and general notions to the mind" and culture, including to American Catholics.[15] This supplied a sense of moral solidarity borrowed from Luther and Calvin, which a democratic society built on the Enlightenment pattern might otherwise have to do without. "Belief in a God All Powerful wise and good," Madison wrote in 1821, "is so essential to the moral order of the World and to the happiness of man that arguments that enforce it cannot be drawn from too many sources"—including those, like Newton's, that found in nature the existence of nature's God.[16] Thomas Jefferson agreed. The author of the Declaration of Independence is the famed progenitor of the idea of separation of Church and State. He was a confirmed Deist, and while he deeply admired the figure of Jesus, he was also deeply suspicious of organized religion as the enemy of liberty. He saw it as another dangerous offshoot of Plato's baneful influence on the West.[17]

The answer was complete religious freedom, including the freedom *not* to believe. "It does me no injury," he wrote in *Notes on the State of Virginia*, "for my neighbor to say that there are twenty gods or no gods. It neither picks my pocket nor breaks my leg." Yet it was also Jefferson who wrote, "Can the liberties of a nation be thought secure when we have removed their only firm basis, a conviction in the minds of people that these liberties are the gift of God?" Later he added, "No nation has ever yet existed or been governed without religion. Nor can be."[18]

So from the start the United States found itself with a constitution founded on a permanent clash between the executive, legislative, and judicial branches and between federal power and states' rights (epitomized by the fierce ideological battles between Jefferson and Alexander Hamilton in the early decades of the Republic) and a sectional split between a commercial-minded North and a slave-owning South. It was also a society delicately balanced between individualism and volunteerism and between a business- and engineer-centered culture of focused practicality and a religious evangelism bordering on mysticism. Clearly, some kind of conceptual glue was going to be needed to hold all these disparate elements together if the new republic was going to survive.

For nearly seventy years, Americans found it in the ideas of Common Sense Realism. It was yet another product of the Scottish Enlightenment, but one with a firmer impress of both Protestant Christianity and Plato's idealism. In America, its principal spokesman was John Witherspoon, longtime president of Princeton University, signer of the Declaration of Independence, and mentor to an entire generation of American politicians and statesmen, among them James Madison.

The Common Sense philosophy (as it was also called) was a shrewd fusion of an empiricism borrowed from Locke and Aristotle and a moral intuitionism—the idea that the human mind has direct access to truths that the senses cannot reach—that can be traced back to Plato. Thomas Jefferson became a convert to it. Thanks to Witherspoon it became the reigning philosophy in every Protestant seminary of note in America. Its assumptions shaped American education from one-room country schoolhouses to Harvard Yard. It shaped American legal thinking from the moment the United States Supreme Court opened its doors (John Marshall was strongly influenced by it). Indeed, from the Constitutional Convention until the Compromise of 1850, Common Sense Realism was virtually the official creed of the American Republic.[19]

So what was it? Its founder, Thomas Reid, was part of the empirical tradition that flowed from Aristotle and John Locke, that all knowledge comes from experience. However, Reid made an important alteration to Locke's theories. Reid said that the mind is not an entirely blank tabula rasa but comes equipped with a set of "natural and original judgments" that enables human beings to separate out internal sensations arising within their own minds from sensations arising from an outside world.

In other words, we know automatically when we see a pencil in a glass of water that it isn't really bent even though it appears to be, just as we know someone's trying to pick our pocket even though he says he's only helping us on with our coat—and that there's a difference between good and evil even when certain philosophers say there isn't.

Reid called this power of judgment "common sense" because it is common to all human beings. Our common sense allows us to distinguish fantasy from reality and truth from falsehood and tell black from white and right from wrong—not by seeing the world as a series of mental images, but by interacting with it through mental *acts*. This power of judging is what enables us to live more fully in the real world, and the beliefs of common sense "are older and of more authority," Reid wrote, "than all the arguments of philosophy." Common sense tells us that the world consists of real objects that exist in real time and space. It also tells us that the more we know about those objects through our experience, the more effectively we can navigate our way through that reality.

More than any previous philosophy, Common Sense Realism had a built-in democratic bias, one reason it was so popular in America. The power of common judgment belongs to everyone, rich or poor, educated or uneducated; indeed, we exercise it every day in hundreds of ways. Of course, ordinary people make mistakes—but so do philosophers. And sometimes they cannot prove what they believe is true, but many philosophers have the same problem. On some things, however, like the existence of the real world and basic moral truths, they know they don't have to prove it. These things are, as Reid put it, self-evident, meaning they are "no sooner understood than they are believed" because they "carry the light of truth itself."

Common sense man turned out to be the enemy of more than just moral relativism. Madison's constitution had ensured that countervailing interests would jam the political doorway, allowing no one to get his agenda through without facing the opposition of others. How to sort it out? The answer was "that degree of judgment which is common," as Reid put it, "to men with whom we can converse and transact business." Common sense would enable people to agree on certain fundamental priorities and truths, so that a solution can be worked out, whether it's over a Supreme Court nomination or a tariff issue or whether America should go to war. In a democratic America where no one was officially in charge, not even philosophers, common sense would have to rule.

But what if it didn't rule? In 1860, it collapsed on the issue of slavery. Reasonable Americans, men who conducted business in Washington and elsewhere on those common sense principles every day, saw the same disaster looming: the secession of the southern states. All agreed it would be a disaster, many appealed to the many compromises struck since 1820 to make the issue go away. Yet no one could do anything to stop it. Some on both sides even welcomed it.

It took Abraham Lincoln to realize that abolitionists like William Lloyd Garrison had seen a higher truth that a common sense man like Stephen Douglas failed to recognize: Slavery wasn't just a national embarrassment or source of sectional friction. It was a deep and pervasive national sin. Lincoln was a prairie product of the American Enlightenment, a reader of Locke and Mill as well as Jefferson and the Founding Fathers. But Lincoln also believed in an Old Testament God who would make the nation pay a terrible price for selling human beings as chattel. Says Saint Paul's letter to the Hebrews (9:22), "Without shedding of blood there is no remission." Lincoln's God told him that the sin could be blotted out not by rational argument and compromise, but only by bloodshed.

As president, Lincoln may have started the Civil War believing that saving the Union and ending slavery were two distinct aims. By the time he issued the Emancipation Proclamation in 1862, he realized they were one and the same. Only then, as he stated in his Gettysburg Address, would America be ready for a new "birth of freedom" and to give a new meaning to the idea of democracy.[20] It took the slaughter of Gettysburg, Atlanta, the Wilderness, and Spotsylvania to convince the rest of the nation that he had been right.

It also meant that the old way of framing intellectual and moral debates in America would have to change. The Civil War of 1861–65 shattered the certainties of Common Sense Realism almost as decisively as the Great War would shatter those of Victorian Europe. Of course, as in the European case, the doubts and counterthrusts had begun years before that. Hegel, Kant, and German Idealism had broken through the Common Sense crust as early as the 1840s. It would branch out with the American Transcendentalists like

Ralph Waldo Emerson. It would grow into full blossom in the Harvard of Josiah Royce and George Santayana, just as Princeton served as the last bastion of Common Sense Realism under its Scottish-born president, James McCosh. Ernst Mach, Auguste Comte, even Karl Marx: all found American converts in the new post–Civil War industrial age.

It was clear some new reassessment of old principles was in desperate order, and the place it happened was in the thriving port city of Baltimore, at the brand-new university founded by a Quaker merchant named Johns Hopkins.

The life of its founder reflected many of the cross-currents of American culture, as well as the vibrancy of its business culture. Born in 1795 on a tobacco plantation, Hopkins was the son of Quakers who, in 1807, freed their slaves in accordance with Quaker doctrine and put their own eleven children, including twelve-year-old Johns, to work in the fields in their place.

Five years later Johns Hopkins left to join his uncle's wholesale grocery business in Baltimore—just in time to witness the British siege of Fort McHenry during the war that same year. After the war, Hopkins struck out to found a dry goods business on his own with his three brothers. Hopkins and Brothers became dealers in the region, and Johns Hopkins became a very rich man as well as a director of the fledgling Baltimore and Ohio Railroad.

The Civil War found him—unlike most Marylanders—a firm supporter of Abraham Lincoln and the abolitionist cause: he even gave the Union Army use of the B&O for free. After the war he poured his fortune into various philanthropic projects, including a college in the District of Columbia for African-American women, an orphanage in Baltimore for black children, and a university in the same town that opened its doors three years after his death, in 1876.

Under its first president, Daniel Coit Gilman, the Johns Hopkins University was the first American academy founded to compete with its European counterparts in the breadth of its learning and depth of its cutting-edge research. Gilman recruited scientific giants such as mathematician James Sylvester and physicists Henry Rowland and Lord Kelvin, inventor of the famous temperature scale but also a major researcher in electromagnetism and atomic theory—the same frontiers James Clerk Maxwell and Ludwig

Boltzmann were exploring on the other side of the Atlantic. Gilman hired famed philosophers George S. Morris and Stanley Hall; and the first Hopkins PhDs in philosophy would go to such future luminaries as Josiah Royce, Thorstein Veblen, and a rumpled, nearsighted youngster from Vermont named John Dewey.

Gilman always said the goal of a university should be "to make less misery for the poor, less ignorance in the schools, less suffering in the hospitals"—in 1893 he would create the Johns Hopkins Medical School, run by the legendary English physician Sir William Osler—"less fraud in business, and less folly in politics."[21] But his most significant contribution was hiring a shy man with a degree in chemistry from Harvard and a background in physics and astronomy who happened to be working for the U.S. Coast and Geodetic Survey, to teach the Hopkins students logic.

He was Charles Sanders Peirce, and together with another visitor to Hopkins who occasionally dropped in from Harvard to lecture there, William James (Gilman tried desperately to hire James full time, but Harvard refused to let him go), he would create America's first homegrown philosophical creed—one, more than any other, that worked to translate the culture's dynamic balance of Plato and Aristotle into a conscious way of understanding the world.

Although Peirce devoted himself to teaching logic, few people in America had better knowledge of the new trends in Western scientific thinking, from Darwin to Maxwell's thermodynamics and Mach's Positivism—as well as the mathematics of probability. That knowledge, however, made him uneasy. It was the same unease that had stirred Henry More in the mid-1600s about the triumph of the new mechanical science, on the eve of Newton's arrival at Cambridge.

In an impersonal world that has finally, definitively banished all final causes from nature and our lives—including, presumably God—what happens to the human factor? "The world . . . is evidently not governed by blind law," Peirce would write, "its leading characteristics are absolutely irreconcilable with that view"—including how we lead our lives in accordance with the basic assumption of free will.[22] Yet the triumph of Darwin and science, and the breakup of Common Sense Realism, had seemed to encourage people to think the opposite, and made them feel as minor cogs in the great impersonal machine of Nature.

A man said to the universe:
"Sir, I exist!"
"However," replied the universe,
"The fact has not created in me
A sense of obligation."

Stephen Crane

No wonder others were being drawn to the nihilistic pessimism already surfacing in the Europe of Friedrich Nietzsche (*Birth of Tragedy* appeared the year after Peirce published his first article in *North American Review*); in the deterministic materialism of Karl Marx (the first American edition of *The Communist Manifesto* appeared in 1871); and in the strange supernatural flights of the mystagogue Baron Swedenborg (one of them was William James's father). Peirce would have argued that Hegel belonged in the same camp.

That disillusionment had already appeared in the works of Mark Twain. The author of *Tom Sawyer* and *The Adventures of Huckleberry Finn* felt a chronic anxiety about the direction the country was headed after the Civil War, a gloom that broke the surface in his late essays, titled *What Is Man?*: "There is no God, no universe, no human race, no earthly life, no heaven, no hell. It is all a dream—a grotesque and foolish dream. Nothing exists but you. And you are but . . . a useless thought, a homeless thought, wandering forlorn among the empty eternities."[23] Discovery of the law of entropy had led historian Henry Adams to conclude that the human race was stuck on a degenerative course that would leave not only civilization but the planet itself a cold, lifeless lump of matter by 2025, yet Adams himself was the grandson of a president, John Quincy Adams, and great-grandson of another, John Adams.[24]

It was precisely this demoralizing despair that Peirce was trying to fight against. Surely there had to be a more secure way to find our place in the world, Peirce believed; a way to rebuild the foundations of both thinking about and living in a universe governed by change, uncertainty, and chance. An America that ceased to believe truth and justice, right and wrong, are as real and important to life as the laws of evolution and physics, was doomed.[25]

In this, Peirce sympathized with Common Sense Realism. Indeed, he considered his new philosophical path as only a deeper furrow in the direction already charted out by Reid, Witherspoon, and their followers. Still, the old Common Sense school had made two fundamental errors. The first was that it confused certainty with objectivity; the second was that it confused doubt with lack of clarity. In fact, common sense judgments, even our most certain and universal ones, are bound to change with the accumulation of new evidence. "Original beliefs only remain indubitable," Peirce wrote, as long as they seem applicable to our current conduct. When they aren't, they can change with a sudden flash of insight.

The classic example is our knowledge that the earth revolves around the sun. At one time, believing the opposite seemed the height of common sense, while those who doubted were deemed either idiots or frauds—as Galileo had found out. Today, however, anyone arguing that the earth is the center of the cosmos would seem the real idiot, as much as the man who insists the earth is flat. Rutherford and Niels Bohr would even apply the heliocentric solar system as their "common sense" model of the atom.

How "flat earthers" (or "global warming deniers") become repellent to our common sense has little to do with objective evidence, Peirce realized. It has everything to do, however, with how we weigh doubt in the balance of outcomes. The more vital the consequences, the less tolerant we are of doubt and the more certain of our judgment. Yet doubt, Peirce pointed out, is the starting point for acquiring all certain knowledge. What Peter Abelard had believed about logic and theology—"Through doubting we come to understand"—Peirce insisted was the basic rule for modern science as well. It is the desire to *clear away doubt* that leads to genuine empirical investigation and to arriving at the truth. But with it comes a realization that some of "our indubitable beliefs may be proved false."[26]

Some beliefs have to remain fixed. We may doubt that the sky is really blue; science teaches us it isn't. But we cannot doubt that it *seems* blue. We cannot doubt that we live in the real world, but we can't be certain all our judgments about it are accurate. What we can know is that they are *our* judgments and that they have inescapable practical consequences. "The Critical Common Senser," Peirce wrote, "holds there is less danger to science in believing too little than believing too much. Yet for all that, the consequences of believing too little may be no less than disaster."[27]

Peirce was the most original American thinker of the 1800s. Yet before his death in 1914, he remained largely unknown and his important writings unpublished. It was left to his friend William James to turn his new way of thinking about the relationship between reason and truth into a philosophical guided missile that would light up the skies of America, and Europe, as well.

. . .

He was born in 1842 in New York City; his father, Henry James Sr., was a celebrated religious figure and his brother a distinguished novelist. His own claim to fame was to translate the traditional problems of philosophy into a distinctive American idiom. James charmed professional and amateur readers alike with vivid phrases like "the buzzing blooming world of reality," the "cash value" of ideas and propositions, and "the bitch goddess success." His gift for putting abstruse problems in ordinary language also allowed him to redefine the old battle between rationalism and empiricism—or ideas versus facts—as essentially a clash between two types of human personality, the "tough-minded" and the "tender-minded."

"Empiricist," he wrote in 1907, "means your lover of facts in all their crude variety, rationalist means your devotee to abstract and eternal principles. . . . The individual rationalist is what is called a man of feeling, [while] the individual empiricist prides himself on being hardheaded."

He drew up their character in two contrasting columns:

THE TENDER-MINDED	THE TOUGH-MINDED
Rationalistic (going by principles)	Empiricist (going by facts)
Intellectualistic	Sensationalistic
Idealistic	Materialistic
Optimistic	Pessimistic
Religious	Irreligious
Freewillist	Fatalistic
Monistic	Pluralistic
Dogmatical	Skeptical

The two philosophers James saw as epitomizing the tender-minded versus tough-minded split were probably Hegel and John Stuart Mill.[28] Still, with the exception of optimism and pessimism (and here James was thinking of the optimism of Hegelians and Marxists in believing history has a final purpose), it's clear he was really talking about the perennial split between Platonists and Aristotelians in a distinctly American guise.

Indeed, he might have been standing in front of Raphael's *School of Athens* when he wrote that the clash between the tough- and tender-minded "has formed in all ages a part of the philosophical atmosphere." Each has a low opinion of the other. "The tough think of the tender as sentimentalists and soft-heads"—in other words, as a collection of weak-willed Percy Shelleys or Walt Whitmans. "The tender feel the tough to be unrefined, callous, or brutal"—a nation of John Waynes.

However, James realized that "most of us have a hankering for the good things on both sides of the line." What was needed instead was a stable blend of the two temperaments.[29] What was needed, William James believed, was an intellectual creed *tender-minded* enough to show us our connection to something outside ourselves; but also *tough* enough to deal with robust reality, whether it's a presidential election, analyzing the behavior of atoms, or driving a locomotive across the Great Plains.

James called his creed Pragmatism. He had borrowed the term from Charles S. Peirce,[30] which was summed up in Peirce's statement that "to understand a proposition means to know what is the case if it is true." Truth, in short, emerges from the *consequences*—what Peirce called the upshot—of what we say or believe.[31] We go back to the example of the earth going around the sun or vice versa. If we wished, the debate could go on endlessly; no matter how indubitable the evidence on paper or in photographs, some margin for doubt could still emerge, no matter how tiny.

But try launching the space shuttle on the assumption that we live in a geocentric universe and see what happens. "Seeing what happens" is not only a factor in figuring out whether a scientific theory is true or not. For William James, it is *the* factor, now and forever, in all forms of knowledge. To know something is not to arrive at a final state of mental being or a form of inner consciousness; or even (as Wittgenstein would soon claim) a certain logical form. It is a constant process involving the perceiving self and "the immediate flux of life which furnishes the material of our later reflection."[32]

It was a groundbreaking insight—possibly the most important of the twentieth century.[33] Scientific truth, Peirce had asserted, was no more a series of breakthroughs to intellectual certainty than predicting the weather. Instead, it is a series of constant laboratory experiments in which we test hypotheses, run the numbers or heat up the test tubes, and see what comes out.[34] William James affirmed the same was true of life. We grope and feel our way along step by step, trying out and sticking to what works and dropping what doesn't. Our knowledge grows in *spots*, James liked to say.[35] It is from this humble process, not from enacting some series of a priori principles or a transcendental *Diktats* à la Hegel, that human progress is made. It was in a profound sense an outgrowth of the old Common Sense Realism—"common sense is less sweeping in its demands than philosophy or mysticism have been wont to be, and can suffer the notion of this world being partly saved and partly lost"—and one perfectly suited, James thought, for America, the Common Sense Nation.

Not that James underestimated its importance to previous thinkers. "Socrates was an adept at it," he wrote. "Aristotle used it methodically. Locke, Berkeley, and Hume made momentous contributions to truth by its means." This part of James's Pragmatism, the tough-minded Aristotelian side of the ledger, was empirical in the sense that data are the ultimate data of truth and utilitarian in Mill's sense of learning by doing.[36] At the same time, James was more insistent than any of his "tough-minded" predecessors that truth is a process *not* just of discovery, but also of intuitive creation.

A modern reader has an easier time grasping what James meant than his Gilded Age contemporaries did, because of our experience of commuter traffic. As a commuter we see the map, we know the rules of the road, and we know where we are headed. We even have the last word in technology over GPS, which is supposed to know all the answers and supply us with all the knowledge we need.

But once we're in our car, we find that the quickest route recommended by GPS is blocked by an accident, while the alternative is temporarily closed for construction. We are forced to try a series of different routes, sometimes relying on our past experience, sometimes asking advice from taxi drivers or passersby, and sometimes based on pure hunch. We decide to cut through a parking lot here or even head back across town there. But we never turn around and give up or abandon the car to hitch a ride to the airport instead. We accept the *consequences of the decisions we make on the move* and keep going until we finally reach our goal.

Once we get to our destination—and this is true whether it's an office building or the truth of a proposition—we can retrace our route on the map and say, "Here's how I got here." But as with most of life, James would argue, how we got there was never according to plan. The journey unfolds instead through a series of deliberate choices, based on what we know has worked in the past and what we think will work now.

The anthropologist Clifford Geertz once quipped, "Life is a bowl of strategies." William James would have agreed, although he put it somewhat differently: "An idea is 'true' so long as to believe it is profitable to our lives."[37]

Understandably, some critics have branded his Pragmatism a squishy form of moral relativism. Others, alternately, see it as an ideology peculiarly suited to a nation of engineers and capitalist entrepreneurs.[38] But James himself could counter that what we call fixed moral principles are themselves the end products of the same experimental process, including the Ten Commandments. What kind of society could exist, after all, where men were free to covet their neighbors' wives and cattle or commit murder on a whim? God's command is one thing, and an important thing. The proof, however, is in the doing.

In fact, James's Pragmatism is inherently *conservative* in Edmund Burke's sense — and Aristotle's. Every subject of knowledge, Aristotle wrote in Book II of the *Ethics,* has its own method. We learn to play the flute by studying the best flute players; we learn to understand mathematics by studying with the best mathematicians. The same is true of our ethical and social life, Aristotle argued: by following the best-tested rules of our predecessors, we can expect the best results.[39]

If others in the past have done what I'm trying to do successfully in a certain way, whether we're talking about self-government or conducting a business deal or a marriage, then I should be inclined (though not necessarily required) to do it that way, too. James's Pragmatism doesn't cut us off from Burke's definition of society as "the partnership of the living, those to come, and those who came before." Far from it. It imbeds us in it, as an active participant in the same perennial search for answers.

Finally, James's Pragmatism was pluralistic. Philosophers since Plato had assumed there was one way out of the cave: *their* way. Now thanks to James it turned out there may be more than one way at any given moment — particularly when at almost the same time, modern physics, including quantum physics, was revealing that the cave itself was constantly changing.

Charles Darwin had made process the basic structure of biology. By the time of William James's death in 1910, Boltzmann, Einstein, and Bohr were showing that an evolutionary process governed the basic structure of the physical world as well. To such a world, James offered a vital message. We need to be open to possibilities, since circumstances might one day prove our assumptions wrong — including circumstances of our own making. The power of the individual to change, not only his own life, but the world, was not diminished but affirmed, by the precepts of Pragmatism.

So instead of Plato's universe of moral absolutes, Pragmatism leaves us with a universe of probable outcomes. "So far as man stands for anything," James wrote, "and is productive or originative at all, his entire vital function may be said to have to deal with maybes." Still, in order for this approach to work, we need a destination—just like the commuter in traffic. The goal of James's Pragmatism was to arrive at a truth that works, not just go with the flow.

And here we come to the other, tender-minded Platonic side of James's thinking, on the issue of religious belief.

His *The Will to Believe* (1897) and *The Varieties of Religious Experience* (1902) drew a sharp differentiation between trying to treat religion as a set of *truths* and seeing it as a set of *beliefs* that give force and meaning to our lives. Truths are ideas we can verify; false ideas are those we can't.[40] We may not be able to *prove* God exists; but believing He does can change our lives and actions in profound ways that, from the Pragmatic standpoint, can actually make that belief true. "There are cases," James said, "where a fact cannot come at all unless a preliminary faith exists in its coming."

James liked to use the example of a train robbery. A pair of bandits rob an entire train of passengers because the robbers believe they can count on each other if they encounter trouble, while each passenger believes resisting means instant death, even though they outnumber the thugs a hundred to one. The result is a robbery. However, "if we believed that the whole carful would rise at once with us, we should each severally rise, and train-robbing would never even be attempted."[41]

Or take the mountain climber who has to leap an immense and deep chasm in order to return home. If he believes he can make it, he can make it. If he hesitates and jumps halfheartedly, he will plunge to his death. Beliefs, James believed, are rules for action, including (or especially) Christianity. Religious belief helps us to overcome the maybes and the self-doubts that lurk in the normal interactions of life. It can inspire a mountain climber to superhuman acts or a drug addict to stop taking heroin. It can inspire people to resist a fearsome tyranny or save others from the same threat.

"The world interpreted religiously," he told a European audience in 1902, "is *not* the materialistic world over again with an altered expression." It looks and *is* different from the one a pure materialist sees and through which he moves, even with the benefit of science. An Aristotelian view allows us to see clear and far. A Platonist belief may help us to see farther.

"St. Paul long ago," he wrote in *Varieties*, "made our ancestors familiar with the idea that every soul is virtually sacred. Since Christ died for us all without exception, St. Paul said, we must despair of no one. This belief in the essential sacredness of everyone," he continued, became the driving force of modern Christianity and its humanitarian offshoots from penal reform to aversion to the death penalty. It is "the tip of the wedge, the cleaver of the darkness."[42]

In America, William James created an entirely new school of philosophy, Pragmatism, which spawned followers in logic, sociology, and the other social sciences. In Europe, however, he had an impact unlike any other American thinker before or since. Henri Bergson hailed James as a soul mate for his celebration of "the immediate flux of life" as the essential grounding of all knowledge. From opposite ends of the political spectrum, Georges Sorel and Max Weber both relied on his demolition of the notion that knowledge is an essentially contemplative activity.

The Logical Positivists, meanwhile, were quick to claim him as one of their own, for seeing life as well as science as a constant process of experiment out of which a unified picture of reality gradually emerges.*[43] This affinity may seem odd, since unlike the men of the Vienna Circle, James had seen the benefits of religion and metaphysical belief in people's lives. He was even open to the possibility that they might in fact be true, including spiritualism and life after death.

At the same time, however, James shared the Vienna Circle's detestation of tyranny and fanaticism in either its intellectual or its political form. He was horrified by those like Hegel and Marx who celebrated conflict and violence as necessary steps in human progress, or those like Nietzsche who saw in man's dark side a source of healing vitality.[44] To despise compassion as weakness is not an expression of the love of life, but its opposite.

From the serene perspective of Gilded Age Harvard Yard, James had been inclined to treat these threats somewhat lightheartedly. "To my personal

---

*His impact on Ludwig Wittgenstein was decisive. Wittgenstein read *The Will to Believe* and *The Varieties of Religious Experience* with his usual laser insight. They helped him to realize that the world he had described in the *Tractatus*, as a matrix of logic and scientific propositions, was missing a key component: real-life experience and how language seeks to describe it, however imperfectly. The next great stage in Wittgenstein's philosophical quest, the analysis of ordinary language, which consumed him until his death in 1951, was at least in part inspired by James.

knowledge," he once wrote, "all Hegelians are not prigs but I somehow feel as if prigs end up, if developed, by becoming Hegelians." But what would keep their ideas at bay, he believed, and keep them from seizing power was a nation of men and women committed to what experience teaches us works. Such a people can afford to be realistic about the challenges of the present, but also optimistic about the multiple possibilities for the future. Like the train passengers defending themselves against the armed thugs, they will be inclined to say to one another: We can do this, and do it together.

These, then, are my last words to you. Be not afraid of life. Believe that life is worth living, and your belief will help create the fact. The scientific proof that you are right may not be clear before the day of judgement (or some stage of being which that expression may serve to symbolize) is reached. But the faithful fighters of this hour, or the be-ings that then and there will represent them, may then turn to the faint-hearted, who here decline to go on, with words with which Henry IV greeted the tardy Crillon after a great victory had been gained: "Hang yourself, brave Crillon! We fought at Arques, and you were not there."[45]

James spoke these words to the Harvard YMCA in October 1895. The movement he and Charles Peirce had founded was about to be hijacked, pulled and dragged in a direction quite contrary to the one they had in mind—and which would disrupt American politics for more than a genera-tion. But forty years later, James's words could serve as a rallying cry, as the forces of barbarism and darkness descended on Europe, from both the West and the East.

Twenty-nine

WORLDS AT WAR:
PLATO AND ARISTOTLE
IN THE VIOLENT CENTURY

*I see more clearly than ever before that even our greatest troubles
spring from something that is as admirable and sound as it is
dangerous—from our impatience to better the lot of our fellows.*
— Karl Popper, *The Open Society and Its Enemies* (1945)

Aristotle's philosophy was the intellect's Declaration of Independence.
—Ayn Rand, *For the New Intellectual* (1961)

You can watch it in the Bundesarchiv newsreel footage. The crowds cheering
along the entire motorcade route, the crowd waving bouquets of flowers;
some weep. Others shout until they are hoarse: "Heil Hitler! Heil Hitler!"

It was March 14, 1938, and the *Anschluss*, the absorption of the nation of
Austria into the Third Reich. Without a doubt it was the most popular event
in Austria's history.[1] The majority of Austrians were tired of being losers; they
wanted to be part of history's winners. The writer Karl Kraus had once predicted that *fin de siècle* Vienna would be "the proving ground of world destruction." The city of Ernst Mach, Sigmund Freud, and the Vienna Circle
was also the city where Adolf Hitler had spent his youth as a starving artist,
nursing his resentments against those he blamed for his personal and professional failures. Now in the spring of 1938 he was returning to Vienna in tri-

umph, surrounded by chanting, adoring crowds and a sea of arms upthrust in the Nazi salute. Hitler later said that on returning, he met a stream of love such as he had never experienced. "I can only describe him," said one eyewitness that afternoon, "as being in a state of ecstasy."[2]

Hitler began his revenge almost at once. Even as his black limousine rolled onto the Ringstrasse on March 14, his henchman Heinrich Himmler was rounding up more than seventy-five thousand "undesirables" in Vienna, meaning Jews. Days later, hundreds of Jewish men and women were on their hands and knees, set to work cleaning Vienna's gutters. SS men gathered around, jeering and kicking their helpless prisoners. Crowds of ordinary Viennese joined in. An American eyewitness called it "an orgy of sadism."[3] What began that week in March 1938 would finish at Dachau and Auschwitz.

From our point of view, Germany's Third Reich was the end product of a Hegelian nation-state taken over by a racialized Nietzschean will to power. The yearning for absolute power to do good had become the tool for doing evil. One by one, the centers of intellectual life in eastern Europe, the new homes of Aristotle, would be devoured by its advance: Vienna and Graz in 1938, Prague in 1939, Warsaw and Lublin the same year. The major figures of Logical Positivism, many of whom were Jews, had sensed what was coming and fled abroad.

One of them was a thirty-six-year-old former high school teacher who had attended several of the circle's meetings in the heyday of the early thirties. He had found refuge even farther away than the others who moved to America or England, in New Zealand. In fact, he was sitting at his desk in Canterbury University College in Christchurch when news of the *Anschluss* reached him.

It wasn't hard for him to visualize the scene. Before he had left Vienna two years earlier, he had seen the groups of swastika-armbanded Nazis wandering the streets. They were young Austrians, drawn to the vision of an Aryan National Socialist state the way young Rousseauians had been drawn to the French Revolution 150 years earlier. Most had been singing Nazi songs and accosting anyone they thought might be a Jew. With a studied brutal hostility, one of them had come up to him and waved a pistol.

Where are you from? Karl Popper asked. Carinthia, the young man replied contemptuously. Popper was about to say something when the young man stuck the pistol under his nose. "What, you want to argue?" he sneered. "I don't argue, I shoot."[4]

Now the memory came back to Popper with a startling power. How could this happen? he asked himself. The hard-won fruits of two thousand years of Western civilization had been reason, tolerance, and individual freedom. It seemed incredible that an entire generation had decided to reject all three, not just in Austria and Nazi Germany, but in Soviet Russia, where Stalin's purges were building to their bloodstained climax.*

How had civilization gotten so off track? The answer, Karl Popper decided, was that it had been betrayed by its intellectual leadership, both past and present. One of the betrayers was clearly Georg Friedrich Hegel, the progenitor of the all-powerful modern state. Another was Karl Marx. But Popper saw another figure lurking deeper in the shadows to whom the blame for the rise of modern totalitarianism could largely be attached.

That figure was Plato.

Popper knew his conclusion would be shocking to scholars and the public alike. They had been conditioned by centuries of humanist education to consider Plato as the most eloquent and sublime of ancient Greek thinkers and, along with Aristotle, one of the twin pillars of Western thought.

From Popper's perspective, that was precisely the problem. Plato's spell was hardly a humanist one. In fact, Popper would assert, it had been Plato in the *Republic* and the *Laws* who first encouraged Western man "to see the individual as a pawn, as a somewhat insignificant instrument in the general development" of society toward virtue. It was Plato's assertion of "the principle of collective unity" and in the *Laws* that "no one should ever be without a leader" that had spawned the succession of would-be Philosopher Rulers who had bathed history in blood, from Plato's friend the tyrant Dion of Syracuse to Stalin and Hitler.[5]

Popper set to work that same day on the book that would eventually bear the title *The Open Society and Its Enemies*. He spent all of World War II writing it. He confessed to friends that he considered it his "war work," as important to saving the West as building ships or manufacturing bombs. In his mind, it was a much needed riposte to a century and a half of philosophical doctrines that had attacked the Aristotelian "open society" of democracy, tol-

---

*Archives show that in 1937 and 1938 alone, Stalin's secret police arrested more than 1.75 million persons. Of those, more than 85 percent would be sentenced to the Gulag; more than half of those would be executed.

erance, pluralism, and free inquiry and celebrated the monistic uniformity, intolerance, and regimentation of the "closed" society for the sake of the ideals of virtue and justice.

Hegel and Marx were Popper's principal foes.* However, the entire first volume was an extended attack on Plato. Popper targeted more than just his political and social doctrines in the *Republic*—pretty fair game from a more pluralist perspective, as Aristotle was the first to show. He also hammered at their larger metaphysical basis. At bottom Popper's thesis was that Plato had passed on to posterity a singularly dangerous vision of history.

Popper dubbed that vision *historicism*. Hegel had shared it; Marx had inherited it. During his years in Vienna, Popper had already written a book on the subject, one that grew out of his interest in the philosophy of science.[6] Popper defined historicism as the doctrine that history is governed by certain evolutionary laws, the discovery of which allows us to prophesy the destiny of mankind.

Why did Popper think Plato's historicism was important? First, because it destroys the notion of free will. It wrecks the notion that the future depends on us and the consequences of our own individual actions—the same principle, in fact, that William James had been arguing for on the other side of the Atlantic. Second, it encourages men to think they can use these laws to build a better future for society than if men are left to themselves. They become tempted to set themselves up as a ruling elite of Platonic Philosopher Rulers based on their knowledge of where History with a capital H is going. "The tendencies of historicism appeal to those who feel a call to be active: to interfere, especially with human affairs, refusing to accept the existing state of affairs as inevitable"—or as the result of human nature.[7]

"The wise shall lead and rule," Plato had written, "and the ignorant shall follow." Reading this passage from the *Laws* in the light of Aristotelian and Enlightenment-based models made it clear that Plato intended to divide society between Those Who Know and Those Who Must Obey.[8] "Never," Popper wrote, "was a man more in earnest in his hostility to the individual" than Plato. Popper pointed to another passage from the *Laws*, written in the con-

---

*Curiously, Popper gives Rousseau little mention. The main reason may have been that the iconoclast from Geneva was an intellectual lightweight compared with the other two. In addition, his influence on German thought, including that of Kant, was never as manifestly malign as Plato's modern successors Hegel and Marx.

Karl Popper (1902–94): He saw in Plato the roots of the
totalitarianism that was engulfing the world.

text of military tactics: "The greatest principle is that nobody, whether male
or female, should be without a leader."[9] It was this same principle that, Popper argued, the Communist Party in Russia, the Fascist Party in Italy, and the
Nazi Party in Germany all embraced and made their own.

Was Popper right? Certainly the men who led Stalinist Russia, Mussolini's Italy, and Nazi Germany saw themselves in historicist terms, as the van-
guard of the future.[10] On the other hand, Popper's underestimation of the
impact of Rousseau and Nietzsche, not to mention the racial doctrines
springing from Darwin and his disciples missed half the target. All the same,
we don't have to accept Popper's assessment of the totalitarian thrust of Plato's philosophy to agree on one point. The twentieth century's greatest ideo-

logical conflicts do mark the violent unfolding of a Platonist versus Aristotelian view of what it means to be free and how reason and knowledge ultimately fit into our lives.

For Aristotle, the locus of rational planning had always been the individual and his *oikos*, or household. In the same way, justice, or who deserves what, pertains to the individual person apart from his or her social or economic function. No notion of individual or natural right can take root without it.[11]

From the very start, Plato had argued the opposite. Justice belongs to the social and economic whole, the community. Indeed, it presupposes it. That community may be perfect (as in the *Republic*) or imperfect, depending on whether it upholds an absolute standard of virtue or goodness. However, the same basic rule applies: To belong is to submit to a definition of virtue and justice that is common to all, whether Philosopher Ruler or Guardian or Worker, because all are part of the whole. It is those who stand outside the system—the ones Plato dubbed foreigners, or *metics*—who receive no justice at all. "In a sense, their very existence as the Other undermines it: a point Rousseau picked up when he said that Spartans' hatred of foreigners sprang from their love and respect for one another.

What had been a theoretical exercise for Plato twenty-four centuries ago, and was obscured for nearly two thousand years by the evolution of Christianity, would become a major exercise in social engineering in the modern age. After Saint Augustine, Plato's community of justice had been expanded and redefined as Christendom. Its sources of law and order and virtue were other-worldly. They were made softer, more broadly accessible and human, by Neoplatonism, in both its medieval and its Renaissance forms. Saint Bernard's devotion to a religion of the heart does not make him appealing to the modern humanist. Conversely, Erasmus was deeply devoted to the welfare and advance of Christendom. But no one would ever accuse either one of being a totalitarian.

When that Neoplatonist frame fell away, however, what was left was a commitment to the community of virtue in a starkly secular form. The Other for medieval Christianity had been preeminently outsiders: the Muslim, the Jew, and the infidel. In modern Europe, the Other suddenly appeared from within the community as dangerous parasites to be exposed and removed. The Other became Robespierre's counterrevolutionaries; then Marx's class enemies; and finally Hitler's useless mouths and racial degenerates, including the Jews.

"The first question we ask," wrote one of Lenin's minions, "is—to what class does he belong, what are his origins, upbringing, education, profession? These questions define the fate of the accused. This," he added, "is *the essence of the Red Terror*."[12] It was not a sentence Plato or Augustine could have written. But Robespierre could, and did. Likewise Lenin and Goebbels. The collapse of Platonized Christianity under the Enlightenment assault, along with the Neoplatonist kingship of Louis XIV, had left certain hostages to fortune. The Romantics rescued some of them. But when men sought absolutes in the political sphere again—as they were bound to do—they found them in a communitarian vision shorn of any compassion or pity.

Karl Popper was a philosopher, not a historian. In Popper's view, it was Hegel and not Rousseau who was the pivotal figure in turning totalitarian theory into practice. Hegel, after all, had been the original inspirer of both Marx and the celebrants of the Prussian state that Hitler took over and fulfilled. More than anything else, it was Hegel's belief that history made society a staging ground for the realization of perfection that united the totalitarians of the Left and the Right in 1939 against everyone else.

At the same time, Popper saw Hegel's role running deeper. The Enlightenment of Voltaire, Hume, and Adam Smith had built its social and political vision, including the role of commerce and free markets, around Aristotle's idea that human nature is uniform and unchanging. Its belief in natural law and the growth of civil society; in the development of natural religion; in the notion of the unity of mankind running from Aquinas to Las Casas and Humboldt and Darwin; and in Thomas Reid's conception of a democratic common sense: All presupposed that human beings will react to things the same way at all times and in all places. This also means they want and desire the same things as human beings, above all individual freedom.

Hegel chose to deny this.[13] Instead, he insisted human nature was itself created and shaped by historical forces, just as society was. It was history as the unfolding of the Absolute that finally determined what we are and who we want to be. This is why Hegel, the ultimate historical determinist, believed there are no "lessons" to be learned from history. Human beings learn nothing from experience. Instead, experience shapes *them*, including their wants and desires—however much they seem "natural" at the time.

The Athenian citizen and the medieval Crusader; the Tuareg tribesman and the white explorer; Martin Luther and John Stuart Mill: In the Hegelian view, all see the world from entirely subjective perspectives determined by their historical time and place.* They have nothing in common beyond their biological needs. Instead, what they do share is being part of the historical process, moving parts on the ascent to the One, even if they are unaware of it.

In this ultimate Big Picture, the self-interested individual of bourgeois capitalism is a temporary aberration. Hegel's nation-state could mold him into something better and more edifying than the self-interested Wal-Mart shopper whom Rousseau and the Romantics had excoriated, but around whom Western civil society had built itself. "In the perfection of the state," Hegel had written, "each and every element . . . [will reach] its free existence" as each human being is molded to fit into that final perfect community.[14]

Plato had created his *Republic* to make men better than they are. The same conceit (it seems) had infected Pythagoras, who attempted to make the citizens of Croton live according to his theory of perfection. They thanked him by driving him from Croton and throwing his works into the sea. The medieval Church inherited the same task, while never assuming it could really change man's basic sinful nature. In the modern secular era, however, that acceptance of a limitation faded.

Rousseau had taken up the Platonic conceit anew: by suppressing the desire of the individual, human beings can realize their moral redemption. Hegel had given Plato's idea of statecraft as soulcraft[15] a new intellectual varnish—one that drew not only extremists on the political left and right, but more moderate men casting around for an alternative to Marxism on one side, and fascism on the other.

This was true even of America. James Madison had said, "If men were angels, no government would be necessary." By 1900, however, certain Americans were beginning to think men *could* become angels, with government helping them to do it.

They called themselves Progressives, and Hegel's influence was profound. One of them was John Dewey, the creator of modern Progressive education and student of the most prominent neo-Hegelian in America, Johns Hopkins University's George Sylvester Morris.[16] Another was Harvard's Josiah Royce,

---

*Or latterly, by their class or race or gender. Hegel stands as the original mentor of multiculturalism as well as deconstruction—that is, the idea that all meaning, like human nature, is relativized.

fierce opponent of the Pragmatic theories of William James. Still another was
Herbert Croly, a former James student until he found headier fodder in the
writings of Hegel. Croly's *Promise of American Life,* published in 1909,
marked the first major breakthrough of Hegel onto the American political
scene.[17] It also signaled the demise of laissez-faire economics as part of American liberalism.

The time had come, Croly argued, to move away from Thomas Jefferson's
version of America with its concept of "democracy as tantamount to extreme
individualism" and of society as a collection of individuals "fundamentally
alike in their abilities and deserts." Such a vision might have worked in the
early days of the American Republic, Croly said. However, the advent of industrial capitalism and its large concentration of wealth in the hands of men
like Morgan, Rockefeller, and Carnegie, along with masses of foreign immi-
grants and an industrial working class, meant that such a simple vision of
agrarian individualism could no longer work.[18]

Croly's solution was to use the power of the federal government to revivify
and reshape American democracy. The "intellectual lethargy, superficiality,
and insincerity" of American political thinking, he declared, must be swept
aside. A new leadership class was needed to remake American institutions
based on "the formative idea" that modern democracy must benefit every
citizen, not just the rich or economically privileged, and that all citizens loving one another and loving their country forms the true core of a national
interest.[19]

"There is no reason why a democracy cannot trust its interests absolutely
to the care of the national interest," Croly concluded, "and . . . every reason
why the American democracy should become . . . frankly, unscrupulously,
and loyally nationalist." In this new arrangement, old-fashioned Jeffersonian
individualism would fade into history. The power of the individual states, the
other half of Madison's constitutional system, would have to give way, too.
The days of Madisonian gridlock would be over. However, "popular interests
have nothing to fear from a measure of Federal centralization."[20] Instead, this
shift would constitute a new Declaration of Independence: essentially, a new
kind of America.[21]

To be sure, any increase in the power of central government would spell
the end of certain aspects of traditional American democracy, in its freewheeling economic life, for example, and its creed of self-reliance. However,
"the fault in that case lies with the democratic tradition; and the erroneous

and misleading tradition must yield before the march of a constructive national democracy"—a Hegelian turn of phrase if ever there was one. Indeed, Croly even quoted Otto von Bismarck on the need for a nation to see its destiny as a single collective purpose. If such a view seemed a heresy in the eyes of a Jefferson or Madison, it was this heresy "whereby alone the American people can obtain political *salvation*."[22]

That word is significant. Just as Hegel saw the nation-state as our better and higher self; a sublunary version of Augustine's City of God, so Croly saw the new America in almost evangelical terms. His own choice for its Moses was Theodore Roosevelt, a kind of elected Philosopher Ruler who would embody the New Nationalism and use his presidential powers to concentrate economic power and responsibility in Washington, "for the ultimate purpose of its more efficient exercise and the better distribution of its fruits."[23] In 1912, President Woodrow Wilson would assume the same Hegelian mantle, and exercise his expanded powers in both peace and war with an appropriately messianic fervor.

As a lawyer and then professor of political science, Wilson was so bowled over by reading Hegel that, as he wrote to his future wife, "Hegel used to search for—and in most cases found seems to me—the fundamental psychological facts of society."[24] Wilson's own work, especially his massive *Constitutional Government*, was not much more than an iteration of Hegel's philosophy of the nation-state, in an American guise. Wielding the power of government to mold human nature, and to reform or strip away those institutions that stood in the way of the forward march of history—including even Madison's delicate system of checks and balances— became Wilson's central mission as president.

Prohibition and the Volstead Act (1920), and the establishment of the Federal Reserve Board and the Federal Trade Commission (1914), were all extensions of Wilson's progressive vision of using the power of government to enhance individual liberty "rightly understood"—that is to say, within the confines of America's larger historic mission.* "These are American principles," Wilson declared in 1915, "American policies. We stand for no others. They are the principles of mankind and must prevail."[25]

---

*That was one reason Wilson was untroubled with passing legislation enforcing segregation against blacks. Like many other Progressives, he believed history was on the side of the white race, not its colored inferiors—an attitude he would later express by supporting national self-determination at the Versailles conferences for whites, but not nonwhites, in Europe's colonies.

It's historically inaccurate, and intellectually misleading, to brand Wilson's version of Progressivism as "liberal fascism." Still, Wilson's America looks a lot like Hegel's Germany: a nation whose historical evolution embodies the universal values of the Absolute. "Here is a great people," he once told an audience, "great with every force that has ever beaten in the lifeblood of mankind. . . . The United States has the distinction of carrying certain lights for the world that the world has never so distinctly seen before . . . of liberty, principle, and justice."

Wilson was speaking in the summer of 1914, just as war was breaking out in Europe. He wanted no part of it; indeed two years later he campaigned for reelection on the slogan, "He Kept Us Out of War." Yet once the United States did become embroiled in that great cataclysm, it was all too easy for Wilson to see "the war to end all wars" as an opportunity to bring America's universalizing mission to the rest of humankind.

He got his chance at the peace table at Versailles in 1919.

Fighting World War I cost America almost 117,000 lives and left it the most powerful nation in the world, with the second greatest naval force after Britain. Wilson found himself leader of an industrial power second to none, whose financial and food aid kept the rest of the civilized world alive, including Lenin's Soviet Union. When he arrived in Paris for the peace conference, adoring crowds treated him almost as their messiah. "Never," wrote a member of the British delegation, economist John Maynard Keynes, "had a philosopher had such weapons whereupon to bond the Princes of the world."[26]

Yet Wilson squandered it all. Another member of the British delegation, Harold Nicolson, started out as an enthusiastic Wilson fan and admirer of the president's vision of a world government freeing men forever from war and oppression: the League of Nations. "I shared with him a hatred of violence in any form," Nicolson later wrote, "and a loathing of despotism in any form." But Nicolson soon realized the college professor's approach to peacemaking was both "simple" and "mystical"—and completely out of touch with the realities of postwar Europe. Someone gave him a book by Wilson, in which he read, "The new things of the world are the things divorced from force. They are the moral compulsions of the human conscience. No man can turn away from these things without turning away from the hope of all the world."[27]

But men did turn away—first at the Versailles Conference and then in his own country, where the Senate rejected joining the new world order of the League of Nations. Wilson's nationwide campaign to reverse its decision broke his health, his presidency, and ultimately the dream of America as the defender of universal values and last best hope of the Absolute.

Far from being a Philosopher Ruler, Wilson had proved to be a muddled and broken prophet. For two decades his dream was driven from the stage. Meanwhile, a new, violent postdemocratic order took root in Russia and Italy, then began its march across the heart of the continent. It would be made worse, ironically, by another decision Wilson had made back in 1914—and it would take another Viennese philosopher, a few years older than Karl Popper, to point the way out.

In 1914, Herbert Croly and his friend Walter Lippman set up the magazine that would become Progressivism's mouthpiece, *The New Republic*. That same year, President Wilson set up the centerpiece of the Hegelianization of the American economy, the Federal Reserve Board.

From now on, it was believed, the federal government would be able to exercise the same kind of farsighted direction over the economy that central banks enjoyed in England, France, and Germany. That egregious product of self-interested capitalism, the business cycle, with its unpredictable investment booms followed by collapse and unemployment, could be coaxed and prodded "secretly, without legislative enactment or control, and without the public knowing and caring"—and without resorting to the iron surgery of full-blown communism or socialism. Indeed, membership in the Federal Reserve Bank system would be voluntary.[28]

The planned economy was about to become the idée fixe of Western political systems. The searing experience of World War I only speeded up the process, especially in Europe. The electoral successes of Mussolini and Hitler were built on that promise. In the twenties and thirties, John Maynard Keynes and his disciples offered to show the Anglo-Saxon democracies how to do the same thing. Later, economic planners under Franklin Delano Roosevelt would be pleased and delighted that so many of their expert policies geared toward taming the business cycle and bringing "full employment" were actually implemented first by Adolf Hitler in Germany in the thirties, with apparent success.[29]

There was only one problem. What if the experts guessed wrong? What if the Philosopher Rulers' assumptions proved fallible, as Peirce and William James had predicted they might?

This was what worried Friedrich August von Hayek. On any given day in 1929, he could be found at his desk or in a Vienna coffeehouse, reading the newspaper with a growing sense of foreboding. It was not the news from Germany or Russia or Italy that disturbed him. It was the news from America.

America's economy was booming, and had been booming at a growth rate of more than 5 percent for nearly five years. Classical economists since Adam Smith had taught that this would inevitably mean a growing rate of inflation of wages and prices, which in turn would trigger a rise in interest rates and a slowdown in investment and in growth. Boom must inevitably slide into bust.

However, the bankers at the Federal Reserve had kept the money flowing into the American economy at a pitch that held interest rates low and kept expanding business and consumer credit, especially in the stock market. Yet in defiance of all classical economic doctrine, there was no rise in prices.

The business cycle, the dreaded beast of capitalist economies, had finally been tamed—or so it seemed. Economists around the world praised the Federal Reserve. Some even predicted that a "new era" in economics had begun, of continuous prosperity and growth with no threat of crisis or depression.[30] Economic growth without growing pains: it seemed a transformative moment worthy of a Georg Friedrich Hegel or even a Saint Augustine.

Hayek, however, was not sure. Born in Vienna in 1899, he had grown up in a family of natural scientists. Like Karl Popper, he had a keen interest in the philosophy of science along the lines of the Vienna Circle. When he first began studying at the University of Vienna, he was as fascinated by the ideas of Ernst Mach as everyone else.[31] But he was dismayed when they talked about organizing the economy "scientifically," as if people were mere counters in a physics experiment instead of real-life human beings.

Although they detested communism, the Logical Positivists, like most liberals of their day, endorsed some form of centralized planning: many were even socialists. Hayek was drawn instead to another Austrian named Carl Menger, an economist and admirer of John Stuart Mill but also the long-forgotten original founder of economics, Aristotle himself.

Menger stood at the opposite pole from the centralized planning school. He and his students had spent their lives trying to break classical economists free from rigid, a priori "models." Menger insisted that the best place to start understanding economics was not David Ricardo's *Principles of Political Economy* or even Adam Smith's *Wealth of Nations*, but Aristotle's *Ethics*, in which the basis of economic life is defined as a process of exchange.[32] By going back to Aristotle, Menger said, economists would begin to think again about how real people behaved, and why they bought and sold things in the first place.

This wasn't easy. Most economists preferred studying reams of statistics and output data, rather than how a store or farmer's market actually worked. However, Menger argued that a nation's economy, like Aristotle's *polis* or any local farmer's market, was the product of individual human action, not collective human design. People buy eggs because they want eggs, not (as David Ricardo would have said) to support land rents in the agricultural sector. They get jobs to feed their family, not to redress the balance between capital and labor.

And as Hayek immediately saw in the twenties, the vaunted experts at America's Federal Reserve Board had somehow forgotten this fact in their understanding of the boom of the Roaring Twenties. By keeping their eye fixed on national prices, the experts had missed the real consequences of injecting huge amounts of money into the economy while keeping interest rates below their natural business level. People had responded by grossly expanding their use of credit to buy things they needed, from farms and office buildings to stocks on Wall Street. Hayek was sure this growing overinvestment would collapse once people realized that paper credit was only that, paper. When that happened and the bottom fell out of the credit market, Hayek said, the result would be a panic and severe depression across America.

Hayek published his first paper criticizing the artificial American boom in 1925. Then in February 1929, he published another paper predicting a coming crisis that would start in the stock and credit markets.[33] The experts scoffed. Eight months later, Hayek was proved right. Within a year, the American Depression spread across the Atlantic to Europe. In Germany, France, Great Britain, even Austria, the economies based on centralized expert planning collapsed, one by one.

The failure of the experts was more than just an economic failure; it had catastrophic political consequences. Men and women lost faith in democratic governments that had promised to protect them from disaster. In Germany and Austria, it would clear the way for totalitarian solutions to problems the dictators blamed on "capitalism" but which, as Hayek had shown, were the results of the democratic experts' own mistakes. In the end, the Federal

Reserve Board's bad policies in one decade had set the stage for the *Anschluss* in the next.

What had gone wrong? Hayek pointed out, the problem had little to do with production or labor or capital or the other big abstractions economists liked to debate and describe. It had primarily to do with *information*. The real puzzle about economic decision making was figuring out why "the spontaneous interaction of a number of people, each possessing only bits of knowledge, brings about a state of affairs . . . which could [only] be brought about by deliberate direction by someone who possessed the combined knowledge of all these individuals"—something that was clearly impossible.[34] And yet, Hayek pointed out, this is *exactly* what happens in the economic marketplace.

Economists and politicians had been wrong about how markets work. They are *not* places where people pursue their self-interest, rational or otherwise, by buying and selling commodities. They are clearinghouses of information, where individuals discover what is useful or valuable to them and then make their preferences known to others by buying them or, alternately, selling those things that are of *lesser* value to them but hopefully not to others.

The result is an endless succession of individual transactions, random and meaningless to those who are obsessed with the Big Picture (why would anyone need thirty brands of toothpaste or want fourteen different colors for the same automobile?) but out of which gradually emerges a rational economic order. However, it is an order put together not from the top down, but from the bottom up, purchase by purchase, car by car, egg by egg.

Friedrich von Hayek had given the Aristotelian insight that knowledge is power a new meaning. It now meant the empowerment of individuals through the exchange of knowledge in the marketplace. In short, the market is an enormous grid for distributing information as well as goods and services. Every individual in the process "possesses unique information of which beneficial use might be made," Hayek would write, based on what they want or need. Prices are one mechanism for communicating that information; the value of money is another. Governments choosing to mess around with one or the other—whether it's wage and price controls or inflating the money supply—will distort the flow of that information as effectively as scrambling a broadcast signal or crossing out every other word in a letter or e-mail.

This is because "central planning . . . cannot take direct account of these circumstances of time and place" in which genuine economic decisions are made.[35] Hegel had argued that historical change ensures that there is no cumulative fund of information available to the individual. Hayek answered, Yes, there is. It's called the marketplace. And the freer the markets, the more people have access to that fund. Thus, "we need decentralization because only thus can we ensure that the knowledge of the particular circumstances [of a given transaction] will be promptly" and efficiently used—and human beings will benefit materially from that freedom.

Hayek's conclusion was that a centrally planned economic policy was *bound* to fail. Its organizers, no matter how bright or well trained, can never keep up with the innumerable bits of information that go into actual economic decisions. Like Achilles in his race with the tortoise, no matter how fast the central planner runs or how much data he collects, people in the marketplace will have always crept a step further, rendering the data useless the moment they are collected.*

The danger is that when the central planners fail, as they must inevitably do, their reaction is bound to be extreme. Instead of admitting their failure or ignorance, Hayek predicted, their impulse will be to exercise even *more* control, to become *more* coercive in their use of government power in order to force the economy to behave in the ways in which they, as opposed to real-life consumers, want it to behave. "Predominant concern with the visible short-run effects," he would later write, "leads to a dirigiste organization of the whole society. Indeed, what will certainly be dead in the long run, if we concentrate on immediate results," since they are the only ones immediately foreseeable, "is freedom."[36]

At this crucial point, Hayek's analysis and Popper's converged. The rise of the totalitarian state was revealed to be the direct consequence of the failure of liberalism in its Platonized form. Progressive heirs of Hegel, in trying to forestall the Marxists and Fascists by guiding society to supposedly higher and more just ends, had simply opened the door for them. They had fallen into the same trap of assuming that the more people are alike, that is, in sharing the same ends and needs, the happier they will be. In fact, the pursuit of equality only generates more conflict, much as Aristotle had predicted in the *Politics*—which requires more direct government action to maintain order. "The passion for 'the collective satisfaction of our needs,'" Hayek wrote, was

---

*Useless, that is, from the point of view of exercising control. From the point of view of providing data that help individuals make their own forecasts of what to do next, Hegel recognized that number crunching in economics can be extremely useful.

how "the socialists [meaning believers in a strong centralized state] have so well prepared the way for totalitarianism." They have done this, Hayek asserted, by "depriving us of [economic] choice, in order to give us what fits best into the plan and at a time determined by the plan."

He then closed his book with this:

> If in the first attempt to create a world of free men we have failed, we must try again. The guiding principle that a policy of freedom for the individual is the only truly progressive policy remains as true today as it was in the nineteenth century.[37]

The year was 1944, and the book was titled *The Road to Serfdom*. Hayek was living in London, a city battered by five years of war and under siege from Hitler's V-2 rockets. On the other side of the world in New Zealand, Karl Popper was writing *The Open Society and Its Enemies*. (It was his friend Hayek who would find the book its London publisher.) At exactly the same time a third man, Eric Blair, was living in London. In a couple of years, under the pen name George Orwell, he would paint a chilling picture of what Hayek's dystopia of modern serfs and masters in which all free choice is banished and whatever is not forbidden is made compulsory, might look like: *1984*.

In the spring of 1944, however, the place to see the future was not in London but on the south coast of England. The D-day invasion was only weeks away. Plato's American offspring had once tried to save the world and failed. Arguably, they had made it worse. Now Aristotle's children were going to take their shot.

In 1944, you found them in places like Richmond, California, and Sparrow Point in Baltimore. These were two of eighteen shipyards building the so-called Liberty ships that in 1941 began sending tons of food, raw materials, and war equipment to embattled Britain and Soviet Russia.

In 1940, none of these yards had even existed. Then buildings, slipways, cranes, and warehouses went up with an explosion of industrial productivity and engineering and managerial skill, from California and Oregon on the West Coast, to Florida, Alabama, and Baltimore on the East Coast. More than 2,700 Liberty ships would be built—and once bombs fell on Pearl Harbor on December 7, 1941, the ten-thousand-ton cargo vessels would also carry and supply American forces fighting in North Africa, Italy, and the south and central Pacific.

The Liberty shipyards were only the leading edge of a massive American wartime production effort that began in 1940 and would continue for the next five years. The old idea that America became "the arsenal of democracy" in World War II because of actions by the federal government is a myth. It was in fact an explosion of productivity by the most capitalist—and Aristotelian—economy on earth.[38]

In Aristotelian terms, its *dyanamis*, or potential for change, was stupefying.

In the fifty years after the Civil War, that economy had grown faster, and become larger, than any nation had ever seen.[39] Once a net importer of capital, America had become a world financial power equal to Great Britain. After World War I, the automotive, electronics, and chemical industries joined giant corporations like U.S. Steel, Standard Oil, Goodyear, and Eastman Kodak as the driving engines of the most productive economy in the world.

Feared and loathed by the New Nationalists, Progressives, Socialists, and various neo-Hegelians, America's capitalist sector had been hit by various waves of legislative restrictions and disruptive regulations, including antitrust laws. Yet it still managed to raise living standards and grow the nation's wealth with cars, radios, washing machines, and other consumer goods in a tsunami of rising industrial output—from 1921 to 1925 by almost 53 percent.

Even the coming of the Great Depression barely slowed it down. The U.S. economy's growth rate from 1933 to 1941 was still the highest of any other peacetime period, compared to every other industrialized country.[40] The Progressive gurus of the New Deal not only failed to lift the country out of economic decline; by 1938 they had deepened it. We now know that it was the coming of war that broke the back of the Great Depression. Few, however, realize that the reason was that war production tapped the pent-up dynamism of American private industry. "Made lean by court battling," as one chronicler put it shortly afterward, "weakened by depression and recession, and starved for new capital by inordinate tax burdens, [American business] still had the strength and means" to equip and arm not only the country's own forces but those of its allies as well.[41]

"Choose any American at random," Alexis de Tocqueville had written, "and he will be a man of burning desires, enterprising, adventurous, and above all, an innovator."[42] As twelve million Americans went into uniform, millions more—including eight million women and three million African-Americans—poured into factories, shipyards, airplane plants, and offices to join the production effort. Already by the time of Pearl Harbor, American war production was approaching that of Hitler's Germany. By the end of 1942, it was equal to that of all three Axis powers; by the end of 1943, it surpassed that of all the other major combatants combined.

Hayek had shown that economic growth was about not production but *productivity*, the release of potential human energy by matching buyers to sellers and means to ends in a chain reaction that rivaled the one scientists would soon be working on for the Manhattan Project. Tocqueville, too, had seen something heroic about the American way of business, and the war brought forward a number of heroic entrepreneurs to match Andrew Carnegie, John D. Rockefeller, and Henry Ford and those who had built the earlier industrial economy.

They were men like Henry Kaiser, wizard of the Richmond and Portland Liberty shipyards and former builder of Hoover Dam as well as the country's most advanced steel plant in California; Roy Grumman, the aircraft engineer who founded Grumman Aircraft in an abandoned garage and built the U.S. Navy fighters and bombers that would command the skies of the Pacific theater; and Andrew Jackson Higgins, the New Orleans–based boat builder who designed 92 percent of the vessels used by the U.S. Navy in World War II— although most were too small to deserve a name or a christening. Higgins landing craft would carry Marines into battle at Guadalcanal and Tarawa, and soldiers onto the beaches of Normandy on D-day. Supreme Allied Commander Dwight Eisenhower called Higgins "the man who won the war for us."[43]

Higgins was hardly alone. By the time of D-day, American factories were building a warplane every five minutes and producing 150 tons of steel every minute. Shipyards were launching eight aircraft carriers a month and fifty merchant ships a day. The country's railroads were moving 142 million carloads, carrying guns, ammunition, parachutes, helmets, rations, and rubber boats produced in the industrial heartland to both coasts for shipping overseas—the most massive cargo lift in history.[44]

And the scientists whom Europe's totalitarianism had chased to America—Albert Einstein from Germany, Enrico Fermi from Italy, Leó Szilárd, Edward Teller, and John von Neumann from Hungary—turned out to be the

Henry Kaiser and fellow businessmen at Hoover Dam, circa 1932:
the capitalist as hero. "*He* is the great liberator," Ayn Rand would
write, who "has released men from bondage to their physical needs."

arsenal of democracy's deadliest secret weapon. They would team up with American physicists like Robert Oppenheimer and Arthur Compton, and American engineers from the chemical giants DuPont and Union Carbide, to turn the unimaginable power buried in the heart of the atom into the world's most destructive device—the atom bombs that would win the world's most destructive conflict in 1945.

"To American production, without which this war would have been lost": that was the ceremonial toast of communism's biggest dictator, Marshal Josef Stalin, at the Tehran summit in 1943. He knew American industry had kept his Red Army on the move with trucks, half-tracks, and fuel, and his people clothed and fed throughout the war—providing almost one-fifth of Soviet GNP. It was also the acknowledgment by Platonism's most potent political offspring—Marxist communism—that economies and societies built around

Aristotle's empirical system were not only wealthier and more productive but better able to meet the stress of crisis better—even the crisis of total war.

This came as a complete surprise to an entire century of social thinkers. The whole premise on which Lenin had built his revolution was that capitalism was in the last stage of collapse. Max Weber had treated the capitalist businessman as the master of routine, representative of a world drained of magic (the term he coined was *charisma*) and spontaneity. Werner Sombart had divided the world into "traders" and "heroes," with only the latter embodying the values of courage, duty, and compassion. "The trader approaches life with the question, what can you give me," Sombart wrote. "The hero approaches life with the question, what can I give you?"

Now it turned out, the trader could give you victory—as well as wealth beyond people's imagining. Far from quailing in the face of danger, he had risen to the occasion. Like modern-day Archimedes, American businessmen and engineers had harnessed the forces of science and technology to the service of freedom—just as he harnessed them to the energies of the free market. *Thymos*, the Platonists' heroic virtue of spirit or courage, turned out to be much the property of the capitalist entrepreneur as it was of the Homeric warrior.

By contrast, none of this came as a surprise to one writer—an exile from Russian communism, as it happened—living in New York City. As the United States and Soviet Union lurched toward the climactic confrontation of the heirs to Plato and Aristotle in the Cold War, she would turn capitalism's new heroic face into a full-blown philosophy—and give credit directly to Aristotle for setting it in motion.

Born in St. Petersburg in 1905, she was the child of nonobservant Jewish chemists. The Russian Revolution forced Alisa Rosenbaum to flee into hiding in the Crimea, while her family remained trapped and starving. She managed in 1925 to obtain a visa to the United States. Her first sight of the skyscrapers of Manhattan led her, as she wrote later, to weep "tears of splendor." She had found her true home, and after changing her name to Ayn Rand, she would spend her life celebrating that home's explosive *dynamis*.

The Aristotelian term is appropriate. As a university student in the 1920s, she had read the works of Plato and Aristotle, as well as Nietzsche and the

German Romantics, and found that while Plato left her cold and dissatisfied, Aristotle seemed a kindred spirit. When she wrote later that "Aristotle's philosophy was the intellect's Declaration of Independence," and that he "should be given the title of the world's first intellectual, in the purest and noblest sense of the word," she was thinking of a far larger historical and philosophical context than simply the United States.

Borrowing from the Enlightenment as well as Nietzsche, she derived her view of premodern societies as dominated by a self-serving priestly class, who used guilt and an ascetic ideal to manipulate the majority to sacrifice their own identities for a false communitarian ideal. Rand refers to them as Witch Doctors, but Plato is their true archetype, along with his followers Plotinus and Saint Augustine.[45]

Far from serving virtue or God, as they claim, the Witch Doctors' real ally is the warlord, designated as Attila, whose entire perspective is shaped by his dependence on brute force. Like the Witch Doctor, he produces nothing, creates nothing. He only steals from those actually growing the crops, raising the livestock, forging the implements, and exchanging the produce of their labor with others.

Together this unholy alliance ruled Europe until Thomas Aquinas and the rediscovery of Aristotle. This, not the Renaissance, marks for Rand the true rebirth of Western civilization: the rediscovery of the "basic principles of a rational view of existence . . . that the task of man's consciousness is to perceive, not to create reality." Everything else, for Rand, flows from this realization that there is only one objective reality, the world perceived through the senses. The Renaissance, the scientific revolution, the Enlightenment, and the industrial revolution are for Rand all perched upon Aristotle's original basic insight.

This was the vision, Rand declared, that had set civilization on its great ascent. "Everything that makes us civilized beings," she wrote, "every rational value that we possess—including the birth of science, the industrial revolution, the creation of America, even the [logical] structure of our language, is the result of Aristotle's influence."[46] Her novels like *The Fountainhead* and *Atlas Shrugged* are much more than a Romantic celebration of laissez-faire capitalism and entrepreneurs like Kaiser and Grumman. They are allegories of how our practical reason can turn us into active producers rather than passive recipients of life's deepest truths.

For Rand, the final product of this burst of Aristotelian enlightenment was the modern free market entrepreneur. He is the field marshal of the army of freedom, Rand insisted in 1960, and his "lieutenant commander-in-chief is the *scientist*." The businessman turns science's discoveries "into material products that fill men's physical needs and expand the comforts of man's existence." The free market becomes a mass market, where millions of people of every income level are able to get the products they want cheaper, faster, and more efficiently.

Aristotle's great-souled man becomes Rand's great-souled entrepreneur:

> By using machines, he increases the productivity of human labor. . . . By organizing human effort into productive enterprises, he creates employment for men of countless professions. *He* is the great liberator who, in the short span of a century and a half, has released men from bondage to their physical needs . . . and released them from famine, from pestilence, from stagnant hopelessness and terror.[47]

For a refugee from Lenin's revolution, the term *terror* had a special significance. Soviet communism, like its Hegelian predecessors, hoped to remold human nature with the same confidence and ease as it would build new factories and hydroelectric dams. The State itself, which Hegel saw as the last stage of human progress, would wither away once everyone understood that "to each according to his need; from each according to his means" was the only just pathway of justice. Law, one Soviet theorist enthusiastically predicted, would be replaced by Plan—including the first Soviet Five-Year Plan in 1928.[48]

But the New Soviet Man never appeared, except in propaganda posters and films.

The first gulags appeared only months after Lenin and Trotsky seized power. Under their successor Stalin, they would swell to the point that at the start of the Cold War in 1948 some twelve million people were in Soviet labor camps. Millions of others had been shot, starved to death, or fled the Communist regime—while tens of millions more were being forced to the same system from East Germany and Poland to Vietnam and China.[49]

Aristotle had been proven right, and Plato and Hegel wrong. What ultimately killed communism—and ended the Cold War—wasn't a great military crusade or a nuclear apocalypse, as so many feared, including many of the inventors of the atomic bomb. It was a triumph of ordinary human nature, backed by Rand's triad of science, technical engineering, and free market productivity. Free creative minds—embodiments of what Aristotle called *energeia* or an impulse toward action—made the mountains of vinyl records and blue jeans that revolutionized youth culture in the fifties and sixties, including the youth of Soviet Russia and Eastern Europe. They formed a military-industrial complex that would shrug off defeat in Vietnam and produce advanced military miracles like the Stealth fighter and the Strategic Defense Initiative. (The Soviet military-industrial complex, by contrast, would produce nuclear submarine meltdowns and Chernobyl.)

Finally, that same creative power spawned a computer industry that would reconnect the world via satellite, fax, television, and the Internet—and enable dissidents in Iron Curtain Europe to defy their Communist masters and rejoin the West.

By 1980, they knew what that Western legacy meant—and what it didn't. Their heroes were very different from the ones whose portraits studded government walls and adorned public squares: Lenin, Stalin, Marx. Most had contraband copies of Popper and Hayek. One leading Czech dissident, Rita Klimova, wrote her officially banned articles on free market economies under the pen name "Adam Kovarc," the Czech for Adam Smith. Another, Václav Havel, actually studied with American free market economist Milton Friedman. And when Russian dissident Alexander Solzhenitsyn told an audience at Harvard in 1975 that Americans had died in Vietnam fighting for freedom, he sent shock waves across Cambridge—but spoke for a generation of Eastern Europeans who knew where the road to serfdom really led and what closed societies really were.

Ayn Rand didn't live long enough to see the fall of the Berlin Wall. But Karl Popper did and sensed that the fall of communism hadn't cleared away all of Plato's political disciples, the avowed enemies of the open society. "Communism is dead," he would point out, but "it's left the hatred of capitalism still alive and well."

Meanwhile, in a snug little house in Freiburg-im-Breisgau in Germany, a frail white-haired man watched the TV images of crowds smashing the Berlin Wall, and other images of crowds in Prague proclaiming what Rita Klimova had dubbed the Velvet Revolution, the peaceful overthrow of Communist Czechoslovakia.

He was Friedrich von Hayek, now ninety years of age and in poor health.

He had almost lost the power of speech. But on that day, his son remembered, Hayek was beaming. He turned away from the television for a moment with a smile on his face, and said:

"I told you so."

So had Aristotle.[50]

Conclusion

FROM THE CAVE TO THE LIGHT

If all were of one mind, the cosmos would stand still.
—Alexander the Great

Just a decade after the fall of the Berlin Wall, three events set the compass for the twenty-first century.

The first, and most spectacular, was the attack on the World Trade Center in New York and the Pentagon on September 11, 2001, which killed three thousand people and triggered a global war on terror that has transformed the West's relations with the Middle East and the Muslim world. As of this writing, it shows no sign of abating.

The second attracted less attention but marked a watershed in the future of science. This was the completion in 2003 of the Human Genome Project, the successful mapping and identification of the 25,000 or so genes that make up the human species. The molecular backbone of the human gene, DNA— which is the molecular basis of *all* life—had been identified back in 1958. But now for the first time all the possible sequences of DNA's chemical base pairings were laid bare— the equivalent of cracking the master code of living nature.[1] The project not only finally opened the door to finding the genetic causes of diseases like cancer; it offered the heady vision of an ability to reorganize the biochemical structure of all life.

The third event was the 2008 global financial meltdown, which pushed the world's economies to the brink of bankruptcy and rammed home the fact that interconnectivity through the Internet, satellite communication, and globalized markets can be a source of frightening vulnerability as well as productive power.

Three events, each opening an entirely new horizon for the future—or so it seems. The post–Cold War era, far from representing the "end of history," as a RAND Corporation analyst named Francis Fukuyama once wrote, has only opened new vistas of dilemmas and dangers. What possible relevance can two philosophers who've been dead for more than twenty-five hundred years have for figuring out what's happening and where we're going?

It turns out, a lot.

Take the war on terror, which turns out to be closely linked to the intellectual fate of Islam since the Middle Ages. From the twelfth century onward, Islamic texts and scholars were the West's principal source for the wisdom of the Greeks, including the works of Plato and Aristotle. Thanks to Muslim scholars like Averroës and Avicennes, for a few precious decades the Muslim and Christian outlooks on the world, especially the natural world, were virtually the same.*

Then for various reasons, the Islamic mind turned its back on Plato. Averroës, for example, made it his task in his commentaries to systematically purge Aristotle's writings of any Neoplatonist taint. Other Arabs followed his lead. So instead of the constant creative tension between speculation and science that arose in the Christian West, Islamic Platonism retreated to the religious sidelines of Sufism, where it contemplated the mystical and divine and little else.

In short, "what went wrong" with Muslim culture, then and later, was that it wound up getting too much Aristotle too soon, which deprived it of growth and dynamism. Aristotle's scientific and logical treatises became the basis of a fossilized orthodoxy in Arab culture, dry and lifeless and unchanging over the centuries. (They are still used as textbooks at Shia seminaries like Qom in Iran.) Aristotle's more humanistic works like the *Politics* and *Nicomachean Ethics* dropped from sight in the Islamic world, since the debate with Plato, of which they were an essential part, had been cut short.

So Islam and the West found themselves set on separate and divergent paths. It was not until the 1700s that Islamic scholars, confronting an aggressive Europe intruding on their home turf, woke up to what had happened.[2] They realized that the West had stolen a march on them, but they could not

*See chapter 14.

understand why. The backlash and resentment that resulted—first in Wahabism and then in other "back to the Koran" reactionary movements—would grow and gather force, as the West and Islamic world continued to diverge—only to collide together once again, horribly, on September 11, 2001.

In the case of the human genome, what the project really revealed was that everything does indeed begin with biology, as Aristotle thought—but not as he imagined. The genome isn't a seed or a substance but a sequential unfolding inside the DNA molecule of a protein chain whose links can number in the millions. Yet each chain link is individually coded by one of four letters in a simple "alphabet" of protein base pairs,* which special enzymes "read" and copy as they split each base pair when cells divide. The DNA molecule is, in short, a minicomputer, whose digital codes are read in sequence in order to give every cell its structure, behavior, and character.[3]

Now, the information that the DNA computer provides, like that of the modern electronic computer, isn't only something to be manipulated and analyzed. As Einstein realized with the quantum, it forms the very structure of perception *and* reality—just as the quantum "exists" only as a moment of probabilities in a field of information. Biological life, it turns out, is about information—just as physical matter turned out to be.

And so is economics. As Friedrich von Hayek and his colleagues realized, markets are more than just a means of conveying physical goods and services. They are fields of information in which—as with the quantum—the moment we perceive the information it conveys (time to buy, time to sell), we also alter its nature and direction. Werner Heisenberg's Principle of Uncertainty proves as valid in international financial markets as it does in the realm of physics—and with about the same results.[4]

The upshot is soberingly clear. The inability of governments and large, centralizing institutions to keep up with the information needed to make the right economic decisions (an inability that Hayek identified more than eighty years ago) grows exponentially with the growth of those global markets—just as the destructive consequences of making the wrong decision expand exponentially as well.

The result is financial collapse.[5] Collapses like that in 1929, which inspired Hayek's original insight, and like that in 2008. Collapses that governments have proven largely incapable of fixing but which individuals, acting

*They are: adenine-thymine, thymine-adenine, cytosine-guanine, and guanine-cytosine.

together over time, do. "Because uncertainty about the future is fundamental," writes one distinguished economist regarding the history of financial meltdowns, "financial mistakes will continue to be made." As Karl Popper would put it, economics are as impervious to prediction or guidance as societies are. Yet "on average over time, the trend is for greater and greater overall economic well-being. While bubbles and crises continue, we cycle in a rising trend"—at least in societies where free markets, along with creativity, are allowed to flourish.[6]

And here Aristotle suddenly hovers at our shoulder. Human beings build their lives around the future, not the past. They forget the mistakes of the past because they must; otherwise they would become powerless to act. Our rational nature is geared toward *energeia*, creative engagement in the world as individuals, not cogs in the collectivity. Perhaps it's our DNA sequences that program us that way—just as some claim they program us with a "God gene."

That prints to a final irony: what if what makes us natural Aristotelians turns out to be embedded in Plato's sacred geometry after all?

So the struggle between Plato and Aristotle, which has always given the West its historical dynamism, is far from over. And if we want to sense where it may be going, we need to revisit Plato's cave—not in the pages of the *Republic* but in real life.

When Plato first dreamed up his allegory, he very probably had in mind an actual cave, which we can still visit today. It's on the island of Eleusis, where it served as the entrance to the sanctuary dedicated to the goddess Demeter. Some fifteen feet deep and forty feet wide, it marked the starting point of the famous Eleusinian mystery rites performed every year by Athenians (very likely including Plato himself) and others from all over Greece, in which initiates made a ritual journey into the underworld and then back again.

Since the Stone Age, every civilization and culture has treated the cave as a place packed with symbolic power, a place for rites of passage and sacred initiation. (In Chinese, for example, the word for cave, *tong*, comes to mean "mysterious, profound, transcendent.") The cave symbolized the primordial womb of Mother Earth into which initiates descended, torches in hand and reciting magic spells, in order to reemerge purified and transformed.[7]

Archaeologists tell us[8] that it was from the cave on Eleusis that initiates passed from the experience of utter darkness—and a sense of fear and even terror, according to the ancient author Plutarch— into a nearby inner sanctuary, where they would suddenly encounter a female figure bearing a torch and casting a blinding dazzling light into the inky blackness. "Happy is he among men upon earth who has seen these mysteries," reads an Eleusinian cult hymn, "but he who is uninitiate . . . is [lost], down in the darkness and gloom."[9]

The cave and the light. Plato's insight was to turn the Eleusinian cave experience from an allegory of death and rebirth into an allegory of the mind's journey from ignorance to truth. For Plato, the answer to the cave's uncertainties lies not with esoteric rituals or magic spells but within ourselves, thanks to our reason: what his teacher Socrates described as the gift of the soul. A properly cultivated mind leads us to the light of truth and knowledge, because in the end they share the same divine nature. Like Socrates in his prison cell, we escape from the shackles of darkness and illusion by turning toward the inner light of the soul, which burns and illuminates until death. "And this state of the soul," Socrates had said, "we call Wisdom"—and Plato agreed.

As we have seen, Aristotle saw things differently. The cave isn't all gloom and darkness and terror. There's an underlying rational plan to this cave, he insisted, which is called nature. It's a plan men can and should observe and follow, in order to organize their individual and communal lives. As he says in the *Metaphysics*, "All men by nature desire to know and the proof is the delight we take in our senses." The light of truth, Aristotle argued, doesn't come at the end of our journey, in a sudden burst of illumination. Nor does it belong to a select handful of initiates, the philosophers. We can all find it if we look hard enough, all along the way.

Aristotle declared that we arrive at the truth through the analysis of the material world—much as the modern scientist does. By contrast, Plato becomes Western civilization's spokesman for a quest for truth and knowledge *outside* and *beyond* our immediate material reality—a reality that Plato taught was really a source of limitation. Truth always lies beyond our conventional limits—those limits imposed by our own mortal nature.

Thanks to that insight, Plato became the godfather of the religious, artistic, intuitive, and mystical side of the Western personality. But he also turns out to have put his finger on the truth of modern quantum physics. Our perception of a world of material solids turns out to be an illusion—there are only bursts and clumps of energy, quanta, in various ordered and disordered

Cave, steps in rear.

Mirthless rock, as seen from rear opening in cave.

Cave, rear opening.

Is this cave on the island of Eleusis the real cave in Plato's *Republic*?

states. If the proponents of string theory are correct and the elementary particles of physics reflect the different oscillation of subatomic loops or strings, Pythagoras's notion that number is the language of nature isn't so far off, either.

Aristotle, in turn, became spokesman for the West's utilitarian scientific side. Reason exists in order to unlock the secrets of nature, not to dismiss them as irrelevant or a distraction. For Aristotle, the life of reason is a constantly unfolding process of inquiry and analysis that serves to reinforce our place as part of a larger natural order. There are no final answers, only more questions and explorations. This makes Aristotle the progenitor not only of sending rockets to the moon but of democratic individualism and free markets.

History shows that too much Plato brings a rigid dogmatism and an elitist arrogance—which, as Karl Popper pointed out and as the world saw in the age of Hitler and Stalin and Mao, easily slides into totalitarianism.* The twentieth-century successors to Aristotle, the voices of enlightened liberal Europe, forgot how to defend themselves and allowed the totalitarians, with their passionate intensity and contempt for debate, to goose-step into power. The catastrophes of the twentieth century arose not because men argued too much but because they gave up arguing at all.

Such are the perils of too much Plato. Too much Aristotle, on the other hand, ends in the narrow-minded sterility that dominated the scholasticism of the Middle Ages, in which everything is reduced to rote formulae and habit and individual creativity is stamped out. A complacent behaviorist calculus begins to govern social and political relationships; fellow human beings become abstract unknowable ciphers to be manipulated at will.

In this Pavlovian moral universe, avoiding pain and maximizing pleasure become the only valid measures of right and wrong: "If it feels good, do it." Aristotle, the brilliant doctor's son, the great Peripatetic who tried to teach his students that the life of virtue is the highest good, would be horrified that his legacy could be reduced to such an empty slogan. However, we recognize it when we enter the credit card culture of the shopaholic and the megamall, of the Kardashians and The Real Housewives of Beverly Hills.

The Enlightenment virtues of affluence can decay into a mindless consumerism devoid of any deeper meaning or spiritual connection to life. Nothing is permanent, including relationships. Everything has returned to the Heraclitean flux; there is no basis for a lasting identity. Human beings be-

*And not just in the West.

come, as Edmund Burke puts it, "flies of a summer" in which "no generation can link with another."[10] The result is a constant, restless boredom. A wildly vacillating self-esteem drifts from one unsatisfying outlet to the next with the click of a mouse or a thumb-flick of an X-Box. The only face that appears when we peer into the pool of self-reflection belongs to Narcissus.[11]

It is the balance between living in the material and adhering to the spiritual that sustains any society's cultural health. Other civilizations and religions—India, Egypt, China, Buddhism, and Islam—have confronted these same issues throughout their histories. They erected their own cultural edifices to deal with them. The problem has been that the West's material drive and dynamism—the product of the same creative tension described in this book—has tended to reach out and pull down those older, more stable edifices, the traditional guarantees for social and psychological survival.

This, far more than any financial meltdown, is the real enduring crisis of the modern global system. As in the title of Chinua Achebe's marvelous novel about life in Nigeria under European colonialism, *Things Fall Apart*, the meaning of things and institutions drains away, and people find themselves adrift. They have been left abandoned in the cave.

Some societies have struggled to overcome this problem, with some success. Japan confronted the issue from the very beginning of its contact with the West. Its rulers sought a top-down solution with their Meiji Restoration, self-consciously fitting Western technology into Japan's traditional political, social, and religious structure. The results have been erratic. When it works, it works—as witness downtown Tokyo. When it doesn't, as during Japan's brutal imperial advance, which led to World War II, the result was catastrophic to its neighbors and deadly to its own people and the rest of the world. The same happened under Mao Zedong in China, with even more horrific results.

Yet people do search out their balance, if only instinctively. With the emergence of a capitalist China since the 1990s, the explosion of dynamic material affluence has triggered a resurgence of traditional Confucianism, which has managed to push itself up like a resilient plant from under the rubble of Maoism and Communist corruption—as well as, even more amazingly, a discovery of Christianity. When Mao took over in 1949, there were perhaps 5 to 6 million Chinese Christians. Today the number is closer to 100 million.

Visiting one of the hubs of the world's technological revolution, Bangalore, India, means being surrounded by landmarks left by Aristotle and his technological and entrepreneurial Western offspring. It is a world of computer engineers and technicians making money, building networks, and opening up channels of communication around the planet.

Still, many of those same engineers are also devout Hindus. They go home to worship at Hindu shrines, participate in traditional festivals, and practice, in the temple of the Hindu god Shiva, some of the oldest surviving religious rites in the world. They will go on to marry and die according to those same ancient rites. These reflections of the Platonist dimension of the human personality are as vital and important to the lives of modern Indians as the Aristotelian side that appears on their computer screens.

In other non-Western societies, however, people have found themselves overwhelmed by this scientific and materialist onslaught. We see the results in the sprawling megaslums of third-world cities like Rio, Karachi, Lagos in Nigeria, Caracas, Mexico City, and Capetown. The floods of displaced persons from traditional rural areas have grown every major city in the poorest parts of the globe by more than a factor of ten. Dhaka in Bangladesh is more than forty times the size it was in 1950.

These are not cities on the Greek city-state model; they are neither Plato's centers of civic identity nor Aristotle's emporiums of commerce. They are rotting "stinking mountains of shit," as urban anthropologist Mike Davis vividly describes them, demographic "volcanos waiting to erupt." They are the new barbarian frontier, where poverty, fear, and violence rule—and where irrational religious fundamentalisms are taking root to feed resentment and rage, from radical Hinduism in the slums of Mumbai and apocalyptic Islamicism in Cairo and Gaza, to wild-eyed Pentecostalists in San Salvador and born-again Marxists in Caracas.[12] The global village turns out to be a shantytown, instead.

These are the breeding grounds of today's and tomorrow's terrorist movements. The answer to them is *not* more prosperity. The attackers of 9/11 like Mohamed Atta did not spring up from the slums or from rural poverty. They were the beneficiaries of middle-class wealth in their home countries. (Atta's father was a lawyer.) They were comfortable with modern technology and were the recipients of a Western-style education. That education, however, had left a cultural and psychological void. Their confrontation with a technological modern pluralist society like ours triggered an incomprehension and rage that radical Islamicism fanned into a nihilistic barbarism.

Terrorists see themselves as warriors of God. They are in fact murderers from the scariest depths of the cave, the cultural underworld that has grown up in societies that have lost their traditional ways and landmarks. That cave is increasingly coming to include our own cultural underclass, whose nihilistic barbarism is reflected on television and in gangsta rap.

The answer is rediscovering that creative tension and sense of balance *not* in the Western image but in Western terms.

Today's affluent, globalized material world was largely made by Aristotle's offspring—and is not so different from the Athens of Socrates's day. It's a world filled with comforts and conveniences, a world of constant change and unimaginable individual freedoms. But it is also riddled with false façades and shoddy superficialities, and it is populated by institutions that have become obsessed with process for its own sake, rather than keeping Western civilization "on message" regarding the larger meaning of freedom and liberty, community and spiritual truth.

Contrary to the pessimists, it's not going away anytime soon. Despite recent economic downturns and resulting gloomy prognostications, the fact is that since 1920 the rate of growth of U.S. gross domestic product has been expanding exponentially, and it shows no sign of slowing down. Even the Great Depression and the most recent turndown represent only very minor deviations from the underlying curve.[13] The trend line is even clearer in other countries, including China and India. Those waiting for the modern technological global system to collapse from its own weight back to "sustainability" are bound to be disappointed.

Still, for all its dynamism and resilience, ours is a world constructed largely around getting and spending. While this has not led to mass spiritual death, as so many critics of consumer culture charge, it has allowed mass consumerism to suffocate and choke off other important forms of human potential.

The modern environmentalist movement has recognized this and exploited it with its austere downsizing appeal. The Greens offer a manifestly Platonist reply to Aristotle's world of technology, individual desire, and convenience, by stressing collective responsibility, self-sacrifice, and moral rather than material comfort and consumer choice.* And whatever their empirical scientific merits or demerits, climate change gurus and advocates of the Gaia thesis do point to an important truth: that a world built on getting and spend-

---

*And what could be more Platonic than its slogan "Think Globally, Act Locally"?

ing is not enough. There are other values, spiritual needs that also require satisfaction and that demand a priority on our agendas. The tens of thousands of congregants who fill Saddleback Church in California every Sunday grasp that as well.

The point is, this kind of contradiction is nothing new in Western culture. History may not repeat itself, but ideas certainly do. The tension between our material and spiritual selves has always been there, embedded in Western history by the legacies of Plato and Aristotle. It has inspired one breakthrough after another, in the clash between Christianity and classical culture; the battle of the books between Renaissance humanists and the schoolmen; and the culture wars between the Romantics and the Enlightenment. And of course it runs all through the current clash over Darwinism and creationism or "intelligent design": a battle founded, in the last analysis, on the irreconcilable contradiction between Plato's God and Aristotle's Prime Mover.

So what the current debates over climate change and economic growth really reveal is that our world still needs its Plato alongside its Aristotle. *Both* are indispensable to our culture and our future—and perhaps all futures. Whether it is called yin and yang or right brain versus left brain,[14] the tense tug-of-war is all-pervasive. But it is peculiarly fundamental to our Western identity. Thanks to Plato and Aristotle, the variation is endless, with one giving rise to the other in a never-ending ever-ascending circle of renewal.

Alexander the Great, Aristotle's most famous pupil, was right. The end result of consensus, of all thinking with one mind, is stagnation and worse. Indeed, tension and renewal *are* our identity. And if those of us in the West can rediscover that identity, perhaps we can then save the world—not by making it richer or alternately by giving it a world government, but by leading by example and showing how to leave the cave and step once more out into the light.

ACKNOWLEDGMENTS

My very first thanks go to my father, who introduced me to the dialogues of Plato at an embarrassingly early age, and whose marvelous library on the history of philosophy supplied something to every chapter. As the book itself took shape, he carefully read early drafts of every chapter and pointed me to materials that helped to flesh out the major argument. My mother also read chapter drafts and offered editorial comments that have helped to make it a better, and more readable, book.

Thanks also go to Professor J. Baird Callicott, who generously allowed me to attend his graduate seminar on Plato back in 1975, and who first introduced me to the intimate connections between Plato's world vision and Pythagoras, and Professor John Billings, who gave me my first primer on Aristotle's logic. At the University of Minnesota, Professor Vicki Harper led me and a small band of students on an intense excursion into Aristotle's metaphysics, and Steven Oberhelman, now at Texas A&M, was my indispensable guide to unraveling the tangled web of the Roman Republic. He will be surprised to see some of his insights reappear in this book thirty-six years later.

I have to extend my gratitude to the Johns Hopkins University's John G. A. Pocock for his help in understanding Aristotle's impact on Western political thinking; to Orest Ranum for encouraging my fascination with Neoplatonist kingship; and to Nancy Struever, who turned me loose on Boethius's translations of Aristotle and showed me their importance to the Middle Ages and the early Renaissance. Maurice Mandelbaum's seminar on Nietzsche and Schopenhauer also made an indelible impression on me that carried through in my first book, *The Idea of Decline in Western History*, and now this one.

Tom Veblen read and commented on the entire manuscript in its first stages, as did Charles Matheson, who also patiently guided me through the mysteries of Pythagorean geometry as well as the Golden Section, while opening up his library on architecture to me. Responsibility for any remaining mistakes lies not with him—or anyone else mentioned here—but with me.

Thanks also go to my two editors at Random House. John Flicker enthusiastically embraced the idea of a book on Plato and Aristotle, and Jonathan Jao saw it through to completion. A similar note of gratitude goes to Molly Turpin for her patient help in getting the book finished, especially with finding images, and Dennis Ambrose and the entire production staff. My agents, Glen Hartley and Lynn Chu, became the book's constant and consistent champions, and their support and advice have been, over fifteen years, of inestimable value.

Peter Schramm of the Ashbrook Center at Ashland University cheered the book's idea from the first time he heard about it, as did Hillsdale College's Larry Arnn. Successive visits with Greg Lindsay at Australia's Center for Independent Studies contributed to several ideas that are central to the book's thesis, including one particular lively conversation with Ayaan Hirsi Ali. Norman Podhoretz, Midge Decter, Neal Kozodoy, and Roger Hertog all listened patiently while I laid out different aspects of the book, while conversations at the American Enterprise Institute with Alex Pollock, Chris DeMuth, Michael Novak, and Arthur Brooks helped with key turning points.

Last but always first, my gratitude goes to my wife, Beth. Her patience during the four years it took for this book to see the light of day was exemplary, and her love and support were indispensable—as they always are.

Prologue: The School of Athens

1. Giorgio Vasari, *Lives of the Artists*, trans. George Bull (Harmondsworth: Penguin, 1987), 1:284.

2. Christiane Joost-Gaugier, *Raphael's Stanza della Segnatura: Meaning and Invention* (Cambridge: Cambridge University Press, 2002), 9.

3. Vasari, *Lives of the Artists*, 292.

4. This is the thesis of Joost-Gaugier, *Raphael's Stanza*, passim. The librarian, Tommaso Inghirami, called the Cicero of his age, was no less an authority than Erasmus of Rotterdam. Inghirami died only five years after Raphael's frescoes were finished, in 1516, when he fell from his mule under the wheels of a bullock cart. A painting of the bizarre accident still exists, in Rome's Church of St. John Lateran.

5. Joost-Gaugier, *Raphael's Stanza*, 93.

6. Usually identified since Vasari's time as Zoroaster. However, Joost-Gaugier argues convincingly (107–10) that the portrait shows the geographer Strabo, who was born around 64 BCE and who was a convinced Aristotelian, as well as heir to the great Alexandrian school of geography.

7. Joost-Gaugier, *Raphael's Stanza*, 87–88, 90.

8. Coleridge quoted in John Stuart Mill, "Coleridge" (1840), in *The Collected Works of John Stuart Mill* (Toronto: University of Toronto Press, 1985), 10:118.

Chapter 1: The First Philosopher

1. Plato, *Phaedo*, in Plato, *The Last Days of Socrates*, trans. Hugh Tredennick (Harmondsworth: Penguin, 1954), 111.

2. Added good and evil, as implied if not stated in Socrates's statement.

3. Plato, *Crito*, in *Last Days of Socrates*, 88.

4. Ibid., 90.

5. Plato, *Phaedo*, 179.

6. Ibid., 181.

7. Ibid.

8. Plato, *The Symposium*, trans. Christopher Gill (Harmondsworth: Penguin, 1999), 60–61.

9. According to the *Apology* (60), he fought at the battles of Potidaea, Amphipolis, and Delium during the war against Sparta, where "I remained at my post like anyone else and faced death."

10. A. E. Taylor, *Plato: The Man and His Work* (London: Methuen, 1960), 8.

Chapter 2: The Soul of Reason

1. G. S. Kirk and J. E. Raven, *The Presocratic Philosophers* (Cambridge: Cambridge University Press, 1964), 74, 83.

2. Ibid., 90.

3. Bertrand Russell, *A History of Western Philosophy* (1945; repr., New York: Simon & Schuster, 2007), 65.

4. Heraclitus's pupil Cratylus took the next step by declaring, "No one steps into the same river even once."

5. Arthur L. Herman, *The Ways of Philosophy* (Atlanta, Ga.: Scholars Press, 1990), 54.

6. John Burnet, *Early Greek Philosophy* (1892; repr., New York: Meridian, 1958), 174.

7. A. E. Taylor, *Socrates* (1951; repr., Westport, Conn.: Greenwood, 1975), 132.

8. W.K.C. Guthrie, *The Greek Philosophers from Thales to Aristotle* (1950; repr., New York: Harper & Row, 1960), 87.

9. Plotinus quoted in Paul Friedlander, *Plato* (New York: Pantheon, 1958), 1:29.

10. Plato, *Phaedo*, in Plato, *The Last Days of Socrates*, trans. Hugh Tredennick (Harmondsworth: Penguin, 1954), 131.

11. Ibid., 135.

12. Plato, *Apology*, in *Last Days of Socrates*, 51.

13. Plato, *The Republic*, trans. Desmond Lee, 2nd ed. (Harmondsworth: Penguin, 1974), 317–18.

14. Ibid., 317–19.

15. Plato, *Phaedo*, 124.

16. Plato, *Republic*, 264–66 (translator's introduction to bk. V).

17. Plato, *Phaedo*, 492.

18. A point raised by R. M. Hare in his *Plato* (Oxford: Oxford University Press, 1982), 37.

19. Plato, *The Works of Plato*, trans. Benjamin Jowett (New York: Random House, 1956), lii.

20. Russell, *History of Western Philosophy*, 122.

21. *Meno*, in *Collected Dialogues of Plato*, ed. Edith Hamilton and Huntington Cairns (Princeton, N.J.: Bollingen, 1961), 364 (81d–e).

22. Alexander Kohanski, *The Greek Mode of Thought in Western Philosophy* (Rutherford, N.J.: Fairleigh Dickinson University Press, 1984), 38–39.

23. Plato, *Republic*, 342 (VII:532).

24. Taylor, *Socrates*, 100.

25. Xenophon, *Memorabilia*, trans. E. C. Marchant (Cambridge, Mass.: Harvard University Press, 1968), 32 (I:ii).

26. Plato, *Apology*, in *Last Days of Socrates*, 64.

27. Ibid., 62.

28. Ibid., 76.

Chapter 3: The Mind of God

1. A rare exception is I. F. Stone's *The Trial of Socrates* (Boston: Little, Brown, 1988), and perhaps the first volume of Karl Popper's *The Open Society and Its Enemies* (Princeton, N.J.: Princeton University Press, 1966), although Popper paints Plato in far more sinister colors than his deceased teacher.

2. Plato, *Apology*, in Plato, *The Last Days of Socrates*, trans Hugh Tredennick (Harmondsworth: Penguin, 1954), 60.

3. This has stopped scholars from arguing that his notion of the divine and Plato's actually descend from the ancient mystery cults, in particular the Orphic mysteries. In the Renaissance, it was accepted as historical truth. For a modern version, see G.R.S. Meade, *Orpheus* (New York: Barnes & Noble, 1965).

4. Plato, *The Republic*, trans. Desmond Lee, 2nd ed. (Harmondsworth: Penguin, 1974), 449 (X:614–15).

5. Ibid., 450 (X:616b).

6. Francis Cornford, *Before and After Socrates* (Cambridge: Cambridge University Press, 1962), 1.

7. John Burnet, *Early Greek Philosophy* (1892; repr., New York: Meridian, 1958), 106–7.

8. John Strohmeier and Peter Westbrook, *Divine Harmony: The Life and Teachings of Pythagoras* (Albany, Calif.: Berkeley Hills Books, 1999), 67–88.

9. Peter Gorman, *Pythagoras: A Life* (London: Routledge & Kegan Paul, 1979).

10. Burnet, *Early Greek Philosophy*, 287–88.

11. Strohmeier and Westbrook, *Divine Harmony*, 73.

12. G. S. Kirk and J. E. Raven, *The Presocratic Philosophers* (Cambridge: Cambridge University Press, 1964), 229.

13. In 1917, the biologist D'Arcy Thompson showed how the growth of microscopic spores and of liquid crystals followed very much the same progression as in Pythagoras and the *Timaeus*. See D'Arcy Thompson, *On Growth and Form*, ed. John Tyler Bonner (Cambridge: Cambridge University Press, 1992).

14. Paul Friedlander, *Plato* (New York: Pantheon, 1958), 1:27.

15. A. E. Taylor, *Plato: The Man and His Work* (London: Methuen, 1960), 4. Later legends have Plato becoming so fascinated with this sacred geometry, and the notion of number as the language of creation, that he made his own journey to Egypt to explore

its mathematical mysteries. There is no evidence, let alone proof, that he took such a trip. However, some of his accounts in the *Laws* of Egyptian customs suggest he may have known them firsthand.

16. This is Timon of Athens. See Francis Cornford, *Plato's Cosmology: The Timaeus of Plato* (Indianapolis: Bobbs-Merrill, 1975), 3.

17. Plato, *Timaeus and Critias*, trans. Desmond Lee (Harmondsworth: Penguin, 1965), 42.

18. Ibid.

19. Ibid., 43, 73.

20. Ibid., 77.

21. Ibid., 49.

22. As explained in Taylor's analysis of *Timaeus* in *Plato*, 445.

23. Plato, *Timaeus and Critias*, introduction, 11.

24. See for example Raymond Klibansky, *The Continuity of the Platonic Tradition in the Middle Ages* (repr., Milwood, N.Y.: Kraus, 1982).

25. Plato, *Timaeus and Critias*, 40.

26. Ibid., 10 (introduction).

27. Charles Norris Cochrane, *Christianity and Classical Culture* (1940; repr., Oxford: Oxford University Press, 1957), 78–79.

28. Plato, *The Laws*, trans. Trevor J. Saunders (Harmondsworth: Penguin, 1970), (977e–978b).

29. Taylor, *Plato*, introduction to *Philebus*, 39.

30. See Bertrand Russell, *The Wisdom of the West* (New York: Doubleday, 1959), 75.

31. Taylor, *Plato*, 7.

32. According to John Dillon, *The Heirs of Plato: A Study of the Old Academy (347–274 B.C.)* (Oxford: Oxford University Press, 2003), 2–5.

33. Friedlander, *Plato*, 1:102.

Chapter 4: The Doctor's Son

1. Aristotle, *The Politics of Aristotle*, trans. and ed. Ernest Barker (1946; repr., Oxford: Oxford University Press, 1979), xxvii.

2. Diogenes Laertius, quoted in Werner Jaeger, *Aristotle: Fundamentals of the History of His Development* (1934; repr., Oxford: Oxford University Press, 1962), 33.

3. Ibid., 111.

4. On Aristotle on the Pythagoreans, see Burnet, *Early Greek Philosophy* (1892; repr., New York: Meridian, 1958), 291.

5. Aristotle, *Metaphysics*, in *Basic Works of Aristotle*, ed. Richard McKeon (New York: Modern Library, 1951).

6. Paul Friedlander, *Plato* (New York: Pantheon, 1958), 1:172.

7. Quoted in G.E.R. Lloyd, *Aristotle: The Growth and Structure of His Thought* (Cambridge: Cambridge University Press, 1968), 68–79.

8. W. D. Ross, *Aristotle* (1949; repr., London: Methuen, 1966), 1.

9. Aristotle, *Introduction to Aristotle*, ed. Richard McKeon (New York: Modern Library, 1967), xiii.

10. G. S. Kirk, "Greek Science," in Hugh Lloyd-Jones, ed., *The Greek World* (Harmondsworth: Penguin, 1967), 121–22.

11. Leonard Mlodonow, *Euclid's Window: The Story of Geometry from Parallel Lines to Hyperspace* (New York: Free Press, 2002), ix.

12. Bertrand Russell, *A History of Western Philosophy* (1945; repr., New York: Simon & Schuster, 2007), 163.

13. Exemplified by the famous third man argument, which Plato himself had to confront in the *Parmenides*. If a man is a man because he partakes of the ideal Form of Man (or a woman the Form of Woman or a chair the Form of Chair), then there must be a third, even more ideal Form of Man to cover the similarity between the particular man and his ideal Form; and likewise a fourth ideal Form to which both the other Forms and ordinary men are similar; and so on ad infinitum.

14. Russell, *History of Western Philosophy*, 167.

15. Richard Tarnas, *Passion of the Western Mind* (New York: Harmony, 1991), 57.

16. Aristotle, *Posterior Analytics*, in *Introduction to Aristotle*, ed. McKeon, 11.

17. Russell, *History of Western Philosophy*, 169.

18. W.K.C. Guthrie, *The Greek Philosophers from Thales to Aristotle* (1950; repr. New York: Harper & Row, 1960), 139.

19. For instance, see Frank Manuel, *The Eighteenth Century Confronts the Gods* (New York: Atheneum, 1967).

20. W. D. Ross, *Aristotle* (1949; repr. London: Methuen 1966), 186.

21. Russell, *History of Western Philosophy*, 167; Francis Cornford, *Before and After Socrates* (Cambridge: Cambridge University Press, 1962). Admittedly, I use "aspiration" in a slightly different way from Cornford's original formulation.

22. Aristotle, *The Nicomachean Ethics*, trans. J.A.K. Thomson (Harmondsworth: Penguin, 1976), 206, 208.

23. Guthrie, *Greek Philosophers*, 152.

24. Ibid., 191.

25. Ibid., 83.

26. Ibid., 271, 273.

27. Ibid., 101.

28. Plato, *Phaedrus*, trans. W. Hamilton (Harmondsworth: Penguin, 1973), 53.

29. Aristotle, *Nichomachean Ethics*, 93.

Chapter 5: Good Citizen or Philosopher Ruler?

1. Philip Rieff, *The Triumph of the Therapeutic: Uses of Faith After Freud* (New York: Harper & Row, 1966), 67.

2. Plato, *The Republic*, trans. Desmond Lee, 2nd ed. (Harmondsworth: Penguin, 1974), 24–25.

3. Aristotle, *The Politics of Aristotle*, ed. Ernest Barker (1946; repr., Oxford: Oxford Uni-

versity Press, 1979), 258. See John B. Morrall, *Aristotle* (London: Allen & Unwin, 1977), 94.

4. Plato, *Plato's Epistles*, ed. Glenn Morrow (Indianapolis: Bobbs-Merrill, 1962), 123.

5. Plato, *Republic*, introduction, 576.

6. A. E. Taylor, *Plato: The Man and His Work* (London: Methuen, 1960), 109.

7. Plato, *Gorgias*, trans. W. Hamilton (Harmondsworth: Penguin, 1960), 149.

8. Ibid., 126 (513e).

9. Plato, *Republic*, 451 (X:616b–617b).

10. Ibid., 235 (X:45b).

11. In fact, the image of Socrates's political legislator as a doctor of souls runs through all his works and not just the *Republic*.

12. Plato, *Epistles*, Epistle VII.

13. This has led some, like Karl Popper, to see Plato's *Republic* as endorsing a kind of racism.

14. Plato, *Republic*, 261.

15. Ibid., 263.

16. Michael Rostovtzeff, *A History of the Ancient World* (Oxford: Clarendon Press, 1928), 1:204.

17. Antony Andrewes, *The Greek Tyrants* (1956; repr., New York: Harper & Row, 1963), 91. Solon is also a key figure in Plato's *Critias*, where he learns about the laws and institutions of another Platonic utopia, the vanished Atlantis.

18. Plato, *Epistles*, 220.

19. Ibid., 219.

20. Ibid., *Epistles*, 177.

21. Ibid., 229. Plato would expand on this notion of good laws, not good men, as a political principle in the last dialogue he ever wrote, the *Laws*. In general, both the *Laws* and its immediate predecessor, the *Statesman*, give us a very different picture of the Philosopher Ruler from the all-powerful, all-knowing sage in the *Republic*. His aims are more modest, his methods more pragmatic, with a stress on proportion and process. If the discussion is more realistic, it is also less bracing to read.

22. Plato, *Republic*, 263.

23. Aristotle, *Politics of Aristotle*, 52 (II:1264 a16).

24. Aristotle, *Nicomachean Ethics*, trans. J.A.K. Thomson (Harmondsworth: Penguin, 1976), 81 (I:1100a).

25. As noted by C. A. Bates, *Aristotle's "Best Regime": Kingship, Democracy, and the Rule of Law* (Baton Rouge: Louisiana State University Press, 2003), which forcefully argues that Aristotle's ideal political system, or *politeia*, is not an aristocracy, as W. D. Ross and many other critics have claimed, but democracy on the Athenian model.

26. Aristotle, *Politics*, 41.

27. Ibid., 42.

28. Ibid. See J.G.A. Pocock, *The Machiavellian Moment* (Princeton, N.J.: Princeton University Press, 1975), 71.

29. Aristotle, *Politics*, 51.

30. For example, Aristotle, *Politics*, 119.

31. Ibid., 123.

32. Ibid., 126, 127.

33. This is during his remarks on the virtues of ostracism in Greek law. Aristotle, *Politics*, 135.

34. Werner Jaeger, *Aristotle: Fundamentals of the History of His Development* (1934; repr., Oxford: Oxford University Press, 1962), 313.

35. For instance, W.K.C. Guthrie, *The Greek Philosophers from Thales to Aristotle* (1950; repr., New York: Harper & Row, 1960), 113.

36. Jaeger, *Aristotle*, 321.

Chapter 6: The Inheritors: Philosophy in the Hellenistic Age

1. Paul Zanker, *The Mask of Socrates: The Image of the Intellectual in Antiquity* (Berkeley: University of California Press, 1995).

2. Edwyn Bevan, "Hellenistic Popular Philosophy," in J. B. Bury, ed., *The Hellenistic Age: Aspects of Hellenistic Civilization* (1923; repr., New York: Norton, 1970), 81.

3. Alexander Kohanski, *The Greek Mode of Thought in Western Philosophy* (Rutherford, N.J.: Fairleigh Dickinson University Press, 1984), 73–74.

4. P. E. More, *The Greek Tradition*, vol. 3, *Hellenistic Philosophies* (Princeton, N.J.: Princeton University Press, 1923), 19.

5. Gordon Clark, *Selections from Hellenistic Philosophy* (New York: Appleton-Century-Crofts, 1940), 4.

6. Epicurus, "Letter to Menoeceus," in Whitney J. Oates, ed., *The Stoic and Epicurean Philosophers* (New York: Random House, 1940), 33.

7. Seneca quoted in Bertrand Russell, *A History of Western Philosophy* (1945; repr., New York: Simon & Schuster, 2007), 260; Moses Hadas, ed., *The Stoic Philosophy of Seneca* (New York: Doubleday, 1958), 7.

8. The story about Epictetus's leg is from Plotinus's student Celsus. See Origen, *Contra Celsum, Libra VIII*, ed. M. Marcovich (Boston: Brill, 2001), vii, 53.

9. More, *Greek Tradition*, 81.

10. A. E. Taylor, *Platonism and Its Influence* (1924; repr., New York: Cooper Square, 1963), 8–9. This led the Academy's fifth president, Arcesilaus (d. 241 BCE), to embrace a version of Skepticism that left Platonist followers of the time, and scholars since, scratching their heads, but which seems to have been directed to refute the notion that anything we know from our senses is known for certain.

11. More, *Greek Tradition*, 65.

12. Diogenes quoted ibid., 261.

13. There are many versions of the story, but the best comes from Diogenes Laertius.

14. That may have been a deliberately ironic turn of phrase, since Diogenes's father seems to have been charged with counterfeiting: it may even have been why Diogenes was exiled from Sinope. See More, *Greek Tradition*, 260.

15. See E. A. Barber, "Alexandrian Literature," in Bury, *Hellenistic Age*, 67, 69–70.

16. John Dillon, *The Heirs of Plato: A Study of the Old Academy (347–274 B.C.)* (Oxford: Oxford University Press, 2003).

17. Felix Grayeff, *Aristotle and His School* (London: Duckworth, 1974), 52, 57.

18. Cicero, *Academica*, bk. I. See David Sedley, "The Origins of Stoic God," in Dorothea Frede and André Laks, eds., *Traditional Theology: Studies in Hellenistic Theology* (Leiden: Brill, 2011).

19. A point raised by G.E.R. Lloyd in *Greek Science After Aristotle* (New York: Norton, 1973).

20. In Theophrastus's case, Aristotle's assertions about final causes and the Unmoved Mover came to play a less and less prominent part of Aristotelian science, as opposed to Aristotelian philosophy. See Lloyd, *Greek Science After Aristotle*.

21. Theodore Vrettos, *Alexandria: City of the Western Mind* (New York: Free Press, 2001), 6–7.

22. P. M. Fraser, *Ptolemaic Alexandria* (Oxford: Clarendon Press, 1972), 315.

Chapter 7: Knowledge Is Power

1. P. M. Fraser, *Ptolemaic Alexandria* (Oxford: Clarendon Press, 1972), 315–17.

2. Ibid., 320.

3. Athenaeus was an Athenian grammarian of the first century BCE. Theodore Vrettos declares his account "more valid" than the one that has Neleus's heirs burying the library until it was resurrected by one Apellico, whose house in Athens was then looted by the Roman general Sulla in 86 and the books transferred to Rome by Andronicus of Rhodes. See Theodore Vrettos, *Alexandria: City of the Western Mind* (New York: Free Press, 2001), 38–39; and Felix Grayeff, *Aristotle and His School* (London: Duckworth, 1974), 74–75. The Andronicus version was laid to rest by Jonathan Barnes in *Philosophia Togata II: Plato and Aristotle in Rome* (New York: Oxford University Press, 1997). What is beyond dispute is that some of the library, and perhaps some of Aristotle's work in his own handwriting, wound up in the royal library at Pergamum, another center of Peripatetic study in the Hellenistic era.

4. Grayeff, *Aristotle and His School*, 72.

5. Fraser, *Ptolemaic Alexandria*, 319.

6. Ibid., 352–53, 354.

7. G.E.R. Lloyd, *Greek Science After Aristotle* (New York: Norton, 1973), 77.

8. The author was Tertullian, and the work was *De Anima*.

9. Fraser, *Ptolemaic Alexandria*, 348.

10. B. L. van der Waerden, *Science Awakening* (New York: Oxford University Press, 1961), 202–3.

11. Bertrand Russell, *A History of Western Philosophy* (1945; repr., New York: Simon & Schuster, 2007), 217; on Aristotle's celestial spheres, see G. Huxley, "Greek Mathematics and Astronomy," in Hugh Lloyd-Jones, ed., *The Greek World* (Harmondsworth: Penguin, 1965), 147.

12. Alexander Kohanski, *The Greek Mode of Thought in Western Philosophy* (Rutherford, N.J.: Fairleigh Dickinson University Press, 1984), 116.

13. Van der Waerden, *Science Awakening*, 196.

14. Fraser, *Ptolemaic Alexandria*, 391.

15. Van der Waerden, *Science Awakening*, 197.

16. As noted by Jacob Bronowski, *The Ascent of Man* (Boston: Little, Brown, 1974).

17. Lloyd, *Greek Science After Aristotle*, 49.

18. J. B. Bury, "The Hellenistic Age and the History of Civilization," in Bury, *Hellenistic Age*, 21–22.

19. Thomas Kuhn, *Structure of Scientific Revolutions* (Chicago: University of Chicago Press, 1962), 36.

20. According to Plutarch, "Marcellus," in Plutarch, *Makers of Rome*, trans. Ian Scott-Kilvert (Harmondsworth: Penguin, 1965).

21. This is sometimes confused with a catalog of the Library itself: Fraser, *Ptolemaic Alexandria*, 454–55.

22. Ibid., 429.

23. Plutarch, "Marcellus," 99.

24. Fraser, *Ptolemaic Alexandria*, 431; Lloyd, *Greek Science After Aristotle*, 96.

25. Michael Rostovtzeff, *A History of the Ancient World* (Oxford: Clarendon Press, 1928), 360, 363; Van der Waerden, *Science Awakening*, plate facing 216.

26. F. J. Dijksterhuis, *Archimedes* (Copenhagen: E. Munksgaard, 1972), 18–19.

27. Reviel Netz and William Noel, *Archimedes Codex* (Philadelphia: Da Capo Press, 2007), 41.

28. Ibid., 41–43.

29. Dijksterhuis, *Archimedes*, 24.

30. Plutarch, "Marcellus," 99; Van der Waerden, *Science Awakening*, 209.

31. Polybius, *The Rise of the Roman Empire*, trans. F. W. Walbank (Harmondsworth: Penguin, 1979), 365.

32. Ibid., 366.

33. Ibid., 367.

34. Plutarch, "Marcellus," 101.

35. Ibid., 103.

36. Dijksterhuis, *Archimedes*. What problem was he working on when he died? Scholars like to speculate.

37. Plutarch, "Marcellus," 105.

38. Russell, *History of Western Philosophy*, 217.

Chapter 8: Hole in the Soul: Plato and Aristotle in Rome

1. Cicero's account of his discovery of Archimedes's tomb comes from Book II of his *Tusculan Disputations*, trans. C. D. Yonge (London: Henry G. Bohn, 1853).

2. F. R. Cowell, *Cicero and the Roman Republic* (1948; repr., Harmondsworth: Penguin, 1968), 324.

3. Mark Morford, *The Roman Philosophers* (New York: Routledge, 2002).

4. Jonathan Barnes and Miriam Griffin, eds., *Philosophia Togata II: Plato and Aristotle in Rome* (New York: Oxford University Press, 1997), vi–vii.

5. F. W. Walbank, *A Historical Commentary on Polybius* (Oxford: Clarendon Press, 1957), vol. 1.

6. Robert Malcolm Errington, *The Dawn of Empire: Rome's Rise to World Power* (Ithaca, N.Y.: Cornell University Press, 1972), 268.

7. Polybius, *The Rise of the Roman Empire*, trans. Ian Scott-Kilvert (Harmondsworth: Penguin Books, 1979), 41.

8. Walbank, *Historical Commentary on Polybius,* 18.

9. Aristotle, *The Politics of Aristotle*, ed. Ernest Barker (1946; repr., Oxford: Oxford University Press, 1979), 114 (III, vii).

10. Polybius, *Rise of Roman Empire*, 314–15.

11. Ibid., 317.

12. Plato, *The Republic*, trans. Desmond Lee, 2nd ed. (Harmondsworth: Penguin, 1974), 381 (VIII:561d).

13. Ibid., 368 (551d).

14. Polybius, *Rise of Roman Empire*, 310, 350.

15. J.G.A. Pocock, *The Machiavellian Moment* (Princeton, N.J.: Princeton University Press, 1975), 71.

16. J.P.V.D. Balsdon, ed., *Roman Civilization* (Harmondsworth: Penguin, 1965), 39.

17. Plutarch, "Cato the Elder," in Plutarch, *Makers of Rome*, trans. Ian Scott-Kilvert (Harmondsworth: Penguin, 1965), 145–46.

18. Sallust, *Jugurthine War / The Conspiracy of Cataline*, trans. S. A. Handford (Harmondsworth: Penguin, 1963), 177, 180.

19. Ibid., 178. Sallust made his own contribution to that part of the formula with his *Jugurthine War*, an account of Rome's ruthless conquest of the African kingdom of Numidia and its king Jugurtha.

20. Cicero, "On Duties (II)," in *On the Good Life*, trans. Michael Grant (Harmondsworth: Penguin, 1971), p. 135.

21. Neal Wood, *Cicero's Social and Political Thought* (Berkeley: University of California Press, 1988), 66.

22. Cicero, *De Re Publica*, ed. Geoffrey Poyser (Cambridge: Cambridge University Press, 1948), 190 (II).

23. Wood, *Cicero's Social and Political Thought,* 177.

24. Cicero, *De Officiis*, trans. Harry G. Edinger (Indianapolis: Bobbs-Merrill, 1974), 28 (I).

25. Ibid., 112 (II).

26. L. R. Taylor, *Party Politics in the Age of Caesar* (Berkeley: University of California Press, 1948), 99.

27. Plato, *Gorgias*, trans. Walter Hamilton (Harmondsworth: Penguin, 1960), p. 47.

28. In fact, "the more one tries to build up either Dialectic or Rhetoric, not as a faculty,

but as an exact science, the more one will be inadvertently destroying their nature."
Aristotle, *Rhetoric*, trans. Lane Cooper (1932; repr., Englewood Cliffs, N.J.:
Prentice-Hall, 1960), 21.

29. Ibid., 24 (III:19).

30. Elaine Fantham, *The Roman World of Cicero's "De Oratore"*(Oxford: Oxford University Press, 2004), 171.

31. Aristotle, *Rhetoric*, trans. Lane Cooper (1932; repr., Englewood Cliffs, N.J.:
Prentice-Hall, 1960), 23 (I:4).

32. Cicero, *On the Ideal Orator*, trans. James May and Jakob Wisse (New York: Oxford University Press, 2001).

33. Cicero, *De Re Publica*, 129 (I).

Chapter 9: Dancing in the Light: The Birth of Neoplatonism

1. See Hans Baron, *The Crisis of the Early Italian Renaissance* (Princeton, N.J.: Princeton University Press, 1966); and chapter 13 of this book.

2. Caesar quoted in Ronald Syme, *The Roman Revolution* (Oxford: Oxford University Press, 1939), 62.

3. Ibid.

4. Plutarch, "Life of Caesar," in *The Fall of the Roman Republic*, trans. Rex Warner (Harmondsworth: Penguin, 1958), 303.

5. Virgil, *Aeneid*, quoted in Erich Gruen, ed., *The Image of Rome* (Englewood Cliffs, N.J.: Prentice-Hall, 1969), 63; Virgil, *Fourth Ecologue*, ibid., 61.

6. The rhetorician Porcius Latro, quoted in M. L. Clarke, *The Roman Mind* (New York: Norton, 1968), 100.

7. Tacitus, *Agricola*, in *Tacitus on Britain and Germany*, trans. Harold Mattingly (Harmondsworth: Penguin, 1965).

8. R. H. Barrow, *The Romans* (1949; repr., Harmondsworth: Penguin, 1975), 89.

9. Clarke, *Roman Mind*, 110–11.

10. Tacitus, *Germania*, in *Tacitus on Britain and Germany*.

11. Plato, *Critias*, in *Timaeus and Critias*, trans. Desmond Lee (Harmondsworth: Penguin, 1971), 143.

12. As noted by Hegel in *Phenomenology of Spirit*, and quoted in Alexander Kohanski, *The Greek Mode of Thought in Western Philosophy* (Rutherford, N.J.: Fairleigh Dickinson University Press, 1984), 86.

13. A. A. Long, *Hellenistic Philosophy: Stoics, Epicureans, Sceptics*, 2nd ed. (1974; repr., London: Duckworth, 1986), 80–81.

14. Clarke, *Roman Mind*, 39.

15. Seneca, "Of Peace of Mind," in *Minor Dialogs*, trans. Aubrey Stewart (London: George Bell & Sons, 1900), 3.2.

16. Seneca, "Of Anger," ibid., II, 7–8.

17. Tacitus, *The Annals of Tacitus*, trans. Donald Dudley (New York: Mentor Books, 1966), 363–64.

18. Marcus Aurelius, *Meditations*, in Whitney J. Oates, *The Stoic and Epicurean Philosophers* (New York: Modern Library, 1940), 544 (VIII), 584–85 (XII).

19. Peter Brown, *The World of Late Antiquity* (New York: Harcourt Brace Jovanovich, 1971), 22.

20. John Gregory, ed., *The Neoplatonists* (London: Routledge, 1991), 3.

21. See W. R. Inge, *The Philosophy of Plotinus* (1929; repr., New York: Greenwood Press, 1968), 1:41. However, the notion propagated by Inge and others—that Plotinus's mystical philosophy was the result of a fusion of Greco-Roman and Oriental ideas—seems unfounded. As Mark Edwards notes in *Culture and Philosophy in the Age of Plotinus* (London: Duckworth, 2006), there is no evidence that Plotinus joined Gordian's expedition to Persia in hopes of meeting Zoroastrian and Indian mystics, as his student Porphyry claimed, or that "Plotinus gave a thought to either of these races" (31).

22. A. E. Taylor, *Platonism and Its Influence* (1924; repr., New York: Cooper Square, 1963), 12.

23. Plato, *The Republic*, trans. Desmond Lee, 2nd ed. (Harmondsworth: Penguin, 1974), VII, 509B.

24. Arthur L. Herman, *The Ways of Philosophy* (Atlanta, Ga.: Scholars Press, 1990), 83.

25. David Knowles, *The Evolution of Medieval Thought* (New York: Random House, 1962), 24.

26. Taylor, *Platonism*, 13.

27. Quoted in A. O. Lovejoy, *The Great Chain of Being* (1936; repr., New York: Harper & Row, 1965).

28. Especially in the *Sophist* and *Parmenides*. See Plato, *Plato's Epistles*, ed. Glenn Morrow (Indianapolis: Bobbs-Merrill, 1962), 70.

29. Plotinus, *Enneads*, trans. Stephen McKenna, 2nd ed., rev. (London: Faber & Faber, 1956), IV, 8.

30. Knowles, *Evolution of Medieval Thought*, 21.

31. Plotinus, *Enneads*, VI, 9, viii–ix.

32. Ibid., II, 4, quoted in Charles Norris Cochrane, *Christianity and Classical Culture* (1940; repr., Oxford: Oxford University Press, 1957), 172.

33. Gregory, *Neoplatonists*, 6.

Chapter 10: Christ Is Come: Plato and Christianity

1. Acts 17:18. All direct quotations are from the King James Version.

2. Acts 17:26, 28, 31. Outside the account in Acts, very little is known about the Unknown God or where such an altar existed. See Charles Stephan Conway Williams, *Commentary on the Acts of the Apostles* (London: A. & C. Black, 1964).

3. Acts 20:13–15.

4. 2 Corinthians 9:8.

5. 1 Corinthians 15:55.

6. Tacitus, *The Annals of Tacitus*, trans. Donald Dudley (New York: Mentor Books, 1966), 354.

7. Marcus Aurelius, *Meditations*, in Whitney J. Oates, *The Stoic and Epicurean Philosophers* (New York: Modern Library, 1940), 583 (XII).

8. Richard Tarnas, *Passion of the Western Mind* (New York: Harmony, 1991), 103.

9. For example, Charles Freeman, *The Closing of the Western Mind* (New York: Alfred A. Knopf, 2003), and in a more vulgar vein, Richard Dawkins, *The God Delusion* (Boston: Houghton Mifflin, 2008).

10. Heraclitus quoted in Alexander Kohanski, *The Greek Mode of Thought in Western Philosophy* (Rutherford, N.J.: Fairleigh Dickinson University Press, 1984), 92.

11. 1 John 1:9, 14.

12. See John Dillon, "Logos and Trinity: Patterns of Platonist Influence on Early Christianity," in Dillon, *The Great Tradition: Further Studies in the Development of Platonism and Early Christianity* (Brookfield, Vt.: Ashgate, 1997), chap. 8, 3; and Dillon, "Origen and Plotinus: The Platonic Influence on Early Christianity," in Thomas Finan and Vincent Twomey, eds., *The Relationship Between Neoplatonism and Christianity* (Dublin: Four Courts Press, 1992), 11.

13. Tarnas, *Passion of Western Mind*, 475 n.

14. "For Plato says: 'The holy souls shall return to human bodies.' " Augustine, *The City of God*, trans. John Healey (London: Dent, 1945), (XXII:27). Augustine was in effect taking Plato's theory of transmigration of souls as an endorsement of the idea of physical resurrection after death.

15. Ibid., 403–4 (XXII:29).

16. Revelation 22:13, 5.

17. Plato, *Phaedo*, in Plato, *The Last Days of Socrates*, trans. Hugh Tredennick (Harmondsworth: Penguin, 1954), 135.

18. John 20:31.

19. Tarnas, *Passion of Western Mind*, 103.

20. Justin Martyr, *The First Apology* (Edinburgh: J. Grant, 1912), 5, 56.

21. In particular, Porphyry and Iamblichus. See Mark Edwards, *Culture and Philosophy in the Age of Plotinus* (London: Duckworth, 2006).

22. Theodore Vrettos, *Alexandria: City of the Western Mind* (New York: Free Press, 2001), 186, 188. Celsus's work is lost. The arguments and quotations largely come from Origen's refutation, *Against Celsus*, trans. H. Chadwick (Cambridge: Cambridge University Press, 1965).

23. *Adamantius* in Latin. See Henri Crouzel, *Origen* (Edinburgh: T. T. Clark, 1999), 51.

24. Henri Daniel-Rops, *Church of Apostles and Martyrs* (New York: Doubleday, 1960), 2:55.

25. Vrettos, *Alexandria*, 181.

26. The method of the death of his father, Leonidas, has led some scholars to speculate that he must have been a Roman citizen. See Crouzel, *Origen*, and Joseph Wilson Trigg, *Origen* (London: Routledge, 1998).

27. Pierre Hadot, *Philosophy as a Way of Life* (Oxford: Wiley-Blackwell, 1995), 264.

28. Trigg, *Origen*.

29. Charles Norris Cochrane, *Christianity and Classical Culture* (1940; repr., Oxford: Oxford University Press, 1957), 181.

30. Justin Martyr, *The First Apology* (Edinburgh: J. Grant, 1912), 19.

31. Crouzel, *Origen*, 74, 93.

32. Ibid., 100. See also Robert Berchman, *From Philo to Origen: Middle Platonism in Transition* (Chicago: Scholars Press, 1984).

33. Joseph Wilson Trigg, *Origen: The Bible and Philosophy in the Third Century Church* (Atlanta, Ga.: J. Knox, 1983), 10–11.

34. Trigg, *Bible and Philosophy*, 167; Trigg, *Origen*, 36–39.

35. Crouzel, *Origen*, 63; Henry Chadwick, *The Early Church* (1967; repr., Harmondsworth: Penguin, 1982), 105–7.

36. Dorothy Sayers, introduction to Dante Alighieri, *Divine Comedy I: Hell*, trans. Dorothy Sayers (1949; repr., Harmondsworth: Penguin, 1976).

37. E. R. Dodds, *Pagan and Christian in an Age of Anxiety* (New York: Norton, 1970), 120.

38. Crouzel, *Origen*, 53, which calls Origen's devotion to Jesus as a person "unique" in Christian antiquity.

39. Origen, *Commentary on the Gospel According to John*, trans. Ronald E. Heine (Washington, D.C.: Catholic University Press, 1989), 2:267–68.

40. Thomas à Kempis, *Imitation of Christ*, trans. Thomas Kepler (Cleveland: World Publishing, 1952), 35.

41. Quoted in Dodds, *Pagan and Christian*, 120.

42. Trigg, *Bible and Philosophy*, 228.

43. See Dodd, *Pagan and Christian*, 29–36.

44. Ibid., 119.

45. Eusebius, *The History of the Church*, trans. Geoffrey A. Williamson (Harmondsworth: Penguin, 1965).

46. Crouzel, *Origen*, 140–42.

47. A. E. Taylor, *Platonism and Its Influence* (1924; repr., New York: Cooper Square, 1963), 88.

48. Eusebius, *History of the Church*; Theodore Vrettos, *Alexandria: City of the Western Mind* (New York: Free Press, 2001), 192.

49. Chadwick, *Early Church*, 109.

Chapter 11: Toward the Heavenly City

1. This is the account from Lactantius, who was writing only a few years after the event. See Ramsay MacMullen, *Constantine* (New York: Harper Torchbooks, 1970), 72.

2. Noel Lenski, *Cambridge Companion to the Age of Constantine* (Cambridge: Cambridge University Press, 2006), 69.

3. Ibid., 71. The other interpretation is that Constantine himself connected the looped cross with the Christogram, and by making his soldiers paint it on their shields, he was

declaring himself to be a Christian. Peter Weiss, "The Vision of Constantine," *Journal of Roman Archeology* 16 [2003]: 237–59.

4. See Justin Martyr, Apology I, in *The Apologies of Justin Martyr*, trans. Basil Gildersleeve (New York, 1877).

5. Charles Norris Cochrane, *Christianity and Classical Culture* (1940; repr., Oxford: Oxford University Press, 1957), 179.

6. Eusebius, *The History of the Church*, trans. Geoffrey A. Williamson (Harmondsworth: Penguin, 1965), 413.

7. Tertullian, *On Idolatry* (New York: Kessinger, 2004), 18–19.

8. Celsus quoted in Peter Brown, *The World of Late Antiquity* (New York: Harcourt Brace Jovanovich, 1971), 82.

9. On Origen and Eusebius, see Timothy Barnes, *Constantine and Eusebius* (Cambridge, Mass.: Harvard University Press, 1981), 86–95.

10. Eusebius, *History of the Church*.

11. Ibid., 389; *Panegyric*, quoted in Cochrane, *Christianity and Classical Culture*, 185.

12. Eusebius, *The Life of Constantine*, trans. A. Cameron and Stuart Hall (Oxford: Clarendon Press, 1999), 87.

13. Noel Lenski, *Cambridge Companion to the Age of Constantine* (Cambridge: Cambridge University Press, 2006).

14. Walter Ullmann, *A History of Political Thought: The Middle Ages* (Harmondsworth: Penguin, 1970), 35.

15. C. M. Odahl, *Constantine and the Christian Empire* (New York: Routledge, 2004), 136.

16. Cochrane, *Christianity and Classical Culture*, 39.

17. Lactantius, *Divine Institutes*, trans. A. Bowen and P. Garnsey (Liverpool: University of Liverpool Press, 2003).

18. Cochrane, *Christianity and Classical Culture*, 195.

19. Ibid., 194.

20. Eusebius, *Life of Constantine*, bk. II, 24, 28.

21. Ibid., bk. IV, 25.

22. See James Carroll, *Constantine's Sword: The Church and the Jews: A History* (New York: Houghton Mifflin, 2001).

23. Richard Krautheimer, *Three Christian Capitals: Topology and Politics* (Berkeley: University of California Press, 1983); Odahl, *Constantine and Christian Empire*, 262.

24. Edward Gibbon, *Decline and Fall of the Roman Empire* (Harmondsworth: Penguin, 1994), 1:863.

25. Quoted in ibid., 1:994.

26. Ibid., 1:869.

27. Ibid., 1:946.

28. J. M. Wallace-Hadrill, *The Barbarian West: The Early Middle Ages A.D. 400–1000* (1952; repr., New York: Harper & Row, 1962), 21–22.

29. Augustine quoted in David Knowles, *The Evolution of Medieval Thought* (New York: Random House, 1962), 37.

30. See Richard Enos, *The Rhetoric of Saint Augustine of Hippo* (Waco, Tex.: Baylor University Press, 2008).

31. Cochrane, *Christianity and Classical Culture*, 195.

32. Augustine, *Confessions*, trans. R. S. Pine-Coffin (Harmondsworth: Penguin, 1961), 47.

33. Jerome quoted in Peter Brown, *Augustine of Hippo: A Biography* (Berkeley: University of California Press, 1969), 289.

34. Augustine quoted ibid., 293, 298.

35. Augustine, *The City of God*, 94 (III:17).

36. Ibid., 64 (II:21).

37. Ibid., 235–36 (VIII:9).

38. Which is why, for Augustine, animals are incapable of true knowledge. See Bruce Bubacz, *St. Augustine's Theory of Knowledge* (New York: E. Mellen Press, 1981), 101.

39. See the discussion in Knowles, *Evolution of Medieval Thought*, 41–43, and compare Étienne Gilson, *The Christian Philosophy of Saint Augustine* (1960; repr., New York: Octagon, 1983), chap. 5, esp. 107–11.

40. Étienne Gilson, *Reason and Revelation in the Middle Ages* (New York: Charles Scribner's Sons, 1939), 18–19.

41. Augustine, *City of God*, 404 (XXII:30).

Chapter 12: Inquiring Minds: Aristotle Strikes Back

1. Boethius, *The Consolation of Philosophy*, trans. Victor E. Watts (Harmondsworth: Penguin, 1969), 11 (introduction).

2. Theodoric quoted in Jonathan Barnes, "Boethius and the Study of Logic," in Margaret Gibson, ed., *Boethius: His Life, Thought, and Influence* (Oxford: Basil Blackwell, 1982), 73.

3. Boethius, *Consolation of Philosophy*, I, 35, 36, 38.

4. John Marenbon, *The Cambridge Companion to Boethius* (Cambridge: Cambridge University Press, 2009), 77–79.

5. Boethius, *Consolation of Philosophy*, III, 113.

6. R. W. Southern, *The Making of the Middle Ages* (1953; repr., New Haven, Conn.: Yale University Press, 1967), 171.

7. Ultimately, Boethius's distinction between simple and conditional necessity, which allows for free choice, rested on his reading of Aristotle. H. R. Patch, "Fate in Boethius and the Neoplatonists," *Speculum* 4, no. 1 (1929), 62–72.

8. Boethius, *Consolation of Philosophy*, I, 39.

9. Boethius, *Commentaries on Aristotle's "De Interpretatione,"* ed. H. F. Campenhausen (Tübingen: Mohr, 1988), 285–86.

10. See Richard Rubenstein, *Aristotle's Children* (Orlando, Fla.: Harcourt, 2003), and chapter 14 of this book.

11. Thomas Cahill, *How the Irish Saved Civilization* (New York: Anchor, 1996).

12. Plato, *Theaetetus*, 189e–190a. On the Neoplatonist attitude contrasted with Aristotle, see Henry Chadwick, *Boethius: The Consolation of Music, Logic, Theology, and Philosophy* (Oxford: Clarendon Press, 1981), 108–9.

13. Bertrand Russell, *A History of Western Philosophy* (1945; repr., New York: Simon & Schuster, 2007), 199.

14. Henri Focillon, *The Year 1000* (New York: Ungar, 1970).

15. R. W. Southern, *The Making of the Middle Ages* (1953; repr., New Haven, Conn.: Yale University Press, 1967), 174–75.

16. David Wagner, ed., *The Seven Liberal Arts in the Middle Ages* (Bloomington: Indiana University Press, 1983).

17. Southern, *Making of the Middle Ages*, 177; James Morrison, *The Astrolabe* (London: Janus, 2007).

18. Southern, *Making of the Middle Ages*, 175–76.

19. David Knowles, *The Evolution of Medieval Thought* (New York: Random House, 1962), 95.

20. R. W. Southern, *Saint Anselm and His Biographer* (Cambridge: Cambridge University Press, 1963).

21. Originally stated in Anselm, *Proslogium*, chapter 3. The key to the argument is the notion that a being so obviously perfect as the God we imagine in our minds would never *not* exist, because existence is part and parcel of perfection. For a quick summary of the philosophical issues involved, check W. T. Jones, *A History of Western Philosophy*, vol. 2, *The Medieval Mind* (New York: Harcourt Brace & World, 1971), 203–4.

22. D. W. Robertson, *Abelard and Heloise* (New York: Dial Press, 1972), 6.

23. Later, Abelard probably knew some additional Aristotle texts on logic that were being translated from Arab sources, like the *Topics*, but the *Categories* remained the heart of his own system, along with Boethius's own two treatises on the subject; and Porphyry's *Isagoge*, which was still considered the best introduction to logic for young minds. See Jeffrey Brower, *The Cambridge Companion to Abelard* (New York: Cambridge University Press, 2004).

24. Peter Abelard, *History of My Calamities*, quoted in Robertson, *Abelard and Heloise*, 11.

25. Ibid., 27.

26. Russell, *History of Western Philosophy*, 438–39.

27. Knowles, *Evolution of Medieval Thought*, 126; Jones, *Medieval Mind*, 191.

28. Russell, *History of Western Philosophy*, 437.

29. *Sic et Non*, quoted in Georges Duby, Eleanor Levieux, and Barbara Thompson, *The Age of the Cathedrals: Art and Society 980–1420* (Chicago: University of Chicago Press, 1981), 115.

30. Knowles, *Evolution of Medieval Thought*, 125.

31. Ibid.

32. Abelard, *History of My Calamities*, quoted in Robertson, *Abelard and Heloise*, 44.

33. Ibid., 56.

34. Peter Abelard, *Letters of Abelard and Heloise*, trans. Betty Radice (Harmondsworth: Penguin, 1974).

35. Russell, *History of Western Philosophy*, 437, 199.

36. Knowles, *Evolution of Medieval Thought*, 123.

Chapter 13: Celestial Harmonies: Plato in the Middle Ages

1. Glauber quoted in Alain Erlande-Brandenburg, *The Cathedral Builders of the Middle Ages* (London: Thames & Hudson, 1995), 13.

2. Augustine, *Confessions*, trans. J. M. Cohen (Harmondsworth: Penguin, 1954), VIII:i, 1 and 2.

3. Bernard of Clairvaux, *Letters of Saint Bernard of Clairvaux*, trans. Bruno Scott James (Kalamazoo, Mich.: Cistercian Publications, 1998), 249, 328.

4. Ibid., 318, 324.

5. Ibid., 239, 318.

6. G. R. Evans, *Bernard of Clairvaux* (New York: Oxford University Press, 2000), 121.

7. Bernard of Clairvaux, *Letters*, 319.

8. Ibid., 328.

9. Étienne Gilson, *Reason and Revelation in the Middle Ages* (New York: Charles Scribner's Sons, 1939).

10. Bernard of Clairvaux, *Letters*, 163.

11. In a letter to the pope, he said he wanted Abelard "exterminated." Ibid., 324, 320.

12. R. W. Southern, *Western Society and the Church in the Middle Ages* (Harmondsworth: Penguin, 1970), 314–15.

13. Bernard of Clairvaux, *Letters*, 162.

14. Ibid.

15. Knowles, *Evolution of Medieval Thought*, 147.

16. Bernard of Clairvaux, *Letters*, 161.

17. Ibid.,162.

18. Southern, *Making of the Middle Ages*.

19. Augustine declared that the perfect consonance of the major octave, based on the ratio 1:2, conveyed to human ears the mystery of redemption. Augustine, *On the Trinity*, trans. Stephen McKenna (Washington, D.C.: Catholic University of American Press, 1963), IV:2, 4.

20. Augustine quoted in David Wagner, ed., *The Seven Liberal Arts in the Middle Ages* (Bloomington: Indiana University Press, 1983), 40.

21. Otto G. von Simson, *The Gothic Cathedral* (1956; repr., Princeton, N.J.: Princeton University Press, 1974), 41.

22. Fran O'Rourke, "Being and Non-Being in the Pseudo-Dionysius," in Thomas Finan, and Vincent Twomey, eds., *The Relationship Between Neoplatonism and Christianity* (Dublin: Four Courts Press, 1992), 56.

23. Eric Perl, *Theophany: The Neoplatonic Philosophy of Dionysius the Areopagite* (Albany: SUNY Press, 2007).

24. See M. D. Chenu, *Nature, Man, and Society in the Twelfth Century* (Chicago: Chicago University Press, 1979).

25. Dionysius the Areopagite, *Celestial Hierarchy* (Fintry, U.K.: Shrine of Wisdom Press, 1965).

26. Especially the Gnostics. See Elaine Pagels, *The Gnostic Gospels* (New York: Vintage Books, 1979).

27. Dionysius the Areopagite, *Celestial Hierarchy.*

28. Plato, *The Republic*, trans. Desmond Lee, 2nd ed. (Harmondsworth: Penguin, 1974), VI, 517c.

29. Simson, *Gothic Cathedral*, 53–55.

30. Dionysius himself almost certainly knew nothing about Saint Augustine or Plotinus's theory of divine illumination. He came out of the Neoplatonist tradition of the Eastern Church derived from figures like Origen and Saint Gregory of Nyssa. See John Dillon, *The Great Tradition: Further Studies in the Development of Platonism and Early Christianity* (Brookfield Vt.: Ashgate, 1997).

31. Simson, *Gothic Cathedral*, 143–44.

32. As noted by Jacob Bronowski, *The Ascent of Man* (Boston: Little, Brown, 1974), 112.

33. Conrad Rudolph, *Artistic Change at Saint Denis* (Princeton, N.J.: Princeton University Press, 1990), 8–11.

34. Quoted in Gordon Strachan, *Sacred Geometry, Sacred Space* (Edinburgh: Floris, 2003), 52.

35. Ibid., 45.

36. A. Katzenellenbogen, *The Sculptural Programs of Chartres Cathedral* (New York: Norton, 1964), 27.

37. D. W. Robertson, *Abelard and Heloise* (New York: Dial Press, 1972).

38. John Sarracenus to Abbot Odo, Suger's successor; quoted in Simson, *Gothic Cathedral*, 103.

39. This was the assertion of a Pseudo-Dionysius disciple named Maximus the Confessor. On his influence on Saint Bernard, see Étienne Gilson, *The Mystical Theology of Saint Bernard* (1940; repr., Kalamazoo, Mich.: Cistercian Publications, 1990).

40. Quoted in Richard Viladesau, *Theological Aesthetics: God in Imagination, Beauty, and Art* (Oxford: Oxford University Press, 1999), 109–10.

41. Bernard's initial reaction was less than enthusiastic.

42. Simson, *Gothic Cathedral.*

43. Francis Cornford, *Plato's Cosmology: The Timaeus of Plato* (Indianapolis: Bobbs-Merrill, 1975).

44. John James, *The Master Masons of Chartres* (1982; repr., Sydney, Australia: West Grimstead, 1990).

45. Ibid., quoted in Strachan, *Sacred Geometry*, 65.

46. Simson, *Gothic Cathedral*, 55.

47. Ernst Mösel, *Von Geheimnis der Form und der Urform des Seins* (Stuttgart: Deutsche Verlagsanstalt, 1938).

48. Hugh of St. Victor, *Didasclion*, quoted in Knowles, *Evolution of Medieval Thought*.

49. Quoted in Southern, *Making of the Middle Ages*, 229.

Chapter 14: At the Summit: Arabs, Aristotle, and Saint Thomas Aquinas

1. See Charles H. Haskins, *Renaissance of the Twelfth Century* (1927; repr., New York: Meridian, 1968), 285–86.

2. Aristotle, *On the Heavens*, in *Basic Works of Aristotle*, ed. Richard McKeon (New York: Modern Library, 1947), 436.

3. C. Warren Hollister, *Medieval Europe: A Short History* (New York: Wiley, 1978).

4. J. R. Roberts, *The Pelican History of the World* (Harmondsworth: Penguin, 1980), 326.

5. Haskins, *Renaissance of the Twelfth Century*.

6. David Knowles, *The Evolution of Medieval Thought* (New York: Random House, 1962), 187–88.

7. Bernard Lewis, *Islam and the West* (New York: Oxford University Press, 1994).

8. Averroës, *Commentary on Aristotle's De Anima*, quoted in Knowles, *Evolution of Medieval Thought*, 200.

9. Richard Rubenstein, *Aristotle's Children* (Orlando, Fla.: Harcourt, 2003), 79.

10. Étienne Gilson, *Reason and Revelation in the Middle Ages* (New York: Charles Scribner's Sons, 1939), 45.

11. Knowles, *Evolution of Medieval Thought*, 200–1.

12. Gilson, *Reason and Revelation in the Middle Ages*.

13. Josef Pieper, *Guide to Thomas Aquinas* (New York: New American Library, 1962), 40.

14. Jacques Maritain, *Saint Thomas Aquinas* (New York: Meridian, 1958), 29.

15. Ibid., 31.

16. Pieper, *Guide to Thomas Aquinas*, 84.

17. Quoted in Donald Attwater and C. R. John, *The Penguin Dictionary of Saints*, rev. ed. (Harmondsworth: Penguin Books, 1983), 316.

18. Knowles, *Evolution of Medieval Thought*, 164.

19. Gilson, *Reason and Revelation in the Middle Ages*, 80.

20. Knowles, *Evolution of Medieval Thought*.

21. The military treatise was one of his most sought after during and after his lifetime. Walter Ong, *Ramus: Method and the Decay of Dialogue* (Cambridge, Mass.: Harvard University Press, 1963), 143.

22. Albertus quoted in Maritain, *Saint Thomas Aquinas*.

23. McKeon, *Basic Works of Aristotle*, 151.

24. Aquinas, *Summa Contra Gentiles*, in *Introduction to Saint Thomas Aquinas*, ed. Anton C. Pegis (New York: Random House, 1948), 466.

25. Ibid., 27.

26. Aristotle, *On the Heavens*; Aquinas, *Summa Theologica*, 466.

27. Aquinas quoted in A. O. Lovejoy, *The Great Chain of Being* (1936; repr., New York: Harper & Row, 1965), 79.

28. The translator was Robert Grosseteste. For more on Grosseteste and the later fate of Aristotle in the Middle Ages, see chapter 15 of this book.

29. Anthony Kenny, *Medieval Philosophy* (Oxford: Clarendon Press, 2005), 160.

30. Aquinas, *Summa Theologica, Question 1, Section 1,* in Pegis, *Introduction to Saint Thomas Aquinas,* 4.

Chapter 15: The Razor's Edge

1. David Knowles, *The Evolution of Medieval Thought* (New York: Random House, 1962), 244, 233.

2. A. C. Crombie, *Medieval and Early Modern Science* (1953; repr., New York: Double-day Anchor, 1959), 1:207, 218.

3. "Biblical history is lost," Bacon once wrote in frustration. "Numberless books of Hebrew and Greek expositors are wanting [translators]. . . . It is an amazing thing, this negligence of the Church." Quoted in Jean Gimpel, *The Medieval Machine: The Industrial Revolution of the Middle Ages* (New York: Penguin, 1976), 189.

4. W. T. Jones, *A History of Western Philosophy,* vol. 2, *The Medieval Mind* (New York: Harcourt Brace & World, 1971).

5. Knowles, *Evolution of Medieval Thought,* 285.

6. Bacon quoted in Gimpel, *Medieval Machine,* 192.

7. Jones, *Medieval Mind.*

8. Crombie, *Medieval and Early Modern Science,* 1:102–5.

9. Gilson, *Reason and Revelation in the Middle Ages* (New York: Charles Scribner's Sons, 1939), 87.

10. Bertrand Russell, *A History of Western Philosophy* (1945; repr., New York: Simon & Schuster, 2007), 473.

11. Ernest A. Moody, *The Logic of William of Ockham* (New York: Sheed & Ward, 1935).

12. Ibid.

13. Gilson, *Reason and Revelation in the Middle Ages,* 86–87.

14. Richard Rubinstein, *Aristotle's Children* (Orlando, Fla.: Harcourt, 2003), 79.

15. Walter Ullmann, *A History of Political Thought: The Middle Ages.* (Baltimore: Penguin Books, 1965), 51.

16. Papal bull *Unam Sanctam,* in Brian Tierney, ed., *The Crisis of Church and State 1050–1300* (Englewood Cliffs, NJ: Prentice-Hall, 1964), 188–89.

17. William of Ockham, *A Short Discourse on Tyrannical Government,* ed. A. S. McGrade (Cambrdige: Cambridge University Press, 1992), xvii.

18. A brief account of the power of the pope, quoted in Quentin Skinner, *The Foundations of Modern Political Thought* (Cambridge: Cambridge University Press, 1978), 2:38.

19. Dialogue, in Evart Lewis, *Medieval Political Ideas* (1954; repr., New York: Cooper Square, 1974), 2:399–400.

20. William of Ockham, *Short Discourse*, 60.

21. Ibid.

22. Ibid., 124.

23. Dialogue quoted in Skinner, *Foundations of Modern Political Thought*, 38.

24. Hwa-Yong Lee, *Political Representation in the Middle Ages: Marsilius in Context* (Frankfurt: Peter Lang, 2008).

25. Heiko Oberman, *The Harvest of Late Medieval Theology* (1963; repr., Durham, N.C.: Labyrinth, 1983).

26. Almain quoted in Skinner, *Foundations of Modern Political Thought*, 45.

27. See for example Gerald Christianson, Thomas M. Izbicki, and Christopher M. Belitto, *The Church, the Councils, and Reform: The Legacy of the Fifteenth Century* (Washington, D.C. Catholic University Press, 2008), 17–18.

28. Stillman Drake, *Galileo* (New York: Oxford University Press, 1980), 8.

Chapter 16: Aristotle, Machiavelli, and the Paradoxes of Liberty

1. Georges Duby, Eleanor Levieux, and Barbara Thompson, *The Age of the Cathedrals: Art and Society 980–1420* (Chicago: University of Chicago Press, 1981), 232.

2. Erasmus was educated at a Brethren of the Common Life school in Deventer. See Johan Huizinga, *Erasmus and the Age of Reformation* (1924; repr., New York: Harper & Row, 1957), and chapter 18 of this book.

3. Hans Baron, *The Crisis of the Early Italian Renaissance* (Princeton, N.J.: Princeton University Press, 1966), 35.

4. Ibid., 38.

5. Aristotle, *The Politics of Aristotle*, trans. and ed. Ernest Barker (1946; repr., Oxford: Oxford University Press, 1979), 134 (III:13, 1283b).

6. Ibid., 118 (III:9, 1280a).

7. J.G.A. Pocock, *The Machiavellian Moment* (Princeton, N.J.: Princeton University Press, 1975), 68.

8. Baron, *The Crisis of the Early Italian Renaissance*, 35.

9. Ibid., 43.

10. Ibid., 188.

11. Quentin Skinner, *The Foundations of Modern Political Thought* (Cambridge: Cambridge University Press, 1978). The link between rhetoric and liberty went back in cities like Padua as well as Florence to the 1100s. At one point, the poet Petrarch had even dreamed of restoring the Roman republic through the power of civic eloquence.

12. Ibid.

13. Otto von Gierke, *Political Theories of the Middle Ages*, trans. F. W. Maitland (Boston: Beacon Press, 1958).

14. Pocock, *Machiavellian Moment*; Benjamin Kohl and Ronald G. Witt, *The Earthly Republic: The Italian Humanists on Government and Society* (Philadelphia: University of Pennsylvania Press, 1978).

15. Bruni quoted in Baron, *Crisis of the Early Italian Renaissance*, 419.

16. Giorgio Vasari, *Lives of the Artists*, trans. George Bull (Harmondsworth: Penguin, 1987).

17. Vespasiano da Bisticci, *Renaissance Princes, Popes, and Prelates: The Vespasiano Memoirs: Lives of the Illustrious Men of the Fifteenth Century*, trans. William George Waters and Emily Waters (New York: Harper, 1963), 372.

18. Paul Kristeller, *Renaissance Thought* (1955; repr., New York: Harper & Row, 1961).

19. Leon Battista Alberti, *Autobiography*, quoted in Kenneth Clark, *Civilisation* (New York: Harper & Row, 1969), 89.

20. Lauro Martines, *April Blood: Florence and the Plot Against the Medici* (New York: Oxford University Press, 2003).

21. Pasquale Villari, *The Life and Times of Girolamo Savonarola* (New York: Charles Scribner's Sons, 1888), 753–54.

22. Girolamo Savonarola, "Treatise on the Constitution and Government of Florence," in Renée Neu Watkins, ed., *Humanism and Liberty: Writings on Freedom from Fifteenth-century Florence* (Columbia: University of South Carolina Press, 1978), 238.

23. Jacob Burckhardt, *The Civilization of the Renaissance in Italy* (1929; repr., New York: Harper & Row, 1958), 1:305.

24. Pasquale Villari, *The Life and Times of Girolamo Savonarola* (New York: Charles Scribner's Sons, 1888), 759.

25. Niccolò Machiavelli, *The Prince*, trans. George Bull (Harmondsworth: Penguin, 1981), 9.

26. On Machiavelli's education, see Herbert Butterfield, *The Statecraft of Machiavelli* (New York: Collier Books, 1962).

27. Aristotle quoted in Baron, *Crisis of the Early Italian Renaissance*, 432–33.

28. Machiavelli, letter of September 1512, in *The Letters of Machiavelli*, ed. Felix Gilbert (New York: Capricorn Books, 1961), 91–92.

29. Roberto Ridolfi, *The Life of Niccolò Machiavelli*, trans. C. Grayson (Chicago: University of Chicago Press, 1963), 129.

30. Machiavelli, letter of September 1512, in Gilbert, *Letters of Machiavelli*, 94.

31. Machiavelli's account of his imprisonment is in the form of a sonnet, "Io ho, Guiliano, in gamba un paio di geti," quoted in Ridolfi, *Life of Machiavelli*.

32. Machiavelli to F. Vettori, December 10, 1513, in Gilbert, *Letters of Machiavelli*, 142.

33. Butterfield, *Statecraft of Machiavelli*, 28, 64; Pocock, *Machiavellian Moment*, 22.

34. Pocock, *Machiavellian Moment*, 185–87.

35. Niccolò Machiavelli, *Discourses*, trans. Leslie Walker (Harmondsworth: Penguin, 1974), 123 (I:6).

36. Ibid., 113 (I:4).

37. Ibid., 223–25 (I:46–47).

38. Ibid., 123 (I:6).

39. Ibid.

40. Ibid., 163 (I:18).

41. Ibid.

42. Niccolò Machiavelli, *The Prince*, trans. Russell Price (Cambridge: Cambridge University Press, 1988), 50 (VI).

43. Ibid., 89 (XIV), 99 (XVIII).

44. Machiavelli, *The Prince*, 62 (XVIII).

45. Ibid., 90–91 (XXVI).

46. Machiavelli, *Discourses*, 137–38 (I.10).

47. Machiavelli, *The Prince*, 99 (XVIII).

Chapter 17: The Creative Ascent: Plato and the High Renaissance

1. Edward Gibbon, *Decline and Fall of the Roman Empire* (Harmondsworth: Penguin, 1994), vol. 1; Jason Goodwin, *Lords of the Horizons: A History of the Ottoman Empire* (New York: Henry Holt, 1998), 32.

2. Gibbon, *Decline and Fall*, 968.

3. Marsilio Ficino, *Letters* (London: Shepheard-Walwyn, 1975); Arthur Field, *Origins of the Platonic Academy in Florence* (Princeton, N.J.: Princeton University Press, 1988).

4. In a famous passage in the dialogue *Theatetus* (150b–d), Socrates describes himself as an intellectual midwife.

5. Paul Kristeller, *Renaissance Thought* (1955; repr., New York: Harper & Row, 1961), 58.

6. Sem Dresden, *Renaissance Humanism* (London: Weidenfeld & Nicolson, 1968), 24.

7. Christine Raffini, *Marsilio Ficino, Pietro Bembo, Baldassare Castiglione: Philosophical, Aesthetic, and Political Approaches in Renaissance Platonism* (New York: Peter Lang, 1998).

8. Ficino, *Letters*; Raffini, *Marsilio Ficino*, 27–28.

9. Plato, *The Symposium*, trans. Christopher Gill (Harmondsworth: Penguin, 1999), (210d).

10. Ibid., (211c, 212b).

11. Its doctrines are also consistent with the discussion of love in another later Platonic dialogue, the *Phaedrus*.

12. Marsilio Ficino, *Platonic Theology* (Cambridge, Mass.: Harvard University Press, 2004), 1:9.

13. Paul Kristeller, ed., *Eight Philosophers of the Renaissance* (Stanford, Calif.: Stanford University Press, 1964), 47.

14. Plato, *Symposium*, (212a).

15. Ficino, *Platonic Theology*, 4:225.

16. Ibid., 4:183.

17. Edgar Wind, *Pagan Mysteries of the Renaissance* (New York: Norton, 1968).

18. Ficino, Commentary on the *Symposium*, quoted in John Nelson, *The Renaissance Theory of Love: The Context of Giordano Bruno's "Eroici Furori"* (New York: Columbia University Press, 1958), 77.

19. The quotation is from Saint Augustine but was extremely well known to Ficino, Pico, and other Renaissance scholars. Wind, *Pagan Mysteries*, 21.

20. Giovanni Pico della Mirandola, *Syncretism in the West: Pico's 900 Theses (1486)*, trans.

S. A. Farmer (Tempe, Ariz.: Medieval and Renaissance Texts and Studies, 1998), 337, 245, 295.

21. Frances A. Yates, *Giordano Bruno and the Hermetic Tradition* (1964; repr., Chicago: University of Chicago Press, 1977).

22. Pico, Commentary on Beniveni's *Canzona d'Amore,* quoted in Wind, *Pagan Mysteries,* 17.

23. D. P. Walker, *Spiritual and Demonic Magic from Ficino to Campanella* (London: Warburg Institute, 1958); Frances A. Yates, *The Rosicrucian Enlightenment* (London: Routledge & Kegan Paul, 1972).

24. "On the Dignity of Man," in Paul Kristeller, ed., *The Renaissance Philosophy of Man* (1948; repr., Chicago: University of Chicago Press, 1956), 224–25.

25. Kristeller, *Eight Philosophers.*

26. Christiane Joost-Guignier, *Raphael's Stanza della Segnatura: Meaning and Invention* (Cambridge: Cambridge University Press, 2002), 73–77.

27. The parallels between Faust and Pico are explored in Harold Jantz, *Goethe's Faust as a Renaissance Man: Parallels and Prototypes* (Princeton, N.J.: Princeton University Press, 1951).

28. Joost-Guignier, *Raphael's Stanza,* 91, 92–93.

29. Kristeller, *Eight Philosophers,* 63. Pico specifically said that Moses anticipated many of the doctrines of the *Timaeus.* Joost-Gaugier, *Raphael's Stanza,* 150.

30. Joost-Guignier, *Raphael's Stanza,* 90.

31. Charles de Tolnay, *The Art and Thought of Michelangelo* (New York: Pantheon, 1964), 32.

32. "The best of artists never has a concept / A single block of marble does not contain": Michelangelo, Sonnet 149, *Complete Poems and Letters of Michelangelo,* ed. Creighton Gilbert (New York: Vintage, 1963), 100.

33. Lauro Martines, *Scourge and Fire: Savonarola and the Republic of Florence* (London: Jonathan Cape, 2006).

34. Michelangelo, letter of September 18, 1512, in *Complete Poems and Letters,* 211.

35. Michelangelo, Sonnet 10, ibid., 8.

36. Michelangelo, Sonnet 60, ibid., 39–40.

37. Michelangelo, letter to G. F. Fatucci, December 1523, ibid., 237.

38. Plato's discussion of prophecy as "divine madness" is in the *Phaedrus.*

39. Quoted in Sydney J. Freedberg, "Michelangelo: The Sistine Ceiling," in Charles Seymour Jr., ed. *Michelangelo: The Sistine Chapel Ceiling* (New York: Norton, 1972), 193.

40. Ibid., 201.

41. Ficino, *Platonic Theology,* 1:9.

Chapter 18: Twilight of the Scholastics: The Reformation and the Doom of Aristotle

1. Michelangelo, sonnet to John of Pistoia, in *Complete Poems and Letters of Michelangelo,* ed. Creighton Gilbert (New York: Vintage, 1963), 6.

2. Heinrich Boehmer, *Road to Reformation: Martin Luther to the Year 1521* (Philadelphia: Muhlenberg Press, 1946), 64–65.

3. Erik H. Erikson, *Young Man Luther* (New York: Norton, 1962), 173.

4. Boehmer, *Road to Reformation*, 64.

5. "The chief end of the Apostle in this letter is to destroy all Righteousness and wisdom of our own [and] that Christ and his Righteousness are necessary for us, for [the] genuine extermination" of our sins. Luther quoted in E. Gordon Rupp, *The Righteousness of God: Luther Studies* (London: Hodder & Stoughton, 1968), 160–61.

6. Martin Luther, "Appeal to the German Nobility," in *Martin Luther: Selections from His Writings*, ed. John Dillenberger (New York: Doubleday, 1961), 471.

7. Ibid., 470, 471.

8. Diarmaid MacCulloch, *The Reformation: A History* (New York: Penguin, 2004).

9. George Sarton, *Appreciation of Ancient and Modern Science During the Renaissance* (Philadelphia: University of Pennsylvania Press, 1955); Elizabeth Eisenstein, *The Printing Revolution in Early Modern Europe* (Cambridge: Cambridge University Press, 1993), 51–52.

10. François Rabelais, *Pantagruel*, ed. Jean Plattard (Paris: Société des Belles-Lettres, 1959), VII, 42.

11. Eisenstein, *Printing Revolution*, 43.

12. Ibid., 44.

13. Johan Huizinga, *Erasmus of Rotterdam* (London: Phaidon Press, 1952), 3, 7.

14. Desiderius Erasmus, *The Epistles of Erasmus*, trans. F. M. Nichols, 3 vols. (London: Longmans, 1901–18).

15. Paul Kristeller, ed., *Eight Philosophers of the Renaissance* (Stanford, Calif.: Stanford University Press, 1964), 51; editor's introduction, Desiderius Erasmus, *In Praise of Folly*, ed. A.H.T. Levi (Harmondsworth: Penguin, 1971), 23.

16. Huizinga, *Erasmus*, 62.

17. Ibid., 64.

18. Ibid. Erasmus had published an earlier version of the *Adagia*, using only Latin authors, in 1500. However, with Greek now under his belt, he could comb through the offerings of various Venetian scholars from authors like Plato, Plutarch, and Pindar.

19. Erasmus, letter to Martin Dorp, 1515, in *In Praise of Folly*, 230.

20. Hastings Rashdall, *The Universities of Europe in the Middle Ages*, 3 vols. (Oxford: Oxford University Press, 1958); Walter Ong, *Ramus: Method and the Decay of Dialogue* (Cambridge, Mass.: Harvard University Press, 1963), 133–35.

21. Ong, *Ramus*, 143.

22. François Rabelais, *Gargantua and Pantagruel*, trans. J. M. Cohen (Harmondsworth: Penguin, 1955), 70.

23. Huizinga, *Erasmus*, 107.

24. As implied in Anthony Grafton and Lisa Jardine, *From Humanism to the Humanities: Education and the Liberal Arts in Fifteenth- and Sixteenth-Century Europe* (Cam-

bridge, Mass.: Harvard University Press, 1986); and Martin J. Wiener, *English Culture and the Decline of the Industrial Spirit, 1850–1980* (Cambridge: Cambridge University Press, 1981).

25. David McNeil, *Guillaume Budé and Humanism in the Reign of Francis I* (Geneva: Droz, 1975).

26. Quoted in Huizinga, *Erasmus*, 103.

27. Boehmer, *Road to Reformation*, 370.

28. Albrecht Dürer, *Dürer's Record of Journeys to Venice and the Low Countries*, ed. Roger Fry (1913; repr., New York: Dover Books, 1995).

29. Heiko Oberman, *The Harvest of Late Medieval Theology* (1963; repr., Durham, N.C.: Labyrinth, 1983); and Roland Bainton, *The Reformation of the Sixteenth Century* (1952; repr., Boston: Beacon Press, 1980).

30. John Bossy, *Christianity in the West 1400–1700* (Oxford: Oxford University Press, 1985).

31. Martin Luther, "Bondage of the Will," in Dillenberger, *Martin Luther*, 203.

32. Martin Luther, "Preface to Romans," ibid., 20.

33. Martin Luther, "Pagan Servitude of the Church," ibid., 268.

34. Martin Luther, "Bondage of the Will," ibid., 171.

35. Martin Luther, "Pagan Servitude," ibid., 343.

36. Martin Luther, "Institutes," ibid., 361.

37. Martin Luther, "Freedom of the Christian Man," ibid., 73.

38. Martin Luther, "On Corruption and Grace," quoted in Charles Norris Cochrane, *Christianity and Classical Culture* (1940; repr., Oxford: Oxford University Press, 1957), 504.

Chapter 19: Secrets of the Heavens: Plato, Galileo, and the New Science

1. "The Publisher to the Reader," in Galileo Galilei, *Dialogues Concerning Two New Sciences*, trans. Henry Crew (1914; repr., New York: Dover, 1954), xx.

2. Alexander Kohanski, *The Greek Mode of Thought in Western Philosophy* (Rutherford, N.J.: Fairleigh Dickinson University Press, 1984), 42.

3. Plato, *The Republic*, trans. Desmond Lee, 2nd ed. (Harmondsworth: Penguin, 1974), (510d–511b).

4. Ibid., (511c–d).

5. Jacopo Zabarella, *De Natura Logicae*, quoted in John Herman Randall, "The Development of Scientific Method in the School of Padua," in Paul Kristeller and Philip Wiener, eds., *Renaissance Essays* (New York: Harper & Row, 1968), 240.

6. As in John Herman Randall, *The Making of the Modern Mind* (New York: Houghton Mifflin, 1940). But see Stillman Drake, *Galileo at Work: His Scientific Biography* (Chicago: University of Chicago Press, 1978), 47–48, who points out that Zabarella steadfastly opposed the use of mathematics in science, and that his successors fought Galileo every step of the way.

7. Randall, "School of Padua," 224.

8. What chiefly kept him there for more than a decade was a salary three times what he could get at any other university. Stillman Drake, *Galileo* (New York: Oxford University Press, 1980), 27.

9. Vincenzo Galilei, *"Dialogo della musica antica et della moderna" of Vincenzo Galilei: Translation and Commentary*, ed. R. H. Herman, PhD thesis, North Texas State University, 1973.

10. Robert Lawlor, *Sacred Geometry: Philosophy and Practice* (London: Thames & Hudson, 1982), 13.

11. John Burnet, *Early Greek Philosophy* (1892; repr., New York: Meridian, 1958), 284.

12. R. A. Schwaller de Lubicz, *Symbol and the Symbolic* (Rochester, Vt.: Inner Tradition, 1981).

13. Drake, *Galileo at Work*, 2–3.

14. Mario Biagioli, *Galileo, Courtier* (Chicago: University of Chicago Press, 1993), 7.

15. Alexandre Koyré, *From the Closed World to the Infinite Universe* (Baltimore: Johns Hopkins University Press, 1957).

16. Biagioli, *Galileo, Courtier*, 105–6.

17. Quoted in Drake, *Galileo*.

18. For example, Aristotle, *Physics*, VII:3.

19. Galileo mentioned *De Revolutionibus* in his 1591–92 treatise on motion, *De Motu*, but only regarding its mathematical calculations, never its heliocentric theory. Drake, *Galileo at Work*, 27.

20. Galileo to Kepler, August 4, 1597, in *Johannes Kepler: Life and Letters*, ed. Carola Baumgardt (London: V. Gollancz, 1952), 38.

21. Galileo Galilei, *Dialogue Concerning the Two World Systems*, quoted in Drake, *Galileo*, 46.

22. V. Galilei, *"Dialogo della musica antica."*

23. The full account is in Galileo's *The Assayer* (1623), quoted in Stillman Drake, *Galileo: Pioneer Scientist* (Toronto: University of Toronto Press, 1990), 132.

24. Galileo to Kepler, August 19, 1610, in Baumgardt, *Kepler*, 86.

25. Drake, *Galileo*, 44–45.

26. Galileo-Kepler correspondence, quoted in Mario Livio, *The Golden Ratio* (London: Review, 2003), 148.

27. Thomas Kuhn, *The Copernican Revolution* (Cambridge, Mass.: Harvard University Press, 1957), 214–19.

28. Benoît Mandelbrot, *Les objets fractals: Forme, hasard et dimension* (1975; repr., Paris: Flammarion, 1989).

29. Quoted in Lawlor, *Sacred Geometry*, 10.

30. Livio, *Golden Ratio*, 136. See also Fritjof Capra, *The Science of Leonardo: Inside the Mind of the Great Genius of the Renaissance* (New York: Anchor, 2007), 148–49.

31. Charles Carman, *Images of Humanist Ideals in Italian Renaissance Art* (Lewiston, N.Y.: Edwin Mellen Press, 2000), 74–76, 81.

32. Frances A. Yates, *Giordano Bruno and the Hermetic Tradition* (1964; repr., Chicago: University of Chicago Press, 1977), 272–73.

33. Ibid., 24.

34. Drake, *Galileo*, 29; Galileo did add, "No one doubts that the Supreme Pontiff has always an absolute power to approve or condemn" on matters of faith, "but it is not in the power of any created being to make things true or false."

35. Kuhn, *Copernican Revolution*; Livio, *Golden Ratio*, 147–48.

36. Galileo Galilei, *Dialogue Concerning the Two Chief World Systems* (1632), quoted in Drake, *Galileo*, 91.

37. Galileo Galilei, *The Assayer* (1623), quoted in Stillman Drake, ed., *Discoveries and Opinions of Galileo* (New York: Anchor Books, 1957), 237–38.

38. With apologies to Thomas Kuhn's masterpiece, *The Structure of Scientific Revolutions* (Chicago: University of Chicago Press, 1962).

39. Galileo Galilei, *Dialogue Concerning the Two Chief World Systems*, trans. Stillman Drake (Berkeley: University of California Press, 1967), 110.

40. Giorgio de Santillana, *The Crime of Galileo* (Berkeley: University of California Press, 1955), 187.

41. Dated February 25, 1616, reprinted in Maurice E. Finocchiaro, ed., *The Galileo Affair: A Documentary History* (Berkeley: University of California Press, 1989), 147.

42. Quoted in ibid., 213.

43. Deposition of April 12, 1633, ibid., 259.

44. Ibid.

45. By their own rules of evidence, as Stillman Drake points out. Drake, *Galileo*, 78.

46. Santillana, *Crime of Galileo*.

47. Ibid., 310–11.

48. According to a 1639 letter, quoted in Arthur Koestler, *The Sleepwalkers* (New York: Macmillan, 1968).

49. See R. Hooykaas, *Religion and the Rise of Modern Science* (London: Regent College Publishing, 2000).

50. John Milton, *Paradise Lost*, in *Complete Poetry and Major Prose*, ed. Merritt Hughes (New York: Odyssey, 1957), 1:287–290.

51. John Milton, *Areopagitica*, ibid., 1:738.

Chapter 20: God, Kings, and Philosophers in the Age of Genius

1. Richard Westfall, *Never at Rest: A Biography of Isaac Newton* (Cambridge: Cambridge University Press, 1980), 15.

2. Bacon's quotation is that Greek philosophy "abounds in words but is barren of works." Francis Bacon, *Novum Organum* (Chicago: Encyclopedia Britannica Press, 1952), 1:81.

3. Bacon quoted in Ernst Cassirer, *The Platonic Renaissance in England* (New York: Gordian, 1970), 48.

4. Theo Verbeek, *Descartes and the Dutch: Early Reactions to the Cartesian Philosophy, 1637–1650* (Carbondale: Southern Illinois University Press, 1992).

5. Henry More, letter to Samuel Hartlib, in Henry More, *Letters on Several Subjects* (London: 1694).

6. René Descartes, *Philosophical Works*, trans. E. S. Haldane and G.R.T. Ross (1911; repr. Cambridge: Cambridge University Press, 1977), vol. 1.

7. Westfall, *Never at Rest*, 102–3.

8. It was Gottfried Leibnitz's unveiling of his own discovery of the principles of calculus that finally compelled Newton to come clean. Characteristically, Newton assumed the German philosopher had somehow stolen the secret from him. See Westfall, *Never at Rest*.

9. Isaac Newton, "On the Gravity and Equilibrium of Fluids" and "Optics," quoted in Westfall, *Never at Rest*, 302, 395–96.

10. Ibid., 303.

11. Isaac Newton, *Principia Mathematica*, in Isaac Newton, *Newton's Philosophy of Nature: Selections from His Writings*, ed. H. S. Thayer (1953; repr. New York: Macmillan, 1974), 45; Isaac Newton, letter to Dr. Bentley, February 1692–93, ibid., 54.

12. Newton, *Principia Mathematica*, 42–43.

13. Ibid., 44.

14. Duke de la Force, *Louis XIV et sa cour*, in John B. Wolf, ed., *Louis XIV* (New York: Norton, 1974), 74.

15. Ibid., 75; Saint-Simon, *Memoirs* (New York: Brentano, 1915–18).

16. La Force, *Louis XIV et sa cour*, 79.

17. Quoted in Wolf, *Louis XIV*, 373.

18. La Force, *Louis XIV et sa cour*, 81.

19. Bishop Bossuet, *Politique tirée de l'écriture sainte*, quoted in Wolf, *Louis XIV*, 373.

20. Pierre Goubert, *Louis XIV et quarante million français* (1966; repr., Paris: Fayard, 1977).

21. Maurice Cranston, *John Locke: A Biography* (1957; repr., London: Longmans, 1959), 229–30.

22. Westfall, *Never at Rest*, 489.

23. Cranston, *John Locke*, 210.

24. John Locke, *Essays on the Law of Nature*, quoted in Francis Oakley, *Natural Law, Laws of Nature, Natural Rights* (New York: Continuum, 2005), 83–84.

25. Aristotle, *The Nicomachean Ethics*, trans. J.A.K. Thomson (Harmondsworth: Penguin, 1976), V, vii (1134b8–24), 189.

26. Ernest Barker, "Translator's Introduction," in Otto Gierke, *Natural Law and the Theory of Society, 1500 to 1800* (Cambridge: Cambridge University Press, 1934), xxxviii. Aquinas actually had a fourth category, *lex aeterna*, which was the law inherent in God's purposes for all His creation. However, most commentators incorporated this teleological aspect of creation under *lex divina*.

27. Gierke, *Natural Law*.

28. Suárez quoted in Quentin Skinner, *The Foundations of Modern Political Thought* (Cambridge: Cambridge University Press, 1978),156.

29. See Richard Tuck, *Natural Rights Theories: Their Origin and Development* (Cambridge: Cambridge University Press, 1979).

30. Skinner, *Foundations of Modern Political Thought.*

31. Thomas Hobbes, *Leviathan*, ed. C. B. MacPherson (Harmondsworth: Penguin, 1968), 257 (II:20).

32. For Hobbes on Aristotle, see ibid., 267 (II:22), 369 (II:29). The quotation is at 264 (II:22).

33. John Locke, *Second Treatise*, in *Two Treatises of Government*, ed. Peter Laslett (Cambridge: Cambridge University Press, 1960), I:6.

34. Ibid., IV:27–28. See James Tully, *A Discourse of Property: John Locke and His Adversaries* (Cambridge: Cambridge University Press, 1980).

35. Westfall, *Never at Rest*, 491.

36. Locke, *Second Treatise*, in *Two Treatises of Government*, III:21.

37. Ibid., III:17.

38. Ibid., XIX:220.

39. See Algernon Sidney, *Discourses Concerning Government* (1698; repr., Indianapolis: Liberty Fund, 1996); and Zera Silver Fink, *The Classical Republicans* (Chicago: Northwestern University Press, 1962).

40. See Martyn Thompson, *Ideas of Contract in English Political Thought in the Age of John Locke* (New York: Garland, 1987).

41. John Locke, *The Reasonableness of Christianity*, ed. I. T. Ramsey (Stanford, Calif.: Stanford University Press, 1958), 61.

Chapter 21: Aristotle in a Periwig: The Culture of the Enlightenment

1. J.G.A. Pocock, *Virtue, Commerce, and History: Essays on Political Thought and History, Chiefly in the Eighteenth Century* (Cambridge: Cambridge University Press, 1985).

2. See John Locke, *An Essay Concerning Human Understanding* (1689; repr., London: G. Bell, 1903), on substance and essence. But, Locke uses these words in a sense very different from the way Aristotle had coined them in his *Metaphysics.*

3. Maurice Cranston, *John Locke: A Biography* (1957; repr., London: Longmans, 1959), 245, 428.

4. John Adams to Thomas Jefferson, July 16, 1814, quoted in Jeffrey Morison, *John Witherspoon and the Founding of the American Republic* (Notre Dame, Ind.: University of Notre Dame Press, 2005), 116.

5. Jefferson to Adams, July 5, 1814, quoted in ibid., 2:252–53. Voltaire's article on the Chain of Being in *Dictionnaire philosophique* is quoted in A. O. Lovejoy, *The Great Chain of Being* (1936; repr., New York: Harper & Row, 1965), 253.

6. Voltaire, "Letter on Pascal," in *Voltaire. Candide and Philosophical Letters* (New York: Modern Library, 1992).

7. Adams to Jefferson, July 16, 1814, quoted in Morison, *John Witherspoon*.

8. Quoted in ibid.,117. Witherspoon was a founding member of the American Philosophical Society, along with another confirmed neo-Aristotelian, Benjamin Franklin.

9. See René Descartes, Meditation III, in Descartes, *Philosophical Works*, trans. E. S. Haldane and G.R.T. Ross (1911; repr. Cambridge: Cambridge University Press, 1977).

10. John Locke, *An Essay Concerning Human Understanding*, quoted in Bertrand Russell, A *History of Western Philosophy* (1945; repr., New York: Simon & Schuster, 2007), 610.

11. It was one that many philosophers who accepted Locke's assertion that all knowledge comes from observation, including Thomas Reid, were unwilling to take. See Thomas Reid's critique on Locke in *Essays on the Intellectual Powers of Man* (Cambridge, Mass.: MIT Press, 1969).

12. Locke, *An Essay Concerning Human Understanding*, IV:15.

13. Quoted in Russell, *History of Western Philosophy*, 609.

14. See Keith Thomas, *Religion and the Decline of Magic: Studies in Popular Beliefs in Sixteenth- and Seventeenth-Century England* (New York: Oxford University Press, 1997); Lovejoy, *Great Chain of Being*, esp. chapter 9.

15. Alexander Pope, *Essay on Man, in Alexander Pope: Selected Poetry and Prose*, ed. Robin Sowerby (London: Routledge, 1988), 157 (IV:29–34).

16. Thomas Hankins, *Science and the Enlightenment* (Cambridge: Cambridge University Press, 1985).

17. Locke quoted in Russell, *History of Western Philosophy*, 613.

18. See Pocock, *Virtue, Commerce, and Liberty*; and Pocock, *The Machiavellian Moment* (Princeton, N.J.: Princeton University Press, 1975), passim.

19. For example, Daniel Defoe, *The Complete English Tradesman* (1726; repr., Gloucester: Alan Sutton, 1987), chapters 4, 5.

20. Nathan Rosenberg and L. E. Birdzell, *How the West Grew Rich: The Economic Transformation of the Industrial World* (New York: Basic Books, 1986), 18–19.

21. Adam Smith, *An Inquiry into the Nature and Causes of the Wealth of Nations*, ed. Edwin Cannan (Chicago: University of Chicago Press, 1976), 1:90, 2:413.

22. Shaftesbury,"Freedom of Wit and Humor," in *Characteristics of Men, Manners, Opinions, Times* (Indianapolis: Bobbs-Merrill, 1964), 46.

23. Aristotle, *The Nicomachean Ethics*, trans. J.A.K. Thomson (Harmondsworth: Penguin, 1976), 154–55.

24. "The necessity of believing without knowledge, nay often upon very slight grounds . . . should make us more busy and careful to inform ourselves than constrain others." Locke adds, "For where is the man that has incontestable evidence of the truth of all he holds, or the falsehood of all he condemns?" John Locke, *An Essay Concerning Human Understanding*, IV:16.

25. Voltaire, *Letters on England*, trans. Leonard Tancock (Harmondsworth: Penguin, 1980), 51.

26. Ibid.

27. Ibid., 62, 57.

28. Ibid., 112.

29. Ibid., 52.

30. See Richard Langford, *A Polite and Commercial People: England 1727–1783* (Oxford: Clarendon Press, 1989).

31. The parallels with Newton are made plain in Duncan Forbes, *Hume's Philosophical Politics* (Cambridge: Cambridge University Press, 1975).

32. Henry Home, Lord Kames, *Historical Law Tracts* (1761), quoted in Arthur Herman, *How the Scots Invented the Modern World* (New York: Crown, 2001), 98.

33. William Robertson, *The Progress of Society in Europe* (Chicago: University of Chicago Press, 1972), 31.

34. Robertson, *Progress of Society in Europe*, 67.

35. Montesquieu, *The Spirit of the Laws*, trans. Thomas Nugent (New York: Macmillan, 1949), XXIII:22.

36. Robertson, *Progress of Society in Europe*, 8.

37. Of course, both Francis Bacon and René Descartes had deprecated the *intellectual* achievements of the ancients, especially in the realm of science; and the French academician Charles Perrault had launched the famous battle of the "ancients" and "moderns" in 1687 when he questioned the assumption that classical culture was necessarily superior to its successors. See the classic J. B. Bury, *The Idea of Progress: An Inquiry into Its Origin and Growth* (New York: Macmillan, 1932). However, it was the Enlightenment that explained *why* both assertions were true—that is, because of the relative backward nature of ancient society.

38. David Hume, "Of Commerce," in Hume, *Essays Moral, Political, and Literary*, ed. Eugene F. Miller (Indianapolis: Liberty Fund, 1985), 264.

39. Smith, *Inquiry into Wealth of Nations*, 208 (IV:9).

40. Ibid., 308 (V:1).

Chapter 22: Starting Over: Plato, Rousseau, and Revolution

1. Jean-Jacques Rousseau, *Julie, ou La Nouvelle Héloïse* (Paris: Garnier, 1973), part 2, letter 14.

2. Lester Crocker, *Jean-Jacques Rousseau* (London: Macmillan, 1968), 1:141–42.

3. Jean-Jacques Rousseau, *The Confessions*, trans. J. M. Cohen (Harmondsworth: Penguin, 1954), 270.

4. Rousseau, *Nouvelle Héloïse*, part 2, letter 17.

5. Jean-Jacques Rousseau, *The First and Second Discourses [Discourse on Arts and Sciences]*, trans. Victor Gourevitch (New York: Harper & Row, 1990), 6.

6. Ibid., 22, 11.

7. Ibid., 17, 19, 25.

8. Diderot quoted in Crocker, *Rousseau*, 1:220.

9. In Jean-Jacques Rousseau, *Émile, or Education*, trans. Barbara Foxley (New York: Dutton, 1911), I:8.

10. According to Paul Shorey, *Platonism Ancient and Modern* (Berkeley: University of California Press, 1938), 86.

11. Montesquieu, *The Spirit of the Laws*, trans. Thomas Nugent (New York: Macmillan, 1949), 1:316 (XX:1).

12. Jean-Jacques Rousseau, *A Discourse on Inequality*, trans. Maurice Cranston (Harmondsworth: Penguin, 1984), 109.

13. Ibid., 115.

14. Ibid., 116.

15. Drawn largely from his adolescent fascination with Plutarch's *Lives*, which, at least as much as Plato, shaped his picture of the ancient world and its virtues. See Maurice Cranston, *John Locke: A Biography* (1957; repr., London: Longmans, 1959), 25.

16. Plato, *The Laws*, trans. Trevor J. Saunders (Harmondsworth: Penguin, 1970), 162 (739d); 448 (942b).

17. Rousseau, *Discourse on Inequality*, 82.

18. Rousseau, *Émile*, I:8.

19. For instance, David Hume cites the Spartans' "peculiar laws" as an example of how the ancient polis "was violent, and contrary to the more natural course of things." Hume, *Essays Moral, Political, and Literary*, ed. Eugene F. Miller (Indianapolis: Liberty Fund, 1985), 259.

20. Rousseau, *Discourse on Political Economy*, quoted in Norman Hampson, *Will and Circumstance: Montesquieu, Rousseau, and the French Revolution* (London: Duckworth, 1983), 33.

21. Rousseau quoted in Carol Blum, *Rousseau and the Republic of Virtue* (Ithaca, N.Y.: Cornell University Press, 1986), 175.

22. Roger Masters, *The Political Philosophy of Rousseau* (Princeton, N.J.: Princeton University Press, 1968), 362.

23. Jean-Jacques Rousseau, *The Government of Poland*, trans. Willmoore Kendall (Indianapolis: Hackett, 1985), 3. The use of mathematical formulae extends to the *Social Contract* as well, especially Book III; see Masters, *Political Philosophy of Rousseau*, 340–45.

24. Rousseau, *Government of Poland*, 8.

25. Ibid., 68–69.

26. Ernst Cassirer, *Rousseau, Kant, Goethe: Two Essays* (1945; repr., Princeton, N.J.: Princeton University Press, 1970), 20.

27. Immanuel Kant, "Conjectural Beginning of Human History," in *Kant on History*, ed. L. W. Beck (Indianapolis: Bobbs-Merrill, 1963), 68.

28. See Immanuel Kant, *Groundwork of the Metaphysics of Morals*, trans. H. J. Paton (New York: Harper & Row, 1964), passim.

29. Immanuel Kant, "Perpetual Peace," in *Kant on History*, 106.

30. Immanuel Kant, "Idea for a Universal History," ibid., 21.

31. See the letter from Baron de Grimm from 1752, quoted in Maurice Cranston,

Jean-Jacques: The Early Life and Work of Jean-Jacques Rousseau, 1712–1754 (New York: Norton, 1982), 234.

32. Quoted in Crocker, *Rousseau*, vol. 2.

33. Hampson, *Will and Circumstance*, 44.

34. For the success of *The Confessions*, see Huntington Williams, *Rousseau and Romantic Autobiography* (Oxford: Oxford University Press, 1983); and Eugene Stelzig, *The Romantic Subject in Autobiography: Rousseau and Goethe* (Charlottesville: University of Virginia Press, 2000).

35. Gita May, *Madame Roland and the Age of Revolution* (New York: Columbia University Press, 1970), 58.

36. Madame Roland quoted in ibid., 162.

37. Christopher Kelly, *Rousseau's Exemplary Life: The "Confessions" as Political Philosophy* (Ithaca, N.Y.: Cornell University Press, 1987), 49–52.

38. Kenneth Clark, *The Romantic Rebellion: Romantic Versus Classic Art* (New York: Harper & Row, 1973), 25.

39. Roger Barny, *Rousseau dans la revolution: Le Personnage de Jean-Jacques et les debuts du culte revolutionaire (1787–1791)* (Oxford: Voltaire Foundation, 1986), 135–36.

40. Astonishingly, this "political reverie" was penned in the mid-1770s; quoted in May, *Madame Roland*, 72.

41. Georges Lefebvre, *The Coming of the French Revolution*, trans. R. R. Palmer (Princeton, N.J.: Princeton University Press, 1947), 21–22.

42. Ibid., 22.

43. Quoted in Lewis Namier, *1848: The Revolt of the Intellectuals* (1944; repr., New York: Doubleday, 1964), 8.

44. Jean-Jacques Rousseau, *The Social Contract*, trans. Maurice Cranston (Harmondsworth: Penguin, 1968), 84, 87.

45. Quoted in Hampson, *Will and Circumstance*, 143.

46. Quoted in ibid., 257.

47. As noted by William Doyle, *The Oxford History of the French Revolution* (New York: Oxford University Press, 1989).

48. May, *Madame Roland*, 291–92.

49. Edmund Burke, *Letter to a Member of the National Assembly* (1791); see Peter Stanlis, *Edmund Burke: The Enlightenment and Revolution* (New Brunswick, N.J.: Transaction Books, 1991), 175; Edmund Burke, *Reflections on the Revolution in France*, ed. J.G.A. Pocock (Indianapolis: Hackett, 1987), 68.

Chapter 23: "Feeling Is All": The Triumph of the Romantics

1. Edmé Champion, *J.-J. Rousseau et la révolution française* (Paris: A. Colin, 1909), 120.

2. This is the official count, largely accepted by scholars, in Donald Greer, *The Incidence of the Terror During the French Revolution: A Statistical Interpretation* (Cambridge,

Mass.: Harvard University Press, 1935). The full count, including unofficial roundups and executions, may be much higher.

3. The best account of Robespierre's execution is by Irish exile Hamilton Rowan, in J. M. Thompson, *English Eye-Witnesses to the French Revolution* (Oxford: Basil Blackwell, 1938), 257–58.

4. Stephen Gill, *William Wordsworth: A Life* (Oxford: Clarendon Press, 1989).

5. This famous passage is from Book IX of *The Prelude*, lines 108–9.

6. Hölderlin quoted in Irving Babbitt, *Rousseau and Romanticism* (1919; repr., Boston: Houghton Mifflin, 1979), 82.

7. Friedrich Schiller, *On the Aesthetic Education of Man*, trans. R. Snell (1954; repr., New York: Ungar, 1971), 39.

8. Denis Diderot, *Supplément au Voyage de Bougainville* (1778; Gutenberg Project, 2002).

9. William Wordsworth, "Remembrance of Collins, Composed Upon the Thames at Richmond."

10. Jean-Jacques Rousseau, *The Reveries of the Solitary Walker* (Indianapolis: Hackett, 1992), 362.

11. See Anand Chitnis, *The Scottish Enlightenment: A Social History* (London: Croom Helm, 1976).

12. See Meyer H. Abrams, *The Mirror and the Lamp: Romantic Theory and the Critical Tradition* (1953; repr., New York: Norton, 1958), 72–73.

13. Edmund Burke, *A Philosophical Enquiry into the Origins of Our Ideas of the Sublime and Beautiful* (London: Abraham Mills, 1889).

14. Johann Wolfgang von Goethe, *Faust, Part One*, trans. Philip Wayne (Harmondsworth: Penguin, 1949), 43–44.

15. The best summary of the arguments is still Jacques Barzun's *Classic, Romantic, and Modern* (Boston: Little, Brown, 1943).

16. Abrams, *Mirror and the Lamp*, 10.

17. The classic work by Eric Auerbach, *Mimesis: The Representation of Reality in Western Literature* (Princeton, N.J.: Princeton University Press, 1953).

18. Aristotle, *Poetics*, in *Introduction to Aristotle*, ed. Richard McKeon (New York: Modern Library, 1967), 4 (1448b).

19. Ibid., 13 (1453–1453b).

20. R. W. Lee, *Ut Pictura Poesis: The Humanistic Theory of Painting* (New York: Norton, 1963). For the influence of Aristotle's *Poetics* (via the Hellenistic critic Neoptolemus of Parium) on Horace's *Ars Poetica*, see C. O. Brink, *Horace on Poetry* (Cambridge: Cambridge University Press, 1963); and John Boyd, *The Function of Mimesis and Its Decline* (Cambridge, Mass.: Harvard University Press, 1968), 38–39. See also Aristotle, *Poetics*, 25 (1460b).

21. For instance, Charles Batteux's *Les Beaux-Arts réduits à un même principe* (1747; repr., New York: Johnson Reprint Corp., 1988). The principle was that by selecting the best parts of nature, the artist produces a whole more perfect than nature. Sir

Joshua Reynolds wrote in his *Discourses on Painting* that the painter forms an abstract ideal of nature "more perfect than any original."

22. Winckelmann quoted in R. Wittkower, "Imitation, Eclecticism, and Genius," in Earl Wasserman, ed., *Aspects of the Eighteenth Century* (Baltimore: Johns Hopkins University Press, 1965), 145.

23. Percy Bysshe Shelley, letter to T. L. Peacock, 1821, quoted in Newman Ivey White, *Shelley* (New York: Alfred A. Knopf, 1940), 2:333–34.

24. Ibid., 2:22–23. This was in 1818.

25. *Ion*, in *Collected Dialogues of Plato*, ed. Edith Hamilton and Huntington Cairns (Princeton, N.J.: Bollingen, 1961), 219, 220.

26. Immanuel Kant, *Critique of Judgment* (1790), quoted in Abrams, *Mirror and the Lamp*, 207.

27. See Nowell Smith, ed., *Wordsworth's Literary Criticism* (1905; repr., Bristol: Bristol Classical Press, 1980).

28. Percy Bysshe Shelley, "A Defence of Poetry," in David Lee Clark, ed., *Shelley's Prose* (Albuquerque: University of New Mexico Press, 1954), 281.

29. Ibid., 282.

30. Ibid., 294.

31. Ibid., 294, 295.

32. Noted by Babbitt, *Rousseau and Romanticism*, 70.

33. Schiller, *On the Aesthetic Education*, 21, 40: and especially Letter 6.

34. Shelley, "Defence of Poetry," 297.

35. Shelley quoted in Carl Pletsch, *Young Nietzsche: Becoming a Genius* (New York: Free Press, 1991), 5.

36. Friedrich Nietzsche, "On the Uses and Disadvantages of History for Life," in *Untimely Meditations*, trans. R. J. Hollingdale (Cambridge: Cambridge University Press, 1983), 111.

37. Shelley, "Defence of Poetry," 296.

38. White, *Shelley*, 2:377.

39. Mary Shelley, letter of April 1821, quoted in ibid., 2:282.

40. Benita Eisler, *Byron: Child of Passion, Fool of Fame* (New York: Alfred A. Knopf, 1999); Harold Spender, *Byron and Greece* (London: G. Murray, 1924).

Chapter 24: Victorian Crossroads: Hegel, Marx, and Mill

1. Alexis de Tocqueville, *The Recollections of Alexis de Tocqueville*, trans. Alexander Teixeira de Mattos (New York: Columbia University Press, 1949).

2. Peter Stearns, *1848: The Revolutionary Tide in Europe* (New York: Norton, 1974), 76–77.

3. A.J.P. Taylor, *Napoleon to Lenin: Historical Essays* (New York: Harper & Row, 1966), 26.

4. Georges Duveau, *1848: The Making of a Revolution* (New York: Pantheon, 1967).

5. Tocqueville, *Recollections*; Karl Marx, "The Class Struggles in France 1848–1850," in *Karl Marx on Revolution*, trans. and ed. Saul Padover (New York: McGraw-Hill, 1971), 173.

6. Karl Marx and Friedrich Engels, *The Revolution of 1848–49: Articles from the Neue Rheinische Zeitung* (New York: International Publishers, 1972), 44–45.

7. Robert Payne, *Marx* (New York: Simon & Schuster, 1968), 67.

8. In Karl Popper, *The Open Society and Its Enemies* (Princeton, N.J.: Princeton University Press, 1966), 2:49.

9. In his *De Orbis Planetarum* of 1801, he attempted to prove by a priori deduction that there was not, and never could be, any planet or heavenly body between Mars and Jupiter. He did not know that the asteroid Ceres had been discovered just months earlier.

10. As noted by Popper, *Open Society*, 2:36–37.

11. Georg Friedrich Hegel, *Phenomenology of Spirit*, trans. A. V. Miller (Oxford: Clarendon Press, 1977).

12. For example, Charles Taylor, *Hegel* (Cambridge: Cambridge University Press, 1975).

13. Georg Friedrich Hegel, *The Philosophy of History*, trans. J. Sibree (New York: Dover, 1956), 381–83.

14. Ibid., 452.

15. See Jerry Z. Muller, *The Mind and the Market: Capitalism in Modern European Thought* (New York: Alfred A. Knopf, 2002), 164–65.

16. Georg Friedrich Hegel, *The Philosophy of Right*, trans. T. N. Knox (New York: Oxford University Press, 1967), 331.

17. Hegel, *Philosophy of History*, 40–41.

18. Quoted in Popper, *Open Society*, 2:75.

19. Compare Marx's *The German Ideology* and Engels's *Letter to Mehring* (1893). Also see Terry Eagleton, *Ideology: An Introduction* (New York: Verso, 1991).

20. The phrases come from an early draft of *The German Ideology*, written before the June Days in 1844–45; see Payne, *Marx*, 127–28.

21. Quoted in Paul Johnson, *The Intellectuals* (New York: Harper & Row, 1988), 71.

22. As was pointed out shortly after its publication in 1848 by the economist Bruno Hildebrand, and in more damning detail in the Henderson and Chaloner 1958 edition of *Condition*. Yet while the fallacious basis of Marx's economics (for instance, his surplus or labor theory of value) has been steadily exposed, Engels's deceptive (at times deliberately so) account of the effects of industrialization has survived as a persistent myth.

23. Payne, *Marx*, 356.

24. Friedrich Engels, *Anti-Dühring*, in *Marx and Engels: Basic Writings on Politics and Philosophy*, ed. Lewis Feuer (New York: Doubleday, 1959), 111.

25. Karl Marx, *Das Kapital*, vol. 3., quoted in Popper, *Open Society*, 103.

26. John Stuart Mill, *Autobiography of John Stuart Mill* (1924; repr., New York: Columbia University Press, 1960), 4–7; Michael St. John Packe, *The Life of John Stuart Mill* (London: Secker & Warburg, 1954), 20–23.

27. As noted by Bertrand Russell, *A History of Western Philosophy* (1945; repr., New York: Simon & Schuster, 2007), 774–75.

28. Nicholas Capaldi, *John Stuart Mill: A Biography* (Cambridge: Cambridge University Press, 2004), 26–27.

29. Mill, *Autobiography*, 94.

30. Ibid., 103.

31. See Samuel Taylor Coleridge, *On the Constitution of Church and State* (1838; repr., London: Dent, 1972).

32. Mill, *Autobiography*, 113–14.

33. As noted in William Thomas, *Mill* (Oxford: Oxford University Press, 1985), 71–73.

34. John Stuart Mill, *On Liberty* (Harmondsworth: Penguin, 1974), 132.

35. Gertrude Himmelfarb, *Liberty and Liberalism: The Case of John Stuart Mill* (San Francisco: ICS Press, 1974), 297.

36. Mill, *On Liberty*, 72.

37. See Capaldi, *Mill*, 283.

38. Mill, *On Liberty*, 136–37.

39. Ibid., 136.

40. Here Mill relied on Alexis de Tocqueville's analysis in *Democracy in America*. See Alan S. Kahan, *Aristocratic Liberalism: The Social and Political Thought of Jacob Burckhardt, John Stuart Mill, and Alexis de Tocqueville* (New York: Oxford University Press, 1992).

41. Mill, *On Liberty*, 105.

42. Ibid., 136.

43. Ibid., 63.

44. Capaldi, *Mill*, 210–17.

45. Quoted in Thomas, *Mill*, 89–90.

46. John Stuart Mill, *Principles of Political Economy*, quoted in Capaldi, *Mill*, 208.

47. Mill, *On Liberty*, 59.

48. See Andrew Vincent and Raymond Plant, *Philosophy, Politics and Citizenship: The Life and Thought of the British Idealists* (Oxford: Basil Blackwell, 1984).

Chapter 25: The Scale of Nature: Darwin, Evolution, and Aristotle's God

1. Edward Dolan, *Green Universe: The Story of Alexander von Humboldt* (New York: Dodd & Mead, 1959), 62–63.

2. Humboldt quoted in Val Gendron, *The Dragon Tree: A Life of Alexander von Humboldt* (London: Longmans, Green, 1961), 76.

3. Dolan, *Green Universe*, 71.

4. Gendron, *Dragon Tree*, 78.

5. Alexander von Humboldt, *Cosmos: A Sketch of the Physical Description of the Universe* (1845; repr., Baltimore: Johns Hopkins University Press, 1997), vol. 1, introduction.

6. Ibid.

7. Gendron, *Dragon Tree*, 72.

8. Charles Darwin, *Autobiography of Charles Darwin* (New York: H. Schuman, 1950), 33.

9. Darwin quoted in Gertrude Himmelfarb, *Darwin and the Darwinian Revolution* (Garden City, N.Y.: Doubleday, 1959).

10. Jacques Barzun, *From Grandeur to Decadence* (New York: Harper & Row, 2000), 501.

11. Thomas Hankins, *Science and the Enlightenment* (Cambridge: Cambridge University Press, 1985), 113.

12. Barry Gower, *Scientific Method: A Historical and Philosophical Introduction* (London: Routledge, 1997), 110–11.

13. John Locke, *Essay Concerning Human Understanding*, ibid., 83.

14. Humboldt, *Cosmos*, vol. 1, introduction.

15. Henry Kamen, *Imperial Spain 1469–1714* (London: Longmans, 1983).

16. Lewis Hanke, *Aristotle and the Indians* (Bloomington: Indiana University Press, 1959), 31.

17. Quoted in ibid., 47.

18. This almost certainly came from the greatest neo-Thomist natural law thinker of the sixteenth century, Francisco de Vitoria, who in the 1530s penned *The Recently Discovered Indies*, which stated that "there can be doubt that the Indians possessed true dominion both in public and private affairs" and that "there is no case at all for deposing either their rulers or their subjects of their property." No one listened except, presumably, Las Casas. It was not enough to save the indigenous peoples of Latin America, but it did live on in Las Casas's arguments at Valladolid. See Quentin Skinner, *The Foundations of Modern Political Thought* (Cambridge: Cambridge University Press, 1978), 168–69.

19. Hanke, *Aristotle*, 55.

20. Skinner, *Foundations of Modern Political Thought*, 170.

21. Las Casas quoted in Hanke, *Aristotle*, 112.

22. Quoted in Stephen Jay Gould, *The Mismeasure of Man* (New York: Norton, 1981).

23. Peter Bowler, *Evolution: The History of an Idea*, rev. ed. (Berkeley: University of California Press, 1989), 5, 20.

24. Bentley Glass, Owsei Temkin, and William L. Straus, Jr. eds., *Forerunners of Darwin* (Baltimore: Johns Hopkins University Press, 1959).

25. Erasmus Darwin, *Temple of Nature* (1803), quoted in Roy Porter, *The Creation of the Modern World* (New York: Norton, 2000), 443.

26. Ibid., 444.

27. Darwin, *Autobiography*, 17.

28. Gower, *Scientific Method*, 124–25.

29. See Charles Darwin, *The Voyage of the Beagle* (New York: Penguin, 1989), 16–17; and Arthur Herman, *To Rule the Waves: How the British Navy Shaped the Modern World* (New York: HarperCollins, 2004), 436–38.

30. Darwin quoted in Himmelfarb, *Darwin*, 75–76.

31. In *The Voyage of the Beagle*, Darwin called them "savages of the lowest grade" and noted that "the perfect equality" that prevailed among Fuegians doomed them to perpetual savagery. "As we see with those animals, whose instinct compels them to live in society and obey a chief, are most capable of improvement, so is it with the races of mankind." It would be hard to find a better example of how Aristotle's concept of the political animal collides with Rousseau's noble savage: in a clash not over the facts of socialization but over the value of their consequences. Darwin, *Beagle*, 181, 183.

32. Ibid., 275, 276–77.

33. As Himmelfarb notes, he went to write not one but three books on geology in the 1840s, including *Geological Observations on South America* (1846). Himmelfarb, *Darwin*, 86.

34. Darwin notebook, July 1837–February 1838, quoted in Himmelfarb, *Darwin*, 147, 155.

35. Darwin quoted in ibid., 151.

36. A. O. Lovejoy, *The Great Chain of Being* (1936; repr., New York: Harper & Row, 1965), 55–58.

37. Rom Harré, *The Philosophies of Science* (Oxford: Oxford University Press, 1972), 176.

38. Darwin quoted in Himmelfarb, *Darwin*, 149.

39. See Donald Winch, *Malthus* (Oxford: Oxford University Press, 1978).

40. Darwin, *Autobiography*, 54.

41. However, as the historian Gertrude Himmelfarb has pointed out, Malthus was not just an economist but a keen student of the natural sciences, which included membership in the Royal Society and the Geological Society. His entire model for human population growth came directly from the plant and animal kingdom, where "Nature has scattered the seeds of life abroad with the most profuse and liberal hand; but has been comparatively sparing in the room and nourishment necessary to rear them." Plants and animals face limits on their ability to expand and grow, Malthus wrote. He believed humanity could not escape from the same "great restrictive law." Quoted in Himmelfarb, *Darwin*, 158.

42. Jacob Bronowski describes the chronology in *The Ascent of Man* (Boston: Little, Brown, 1974), 305–8.

43. Quoted in Himmelfarb, *Darwin*, 151.

44. Darwin, *Autobiography*, 122.

45. W.K.C. Guthrie, *The Greek Philosophers from Thales to Aristotle* (1950; repr. New York: Harper & Row, 1960), 140.

Chapter 26: Unseen Worlds: Physics, Relativity, and the New World Picture

1. Isaac Newton, "Questions from the *Opticks*," in *Newton's Philosophy of Nature: Selections from His Writings*, ed. H. S. Thayer (1953; repr., New York: Macmillan, 1974), 175.

2. David Lindley, *Boltzmann's Atom* (New York: Free Press, 2001), 78.

3. George Gilder, *Microcosm* (New York: Touchstone Books, 1989), 22.

4. Jacob Bronowski, *The Ascent of Man* (Boston: Little, Brown, 1974), 353–54.
5. Maxwell's full quotation, which leads this chapter, is from Lindley, *Boltzmann's Atom*, 69.
6. Ibid., 69–71.
7. Gilder, *Microcosm*, 22.
8. G. S. Kirk and J. E. Raven, *The Presocratic Philosophers* (Cambridge: Cambridge University Press, 1964), 417.
9. Lindley, *Boltzmann's Atom*, 81.
10. Arthur Herman, *The Idea of Decline in Western History* (New York: Free Press, 1997), 174.
11. Bronowski, *Ascent*, 347–48.
12. The example appears in Erwin Schrödinger, *What is Life? & Mind and Matter* (Cambridge: Cambridge University Press, 1967), 162–63.
13. Bronowski, *Ascent*, 348.
14. Gilder, *Microcosm*, 182.
15. Mach quoted in Philipp Frank, *Modern Science and Its Philosophy* (1949; repr., New York: Collier Books, 1961), 70.
16. A. J. Ayer, ed., *Logical Positivism* (New York: Free Press, 1959), 4.
17. Frank, *Modern Science and Its Philosophy*, 47.
18. Otto Neurath, *Wissenschaftliche Weltauffassung der Wiener Kreis* (1929), quoted in Frank, *Modern Science and Its Philosophy*, 49.
19. Gilder, *Microcosm*, 182.
20. Boltzmann quoted in Lindley, *Boltzmann's Atom*, 215.
21. Ibid., 217.
22. The issue was the mysterious substance known as ether, which physicists since Newton had believed enabled light particles to travel through space. Michelson's experiment proved the doom of ether as well as Newton; the term still survives in everyday language, as when we talk about a poem or concept as being "ethereal." See Barry Gower, *Scientific Method: A Historical and Philosophical Introduction* (London: Routledge, 1997).
23. As described in Bronowski, *Ascent*, 247–48.
24. Albrecht Folsing, *Einstein: A Biography* (New York: Viking, 1997), 208–9. According to Folsing, it was Max Planck who first dubbed it "relativity theory."
25. Einstein quoted in Lindley, *Boltzmann's Atom*, 207.
26. H. Stuart Hughes, *Consciousness and Society: The Reorientation of European Social Thought 1890–1930*, rev. ed. (New York: Vintage, 1971), 183.
27. They included Thomas Hill Green and his disciples at Cambridge, along with J. E. McTaggart, and F. H. Bradley at Oxford. See A. J. Ayer, *Philosophy in the Twentieth Century* (1982; repr., New York: Vintage Books, 1984), 20, and Herman, *Idea of Decline*.
28. Hughes, *Consciousness and Society*, 62–65.

29. Victoria Frede, *Doubt, Atheism, and the Nineteenth-Century Russian Intelligentsia* (Madison: University of Wisconsin Press, 2011).

30. Georg Friedrich Hegel, *The Philosophy of Right*, trans. T. N. Knox (New York: Oxford University Press, 1967).

31. Hegel quoted in Bertrand Russell, *A History of Western Philosophy* (1945; repr., New York: Simon & Schuster, 2007), 740.

32. Georg Friedrich Hegel, *The Philosophy of History*, trans. J. Sibree (New York: Dover, 1956); Leonard Krieger, *The German Idea of Freedom: History of a Political Tradition* (Boston: Beacon Press, 1957).

33. For Hegel's influence on the so-called Historical School in Germany, see George Peabody Gooch, *History and Historians in Nineteenth-Century Europe* (1913; repr., Boston: Beacon Press, 1959), esp. chapter 8.

34. For a time after the Franco-Prussian War, West Point dressed its cadets in Prussian-style spiked helmets or *Pickelhauben*.

35. Disraeli quoted in Norman Rich, *The Age of Nationalism and Reform 1850–1890* (New York: Norton, 1976), 1206.

36. This thesis was first developed by L.T. Hobhouse in *The Metaphysical Theory of the State* (1918; repr., London: Allen & Unwin, 1960).

37. Barry Smith, "Austrian Origins of Logical Positivism," in Klemens Szaniawski, *The Vienna Circle and the Lvov-Warsaw School* (Dordrecht, Netherlands: Kluwer Academic, 1989), 28–29.

38. Gilder, *Microcosm*, 25.

39. Einstein quoted in Folsing, *Einstein*, 408–9.

Chapter 27: Triumph of the Will: Nietzsche and the Death of Reason

1. Friedrich Nietzsche, *Philosophy in the Tragic Age of the Greeks*, trans. M. Cowan (Chicago: H. Regnery, 1962), 4.

2. Ibid., 31.

3. Ibid., 52, 54, 69.

4. Ibid., 68.

5. Carl Pletsch, *Young Nietzsche: Becoming a Genius* (New York: Free Press, 1991), chapters 1, 2.

6. Friedrich Nietzsche, quoted in introduction to *Tragic Age*, 13.

7. Nietzsche's view of Socrates was ambivalent. Nietzsche was never consistent; he certainly identified with Socrates's role as the gadfly and the outsider (for instance, in *Genealogy of Morals*). However, his characterization of Socrates's influence, related to but distinct from Plato's and that of Platonism proper, never softened. See Victor Tejera, *Nietzsche and Greek Philosophy* (Dordrecht, Netherlands: M. Nijhoff, 1987).

8. Friedrich Nietzsche, *On the Genealogy of Morals/Ecce Homo*, trans. Walter Kaufmann (New York: Vintage: 1967), 271, 223.

9. Ibid., 154.

10. Ibid.

11. Quoted in Arthur Herman, *The Idea of Decline in Western History* (New York: Free Press, 1997), 99–101.

12. For example, compare Friedrich Nietzsche, *Beyond Good and Evil*, trans. Walter Kaufmann (New York: Vintage, 1966), 22, with Ludwig Wittgenstein, *Tractatus Logico-Philosophicus* (1922; repr., London: Routledge, 1981), 7.0.

13. Nietzsche, *On the Genealogy of Morals*, 154.

14. Friedrich Nietzsche, *Thus Spoke Zarathustra*, trans. Walter Kaufmann (1954; repr., New York: Penguin, 1966).

15. Ibid., 288.

16. Ibid., 327.

17. Aristotle, *Physics*, VI 239a–b.

18. H. Stuart Hughes, *Consciousness and Society: The Reorientation of European Social Thought 1890–1930*, rev. ed. (New York: Vintage, 1971), 116.

19. Bertrand Russell, A *History of Western Philosophy* (1945; repr., New York: Simon & Schuster, 2007), 798.

20. It is striking how Bergson's theory of memory overlaps with Freud's, and how intuition bears a certain resemblance to Freud's theory of the unconscious and the id. However, Freud knew nothing of Bergson's work and Bergson read Freud only after World War I. Hughes, *Consciousness and Society*, 124.

21. Bergson quoted in Russell, *History of Western Philosophy*, 796.

22. Henri Bergson, *Creative Evolution*, quoted in Hughes, *Consciousness and Society*, 118.

23. Ibid., 119.

24. Ibid., 170.

25. Did Nietzsche mean this in a racial, even proto-Nazi sense? Probably not. However, he was an admirer of the Aryan racial theorist Arthur de Gobineau, who also inspired the Aryanist race supremacy myths of Hitler's mentor Houston Stewart Chamberlain; and he did specifically link the cleansing barbarism in history to an Aryan race. For more discussion, see Herman, *Idea of Decline*, chapter 3.

26. Georges Sorel, *Reflections on Violence*, ed. J. Jennings (Cambridge: Cambridge University Press, 1999).

27. "War is the father of all and king of all; some he has made gods and others men, and some bonded and some free." John Burnet, *Early Greek Philosophy* (1892; repr., New York: Meridian, 1958), 136.

28. Bergson quoted in Hughes, *Consciousness and Society*, 118.

29. As described in Edmund Wilson, *To the Finland Station* (New York: Doubleday, 1940), 468–69.

30. Nikolai Sukhanov, quoted in ibid., 469.

31. Vladimir Ilyich Lenin, *Materialism and Empirio-Criticism* (London: International Publishers, 1940).

32. Steven E. Ascheim, *The Nietzsche Legacy in Germany 1890–1990* (Berkeley, CA: University of California Press, 1994), 23.

33. Allan Bloom, *The Closing of the American Mind* (New York: Simon & Schuster, 1987).

34. Martin Heidegger, *Being and Time*, trans. Joan Stambaugh (Albany: SUNY Press, 1996); and *An Introduction to Metaphysics*, trans. Ralph Manheim (New York: Doubleday, 1961).

35. A. Herman, *Idea of Decline*, 223.

36. Croce eventually reversed himself and disavowed Mussolini. Still, the move was significant.

37. A. J. Ayer, ed., *Logical Positivism* (New York: Free Press, 1959), 6–7 (introduction).

38. Victor Farias, *Heidegger and Nazism*, trans. G. Ricci (Philadelphia: Temple University Press, 1989), 104, 108.

Chapter 28: Common Sense Nation: Plato, Aristotle, and American Exceptionalism

1. Alexis de Tocqueville, *Democracy in America*, abridged ed. (New York: Mentor Books, 1956), 163, 143, 58.

2. Ibid., 48.

3. Ernest Tuveson, *The Redeemer Nation: The Idea of America's Millennial Role* (1968; repr., Chicago: University of Chicago Press, 1980).

4. As summarized in J.G.A. Pocock, *The Machiavellian Moment: Florentine Political Thought and the Atlantic Republican Tradition* (Princeton, N.J.: Princeton University Press, 1975).

5. See Adams's remarks on America's fate to be corrupted by its own prosperity, quoted in Gordon S. Wood, *The Creation of the American Republic 1776–1787* (New York: Norton, 1969), 570–71.

6. James Madison, Alexander Hamilton, and John Jay, *The Federalist Papers* (Harmondsworth: Penguin, 1987), 319.

7. For example, George Will, *Statecraft as Soulcraft: What Government Does* (New York: Simon and Schuster, 1983), 37–41.

8. Madison, *Federalist Papers*, 320; Hume, "Idea of a Perfect Commonwealth" in David Hume, *Essays Moral, Political, and Literary*, 529.

9. Ibid., 321.

10. Tocqueville, *Democracy in America*, 198.

11. Ibid., 201.

12. Ibid., 201–2.

13. Michael Novak, *The Fire of Invention* (Oxford: Rowman and Littlefield, 1997), 35.

14. Tocqueville, *Democracy in America*, 52, 42.

15. Ibid., 154.

16. Madison quoted in Roger Ketcham, *James Madison: A Biography* (Charlottesville: University of Virginia Press, 1990), 667.

17. For example, Thomas Jefferson, letter to John Adams, October 13, 1813, in *The Life and Selected Writings of Thomas Jefferson*, ed. Adrienne Koch and William Peden (New York: Modern Library, 1944), 632.

18. Jefferson quoted in Gertrude Himmelfarb, *The Roads to Modernity: The British, French, and American Enlightenments* (New York: Alfred A. Knopf, 2004).

19. E.g., Brooks Holifield, *Theology in America: Christian Thought from the Age of the Puritans to the Civil War* (New Haven, Conn.: Yale University Press, 2003), 175.

20. See Mark Noll, *America's God from Jonathan Edwards to Abraham Lincoln* (Oxford: Oxford University Press, 2002); and Michael Knox Beran, *Forge of Empires 1861–1871* (New York: Free Press, 2007), 199–200.

21. Abraham Flexner, *Daniel Coit Gilman: Creator of the American Type of University* (New York: Harcourt Brace,1946).

22. Charles S. Peirce, "First Principles," in Peirce, *Values in a Universe of Chance: Selected Writings*, ed. Philip P. Wiener (New York: Doubleday, 1958), 349.

23. Twain quoted in Alfred Kazin, *An American Procession* (New York: Alfred A. Knopf, 1984), 255.

24. Herman, *Idea of Decline*, 174.

25. Charles S. Peirce, *Values in a Universe of Chance: Selected Writings (1839–1914)*, ed. Philip P. Wiener (New York: Doubleday, 1958), xvi.

26. Charles S. Peirce "Issues of Pragmatism," ibid., 214.

27. Ibid.

28. William James, *Pragmatism and Other Essays*, ed. Giles Gunn (New York: Penguin, 2000), 10–11.

29. Ibid., 11, 14.

30. Peirce's actual term was "pragmaticism," but the identification was clear enough.

31. Charles S. Peirce, "What Pragmatism Is," in Peirce, *Values in a Universe*, 183–85.

32. William James, "Does Consciousness Exist?" in James, *Writings, 1902–1910* (New York: Viking, 1987), 1141–58.

33. Bertrand Russell, *A History of Western Philosophy* (1945; repr., New York: Simon & Schuster, 2007), 812.

34. The weather was Chauncey Wright's favorite example. See Louis Menand, *The Metaphysical Club* (New York: Farrar, Straus & Giroux, 2001), and Peirce, "What Pragmatism Is," 182–83.

35. William James, "Pragmatism and Common Sense," in Bruce Kuklick, ed., *William James: Writings 1902–1910* (New York: Viking, 1987), 559.

36. James, *Pragmatism*, 27. However, James also saw Socrates as the ancestor of pragmatism, with this restless probing of the meaning of words like *courage, justice,* and *piety* in concrete situations.

37. Ibid.

38. For instance, Russell, *History of Western Philosophy*, 683–84.

39. Aristotle, *The Nicomachean Ethics*, trans. J.A.K. Thomson (Harmondsworth: Penguin, 1976), II, 91–92.

40. James, *Pragmatism*, 97.

41. William James, *The Will to Believe and Other Essays in Popular Philosophy* (1897; repr., New York: Dover, 1956), 25.

42. William James, *The Varieties of Religious Experience* (New York: Random House, 1952), 283.

43. Philipp Frank, *Modern Science and Its Philosophy* (1949; repr., New York: Collier Books, 1961), 106–8, and Ayer, *Logical Positivism*, 12–13. For James's impact on Wittgenstein, see Russell Goodman, *Wittgenstein and William James* (Cambridge: Cambridge University Press, 2002).

44. Noted by A. J. Ayer, *Philosophy in the Twentieth Century* (1982; repr., New York: Vintage, 1984), 71.

45. William James, "Is Life Worth Living?" in James, *Pragmatism*, 239; James quoted Ayer, *Logical Positivism*, 72.

Chapter 29: Worlds at War: Plato and Aristotle in the Violent Century

1. The referendum that approved it by 99 percent was "a genuine reflection of German feeling" in both countries. A.J.P. Taylor, *The Origins of the Second World War* (New York: Fawcett, 1966), 145.

2. The eyewitness was Germany's ambassador Franz von Papen, quoted in William Shirer, *The Rise and Fall of the Third Reich* (New York: Fawcett, 1960), 473.

3. Ibid., 477.

4. Karl Popper, *Unended Quest: An Intellectual Autobiography*, quoted in David Edmonds and John Eidinow, *Wittgenstein's Poker* (New York: HarperCollins, 2001), 86.

5. Karl Popper, *The Open Society and Its Enemies* (Princeton, N.J.: Princeton University Press, 1966), 7.

6. Karl Popper, *Logik der Forschung* (1934); translated into English as *The Logic of Scientific Discovery* (1959; repr., New York: Harper & Row, 1965).

7. Karl Popper, *The Poverty of Historicism* (New York: Harper & Row, 1961), 8.

8. Plato, *The Laws*, trans. Trevor J. Saunders (Harmondsworth: Penguin, 1970), 93 (690b).

9. Ibid., 448.

10. Popper, *Open Society*, 1:199.

11. See Aristotle, *The Politics of Aristotle*, trans. and ed. Ernest Barker (1946; repr., Oxford: Oxford University Press, 1979), III, 12, 1 (1282b): "Justice is something that pertains to persons."

12. The Chekist M. Y. Latsis, quoted in Paul Johnson, *Modern Times: The World from the Twenties to the Nineties*, rev. ed. (New York: Harper Perennial, 2001), 71.

13. See Francis Fukuyama, *The End of History and the Last Man* (New York: Free Press, 1992), 63.

14. Quoted in Popper, *Open Society*, 45.

15. Borrowing the title, if not the theme, from George Will, *Statecraft as Soulcraft: What Government Does* (New York: Simon & Schuster, 1983).

16. Bruce Kuklick, *Churchmen and Philosophers: From Jonathan Edwards to John Dewey* (New Haven, Conn.: Yale University Press, 1985), 233–39. Dewey is usually described as a follower of William James. However, Kuklick shows that the formative influence on Dewey's thought was Hegelian long before he read any of James's works. Dewey saw his own philosophy as a fusion of Idealism and Pragmatism, or Instrumentalism, as he called it.

17. David Noble, *The Paradox of Progressive Thought* (Minneapolis: University of Minnesota Press, 1958).

18. In fact, Croly argued, it was this American shibboleth of individualism that allowed this unjust concentration of wealth to take place. Herbert Croly, *The Promise of American Life* (1909; repr., Boston: Northwest University Press, 1989), 147.

19. Ibid., 50.

20. Ibid., 266, 274.

21. Ibid., 278.

22. Ibid., 280, 267.

23. Ibid., 169, 202.

24. Wilson quoted in Ronald Pestrilto, *Woodrow Wilson and the Roots of Modern Liberalism* (Lanham, Md.: Rowman & Littlefield, 2005).

25. Wilson quoted in John M. Cooper, *The Warrior and the Priest: Woodrow Wilson and Theodore Roosevelt* (Cambridge, Mass.: Belknap Press, 1983).

26. John Maynard Keynes, *Economic Consequences of the Peace* (1919; Project Gutenberg eBook, 2005), chapter III.

27. Harold Nicolson, *Peacemaking 1919* (New York: Grosset and Dunlap, 1965), 36–37.

28. Johnson, *Modern Times*, 233, 235.

29. See John Kenneth Galbraith, *The Age of Uncertainty* (Boston: Houghton Mifflin, 1977).

30. Fritz Machlup, "Hayek's Contribution to Economics," in Machlup, ed., *Essays on Hayek* (Hillsdale, Mich.: Hillsdale College Press, 1976), 17.

31. Friedrich von Hayek, "Ernst Mach and Vienna Social Science, " in J. T. Blackmore, R. Itagaki, and S. Tanaka, eds., *Ernst Mach's Vienna* (Dordrecht, Netherlands: Kluwer Academic, 2001), 123–24.

32. See Max Alter, *Carl Menger and the Origins of Austrian Economics* (Boulder, Colo.: Westview Press, 1990), 112–20.

33. Machlup, "Hayek's Contribution," 17–18.

34. Friedrich von Hayek, *Individualism and Economic Order* (Chicago: University of Chicago Press, 1948), 79.

35. Ibid., 83–85.

36. Friedrich von Hayek, *Law, Legislation, and Liberty* (Chicago: University of Chicago Press, 1976), 2:29.

37. Friedrich von Hayek, *The Road to Serfdom* (Chicago: University of Chicago Press, 1944).

38. See Arthur Herman, *Freedom's Forge: How American Business Produced Victory in World War II* (New York: Random House, 2012).

39. John Steele Gordon, *An Empire of Wealth: The Epic History of American Economic Power* (New York: HarperCollins, 2004), 205.

40. Robert Barro, *Getting it Right: Markets and Choices in a Free Society* (Cambridge, Mass.: MIT Press, 1996), 111.

41. Francis Walton, *Miracle of World War II: How American Industry Made Victory Possible* (New York: Macmillan, 1956), 550.

42. Quoted in Michael Novak, *The Fire of Invention* (Lanham, Md.: Rowman & Littlefield, 1997), 6.

43. Quoted in Herman, *Freedom's Forge*, 206.

44. Walton, *Miracle of World War II*, 540–41.

45. Ayn Rand, *For the New Intellectual* (New York: Random House, 1961), 23.

46. Ibid.

47. Ibid., 27.

48. Quoted in Paul Johnson, *Modern Times: The World from the Twenties to the Nineties*, rev. ed. (New York: Harper Perennial, 2001).

49. Stéphane Courtois et al., *The Black Book of Communism: Crimes, Terror, Repression* (Cambridge, Mass.: Harvard University Press, 1999), *passim*.

50. Aristotle, *The Politics of Aristotle*, trans. and ed. Ernest Barker (1946; repr., Oxford: Oxford University Press, 1979), 48–55 (bk. II, chap. 5).

Conclusion: From the Cave to the Light

1. Victor McElheny, *Drawing the Map of Life: Inside the Human Genome Project* (New York: Basic Books, 2010).

2. Bernard Lewis, *What Went Wrong: The Clash Between Islam and Modernity in the Middle East* (New York: Harper Collins, 2003).

3. Ray Kurzweil, *The Singularity is Near: When Humans Transcend Biology* (New York: Penguin, 2003), 208.

4. A point explored at length, from a slightly different angle, in Nassim Taleb, *The Black Swan: The Impact of the Highly Improbable* (New York: Random House, 2010).

5. Alex Pollock, *Boom and Bust: Financial Cycles and Human Prosperity* (Washington, D.C.: American Enterprise Institute Press, 2011).

6. Ibid., 82, 7.

7. Mircea Eliade, *Rites and Symbols of Initiation* (New York: Harper & Row, 1958), 58–9; Victor Turner, *The Ritual Process* (University of Chicago Press, 1979).

8. Kevin Clinton, *Myth and Cult: The Iconography of the Eleusinian Mysteries* (Stockholm, 1992), 17–8, 84–5.

9. George Mylonas, *Eleusis and the Eleusinian Mysteries* (Princeton, N.J.: Princeton University Press, 1961), 266–68. Plato was very much aware of the Eleusinian mysteries and its Orphic rites, even if he never became an adept himself. His descriptions of

the underworld in the *Republic* and elsewhere closely correspond to the descriptions in the Eleusinian Hymn to Demeter and other sources.

10. Edmund Burke, *Reflections on the Revolution in France*, ed. J.G.A. Pocock (1790; repr., Indianapolis: Hackett, 1987), 83.

11. Christopher Lasch, *The Culture of Narcissism* (New York: Norton, 1978).

12. Mike Davis, *A Planet of Slums* (London: Verso, 2006); Robert Neuwirth, *Shadow Cities* (London: Routledge, 2006).

13. Kurzweil, *Singularity*, 98–99.

14. For example, Iain McGilchrist, *The Master and His Emissary: The Divided Brain and the Making of the Western World* (New Haven, Conn.: Yale University Press, 2009).

SELECT BIBLIOGRAPHY

Abelard, Peter. *Letters of Abelard and Heloise*. Translated by Betty Radice. Harmondsworth: Penguin, 1974.

———. *The Story of Abelard's Adversities* [*Historia Calamitatum*]. Translated by J. T. Muckle. Toronto: Pontifical Institute of Medieval Studies, 1964.

Abrams, Meyer H. *The Mirror and the Lamp: Romantic Theory and the Critical Tradition*. 1953. Reprint, New York: Norton, 1958.

Adcock, Frank Ezra. *Roman Political Ideas and Practice*. Ann Arbor: University of Michigan Press, 1959.

Alighieri, Dante. *Divine Comedy I: Hell*. Translated by Dorothy L. Sayers. 1949. Reprint, Harmondsworth: Penguin, 1976.

Alter, Max. *Carl Menger and the Origin of Austrian Economics*. Boulder, Colo.: Westview Press, 1990.

Andrewes, Antony. *The Greek Tyrants*. 1956. Reprint, New York: Harper & Row, 1963.

Aristotle. *The Basic Works of Aristotle*, ed. Richard McKeon. New York: Modern Library, 1947.

———. *Introduction to Aristotle*, ed. Richard McKeon. New York: Modern Library, 1967.

———. *Nicomachean Ethics*. Translated by J.A.K. Thomson. Harmondsworth: Penguin, 1976.

———. *Rhetoric*. Translated by Lane Cooper. 1932. Reprint, Englewood Cliffs, N.J.: Prentice-Hall, 1960.

———. *The Politics of Aristotle*. Edited by Ernest Barker. 1946. Reprint, Oxford, U.K.: Oxford University Press, 1979.

Attwater, Donald, and C. R. John. *The Penguin Dictionary of Saints*. Rev. ed. Harmondsworth: Penguin, 1983.

Auerbach, Eric. *Mimesis: The Representation of Reality in Western Literature.* Princeton, N.J.: Princeton University Press, 1953.

Augustine. *The City of God.* 2 vols. London: Dent, 1945.

——. *Confessions.* Translated by R. S. Pine-Coffin. Harmondsworth: Penguin, 1961.

——. *On the Trinity.* Translated by Stephen McKenna. Washington, D.C.: Catholic University of American Press, 1963.

Averroës. *Averroes' Middle Commentaries on Aristotle's "Categories" and "De Interpretatione."* Translated by Charles Butterworth. Princeton, N.J.: Princeton University Press, 1983.

Ayer, A. J. *Philosophy in the Twentieth Century.* 1982. Reprint, New York: Vintage, 1984.

——, ed. *Logical Positivism.* New York: Free Press, 1959.

Babbitt, Irving. *Rousseau and Romanticism.* 1919. Reprint, Boston: Houghton Mifflin, 1979.

Bacon, Francis. *Novum Organum.* Chicago: Encyclopaedia Britannica Press, 1952.

Bainton, Roland. *The Reformation of the Sixteenth Century.* 1952. Reprint, Boston: Beacon Press, 1980.

Balsdon, J.P.V.D., ed. *Roman Civilization.* Harmondsworth: Penguin, 1965.

Barnes, Jonathan. "Boethius and the Study of Logic." In Margaret T. Gibson, ed. *Boethius: His Life, Thought, and Influence.* Oxford: Basil Blackwell, 1981.

Barnes, Jonathan, and Miriam Griffin, eds. *Philosophia Togata II: Plato and Aristotle in Rome.* New York: Oxford University Press, 1997.

Barnes, Timothy. *Constantine and Eusebius.* Cambridge, Mass.: Harvard University Press, 1981.

Barny, Roger. *Rousseau dans la révolution: Le Personnage de Jean-Jacques et les debuts du culte révolutionaire (1787–1791).* Oxford: Voltaire Foundation, 1986.

Baron, Hans. *The Crisis of the Early Italian Renaissance.* Princeton, N.J.: Princeton University Press, 1966.

Barrow, R. H. *The Romans.* 1949. Reprint, Harmondsworth: Penguin, 1975.

Barzun, Jacques. *Classic, Romantic, and Modern.* Boston: Little, Brown, 1943.

——. *From Grandeur to Decadence.* New York: Harper & Row, 2000.

Bates, C. A. *Aristotle's "Best Regime": Kingship, Democracy, and the Rule of Law.* Baton Rouge: Louisiana State University Press, 2003.

Beller, Stephen. *Vienna and the Jews 1867–1938: A Cultural History.* Cambridge: Cambridge University Press, 1989.

Beran, Michael Knox. *Forge of Empires 1861–1871.* New York: Free Press, 2007.

Berchman, Robert. *From Philo to Origen: Middle Platonism in Transition.* Chicago: Scholars Press, 1984.

Bergson, Henri. *Creative Evolution.* Translated by A. Mitchell. Westport, Conn.: Greenwood Press, 1975.

Bernard of Clairvaux. *Letters of Saint Bernard of Clairvaux.* Translated by Bruno Scott James. Kalamazoo, Mich.: Cistercian Publications, 1998.

Biagioli, Mario. *Galileo, Courtier.* Chicago: University of Chicago Press, 1993.

Bisticci, Vespiano de. *Renaissance Princes, Popes and Prelates.* Translated by William George and Emily Waters. New York: Harper & Row, 1963.

Blackmore, J. T., R. Itagaki, and S. Tanaka, eds. *Ernst Mach's Vienna.* Dordrecht, Netherlands: Kluwer Academic, 2001.

Bloom, Allan. *The Closing of the American Mind.* New York: Simon & Schuster, 1987.

Blum, Carol. *Rousseau and the Republic of Virtue.* Ithaca, N.Y.: Cornell University Press, 1986.

Boehmer, Heinrich. *Road to Reformation: Martin Luther to the Year 1521.* Philadelphia: Muhlenberg Press, 1946.

Boethius. *Commentarii in librum Aristotelis.* Leipzig: Teubner, 1877–80.

———. *The Consolation of Philosophy.* Translated by V. E. Watts. Harmondsworth: Penguin, 1969.

Bossy, John. *Christianity in the West 1400–1700.* Oxford: Oxford University Press, 1985.

Bowler, Peter. *Evolution: The History of an Idea.* Rev. ed. Berkeley: University of California Press, 1989.

Boyd, John. *The Function of Mimesis and Its Decline.* Cambridge, Mass.: Harvard University Press, 1968.

Brink, C. O. *Horace on Poetry.* Cambridge: Cambridge University Press, 1963.

Bronowski, Jacob. *The Ascent of Man.* Boston: Little, Brown, 1974.

Brower, Jeffrey. *The Cambridge Companion to Abelard.* New York: Cambridge University Press, 2004.

Brown, Elizabeth A. R. *Saint Denis: La Basilique.* Paris: Zodiaque, 2001.

Brown, Peter. *Augustine of Hippo: A Biography.* Berkeley: University of California Press, 1969.

———. *The World of Late Antiquity.* New York: Harcourt Brace Jovanovich, 1971.

Bubacz, Bruce. *St. Augustine's Theory of Knowledge.* Lewiston, N.Y.: Edwin Mellen Press, 1981.

Burckhardt, Jacob. *The Civilization of the Renaissance in Italy.* Vol. 1. 1929. Reprint, New York: Harper & Row, 1958.

Burke, Edmund. *A Philosophical Enquiry into the Origins of Our Ideas of the Sublime.* London: Abraham Mills, 1889.

———. *Reflections on the Revolution in France.* Edited by J.G.A. Pocock. Indianapolis: Hackett, 1987.

Burnet, John. *Early Greek Philosophy.* 1892. Reprint, New York: Meridian, 1958.

Bury, J. B. *The Idea of Progress: An Inquiry into Its Origin and Growth.* New York: Macmillan, 1932.

———, ed. *The Hellenistic Age: Aspects of Hellenistic Civilization.* 1923. Reprint, New York: Norton, 1970.

Butterfield, Herbert. *The Statecraft of Machiavelli.* New York: Collier Books, 1962.

Cahill, Thomas. *How the Irish Saved Civilization.* New York: Anchor Books, 1996.

Capaldi, Nicholas. *John Stuart Mill: A Biography.* Cambridge: Cambridge University Press, 2004.

Capra, Fritjof. *The Science of Leonardo: Inside the Mind of the Great Genius of the Renaissance.* New York: Anchor, 2007.

Carman, Charles. *Images of Humanist Ideals in Italian Renaissance Art.* Lewiston, N.Y.: Edwin Mellen Press, 2000.

Carroll, James. *Constantine's Sword: The Church and the Jews: A History.* New York: Houghton Mifflin, 2001.

Cassirer, Ernst. *Rousseau, Kant, Goethe: Two Essays.* 1945. Reprint, Princeton, N.J.: Princeton University Press, 1970.

——. *The Platonic Renaissance in England.* New York: Gordian, 1970.

Chadwick, Henry. *Boethius: The Consolation of Music, Logic, Theology, and Philosophy.* Oxford: Clarendon Press, 1981.

——. *The Early Church.* 1967. Reprint, Harmondsworth: Penguin, 1982.

Champion, Edmé. *J.-J. Rousseau et la révolution française.* Reims: Editions A. l'Ecart, 1989.

Chenu, M.-D. *Nature, Man, and Society in the Twelfth Century.* Chicago: Chicago University Press, 1979.

——. *St. Thomas d'Aquin et la théologie.* Paris: Editions du Seuil, 1959.

Chitnis, Anand. *The Scottish Enlightenment: A Social History.* London: Croom Helm, 1976.

Cicalese, Marialuisa. *Democrazia in Cammino: La Formazione del pensiero politico di Stuart Mill nel dialogo con Tocqueville.* Milan: E. Angeli, 1988.

Cicero. *De Officiis.* Translated by Harry G. Edinger. Indianapolis: Bobbs-Merrill, 1974.

——. *De Re Publica.* Edited by Geoffery Poyser. Cambridge: Cambridge University Press, 1948.

——. *On the Ideal Orator.* Translated by James May and Jakob Wisse. New York: Oxford University Press, 2001.

——. *Tusculan Disputations.* Translated by C. D. Yonge. London: Henry G. Bohn, 1853.

Clark, David Lee, ed. *Shelley's Prose.* Albuquerque: University of New Mexico Press, 1954.

Clark, Gordon. *Selections from Hellenistic Philosophy.* New York: Appleton-Century-Crofts, 1940.

Clark, Kenneth. *Civilisation.* New York: Harper & Row, 1969.

——. *The Romantic Rebellion: Romantic Versus Classic Art.* New York: Harper & Row, 1973.

Clarke, M. L. *The Roman Mind.* New York: Norton, 1968.

Clinton, Kevin. *Myth and Cult: The Iconography of the Eleusinian Mysteries.* Stockholm: Paul Arstroms Forlag, 1992.

Cochrane, Charles Norris. *Christianity and Classical Culture.* 1940. Reprint, Oxford: Oxford University Press, 1957.

Coleridge, Samuel Taylor. *On the Constitution of Church and State.* London: Dent, 1972.

Collini, Stefan, Donald Winch, and John Burrow. *That Noble Science of Politics: A Study in Nineteenth-Century Intellectual History.* Cambridge: Cambridge University Press, 1983.

Cornford, Francis. *Before and After Socrates.* Cambridge: Cambridge University Press, 1962.

———. *Plato's Cosmology: The Timaeus of Plato.* Indianapolis: Bobbs-Merrill, 1975.

Cowell, F. R. *Cicero and the Roman Republic.* 1948. Reprint, Harmondsworth: Penguin, 1968.

Craig, Gordon A. *The Battle of Königgrätz.* Philadelphia: University of Pennsylvania Press, 2003.

Cranston, Maurice. *Jean-Jacques: The Early Life and Work of Jean-Jacques Rousseau 1712–1754.* New York: Norton, 1982.

———. *John Locke: A Biography.* 1957. Reprint, London: Longmans, 1959.

Crocker, Lester. *Jean-Jacques Rousseau: The Quest (1712–1758).* London: Macmillan, 1968.

Croly, Herbert. *The Promise of American Life.* 1909. Reprint, Boston: Northeastern University Press, 1989.

Crombie, A. C. *Medieval and Early Modern Science.* Vol. 2. 1953. Reprint, New York: Doubleday Anchor, 1959.

Crouzel, Henri. *Origen.* Edinburgh: T. T. Clark, 1999.

Cumings, Bruce. *Dominion from Sea to Sea: Pacific Ascendancy and American Power.* New Haven: Yale University Press, 2009.

Daniel-Rops, Henri. *Church of Apostles and Martyrs.* Vol. 2. New York: Doubleday, 1960.

Darwin, Charles. *Autobiography of Charles Darwin.* New York: H. Schuman, 1950.

———. *The Voyage of the Beagle.* New York: Penguin, 1989.

Davis, Mike. *A Planet of Slums.* London: Verso, 2006.

Dawkins, Richard. *The God Delusion.* Boston: Houghton Mifflin, 2008.

Deane, Herbert. *The Political and Social Ideas of Saint Augustine.* New York: Columbia University Press, 1963.

Defoe, Daniel. *The Complete English Tradesman.* 1726. Reprint, Gloucester: Alan Sutton, 1987.

Descartes, René. *Philosophical Works.* Vol. 1. Translated by E. S. Haldane and G.R.T. Ross. 1911. Reprint, Cambridge: Cambridge University Press, 1977.

Diderot, Denis. *Supplément au voyage de Bougainville.* Geneva: Droz, 1955.

Dijksterhuis, F. J. *Archimedes.* Copenhagen: E. Munksgaard, 1972.

Dillon, John. "Origen and Plotinus." In Thomas Finan, ed., *The Relationship Between Neoplatonism and Christianity.* Dublin: Four Courts Press, 1992.

———. *The Great Tradition: Further Studies in the Development of Platonism and Early Christianity.* Brookfield, Vt.: Ashgate, 1997.

———. *The Heirs of Plato: A Study of the Old Academy (347–274 B.C.).* Oxford: Oxford University Press, 2003.

Diogenes Laertius. *Lives of Eminent Philosophers.* 3 volumes. Translated by R. D. Hicks. Cambridge, Mass.: Loeb Classical Library, 1925.

Dionysius the Areopagite. *Celestial Hierarchy.* Fintry, U.K.: Shrine of Wisdom Press, 1965.

Dodds, E. R. *Pagan and Christian in an Age of Anxiety.* New York: Norton, 1970.

Dolan, Edward. *Green Universe: The Story of Alexander von Humboldt.* New York: Dodd, Mead, 1959.

Doyle, William. *The Oxford History of the French Revolution.* New York: Oxford University Press, 1989.

Drake, Stillman. *Galileo at Work: His Scientific Biography.* Chicago: University of Chicago Press, 1978.

———. *Galileo.* New York: Oxford University Press, 1980.

———. *Galileo: Pioneer Scientist.* Toronto: University of Toronto Press, 1990.

Dresden, Sem. *Renaissance Humanism.* London: Weidenfeld & Nicolson, 1968.

Duby, Georges, Eleanor Levieux, and Barbara Thompson. *The Age of the Cathedrals: Art and Society 980–1420.* Chicago: University of Chicago Press, 1981.

Dürer, Albrecht. *Dürer's Record of Journeys to Venice and the Low Countries.* Edited by Roger Fry. 1913. Reprint, New York: Dover Books, 1995.

Duveau, George. *1848: The Making of a Revolution.* New York: Pantheon, 1967.

Eagleton, Terry. *Ideology: An Introduction.* New York: Verso, 1991.

Edmonds, David, and John Eidinow. *Wittgenstein's Poker.* New York: HarperCollins, 2001.

Edwards, Mark. *Culture and Philosophy in the Age of Plotinus.* London: Duckworth, 2006.

Eisenstein, Elizabeth. *The Printing Revolution in Early Modern Europe.* Cambridge: Cambridge University Press, 1993.

Eisler, Benita. *Byron: Child of Passion, Fool of Fame.* New York: Alfred A. Knopf, 1999.

Eliade, Mircea. *Rites and Symbols of Initiation.* New York: Harper & Row, 1958.

Elphick, Peter. *Liberty: The Ships That Won the War.* Annapolis, Md.: Naval Institute Press, 2006.

Enos, Richard. *The Rhetoric of Saint Augustine of Hippo.* Waco, Tex.: Baylor University Press, 2008.

Erasmus, Desiderius. *In Praise of Folly.* Edited by A.H.T. Levi. Harmondsworth: Penguin, 1971.

———. *The Epistles of Erasmus.* Translated by F. M. Nichols. 3 vols. London: Longmans, 1901–18.

Erikson, Erik H. *Young Man Luther.* New York: Norton, 1962.

Erlande-Brandenburg, Alain. *The Cathedral Builders of the Middle Ages.* London: Thames & Hudson, 1995.

Errington, Robert Malcolm. *The Dawn of Empire: Rome's Rise to World Power.* Ithaca, N.Y.: Cornell University Press, 1972.

Eusebius. *The History of the Church.* Translated by G. A. Williamson. Harmondsworth: Penguin, 1965.

———. *The Life of Constantine.* Translated by A. Cameron and Stuart Hall. Oxford: Clarendon Press, 1999.

Evans, G. R. *Bernard of Clairvaux.* New York: Oxford University Press, 2000.

Farias, Victor. *Heidegger and Nazism.* Translated by G. Ricci. Philadelphia: Temple University Press, 1989.

Feuer, Lewis, ed. *Marx and Engels: Basic Writings on Politics and Philosophy.* New York: Doubleday, 1959.

Ficino, Marsilio. *Letters.* 7 vols. London: Shepheard-Walwyn, 1975.

——. *Platonic Theology.* Cambridge, Mass.: Harvard University Press, 2004.

Field, Arthur. *Origins of the Platonic Academy in Florence.* Princeton, N.J.: Princeton University Press, 1988.

Fife, Graeme. *The Terror: The Shadow of the Guillotine: France 1792–4.* New York: St. Martin's Press, 2004.

Fink, Zera Silver. *The Classical Republicans.* Evanston, Ill.: Northwestern University Press, 1962.

Finocchiaro, Maurice E., ed. *The Galileo Affair: A Documentary History.* Berkeley: University of California Press, 1989.

Focillon, Henri. *The Year 1000.* New York: Ungar, 1970.

Forbes, Duncan. *Hume's Philosophical Politics.* Cambridge: Cambridge University Press, 1975.

Frank, Philipp. *Modern Science and Its Philosophy.* 1949. Reprint, New York: Collier Books, 1961.

Fraser, P. M. *Ptolemaic Alexandria.* Oxford: Clarendon Press, 1972.

Freeman, Charles. *The Closing of the Western Mind.* New York: Alfred A. Knopf, 2003.

Friedlander, Paul. *Plato.* Vol. 1. New York: Pantheon Books, 1958.

Frosini, Fabio, ed. *Leonardo e Pico: Analogie, Contatti, confronti: Atti del convegno di Mirandola, 10 Maggio 2003.* Rome: Leo Olschki, 2005.

Fukuyama, Francis. *The End of History and the Last Man.* New York: Free Press, 1992.

Galbraith, John Kenneth. *The Age of Uncertainty.* Boston: Houghton Mifflin, 1977.

Galilei, Galileo. *Dialogue Concerning the Two Chief World Systems.* Translated by Stillman Drake. Berkeley: University of California Press, 1967.

——. *Dialogues Concerning Two New Sciences.* Translated by Henry Crew. 1914. Reprint, New York: Dover, 1954.

——. *Discoveries and Opinions of Galileo.* Edited by Stillman Drake. New York: Anchor, 1957.

Gendron, Val. *The Dragon Tree: A Life of Alexander von Humboldt.* London: Longmans, Green, 1961.

Gibbon, Edward. *Decline and Fall of the Roman Empire.* Vol. 1. Harmondsworth: Penguin, 1994.

Gierke, Otto von. *Natural Law and the Theory of Society 1500 to 1800.* Cambridge: Cambridge University Press, 1934.

——. *Political Theories of the Middle Ages.* Translated by F. W. Maitland. Boston: Beacon Press, 1958.

Gill, Stephen. *William Wordsworth: A Life*. Oxford: Clarendon Press, 1989.

Gillespie, Neal. *Charles Darwin and the Problem of Creation*. Chicago: University of Chicago Press, 1979.

Gilson, Étienne. *The Christian Philosophy of Saint Augustine*. 1960. Reprint, New York: Octagon Books, 1983.

———. *The Mystical Theology of Saint Bernard*. 1940. Reprint, Kalamazoo, Mich.: Cistercian Publications, 1990.

———. *Reason and Revelation in the Middle Ages*. New York: Charles Scribner's Sons, 1939.

Gimpel, Jean. *The Medieval Machine*. New York: Penguin, 1977.

Glass, Bentley, Owsei Temkin, and William Straus, eds. *Forerunners of Darwin*. Baltimore: Johns Hopkins University Press, 1959.

Goethe, Johann Wolfgang von. *Faust, Part One*. Translated by Philip Wayne. Harmondsworth: Penguin, 1949.

Gooch, George Peabody. *History and Historians in Nineteenth-Century Europe*. 1913. Reprint, Boston: Beacon Press, 1959.

Goodman, Russell. *Wittgenstein and William James*. Cambridge: Cambridge University Press, 2002.

Goodwin, Jason. *Lords of the Horizons: A History of the Ottoman Empire*. New York: Henry Holt, 1998.

Gorman, Peter. *Pythagoras: A Life*. London: Routledge & Kegan Paul, 1979.

Goubert, Pierre. *Louis XIV et quarante millions français*. 1966. Reprint, Paris: Fayard, 1977.

Gould, Stephen Jay. *The Mismeasure of Man*. New York: Norton, 1981.

Gower, Barry. *Scientific Method: A Historical and Philosophical Introduction*. London: Routledge & Kegan Paul, 1997.

Grafton, Anthony, and Lisa Jardine. *From Humanism to the Humanities: Education and the Liberal Arts in Fifteenth- and Sixteenth-Century Europe*. Cambridge, Mass.: Harvard University Press, 1986.

Grayeff, Felix. *Aristotle and His School*. London: Duckworth, 1974.

Greer, Donald. *The Incidence of the Terror During the French Revolution: A Statistical Interpretation*. Cambridge, Mass.: Harvard University Press, 1935.

Gruen, Erich, ed. *The Image of Rome*. Englewood Cliffs, N.J.: Prentice-Hall, 1969.

Guthrie, W.K.C. *The Greek Philosophers from Thales to Aristotle*. 1950. Reprint, New York: Harper & Row, 1960.

Hadas, Moses, ed. *The Stoic Philosophy of Seneca*. New York: Doubleday, 1958.

Hadot, Pierre. *Philosophy as a Way of Life*. Oxford: Wiley-Blackwell, 1995.

———. *Qu'est-ce que la philosophie antique?* Paris: Gallimard, 1995.

Hampson, Norman. *Will and Circumstance: Montesquieu, Rousseau, and the French Revolution*. London: Duckworth, 1983.

Hanke, Lewis. *Aristotle and the Indians*. Bloomington: Indiana University Press, 1959.

Hankins, Thomas. *Science and the Enlightenment.* Cambridge: Cambridge University Press, 1985.

Hare, R. M. *Plato.* Oxford: Oxford University Press, 1982.

Harré, Rom. *The Philosophies of Science.* Oxford: Oxford University Press, 1972.

Harrison, Brian. *The Bible, Protestantism, and Natural Science.* Oxford: Oxford University Press, 1998.

Haskins, Charles H. *The Renaissance of the Twelfth Century.* 1927. Reprint, New York: Meridian, 1968.

Hayek, Friedrich von. *Individualism and Economic Order.* Chicago: University of Chicago Press, 1948.

——. *The Road to Serfdom.* Chicago: University of Chicago Press, 1944.

Hegel, Georg Friedrich. *Phenomenology of Spirit.* Translated by A. V. Miller. Oxford: Clarendon Press, 1977.

——. *The Philosophy of History.* Translated by J. Sibree. New York: Dover, 1956.

——. *The Philosophy of Right.* Translated by T. N. Knox. New York: Oxford University Press, 1967.

Heidegger, Martin. *Being and Time.* Translated by Joan Stambaugh. Albany: SUNY Press, 1996.

——. *An Introduction to Metaphysics.* Translated by Ralph Manheim. New York: Doubleday, 1961.

Herman, A. L. *The Ways of Philosophy.* Atlanta, Ga.: Scholars Press, 1990.

Herman, Arthur. *The Idea of Decline in Western History.* New York: Free Press, 1997.

——. *To Rule the Waves: How the British Navy Shaped the Modern World.* New York: HarperCollins, 2004.

Himmelfarb, Gertrude. *Darwin and the Darwinian Revolution.* Garden City, N.Y.: Doubleday, 1959.

——. *Liberty and Liberalism: The Case of John Stuart Mill.* San Francisco: ICS Press, 1974.

——. *The Roads to Modernity: The British, French, and American Enlightenments.* New York: Alfred A. Knopf, 2004.

Hobbes, Thomas. *Leviathan.* Edited by C. B. MacPherson. Harmondsworth: Penguin, 1968.

Hobhouse, L. T. *The Metaphysical Theory of the State.* 1918. Reprint, London: Allen & Unwin, 1960.

Hollister, C. Warren. *Medieval Europe: A Short History.* New York: John Wiley & Sons, 1978.

Hughes, H. Stuart. *Consciousness and Society: The Reorientation of European Social Thought 1890–1930.* Rev. ed. New York: Vintage, 1971.

Huizinga, Johan. *Erasmus and the Age of Reformation.* 1924. Reprint, New York: Harper & Row, 1957.

——. *Erasmus of Rotterdam.* London: Phaidon Press, 1952.

Humboldt, Alexander von. *Cosmos: A Sketch of the Physical Description of the Universe.* Vol. 1. Baltimore: Johns Hopkins University Press, 1997.

Hume, David. *Essays, Moral, Political and Literary.* Indianapolis: Liberty Fund, 1985.

Hwa Yong Lee. *Political Representation in the Later Middle Ages: Marsilius in Context.* New York: Peter Lang, 2008.

Inge, W. R. *The Philosophy of Plotinus.* 2 vols. 1929. Reprint, New York: Greenwood Press, 1968.

Jaeger, Werner. *Aristotle: Fundamentals of the History of His Development.* 1934. Reprint, Oxford: Oxford University Press, 1962.

James, John. *The Master Masons of Chartres.* 1982. Reprint, Sydney, Australia: West Grimstead, 1990.

James, William. *Pragmatism and Other Essays.* Edited by Giles Gunn. New York: Penguin, 2000.

———. *Varieties of Religious Experience.* New York: Random House, 1952.

———. *The Will to Believe and Other Essays in Popular Philosophy.* 1897. Reprint, New York: Dover, 1956.

Johnson, Paul. *The Intellectuals.* New York: Harper & Row, 1988.

———. *Modern Times: The World from the Twenties to the Nineties.* Rev. ed. New York: Harper Perennial, 2001.

Jones, Howard Mumford. *The Age of Energy: Varieties of American Experience 1865–1915.* New York: Viking Press, 1971.

Jones, W.T.A. *History of Western Philosophy.* Vol. 2: *The Medieval Mind.* New York: Harcourt Brace & World, 1971.

Joost-Gaugier, Christiane. *Raphael's Stanza della Segnatura: Meaning and Invention.* Cambridge: Cambridge University Press, 2002.

Justin Martyr. *The First Apology.* Edinburgh: J. Grant, 1912.

Kamen, Henry. *Imperial Spain 1469–1714.* London: Longmans, 1983.

Kant, Immanuel. *Groundwork of the Metaphysics of Morals.* Translated by H. J. Paton. New York: Harper & Row, 1964.

———. *On History.* Indianapolis: Bobbs-Merrill, 1957.

Katzenellenbogen, A. *The Sculptural Programs of Chartres Cathedral.* New York: Norton, 1964.

Kelly, Christopher. *Rousseau's Exemplary Life: The "Confessions" as Political Philosophy.* Ithaca, N.Y.: Cornell University Press, 1987.

Kempis, Thomas à. *Imitation of Christ.* Translated by Thomas Kepler. Cleveland: World, 1952.

Kenny, Anthony. *Medieval Philosophy.* Oxford: Clarendon Press, 2005.

Kepler, Johannes. *Kepler's Conversation with Galileo's Sidereal Messenger.* New York: Johnson Reprint, 1965.

Kepler, Thomas, ed. *The Table Talk of Martin Luther.* New York: World, 1952.

Ketcham, Roger. *James Madison: A Biography.* Charlottesville: University of Virginia Press, 1990.

Kirk, G. S., and J. E. Raven. *The Presocratic Philosophers*. Cambridge: Cambridge University Press, 1964.

Knowles, David. *The Evolution of Medieval Thought*. New York: Random House, 1962.

Koestler, Arthur. *The Sleepwalkers*. New York: Macmillan, 1968.

Kohanski, Alexander. *The Greek Mode of Thought in Western Philosophy*. Rutherford, N.J.: Fairleigh Dickinson University Press, 1984.

Kohl, Benjamin, and Ronald G. Witt. *The Earthly Republic: The Italian Humanists on Government and Society*. Philadelphia: University of Pennsylvania Press, 1978.

Koyré, Alexandre. *From the Closed World to the Infinite Universe*. Baltimore: Johns Hopkins University Press, 1957.

Krautheimer, Richard. *Three Christian Capitals: Topology and Politics*. Berkeley: University of California Press, 1983.

Krieger, Leonard. *The German Idea of Freedom*. Boston: Beacon Press, 1957.

Kristeller, Paul. *Eight Philosophers of the Renaissance*. Stanford, Calif.: Stanford University Press, 1964.

——. *Renaissance Thought*. 1955. Reprint, New York: Harper & Row, 1961.

——, ed. *The Renaissance Philosophy of Man*. 1948. Reprint, Chicago: University of Chicago Press, 1956.

Kristeller, Paul, and Philip Wiener, eds. *Renaissance Essays*. New York: Harper & Row, 1968.

Kuhn, Thomas. *The Copernican Revolution*. Cambridge, Mass.: Harvard University Press, 1957.

——. *Structure of Scientific Revolutions*. Chicago: University of Chicago Press, 1962.

Kuklick, Bruce. *Churchmen and Philosophers: From Jonathan Edwards to John Dewey*. New Haven: Yale University Press, 1985.

Lactantius. *Divine Institutes*. Translated by A. Bowen and P. Garnsey. Liverpool: University of Liverpool Press, 2003.

Langford, Richard. *A Polite and Commercial People: England 1727–1783*. Oxford: Clarendon Press, 1989.

Lasch, Christopher. *The Culture of Narcissism*. New York: Norton, 1978.

Lawlor, Robert. *Sacred Geometry: Philosophy and Practice*. London: Thames & Hudson, 1982.

Lee, R. W. *Ut Pictura Poesis: The Humanistic Theory of Painting*. New York: Norton, 1963.

Lefebvre, Georges. *The Coming of the French Revolution*. Translated by R. R. Palmer. Princeton, N.J.: Princeton University Press, 1947.

Leff, Gordon. *William of Ockham: The Metamorphosis of Scholastic Discourse*. Manchester: University of Manchester Press, 1975.

Leinkauf, Thomas. *Platons Timaios als Grundtext der Kosmologie in Spätantike, Mittelalter, und Renaissance*. Leuven: Leuven University Press, 2005.

Lenin, Vladimir Ilyich. *Materialism and Empirio-Criticism*. London: International, 1940.

Lenski, Noel. *Cambridge Companion to the Age of Constantine*. Cambridge: Cambridge University Press, 2006.

Lewis, Bernard. *Islam and the West.* New York: Oxford University Press, 1994.

Lewis, Evart. *Medieval Political Ideas.* Vol. 2. 1954. Reprint, New York: Cooper Square, 1974.

Livio, Mario. *The Golden Ratio.* London: Review, 2003.

Lloyd, G.E.R. *Aristotelian Explorations.* New York: Cambridge University Press, 1993.

———. *Aristotle: The Growth and Structure of His Thought.* Cambridge: Cambridge University Press, 1968.

———. *Greek Science After Aristotle.* New York: Norton, 1973.

Lloyd-Jones, Hugh, ed. *The Greek World.* Harmondsworth: Penguin, 1965.

Locke, John. *Essay Concerning Human Understanding.* 2 vols. London, 1903.

———. *Two Treatises of Government.* Edited by Peter Laslett. Cambridge: Cambridge University Press, 1960.

Long, A. A. *Hellenistic Philosophy: Stoics, Epicureans, Sceptics.* 2nd ed. 1974. Reprint, London: Duckworth, 1986.

Lovejoy, A. O. *The Great Chain of Being.* 1936. Reprint, New York: Harper & Row, 1965.

Luther, Martin. *Martin Luther: Selections from His Writings.* Edited by John Dillenberger. New York: Doubleday, 1961.

MacCulloch, Diarmid. *The Reformation.* New York: Penguin, 2004.

Machiavelli, Niccolò. *The Discourses.* Translated by Leslie Walker. Harmondsworth: Penguin, 1974.

———. *The Letters of Machiavelli.* Edited by Felix Gilbert. New York: Capricorn Books, 1961.

———. *The Prince.* Translated by George Bull. Harmondsworth: Penguin, 1981.

———. *The Prince.* Translated by Russell Price. Cambridge: Cambridge University Press, 1988.

Machlup, Fritz, ed. *Essays on Hayek.* Hillsdale, Mich.: Hillsdale College Press, 1976.

MacMullen, Ramsay. *Constantine.* New York: Harper Torchbooks, 1970.

Madison, James, Alexander Hamilton, and John Jay. *The Federalist Papers.* Edited by Isaac Kramnick. London: Penguin, 1987.

Magee, Bryan, ed. *Modern British Philosophy.* New York: St. Martin's Press, 1981.

Mandelbrot, Benoit. *Les Objets Fractals: Forme, Hasard et Dimension.* 1975. Reprint, Paris: Flammarion, 1989.

Manuel, Frank. *The Eighteenth Century Confronts the Gods.* New York: Atheneum, 1967.

Marenbon, John. *The Cambridge Companion to Boethius.* Cambridge: Cambridge University Press, 2009.

Maritain, Jacques. *Saint Thomas Aquinas.* New York: Meridian, 1958.

Marshall, John. *John Locke: Resistance, Religion and Responsibility.* Cambridge: Cambridge University Press, 1994.

Martines, Lauro. *April Blood: Florence and the Plot Against the Medici.* New York: Oxford University Press, 2003.

———. *Scourge and Fire: Savonarola and the Republic of Florence.* London: Jonathan Cape, 2006.

Marx, Karl. *Karl Marx on Revolution*, Translated and edited by Saul Padover. New York: McGraw-Hill, 1971.

Marx, Karl, and Friedrich Engels. *The Revolution of 1848–49: Articles from the Neue Rheinische Zeitung*. New York: International, 1972.

May, Gita. *Madame Roland and the French Revolution*. New York: Columbia University Press, 1970.

McGilchrist, Iain. *The Master and His Emissary: The Divided Brain and the Making of the Western World*. New Haven: Yale University Press, 2009.

McGrade, Arthur Stephen. *The Political Thought of William of Ockham*. Cambridge: Cambridge University Press, 1974.

McKeon, Richard, ed. *Selections from Medieval Philosophers*. Vol. 1. New York: Charles Scribner's Sons, 1929.

McNeil, David. *Guillaume Budé and Humanism in the Reign of Francis I*. Geneva: Droz, 1975.

Mead, G.R.S. *Orpheus*. New York: Barnes & Noble, 1965.

Menand, Louis. *The Metaphysical Club*. New York: Farrar, Straus & Giroux, 2001.

Michelangelo. *Complete Poems and Selected Letters of Michelangelo*. Edited by Creighton Gilbert. New York: Vintage Books, 1963.

Mill, John Stuart. *Autobiography of John Stuart Mill*. 1924. Reprint, New York: Columbia University Press, 1960.

———. *On Liberty*. Harmondsworth: Penguin, 1974.

———. *Utilitarianism*. London: Dent, 1910.

Milton, John. *Complete Poetry and Major Prose*. Edited by Merritt Hughes. New York: Odyssey, 1957.

Mlodonow, Leonard. *Euclid's Window: The Story of Geometry from Parallel Lines to Hyperspace*. New York: Free Press, 2002.

Monk, Ray. *Wittgenstein: The Duty of Genius*. New York: Free Press, 1990.

Montesquieu, Charles de. *The Spirit of the Laws*. 2 vols. Translated by Thomas Nugent. New York: Macmillan, 1949.

Moody, Ernest A. *The Logic of William of Ockham*. New York: Sheed & Ward, 1935.

More, Henry. *Letters on Several Subjects*. London: 1694.

More, P. E. *The Greek Tradition*. Vol. 3. *Hellenistic Philosophies*. Princeton, N.J.: Princeton University Press, 1923.

Morford, Mark. *The Roman Philosophers*. New York: Routledge, 2002.

Morison, Jeffrey. *John Witherspoon and the Founding of the American Republic*. Notre Dame, Ind.: University of Notre Dame Press, 2005.

Morrall, John B. *Aristotle*. London: Allen & Unwin, 1977.

Morris, Charles. *The Pragmatic Movement in American Philosophy*. New York: Brazillier, 1970.

Mösel, Ernst. *Von Geheimnis der Form und der Urform des Seins*. Stuttgart: Deutsche Verlagsanstalt, 1938.

Mosse, George. *Nationalization of the Masses*. New York: Meridian, 1975.

Muller, Jerry Z. *The Mind and the Market: Capitalism in Modern European Thought.* New York: Alfred A. Knopf, 2002.

Murray, Linda. *Michelangelo.* New York: Oxford University Press, 1980.

Mylonas, George. *Eleusis and the Eleusinian Mysteries.* Princeton, N.J.: Princeton University Press, 1961.

Namier, Lewis. *1848: The Revolt of the Intellectuals.* 1944. Reprint, New York: Doubleday, 1964.

Nelson, John. *The Renaissance Theory of Love: The Context of Giordano Bruno's "Eroici Furori."* New York: Columbia University Press, 1958.

Netz, Reviel, and William Noel. *The Archimedes Codex: How a Medieval Prayer Book Is Revealing the True Genius of Antiquity's Greatest Scientist.* Philadelphia: Da Capo Press, 2007.

Neuwirth, Robert. *Shadow Cities.* London: Routledge, 2006.

Newton, Isaac. *Newton's Philosophy of Nature: Selections from His Writings.* Edited by H.S. Thayer. 1953. Reprint, New York: Macmillan, 1974.

Nicolson, Harold. *Peacemaking 1919.* New York: Grosset and Dunlap, 1965.

Nietzsche, Friedrich. *Thus Spoke Zarathustra.* Translated by Walter Kaufmann. 1954. Reprint, New York: Penguin, 1966.

———. *Beyond Good and Evil.* Translated by Walter Kaufmann. New York: Vintage, 1966.

———. *Genealogy of Morals/Ecce Homo.* Translated by Walter Kaufmann. New York: Vintage, 1967.

———. *Philosophy in the Tragic Age of the Greeks.* Translated by M. Cowan. Chicago: H. Regnery, 1962.

———. *Untimely Meditations.* Translated by R. J. Hollingdale. Cambridge: Cambridge University Press, 1983.

Noble, David. *The Paradox of Progressive Thought.* Minneapolis: University of Minnesota Press, 1958.

Noll, Mark. *America's God from Jonathan Edwards to Abraham Lincoln.* Oxford: Oxford University Press, 2002.

O'Rourke, Fran. "Being and Non-Being in the Pseudo-Dionysius." In Thomas Finan, ed., *The Relationship Between Neoplatonism and Christianity.* Dublin: Four Courts Press, 1992.

Oakley, Francis. *The Conciliarist Tradition: Constitutionalism in the Catholic Church 1300–1870.* Oxford: Oxford University Press, 2003.

———. *Natural Law, Laws of Nature, Natural Rights.* New York: Continuum, 2005.

Oates, Whitney J., ed. *The Stoic and Epicurean Philosophers.* New York: Random House, 1940.

Oberman, Heiko. *The Harvest of Late Medieval Theology.* 1963. Reprint, Durham, N.C.: Labyrinth, 1983.

Odahl, C. M. *Constantine and the Christian Empire.* New York: Routledge, 2004.

Ong, Walter. *Ramus: Method and the Decay of Dialogue.* Cambridge, Mass.: Harvard University Press, 1963.

Orel, Vitezslav. *Gregor Mendel: The First Geneticist*. Translated by S. Finn. Oxford: Oxford University Press, 1996.

Origen. *Contra Celsum, Libri VIII*. Edited by M. Marcovich. Boston: Brill, 2001.

Overy, Ricard. *Why the Allies Won*. New York: Norton, 1995.

Packe, Michael St. John. *The Life of John Stuart Mill*. London: Secker & Warburg, 1954.

Patch, H. R. "Fate in Boethius and the Neoplatonists." *Speculum* 4, no. 1 (1929), 62–72.

Patrides, C. A., ed. *The Cambridge Platonists*. Cambridge, Mass.: Harvard University Press, 1970.

Payne, Robert. *Marx*. New York: Simon & Schuster, 1968.

Pegis, Anton. *Introduction to St. Thomas Aquinas*. New York: Random House, 1948.

Pennington, M. Basil. *Saint Bernard of Clairvaux*. Kalamazoo, Mich.: Cistercian Publications, 1977.

Perl, Eric. *Theophany: The Neoplatonic Philosophy of Dionysius the Areopagite*. Albany: SUNY Press, 2007.

Pico della Mirandola, Giovanni. *Syncretism in the West: Pico's 900 Theses (1486)*. Translated by S. A. Farmer. Tempe, Ariz.: Medieval and Renaissance Texts and Studies, 1998.

Pieper, Josef. *Guide to Thomas Aquinas*. New York: New American Library, 1962.

Plato. *The Collected Dialogues of Plato*. Edited by Edith Hamilton and Huntington Cairns. Princeton, N.J.: Bollingen, 1961.

———. *The Dialogues of Plato*. Translated by Benjamin Jowett. New York: Random House, 1937.

———. *Gorgias*. Translated by Walter Hamilton. Harmondsworth: Penguin, 1960.

———. *The Last Days of Socrates: Euthyphro, Apology, Crito, Phaedo*. Translated by Hugh Tredennick and Harold Tarrant. Harmondsworth: Penguin, 1954.

———. *Plato's Epistles*. Edited by Glenn Morrow. Indianapolis: Bobbs-Merrill, 1962.

———. *The Republic*. Translated by Desmond Lee. Harmondsworth: Penguin, 1975.

———. *The Symposium*. Translated by Christopher Gill. Harmondsworth: Penguin, 1999.

———. *Timaeus and Critias*. Translated by Desmond Lee. Harmondsworth: Penguin, 1977.

———. *The Works of Plato*. Translated by Benjamin Jowett. New York: Modern Library, 1956.

Pletsch, Carl. *Young Nietzsche: Becoming a Genius*. New York: Free Press, 1991.

Plotinus. *Enneads*. Translated by Stephen McKenna. 2nd rev. ed. London: Faber & Faber, 1956.

Plutarch. *The Fall of the Roman Republic*. Translated by Rex Warner. Harmondsworth: Penguin, 1958.

———. *The Makers of Rome*. Translated by Ian Scott-Kilvert. Harmondsworth: Penguin, 1965.

Pocock, J.G.A. *The Machiavellian Moment*. Princeton, N.J.: Princeton University Press, 1975.

———. *Virtue, Commerce, and History: Essays on Political Thought and History, Chiefly in the Eighteenth Century*. Cambridge: Cambridge University Press, 1985.

Poincaré, Henri. *The Value of Science.* Translated by G. B. Halsted. 1905. Reprint, New York: Science Press, 1907.

Polybius. *The Rise of the Roman Empire.* Translated by F. W. Walbank. Harmondsworth: Penguin, 1979.

Popper, Karl. *The Logic of Scientific Discovery.* 1959. Reprint, New York: Harper & Row, 1965.

——. *The Open Society and Its Enemies.* 2 vols. Princeton, N.J.: Princeton University Press, 1962–66.

——. *The Unended Quest: An Intellectual Autobiography.* LaSalle, Ill.: Open Court, 1976.

Porter, Roy. *The Creation of the Modern World.* New York: Norton, 2000.

Rabelais, François. *Pantagruel.* Edited by Jean Plattard. Paris: Société des Belles-Lettres, 1959.

Raffini, Christine. *Marsilio Ficino, Pietro Bembo, Baldassare Castiglione: Philosophical, Aesthetic, and Political Approaches in Renaissance Platonism.* New York: Peter Lang, 1998.

Rand, Ayn. *For the New Intellectual.* New York: Random House, 1961.

Rand, E. K. *Founders of the Middle Ages.* 1928. Reprint, New York: Dover, 1957.

Randall, John Herman. *The Making of the Modern Mind.* New York: Houghton Mifflin, 1940.

Rashdall, Hastings. *The Universities of Europe in the Middle Ages.* 3 vols. Oxford: Oxford University Press, 1958.

Reid, Thomas. *Essays on the Intellectual Powers of Man.* Cambridge, Mass.: MIT Press, 1969.

Repcheck, Jack. *Copernicus' Secret: How the Scientific Revolution Began.* New York: Simon & Schuster, 2007.

Reynolds, Joshua. *Discourses on Art.* Edited by Robert Wark. New Haven: Yale University Press, 1997.

Rich, Norman. *The Age of Nationalism and Reform 1850–1890.* New York: Norton, 1976.

Ridolfi, Roberto. *The Life of Niccolò Machiavelli.* Translated by C. Grayson. Chicago: University of Chicago Press, 1963.

Rieff, Philip. *Freud: The Mind of the Moralist.* New York: Doubleday, 1961.

——. *The Triumph of the Therapeutic: Uses of Faith After Freud.* New York: Harper & Row, 1966.

Roberts, J. R. *The Pelican History of the World.* Harmondsworth: Penguin, 1980.

Robertson, D. W. *Abelard and Heloise.* New York: Dial Press, 1972.

Robertson, William. *The Progress of Society in Europe.* Edited by Felix Gilbert. Chicago: University of Chicago Press, 1972.

Ross, W. D. *Aristotle.* 1949. Reprint, London: Methuen, 1966.

Rostovtzeff, Michael. *A History of the Ancient World.* 2 vols. Oxford: Clarendon Press, 1928.

Rousseau, Jean-Jacques. *The Confessions.* Translated by J. M. Cohen. Harmondsworth: Penguin, 1954.

——. *A Discourse on Inequality.* Translated by Maurice Cranston. Harmondsworth: Penguin, 1984.

——. *Émile, or Education.* Translated by Barbara Foxley. New York: E. P. Dutton, 1911.

——. *The First and Second Discourses [Discourse on Arts and Sciences].* Translated by Victor Gourevitch. New York: Harper & Row, 1990.

——. *The Government of Poland.* Translated by Willmoore Kendall. Indianapolis: Hackett, 1985.

——. *Julie, ou La Nouvelle Héloïse.* Paris: Garnier, 1973.

——. *The Reveries of the Solitary Walker.* Indianapolis: Hackett, 1992.

——. *The Social Contract.* Translated by Maurice Cranston. Harmondsworth: Penguin, 1968.

Rubenstein, Richard. *Aristotle's Children.* Orlando, Fla.: Harcourt, 2003.

Rudolph, Conrad. *Artistic Change at Saint Denis.* Princeton, N.J.: Princeton University Press, 1990.

Rupp, E. Gordon. *The Righteousness of God: Luther Studies.* London: Hodder & Stoughton, 1968.

Russell, Bertrand. *A History of Western Philosophy.* 1945. Reprint, New York: Simon & Schuster, 2007.

——. *Wisdom of the West.* New York: Doubleday, 1959.

Saint-Simon, *Memoirs.* 6 vols. New York: Brentano's, 1915–18.

Sallust. *The Jugurthine War/The Conspiracy of Cataline.* Translated by S. A. Handford. Harmondsworth: Penguin, 1963.

Santillana, Giorgio de. *The Crime of Galileo.* Berkeley: University of California Press, 1955.

Sarton, George. *Appreciation of Ancient and Modern Science During the Renaissance.* Philadelphia: University of Pennsylvania Press, 1955.

Schiller, Friedrich. *On the Aesthetic Education of Man.* Translated by R. Snell. 1954. Reprint, New York: Ungar, 1971.

Schorske, Carl. *Fin-de-Siècle Vienna: Politics and Culture.* New York: Vintage Books, 1981.

Schwaller de Lubicz, R. A. *Symbol and the Symbolic.* Rochester, Vt.: Inner Tradition, 1981.

Seymour, Charles, ed. *Michelangelo: The Sistine Chapel Ceiling.* New York: Norton, 1972.

Shaftesbury, Anthony Ashley Cooper. *Characteristics.* Indianapolis: Bobbs-Merrill, 1964.

Shelley, Mary. *Letters.* 2 vols. Baltimore: Johns Hopkins University Press, 1980.

Shirer, William. *The Rise and Fall of the Third Reich.* New York: Fawcett, 1960.

Shorey, Paul. *Platonism Ancient and Modern.* Berkeley: University of California Press, 1938.

——. *What Plato Said.* 1933. Reprint, Chicago: University of Chicago Press, 1978.

Sidney, Algernon. *Discourses Concerning Government.* Indianapolis: Liberty Fund, 1996.

Simson, Otto G. von. *The Gothic Cathedral.* 1956. Reprint, Princeton, N.J.: Princeton University Press, 1974.

Skinner, Quentin. *The Foundations of Modern Political Thought.* Vol. 2. Cambridge: Cambridge University Press, 1978.

Smith, Adam. *An Inquiry into the Nature and Causes of the Wealth of Nations*. Edited by Edwin Cannan. Chicago: University of Chicago Press, 1976.

Snow, Edgar. *The Two Cultures and the Scientific Revolution*. Cambridge: Cambridge University Press, 1959.

Sorel, Georges. *Reflections on Violence*. Edited by J. Jennings. Cambridge: Cambridge University Press, 1999.

Southern, R. W. *The Making of the Middle Ages*. 1953. Reprint, New Haven: Yale University Press, 1967.

———. *Saint Anselm and His Biographer*. Cambridge: Cambridge University Press, 1963.

———. *Western Society and the Church in the Middle Ages*. Harmondsworth: Penguin, 1970.

Spender, Harold. *Byron and Greece*. London: G. Murray, 1924.

Stanlis, Peter. *Edmund Burke: The Enlightenment and Revolution*. New Brunswick, N.J.: Transaction Books, 1991.

Stearns, Peter. *1848: The Revolutionary Tide in Europe*. New York: Norton, 1974.

Strachan, Gordon. *Sacred Geometry, Sacred Space*. Edinburgh: Floris, 2003.

Strohmeier, John, and Peter Westbrook. *Divine Harmony: The Life and Teachings of Pythagoras*. Albany, Caif.: Berkeley Hills, 1999.

Syme, Ronald. *The Roman Revolution*. Oxford: Oxford University Press, 1939.

Szaniawski, Klemens, ed. *The Vienna Circle and the Lvov-Warsaw School*. Dordrecht, Netherlands: Kluwer Academic, 1989.

Tacitus. *Annals*. Translated by Donald Dudley. New York: Mentor Books, 1966.

———. *On Britain and Germany*. Translated by H. Mattingly. 1948. Reprint, Harmondsworth: Penguin, 1965.

Tarnas, Richard. *Passion of the Western Mind*. New York: Harmony, 1991.

Taylor, A. E. *Plato: The Man and His Work*. London: Methuen, 1960.

———. *Platonism and Its Influence*. 1924. Reprint, New York: Cooper Square, 1963.

———. *Socrates*. 1951. Reprint, Westport, Conn.: Greenwood, 1975.

Taylor, A.J.P. *Napoleon to Lenin: Historical Essays*. New York: Harper & Row, 1966.

———. *The Origins of the Second World War*. New York: Fawcett, 1966.

Taylor, Charles. *Hegel*. Cambridge: Cambridge University Press, 1975.

Taylor, L. R. *Party Politics in the Age of Caesar*. Berkeley: University of California Press, 1948.

Tejera, Victor. *Nietzsche and Greek Philosophy*. Dordrecht, Netherlands: M. Nijhoff, 1987.

Terra, Helmut de. *Humboldt: The Life and Times of Alexander von Humboldt 1769–1859*. New York: Knopf, 1955.

Tertullian. *On Idolatry*. New York: Kessinger, 2004.

Thomas, Keith. *Man and the Natural World: Changing Attitudes in England 1500–1800*. 1983. Reprint, New York: Oxford University Press, 1996.

———. *Religion and the Decline of Magic: Studies in Popular Beliefs in Sixteenth- and Seventeenth-Century England*. New York: Oxford University Press, 1997.

Thomas, William. *Mill*. Oxford: Oxford University Press, 1985.

Thompson, D'Arcy. *On Growth and Form.* Edited by John Tyler Bonner. Cambridge: Cambridge University Press, 1992.

Thompson, Martyn. *Ideas of Contract in English Political Thought in the Age of John Locke.* New York: Garland, 1987.

Thruelson, Richard. *The Grumman Story.* New York: Praeger, 1976.

Tierney, Brian, ed. *The Crisis of Church and State 1050–1300.* Englewood Cliffs, N.J.: Prentice-Hall, 1964.

Tocqueville, Alexis de. *Democracy in America.* Abridged ed. New York: Mentor Books, 1956.

———. *The Recollections of Alexis de Tocqueville.* Translated by Alexander Teixeira de Mattos. New York: Columbia University Press, 1949.

Tolnay, Charles de. *The Art and Thought of Michelangelo.* New York: Pantheon, 1964.

Torrance, John. *Karl Marx's Theory of Ideas.* Cambridge: Cambridge University Press, 1995.

Trigg, Joseph. *Origen.* London: Routledge & Kegan Paul, 1998.

———. *Origen: The Bible and Philosophy in the Third-Century Church.* Atlanta, Ga.: J. Knox, 1983.

Tuck, Richard. *Natural Rights Theories: Their Origin and Development.* Cambridge: Cambridge University Press, 1979.

Tully, James. *A Discourse on Property: John Locke and His Adversaries.* Cambridge: Cambridge University Press, 1980.

Turner, Victor. *The Ritual Process.* Chicago: University of Chicago Press, 1979.

Tuveson, Ernest. *The Redeemer Nation: The Idea of America's Millennial Role.* 1968. Reprint, Chicago: University of Chicago Press, 1980.

Ullmann, Walter. *A History of Political Thought: The Middle Ages.* Baltimore: Penguin Books, 1965.

———. *Medieval Papalism: The Political Theory of the Medieval Canonists.* 1949. Reprint, Westport, Conn.: Hyperion, 1979.

Vasari, Giorgio. *Lives of the Artists.* Translated by George Bull. Vol. 1. Harmondsworth: Penguin, 1987.

Villari, Pasquale. *The Life and Times of Savonarola.* New York: Scribner's, n.d.

Vincent, Andrew, and Raymond Plant. *Philosophy, Politics and Citizenship: The Life and Thought of the British Idealists.* Oxford: Basil Blackwell, 1984.

Voltaire. *Candide and Philosophical Letters.* New York: Modern Library, 1992.

———. *Letters on England.* Translated by Leonard Tancock. Harmondsworth: Penguin, 1980.

Vrettos, Theodore. *Alexandria: City of the Western Mind.* New York: Free Press, 2001.

Waerden, B. L. Van der. *Science Awakening.* New York: Oxford University Press, 1961.

Wagner, David, ed. *The Seven Liberal Arts in the Middle Ages.* Bloomington: Indiana University Press, 1983.

Walbank, F. W. *A Historical Commentary on Polybius.* Vol. 1. Oxford: Clarendon Press, 1957.

Walker, D. P. *Spiritual and Demonic Magic from Ficino to Campanella*. London: Warburg Institute, 1958.

Wallace-Hadrill, J. M. *The Barbarian West: The Early Middle Ages A.D. 400–1000*. 1952. Reprint, New York: Harper & Row, 1962.

Wasserman, Earl, ed. *Aspects of the Eighteenth Century*. Baltimore: Johns Hopkins University Press, 1965.

Watkins, Renée Neu, ed. *Humanism Liberty: Writings on Freedom from Fifteenth-Century Florence*. Columbia: University of South Carolina Press, 1978.

Weiss, P. "The Vision of Constantine." *Journal of Roman Archaeology* 16 (2003): 237–59.

Westfall, Richard. *Never at Rest: A Biography of Isaac Newton*. Cambridge: Cambridge University Press, 1980.

White, Newman Ivey. *Shelley*. 2 vols. New York: Alfred A. Knopf, 1940.

Whitehead, Alfred North. *Science and the Modern World*. 1925. Reprint, New York: Free Press, 1967.

Wiener, Martin J. *English Culture and the Decline of the Industrial Spirit, 1850–1980*. Cambridge: Cambridge University Press, 1981.

Wiener, Philip P., ed. *Values in a Universe of Chance: Selected Writings of Charles S. Peirce (1839–1914)*. New York: Doubleday, 1958.

William of Ockham. *A Short Discourse on Tyrannical Government*. Edited by A. S. McGrade. Cambridge: Cambridge University Press, 1992.

Williams, Charles Stephan Conway. *Commentary on the Acts of the Apostles*. London: A. & C. Black, 1964.

Wilson, Edmund. *To the Finland Station*. New York: Doubleday, 1940.

Winch, Donald. *Malthus*. Oxford: Oxford University Press, 1978.

Wind, Edgar. *Pagan Mysteries of the Renaissance*. New York: Norton, 1968.

Wittgenstein, Ludwig. *Tractatus Logico-Philosophicus*. 1922. Reprint, London: Routledge & Kegan Paul, 1981.

Wolf, John B., ed. *Louis XIV*. New York: Norton, 1974.

———. *Louis XIV: A Profile*. New York: Hill & Wang, 1972.

Wood, Gordon S. *The Creation of the American Republic 1776–1787*. New York: Norton, 1969.

Wood, Neal. *Cicero's Social and Political Thought*. Berkeley: University of California Press, 1988.

Xenophon. *Memorabilia*. Translated by E. C. Marchant. Cambridge, Mass.: Harvard University Press, 1968.

Yates, Frances A. *Giordano Bruno and the Hermetic Tradition*. 1964. Reprint, Chicago: University of Chicago Press, 1977.

———. *The Rosicrucian Enlightenment*. London: Routledge & Kegan Paul, 1972.

Zanker, Paul. *The Mask of Socrates: The Image of the Intellectual in Antiquity*. Berkeley: University of California Press, 1995.

PHOTO: © BETH HERMAN

ARTHUR HERMAN is the bestselling author of *The Cave and the Light, Freedom's Forge, How the Scots Invented the Modern World, The Idea of Decline in Western History, To Rule the Waves,* and *Gandhi & Churchill,* which was a 2009 finalist for the Pulitzer Prize. Dr. Herman taught the Western Heritage Program at the Smithsonian's Campus on the Mall, and he has been a professor of history at Georgetown University, The Catholic University of America, George Mason University, and The University of the South at Sewanee.

About the Type

This book was set in Electra, a typeface designed for Linotype by renowned type designer W. A. Dwiggins (1880–1956). Electra is a fluid typeface, avoiding the contrasts of thick and thin strokes that are prevalent in most modern typefaces.